THEGREENGUIDE
French Alps

House in Courchevel © Pierre Jacques/hemis.fr

MICHELIN

THEGREENGUIDE **FRENCH ALPS**

Editor	Martha Burley
Principal Writers	Wink Lorch and Lyn Parry
Production Manager	Natasha G. George
Cartography	John Dear
Photo Editor	Yoshimi Kanazawa
Proofreader	Karolin Thomas
Interior Design	Chris Bell
Cover Design	Chris Bell, Christelle Le Déan
Layout	Michelin Apa Publications Ltd., Alison Rayner
Cover Layout	Michelin Apa Publications Ltd.

Contact Us
The Green Guide
Michelin Travel and Lifestyle
One Parkway South
Greenville, SC 29615
USA
www.michelintravel.com

Michelin TravelPartner
Hannay House
39 Clarendon Road
Watford, Herts WD17 1JA
UK
℘01923 205240
www.ViaMichelin.com
travelpubsales@uk.michelin.com

Special Sales
For information regarding bulk sales,
customized editions and premium sales,
please contact our Customer Service
Departments:
USA   1-800-432-6277
UK   01923 205240
Canada 1-800-361-8236

HOW TO USE THIS GUIDE

PLANNING YOUR TRIP

The blue-tabbed PLANNING YOUR TRIP section gives you **ideas for your trip** and **practical information** to help you organize it. You'll find tours, practical information, a host of outdoor activities, a calendar of events, information on shopping, sightseeing, kids' activities and more.

INTRODUCTION

The orange-tabbed INTRODUCTION section explores **Nature** and geology of the French Alps. The **History** section spans from The Celts and Romans to the modern day. The **Art and Culture** section covers architecture, art, literature and music, while **French Alps Today** delves into the modern region.

DISCOVERING

The green-tabbed DISCOVERING section features Principal Sights by region, featuring the most interesting local **Sights**, **Walking Tours**, nearby **Excursions**, and detailed **Driving Tours**. Admission prices shown are normally for a single adult.

ADDRESSES

We've selected the best hotels, restaurants, cafes, shops, nightlife and entertainment to fit all budgets. See the Legend on the cover flap for an explanation of the price categories. See the back of the guide for an index of hotels and restaurants.

Sidebars

Throughout the guide you will find blue, orange and green-coloured text boxes with lively anecdotes, detailed history and background information.

😊 A Bit of Advice 😊

Green advice boxes found in this guide contain practical tips and handy information relevant to your visit or to a sight in the Discovering section.

STAR RATINGS★★★

Michelin has given star ratings for more than 100 years. If you're pressed for time, we recommend you visit the ★★★ or ★★ sights first:

★★★   **Highly recommended**

★★   **Recommended**

★   **Interesting**

MAPS

😊 Regional Geology maps.

😊 Region maps.

😊 Maps for major cities and villages.

😊 Local tour maps.

All maps in this guide are oriented north, unless otherwise indicated by a directional arrow. The term "Local Map" refers to a map within the chapter or Tourism Region. A complete list of the maps found in the guide appears at the back of this book.

CONTENTS

Welcome to the French Alps

The southeastern quarter of France is dominated by the Alps, beloved by winter sports fans, but also a source of dramatic and beautiful mountain landscapes to explore when the snow is confined to the highest peaks. Visitors to the French Alps can partake in increasingly varied sports, relax by the glistening blue lakes or learn about the region's chequered history.

ANNECY, THE LAKE AND MASSIF DES ARAVIS *(pp97–126)*

Wonderful for a summer trip, Lake Annecy makes a good starting point for the underrated Aravis mountains. The colourful town of Annecy is known as a "little Venice" of the Alps.

ÉVIAN AND LE CHABLAIS *(pp127–148)*

On the southern shores of Lake Geneva, the old spa towns of Évian and Thonon host many cultural events. The Chablais mountains above include the pretty resort of Morzine reached via the Dranse gorges.

MONT-BLANC AND LE FAUCIGNY *(pp149–180)*

The highest point in the Alps, Mont-Blanc holds a mythical status amongst all mountain lovers. The whole region is full of spectacular viewpoints, drives and hikes.

CHAMBÉRY, AIX-LES-BAINS, BAUGES AND BEAUFORTAIN *(pp181–212)*

Savoie's capital, Chambéry and nearby Aix les Bains are within easy reach of vineyards and pastures. The Bauges and Beaufortain massifs offer a more Alpine environment.

LA TARENTAISE AND LA VANOISE *(pp213–244)*

Within the Vanoise National Park are legendary ski resorts of the Tarentaise, like Val d'Isère and Courchevel.

Visitors will also discover the wild landscape of the park in summer.

LA MAURIENNE *(pp245–266)*

On the hillsides above the busiest thoroughfare to Italy the historically important Maurienne Valley includes many authentic mountain villages.

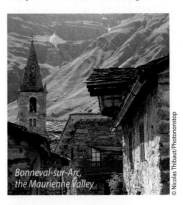

Bonneval-sur-Arc, the Maurienne Valley

© Nicolas Thibaut/Photononstop

GRENOBLE, CHAMROUSSE AND LA CHARTREUSE *(pp267–292)*

The largest city in the French Alps, Grenoble is surrounded by mountain ranges. Discover why the monks of the Chartreuse Abbey chose to settle in this hidden landscape.

L'OISANS AND LES ÉCRINS *(pp293–308)*

The Oisans is much revered by fans of the Tour de France for the gruelling rides here. Drivers can expect vertiginous routes too in the mountainous Écrins park.

LE VERCORS AND LE TRIÈVES
(pp309–331)

Southwest of Grenoble, you can find the desolate Vercors, wonderful for nature lovers to visit, but don't get lost in the caves. This is an Alpine area steeped in history.

BRIANÇON AND LE BRIANÇONNAIS *(pp333–346)*

This region, with its blue skies, soaring summits and sunny disposition is a popular tourist destination and major ski centre.

THE PAYS DES ÉCRINS, CHAMPSAUR AND VALGAUDEMAR *(pp347–360)*

Fertile peaks and valleys, alpine pastures and Mediterranean blue skies draw tourists to the region all year round. Devotees of extreme sports will love it here too.

LE QUEYRAS *(pp361–380)*

An unspoilt region, scattered with quaint villages characterized by fuste-style houses and sundials with quirky mottos. It boasts two examples of military architecture at Château Queyras and Mont-Dauphin.

LAC DE SERRE PONÇON, GAPENÇAIS AND DÉVOLUY *(pp381–395)*

The lively town of Gap is a good base for exploring the surrounding countryside, especially the giant of a lake at Serre-Ponçon.

L'UBAYE *(pp396–404)*

This patchwork landscape forms the most northern region of the Provençal Alps. The former base of the Count of Barcelona, Barcelonnette, is the hub of this isolated valley.

Colourful houses of Buis-les-Baronnies

© Camille Moirenc/hemis.fr

DE DIOIS, LE BUËCH AND LES BARONNIES *(pp405–422)*

North meets south, at this surprisingly lesser known region of the Alps. Picturesque villages, lavender fields and olive groves contrast with high-altitude passes and craggy peaks.

LA MOYENNE DURANCE AND LES PRÉALPES DE DIGNE *(pp423–448)*

This region has a distinct southern appeal with swathes of lavender and olive trees. The Sisteron citadel, at the gateway to Provence, is now used for a summer festival. The Durance and its tributaries are great for water sports.

THE PAYS DU VERDON *(pp449–472)*

A tour of the spectacular Verdon canyon, with its vertiginous views, offers a plethora of pretty villages such as Riez and Castellane. The steep limestone gorge cliffs are a mountaineer's delight.

THE ALPES DU MERCANTOUR *(pp473–500)*

Rugged peaks, glacial valleys and tranquil lakes contribute to rich diversity here. The perched villages, dotted around the perimeter, hide architectural treasures. A haven for walking, mountaineering and skiing.

La Saulire, la Tarentaise, Savoie
© Pierre Jacques/hemis.fr

Michelin Driving Tours

1 ROUTE DES GRANDES ALPES

La Route des Grandes Alpes starts on Lake Geneva at Thonon-les-Bains and crosses the Alps to Menton on the Mediterranean coast. The length of the route is approximately 700km/435mi.

2 THE CHABLAIS TO THE VALAIS REGION

Offering a chance to explore the Abondance Valley, this route begins on the shores of Lake Geneva and heads for the attractive town of Thonon before setting off on a delightful tour through the Abondance pastures, and climbing to the Pas de Morgins, where you cross into Switzerland for a while.

3 THE ARAVIS RANGE

Linking Annecy and Chamonix, this tour of the Aravis mountains is continuously spectacular, and with numerous places at which to take a break for coffee or a snack. Wait for a sunny day for best effect.

4 THE CHARTREUSE RANGE

In effect two loops that join the great city of Grenoble with the equally fascinating Chambéry. Take time out to explore Les Échelles in particular.

5 VERCORS

The Vercors was one of the first regional parks of France to gain recognition for its rich natural heritage. Within the park there are 85 different communities who are responsible for the protection of the natural habitat and maintain the balance between culture, development and the environment.

6 DRAC AND ROMANCHE, CORNICES AND GORGES

Exploring steep-sided river valleys in a wild landscape cut through by mountain rivers, this tour also takes in the civilised Château de Vizille with its large park that includes both elegant gardens and an intriguing maze.

7 DURANCE AND UBAYE

East of Gap, the Lac de Serre-Ponçon is an especial delight, set against the wooded slopes of the Forêt de Boscodon, but beyond lies a spectacular mountain drive between Barcelonnette and Guillestre.

8 ROUTE NAPOLÉON

The Route Napoléon runs from Golfe Juan, the sandy cove on the Mediterranean where Napoleon landed after returning from Elba, via Cannes and northwards through Grasse, Castellane, Sisteron and Gap to Grenoble. Parts of the road are winding and narrow, but all of it is beautiful.

9 HAUTE-PROVENCE BETWEEN VERDON AND DURANCE

This tour of the Verdon offers a surfeit of picturesque villages, visiting Riez, Castellane, Annot, Thorame, St André-les-Alpes and Valensole. Spring and early summer are good times to visit.

10 VINEYARDS AND TREES OF THE DIOIS REGION

This tour visits numerous picturesque villages in a region that is surprisingly less well known than other parts of the Alps. Be sure to include the diversion to Die and the Cirque d'Archiane.

11 LOCAL DRIVING TOURS

Listed below are the sights within the *Discovering the French Alps* section of the guide where you can find local driving tours.

- **Allevard** *p282*
- **Annecy** *p105*
- **Annot** *p482*

- **Massif des Aravis** *p119*
- **Route de la Bonette** *p499*
- **Bonneval-sur-Arc** *p266*
- **Lac du Bourget** *p197*
- **Le Briançonnais** *p340*
- **Buis-les-Baronnies** *p420*
- **Chambéry** *p188*
- **Gorges du Cians** *p488*
- **Colmars** *p476*
- **Cluses** *p175*
- **Diois** *p409*
- **Évian-les-Bains** *p132*
- **Route du Galibier** *p252*
- **Le Grésivaudan** *p279*
- **Route de L'Iseran** *p242*
- **Lacs de Laffrey** *p327*
- **Moustiers-Ste-Marie** *p467*
- **Route Napoléon** *p391 & 446*
- **Pont-en-Royans** *p324*
- **Puget-Théniers** *p483*
- **Le Queyras** *p364*
- **Samoëns** *p179*
- **Barrage and Lac de Serre-Ponçon** *p385*
- **Sisteron** *p429*
- **Ste-Jean-de-Maurienne** *p249*
- **La Tarentaise** *p233*
- **Thonon-les-Bains** *p136*
- **Vallée de la Tinée** *p492*
- **L'Ubaye** *p401*
- **Plateau de Valensole** *p463*
- **Le Valgaudemar** *p358*
- **La Vallouise** *p351*
- **Grand Canyon du Verdon** *p453*
- **Villars-sur-Var** *p485*

THEMED TOURS

Themed circuits – La Fondation pour l'action culturelle internationale en montagne (FACIM) has developed five thematic circuits for the northern French Alps: **Les Chemins du baroque**, which includes 60 Baroque sites and 500km/311mi of roads in the Savoie; **Les Pierre Fortes**, which takes you around castles and fortresses, often on vertiginous mountain faces, along the French–Italian frontier; **Terre des Alpes**, which explores alpine farms and pastures and rural traditions; **Archipels d'altitude**, which looks at ski resorts and their often innovative designs; and

Voyages Autour de la Table, which guides you to the best production areas for local food and drink. FACIM – 59 rue du Commandant Perceval, 73000 Chambéry ℘04 79 60 59 00; www.fondation-facim.fr.

Route des fruits et des vins – In the Hautes-Alpes, this itinerary stretches from the Pays du Buëch to the Durance and Avance valleys with opportunities for tastings *(dégustations)* in various wine and fruit cooperatives, according to the season. Local tourist offices will provide a list of orchards and wine cellars to visit or contact the **Comité départemental du tourisme de Hautes-Alpes**, www.holidays-alps.com.

Route de l'Olivier – A number of routes in the Bouches-du-Rhône and Drôme *départements* are devoted to the symbol of Provence and Provençal cuisine, the olive. An itinerary around Les Barronies and the Plateau de Valensole takes in mills where oil is produced and sold as well as restaurants which make a point of using local produce. Further information is available from the **Association Française Interprofessionelle de l'Olive (Afidol)** ℘04 42 23 01 92; www.afidol.org.

La route des Grandes Alpes – Linking the French Alps north to south from Thonon-les-Bains to Menton, this route was first conceived in 1937 and many variations are feasible. The route crosses 16 passes, so is only practicable from June to mid-October (due to snow closures). It also goes through several important parks and some of the finest sites of the Alps.

Association Grande Traversée des Alpes – 14 rue de la République, BP 227, 38000 Grenoble ℘ 04 76 42 08 31; www.routedesgrandesalpes.com or www.grande-traversee-alpes.com.

When to Go

CLIMATE

Sport and leisure in the French Alps change with the seasons.

The region's resorts are at their liveliest in winter, when snowy villages and landscapes offer the best-known images of alpine holidays.

Weather in spring and autumn, while lovely and mild, is more unpredictable, with sometimes violent storms and, in the south, the notorious springtime mistral wind. In the summer, the south generally remains drier than the lush north, but is also considerably hotter, except in the higher hills. Climbers and walkers flock to the area in search of striking panoramas and clean mountain air. Be aware, however, that heat haze may obscure some of the best views in the height of summer.

For any outdoor activity on sea or land, it is useful to have reliable weather forecasts.

For **Metéo France** (national weather bureau, www.meteo.fr) reports in French, dial 3250, then select from the recorded choices (0.34€/min).

For **départemental reports**, dial 08 92 68 02 followed by the two-digit number of the *département*:

Alpes-de-Haute-Provence 📞04
Alpes-Maritimes 📞06
Drôme 📞26
Haute-de-Savoie 📞74
Hautes-Alpes 📞05
Isère 📞38
Savoie 📞73
Var 📞83
Vaucluse 📞06

WHAT TO PACK

As little as possible! Cleaning and laundry services are available everywhere, and most personal items can be replaced at a reasonable cost. Try to pack everything into one suitcase. Take a day sack for carrying new purchases or for shopping at open-air markets, for carrying a picnic, etc. Be sure luggage is clearly labelled and old travel tags removed.

Do not pack medication in checked luggage, but keep it with you; be sure the prescription is with the medication.

Carry-on luggage is restricted; make sure you have room in your checked luggage for purchases. To avoid last-minute drama, find out from your airline exactly what is permitted in both your carry-on and checked luggage, and any other security restrictions, which are different on continental Europe from those in Britain or the USA.

Where to Go

ONE WEEK

Even as a recreational visitor it makes sense to acclimatise yourself to the altitude before going up to the high mountains, so for a summer visit, consider a two-centre base, first around Annecy, and later in a mountain resort.

On Day 1 visit the old town of **Annecy**★★★ in the morning and later, relax on one of the lake beaches, take a boat trip or drive around the lake. On Day 2 drive up to the forested **Semnoz** and take the road through the **Bauges** down to **Aix-les-Bains** for lunch in the old spa town, then explore the magnificent **Lac du Bourget**. Plan to move on to your mountain resort on Day 3. Drive up through the **Aravis** over either the **Col des Aravis** or the **Col de la Colombière** depending where you plan to stay. For days 4–6, check the weather forecast and reserve the finest day to go up to the **Aiguille du Midi** in **Chamonix** to see the glaciers and **Mont Blanc** up close. On other days, ride the ski lifts, go hiking, taste the local **reblochon cheese** from a farm and visit a village heritage (*patrimoine*) museum to understand how life used to be in the Alps.

TWO WEEKS

Ambitious travellers may wish to drive the **Route des Grandes Alpes** from Thonon-les-Bains to Menton or vice versa, staying in a different place every 1–2 nights.

Alternatively, **Grenoble**, between northern and southern Alps, would be a good base for the first week. Explore first the vibrant town itself, then try excursions to cycling territory at **Alpe d'Huez**, the historic **Maurienne Valley**, or into the **Chartreuse** and **Vercors** national parks. The second week you could follow the one-week itinerary on p12, discovering **Annecy** and the **Mont Blanc** Massif, or make a base close to **Briançon**, Europe's highest town. Not only will you find fascinating history there, but you can explore the characterful **Queyras** region nearby.

SIGHTSEEING ACROSS THE BORDER
SWITZERLAND

Swiss Tourist Offices

♦ **United Kingdom**: Swiss Centre, 1st floor, 30 Bedford St, London WC2E 9ED ℘0800 100 200 30; www.myswitzerland.com.

♦ **United States**: Swiss Center, 608 Fifth Ave., New York City, NY 10020–2303 ℘(212) 757 5944; www.myswitzerland.com.

There are also SNTO locations in the following cities: Amsterdam, Brussels, Frankfurt, Madrid, Milan, Paris, Rome, Stockholm, Tokyo and Vienna.

The **Green Guide Switzerland**, the **Michelin Hotel and Restaurant Guide Switzerland** and **Michelin Map 729** provide all the information you need for a visit.

Formalities

For a stay of less than three months, citizens of an EU member state require a valid ID card (or in the case of UK visitors, a passport). Travellers from outside the European Union must be in possession of a passport. When

View of Briançon with Collégiale Notre-Dame

© Franck Guiziou/hemis.fr

travelling by car, drivers should be prepared to present a driving licence, international driving permit and car registration papers. Motorcyclists will require the same documents and must wear helmets. Owners of pets brought into the country will be required to prove that the animal has been vaccinated against rabies in the past year, but more than a month before their entry into Switzerland.

Excursions
Vallorcine to Emosson

(☞see GREEN GUIDE SWITZERLAND) – Travellers may like to continue the route from Chamonix to Vallorcine as far as Martigny and then on to the Emosson Dam *(☉exterior open May–Oct; for further information, contact the Parc d'attractions on ℘(0)27 769 11 11)*; the approach to the lake offers a superb view of the north face of Mont Blanc. From the resort of Châtelard at the bottom of the valley, a three-stage rail journey takes visitors to a height of 1 961m/6 434ft in about 40 minutes *(operates Jun–mid-Oct 9.30am–12.30pm, 1.30–5.30pm; fare there and back 44CHF; ℘(0)27 769 11 11; www.chatelard.net)*.

The first section funicular is the steepest in Europe, rising at a dizzying gradient of 87 percent. Experienced walkers can return on foot in about two hours 30 minutes.

On the water – Avoid the traffic jams and cruise across Lake Geneva. The Compagnie Générale de Navigation (*℘+41 (0)848 811 848*) offers regular sailings between France and Geneva, Vevey, Nyon and its headquarters in Lausanne.

ITALY

Italian State Tourist Board

- **United Kingdom**: 1 Princes Street, London W1B 2AY *℘+44 (0)207 399 3562*; www.italiantouristboard.co.uk.
- **Canada**: 175 Bloor Street, Suite 907 South Tower, Toronto, Ontario M4W 3R8 *℘001 416 925 4882*; www.italiantourism.com.
- **United States**: (New York) 630 Fifth Avenue, Suite 1565, New York City, NY 10111 *℘001 212 245 5618*; (Los Angeles) 12400 Wilshire Boulevard, Suite 550, Los Angeles, CA 90025 *℘001 310 820 1898*; (Chicago) 500 North Michigan Avenue 506, Chicago, IL 60611 *℘001 312 644 0996*; www.italiantourism.com.

The **Green Guide Italy**, the **Michelin Guide Italia** and **Michelin Map 562 Italy North West** provide further in-depth information on the western Italian Alps and the northwest coast.

Via the Mont Blanc Tunnel

Val d'Aoste – *After the tunnel, continue on A 5 or follow S 26 towards Turin (see Massif du Mont-Blanc).* The valley of the Dora Baltea and its tributaries is surrounded by the highest peaks of the French and Swiss Alps, including the Matterhorn, Mont Blanc, Monte Rosa, Grand Combin, Dent Hérens, Gran Paradiso and Grande Sassière.

Countless excursions by car and cable car or on foot, quiet valleys, picturesque villages and above all the superb **views**★★★ make the Aosta Valley one of northern Italy's most popular holiday destinations.

Aosta, the capital, has preserved relics from Roman and medieval times.

Aoste tourist office – Piazza Chanoux, 2 *℘0165 23 66 27*; www.regione.vda.it.

Via the Tunnel de Fréjus

Susa★ – *Via A 32*. Marking the intersection of the two main roads to France, Susa, the "gateway to Italy" and site of the 2006 Winter Olympic games, lies at the foot of a colossal massif, crowned by the Rocciamelone (3 538m/11 608ft). Besides its best-known landmark, the 4C **Savoy Gate**★ (Porta Savoia), the town also boasts a fine **Romanesque campanile** on the south side of the Gothic **cathedral** and the elegant **Arco di Augusto**★, the oldest monument in the city (8C BC).

Further along the road to Turin, perched high on a hill, stands the Benedictine **abbey Sacra di San Michele**★★★ *(A 32 then S 25)*. The great staircase leads up to the **Zodiac Door** with its decorated capitals and pilasters. The Romanesque–Gothic abbey church, built on top of the rocky eminence, has fine 16C frescoes. From the esplanade there is a lovely **view**★★★ of the Alps, the Dora Valley, the Po and Turin plains.

THEMED ITINERARIES
HISTORICAL AND CULTURAL

Villes et Pays d'Art et d'Histoire

Tours led by guides approved by the Ministry of Culture and Communication are offered in important cities and sites throughout the region. Contact the local tourist offices, or go to www.vpah.culture.fr (French only).

In Vauban's Footsteps

The comprehensive defence system designed by Vauban during Louis XIV's reign is unique in the history of military architecture. Some of these former strategic sites can be visited: citadels in Mont-Dauphin and Briançon, the castle in Château-Queyras, the citadel in Seyne-les-Alpes and the two forts in Colmars-les-Alpes are the finest examples of Vauban's work.

How to Tell the Time by Looking at a Sundial

A vertical sundial consists of a panel, usually facing south, and of a metal rod, or gnomon, representing the Earth's axis. Its length must not extend the shadow beyond the panel at the time of the summer solstice and be sufficient for the shadow to be visible at the time of the winter solstice. Reading the time on a sundial is relatively easy but the conversion into accepted, "normal" time is rather involved and requires three factors to be taken into account: the longitude, which, in the south of France, results in a 20- to 30-minute difference from Paris;

Sundial in Saint-Véran

© Jean-Pierre Degas/hemis.fr

real time (solar time) and average time (24-hour day) corresponding to the variation in the Earth's rotating speed (in summer, it can vary from +3minutes to –6minutes); and finally, the difference between summer and winter time.

Later military fortifications by Vauban's successors are also open to the public: 18C works are centred round Briançon whereas 19C defences are situated further afield.

A fort by Maginot, known as Janus, can be visited by appointment. For detailed information, contact the **Office du Tourisme** in Briançon: 1, Place du Temple, 05105 Briançon ℘04 92 21 08 50; www.ot-briancon.fr.

In Jean Giono's Footsteps

The Jean Giono Centre at Manosque organises walks all year long, led by qualified guides, around natural sites that inspired the famed novelist. The itinerary is wheelchair-accessible. **Centre Jean Giono**, 3 boulevard Élémir-Bourges, Manosque ℘04 92 70 52 54; www.centrejeangiono.com.

Sundials

The **Briançonnais** offers a variety of mostly 18C sundials; there are 20 in Briançon alone as well as in the villages of Prelles, Puy-St-Vincent, Les Alberts, Val-des-Prés, Plampinet, La Salle-les-Alpes and Névache.

In the **Queyras**, sundials are often decorated with exotic birds. There are also interesting sundials in the **Pays du Buëch** to the west and in the **Ubaye** Valley to the south; contact the **Office de Tourisme**, place Frédéric Mistral, 04400 Barcelonnette ℘04 92 81 04 71; www.barcelonnette.com.

ON THE WATER

Several large lakes situated in shallow valleys, such as the Lac du Bourget, Lac d'Annecy, Lac Léman (Lake Geneva) and Lac d'Aiguebelette offer a wide range of outdoor activities (sailing, waterskiing, diving, wind-surfing, etc.). The mildness of the climate is underlined by the presence of vineyards and fruit trees.

Lake Geneva cruises – There are 30 landings around the French and Swiss shores of the lake, with many boat trips and cruises (restaurants on board) available. All year long, a daily (35-minute) route links **Évian** and **Lausanne** in Switzerland and a daily service (20 minutes) links **Yvoire** and **Nyon**. By taking a boat, you can pass time in Vevey, Lausanne and Geneva while avoiding road traffic. In summer, there are also round trips at night. Information from the tourist office in Yvoire, place de la Mairie, 74140 Yvoire *04 50 72 80 21; www.ot-yvoire.fr. Several clubs offer **yachting facilities and sailing courses**: Société nautique du Léman français, port de Rives, 74200 Thonon-les-Bains *04 50 71 07 29; www.voilethonon.com and Cercle de la voile d'Évian, port des Mouettes, BP 103, 74500 Évian-les-Bains *04 50 75 06 46; www.cercle-voile-evian. com. There is a colourful yacht race on the lake in mid-June, called the Bol d'Or, when 600 boats compete for the golden cup. www.boldormirabaud. com.

Lac du Bourget – The largest natural lake in France also offers a variety of water-based activities. Cruises starting from the Grand Port in Aix-les-Bains, Le Bourget-du-Lac, Portout-Chanaz, Lavours or Belley include a choice of trips from a one-hour tour of the lake to a day trip to the Savière Canal and the River Rhône. The cruises are organised by the **Compagnie des Bateaux du Lac du Bourget et du Haut-Rhône**, Le Grand Port, 73100 Aix-les-Bains *04 79 63 45; www.gwel.com.

The lake is exposed to high winds and sailing conditions are similar to those encountered at sea, so ideal for windsurfing. There are also several sailing clubs in Aix-les-Bains and Le Bourget-du-Lac. The best period to sail on the lake is from March to early November.

Lac d'Annecy – The superb scenery is the major attraction of the lake. There is a tour of the lake starting from the Thiou pier in Annecy.

Monteynard – In high season, the cruises on this charming lake on the edge of the Parc régional du Vercors also take in the breathtaking gorges of the Drac and the Ebron, which can be seen only from the water. Ask about sailing times at **Bateau-Crosières La Mira**, 38650 Treffort *04 76 34 14 56.

Lac d'Esparron-de-Verdon – Cruises tour the lake in season, and the local yachting club offers sailing courses and rentals. The lake is especially renowned for canoes and kayaks. For information contact the **tourist office at Hameau du Port**, 04800 Esparron-de-Verdon *04 92 77 15 97; www.esparrondeverdon.com.

TOURIST TRAINS

Chemin de fer de la Mure – Currently closed after a landslide (check www.trainlamure.com for updates) the 30km/18.6mi itinerary of this former mining railway between St-Georges-de-Commiers and La Mure includes an impressive number of engineering works and offers exceptional views of the Drac gorges.

Chemin de fer du Montenvers – This line, opened in 1908, transports you from the valley of Chamonix to the Mer de Glace Glacier high on Mont Blanc (1 913m/6 276ft), through exhilarating scenery. From the terminus, you can follow a footpath or take a gondola down to sites on the glacier.

Chemins de Fer de Provence – The famous **Train des Pignes** – so-called because the old steam locomotives used to burn pine cones – links Nice and Digne-les-Bains, covering a distance of 150km/93.2mi via Puget-Théniers, Entrevaux, Annot and St-André-les-Alpes, along a route which once continued to Toulon on the coast.

The line, built between 1890 and 1911, includes some 60 metal bridges, viaducts, tunnels and other daring works of engineering. A three-hour journey through five mountain valleys opens up a world of magnificent landscapes, dotted with hilltop villages. For **hikers and ramblers**, designated stopping points, in addition to the stations, allow walkers to strike off into open countryside and rejoin the train further along the line. In winter the **Train des Neiges** runs daily to the resorts in the Val d'Allos. Information about the **Chemins de Fer de Provence**, 4 bis rue Alfred Binet, 06000 Nice *04 97 03 80 80; www.trainprovence.com.

Tarines cows on the pastures of the Beaufortain

© Franck Guiziou/hemis.fr

INDUSTRIAL SITES

Some still operational, some now preserved as cultural monuments, these sites offer an insight into the industries in the French Alps.

- **Caves de la Chartreuse** – The famous liqueur distillery; 10 boulevard Kofler, BP 102, 38500 Voiron. ℘04 76 05 81 77; www.chartreuse.fr (*see Massif de la Chartreuse*).

- **Coopérative laitière de haute Tarantaise** – Cooperative dairy; ZA des Colombières, 73700 Bourg-St-Maurice ℘04 79 07 08 28; www.fromagebeaufort.com (*see Bourg-St-Maurice*).

- **Coopérative laitière du Beaufortain** – Cooperative dairy; 73270 Beaufort ℘04 79 38 33 62; www.cooperative-de-Beaufort.com (*see Le Beaufortain*).

- **Eaux minérales d'Évian** – Mineral water bottling plant (*See Évian-les-Bains*).

- **Centre scientifique et technique de Grenoble** – Tours and temporary exhibits in a science and technology centre; La Casemate, 1 place Laurent, Grenoble ℘04 76 44 88 80; www.ccsti-grenoble.org.

- **Musée Opinel** – Museum devoted to the famous Savoyard knife (*See St-Jean-de-Maurienne*).

- **Hydrelec** – EDF Museum showing the workings of this huge dam used for hyrdoelectricity; Hydrelec, Le Verney, 38014 Vaujany ℘04 76 80 78 00; www.musee-hydrelec.fr.

- **La Mine-Image** – Coal mine; 38770 La Motte-d'Aveillans ℘04 76 30 68 74; www.mine-image.com (*see Lacs de Laffrey*).

- **Centrale hydroéléctrique de La Bâthie** (beneath the Roselend Dam in the Beaufortain) – Celebrates 50 years in 2011; visits by appointment; ℘04 79 31 06 60; www.50-ans-roselend.com.

FOR NATURE LOVERS

A number of organisations offer natural history excursions in the Alps; a list of locations is available from *UNCPIE* (Centre permanent d'initiatives pour l'environnement), 26, rue Beaubourg, 75003 Paris ℘01 44 61 75 35; www.cpie.fr.
On **Mont Blanc**, 50 footpaths have been developed along alpine themes such as pastures, marshes, lakes, animal life, agriculture, daily life, industry, etc. Explanatory panels

follow the trails, which are generally very easy and short, so ideal for families. For a booklet contact **Espace Mont-Blanc**, 175 rue Paul-Corbin, 74190 Passy-Chedde *℘*04 50 93 66 73; www.espace-mont-blanc.com.

Nature Parks and Reserves

The protected areas, parks and reserves of the French Alps offer wonderful opportunities for ramblers, cyclists and other nature lovers. The parks have visitor centres, called "Maisons" at several sites; these are noted in the Discovering section. You will find organised nature walks, exhibits and other activities for adults and children.

◆ **Parc naturel régional des Bauges** – Maison du Parc, 73630 Le Châtelard *℘*04 79 54 86 40; www.parcdesbauges.com.

◆ **Parc naturel régional de la Chartreuse** – Maison du Parc, 38380 St-Pierre-de-Chartreuse *℘*04 76 88 75 20; www.parc-chartreuse.net.

◆ **Parc national des Écrins** – Domaine de Charance, 05000 Gap *℘*04 92 40 20 10; www.ecrins-parcnational.fr *(seven maisons du parc ☙ see Briançon, L'Embrunais, Valouise, Valgaudemar, Champsaur, Oisans, Valbonnais).*

◆ The **Parc national du Mercantour** – 23 rue d'Italie, BP 1316, 06006 Nice *℘*04 93 16 78 78; www.mercantour.eu *(Maison du parc at ☙ Barcelonnette).*

◆ **Parc naturel régional du Queyras** – La Ville, 05350 Arvieux *℘*04 92 46 88 20; www.pnr-queyras.com.

◆ **Parc national de la Vanoise** – 135 rue du Docteur-Julliand, BP 705, 73007 Chambéry *℘*04 79 62 30 54; www.vanoise.com.

◆ **Parc naturel régional du Vercors** – Maison du Parc, 255 chemin des Fusiliés, 38250 Lans-en-Vercors *℘*04 76 94 38 26; www.parc-du-vercors.fr.

◆ **Parc naturel régional du Verdon** – BP 14, 04360 Moustiers-Ste-Marie *℘*04 92 74 68 00; www.parcduverdon.com *(☙ see Gorges du Verdon).*

◆ **Réserve naturelle géologique de Haute-Provence** – 10 montée Bernard Dellacasagrande, 04005 Digne-les-Bains *℘*04 92 36 70 70; www.resgeol04.org *(☙ see Dignes-les-Bains).*

◆ **La Maison des Gorges de Verdon** – Le Château, 04120 La-Palud-sur-Verdon *℘*04 92 77 32 02; www.lapaludsurverdon.com *(☙ see Verdon).* In the summer, outings are organised to observe **Verdon's famous vulture colony**. Contact *℘*04 92 83 69 55; http://verdon.lpo.fr.

What to See and Do

WINTER SPORTS

SKIING

♿Refer to Mountain Safety p50 for details on safety in the mountains.
The Alps are the most important winter-sports area in Europe, and resorts in the French Alps are at the cutting edge in providing equipment and facilities for all the various sports possibilities.

For up-to-date information, contact the **France Montagnes**, Alpespace, 24 voie St Exupéry, 73800 Francin ✆04 79 65 06 75; http://en.france-montagnes.com.

Downhill skiing – This is the most popular form of skiing, available in all the alpine resorts. The French champion Émile Allais founded the first French ski school (École de Ski Français) in 1935.

Cross-country or nordic skiing – This type of skiing is ideal on fairly level terrain; skis are long and narrow, boots are low and fixed at the point only. Skiers either glide forward in a stride (traditional style), or skate in modern racing style with different equipment appropriate for each technique. There are marked tracks of various lengths and difficulties in most resorts.

This form of skiing can be practised at any age, each skier going at his or her own pace. The **Vercors** region is particularly suitable for cross-country skiing, with marked tracks, mountain refuges and shelters. Information is available from the Parc naturel régional du Vercors (*♿Le Vercors*). Hard-core skiers can try the **Haute Trace des Escartons** between St Véran and Névache.

The **Parc naturel régional du Queyras**, which combined with the **Guisane** Valley boasts some of the best cross-country skiing in the south, offers similar facilities; www.pnr-queyras.com.

For more information, contact **Hautes-Alpes Ski de Fond**, 1 avenue Vauban, 05100 Briançon ✆04 92 20 15 09; www.skidefond05.com.

Ski touring – This form of skiing is suitable for experienced skiers with plenty of stamina as it combines the technique of cross-country skiing for uphill sections and that of off-piste skiing for downhill sections. Skiers should be accompanied by a qualified guide, and special equipment is necessary: skis able to be fitted with seal skins for climbing. There are several famous itineraries across the Alps: the **Grande Traversée des Alpes** (GTA), which follows footpath GR 5 from Lake Geneva to the Mediterranean. For more information,

Val Thorens – one of the great French resorts

S. Sauvignier/MICHELIN

contact the **Bureau Information Montagne/GTA** – Maison de la Montagne, 3 rue Raoul-Blanchard, 38000 Grenoble ℘04 76 44 67 03; www.grenoble-montagne.com.

Ski touring is also popular in the Alpes-de-Haute-Provence region, where there are more than 1 000km/ 622mi of trails in the upper Ubaye, the upper Verdon (and the pays d'Annot), and also in more southern regions such as the slopes of Contadour. Contact a guiding centre if you want to be accompanied (see list p22).

Monoskiing – Requires a good sense of balance because both feet are fixed to a single ski, facing downhill. It is mostly practised off-piste. An ancestor of snowboarding, it was abandoned for a time but is now back in vogue. Association française de Monoski – Les Verdoux, 38250 Villard-de-Lans; www.monoski-france.com.

Mogul skiing – This acrobatic form of skiing is an Olympic event; it consists of skiing down very steep bumpy runs.

Ski-joering – Some resorts now offer this old Scandinavian means of transport: riding on skis while attached to a horse or sled dogs.

Telemark skiing – This Norwegian technique is the ancestor of modern skiing: ski boots are attached at the heel by a cable that leaves the heel free, permitting the skier to execute elegant turns by genuflecting over one ski and bringing the tail of the other up and around: **Association française de télémark**, 50 rue des Marquisats, 74011 Annecy ℘04 50 51 40 34; www.ffs.fr.

Handiski – It's possible to ski even if you have a disability. Special teams, infrastructure and equipment are available at many ski areas. Ski sleds allow people to ski seated, while those with sight or hearing difficulties can also ski, accompanied by qualified personnel. Often there are discounted lift tickets for the disabled and their companion; all equipment, of course, must be approved by ski technicians and by the French Fédération Handisport. Information about special ski instruction through Handiski is found at http://ski.handisport.free.fr.

SNOWBOARDING

Very popular in the French Alps, snowboarders use a single board usually with softer boots than downhill skiers. Boarders use the same slopes as skiers but especially favour fresh powder snow on steep slopes, and off-piste when conditions allow. Techniques and equipment are constantly evolving and most resorts have "snowparks" where boarders can enjoy jumps and pipes.

OFF-PISTE

This is intended for very experienced skiers and boarders who ski or ride outside marked runs at their own risk. The presence and advice of a guide or instructor with a comprehensive knowledge of dangerous areas is highly recommended.

SNOWSHOEING

This old-fashioned winter sport has become popular again with the introduction of smaller, lightweight plastic snowshoes that can be used with sturdy walking or mountain boots. The sport is enjoyed by people of all ages and abilities who want to experience untrammelled nature far from crowds. It is best to begin with a lesson on how to walk lightly on the snowshoes and how to use poles.

DOG SLEDGING

A wonderful chance to try out being a "musher", sledging with a team of dogs. Courses and single experiences are available in certain winter-sports areas, in particular at Le Grand Revard, Lans-en-Vercors, La Croix Chabaud and Royan-Vercors.

La Grande Odysée is a 1 000km/ 622mi international dog-sledging race across the Alps with around 250 dogs of various breeds pulling beautiful sledges. It is possible to watch the various stages.

For details of this annual event, visit www.grandeodyssee.com.

RESORTS

All the resorts mentioned offer accommodation listed in the Michelin Guide France.

The Alps boast a great variety of resorts. Beside internationally famous resorts such as Tignes, Val d'Isère, Courchevel and Chamonix, there are a great number of more modest ones which have retained their village character and attract a family clientele.

Over the years, many individual resorts have linked together. Those that reach high up into glacier areas may offer summer skiing.

Summer Skiing Resorts

Six resorts offer summer skiing, depending on snow conditions, as well as offering more traditional summer activities. The most important areas are Les Deux Alpes and Tignes. Some snow-making equipment is used to ensure opening, but it is still worth checking with each resort to verify opening dates.

- **L'Alpe-d'Huez** – June to late July on the Sarennes Glacier (3 000m/9 843ft).
- **Les Deux Alpes** – Mid-June to August on the Mont-de-Lans Glacier (3 420m/11 220ft).
- **La Plagne** – July to August on the Bellecôte Glacier (3 416m/11 207ft).
- **Tignes** – Mid-June to August on the Grande Motte Glacier (3 430m/11 253ft).
- **Val d'Isère** – Late June to mid-August.
- **Val Thorens** – July to August on the Péclet Glacier (3 400m/11 155ft).

Linked Skiing Areas

A number of individual resorts have joined together to form extensive ski areas. Note that the term *domaines reliés*, or linked resorts such as Portes du Soleil, means you can ski from one resort to another, while *domaine skiable* means that, while you can ski all the areas with one ticket, you may have to take a bus or car among areas.

- **Les Aravis** – St-Jean-de-Sixt, La Clusaz, Le Grand Bornand, Manigod
- **Les Deux Alpes** – La Grave, La Meije, Les Deux Alpes, Vénoesc-Vénéon
- **Espace Diamant** – Crest-Voland, Cohennoz, Les Saises, Flument, Notre-Dame de Bellecombe
- **Espace Killy** – Tignes, Val d'Isère
- **Espace San Bernardo** – Séez-St-Bernard, La Rosière; Italian resort: La Thuile
- **Évasion Mont-Blanc** – Combloux, La Giettaz, Megève, St-Gervais, St-Nicolas-de-Véroce, Les Contamines-Montjoie, Les Houches
- **Grand Domaine** – St-François-Longchamp, Valmorel, Doucy-Combelouvière
- **Le Grand Massif** – Les Carroz-d'Arâches, Flaine, Morillon, Samoëns, Sixt-Fer-à-Cheval
- **Les Grandes Rousses** – Allemont, L'Alpe-d'Huez, Auris-en-Oisans, Oz-en-Oisans, Vaujany, Villard-Reculas
- **Paradiski** – La Plagne, Plagne-Montalbert, Les Arcs/Bourg-St-Maurice, Peisey-Vallandry, Nancroix, Champagny-en-Vanoise, Montchavin-les-Coches, Villaroger
- **Les Portes du Soleil** – Abondance, Avoriaz, La Chapelle d'Abondance, Châtel, Les Gets, Montriond-Morzine, Morzine St-Jean-d'Aulps; Swiss resorts: Champéry, Morgins, Torgon, Val d'Illiez
- **Savoie Grand Revard** – La Féclaz, Le Revard, St-François-de-Sales
- **Les Sybelles** – Les Bottières-Jarrier, St-Colomban, St-Alban-des-Villards, La Toussuire, Le Corbier, St-Jean-d'Arves, St-Sorlin-d'Arves
- **Les Trois Vallées** – Les Ménuires, Courchevel, Val Thorens, La Tania, Méribel, St-Martin-de-Belleville, Brides-les-Bains, Orelle
- **Valée-Verte** – St-Jean-d'Aulps, Bellevaux, Hirmentaz, Les Habères
- **Valloire/Valmeinier** – Valloire, Valmeinier

OUTDOOR FUN
ANGLING

Trout is the prize catch in mountain areas; it can be caught with live insects or larvae (in mountain streams with steep banks) or with artificial flies and a rod and reel in wider streams and mountain lakes. Other common fish found in alpine streams and lakes are grayling, barbel, chub and perch. In France, fishing permits are only available to members of a local angling club; tourists must generally pay for a year's club membership, although day permits may be available in some areas.

Seasons vary according to species and the type of water being fished. Any catches under the permitted size (50cm/19.7in for pike and 23cm/9.1in for trout) must be released at once. Be aware that many rivers are dammed, and that water can be released unexpectedly; many sites are unsuitable for children.

Special regulations apply to fishing in some of the large lakes. For more information, look at the website of the **Union nationale pour la pêche, www.unpf.fr**.

In the **Savoie and Haute-Savoie**, more than 70 fishing sites (lakes, rivers, ponds) have been listed for fishing. The largest variety of fish are found in the rivers Giffre, Arve and Ménoge, while the Fier is one of the best fishing rivers in an area known for its waterfalls and impressive scenery.

In the **Isère region**, the rivers Drac and Isère and their many tributaries, as well as the lakes (Laffrey, the Belledonne Massif and Les Sept Laux), offer excellent sport. Eighteen sites are equipped to permit **disabled access**.

Lac du Bourget – White-fish angling along the shore is only allowed near harbours (Aix-les-Bains, St-Innocent), but it is possible to hire a boat; besides perch and pike, you sometimes find salmon-type fish named *lavaret*. The availability of zander or pike-perch is also expanding.

In the south there are more than 40 mountain lakes, as well as numerous

---

Hiking, Canyoning and Mountaineering Guides

Le Club alpin français publishes guides and brochures: 24 rue de Laumière, 75019 Paris ℘01 53 72 87 00; www.ffcam.fr.

La Fédération française de la montagne et de l'escalade, 8–10 quai de la Marne, 75019 Paris ℘01 40 18 75 50; www.ffme.fr. The FFME publishes a *Guide des sites naturels d'escalade en France* by D. Taupin, where you will find climbing sites throughout France. Guides can be hired though local *bureaux*.

The Conseil général des Alpes-Maritimes produces guides on *via ferrata*, canyoning and other outdoor sports: Route de Grenoble, BP 3007, 06201 Nice ℘04 97 18 60 00; www.cg06.fr (look under "Guides randoxygène").

The tourist office of **Alpes-de-Haute-Provence** publishes a guide, *Canyoning, escalade, via ferrata*: Immeuble François-Mitterrand BP 170, 04005 Digne-les-Bains ℘04 92 31 57 29; www.alpes-haute-provence.com.

◆ **Bureau des Guides de Briançon**, Place Suze ℘04 92 20 15 73; www.guides-briancon.fr.

◆ **Bureau des Guides des Écrins**, 05290 Vallouise ℘04 92 23 32 29; www.guides-ecrins.com.

◆ **Bureau des Guides de Serre-Chevalier**, Maison de la Montagne, Pré Long Villeneuve, 05240 La Salle-des-Alpes ℘04 92 24 75 90; www.guides-serrechevalier.com.

◆ **Bureau des Guides de l'Ubaye**, ℘04 92 81 20 76; www.guides-montagne-ubaye.com.

◆ **Bureau des Guides de Verdon**, rue Grande, 04120 La Palud-sur-Verdon ℘04 92 77 30 50; www.escalade-verdon.fr.

mountain streams and rivers ideal for fishing. The **Pays du Buëch** offers an infinite variety of fishing in fast streams. The bridge at Serre is in the top category, where you find trout, dace and barbel. Note that fishing on the **Lac de Serre-Ponçon** is subject to special regulations.
The Parc naturel régional du Verdon offers a map of all its fishing sites and their particularities *(Pêche nature dans le Verdon)*.

CANYONING

A good knowledge of potholing (caving), diving and rock-climbing techniques is necessary to abseil (rappel) or jump down tumultuous mountain streams and to follow their course through narrow gorges and down steep waterfalls. The appeal of this sport lies in the variety of the terrain. Summer is the best period to practise canyoning: the water temperature is bearable and the rivers are not so high. However, the weather forecast plays a crucial role in deciding whether to go canyoning, as a storm upriver can make it dangerous to go through a gorge and cause basins to fill up with alluvial sediments. In any case, it is preferable to leave early in the morning (storms often occur during the afternoon) to allow yourself time to overcome any unforeseen minor problems.
The main canyoning areas are the Vallée d'Abondance in the **Chablais**, La Norma and Valfréjus in the **Haute-Maurienne**, the Canyon des Écouges and Gorges du Furon in the **Vercors**, the **Ubaye Valley** between Les Thuiles and Le Lauzet, in particular the Ravin de Sauze, the **upper Var and the Cians valleys**, and, of course, the **Verdon** (Ravin du Four near Beauvezer). The Vallon du Fournel (**Briançonnais**) and the Vallon du Pas de La Tour (**Ubaye**) are best for beginners. Remember that, in spite of appearances, river gorges are no less dangerous in summer, when the river's flow is slower, than at other times. Long, narrow ravines, sometimes with

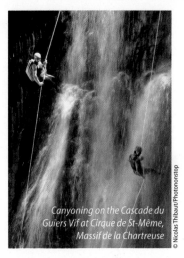

Canyoning on the Cascade du Guiers Vif at Cirque de St-Même, Massif de la Chartreuse

© Nicolas Thibaut/Photononstop

no way out to higher ground, can be filled by a rush of water if a sudden cloudburst swells the river.

CAVING AND POTHOLING

This activity requires thorough training if participants wish to explore caves left in their natural state. However, several sites are accessible to amateurs on the condition that they are accompanied by instructors from potholing clubs. The necessary equipment is sophisticated: reinforced suit, rock-climbing equipment, inflatable dinghy, helmet, waterproof bag, carbide and halogen lamps.
Vercors Massif – This is one of the best areas for potholing: there are more than 1 500 caves or entrances marking the beginning of itineraries, often situated along hiking itineraries. It is therefore essential to remain cautious particularly when attempting an unplanned exploration.
The following sites offer the opportunity to spend a day discovering underground exploration: the Goule Blanche and Goule Noire, the Grotte de Bournillon, the Scialet de Malaterre (near Villard-de-Lans), the Trou qui souffle (dry cave) near Méaudre, the Grotte de la Cheminée and the Scialets d'Herbouvilly.
The **Grotte du Gournier** (above the Grotte de Choranche) is particularly

Useful Canyoning Terms

- **Bassin**: basin filled with water, deep enough to swim in; if no depth is indicated, it is less than 10m/6.2mi.

- **Chenal**: area where the water flows along a large "gutter" requiring a special technique to tackle it; a small gutter is called a **goulotte**.

- **Échappatoire**: exit making it possible to shorten the course.

- **Escalier de géant**: a succession of rocky ledges forming a flight of steps several metres high.

- **Durée parcours amont** (or **aval**): the estimated time to complete the course upstream (or downstream), allowing time to gain access + time to go through the canyon (upstream or downstream of the signs) + time to return on foot to the starting point.

- **Longueur de nage**: indicates the total distance that has to be swum.

- **Marmite**: hollow filled with water into which it is possible to jump (after checking the depth).

- **Vasque**: shallow basin.

good for supervised beginners; the passage allows them to practise a number of different techniques while moving horizontally through a fossil cave. The whole network covers a distance of 18km/11.2mi.

Savoie – There are more than 2 000 caves listed in the area; the temperature inside these caves remains constant throughout the year, around 4°C/39°F.

The highest chasms are situated in the Vanoise Massif, at Pralognan and Tignes (3 000m/9 843ft) whereas the Gouffre Jean-Bernard in Haute-Savoie holds the depth record (–1 600m/ 5 249ft).

- **Fédération française de Spéléologie**, 28 rue Delondine, 69002 Lyon ℘04 72 56 09 63; www.ffspeleo.fr.

- **Maison de l'aventure**, 26420 La Chapelle-en-Vercors ℘04 75 48 22 38; www.maison-aventure.com.

CYCLING AND MOUNTAIN BIKING

The Route des Grands Cols (Galibier, Croix de Fer, Iseran,La Madeleine, Granier) was made famous by the Tour de France. In summer many cycle and mountain-bike races take place throughout the region, in particular in the area around Vars, which plays host

to the "Six jours de Vars", an annual week-long cycling event.

Tourist offices have lists of establishments providing a rental service.

Mountain biking (VTT) is extremely popular as it can be practised almost anywhere, in particular along forest roads, mule tracks and cross-country skiing tracks; some ski areas open their lifts to mountain bikes, giving access to downhill ski trails.

Look for signs referring to VTT (*vélo tout-terrain*) or FCC (Fédération française de cyclisme) trails.

Some areas offer a choice of marked itineraries, such as Aussois, Bourg-St-Maurice, Parc naturel régional du Vercors, Val d'Allos, Serre-Ponçon/Durance, Pays du Buëch, Embrunais/Savinois, Champsaur, Val du Mercantour, Vallée de l'Ubaye, Digne-les-Bains/Pays Dignois, Verdon les Collines.

- **Fédération française de cyclisme**, 5 rue de Rome, 93561 Rosny-sous-Bois ℘01 49 35 69 00; www.ffc.fr.

- **Comités départemental de cyclotourisme**:
  Savoie – Maison des Sports, 90 rue Henri-Oreiller, 73000 Chambéry ℘04 79 85 09 09; http://www.comitesavoieffc.com.
  Haute-Savoie – H. Saccani, 10 chemin de la Fruitière, 74960

Meythet ℘04 50 22 16 76;
www.cyclisme-haute-savoie.com.
Isère – M. Costantini, 7 rue de
l'Industrie, 38327 Eybens ℘06 78
51 79 94; www.cyclo38ffct.org.
Alpes-de-Haute-Provence,
M. Manent, avenue Georges-
Pompidou, 04000 Digne-les-Bains
℘06 03 45 42 92;
www.ffcprovence.com.
Var, L'Hélianthe, rue Emile-Ollivier,
83000 Toulon; ℘04 94 36 04 09;
www.cyclotourisme83-ffct.org.

HIKING

Hiking is the best way to explore
mountain areas and discover
the finest scenery. Footpaths are
extensively described in this guide
and three types of hike are identified.
Rambles are, in principle, suitable
for anyone, including children.
Day hikes require more stamina
and some prior training for a walking
time exceeding four hours and a
vertical rise of 700m/2 297ft.
A few more demanding **itineraries
for experienced hikers** are also
described including extremely steep
or vertiginous sections, but which do
not, however, require any specialised
mountaineering knowledge; these
are worth the extra physical effort for
the exceptional panoramas. Before
leaving, always get the latest weather
forecast and make sure that the length
of the hike is compatible with the time
of departure. In mountain areas, the
estimated length of an excursion is
calculated according to the vertical
rise: 300m/984ft per hour going
up and 500m/1 640ft going down,
excluding stops.
Leave early in the morning if you can,
so that all the climbing can be done
during the cool hours of the morning
and you stand a better chance of
observing the fauna.
Whatever the type of hike, you should
carry a map on a scale of 1:25 000 or
1:50 000 or suitable GPS, 1.5–3 litres
of water per person, energy-building
food, a hat, waterproof clothing,
a pullover or fleece, sunglasses,

sunscreen, a first-aid kit and a plastic
bag for rubbish, which you must carry
down with you as it must not be left
at the refuges. You should also wear
mountain boots (and be prepared
to cross snow at high altitudes).
Take a pair of binoculars to observe
the wildlife.
Mountain-refuge bookings –
Refuges are now equipped with
radio-telephones (numbers available
at tourist offices) and booking is
compulsory during the summer
season. Anyone arriving without a
booking may not find a bed for
the night.
Long-distance footpaths (GR) –
Many footpaths waymarked in red
and white run through the Alps.
Booklets or "topo-guides" published
by the Fédération française de la
randonée pédestre give maps,
detailed itineraries, accommodation
information (refuges and lodges)
and useful advice.

♦ **GR 5** goes across the Alps from
Lake Geneva to Nice, following
the high Alps north to south, and
crossing other footpaths on its way.
♦ The **TMB** (Tour du Mont Blanc)
goes round the massif, entering
Switzerland and Italy.
Allow eight days.
♦ **GR 55** runs through the Parc
national de la Vanoise.
♦ **GR 54** "Tour de l'Oisans" goes
round the Parc national des Écrins
in the Oisans region.
♦ **GR 58** enables hikers to explore
the Queyras region (numerous
refuges and lodges) and can
connect with GR 54.
♦ **GR 56** goes through the
Ubaye region.
**Other footpaths run through
the Préalpes.**
♦ **GR 96** goes through the Chablais,
the Aravis and the Bauges massifs.
♦ **GR 9**, **91**, **93 and 95** criss-cross
the Vercors.
♦ **GR 93** continues across the
Dévoluy and **GR 94** runs through
the Buëch, Bochaine and
Baronnies regions.

- **GR 6** "Alpes-Océan" links the Ubaye and Forcalquier regions via Sisteron.
- **GR 946** runs from Serres to Sisteron, along a ridge above the Buëch Valley.
- **GR 97** connects Châtillon with Brantes.
- **GR 4** "Méditerranée-Océan" goes right through Haute-Provence via Entrevaux, Castellane, Moustiers-Ste-Marie, Riez and Gréoux-les-Bains.

There are also numerous local footpaths offering interesting hikes or linking main itineraries. Shorter routes, known as **Sentiers de Petite Randonnée**, or **PR**, are marked in yellow.

Useful addresses – Topo-guides are published by **La Fédération française de la randonnée pédestre** – 14 rue Riquet, 75019 Paris ☏01 44 89 93 93; www.ffrandonnee.fr.
A very comprehensive hiking guide is published by **Le Comité régional de tourisme Rhône-Alpes FFRP** – 3 hameau de St-Gras, rue de Joigny, 73490 La Ravoire ☏04 79 71 00 08; http://rhone-alpes.ffrandonnee.fr.
In the Alps, contact **L'Association de randonnée en Savoie**, 4 rue du Château, 73000 Chambéry ☏04 79 75 02 01; for the Alpes-de-Haute-Provence region, contact the **Association départementale des Relais et Itinéraires** (ADRI), 19 rue du Docteur-Honnorat, 04000 Digne-les-Bains ☏04 92 31 07 01; www.alpes-haute-provence.com. For a map of shelters, contact the **Comité départemental de randonnée pédestre des Hautes-Alpes**, 12 rue Faure-du-Serre, 05000 Gap ☏04 92 53 65 11; www.ffrandonnee05.net.

IN THE AIR

Brightly coloured paragliders flying slowly and silently over the valleys are a common sight in the French Alps, as thermal updrafts and strong air currents typical of mountainous terrain provide a remarkable site for unpowered flight. Many summer resorts with easy access to nearby summits offer opportunities for paragliding, as well as hang gliding and "kiting". Even old-fashioned kite flying has taken on new popularity as enthusiasts compete with acrobatic, combat and racing kites.

Annecy and the Aravis resorts; Les Saisies and Signal de Bisanne in the Beaufortain; L'Alpe-d'Huez in Oisans; and St-Hilaire on the edge of the Chartreuse Massif are among the most renowned paragliding locations. **Chamonix** still remains one of the main centres, although access to the slopes of Mont Blanc is restricted in July and August (*École de parapente de Chamonix; www. summits.fr/chamonix-paragliding. html*). The **Vercors** is also a favourite area, as its many well-oriented valleys allow a gentle introduction to the sport. Two remarkable sites are worth mentioning: Cornafion, near Villard-de-Lans (500m/1 640ft flights, access forbidden in May and June for the protection of the fauna); and Le Moucherotte (landing in Lans-en-Vercors). Further south, Haute-Provence also has several ideal spots.

Paragliding – This descendant of parachuting has spread to winter-sports resorts for both summer and winter, when paraglider pilots use skis. It has seen an enormous surge in popularity as the paraglider is both cheaper and easier to transport than the hang glider, and the training is faster and cheaper too.

Hang gliding (deltaplane) – A semi-rigid wing carries the pilot, who hangs in a frame and, using his or her body, directs flight by moving the centre of gravity relative to the aerodynamic centre of the wing.

Kiting – Riders skim across water, snow or land attached to a large kite.

To learn the various forms of unpowered flight, it is highly recommended to take one of the many courses offered by schools under the aegis of the Fédération

Mountaineers on the Glacier Jean Gauthier, Parc national des Écrins

© Pierre Jacques/hemis.fr

française de vol libre (FFVL),
(☙*see below for the address*).
A training course of about a week will give you the necessary skills as well as a knowledge of weather necessary to understand appropriate flying conditions. Then you apprentice during a series of 20 flights radio-guided by an instructor on the ground.
Useful addresses: **Le Comité régional de tourisme** publishes a brochure *Parapente*, listing 21 sites: Rhône-Alpes Tourisme (☙*see Tourist Offices*).

♦ **Fédération française de vol libre**, 4 rue de Suisse, 06000 Nice ✆04 97 03 82 82; www.ffvl.fr.

♦ **Fédération française de planeur ultra-léger motorisé**, 96 bis rue Marc Sangnier, 94704 Maisons-Alfort Cedex ✆01 49 81 74 43; www.ffplum.com.

MOUNTAINEERING

The Alps are one of the major mountaineering regions of the world. The sport, which is increasingly popular, requires **good physical condition** and **appropriate equipment**. ♿ It is essential to be accompanied by a qualified mountain guide for any expedition, even a minor one.
The best mountaineering terrain is found in the Mont Blanc, Écrins and Vanoise massifs. Nearby resorts serve as the base for expeditions: Chamonix-Mont-Blanc, St-Gervais-les-Bains, Pralognan-la-Vanoise, Bourg-d'Oisans and St-Christophe (La Bérarde) and La Grave.
Discuss frankly with your guide your level of skill and your preferences (ice climbing, rocks, frozen waterfalls, etc.). You should be aware that your guide is engaged to provide the means to climb, not the result. In other words, guides do all they can to ensure your safety, but they have no obligation to get you to the summit if they judge your abilities insufficient, or the weather conditions unfavourable.
☙*See Mountain Safety p50.*
The official French alpine club is

♦ **Le Club alpin français** – 24 rue de Laumière, 75019 Paris ✆01 53 72 87 00; www.ffcam.fr.

Rock-Climbing

There are an infinite variety of sites and of rock types in the Alps and thus many ideal rock-climbing centres. In the Maurienne region, **Aussois** is the most celebrated and has welcomed several international climbing Open competitions. The cliffs of **Presles** offer the best variety of climbing routes and of canyons in the Vercors range. The cliffs of the **Haute Ubaye**, the sheer rock faces of **Verdon** (notably the cliff at L'Escales) and

Climbing the cliffs of the Grand Canyon du Verdon

© Romain Cintrac/hemis.fr

the abrupt steps of the **Préalpes de Digne**, the sandstone of **Annot** and the rock spurs of **Les Baronnies** (Orpierre) are justly renowned.

Via ferrata – *Via ferrata* climbing, which is a cross between mountaineering and hiking, has become increasingly popular in the past few years.

These rock-climbing courses (you pay a fee to use them) fitted with metal rungs and cables originated in the Dolomites during World War I; they were planned by the Italian army and only discovered by the public in the 1950s. The first *via ferrata* courses were set up in the Briançon region at the beginning of the 1980s. It is imperative that inexperienced climbers are accompanied by a guide or join a group. The routes offer

varying levels of difficulty, but many are not suitable for children, or those with low endurance or susceptibility to altitude sickness or vertigo.

Notable Via Ferrata
At Chamonix, the *via ferrata* of the **Balcon de la Mer de Glace** Glacier is for experienced climbers. In Savoie, you can climb a portion or the whole length of the longest route in France, at **Aussois-La Norma** (3 460m/ 11 352ft). You will find easier routes charging lower fees in **Isère**.

In Grenoble, the **Prise de la Bastille** route offers a spectacular view over the city. In the southern Alps, well-known *via ferrata* are found at Sisteron (the route from **Grande Fistoire to la Motte-du-Caire**), in the L'Argentière-la-Bessée region (**Vignaux** and **Les gorges de la Durance**), at Briançon (La **Croix de Toulouse**), at **Freisnières** and at Serre-Chevalier (**l'aiguillette du Lauzet**).

RIDING

There are many horseriding centres throughout Savoie, Dauphiné and Haute-Provence and numerous touring itineraries – from one-day treks to week-long excursions – identified along the way by orange markings. In addition, tours for beginners and experienced riders are organised by the *associations régionales de tourisme équestre* (ARTE). **Le Comité national de Tourisme équestre** (9 boulevard Macdonald, 75019 Paris ℘01 53 26 15 50;

Hiking with a Pack Donkey

Rest your shoulders for a while and hire a real beast of burden for a day or up to a week. This extra member of the family can carry a 40kg/88-pound pack and trots along willingly at a pace of 4km/h (2.5mph), whatever the terrain. Farms providing the animals, the equipment and the necessary information for a successful tour can be found in Thorens-Glières, Les Carroz, St-Sigismond, St-Martin-en-Vercors, St-Martin-le-Vinoux, Guillaumes, Seyne-les-Alpes and Val-des-Près. A national donkey association, based in Digne-les-Bains, runs a website, available in English, with links to donkey enthusiasts throughout France.

Fédération nationale "âne et randonnées", *13 montée St-Lazare, 04000 Digne-les-Bains* ℘04 92 34 23 11; www.ane-et-rando.com.

www.ffe.com) publishes a brochure, updated annually, called *Cheval nature*, which lists programmes for equestrian tourists as well as lodgings.

WHITE-WATER SPORTS

White-water sports are ever popular in the Alps, which offer a dense network of rivers and streams, pleasant summer temperatures and many outdoor leisure parks, ideal for newcomers or families to try out these activities. Several of these parks are described in the green Address Books in the Discovery section. In every area, the Comité Départemental du Tourisme (⚘ *see Tourist Offices*) has a list of organisations providing group activities.

All participants in white-water sports must be in top physical condition, strong swimmers, and wearing a buoyancy aid and helmet.

Rafting – This is the easiest of all the white-water sports because it is guided and requires no previous experience. It consists of descending turbulent rivers in groups of six or more persons, aboard inflatable rubber rafts manoeuvred with paddles and controlled from the rear by a guide. The technique is simple and team spirit is the key to success. The level of difficulty is graded from I to VI (easy to virtually impossible).

The Alps are the ideal area for rafting, preferably during the thaw (April to June) and in summer along rivers which maintain a constant flow. Among the rivers particularly suitable for rafting are the upper Isère (between Bourg-St-Maurice and Centron, grade III), the Doron de Bozel in the Vanoise region (between Brides-les-Bains and Moûtiers, grades IV and V), the Giffre and the Dranses de Savoie. The lower Ubaye is a popular rafting river, as are many of the rivers of the Durance basin.

Hydrospeed – A sport similar to bodyboarding down mountain streams. Participants propel themselves with flippers, wear a wetsuit, and lie on a tough streamlined float, called a "hydrospeed".

Canoeing and kayaking – Canoes, originally from North America, are manoeuvred with a single paddle. They are ideal for family trips along rivers. In kayaks, paddlers use a double-bladed paddle and a spraydeck (jupe) covering the cockpit. There are canoeing-kayaking schools in white-water sports centres throughout the Alps and touring takes place on the lakes and the lower courses of most rivers, particularly the the Giffre, the Chéran, the Arly, the Doron de Bozel, the Guiers Vif et Mort,

Rafting in the Guil gorges, the Queyras

© Franck Guiziou/hemis.fr

the Isère (Les Arcs), the Ubaye and the Verdon, and also on the Clarée, the Guisane, the Gyronde, the Biaisse, the Durance, the Guil, the Buëch, the Méouge, the Drac, the Souloise and the Séveraisse.

The **Fédération française de canoë-kayak** publishes an annual guide called *France canoë-kayak et sports d'eaux-vives* as well as a map, *Les Rivières de France*, of all suitable rivers: 87 quai de la Marne, BP 48, 94344 Joinville-le-Pont ℘01 1 45 11 08 50; www.ffck.org.

ACTIVITIES FOR KIDS 👥

Throughout this guide, sights of particular interest to children are indicated with a 👥 symbol. There are many family-oriented resorts in the Alps offering specific activities for children during school holidays.

"**Famille Plus Montagne**" resorts pay particular attention to the welcome they extend to families and children, and provide especially adapted facilities and activities. For more information and a list of resorts see www.familleplus.fr.

SHOPPING

Woodcarving and painting – In the south, the **Queyras** is undoubtedly the most famous of alpine regions for the skill of its woodcarvers.

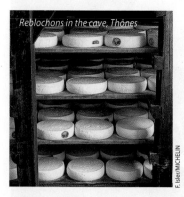
Reblochons in the cave, Thônes

F. Isler/MICHELIN

The Maison de l'Artisanat, 05350 Ville-Vieille ℘04 92 46 72 76; www.meubles-queyras.com has a fine selection of wooden objects as well as other handicraft samples. In the north, the **Bauges** is known for its carved bowls turned from maple. Wood painting is the speciality of the **Chartreuse** region, in the area of Entremont-le-Vieux.

Earthenware and santons – These are the speciality of the **Alpes-de-Haute-Provence** region. **Faïences de Moustiers** are world famous, but there are other earthenware workshops in Barcelonnette, Reillanne and St-Michel-l'Observatoire. Fine pottery is manufactured in the nearby towns of Forcalquier and Castellane.

Santons (human and animal figures which make up a Provençal Christmas crib) are handmade and painted in Gréoux-les-Bains, Champtercier and Manosque.

Cheeses – Cheese lovers should make time for a visit to a Savoyard dairy like the one in **St-François-de-Longchamp**, where it is possible to watch beaufort – the "prince of gruyère cheeses" – being made in high-pasture chalets at the **Col de la Madeleine**. Among the other varieties to bear the Appellation d'Origine Contrôlée (AOC) are **abondance** from the Val d'Abondance, **tomme de savoie**, **bleu de termignon** and **reblochon** from the Aravis. This last is also one of the main ingredients of Savoie's most famous dish, tartiflette, a rich potato dish baked with onions, crème fraîche and bacon.

Wines – Wines can be purchased directly from the producers in many areas *(for details about wine styles see p64).*

The **Maison de la Vigne et du Vin** in Apremont near Chambéry in Savoie has an *oenotheque* (wine shop), ℘04 79 33 44 16; www.vindesavoie.net. Wine tastings are offered and purchases can be made at cellar door prices; the centre also provides information of producers to visit.

In the south, Die is known for its delicate semi-sweet sparkling Clairette de Die, made from a blend of Clairette and Muscat grapes, and available to buy at the large wine cooperative near the town and from smaller growers close by. A brut is also sold.

There are many scattered vineyards throughout Provence including **Coteaux de Pierrevert** AOC.

From the north come powerful herbal liqueurs like chartreuse (in yellow, green or other styles), Cherry-Rocher and aperitifs such as chambéryzette and vermouth. All over the Alps you will find the green-coloured génépi.

Olive oil – The western section of the Alpes-de-Haute-Provence is particularly known for its olive oil with mills selling oil at Oraison (moulin Paschetta) and Peyruis (moulin Mardaric). There is also quality oil from the Baronnies.

Honey – The Haute-Provence region produces large quantities of honey *(miel)* from a variety of plants; lavender honey comes essentially from the Alpes-de-Haute-Provence *département*. Honey from Savoie is produced between July and September; Vercors honey comes from around the regional park. There are two official seals of origin, namely *miel de lavande* and *miel toutes fleurs de Provence*.

Also look out for **croquants de Queyras**, little crunchy honey and almond cakes, and **confiture de genièvre**, a juniper conserve sold in the markets of the Ubaye.
 Other treats include **biscuits de Savoie**, **rissoles aux poires** (pastry filled with pears), pralines known as **cloches** or **roseaux d'Annecy** and **sabayon**, a sweet egg cream which takes its name and inspiration from the Italian *zabaglione*.

BOOKS

100 Hut Walks in the Alps – Kev Reynolds

Another Long Day on the Piste: A Season in the French Alps – Will Randall

Cycling in the French Alps – Paul Henderson

The Écrins National Park (French Alps): A Walking Guide – Kev Reynolds

Freeheel Skiing: Telemark and Parallel Technique – Paul Parker

The GR5 Trail – Paddy Dillon

How the English Made the Alps – Jim Ring

The Man Who Planted Trees – Jean Giono

Queyras Tour GR58 – Alan Castle

Savage Snows: The Story of Mont Blanc – Walt Unsworth

Summits for All: The French Alps – Edouard Prevost

Walking in the Haute Savoie – Janette Norton

FILMS

There are many extreme ski and mountaineering films shot in the French Alps, especially in the Chamonix Massif. One feature-length films stands out:

The Edge of Never (2009) – The exciting, true story of a 15-year-old who returns to ski on the extreme slope in Chamonix where his father died.

There are few other feature-length films from the French Alps. The following may be of interest:

Jean de Florette and Manon des Sources (1986) – Two films, one set about 15 years after the other, tell a wonderful story full of period and regional detail; set in Provence in the early 20C.

Malabar Princess (2006) – A French film shot in Mont Blanc, it relates the story of a young boy who finds the wreckage of the Air India plane that crashed in 1950.

Napoleon and Me (2006) – The emperor (Daniel Auteuil) plots his return from Elba.

Calendar of Events

JANUARY
Valloire – International ice-sculpture competition 📞04 79 59 03 96

MARCH
Courchevel – Les Musicîmes, chamber music 📞04 79 08 00 29
Grenoble – Spring Fair 📞04 76 39 66 00; www.alpexpo.com
St-Gervais – International humour festival 📞04 50 47 76 08

APRIL–MAY
Avoriaz – Festival Jazz d'up Avoriaz 📞04 50 74 02 11
Évian-les-Bains – Escales Musicales, classical music festival 📞04 50 26 85 00; www.royalparcevian.com
Orcières – Jazz festival 📞04 92 55 89 89; www.orcieres.com

JUNE
Annecy – Animated Film Festival 📞04 50 10 09 00; www.annecy.org
Chambéry – Estivales du Château des ducs: music, dance, theatre, sculpture 📞04 79 70 63 55

Escales Musicales, Évian-les-Bains

Olivier Chambion/Evian Resort

JULY
Aix-les-Bains – Festival Musilac, international pop festival 📞04 79 88 09 99; www.musilac.com
Annecy – Les Noctibules, festival of street arts 📞04 50 33 44 00
Les Arcs – International folklore festival 📞04 79 17 12 57
Barcelonnette – Jazz festival 📞04 92 81 04 71; www.barcelonnette.com
Le Bourget-du-Lac – Fireworks and medieval festival 📞04 79 25 01 99; www.bourgetdulac.com
Les Gets – Festival of mechanical music (even-numbered years); Festival of wood (odd-numbered years) 📞04 50 79 85 75
La Grave – Festival of the Music of Messiaen 📞04 76 79 90 05; www.festival-messiaen.com
Serres – Jazz festival 📞04 92 67 01 04; www.festivaldejazzdeserres.com

JULY–AUGUST
Albertville – Festival de rencontres musicales de Savoie 📞04 79 06 06 60
Combloux – Musical Hours (Mondays) 📞04 50 58 60 49; www.combloux.com
Cordon – Festival of Baroque music (over eight days the first two weeks of month) 📞04 50 58 01 57; www.cordon.fr
St-Disdier-en-Dévoluy – Classical and traditional music 📞04 92 58 91 91; www.musiqueendevoluy.fr
Sisteron – Nights of the Citadel 📞04 92 67 06 00; www.nuitsdelacitadelle.fr

AUGUST
Aix-les-Bains – NavigAix' gathering of vintage boats on the lake 📞04 79 88 68 00; www.aixlesbains.com
Barcelonnette – Latin American and Mexican festival 📞04 92 81 04 71; www.barcelonnette.com
Briançon – Chamber Music Festival 📞04 92 21 08 50; www.festival-musique-briancon.com

Festival of transhumance, Riez

Bureau du Tourisme de Riez

Colmars – Medieval Festival
📞04 92 83 41 92;
www.colmars-les-alpes.fr

La Côte-St-André – Hector Berlioz
music festival 📞04 74 20 61 43;
www.festivalberlioz.com

Le Grand-Bornand – European
festival of children's theatre
📞04 50 02 78 00; www.
aubonheurdesmomes.com

Orcières – Festival of the mountains
with traditional music 📞04 92 55
89 89; www.orcieres.com

Simiane-la-Rotonde
Festival of Ancient Music
📞04 92 75 90 14;
www.festival-simiane.com

SEPTEMBER

Aix-les-Bains – Festival des nuits
romantiques, classical music
📞04 79 88 68 00

Gréaux-les-Bains – Classical singing
"Les Courants d'airs" (1st week of
month); events also at Manosque
and Valensole 📞04 92 78 01 08

Moustier-Ste-Marie
Festival of the "Diane", traditional
Provençal musical groups
📞04 92 74 67 84

OCTOBER

Chambéry – Festival of comic books
📞04 79 33 95 89;
www.chamberybd.fr

TRADITIONAL FESTIVALS AND FAIRS

JANUARY–MARCH

Abriès – Winter carnival
📞04 92 46 72 26

Annecy – Venetian carnival
📞04 50 33 44 00

Ceillac – Festival of Queyras traditions
📞04 92 45 05 74;
www.queyras.com

Many resorts hold a carnival during
the Lent week.

JUNE

Riez – Festival of alpine pastoral
traditions *(transhumance)*
📞04 92 77 99 09; www.ville-riez.fr

JULY

Les Arcs/Bourg-St-Maurice –
International folklore
festival of the Haute Tarentaise
📞04 79 07 12 57

Briançon – Grand Escarton crafts and
medieval fair 📞04 92 21 08 50

Forcalquier – Potters' fair
📞04 92 77 00 61

15 AUGUST

Bramans – Traditional 15 August
celebration 📞04 79 05 03 45

Chamonix – Festival of guides (sound
and light show 14 August, blessing
of ropes and ice-axes 15 August)
📞04 50 53 00 88

Les Contamines-Montjoie –
Pilgrimage to Notre-Dame de
la Gorge (sound and light show
in evening)
La Grave – Festival of guides, Mass
and blessing of the mountain
☏04 76 79 90 21
Peisey-Nancroix – Festival of
traditional costumes
☏04 79 07 94 28;
www.peisey-vallandry.com
Tignes – Festival of the lake
☏04 79 40 25 80; www.tignes.net

AUGUST
Annecy – Fête du Lac
☏04 50 33 44 00
Castellane – Crafts fair
☏04 92 83 61 14
Châtel – Festival of alpine pastures
☏04 50 73 22 44
La Clusaz – Reblochon cheese
festival. ☏04 50 32 65 00;
www.laclusaz.com
Cruis – Pottery fair (1st Sunday of
month) ☏04 92 77 00 61
Digne-les-Bains – Parade of lavender
floats ☏04 92 36 62 62; Lavender
Festival ☏04 92 31 05 20
Flumet – Mule fair (1st Tuesday of
month) ☏04 79 31 61 08;
www.flumet-montblanc.com
La Rosière-Montvalezan, **Séez**
St-Bernard – Traditional festival of
shepherds (3rd Sunday of month)

☏04 79 41 00 15;
www.seezsaintbernard.com
St-Gervais – Festival of guides
☏04 50 47 76 08
Ugine – Festival of the mountains
☏04 79 37 56 33

SEPTEMBER–OCTOBER
Beaufort – Salon of French
gastronomic products
☏04 79 38 15 33;
www.areches-beaufort.com
Moustiers-Ste-Marie – Fête de Diane
(31 August–8 September)
☏04 92 74 67 84
Sisteron – Regional fair (lasts 4 days)

NOVEMBER–DECEMBER
Chambéry – Saveurs et terroirs:
market of gourmet products
☏04 79 33 42 47
Champtercier – Fair of Santons
☏04 92 31 10 37; www.foire
santonschamptercier.com

SPORTING EVENTS
JANUARY
Autrans – La Foulée blanche (the
white rush) cross-country ski
competition ☏04 76 95 37 37;
www.lafouleeblanche.com
Bessans – International marathon
of cross-country skiing
☏04 79 05 96 52;
www.marathondebessans.com

La Foulée Blanche, Autrans

Sylvie Chappaz/La Foulée Blanche

Transmaurienne, St-Jean-de-Maurienne

Ludovic Valentin Organisation

Chamonix – Le Kandahar downhill ski race ☎04 50 53 00 24; www.chamonixworldcup.com

Megève – International competition of polo on snow ☎04 50 21 27 28; www.megeve.com

Serre-Chevalier – Trail Blanc, running race on snow ☎04 92 24 98 98

FEBRUARY

Arêches-Beaufort – La Pierre Menta, extreme ski-touring race ☎04 79 38 15 33; www.pierrementa.com

MARCH

Villard de Lans – Traversée du Vercors cross-country ski race ☎06 17 08 82 83; www.transvercors.com

APRIL

La Clusaz – Défi Foly, madcap competition on a mountain lake ☎04 50 32 65 00

JUNE

Embrun – Rafting on the Durance river ☎04 92 43 72 72

Les Gets, **Morzine**, **Chatel** – La Pass'Portes, meeting of mountain bikes ☎04 50 75 80 80

JULY

Évian – Évian Masters Ladies golf tournament ☎04 92 43 72 72

AUGUST

Chamonix – Ultra Trail Tour du Mont Blanc, running race ☎04 50 53 00 24; www.chamonix.com

Courchevel – World cup of summer ski-jumping ☎04 79 08 00 29

St-Jean-de-Maurienne – Trans'Maurienne, mountain-bike competition ☎04 50 23 19 58; www.transmaurienne.com

SEPTEMBER

Vercors – Transvercors, crossing the massif on mountain bikes ☎06 17 08 82 83; www.transvercors.com

DECEMBER

Pays du Mont-Blanc – International ice-hockey competition ☎04 50 47 08 08

Val Thorens – Andros Trophy, snow and ice-driving competitions ☎04 79 00 08 08; www.valthorens.com

Val Thorens – Boarderweek, international snowboarding competition and concerts ☎04 79 00 08 08

Know Before You Go

USEFUL WEBSITES

www.franceguide.com
The French Government Tourist Office site has practical information and links to more specific guidance, for American or Canadian travellers, for example. The site includes information on everything you need to know about visiting France.

www.visiteurope.com
The European Travel Commission provides useful information on travelling in 30 European countries, and includes links to commercial services, rail schedules, weather reports, etc.

www.holidayfrance.org.uk
The Association of British Travel Organisers to France has created this tidy site which covers just about everything.

www.ambafrance-uk.org
www.ambafrance-us.org
The websites for the French Embassy in the UK and the USA provide a wealth of information and links to other French sites (regions, cities, ministries).

www.skiinfo.co.uk
Select France from the map of Europe on the right-hand start to take you to the right section of this huge skiing information portal. You will find details of hundreds of ski resorts and useful information on all snow sports and other activities.

www.rhonealpes-tourisme.com
The Rhône-Alpes regional tourist office website includes information for Haute- Savoie, Savoie and Isère *départements*, and links for planning your trip to the northern Alps.

www.discover-southoffrance.com
The Provence-Alpes-Côte d'Azur regional tourist office website is the information portal for the southern Alps covering all the *départements* south of Isère.

TOURIST OFFICES
ABROAD

For information, brochures, maps and assistance in planning a trip to France you should apply to the French Tourist Office in your own country:

♦ **Australia – New Zealand**
Maison de la France (Australia and New Zealand), Level 13, 25 Bligh Street 2000 NSW, Sydney, Australia ☎+61 (0)2 9231 5244; http://au.franceguide.com.

♦ **Canada**
1800 Avenue McGill College, Suite 1010, Montreal H3A 3J6 ☎(514) 288-2026; http://ca.franceguide.com.

♦ **Eire**
No office ☎+15 60 235 235 (Irish information line); http://ie.franceguide.com.

♦ **South Africa**
3rd floor, Village Walk, Office Tower, cnr Maude and Rivonia, Sandton ☎+27 (0) 11 523 82 92; http://za.franceguide.com.

♦ **United Kingdom**
Lincoln House, 300 High Holborn, London WC1V 7JH ☎09068 244 123; http://uk.franceguide.com.

♦ **United States**
http://us.franceguide.com.
New York – 825 Third Avenue, 29th floor (entrance on 50th Street), New York, NY 10022 ☎1 (514) 288 1904.
Chicago – Consulate General of France, 205 North Michigan Avenue, Suite 3770, Chicago, IL 60601 ☎1 (312) 327 0290.
Los Angeles – 9454 Wilshire Boulevard, Suite 210, Los Angeles, CA 90212 ☎1 (310) 271 6665.

IN FRANCE

Visitors will find information through the network of tourist offices in France. The addresses and telephone numbers of local tourist offices, called *syndicats d'initiative* in smaller

towns, are listed after the symbol
🔲 in the introductions to individual
sights. Regional tourist offices
(covering several *départements*) and
départements covered in this guide
are listed here:

Regional: Comité Régional du
Tourisme (CRT)

Departmental: Comité
Départemental du Tourisme (CDT)

- ◆ **Rhône-Alpes** (CRT) – 104 route
  de Paris, 69260 Charbonnières-les-
  Bains 𝒞04 72 59 21 59;
  www.rhone-alpes-tourisme.com.
- ◆ **Drôme** (CDT) – 8 rue Baudin,
  26005 Valence 𝒞04 75 82 19 26;
  www.drometourism.com.
- ◆ **Isère** (CDT) – 14 rue de la
  République, 38019 Grenoble
  𝒞04 76 54 34 36;
  www.isere-tourisme.com.
- ◆ **Savoie Mont-Blanc Tourisme**
  (CDT) – 24 boulevard de la
  Colonne, 73025 Chambéry
  𝒞04 50 23 96 00;
  www.savoie-mont-blanc.com.
- ◆ **Provence-Alpes-Côte d'Azur**
  (CRT) – Les Docks, 10 place de la
  Joliette, 13567 Marseille 𝒞04 91
  56 47 00; www.discover-southof
  france.com.
- ◆ **Alpes-de-Haute-Provence** (CDT)
  – Immeuble François-Mitterrand,
  04005 Digne-les-Bains
  𝒞04 92 31 57 29;
  www.alpes-haute-provence.com.
- ◆ **Hautes-Alpes** (CDT) – 8 bis rue
  Capitaine-de-Bresson,
  05002 Gap 𝒞0 810 10 11 11;
  www.hautes-alpes.net.
- ◆ **Var** (CDT) – 1 boulevard Foch,
  83003 Draguignan 𝒞04 94 50
  55 50; www.visitvar.fr.

INTERNATIONAL VISITORS
EMBASSIES

Australia
4 rue Jean-Rey, 75724 Paris
𝒞01 40 59 33 00;
www.france.embassy.gov.au.

Canada
35 avenue Montaigne,
75008 Paris 𝒞01 44 43 29 00;
www.amb-canada.fr.

Eire
4 rue Rude, 75116 Paris
𝒞01 44 17 67 00;
www.embassyofireland.fr.

New Zealand
7 ter rue Léonard-de-Vinci,
75116 Paris 𝒞01 45 01 43 44;
www.nzembassy.com.

South Africa
59 quai d'Orsay, 75343 Paris
𝒞01 53 59 23 23;
www.afriquesud.net.

UK
35 rue du Faubourg St-Honoré,
75383 Paris 𝒞01 44 51 31 00;
www.britishembassy.gov.uk.
UK Consulates: 24 rue Childebert,
69002 Lyon 𝒞04 72 77 81 70;
24 avenue du Prado, 13006
Marseille 𝒞04 91 15 72 10.

USA
2 avenue Gabriel, 75382 Paris
𝒞01 43 12 22 22; www.amb-usa.fr.
USA Consulates: 1 quai Jules
Courmont, 69002 Lyon 𝒞04 78
38 36 88; Place Varian Fry, 13286
Marseille 𝒞04 91 54 92 00.

DOCUMENTS

Passport – Nationals of countries
within the European Union entering
France need only a national identity
card (or in the case of the British, a
passport). Nationals of other countries
must have a valid national passport.

Visa – No **entry visa** is required for
Canadian, US or Australian citizens
travelling as tourists and staying less
than 90 days, except for students
planning to study in France. If in doubt,
apply to your local French consulate.
General passport information is
available by phone to US citizens toll-
free from the **Federal Information
Center**, 𝒞800-688-9889. US passport
application forms can be downloaded
from http://travel.state.gov.

CUSTOMS

In Britain, go to the Customs Office
(UK) website at www.hmrc.gov.
uk for information on allowances,
travel safety tips, and to consult and
download documents and guides.

SPIRITS (whisky, gin, vodka, etc)	10l
FORTIFIED WINES (vermouth, port, etc.)	20l
WINE (not more than 60l sparkling)	90l
BEER	110l
CIGARETTES	3 200
TOBACCO PRODUCTS (other than cigarettes)	3kg
CIGARS	200
SMOKING TOBACCO	3kg

Persons living in a Member State of the European Union are not restricted in regard to goods for private use; recommended allowances for alcohol and tobacco are shown in the table – see website for more details.

The **US Customs Service** offers a publication *Know Before You Go* for US citizens, to consult and download at www.customs.ustreas.gov (click on Travel).

Australians will find customs information at www.customs.gov.au; for **New Zealanders** Advice for Travellers is at www.customs.govt.nz.

HEALTH

First aid, medical advice and chemists' night service rota are available from chemists/drugstores *(pharmacies)* identified by the green cross sign. You should take out comprehensive insurance coverage as the recipient of medical treatment in French hospitals or clinics must pay.

Nationals of non-EU countries should check with their insurance companies about policy limitations. All prescription drugs must be labelled; it is essential that you carry the prescription.

British and Irish citizens (and all EU citizens) should apply for a European Health Insurance Card (EHIC), which has replaced the E111 and entitles the holder to treatment for accident or unexpected illness in EU countries.

British citizens apply online at www.dh.gov.uk/travellers, or call ℘0845 606 2030, or pick up an application at a post office.

Irish citizens should consult www.ehic.ie.

Americans and Canadians can contact the International Association for Medical Assistance to Travelers: ℘for the USA (716) 754-4883 or for Canada (416) 652-0137 or (519) 836-0102; www.iamat.org.

The **American Hospital of Paris** is open 24hr for medical and dental emergencies as well as consultations, with English-speaking staff, at 63 boulevard Victor-Hugo, 92200 Neuilly sur Seine ℘01 46 41 25 25; www.american-hospital.org.

The **Hertford British Hospital** is just outside Paris at 3 rue Barbès, 92300 Levallois-Perret ℘01 46 39 22 22; www.british-hospital.org.

ACCESSIBILITY

Sights described in this guide that are easily accessible to people of reduced mobility are indicated in the *Admission times and charges* by the symbol ♿. Since 2001, the designation **Tourisme et Handicap** has applied to a thousand sites accessible to the disabled: go to **www.france guide.com**.

The principal French source for information on facilities is the **Association des Paralysés de France**; www.apf.asso.fr.

The **Michelin Guide France** and the **Michelin Camping Caravanning France** indicate hotels and campsites with facilities suitable for the disabled. The **French railways** (SNCF) (www.voyages-sncf.com), **Air France** (www.airfrance.fr) and major ski resorts, through **Handi-Ski** (found at www.esf.net), offer facilities for the disabled. The French federation for **Handisport** has a website at www.handisport.org.

Getting There and Getting Around

BY PLANE

Various national and independent airlines operate services to Paris (Roissy-Charles-de-Gaulle and Orly airports).

Major companies offering regularly scheduled flights from the UK and the USA to one of the key gateway airports (Geneva, Lyon-St-Exupéry, Chambéry and Grenoble) include Air France, Swiss, American Airlines, Delta and British Airways.

Budget flights within Europe offer wide choice, but conditions change often, so check the websites. These include:

*   **Ryanair** www.ryanair.com;
*   **Easyjet** www.easyjet.com;
*   **Flybe** www.flybe.com;
*   **Jet2.com** www.jet2.com.

Within France, air travel generally compares unfavourably with rail, for both price and time, especially when you consider transport to and from airports.

AIR TRAVEL FOR DISABLED PASSENGERS

Air France offers "Saphir" services for disabled passengers ℹ08 20 01 24 24; www.airfrance.fr.

BY FERRY

There are numerous **cross-Channel passenger and car** ferry services from the United Kingdom and Ireland. To choose the most suitable route between your port of arrival and your destination use the Michelin Tourist and Motoring Atlas France, Michelin Map 911 (which gives travel times and mileages) or Michelin maps from the 1:200 000 series (yellow cover).

*   **P & O Ferries**
    Channel House, Channel View Road, Dover, Kent CT17 9TJ
    ℹ08716 645 645 (in the UK)

or 0825 120 156 (0.15€/min) (in France); www.poferries.com. Service between Dover and Calais.

*   **Norfolk Line**
    Norfolk House, Eastern Docks, Dover, Kent CT16 1JA ℹ870 870 10 20 (in the UK) or 03 28 59 01 01 (in France); www.norfolkline-ferries.com. Service between Dover and Dunkerque.

*   **Brittany Ferries**
    Millbay Docks, Plymouth, Devon PL1 3EW ℹ0870 9 076 103 (in the UK) or 825 828 828 (in France); www.brittany-ferries.com. Service between Portsmouth, Poole and Plymouth and ports in France and Spain.

*   **Irish Ferries**
    PO Box 19, Alexandra Road, Dublin 1 ℹ8705 17 17 17 (in the UK), 00 353 818 300 400 (Northern Ireland) or 0818 300 400 (Republic of Ireland); www.irishferries.com. Service between Dublin and Rosslane and Roscoff and Cherbourg.

*   **Seafrance Ferrries Ltd**
    Whitfield Court, Honeywood Close, Whitfield, Kent CT16 3PX ℹ0870 443 1653; www.seafrance.com. Service between Dover and Calais.

*   **www.ferries.co.uk**
    Online ferry booking through 12 companies as well as accommodation, travel insurance, coverage for vehicle breakdowns ℹ0871 222 3312.

BY RAIL

Eurotunnel operates a 35-minute rail trip for passengers with a car through the Channel Tunnel between Folkestone and Calais ℹ08705 35 35 35 (in the UK) or 08 10 63 03 04 (in France); www.eurotunnel.com. The **Eurostar Group**, composed of British, French and Belgian railways, operates a 3-hour passenger service between **London** (St Pancras International Station) and **Paris** (Gare du Nord), with up to 16 trains daily taking 2 hours 15 minutes.

Eurostar passengers can connect to the high-speed TGV train at either Lille or Paris. The TGV, speeding at up to 297km/h (185mph), travels from Paris to Albertville in approximately 4 hours (3 hours 40 minutes in winter), to Annecy in 3 hours 45 minutes, to Chambéry in 3 hours, to Grenoble in 3 hours, to Thonon-les-Bains in 4 hours 30 minutes, to Moutiers in 4 hours. From Lille, add one hour. From Lille and Paris, there are direct TGV connections to Bourg-St-Maurice and St-Jean-de-Maurienne.

For French railways (SNCF) reservations and information; **www.voyages-sncf.com**. Regional trains, called TER, and SNCF buses link the whole region in an efficient network. However, you will often have to transfer between lines if you want to go from the Tarentaise to the Maurienne regions, or to Faucigny. During the winter, special ski trains leave from St Pancras on Friday evening, and Saturday and Sunday mornings, direct to Moûtiers, Aime la Plagne and Bourg-St-Maurice, serving the Tarentaise resorts, to which you can transfer by bus: www.altibus.com. In summer, direct Eurostar service connects London St Pancras to Avignon on Saturdays. For all **Eurostar** bookings 🖉08432 186 186 or if calling from outside the UK +44 (0)1233 617 575; www.eurostar.com.

Eurailpass, **Flexipass**, **Eurailpass Youth**, **EurailDrive Pass** and **Saverpass** are travel passes which may be purchased by residents of countries outside the European Union. Go to www.raileurope.com. In the **USA**, contact your travel agent or **Rail Europe** 🖉1 877 257 2887. In **Canada**, contact 1 800 361 RAIL. **Australians** go to www.railplus.com. au; 🖉1300 555 003, and for **New Zealanders**, go to www.railplus. com.nz; 🖉649 377 5415.

European residents can buy an individual country pass if not a resident of the country where you plan to use it. In the **UK**, contact **Rail Europe Ltd**, Rail Europe House, 34

Tower View, Kings Hill, West Malling, Kent ME19 4ED 🖉08448 484 064; www.raileurope.co.uk.
At the SNCF (French railways) site, **www.sncf.fr**, you can book ahead, pay with a credit card, and receive your ticket in the mail at home.
There are numerous **discounts** available, 25–50 percent below the regular rate. These include discounts for using senior cards and youth cards, group rates and seasonal promotions. You can procure special passes and ID cards in all SNCF stations and boutiques; bring an ID photo. The SNCF also operates a **travel service** for accommodation, car rentals and holiday packages. Remember to validate (composter) tickets using the orange automatic date-stamping machines at the platform entrance. Failure to do so may result in a fine. SNCF also operates a **telephone information, reservation and prepayment service in English** from 7am to 10pm (French time) 🖉08 36 35 35 39.

RAIL TRAVEL FOR THE DISABLED

Details of services available to welcome and accompany disabled travellers at French railway (SNCF) stations can be found at www. accessibilite.sncf.com.
Or telephone 🖉0890 640 650.

BY COACH/BUS

The Alps can also be reached by coach via Paris. **Eurolines**, Europe's largest regular coach network, operates ski season services to Chamonix, Grenoble, Chambéry, Valence and Lyon.

◆ **London: National Express Ltd**, Ensign Court, 4 Vicarage Road, Edgbaston, Birmingham B15 3ES 🖉08717 81 81 81; **Disabled Persons Help Line** 🖉08717 81 81 79. A textphone is provided for customers who are deaf or hard of hearing on 🖉0121 455 0086; www.eurolines.co.uk.

◆ **Paris: Gare Routière internationale de Paris Gallieni,**

Boite 313, 28 avenue du Général-de-Gaulle, 93541 Bagnolet 📞01 49 72 51 52; www.eurolines.fr.

BY CAR

The area covered in this guide is easily reached by main motorways and national routes. Refer to the listing of Michelin maps and plans at the back of the guide. The latest Michelin route-planning service is available on the internet at **www.ViaMichelin.co.uk**. Travellers can work out a precise route using such options as shortest route, scenic route, route avoiding toll roads or the Michelin-recommended route. The site also provides tourist information (hotels, restaurants and attractions).

The roads are very busy during the holiday period, particularly at weekends in July and August, and to avoid traffic congestion it is advisable to follow the recommended secondary routes (signposted as *Bison Futé – itinéraires bis*).

DOCUMENTS

Travellers from other European Union countries and North America can drive in France with a valid national or home-state **driving licence**. An **international driving licence** is advisable, however. **In the USA**, contact the National Automobile Club 📞650 294 7000 or 1 800 622 2136, www.nationalautoclub.com; or contact your local branch of the American Automobile Association 📞1 866 968 7222; www.aaa.com. **In Canada**, contact www.caa.ca for provincial clubs.

The **Australian Automobile Association** at www.aaa.asn.au and the **New Zealand Automobile Association** at www.aa.co.nz; 📞0800 500 444 also provide the IDP. Most car rental agencies will ask for it, even if not required, and it is useful identification even for those not planning to drive. For the vehicle, it is necessary to have the registration papers (logbook) and a nationality plate of the approved type. Certain motoring organisations (AAA, CAA, AA, RAC) offer accident **insurance** and breakdown service schemes for members. Check with your current insurance company in regard to cover while abroad, but be aware that breakdown cover does not apply on autoroutes, which are privately owned. If you plan to hire a car using your credit card, check with the company, which may provide liability insurance automatically.

HIGHWAY CODE

The minimum driving age is 18. Traffic drives on the right. All passengers, front and back, must wear **seat belts**. Children under age 10 must ride in the back seat, unless in a specially approved seat facing backwards. Headlights must be switched on in poor visibility and at night.

In the case of a **breakdown**, a red warning triangle or hazard warning lights are obligatory.

In the absence of stop signs at intersections, cars must **yield to the right**. Vehicles must stop when the lights turn red at road junctions and may filter to the right only when indicated by an amber arrow.

The regulations on **drinking and driving** (limited to .05 percent or 0.50g/l, two glasses of wine) and **speeding** are strictly enforced – usually by an on-the-spot fine and/or confiscation of the vehicle.

Remember that on **steep**, **single-lane roads in the Alps**, as elsewhere in France, the driver heading downhill is expected to pull over or reverse to allow oncoming vehicles to pass.

Further regulations – It is obligatory to carry spare lightbulbs, and yellow fluorescent jackets in case of breakdown. UK left-hand drive cars must use headlight adaptors. When driving in the mountains in winter, on some roads carrying chains is obligatory. For further information on mountain driving 🕭*see p48*.

Parking regulations – In town there are zones where parking is either restricted or subject to a fee; tickets

Driving along the Lac du Mont-Cenis, La Maurienne

© Charles Bowman/Robert Harding/age fotostock

should be obtained from the ticket machines (*horodateurs* – small change necessary) and displayed inside the windscreen on the driver's side; failure to do so may result in a fine, or towing away and impoundment. Other parking areas may require you to take a ticket when passing through a barrier. To exit, you must pay the parking fee (usually there is a machine located by the exit – *sortie*) and insert the paid-up card in another machine which will lift the exit gate.

Where a blue parking zone is marked by a blue line on the road and a 🅿 sign, a cardboard disc *(disque de stationnement)* gives 1 hour 30 minutes' parking, or 2 hour 30 minutes over lunchtime. Discs are available in supermarkets or petrol stations and are occasionally given away free.

Tolls – In France, most motorway sections are subject to a toll *(péage)*. You can pay everywhere with a credit card (Visa, MasterCard), but a few smaller exits have only automated credit card tolls and these do not accept cash.

Petrol (USA: gas) – French service stations dispense: *sans plomb* 98 (super unleaded 98), *sans plomb* 95 (super unleaded 95), *diesel/gazole* (diesel) and *GPL* (LPG). Fuel in France costs about the same as in the UK, but is more expensive than in the USA. It is usually cheaper at the large hypermarkets on the outskirts of town.

CAR RENTAL

There are car rental agencies at airports, railway stations and in all large towns throughout France. Most European cars have manual transmission; automatic cars are available only if an advance reservation is made. Drivers must be over 21; between ages 21–25, drivers are required to pay an extra daily fee; some companies allow drivers under 23 only if the reservation has been made through a travel agent. Rental agencies have offices all over France; to find the one near where you want to rent, consult these websites:

- **Avis** www.Avis.fr
- **Budget France** www.budget.fr
- **Europcar** www.europcar.fr
- **Hertz France** www.hertz.fr
- **National-CITER** www.citer.fr
- **SIXT-Eurorent** www.e-sixt.com
- **Worldwide Motorhome Rentals** www.mhrww.com

Where to Stay and Eat

WHERE TO STAY
FINDING A HOTEL

Turn to the Address Books in the *Discovering the French Alps* section for descriptions and prices of typical places to stay and eat with local flair. For an even greater selection, use the red-cover **Michelin Guide France**, with its famously reliable star-rating system and hundreds of establishments all over France.

For further assistance, **La Fédération Loisirs Accueil**, 280 boulevard St-Germain, 75007 Paris ☎01 44 11 10 44; www.loisirsaccueilfrance.com offers booking services. The website gives the addresses and telephone numbers of Fédération offices in 55 *départements*.

La Fédération nationale Clévacances offers a list of rental properties and rooms in 79 *départements*; www.clevacance.com. A guide to good-value, family-run hotels, **Logis et Auberges de France**, is available from the French Tourist Office; www.tourisme.fr. The website gives an extensive list of accommodation for each *département*, as well as links for making reservations, and a list of tourist offices all over France.

Relais et châteaux provides information on luxury hotels with character. The guide can be ordered or downloaded online; www.relais chateaux.com.

Chain hotels – If you need a place to stop en route, these can be useful, as they are inexpensive and generally located near the main road. While breakfast is available, there may not be a restaurant; rooms are small and simple, with a television and bathroom.

Rather than sort through hotels yourself, you can go to websites that cover several chains, from modest to luxurious. These sites allow you to select your hotel based on geographical location, price and level of comfort, and to book online.

- **www.viamichelin.com** covers hotels in France, including famous selections from the Michelin Guide as well as lower-priced chains
- **www.activehotels.com** covers a wide range of hotels, and offers customer reviews
- **Akena** ☎01 69 84 85 17; www.hotels-akena.com
- **B&B** ☎(+33) 1 72 36 51 06; www.hotel-bb.com
- **Mister Bed** ☎01 46 14 38 00. You book through a bigger website such as http://en. venere.com
- **Best Hôtel** ☎03 28 27 46 69; www.besthotel.fr
- **Campanile, Kyriad, Bleu Marine, Première Classe, Louvre** ☎01 64 62 46 46; www.envergure.fr
  - www.ichotelsgroup.com (Holiday Inn)
  - www.choicehotels.com (Comfort)
  - www.bestwestern.fr (Best Western)
  - www.etaphotel.com (Étap Hotels)
  - www.ibishotel.com (Ibis Hotels)

RENTING A COTTAGE OR BED AND BREAKFAST

The **Maison des Gîtes de France** lists self-catering cottages or apartments, or bed and breakfast accommodation *(chambres d'hôtes)* at a reasonable price: 59 rue St-Lazare, 75439 Paris ☎01 49 70 75 75; www.gites-de-france.com.

La Fédération des Stations Vertes BP 71698, 21016 Dijon ☎03 80 54 10 50; www.stationsvertes.com lists some 600 country and mountain sites ideal for families.

The Association of British Travel Organisers to France, www.holiday france.org.uk, lists companies offering self-catering apartments or houses. There is also **Bed and Breakfast France**, PO Box 47085, London SW18 9AB ☎0871 781 0834; www.bedbreak.

com, and Mountain Base specialising in self-catering apartments and chalets in the Chamonix Valley ℘(UK) 020 7099 5727, (France) 04 50 90 67 45; www.mountain-base.com.

The **Fédération des Logis de France** offers hotel-restaurant packages geared to hiking, fishing, biking, skiing, wine-tasting and enjoying nature ℘01 45 84 83 84; www.logis-de-france.fr.

The adventurous can consult **www.gites-refuges.com**, where you can order a guidebook, *Gîtes d'étapes et refuges*, listing some 4 000 shelters for hikers, mountaineers, rock-climbers, skiers, canoe/kayakers, etc.: 74 rue A. Perdreaux, 78140 Vélizy ℘01 34 65 11 89.

HOSTELS AND CAMPING

To obtain an International Youth Hostel Federation (Hosteling International) card (there is no age requirement), contact the IYHF in your own country:

- **Australia** ℘61-2-9565-1669; www.yha.com.au
- **Canada** ℘(613) 273 7884; www.hihostels.ca
- **UK** ℘01707 324 170; www.hihostels.com
- **USA** ℘(202) 783-6161; www.hiusa.org

Camping with a splendid view

© cschoeps/iStockphoto.com

In France, the **Fédération Unie des Auberges de Jeunesse** (FUAJ) is associated with Hosteling International: 27 rue Pajol, 75018 Paris ℘01 44 89 87 27; www.fuaj.org.

The **Ligue Française pour les Auberges de la Jeunesse** (LFAJ) can be contacted at 67 rue Vergniaud, Bât. K, 73013 Paris ℘01 44 16 78 78; www.auberges-de-jeunesse.com.

The **Michelin Camping Caravanning France** guide lists a selection of campsites. The Alps are popular with campers in the summer months, particularly the areas around Chamonix, Lac d'Aiguebelette and Lac d'Annecy, so it is wise to reserve in advance.

WHERE TO EAT

For an overview of regional specialities and produce, refer to the Food and Drink section of the *Introduction*.

Turn to the Address Books in the *Discovering the French Alps* section for descriptions and prices of selected places to eat. Use the red-cover **Michelin Guide France**, with its famously reliable star-rating system for an even greater choice.

If you would like to dine at a highly rated restaurant from the Michelin Guide, book ahead! In the countryside, lunch is served between noon and 2pm and dinner between 7.30 and 10pm. However, a hungry traveller can usually get a sandwich in a café, and ordinary hot dishes may be available in a brasserie.

Restaurants usually charge for meals in two ways: a fixed-price *menu*, with two or three courses and sometimes a small pitcher of wine, or the more expensive *à la carte*, with each course ordered separately.

Cafés have different prices, depending on location. The price is cheaper if you stand at the counter *(au comptoir)* than if you sit down in the main room *(dans la salle)*, and often it is even more expensive outdoors *(sur la terrace)*.

Useful Words and Phrases

Sights

	Translation
Abbey	Abbaye
Bridge	Pont
Cable Car	Téléphérique
Castle	Château
Cemetery	Cimetière
Chair lift	Télésiège
Chapel	Chapelle
Church	Église
Cloisters	Cloître
Convent	Couvent
Courtyard	Cour
Fountain	Fontaine
Garden	Jardin
Gateway	Porte
Gondola	Télécabine
House	Maison
Ice Cave	Grotte de glace
Ice Rink	Patinoire
Monastery	Monastère
Museum	Musée
Park	Parc
Port/harbour	Port
Ramparts	Remparts
Ruins	Ruines
Ski Lift	Rémontée Mécanique
Square	Place
Statue	Statue
Street	Rue
Tower	Tour
Town Hall	Mairie

Natural Sites

	Translation
Abyss	Abîme
Beach	Plage
Cave	Grotte
Coast, Hillside	Côte
Dam	Barrage
Forest	Forêt
Lake	Lac
Pass	Col
Ridge	Crête, arête, corniche

	Translation
River	Rivière, fleuve
Spring	Source
Stream	Ruisseau, torrent
Valley	Vallée
Viewpoint	Belvédère, point de vue
Waterfall	Cascade

On the Road

	Translation
Car Park	Parking
Diesel	Gazole
Driving Licence	Permis de conduire
East	Est
Garage (For Repairs)	Garage
Left	Gauche
Motorway/highway	Autoroute
North	Nord
Parking Meter	Horodateur
Petrol/gas	Essence
Petrol/gas Station	Station essence
Pedestrian Crossing	Passage piéton
Right	Droite
South	Sud
Toll	Péage
Traffic Light	Feu
Tyre	Pneu
West	Ouest

Time

	Translation
Today	Aujourd'hui
Tomorrow	Demain
Yesterday	Hier
Winter	Hiver
Spring	Printemps
Summer	Été
Autumn/fall	Automne
Week	Semaine
Monday	Lundi
Tuesday	Mardi
Wednesday	Mercredi
Thursday	Jeudi
Friday	Vendredi
Saturday	Samedi
Sunday	Dimanche

Shopping

	Translation
Baker's	Boulangerie
Bank	Banque
Butcher's	Boucherie
Chemist's	Pharmacie
Closed	Fermé
Cough Mixture	Sirop pour la toux
Cough Sweets	Cachets pour la gorge
Entrance	Entrée
Exit	Sortie
Fishmonger's	Poissonnerie
Grocer's	Épicerie
Market	Marché
Newsagent, Bookshop	Librairie
Open	Ouvert
Post Office	Poste
Shop	Magasin
Small	Petit
Stamps	Timbres
Supermarket	Supermarché

Food and Drink

	Translation
Beef	Bœuf
Beer	Bière
Bread	Pain
Breakfast	Petit-déjeuner
Butter	Beurre
Cake	Gateau
Cheese	Fromage
Chicken	Poulet
Childrens' Menu	Menu Enfant
Chips	Frites
Dessert	Dessert
Dinner	Dîner
Duck	Canard
Fish	Poisson
Fork	Fourchette
Fruit	Fruits
Fruit Juice	Jus de fruits
Glass	Verre
Green salad	Salade verte
Ham (smoked)	Jambon (fumé)
Hamburger	Steak haché
Herbal Tea	Tisane
Honey	Miel

Ice cream	Glace
Jam	Confiture
Jug of tap water	Carafe d'eau
Carafe of wine	Pichet de vin
Knife	Couteau
Lamb	Agneau
Lunch	Déjeuner
Meat	Viande
Mineral water	Eau minérale
Mixed salad	Salade composée
Olive oil	Huile d'olive
Pasta	Pêtes
Pastries	Patisseries
Pepper	Poivre
Plate	Assiette
Pork	Porc
Rabbit	Lapin
Red wine	Vin rouge
Salmon	Saumon
Salt	Sel
Seafood	Fruits de Mer
Still/sparkling water	Eau plate/gazeuse
Sugar	Sucre
Trout	Truite
Veal	Veau
Vegetables	Légumes
Wine (white/red/rosé)	Vin (blanc/rouge/rosé)
Yoghurt	Yaourt

Typical French Alps Menu

(See also p63)

Starters

Beignet	Potato fritter
Charcuterie	Cold cured meats
Salade de chèvre chaud	Goat's cheese salad

Main Courses

Boudin	Blood sausage
Diot	Local sausage
Fondue Savoyard	Cheese fondue
Polente	Polenta
Poissons du Lac	Lake fish
Pâtes aux pistou	Pasta with pesto
Tartiflette	Baked reblochon cheese and potato

Cheese and Desserts

Fromage Blanc	Fromage frais
Fromage Sec	Cheese selection
Tarte aux fruits	Fruit tart

Basic Information

BUSINESS HOURS

Most of the larger shops are open Mondays to Saturdays from 9am to 6.30 or 7.30pm. Smaller, individual shops may close during the lunch hour. Food shops – grocers, wine merchants and bakeries – are generally open from 7am to 6.30 or 7.30pm; some open on Sunday mornings. Many food shops close between noon and 2pm, or for longer in holiday resorts, and in some smaller towns they close on Mondays. A few bakers close on Wednesdays. Hypermarkets usually stay open non-stop until 9pm or later.

ELECTRICITY

The electric current is 220 volts. Circular two-pin plugs are the rule. Adapters and converters (for hair dryers, for example) should be bought before you leave home; they are on sale in most airports. If you have a rechargeable device (video camera, portable computer, battery recharger), read the instructions carefully or contact the manufacturer or shop. Sometimes these items only require a plug adapter; in other cases you must use a voltage converter as well or risk ruining your device.

EMERGENCIES

Police: 🖉 17
Fire (*Pompiers*): 🖉 18
SAMU (*Paramedics*): 🖉 15

MAIL

Main post offices open Monday to Friday 9am to 6.30pm, Saturday 9am to noon. However, many post offices, especially smaller ones, close at lunchtime between noon and 2pm, and some may close early in the afternoon; in short, opening hours vary widely. Stamps are also available from newsagents and tobacconists (*tabacs*). Stamp collectors should ask for *timbres de collection* in any post office.

MONEY

Along with most EU countries, France uses the euro (€).
There are no restrictions on the amount of currency visitors can take into France. However, visitors carrying a lot of cash are advised to complete a currency declaration form on arrival, because there are restrictions on currency export.

BANKS

Bank opening hours vary widely. Generally, they are open from 9am to noon and 2pm to a variety of afternoon closing times; branches are closed either on Monday or Saturday; if open on these days, it is often only for the morning. Banks close early on the day before a bank holiday. So don't count on a bank being open when you need it. A passport is necessary as identification when cashing travellers' cheques in banks. Commission charges vary, and hotels usually charge more than banks for cashing cheques.

CREDIT AND DEBIT CARDS

One of the most economical ways to use your money in France is by using **ATM machines** to get cash directly from your bank account or to use your credit cards to get cash advances. Be sure to remember your PIN number; you will need it to use cash dispensers and to pay with your card in most shops, restaurants, etc. Code pads are numeric; use a telephone pad to translate a letter code into numbers. PIN numbers have four digits in France; enquire with the issuing company or bank if the code you usually use is longer.
Visa and MasterCard credit networks have merged in France, so merchants

American Express	🖉 01 47 77 72 00
Visa	🖉 0 800 90 13 87
MasterCard/Euro-card/Cirrus/Maestro	🖉 0 800 90 13 87
Diners Club	🖉 01 49 06 17 50

take both interchangeably. However, the cash advance functions have not merged, and Visa is more widely accepted for this than MasterCard; other cards, credit and debit (Diners Club, Plus, Cirrus, etc.) are also accepted in some cash machines. American Express is accepted only in premium establishments.

Most places post signs indicating the cards they accept; if you don't see such a sign, and want to pay with a card, ask before ordering or making a selection. Cards are widely accepted in shops, hypermarkets, hotels and restaurants, at tollbooths and in petrol stations.

Your bank's hotline will be printed on the back of your card: make a note of it in case of its being lost or stolen. The major card company hotlines are listed above.

If your card is stolen, you can call a 24-hour helpline to make a report: ✆08 36 69 08 80. You must report any loss or theft of credit cards or travellers' cheques to the local police, who will issue you with a certificate (useful proof to show the issuing company).

TAXES

There is a Value Added Tax in France (TVA) of 19.6 percent on almost every purchase (books and some foods are subject to a lower rate).

However, non-European visitors who spend at least 175€ in any one participating store on the same day can apply for a refund of the VAT; the VAT cannot be reimbursed for items shipped.

Usually, you fill out a form at the store, showing your passport. Upon leaving the country, you submit all forms to customs for approval (they may want to see the goods, so if possible don't pack them in checked luggage). The refund is usually paid directly into your bank or credit card account, or it can be sent by mail.

Big department stores that cater to tourists provide special services to help you; be sure to mention that you plan to seek a refund before you pay for goods (no refund is possible for tax on services). If you are visiting two or more countries within the European Union, you submit the forms only on departure from the last EU country. The refund is worth while for those visitors who would like to buy fashions, furniture or other fairly expensive items, but remember, the minimum amount must be spent in a single shop.

People travelling to the USA cannot import plant products or fresh food, including fruit, cheeses and nuts. It is acceptable to carry tinned products or preserves.

PUBLIC HOLIDAYS

Museums and other monuments may be closed or may vary their hours of admission on the public holidays in the table below.

National museums and art galleries are closed on Tuesdays; municipal museums are generally closed on Mondays. In addition to the usual school holidays at Christmas and in the spring and summer, there are long mid-term breaks (usually two weeks in February or early March, and one week late October and early

1 January	New Year's Day (Jour de l'An)
Easter	Easter Day and Easter Monday (Pâques)
1 May	May Day
8 May	VE Day
Thursday 40 days after Easter	Ascension Day (Ascension)
7th Sun–Mon after Easter	Whit Sunday and Monday (Pentecôte)
14 July	France's National Day (Bastille Day)
15 August	Assumption (Assomption)
1 November	All Saints' Day (Toussaint)
11 November	Armistice Day
25 December	Christmas Day (Noël)

CONVERSION TABLES

Weights and Measures

	🇪🇺	🇺🇸	🇬🇧	
	1 kilogram (kg)	**2.2 pounds (lb)**	**2.2 pounds**	*To convert*
	6.35 kilograms	14 pounds	1 stone (st)	*kilograms*
	0.45 kilograms	16 ounces (oz)	16 ounces	*to pounds,*
	1 metric ton (tn)	**1.1 tons**	**1.1 tons**	*multiply by 2.2*
	1 litre (l)	**2.11 pints (pt)**	**1.76 pints**	*To convert litres*
	3.79 litres	1 gallon (gal)	0.83 gallon	*to gallons, multiply*
	4.55 litres	1.20 gallon	1 gallon	*by 0.26 (US)*
				or 0.22 (UK)
	1 hectare (ha)	**2.47 acres**	**2.47 acres**	*To convert*
	1 sq kilometre	**0.38 sq. miles**	**0.38 sq. miles**	*hectares to*
	(km²)	**(sq mi)**		*acres, multiply*
				by 2.4
	1 centimetre (cm)	**0.39 inches (in)**	**0.39 inches**	*To convert metres*
	1 metre (m)	**3.28 feet (ft) or 39.37 inches**		*to feet, multiply*
		or 1.09 yards (yd)		*by 3.28; for*
	1 kilometre (km)	**0.62 miles (mi)**	**0.62 miles**	*kilometres to miles,*
				multiply by 0.6

Clothing

Women	🇪🇺	🇺🇸	🇬🇧
	35	4	2½
	36	5	3½
	37	6	4½
Shoes	38	7	5½
	39	8	6½
	40	9	7½
	41	10	8½
	36	6	8
	38	8	10
Dresses	40	10	12
& suits	42	12	14
	44	14	16
	46	16	18
	36	6	30
	38	8	32
Blouses &	40	10	34
sweaters	42	12	36
	44	14	38
	46	16	40

Men	🇪🇺	🇺🇸	🇬🇧
	40	7½	7
	41	8½	8
	42	9½	9
Shoes	43	10½	10
	44	11½	11
	45	12½	12
	46	13½	13
	46	36	36
	48	38	38
Suits	50	40	40
	52	42	42
	54	44	44
	56	46	48
	37	14½	14½
	38	15	15
Shirts	39	15½	15½
	40	15¾	15¾
	41	16	16
	42	16½	16½

Sizes often vary depending on the designer. These equivalents are given for guidance only.

Speed

KPH	10	30	50	70	80	90	100	110	120	130
MPH	6	19	31	43	50	56	62	68	75	81

Temperature

Celsius (°C)	0°	5°	10°	15°	20°	25°	30°	40°	60°	80°	100°
Fahrenheit (°F)	32°	41°	50°	59°	68°	77°	86°	104°	140°	176°	212°

To convert Celsius into Fahrenheit, multiply °C by 9, divide by 5, and add 32.
To convert Fahrenheit into Celsius, subtract 32 from °F, multiply by 5, and divide by 9.

NB: Conversion factors on this page are approximate.

Mountain Safety

Mountain areas are potentially dangerous, even for the most experienced enthusiasts. Avalanches, falling rocks, bad weather, fog, treacherous terrain and snowfields, icy water, loss of one's bearings and wrong assessment of distances are the dangers threatening mountaineers, skiers and hikers.

Driving in Mountain Areas

Unaccustomed drivers may be overawed by the experience and it is essential to take certain precautions. Cars must be in good working order (brakes and tyres particularly; snow tyres and chains in winter) and drivers must abide rigorously by the highway code. For instance, horns must be sounded on twisting roads with reduced visibility and along narrow roads and cars going downhill must give way to those climbing. When climbing continuously, it is advisable to watch the oil and cooling liquid levels. Purchase a screen wash suitable for very low temperatures. In addition, it is recommended to avoid driving in bad weather, getting caught by nightfall or stopping beneath a cliff (falling rocks are frequent).

Tricky scenic roads – Michelin maps on a scale of 1:200 000 show very narrow roads (where passing is difficult or impossible), unusually steep ones, difficult or dangerous sections, tunnels and the altitude of major passes.

Snow cover – Maps nos. 916, 919 and 989 on a scale of 1:1 000 000 show major roads with passes that are always closed in winter with their probable closing dates and those which are sometimes closed, but cleared within 24 hours. Access roads to resorts are normally cleared several times a day.

A Few Words of Advice

Advice given to off-piste skiers also applies to hikers and mountaineers. However, a prolonged stay above 3 000m/9 843ft calls for special precautions. Atmospheric pressure is one-third lower and the heart beats faster to compensate for the lack of oxygen. It takes roughly a week to get used to it as the production of red cells in the blood is intensified so that as much oxygen can be carried as at lower altitudes. It is essential to keep hydrated even at moderate altitudes; drink much more water than usual, even if the weather remains cool and you are not being very active. This mitigates all but the worst effects of altitude.

The main dangers are the following: **Mountain sickness** or hypoxaemia (symptoms: digestive problems, breathing difficulty, severe headache), which can normally be treated with appropriate medicine that tourists are advised to take with them; the more serious cases (pulmonary oedema) have to be treated in hospital. **Hypothermia** is also a danger in mountain areas for people caught by a sudden change in the weather such as fog, for instance, which always brings a cold snap. **Frostbite** is less obvious as symptoms appear progressively: loss of feeling in the hands and feet, numbness and paleness of the skin. The danger lies in the wrong treatment being applied on the spot: never try to heat up the affected part of the body, by whatever means, unless you can keep it warm until the doctor arrives, as a new attack of frostbite on a partially rewarmed limb would cause even more damage.

Accidents can be avoided or their consequences lessened by following these simple rules; never go hiking or mountaineering on your own, and let someone know of your planned itinerary and when you intend to return.

Weather forecast – Up-to-date recorded information about regional weather is available to hikers *(for telephone numbers, 👆 see When to Go p12)*. In addition, more specific information can be obtained:

👆 **Risk of avalanche:** 📞*08 92 68 10 20. www.meteo.fr* offers avalanche predictions; English version at *www.henrysavalanchetalk.com*.

Avalanches – Whether they happen naturally or are started by passing skiers, they represent a permanent danger which must not be dismissed lightly.

Bulletins Neige et Avalanche (BNA), posted in every resort and hiking base, warn of the risks that must be taken into consideration by anyone planning an excursion.

A scale of potential risks (👆*see box below)* has been devised for the benefit of those who ski or board off-piste, but also for cross-country skiers and snowshoe walkers. This is only a general guideline which needs to be supplemented with more precise information concerning the planned itinerary. In addition, it is advisable to be fairly flexible and evaluate the risks incurred in each case.

Lightning – Violent gusts of wind are the warning signs of an imminent thunderstorm, which brings with it the danger of being struck by lightning. Avoid walking along ridges, taking shelter beneath overhanging rocks or isolated trees, at the entrance of caves or hollows in the rock and near metallic fences. Try to distance yourself from any large metallic objects such as an ice-axe and crampons that you may be carrying.

Do not huddle under a metallic-framed shelter. Stand more than 15m/yds from any high point (rock or tree) and adopt a crouching position, keeping your hands and any bare parts of your body away from the surface of the rock. Before lightning strikes, the atmosphere often becomes electrified and a sound like the humming of a swarm of bees can sometimes be heard, well known to mountain-dwellers. Finally, remember that a car provides a safe shelter during a storm as it makes an excellent Faraday cage.

Assistance – Telephone the Europe-wide assistance number 112. Before going on an excursion, note the contact numbers for the local mountain rescue service.

Who pays for it? – The cost can be very high, especially if a rescue helicopter is called out, and the person rescued or his or her family are normally expected to pay. It is therefore advisable to take out insurance to cover such risks.

😊 Avalanche-Risk Scale 😊

1   **Low**: (Yellow flag) Snow cover is stable and there are only rare avalanches on very steep slopes.

2   **Limited**: (Yellow flag) Snow cover is again stable but avalanches may be started in specific areas by an excessive number of skiers or hikers.

3   **Medium**: (Black and yellow flag) Snow cover is only moderately stable and avalanches may be started in many places by individuals; avalanches are also likely to start naturally as for 4 on the scale.

4   **High**: (Black and yellow flag) Snow cover is unstable on steep slopes and avalanches are very likely to occur, set off by people, or even spontaneously.

5   **Very high**: (Black flag) Snow cover is very unstable following a heavy snow fall and major avalanches will occur even on gentle slopes.

November). The two-week February and spring holidays are staggered across three zones.

REDUCED RATES

Significant discounts are available for senior citizens, students, young people under 25, teachers, and groups for public transport, museums and monuments and for some leisure activities such as movies (at certain times of day).

Bring student or senior cards with you, and bring along some extra passport-size photos for discount travel cards.

The **International Student Travel Conference** (www.istc.org), global administrator of the International Student and Teacher Identity Cards, negotiates benefits with airlines, governments, and providers of other goods and services.

The non-profit association sells international ID cards for full-time students over age 12, young people under 25 and teachers.

⌖ *See the section on travelling by rail for discounts on public transport.*

The tourist office of Alpes-de-Haute-Provence sells a **museum passport** giving reductions or free entry to museums and parks in the *département*.

SMOKING

France has joined several other European countries and has banned smoking in all public places including in bars, cafés and restaurants. Many privately owned hotels no longer accept smokers.

TELEPHONE AND INTERNET

Public telephones – Most public phones in France use pre-paid phone cards *(télécartes)*, rather than coins. Some telephone booths accept credit cards (Visa, MasterCard/Eurocard). *Télécartes* (50 or 120 units) can be bought in post offices, branches of France Télécom, *tabacs* (cafés or shops

INTERNATIONAL DIALLING CODES (00 + code):	
Australia	☎61
Canada	☎1
Eire	☎353
New Zealand	☎64
United Kingdom	☎44
United States	☎1

that sell cigarettes) and newsagents and can be used to make calls in France and abroad. Calls can be received at phone boxes where the blue bell sign is shown; the phone will not ring, so keep your eye on the little message screen.

National calls – French telephone numbers have 10 digits. Paris and Paris region numbers begin with 01; 02 in northwest France; 03 in northeast France; 04 in southeast France and Corsica; 05 in southwest France.

International calls – To call France from abroad, dial the country code (0033) + 9-digit number (omit the initial 0). When calling abroad from France, dial 00, then dial the country code followed by the area code and number of your correspondent.

To use your **personal calling card** dial:

- **AT&T** ☎0-800 99 00 11
- **Canada Direct**
  ☎0-800 99 00 16
  or ☎0-800 99 02 16
- **MCI** ☎0-800 99 00 19
- **Sprint** ☎0-800 99 00 87

Some shops sell phonecards for overseas calls that can be used from both public and private phones. These are cheaper than using a regular phonecard at a public booth.

- **International information**: USA/Canada: 00 33 12 11
- **International operator**: 00 33 12 + country code
- **Local directory assistance**: 12

Minitel – France Télécom operates a system offering directory enquiries (free of charge up to three minutes), travel and entertainment reservations, and other services (cost per minute varies). These small computer-like terminals can be found in some post offices, hotels and France Télécom agencies and in many French homes. 3614 PAGES E is the code for **directory assistance in English** (turn on the unit, dial 3614, hit the connection button when you get the tone, type in "PAGES E" and follow the instructions on the screen).

Internet – Internet use is now widespread in France and has supplanted Minitel for most purposes. E-mails are the cheapest way to communicate overseas. Many post offices and some tourist offices have public Internet terminals and cybercafés are quite widespread. For an updated list of cybercafés, go to www.world66.com/netcafeguide. In major cities, France Télécom has Internet kiosks on the street. Better hotels have business centres where you can access computers, and often hotel rooms have Wifi access. French websites, especially those for tourists or offering commercial services, often are multilingual: just click on the little British or American flag on the home page.

Mobile phones in France and across Europe operate on the GSM standard, which is not widespread in the USA. Those with GSM phones can often arrange with their service providers to take with them a phone equipped with an international SIM (Subscriber Information Module) card that allows them to keep their regular phone number and to be billed by their provider.

This can be expensive, however, so if you plan to place calls frequently, it is cheaper to rent or buy a phone for the trip. Phone shops for purchase or rental are found at airports and around France. By consulting websites, you can research phone rentals before you go, often with delivery or airport pickup. Try www.cellularabroad.com for information as well as service offers. Also available on the French mobile phone market are *Mobicartes,* pre-paid phonecards that fit into mobile units and that can be purchased in different denominations in convenience stores.

TIME

France is one hour ahead of Greenwich Mean Time (GMT). France moves to daylight saving time from the last Sunday in March to the last Sunday in October.

WHEN IT IS NOON IN FRANCE, IT IS
3am in Los Angeles
6am in New York
11am in Dublin
11am in London
7pm in Perth
9pm in Sydney
11pm in Auckland
In France "am" and "pm" are not used but the 24-hour clock is widely applied.

TIPPING

Since a service charge is automatically included in the price of meals and accommodation in France, any additional tip *(pourboire)* is up to the visitor, generally small change, and generally not more than 5 percent. Taxi drivers and hairdressers are usually tipped 10–15 percent. Prices for hotels and restaurants as well as for other goods and services may be significantly less expensive in the French regions than in Paris, but this is not the case in some of the major tourist destinations of the Alps.

The French Alps Today

Once a strategic thoroughfare, passed through by Hannibal and Napoleon, and later a Resistance stronghold, today, preservation of this fragile mountain environment provides the main battle to be fought in the French Alps. Tourism, agriculture and technology continue to learn to live side by side. These alpine regions were extremely impoverished with a declining population in the 19C, and yet by the 20C the region included some of the most important tourist attractions in the world, and had become a leader in technological industries. In the 21C, the region is confronting changes in tourism patterns, as well as climate change issues, and is increasingly concerned to protect its historical heritage.

WINTER SPORTS

There is no question that ski resorts, the sporting and touristic activities they offer, and the infrastructure they require dominate life in the French Alps for five months every year. The region is proud of its Olympic history, both as a host of the winter games and as the birthplace of many winter-sports champions, who become role models to the regions' youth.

GOVERNMENT

Decision-making in France was once highly centralised, each *département* headed by a government-appointed prefect, in addition to a locally elected general council *(conseil général)*. But in 1982, the national government decided to decentralise authority by devolving a range of administrative and fiscal powers to local level. Regional councils were directly elected for the first time in 1986.

Administrative units with a local government consist of 36 779 communes, headed by a municipal council and a mayor, grouped in 96 *départements*, headed by a *conseil général* and its president, grouped in 22 regions, headed by a regional council and its president. The centre of administration of a *département* is called a *préfecture* or *chef-lieu de département*, which is usually geographically central to the *département*.

The *conseil général* as an institution was created in 1790 by the French Revolution in each of the newly created departments (they were suppressed from 1942 to 1944). A *conseiller général* (effectively a local councillor) must be at least 21 years old and either live or pay taxes in the locality from which he or she is elected.

The *conseil général* discusses and passes laws on matters that concern the department; it is administratively responsible for departmental employees and land, manages subsidised housing, public transportation and school subsidies, and contributes to public facilities. The council meets at least three times a year and elects its president for a term of three years, who presides over its "permanent commission", usually up to 10 other departmental councillors. The *conseil général* has accrued new powers in the course of the political decentralisation that has occurred in France during the past 30 years.

Different levels of administration have different duties, and shared responsibility is common; for instance, in the field of education, communes run public elementary schools, while *départements* run public junior high schools and regions run public high schools, but only for the building and upkeep of buildings; curricula and teaching personnel are supplied by the national Ministry of Education.

In the French Alps, the regions are Rhône-Alpes in the north, and Provence-Alpes-Côte d'Azur in the south. The main *départements* are, north to south: Haute Savoie (*préfecture*, Annecy); Savoie (Chambéry); Isère (Grenoble); Hautes-Alpes (Gap) and Alpes-de-Haute-Provence (Digne-les-Bains). Parts of the departments of Drôme (Valence), Var (Toulon) and Alpes-Maritimes (Nice) are also included in the alpine area.

ECONOMY

For hundreds of years, alpine economy was based on agriculture and handicraft until the region witnessed two economic revolutions: the first happened as a result of the discovery of hydroelectric power, and led to the industrialisation and urbanisation of the valleys; the second was the rapid development of tourism, and led to drastic changes in high-mountain landscapes. These two phenomena, however, saved the region from the population drift to the cities, which threatened its future prosperity. Today, the northern Alps are already a very dynamic region with important towns such as Grenoble and Annecy, whereas the southern Alps are changing at a slower pace and retain a strong economy centred on small and medium-sized towns such as Briançon, Sisteron and Digne. The creation of large nature reserves has not only protected native plants and animals, but contributed to the strong growth of all-year tourism.

AGRICULTURE

Forestry and cattle farming have long been the mainstays of rural life in the Alps. Farms, fewer in number, are growing larger and must share space with tourist resorts. Farming in this reduced space has become highly specialised. Orchards and nut groves dot the landscape and the broad valleys of the Combe de Savoie and Grésivaudan are given over to cereals, as are the Gapençais, Embrunais, Buëch Valley and Plateau de Valensole to the south. Vegetables and flowers are grown around Grenoble, in Bièvre-Valloire and in the lower Arve Valley. In the valleys where dairy production is traditional, the only crop grown today is hay; in many areas, especially on the steeper slopes, farmers still make hay by hand, scything grasses and binding up bales. Coniferous forests, rapidly taking over from pastures, are exploited for pulp, lumber and speciality furniture wood.

In mountainous regions, south-facing slopes are devoted to pastures and farming whereas north-facing slopes are covered with forests. For a period it seemed that the dairy industry would abandon the high Alps, but determined effort has saved this tradition. Seasonal migration of cows from the villages to high-mountain pastures is now mostly by truck, although some cattle still make the trek, called *transhumance* from low prairie to mid-level pastures and finally, in June, to the high Alps. High-altitude chalets dot the mountains, where cheese is made according to old traditions. High-quality cheese is also produced in the *fruitières* (cheese cooperatives): reblochon from the Aravis, vacherin from the Bauges, beaufort from the Beaufortain, tomme from Savoie, bleu de sassenage and St-Marcellin from Dauphiné.

Cattle – Alpine cattle, famous for their sturdiness and ability to walk long distances, are also generous milk-producers. The most traditional breeds are the **Tarine** and the red-and-white **Abondance**, whose milk is essential to the best traditional cheeses. These breeds co-exist, however, with the black-and-white **Holstein**, the blond **Aquitaine**, and particularly the **Montbéliarde** from nearby Franche-Comté.

Sheep – Sheep farming is one of the main economic activities of the Alpes du Sud and Haute-Provence *départements*. These specialise in the production of lambs fattened quickly and sold when they reach the age of three months. In summer, the resident population is joined by sheep (led, traditionally, by goats, with donkeys to carry the lambs) migrating from lower Provence in search of greener grass. This migration, known

Tarine cow

F. Isler/MICHELIN

as *transhumance*, begins around mid-summer until the end of September. Transhumance inspires many festivals, where the traditional Provençal shepherd skills are celebrated.

Sheep from Haute-Provence do not migrate since they can roam freely over vast areas during the warm season and take shelter in large sheds known as *jas* when winter approaches.

Forestry – In recent years, the policy of reforestation, which is intensive in some areas, has been helped by the restrained use of high pastures and the discontinuation of mowing at high altitude. In fact, forests now cover more than a third of all usable land, and even half in the Préalpes and the northern Alps. They are essentially made up of conifers with deciduous trees at low altitude.

Even though the northern Préalpes boast some splendid specimens of beech, which thrive in humid countries, forests of conifers predominate as in the rest of the alpine region. Spruce is the most common conifer of the Salève, Faucigny, Aravis and Bauges areas, whereas fir trees grow most happily in the Chartreuse, Vercors, Beaufortain, Maurienne and Grésivaudan, as well as in the Diois and Préalpes de Digne; in the high-mountain areas of the southern Alps, such as the Briançonnais, Queyras, Embrunais, Ubaye and Mercantour areas, there are mixed forests of fir trees, spruce and larch.

Many alpine areas owe their prosperity to their forests; some have retained the traditional practice of *affouage,* which consists in allotting a certain quantity of wood to each household within the precinct of a given municipality.

Whole areas of Haute-Provence have been reforested since the middle of the 19C and forests, which are now protected, are not used for industrial purposes.

Lavender and lavandin – The delicate scent of lavender is characteristic of Haute-Provence. At the beginning of the 20C, the picking of the flowers of this wild plant represented an extra income. Then, when it became necessary to replace cereal crops, lavender was cultivated on the plateaux and high slopes. Well adapted to the climate and calcareous soils of Provence, this plant helped many farmers to survive when they were about to give up.

Later on, *lavandin*, a more productive but less fragrant hybrid, was cultivated on the lower slopes and in the valleys. Superb fields of *lavandin* can be spotted on the Plateau de Valensole and along the road from Digne to Gréoux-les-Bains. The harvest takes place from July to September according to the region: most of the picking is now mechanised but some fields are still picked by hand. After drying for two to three days, the picked lavender is sent to a distillery equipped with a traditional still.

Olive trees and olive oil – Olive groves traditionally mark the northern boundaries of the Mediterranean region. The production of olive oil, which represents more than two-thirds of the national output, comes mainly from the Alpes-de-Haute-Provence and the Luberon area. Following the hard winter of 1956, when almost a quarter of the olive trees growing in the Baronnies area died, olive groves were renewed with hardier species. There are many varieties and the flavour varies accordingly; the type of soil and picking time are also important; tradition holds that several varieties should grow in the same olive grove. The harvest begins as early as the end of August, depending on the area. Olives are picked by hand when they are intended to be eaten whole or, for processing at the mill, gathered with a rake that is run through the branches; formerly, they were shaken into nets. Olives from Nyons *(tanches)* were the first to have been granted an AOC (Appellation d'Origine Contrôlée) designation of origin; other varieties now have this rating. Olive oils from the Baronnies (Nyons) and Alpes-de-Haute-Provence (Digne, Les Mées) are considered among the best.

Truffles – The truffle, or *rabasse* in Provençal, is an edible, subterranean fungus which develops from the mycelium, a network of filaments invisible to the naked eye. They live symbiotically with the root of the downy oak, known in

Provence as the white oak. These small stunted oaks are planted in fields called *truffières*. The Vaucluse *département* is the main producing area of the Mediterranean region, followed by the Luberon, Riez and Forcalquier areas as well as the upper valley of the River Var. Truffles, known as the "black gold" of Haute-Provence, are harvested from mid-October to mid-March, when they are ripe and odorous. Pigs are traditionally used to sniff out truffles, but they are being replaced by dogs, easier to train and less greedy. Once a truffle is found by the animal, it is carefully dug up by hand. A white variety of truffle, harvested between May and mid-July mainly in the upper valley of the River Var, is used as a flavouring in cooking.

HYDROELECTRIC POWER AND INDUSTRY

In the French Alps, industries were at first intended to satisfy local needs, but then they undertook to work for the rest of the country and even for the export trade. This led to the development of clock factories in Cluses, several silk factories in Lyon, paper mills in Dauphiné, cement factories in the Préalpes, glove factories in Grenoble and steel foundries in Ugine.

Hydroelectric power – Known as *houille blanche* (literally "white coal"), this was the fuel which drove alpine industry forwards. During the late 1860s a factory owner called Amable Matussière, who wished to increase the driving power of his mills, called on two engineers, Fredet and **Aristide Bergès**. The latter deserves credit for having harnessed the first waterfall at Lancey in 1869. At first, the power of the turbines was used mechanically, but by 1870 the invention of the dynamo by Gramme, followed by the building of the first power lines on an industrial scale, made the new power stations switch to the production of electricity.

The alpine relief lends itself to the production of hydroelectricity: the combination of high-mountain ranges and deep valleys creates numerous waterfalls. Engineers began by using waterfalls with a low rate of flow, situated high above the main valleys. They then tapped the main valley rivers, which had a much higher rate of flow, thus creating a concentration of industries along these valleys. During the 1950s, engineers conceived complex projects embracing whole massifs and involving water storage. The flow of water, channelled through miles of tunnels and sometimes diverted from the natural river basin, is collected in huge reservoirs like that formed by the Tignes and Roselend dams or ducted into neighbouring, more deeply cleft valleys.

Today virtually all possible hydroelectric sites are being exploited. Most of the turbines are linked to the EDF (Électricité de France) network.

There are basically four main types of dam. **Gravity dams** withstand water pressure by their weight alone; examples include Chambon and Bissorte. **Arch dams**, graceful and economic in design, have a curved structure with its convex side upstream which transfers the pressure of water laterally to the steep sides of the gorge, as at Tignes, Le Sautet, St-Pierre and Monteynard. **Buttressed dams** are used when the width of the dam does not allow the use of an arch; they are a combination of gravity and arch dams and can be seen at Girotte, Plan d'Amont and Roselend. **Riprap dykes**, which simply close off a glacial dam and are barely visible, are found at La Sassière, Mont-Cenis and Grand-Maison.

Industry and water power – **Electrometallurgy** and **electrochemistry** were the two industries that benefited most from the use of hydroelectricity. They settled near the power stations built by the industrialists themselves, but the cost of transport of raw materials is a major handicap in the mountains. In the face of stiff world competition for steel and aluminium, industry has become highly specialised. **Mechanical engineering** and **electrical engineering** have become vital aspects of the industrial landscape of the Alps, while the traditional clock industry is still going strong in Annemasse.

TRADITIONS AND FOLKLORE

In spite of harsh living conditions, the Alps have always been densely populated, with a well-structured social life following the rhythm of the seasons and strongly attached to its traditions, each valley having its own customs, dialect and costume.

TRADITIONAL LIFE

Traditional life in the Alps was regulated in two ways: by the main events of life (birth, marriage and death) and by the impact of the seasons on the environment.

Birth – A mother's first visit after the birth of her child was to the local church to express her gratitude to God, but before the end of her confinement, tradition demanded that she eat several dozen eggs. Children were christened very soon after being born.

Marriage – Many rituals were linked to marriage: in some areas, young maidens prayed to the local saint to provide a husband for them; in Entrevaux, girls would make a clay figure of the ideal partner. There were also all kinds of symbolic customs before a wedding: in the Embrunais area, the young man would offer his fiancée some jewellery on the Sunday preceding the ceremony. In the Hautes-Alpes region, a young man who married someone from another village had to cross a symbolic barrier, usually a ribbon or a decorated log, on the day of the wedding, whereas a young maiden in the same situation had to buy a round of drinks for the young men of her village in order to make amends for not having chosen one of them.

Funerals – When a death occurred, the whole village would take turns to watch over the body while members of local brotherhoods sang the *De profundis* and *Miserere*. A funeral banquet took place after the funeral. In high-mountain areas it was impossible to bury the dead in winter because the ground was frozen, so the bodies were kept covered with snow, on the roof of the house, until the thaw came.

The seasons – In the Alps, the year was divided in two: summertime, when people worked in the fields and looked after the animals, and wintertime, when all outdoor activity ceased.

Summer was a busy time because the haymaking and harvesting season was short. Bread was made once a year by the whole village, the large loaves having to last a whole year; only with the introduction of the potato in the 18C was the fear of food shortages at the end of a hard winter diminished. Cattle and sheep farming were the main sources of wealth; the herds were taken from the stables to the summer pastures, where they were looked after on a private or collective basis.

In winter, village folk usually stayed at home and lived on what had been stored during the summer: wood for heating, bread, dry vegetables, smoked meat, charcuterie (pork sausages, hams, etc.) and cheese. Men would repair their tools and make furniture and other objects such as toys, while women were busy at their spinning-wheels. Many men, however, left their homes to travel from region to region, selling the seeds of alpine plants and herbs, sweeping chimneys, or finding temporary employment in the valleys as masons and builders. The Queyras and Briançonnais regions even had a reputation for "exporting" wandering schoolmasters, hired by villages in return for their food and lodging and a small wage. Those travellers who could read and write wore a feather in their cap, teachers of arithmetic wore two and the few who could teach Latin proudly added a third.

COSTUMES

A shawl, an embroidered bodice and belt, and an apron brightened up the long black skirt women wore, and still do on festive occasions. In St-Colomban-des-Villars, the number of blue stripes sewn onto the dress indicated the size of the dowry which a husband would receive, allowing bachelors to plan the most advantageous match. Headdresses were extremely varied and consisted of a lace or linen bonnet

Detail of Savoyard costume from Saint-Sorlind'Arves

F. Isler/MICHELIN

decorated with ribbons and worn under a felt or straw hat. Most remarkable of all was the **frontière**: worn by women from the Tarentaise area, it was richly adorned with gold and silver braid and had three points framing the face like a helmet. Gold belts and necklaces were the most popular pieces of jewellery; in some areas, women wore a **ferrure**, a gold cross and heart hanging round their neck from a black velvet ribbon, as a token from their betrothed.

Men's costumes were simpler, consisting of a loosely fitting jacket of dark ordinary cloth, a pair of black trousers, a white shirt with a touch of lace around the collar, a black tie, wide woollen belt and a large felt hat.

LEGENDS

The devil of Bessans – For all his proverbial cunning, the devil was outwitted by a native of Bessans who sold his soul to him in exchange for supernatural powers. As death drew close, the man went to see the Pope in Rome and asked for his pardon. He obtained it on the condition that he would hear Mass in Bessans, Milan and St Peter's in Rome on the same day. He therefore used the powers he still had to get from one place to the next in a flash. Since then, Bessans has become known for its woodcarving skills, especially of devils.

The seven wonders of Dauphiné – These seven wonders, which are the pride of the people of Dauphiné, are sites or monuments steeped in mystery and strange myths: Mont Aiguille, known as the Mount Olympus of Dauphiné, is a kind of "table mountain" dominating the Vercors, once believed by local people to be inhabited by angels and supernatural animals. Fairies were thought to live in the **Grottes de Sassenage** near Grenoble, but it was the devil who haunted the **fontaine ardente** near the Col de l'Arzelier.

Between Grenoble and St-Nizier, a ruined keep still bears the name of **Tour sans venin** because, according to the legend, no snake can get near it since the lord of the castle brought back some magic earth from the Crusades. Candidates for the remaining wonders include the remarkable **Pont de Claix**, built by Lesdiguières, the **Grottes de la Balme** and the **Pierre Percée**, a rock shaped like an arch.

Ancient beliefs from Haute-Provence – Legend has it that fairies live in the rocks overlooking Moustiers-Ste-Marie. On the other hand, the people of Arvieux (*see Le Queyras*) were, for a long time, divided into two groups: the *gens du Renom,* who were thought to have gained their wealth through a deal with the devil, and the *gens de la Belle,* who invented all sorts of rituals to protect themselves from the former, marriage between the two groups being, of course, strictly forbidden.

Festivals

Paganism and Christian belief were often combined in the many traditional feasts of the alpine communities, where religious fervour was mixed with superstition. Today, these events have become folk festivals. Most villages still celebrate the feast-day of their own patron saints, as well as various events linked with work in the fields, not forgetting pilgrimages. Non-religious events also form part of the festivities, among them the Provençal **bravade**, which is a kind of mock attack organised by the local youth. The curious sword dance known as **Bacchu Ber**, performed in Pont-de-Cervières every year on 16 August, features young men representing death, the stars and the rising sun. Entrevaux has its feast on Midsummer's Day, when the hero of the day, St John, is carried in effigy from the cathedral to the Chapel of St-Jean-du-Désert, out of town and back.

Every Provençal festival has its costumed musicians, playing the flute and the tambourin. In Moustiers-Ste-Marie, a group of musicians, known as the **Diane**, wakes the community every night around 4am with its lively music, during the nine days of the Moustiers festival. See also Calendar of Events p32.

HANDICRAFT

Woodwork

The densely forested Alps have, for centuries, produced enough wood to keep local craftsmen busy during the winter, thus maintaining a strong woodcarving tradition which blossomed between the 17C and 19C.

Woodcarving in Maurienne – The region was famous for its carved religious furnishings: pulpits, altars, statues. Bessans was known as early as the 17C for the skill of its craftsmen.

Chests and toys from Queyras – Wedding chests are an ancient speciality of the Queyras region. Carved out of larch with chisels and gouges, they are made up of four panels and a lid. Inside, there is often a small compartment meant for silverware and precious objects.

Queyras woodworkers made numerous other pieces of furniture which testify to their considerable skills: dressers, chairs, cots, cupboards and a wealth of objects for daily use such as spinning-wheels, lace hoops, bread seals (which enabled a housewife to identify her own bread baked in the communal oven), and boxes of all shapes and sizes.

Provençal furniture – In Haute-Provence, furniture is mainly made of walnut. In addition to chests, tables and beds, there are dresser cupboards, *crédences* and kneading-troughs.

The massive dresser cupboard has two double doors separated by two drawers and sometimes decorated with foliage, grotesque and diamond motifs. A *crédence* is a kind of sideboard with two drawers, sometimes with an added crockery shelf.

The kneading-trough or bread box was the most common piece of furniture; it was used to store food.

Moustiers Earthenware

The word *faïence* means "earthenware" in French, and comes from the name of an Italian town, Faenza, already renowned for its earthenware production before the 15C.

The earthenware tradition in Moustiers could never have developed without the town's plentiful supplies of clay, water and wood, but the turning point came in the 17C, when a monk brought back from Italy the secret process of earthenware making. Manufacture stopped altogether in 1873 and though later revived in the 1920s, now only serves the tourist trade.

Santons

They are the symbol of Provençal handicraft. These small earthenware figures, intended to represent the villagers of Bethlehem at the time of Christ's birth, are in fact typical Provençal villagers dressed in regional costume and representing 19C village trades.

There is a famous annual fair in the village of **Champtercier** (*see page 34*).

FOOD AND DRINK IN THE ALPS

Alpine cuisine owes much to the quality and freshness of local produce. Cheese from the rich alpine pastures, fish from the lakes and rivers, mushrooms from the forests, crayfish from the mountain streams, pork, game, potatoes and fruit form the basis of most alpine dishes.

As for Provençal cuisine, its main characteristic is the generous use of herbs, garlic and olive oil, the last replacing the butter so liberally used in the north.

REGIONAL PRODUCE

Fish – Fish from the lakes and mountain streams are a must in any gastronomic menu: arctic char, pike and trout are prepared in many different ways: *meunière* (dipped in flour and fried in butter), poached in butter sauce or braised.

Meat – Beef from Dauphiné is particularly famous, and delicious served *en daube* (stewed) with herbs from Provence. Lamb from the Sisteron area is said to be more tender and savoury than anywhere else. There is a whole range of charcuterie available, including hams, salamis and sausages such as gently spiced pork **diots** from Savoie. Rabbit and sometimes hare dishes are often served, such as in the Provençal **lapin en cabessol**, where the rabbit is stuffed.

Cheeses – Made from cow's, ewe's or goat's milk, cheeses vary a great deal according to the manufacturing process. The Savoie *départements* are particularly rich in their choice of cheeses, many designated as Appellation d'Origine Contrôllée (AOC). Alpine pastures of the Beaufortain and Tarentaise areas produce **beaufort**, one of the tastiest kinds of gruyère, whereas **reblochon**, an alpine farmhouse cheese, is a speciality of the Aravis. A similarly made goat's cheese is **chevrotin**.

Among the wide selection of tommes or sometimes tomes – the name means "round cheese" in Savoyard dialect – available in the northern Alps, **tomme de savoie** is the best known and the Bauges has its own AOC for **tome des bauges**. From the Chablais Massif, **abondance** is very tasty, firm cheese.

The small **St-Marcellin** is the most popular cheese of the lower Dauphiné area. Originally made from pure goat's milk, it is now processed from mixed goat's and cow's milk.

In the southern Alps, **picodon** from the Diois area is a sharp goat's cheese matured for at least three months, while **banon** is a rustic, strong-tasting cheese from the Montagne de Lure.

The term **fermier** indicates the cheese has been made at a farm, rather than in a cheese factory.

Herbs – Either growing wild or cultivated on sunny slopes, herbs are essential ingredients of alpine cuisine, especially in Haute-Provence. The general term *herbes de Provence* includes **savory** *(sarriette)* used in the making of goat's and ewe's milk cheeses, **thyme** *(thym)* used to flavour vegetables and grilled meat or fish, **basil** *(basilic)*, **sage** *(sauge)*, **wild thyme** *(serpolet)*, **rosemary** *(romarin)*, **tarragon** *(estragon)*, **juniper berries** *(genièvre)*, used in the preparation of game dishes, **marjoram** *(marjolaine)* and **fennel** *(fenouil)*. Herbs are also used as the basis of many alpine liqueurs.

SPECIALITY DISHES

Gratins – **Gratin dauphinois** is a rich mixture of sliced potatoes and milk; **gratin savoyard**, topped with tomme de savoie, is a similar dish in which milk is replaced by stock.

Tomme de Savoie

© Jean-Daniel Sudres/hemis.fr

Tarte au beaufort – This tart is filled with fresh cream mixed with beaufort cheese and served hot.

Tartiflette – Based on sliced potatoes and reblochon baked in the oven with onions and bacon pieces, with cream, there are a myriad of variations of this dish. *Péla* is a more traditional version made on top of the stove.

Aïoli – From the south, this rich mayonnaise is made with olive oil and flavoured with plenty of crushed garlic, intended to be served with hors-d'œuvre, poached fish and various other dishes.

Fougasse – This kind of flat-bread dough cooked in olive oil and topped with crushed anchovies is sold in most baker's shops in Haute-Provence and served as a snack or hors-d'œuvre.

Raclette and fondue – These simple cooked-cheese dishes are linked in most people's minds with dinner after a hard day's skiing. Raclette (originally from Switzerland) is cheese melted at the table, served with potatoes, pickles and *viande de grisons* (strips of dried beef) or other charcuterie. As for fondue, every home has its own recipe, with a mix of comté, emmenthal, beaufort or vacherin added to white wine to give texture, and garlic rubbed on the pot or a little kirsch added for extra flavour and kick.

Farcement – A delicious "pudding" of potatoes and dried fruit or even chestnuts melded together with strips of bacon on the outside.

Desserts – Strawberries, raspberries and bilberries are used to make delicious tarts. **Gâteau de savoie** is a light sponge cake, unlike the rich **walnut cake** from the Grenoble region.

Fruit is abundant in the southern Alps. Plums are the most popular filling of the traditional tart, known as *tourte*.

Thirteen desserts – Traditionally served for Christmas in Provence, in honour of Christ and the 12 apostles, these desserts include raisins, dried figs, several kinds of nuts, apples, pears, nougat (made from honey), prunes stuffed with marzipan, melons and dry cakes flavoured with orange blossom.

WINES AND LIQUEURS

Vines have been grown in Savoie since Roman times, and Savoie wines today are gaining greater recognition. The vineyard areas enjoy warmer microclimates, such as on the southern slopes of the Bauges mountains in the Combe de Savoie and beneath nearby Mont Granier; and close to the alpine lakes or rivers, such as at Chautagne, north of Lac du Bourget, or the southern shores of Lake Geneva. Several indigenous grape varieties are used – **Jacquère** for light dry whites, **Altesse** for fuller whites, **Roussette de Savoie** and **Mondeuse**, for mediumweight, earthy and fruity reds. Other varieties include **Chasselas** and **Bergeron** (Roussanne) for whites, and **Gamay** and Pinot for reds.

The designations "Vins de Savoie" or "Savoie" AOC may be followed by specific "crus" or village names. Among these are Abymes, **Apremont**, **Chignin**, Cruet and Jongieux for whites, plus the excellent **Chignin-Bergeron**. Roussette de Savoie AOC has its own crus including Marestel (from Jongieux) and Frangy (from the Usses Valley). A separate AOC is used for still white and sparkling **Seyssel**. **Ayze** is a good dry sparkling wine made close to the Arve river. The best reds are from **Chautagne** and, in particular, from **Arbin** for Mondeuse.

The wine production of Haute-Provence has considerably declined, but there are very decent reds from the **Côtes du Ventoux** AOC around the Bédoin area. The **Coteaux de Pierrevert** AOC near Manosque on the right bank of the Durance makes improving reds.

Clairette de Die is a delicious semi-sweet sparkling wine from the Diois.

The most famous **liqueur** in the northern Alps is **chartreuse**, known as the "elixir of life". Available in green or yellow versions, its secret formula, dating from the 16C, includes the essence of 130 different plants.

Other alpine liqueurs include **génepi**, gentian liqueur, marc de savoie, "Origan du Comtat" (from herbs on the slopes of Mont Ventoux) and absinthe, based on a medicinal plant, wormwood (*Artemisia absinthium*), well known in the Alps.

History

It is only just over 150 years ago that Savoie in the northern Alps was definitely annexed by France; before that it was an independent state. The southern Alps was made up originally of two provinces, Provence and Dauphiné, and the enclave of Nice belonged to the House of Savoie. The region has frequently been the scene of border battles between France and Italy, ever since Hannibal and his troops crossed the Alps and in more modern times, the tragic battle scars of World War II are widely in evidence. Today, in more peaceful times, this region of France thrives as an important tourist centre.

TIME LINE

Events in italics indicate milestones in history.

THE CELTS AND THE ROMANS

6–5C BC	The Celts progressively occupy the whole alpine region; the Allobroges settle in the area situated between the River Rhône and River Isère.
218	Hannibal crosses the Alps in spite of the Allobroges' attempt to stop him.
125–122	The Romans conquer southern Gaul.
121	The Allobroges finally accept Roman superiority.
1C BC	During the reign of Augustus, the whole alpine region is pacified.
End of 2C AD	The first Christian communities expand in spite of persecution.
4C	Christianity gets a firm hold on the region and bishoprics are founded.
313	*Proclamation of the Edict of Milan, through which Constantine grants religious freedom to the Christians.*
476	*Fall of the Roman Empire.*

THE FRANKS AND THE KINGDOM OF BURGUNDY

534–36	The Franks seize Burgundy and invade Provence.
8C	Franks and Arabs devastate Provence.
800	*Charlemagne becomes Emperor of the West.*
10C	Provence becomes part of the Kingdom of Burgundy. The Saracens are repelled.
987	*Hugues Capet is crowned King of France.*
1032	The Kingdom of Burgundy is annexed by the Holy Roman Empire. At the same time, the Archbishop of Vienne splits his huge territory into two: the future Savoie to the north and the future Dauphiné to the south.

SAVOIE, DAUPHINÉ AND PROVENCE

11–12C	Expansion of the three provinces. The Count of Savoie becomes the guardian of the alpine passes. The ruler of Dauphiné adopts the title of "Dauphin", and the Count of Provence Raimond Bérenger V inherits Forcalquier, thereafter united with Provence.
1209	*Albigensian Crusade.*
1232	Chambéry becomes capital of Savoie.
1268	The Dauphin Guigues VII marries the daughter of the Count of Savoie.
1270	*Death of King St Louis of France, who was married to the daughter of the Count of Provence.*
14C	Savoie becomes a powerful feudal state under Amadeus VI, VII and VIII.
1337–1453	*Hundred Years War.*
1349	Dauphin Humbert II, being in political and financial difficulties, negotiates the sale of Dauphiné to the King of France. The heir to

The House of Savoie

The House of Savoie was the longest reigning dynasty in Europe: it began with the feudal lord Humbert "White Hands", who became Count of Savoie in 1034 and ended with the last King of Italy, Umberto II, Victor-Emmanuel III's son, who abdicated in 1946. For nine centuries, the House of Savoie ruled over Savoie when it was a county, then a duchy; it governed Piedmont from 1429, Sardinia from 1720 and finally provided Italy's monarchs from 1861 to 1946.

Amadeus VIII

© The Art Gallery Collection/Alamy

How counts became dukes – Their role as "gatekeepers" of the Alps gave the Counts and Dukes of Savoie exceptional power. The history of Savoie amounts to a string of successive occupations, each followed by a treaty returning it to its rightful owner. During the Middle Ages, three of Savoie's rulers, Amadeus VI, VII and VIII, gave the region unprecedented ascendency; their court, held in Chambéry, rivalled in splendour those of the most important sovereigns of Europe. The most illustrious, **Amadeus VIII**, was the first to bear the title of Duke of Savoie and at the end of his life was elected as the last anti-pope under the name of Felix V. In the 16C, the Treaty of Cateau-Cambrésis freed Savoie from French domination, which had lasted 23 years. **Duke Emmanuel-Philibert** reorganised his domains and moved his capital from Chambéry to Turin, which was less easily accessible to French monarchs. His wish to expand on the Italian side of the Alps was accomplished during the reign of Victor-Amadeus II, who gained the kingdom of Sicily by the Treaty of Utrecht, then promptly exchanged it for Sardinia and became the king of that region.

Union with France – The people of Savoie were tired of their government, which they ironically called *il Buon Governo*. Moreover, they were worried by Cavour's anticlerical policy and turned towards France for help. Napoleon III and Cavour met in Plombières in 1858 and decided that, in exchange for France's help against Austrian occupation, Italy would relinquish Nice and Savoie if the populations concerned agreed. This led to the plebiscite of April 1860: by 130 533 votes to 235, the people of Savoie overwhelmingly agreed to become French.

the throne of France, from then on, bears the title of "Dauphin" (&see Grenoble).

1416 Savoie becomes a dukedom.

1419 Unification of Savoie and Piedmont.

1447 Dauphin Louis II (the future King Louis XI) settles on his domains, puts an end to the feudal system and creates the Parliament of Grenoble.

ITALIAN WARS AND WARS OF RELIGION

1461–83 *Louis XI's reign. The king inherits Savoie in 1481.*

1488 Crusade against Vaudois heretics in the alpine valleys.

1489–1564 Life of Guillaume Farel, a native of Gap, who preaches the Reformation.

1494–1559 The Italian Wars reveal the strategic importance of the Dauphiné passes.

1498	*Christopher Columbus finally reaches the American mainland.*
1536	With the Swiss cantons' help François I invades Savoie, which remains under French rule for 23 years.
1543–1626	Life of Lesdiguières, the Protestant governor of Dauphiné, who fights the Duke of Savoie
1559	Treaty of Cateau-Cambrésis: Savoie is returned to the Duke of Savoie who transfers his capital from Chambéry to Turin.
1562–98	Fierce fighting between Catholics and Protestants: Sisteron, Castellane and Seyne are besieged; armies of the rival factions clash at Allemagne-en-Provence.
1589	*Beginning of Henri IV's reign.*
1598	*End of the Wars of Religion; Edict of Nantes: Protestants obtain freedom of worship and guaranteed strongholds.*
17C	Savoie is occupied several times by French troops.
1628	Dauphiné loses its autonomy.

FROM LOUIS XIV TO THE REVOLUTION

1643–1715	*Louis XIV's reign.*
1685	*Revocation of the Edict of Nantes: Protestants flee the country.*
1692	The Duke of Savoie invades the southern Alps. The king sends Vauban to the area in order to build fortresses and strengthen existing ones (Briançon, Mont-Dauphin, Sisteron and Colmars).
1707	Invasion of Provence by Prince Eugène of Savoie.
1713	Treaty of Utrecht: Dauphiné and Provence expand; France loses part of the Briançonnais but receives the Ubaye region in compensation.

1736	Jean-Jacques Rousseau settles in Les Charmettes near Chambéry.
1740–48	War of the Austrian Succession. Eastern Provence is invaded by Austrian and Sardinian troops; Savoie is occupied by the Spaniards, France's allies. The Treaty of Aix-la-Chapelle ends the war; the Spaniards give up Savoie.
1774	*Start of the reign of Louis XVI, deposed by the Revolution less than 20 years later.*
1786	Balmat and Paccard are the first to climb Mont Blanc.
1788	Reaction in Grenoble and Vizille to the closure of the local *parlements* foreshadows the Revolution.
1789	*Bastille Day signals the start of the French Revolution; départements are created the following year.*
1791	Dauphiné is divided into three *départements*: Isère, Drôme and Hautes-Alpes.
1792	French revolutionary troops occupy Savoie, which becomes the "Mont-Blanc *département*".
1793	Creation of the "Alpes-Maritimes *département*" (returned to the Kingdom of Sardinia in 1814).

19C

1811	The route du Mont-Cenis is built by order of Napoleon I.
1815	By the Treaty of Paris, Savoie is given back to King Victor-Emmanuel I of Sardinia. Napoleon I, returning from exile on Elba, lands in Golfe-Juan on the Mediterranean coast and crosses the southern Alps to Grenoble.
1852	*Napoleon III becomes Emperor of France.*
1858	Napoleon III meets the Italian statesman Cavour in Plombières (Vosges region):

67

they agree that France shall help the King of Sardinia to drive the Austrians out of Italy; in exchange, France is to receive Nice and Savoie.

1860 In April a plebiscite is organised in Savoie: an overwhelming majority vote in favour of France's annexation of Savoie.

The new province is divided into two *départements*: Savoie and Haute-Savoie.

1869 Aristide Bergès harnesses the first high waterfall in Lancey thus becoming the "father" of hydroelectric power.

1870 *Proclamation of the Third Republic on 4 September.*

1872 Inauguration of the Fréjus railway tunnel.

End of the 19C Acceleration of the population drift from the mountains to the towns.

20C

1921 Megève becomes the first ski resort in the French Alps.

1924 First Winter Olympic Games held in Chamonix.

1940 The advancing German army is briefly halted by the River Isère. Italian attacks are repelled by border garrisons.

1944 Fierce fighting in the Vercors: Dauphiné is one of the main strongholds of the Resistance. One of the underground fighters' most heroic feats takes place on the Plateau des Glières (see Thorens-Glières).

1945 The Resistance liberates the Ubaye region.

1947 The Treaty of Paris alters the Franco-Italian border in favour of France, which receives the Vallée Étroite (see Le Briançonnais).

1955 Aiguille du Midi cable car inaugurated in Chamonix, making the high peaks accessible to all.

1956 Political regions created: northern French Alps falls into Rhône-Alpes; southern French Alps is part of Provence-Alpes-Côte d'Azur.

1963 Creation of the Parc national de la Vanoise, the first French national park.

1965 Inauguration of the Mont Blanc road tunnel.

1968 Tenth Winter Olympics held in Grenoble.

1973 Creation of the Parc National des Écrins.

1980 Opening of the Fréjus road tunnel, over 100 years after the railway tunnel.

1992 Sixteenth Winter Olympic Games held in Albertville.

1999 Fire in the Mont Blanc tunnel claims 41 lives.

21C

2008 As important Vauban sites, Briançon and Mont-Dauphin become classified as UNESCO world heritage sites.

2009 Annecy becomes the official French candidate to hold the 2018 Winter Olympic Games. Other applicants are Munich (Germany) and PyeongChang (South Korea).

2010 Savoie marks the 150th anniversary of the annexation of Savoie to France.

2010-11 The French Alps suffers its worst ski season, due to lack of snow, for a generation.

2013 Work due to begin on the Lyon–Turin Ferroviaire new train tunnel project.

Famous Natives of the Alps

Scholars and Writers

Savoie, which has belonged to France for just over 100 years, was, strangely enough, the cradle of the French language; the Savoyard humanist **Guillaume Fichet** (1433–78) set up the first printing press in Paris. Almost two centuries later, in 1606, the first French Academy was founded in Annecy; one of its founders was **St François de Sales** (1567–1622), who inspired religious life in his native Savoie and whose works contributed to the blossoming of the French language (*see Annecy*).

[245]

LE ROUGE
ET LE NOIR

CHRONIQUE DU XIXᵉ SIÈCLE.

PAR M. DE STENDHAL.

TOME PREMIER.

PARIS.
A. LEVAVASSEUR, LIBRAIRE, PALAIS-ROYAL.
1831.

©Bettmann/CORBIS

Title page from Le Rouge et le Noir by Stendhal published in 1831

One of the prominent early figures of the southern Alps was another humanist, **Guillaume Farel** (1489–1565), a native of the Gap area, who preached the Reformation with Calvin in Geneva.

At that time, Occitan was the dominant language of the southern Alps, as indeed of the whole of southern France; although its official use was discontinued in the 16C, it continued to be spoken by the people for another three centuries.

Champtercier, in the hills above Digne, was the birthplace of Pierre Gassendi (1592–1655), a philosopher, mathematician and scientist who rose to prominence in the 17C.

During the late 18C and early 19C, the brothers **Joseph** (1753–1821) and **Xavier** (1763–1852) **de Maistre** rejected the ideals of the French Revolution and supported absolute monarchy.

However, the most famous man of letters of the alpine region was undoubtedly the novelist **Henri Beyle** (1783–1842), a native of Grenoble, better known by his pseudonym **Stendhal**. Besides his masterpieces, *Le Rouge et le Noir* (1830) and *La Chartreuse de Parme* (1839), he wrote numerous studies, including *De l'amour* (1822), in which he analysed love, and *Vie d'Henry Brulard*, in which he depicted his childhood and adolescent years in Grenoble.

The 19C also saw the birth of the **Félibrige** movement, a revival of the Occitan language and of Provençal traditions under the leadership of **Frédéric Mistral** (1830–1914). One of his disciples, **Paul Arène** (1853–96), a native of Sisteron, wrote tales and poems in both French and Occitan. Better known was **Jean Giono** (1895–1970), born in Manosque, who celebrated Haute-Provence and its country folk in works such as *Regain* (1930) and *Jean le Bleu* (1932). His contemporary, **Alexandre Arnoux** (1884–1973), also chose Haute-Provence as the setting for most of his works (*Haute-Provence, Rhône mon fleuve*).

Jacques de Vaucanson with his duck automata

© Mary Evans Picture Library/Alamy

Notable Figures

Soldiers and Politicians

Born in Grésivaudan, **Bayard** (1476–1524), known as *le chevalier sans peur et sans reproche* ("the knight who is fearless and above reproach"), has gone down in history as the model soldier of his time. He had the honour of knighting King François I after the Battle of Marignan in 1515.

François de Bonne de Lesdiguières (1543–1626) led the Huguenots from Dauphiné during the Wars of Religion and was given command of the armed forces of his native region by King Henri IV, which led him to fight against the Duke of Savoie. He was the last Constable of France before Richelieu abolished the title in 1627.

In 1788 two natives of Grenoble, judge **Jean-Joseph Mounier** and barrister **Antoine Barnave**, led the peaceful protest of the Assemblée de Vizille, which paved the way for the French Revolution a year later. Another native of Grenoble, **Casimir Perier**, was Prime Minister of France in 1831–32, during the reign of King Louis-Philippe. His grandson was President of the French Republic in 1894–95.

Scientists and Inventors

Among her famous sons, Savoie counts the mathematician **Gaspard Monge** (1746–1818), who devised "descriptive geometry" at the age of 19 and later helped found the École Polytechnique, and the chemist **Claude Louis Berthollet** (1748–1822), who discovered the whitening properties of chlorine, widely used in the manufacture of linen.

Dauphiné on the other hand prides itself on having had several inventors such as **Vaucanson** (1709–82), who built automata and partly mechanised the silk industry, and **Xavier Jouvin** (1800–44), who devised a system of classifying hand sizes and invented a machine for cutting gloves to these sizes.

King François I knighted by Pierre Terrail, Seigneur de Bayard after the Battle of Marignan in 1515

© The Print Collector/age fotostock

Architecture

Religious Architecture

SISTERON – Ground plan of the Église Notre-Dame (12-15C)

The early Romanesque style from northern Italy is characterised by a chancel with three capital apsidal chapels and a single nave. The basilical plan has no transept.

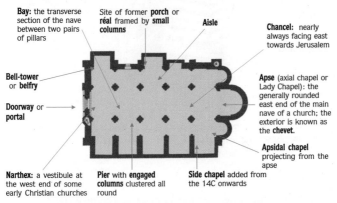

Bay: the transverse section of the nave between two pairs of pillars

Site of former **porch** or **réal** framed by **small columns**

Aisle

Chancel: nearly always facing east towards Jerusalem

Bell-tower or **belfry**

Doorway or **portal**

Apse (axial chapel or Lady Chapel): the generally rounded east end of the main nave of a church; the exterior is known as the **chevet**.

Apsidal chapel projecting from the apse

Narthex: a vestibule at the west end of some early Christian churches

Pier with **engaged columns** clustered all round

Side chapel added from the 14C onwards

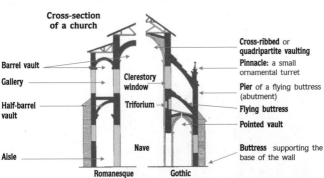

Cross-section of a church

Barrel vault

Gallery

Half-barrel vault

Aisle

Clerestory window

Triforium

Nave

Romanesque

Gothic

Cross-ribbed or **quadripartite vaulting**

Pinnacle: a small ornamental turret

Pier of a flying buttress (abutment)

Flying buttress

Pointed vault

Buttress supporting the base of the wall

GANAGOBIE – Doorway of the Abbey Church (12C)

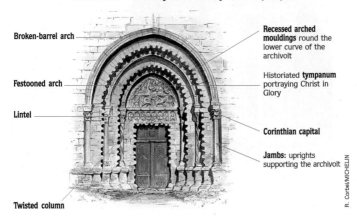

Broken-barrel arch

Festooned arch

Lintel

Twisted column

Recessed arched mouldings round the lower curve of the archivolt

Historiated **tympanum** portraying Christ in Glory

Corinthian capital

Jambs: uprights supporting the archivolt

R. Corbel/MICHELIN

EMBRUN – Porch (14C) of the Cathédrale Notre-Dame

This highly ornamented and elegant feature, usually found on the north side of a church, is common in northern Italy.

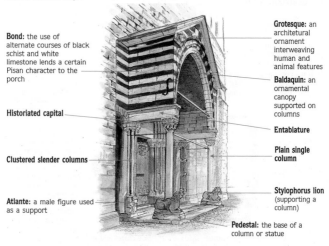

Bond: the use of alternate courses of black schist and white limestone lends a certain Pisan character to the porch

Grotesque: an architetural ornament interweaving human and animal features

Baldaquin: an ornamental canopy supported on columns

Historiated capital

Entablature

Plain single column

Clustered slender columns

Atlante: a male figure used as a support

Stylophorus lion (supporting a column)

Pedestal: the base of a column or statue

EMBRUN – Chancel and crossing of the Cathédrale Notre-Dame (12-13C)

The Romanesque parts (barrel-vaulted aisles and apse) blend harmoniously with the pointed vaulting of the Gothic nave

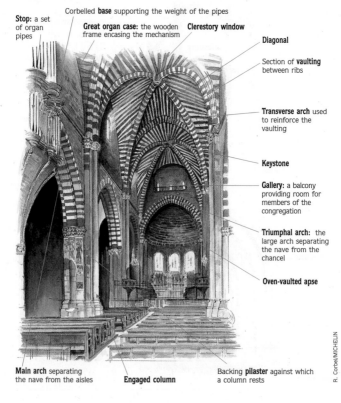

Corbelled **base** supporting the weight of the pipes

Stop: a set of organ pipes

Great organ case: the wooden frame encasing the mechanism

Clerestory window

Diagonal

Section of **vaulting** between ribs

Transverse arch used to reinforce the vaulting

Keystone

Gallery: a balcony providing room for members of the congregation

Triumphal arch: the large arch separating the nave from the chancel

Oven-vaulted apse

Main arch separating the nave from the aisles

Engaged column

Backing **pilaster** against which a column rests

R. Corbel/MICHELIN

ARVIEUX – Nave of Renaissance church (16C) with Baroque altarpiece

Cornice: the third or upper part of an entablature resting on a frieze

Attic: the top part of a structure designed to make it more impressive

Altarpiece

Frieze: a decorative band near the top of an interior wall below the cornice

Entablature: it comprises the architrave, the frieze and the cornice.

Corner piece: the wall section situated between the arch and its frame

Coffer: a sunken panel in a vault or ceiling

Pilaster: an engaged rectangular column

Agrafe: an ornamental element in the form of a mascaron placed on the keystone

NÉVACHE – Baroque altarpiece from the Église St-Marcellin-et-St-Antoine (15-17C)

Modillion: a small console supporting a cornice

Crowning piece

Scroll

Armature: a frame of metal bars supporting and protecting a window

Cartouche: an ornamental tablet often inscribed or decorated

Composite capital combining elements from different classical orders

Saddle-bars fixed into the masonry to maintain stained-glass panels in place

Twisted columns decorated with vine branches

Foliated scrolls: a kind of ornamentation depicting foliage

Niche: recess in a wall, usually meant to contain a statue

Altas

Altascloth

Predella: the bottom tier of an altarpiece divided into several panels

R. Corbel/MICHELIN

Palaces and Castles

GRENOBLE – Façade of the Palais de Justice (16C)

The doorway and chapel of the former palace of the Dauphiné Parliament date from the Late Gothic. The main part of the edifice bearing the Renaissance imprint contrasts with the plainer left-hand extremity which is more recent.

Triangular pediment

Corinthian pilaster

Chimney stack: a structure in which several chimneys are grouped

Table: a flat vertical surface

Mullioned window: a mullion is a vertical post dividing a window

Curved pediment

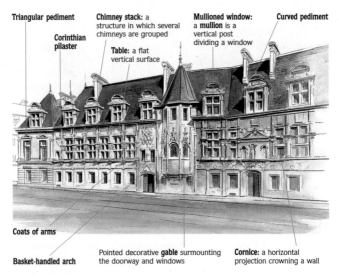

Coats of arms

Basket-handled arch

Pointed decorative gable surmounting the doorway and windows

Cornice: a horizontal projection crowning a wall

ST-GEOIRE-EN-VALDAINE – Château de Longpra (18C)

This former fortified castle, turned into a residential castle in the 18C, has very steep roofs well-suited to the hard winters of the Dauphiné region.

Dormer window

Chimney pot

Central block projecting from the rest of the building

Roof clad with shingles

Wrought-iron balcony

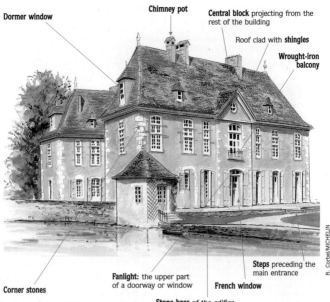

Corner stones

Fanlight: the upper part of a doorway or window

French window

Steps preceding the main entrance

Stone base of the edifice

R. Corbel/MICHELIN

CASTLES AND FORTS

Feudal castles – These, or what is left of them, usually draw the visitors' attention because of the sheer beauty of their ruins standing in picturesque surroundings in isolated spots or overlooking ancient villages. Very few of them offer any real architectural interest, either through their style or state of preservation. Particularly noteworthy, however, are the Château de Simiane, dating from the 12C and 13C, the Château de Bargème (13C) and the Château de Montmaur (14C). Many castles, such as those of Montbrun-les-Bains and Tallard, were badly damaged during the Wars of Religion, which were especially violent in that area. Some castles were entirely rebuilt during the 17C and 18C, while sometimes retaining part of their former structure: such is the case of the castles of Gréoux-les-Bains, Esparron-du-Verdon and Château-Queyras.

Fortifications – Towns had, since antiquity, been protected by walls which often had to be rebuilt or consolidated during the Middle Ages and even later, until the reign of Louis XIV, owing to constant border conflicts. Embrun has retained a 12C tower and Sisteron still boasts four 14C towers and a citadel dating from the end of the 16C. However, most of the border fortifications were built by Vauban, who, from 1693 onwards, endeavoured to "enclose" Haut-Dauphiné.

Sébastien le Prestre de Vauban (1633–1707) took his inspiration from his predecessors, in particular Jean Errard (1554–1610), who is believed to have rebuilt the Sisteron fortifications and wrote a treatise on fortifications. Having observed the numerous sieges which took place during his lifetime, Vauban was able to evolve a series of new types of fortifications, well adapted to the local terrain. In his opinion, Dauphiné was not sufficiently well protected by the natural barrier of the Alps, which could be crossed at certain times of the year. So he studied in great detail the advantages and drawbacks of natural sites such as peaks, passes and valleys in order to choose the best position for his defences. He protected gun sites from enemy fire by means of armoured casings, shielded gunners and soldiers, and made an exact science of defensive features like fortified gates and broken-line walls. The results of his ingenuity can be seen in Briançon, Mont-Dauphin, Château-Queyras, Colmars and Entrevaux, fortresses which were still being used in the 19C.

Residential châteaux – They first appeared in the 16C, when former castles were often remodelled and a Renaissance building was added to the existing structure (Allemagne-en-Provence, Château-Arnoux and Tallard). During the 17C and 18C, the châteaux lost their military aspect, which gave

Ville Haute with Porte Pignerol, Briançon

way to comfort and attractive features. There are practically no constructions of this type in the area with the exception of the Château de Sauvan, designed by Jean-Baptiste Franque in 1719, which is a real gem. The Château de Malijai is another example of the Classical style in the region.

Traces from the past – Most ancient villages, especially in the southern Alps, have retained a wealth of details from the main architectural styles of the past: Romanesque vaults, cellars and doorways; Gothic arches and twin openings; Renaissance lintels, carved jambs decorated with acanthus leaves, mullioned windows and elegant wrought iron; 17C pediments and bosses; 19C Neoclassical buildings and various other imitations.

TRADITIONAL ARCHITECTURE
HOUSES

In the Savoie and Dauphiné mountains, rural dwellings are in harmony with the harsh conditions of their environment: isolation, bad weather and intense cold. Houses are stocky with few large windows. A lot of space is set aside for storage: a wood shed, larders for cheese and for dryng meat, and spaces for hay and grain, often above the living area to insulate it.

All the houses have balconies that enable their occupants to take advantage of the slightest ray of sun; protected by overhanging roofs, these balconies are also used for drying clothes as well as storing wood for winter use, etc.

In areas where snow is abundant, roofs are of prime importance and are always very large and overhanging all round to protect the houses and their immediate surroundings. They are either steep and smooth in order to allow the snow to slide off easily, or less steep, with protective bars in order to allow the snow to remain, forming a protective layer against the cold.

In forested areas, timber is the most common building material; in the past, trees were selected from north-facing slopes, where they grow more slowly and their wood is therefore harder.

Villages are often situated halfway up south-facing mountain slopes with all the houses facing the sun. In flat areas and on plateaux, houses are usually grouped round the church.

In Haute-Provence on the other hand, where climatic conditions are milder in spite of strong winds and a marked contrast between summer and winter, stone and tiles are the traditional building materials. Villages are built on dry rocky south-facing slopes, their houses nestling round the shaded square with the café, church and town hall nearby.

Préalpes de Savoie – In the forested areas of the Chablais, Aravis and Bauges mountains, the most traditional type of house is the wooden chalet built on a stone base with an overhanging roof covered with wood (shingles) or slate tiles and balconies all round. The living

House from the Maurienne region

R. Corbel/MICHELIN

House from the Vercors region

quarters for people and animals as well as the storage space are on the ground floor whereas the hay and grain store is beneath the roof. Traditionally, a little building called a *mazot* stood apart from the farmhouse in case of a serious fire to the main building. It was used for valuables and important storage.

Préalpes du Dauphiné – In Chartreuse, large stone-built farmhouses are surrounded by various outbuildings. In the Vercors area, on the other hand, stone-built gabled houses, two or three storeys high, put everything under one roof.

Oisans region – In this high-mountain area, houses are rustic in appearance and their rather flat roofs are covered with heavy slabs of schist, known as *lauzes*, although these are now often replaced by slates or corrugated metal.

Beaufortain, Tarentaise and Maurienne regions – In forested areas, houses have wooden façades and flat roofs covered with wood. Wherever scree-covered slopes predominate, houses are stone built with wooden balconies, few small windows and relatively flat roofs covered with *lauzes*, which retain a thick layer of snow in winter.

Briançonnais and Vallouise regions – This is an area of scattered stone-built houses: the animals' stalls are on the lower level behind a line of stone arches, the living area, entirely surrounded by wooden balconies, is on the intermediate level, and the barn, accessible from the rear, on the upper level.

Queyras region – Built of stone and wood, the houses of this area are highly original (&see St-Véran). The ground floor, which includes the living area and stalls, is stone built and surmounted by several wooden storeys used for drying and storage. The roofs, overhanging on the balconies, are covered with wood or *lauzes*.

Embrunais and Ubaye regions – This area offers great architectural variety. Houses are rectangular and stocky, stone built with wooden balconies; the steep four-sided roofs are covered with slates. The interior plan is simple: the kitchen and animals' stalls are at ground level, the bedroom and threshing floor above and the barn at the top of the house.

Haute-Provence – Village houses, often built of irregular stones and several storeys high, have a Mediterranean look about them, owing to their rounded tiles covering the roofs and forming under the eaves a decorative frieze known as a *génoise*. Isolated houses, called *granges*, are generally larger, but still fairly high, and surrounded by outbuildings. Outside walls are coated with roughcast and, inside, floors are usually covered with terracotta tiles.

HILLTOP VILLAGES

These hilltop villages and small towns, known as *villages perchés* (Sisteron, Forcalquier, Digne), contain an amazing number of dwellings within a relatively small area, enclosed by a wall.

Their origin is thought to go back to the 9C Arab invasions. In fact, the inhabitants of the region deliberately chose to build their villages on high ground, between the vineyards (which have now disappeared) and other crops. These villages are situated high above the surrounding countryside, on the edge of plateaux or on top of rocky peaks to which they cling.

The steep and twisting streets or lanes are for pedestrians only; they are paved or simply stony, interrupted now and then by flights of steps and often spanned by arches. In some cases, the ground floor of the houses consists of rows of arcades which protect passers-by from the sun and rain. Tiny shaded squares are adorned with attractive fountains and sometimes with a belfry surmounted by a wrought-iron campanile. The high, narrow houses huddle together round the church or the castle which dominates them.

Old studded doors, bronze door knockers and carved lintels show that these were once the residences of the local nobility and wealthy middle class.

During the 19C and 20C, villages moved down into the valleys as peasants chose to live in the middle of their land, where they built their farmhouses. However, places like Montbrun-les-Bains, Lurs, Banon, Bargème, Brantes, Valensole, Auvare, Simiane-la-Rotonde and St-Auban-sur-l'Ouvèze still remind visitors of the old Provençal way of life.

DOVECOTES AND BORIES

There are many **dovecotes** in the southern Alps, particularly in the Diois, Baronnies and Forcalquier areas: pigeons were a precious source of food and their droppings were used as fertiliser for the kitchen garden. There were two basic styles: some dovecotes formed part of a larger structure including a shed and hen house on the lower level; others were separate buildings raised on pillars. The latter were subject to tax.

The drystone huts known as **bories** are typical of the Forcalquier area. Their use was never clearly defined and at times served as sheep pens, tool sheds or shepherds' huts. Whether round or square, they have only one opening, the door. They were built of thick limestone slabs, layered up into distinctive false corbelled vaulting: as the walls were built up, each stone course was laid to overhang the preceding one so that finally the small opening at the top could be closed by placing one slab over it.

CAMPANILES

These metal structures, either simple cages containing a bell, or intricate wrought-iron masterpieces, form part of the Provençal skyline. Campaniles were designed to withstand the assaults of the powerful mistral wind better than the traditional limestone belfries, and today they can be seen on top of church towers, town gates and other public buildings.

Generations of craftsmen have toiled to produce elaborate wrought-iron works, onion or pyramid shaped, spherical or cylindrical. Most remarkable are those on the tower of the Église St-Sauveur in Manosque, the clock tower in Sisteron, the church tower in Mane and that of the Chapelle St-Jean in Forcalquier, not forgetting the lace-like onion-shaped structure surmounting the Soubeyran gate in Manosque.

Belfry on the clocktower in Sisteron

©Brigitte Merle/Photononstop/Tips Images

Sundials on the church in Ville-Vieille, Le Queyras

©Jean-Luc Armand/Photononstop/Tips Images

SUNDIALS

In the southern Alps, from the Briançonnais to the Vallée de la Tinée, numerous buildings, houses, churches and public buildings are decorated with colourful sundials appreciated by lovers of popular art and photographers alike. Considered as a kind of homage to the sun, these dials, mostly from the 18C and 19C, were the work of travelling artists, often natives of Piedmont like Jean-François Zarbula, who travelled the length and breadth of the region for 40 years making many sundials on his way and decorating them with exotic birds. The sundial makers had to be familiar not only with the art of setting up a dial, but also with the art of fresco painting. **Decorations** are often naive yet charming, dials being set within a round, square or oval frame and surrounded by motifs depicting aspects of nature such as flowers, birds, the sky, the sun or the moon. The most elaborate of these sundials include some Baroque features: *trompe-l'œil* decoration, fake marble, scrolls, shells, foliage, fake pilasters; the best example of this type of work can

be seen on the towers of the Collégiale Notre-Dame in Briançon.

Mottos are equally interesting; they express the passing of time: *"Passers-by, remember as you go past that everything passes as I pass"* (Villard-St-Pancrace). Mottos seek to remind us that we must make good use of our time:

"May no hour go by that you would wish to forget", *"Mortal, do you know what my purpose is? To count the hours that you waste"* (Fouillouse).

CONTEMPORARY ARCHITECTURE

During recent years, the economic expansion of the Alps, the rapid development of the towns and the advent and growth of winter-sports resorts have created a need for public and residential buildings. Today the Alps rank as one of the most prominent French regions in the field of modern architecture.

Public buildings – Between 1964 and 1968, Grenoble was turned into a vast building site for the Winter Olympic Games. At the same time, an extensive programme of research into the technical and aesthetic aspects of modern architecture was launched.

Urbanisation was not so systematic in other alpine cities; however, there were some modern achievements such as the sports complex in Chamonix, the Maison des Arts et Loisirs in Thonon, the Palais de Justice in Annecy, the Maison de la Culture in Chambéry, the Dôme in Albertville and Grenoble Museum.

Winter-sports resorts – Rapidly developing resorts tended to follow the general trends of modern urban architecture and serve the demand for comfort and organised entertainment, a combination which was bound to produce its share of functional, unremarkable buildings, yet some of these new creations proved original; for instance, Avoriaz with its strange, rock-like buildings or the triple pyramid of La Plagne, both controversial but defining projects.

Flaine, completed in 1969, was built from scratch as a car-free resort at high altitude, conceived by the American Bauhaus architect Marcel Breuer. The layout of the resort at different levels was designed to blend into the contours of the surrounding mountainsides, and even the colour of the concrete façades of the buildings was planned to match that of the rocks. At the base of the ski slopes, bright sculptures by Picasso, Vasarely and Dubuffet were placed almost to provide a contrasting affront to nature.

The concept of the different resort levels of Les Arcs was originally that of a team of architects led by Charlotte Perriand, a colleague of Le Corbusier. The result was three high-altitude villages, mainly built of wood, combining functionality with respect for the natural environment. A fourth village, Les Arcs 1950, completed in 2003, is deemed to be less austere and perhaps heralds in a more attractive, aesthetic style of ski-resort architecture for the 21C.

Religious Art

Churches and chapels – In the north of the region, churches and chapels are small, but solidly built on steep slopes or summits with thick stone walls pierced by small windows. In Savoie, churches are surmounted by steeples swelling out into onion shapes, whereas in Dauphiné, stone spires are topped by pyramids.

In the south, the majority of churches date from the Romanesque period. The main features of the **Early Romanesque** style, imported from Italy, are the simple plan, massive appearance and rustic aspect of the buildings. The best examples of this early style, in which a minimum of decoration was used, are the Église St-Donat, the crypt of Notre-Dame-du-Dromon and of the Prieuré de Vilhosc near Sisteron. The **Late Romanesque** style flourished during the 12C and 13C, introducing a harmony between spaces, openings and curves as well as the general use of more refined building stones. However, in spite of gaining in height, churches retained their rustic look while the influence from Lombardy and Piedmont could still be felt, particularly in the Briançonnais, Queyras, Ubaye and Embrun regions. Designed like basilicas, these churches were adorned with porches, often supported by squatting lions as in Embrun, Guillestre, St-Véran and La Salle. The slender steeples were surmounted by four-sided pyramids. Exterior ornamentation remained sober owing to the use of hard limestone, difficult to carve. Interior decoration was also rare, with one exception, the Monastère de Ganagobie, which has a beautifully carved pediment and remarkable mosaics. The Romanesque style lasted into the 14C.

The **Gothic** style had only a limited impact on the region and is best represented by the cathedrals built in Embrun and Forcalquier.

The only worthy example of the **Baroque** architectural style in the southern Alps is the Église Notre-Dame de Briançon, built between 1703 and

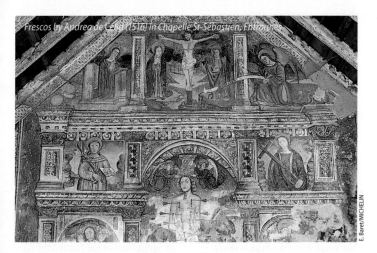

Frescos by Andrea de Cella (1516) in Chapelle St-Sébastien, Entraunes

E. Baret/MICHELIN

1718. However, there is a wealth of Baroque ornamentation, such as wreathed columns, carved pulpits, organ cases, altarpieces and recessed statues, all richly painted and gilded.

In the north, on the other hand, particularly in Savoie, many churches were built or decorated at the time of the Counter-Reformation (a movement which, during the 16C and 17C, tried to counteract Protestant austerity with an abundance of ornamentation, concentrating mainly on decorative altarpiece and pulpit designs).

Artists mostly came from Italy. The best examples of this rich style are Notre-Dame-de-la-Gorge and the church of Champagny-en-Vanoise.

Murals – Pilgrims and travellers crossing the Alps in the 14C and 15C decorated churches and chapels with bright frescoes in a naive style. These illustrated the life of Jesus (Chapelle St-Antoine in Bessans, Chapelle de Puy-Chalvin and Chapelle de Prelles, to name a few) and various saints, as well as many episodes from the Testaments.

An equally popular theme was that contrasting the "**virtues**", represented by beautiful young maidens, and the "**vices**", riding various symbolical animals. In most cases, the connection is still clear to modern eyes, such as pride riding a lion, anger on the back of a leopard and laziness mounted on a donkey, but others, such as the badger

of avarice, lack the same powerful associations today.

The most common technique was tempera painting which used an emulsion of pigment mixed with egg, glue and casein.

Crosses and oratories – Discreet and humble, dotted along paths and on the edge of precipices, crosses and oratories represented an art form which expressed the religious fervour of mountain folk and travellers having to face a hostile natural environment. Oratories were originally mere heaps of stones known as "Montjoie", sometimes with pre-Christian origins, but they gradually became larger, were surmounted by crosses and included a recess which sheltered a small statue. Crosses were erected in the most dangerous places to comfort passersby. The most remarkable of these are situated in the Queyras.

Modern chapels and churches – Due to the development of winter-sports resorts, and the relative wealth in the northern Alps in particular, many churches and chapels have been built in the 20C. The most prolific architect has been Novarina (see *Évian-les-Bains*), with important structures including the church at Vongy near Thonon, the Avoriaz Chapel, and most notably of all Notre-Dame-de-Toute-Grâce at Plateau d'Assy. Its exterior features a mosaic by Léger; interior decoration includes works by Matisse and Chagall.

Nature

The mountain range of the Alps – the highest in Western Europe – stretches along a curved line from Nice on the Mediterranean coast to Vienna in Austria, covering a distance of 1 200km/746mi.
The French Alps extend from Lake Geneva to the Mediterranean, a distance of 370km/230mi, and they are over 200km/124mi wide at their widest point, between the Rhône Valley and the Italian Piedmont.
The highest peak, Mont Blanc, rises to 4 807m/15 771ft, but the altitude gradually decreases towards the south and the range is easily accessible through a series of deep wide valleys.

LANDSCAPES

The region is famed for magnificent views which appear to change with every bend of the steep, winding roads. It is an area full of contrasts, from the colourful shores of Lake Geneva to the glaciers of Mont Blanc, the chalk cliffs of Vercors and the dry Mediterranean landscapes of Haute-Provence.
Geologists divide the French Alps into four main areas:

◆ The **Préalpes**, or alpine foothills, consisting almost entirely of limestone rocks formed during the Secondary Era, except in the Chablais area.

◆ The **alpine trench**, a depression cut through marl, lying at the foot of the central massifs.

◆ The **central massifs**, consisting of very old and extremely hard crystalline rocks. The tectonic upheavals of the Tertiary Era folded the ancient land mass (⌖ see below), creating "needles" and high peaks, which are the highest of the whole alpine range. From north to south, these massifs are the Mont Blanc, Belledonne, Grandes Rousses, Écrins and Mercantour.

◆ The **intra-alpine zone**, forming the axis of the Alps. It consists of sedimentary rocks transformed and folded by the violent upheavals which took place in the area. It includes the Vanoise, the Briançonnais and the Queyras as well as the upper valleys of the Tarentaise, the Maurienne and the Ubaye.

FORMATION OF THE ALPS

Among the "younger" of the Earth's mountains, formed at roughly the same time as the Pyrenees, the Carpathians, the Caucasus and the Himalayas, the Alps are also one of the most geographically complex ranges. Long before the folding of the peaks some 65 million years ago, and the erosion by water, wind and ice which continues to this day, powerful forces were at work beneath the surface.
To explain the phenomenon of geological upheaval that has formed the Alps, we turn to the concept of plate tectonics, which describes the Earth's crust as a series of rigid plates moving in relation to one another. The Alps are situated at the boundary of the African and European plates. During the **Palaeozoic Era**, 540–250 million years BP, a huge folding of the Earth's crust produced the Hercynian mountains, which had a crystalline structure similar to that of the Vosges and the Massif Central today. The luxuriant vegetation, stimulated by the hot and humid climate, produced a huge amount of plant deposits that are the origin of coalfields at La Mure and in the Briançonnais. Erosion followed, and after 200 million years the crystalline foundation was submerged under the sea, and a layer of marine sediments thousands of metres thick was formed.
The **Mesozoic Era**, 250–70 million years BP, saw the land compressed by the African continent, which was moving to the north. The seabed deposits of limestone and sand (which were transformed into sandstone when compressed) as well as clay (which under high pressure often flaked into shale) piled up on the ancient foundation of crystalline rocks. The climate was uniform; forests consisted of pines, oaks, walnut trees, eucalyptus and palm trees. Huge reptiles such as dinosaurs roamed the earth and the first birds appeared.
The **Tertiary Era**, 65–1.8 million years BP, saw the formation of the high range

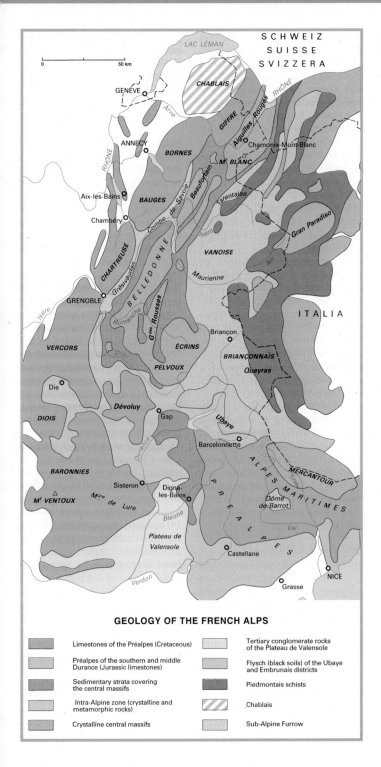

GEOLOGY OF THE FRENCH ALPS

Limestones of the Préalpes (Cretaceous)	Tertiary conglomerate rocks of the Plateau de Valensole
Préalpes of the southern and middle Durance (Jurassic limestones)	Flysch (black soils) of the Ubaye and Embrunais districts
Sedimentary strata covering the central massifs	Piedmontais schists
Intra-Alpine zone (crystalline and metamorphic rocks)	Chablais
Crystalline central massifs	Sub-Alpine Furrow

of mountains we see today. Starting about 30 million years BP, a spur of the African plate, consisting of Italy and part of the Balkans, advanced and collided with Europe, pushing up masses of schist, folding the area like plasticine, and forming the Italian Alps and the Vanoise to the east, Chablais to the west and, to the north, the Swiss Alps.

More recently, 10–5 million years BP, the continuing force of the African plate pushed up the ancient crystalline foundation from under the seabed deposits of limestone, marl and clay; this layer literally came unstuck and began to slide westwards in spectacular folds, creating the Préalpes.

A depression appeared between the crystalline massifs and the Préalpes, which eventually became the alpine trench through the work of erosion. Most recently, in the last few millions of years, the Dauphinois and Savoy areas were covered by shallow inland seas, where a layer of sediment accumulated from erosion of the nearby mountains, forming the gentle, fertile countryside of Albanais and Geneva.

A general cooling of the Earth's atmosphere over the last 2.5 million years caused by the rise of the Himalaya and the Isthmus of Panama, has brought about a series of glacial periods during which the whole alpine region was covered with a huge mantle of ice. Erosion then worked relentlessly on a complete remodelling of the Alps into the mountain range it is today.

REGIONAL LANDSCAPES

These vary considerably according to the different geological structure of each area. So it is logical to adopt the geologists' division of the Alps into four parts (Ⓒsee p82) preceded by what we might call the alpine fringe. From west to east and south to north, they are the Préalpes, the alpine trench, the central massifs and the intra-alpine zone.

Alpine Fringe

The Albanais, the Geneva area and the Bornes Plateau situated on the edge of the northern Alps offer landscapes of green rolling hills dominated by a few moderate mountain ranges such as the **Salève** south of Geneva and the **Mont du Chat** near the Lac du Bourget. The basins left behind by retreating glaciers have been filled in by deep lakes: Lac d'Aiguebelette and Lac du Bourget.

Préalpes

The northern Préalpes lie just beyond the alpine fringe along a north–south axis, forming a barrier which rarely rises above 2 500m/8 202ft.

They consist of five distinct massifs carved out of limestone (except for the Chablais), separated by transverse valleys: the Arve river valley, and the "cluses" of the towns of Annecy, Chambéry and Grenoble.

Overlooking Lake Geneva and drained by the three Dranse rivers, the **Chablais** is backed by the **Giffre** with its lively winter resorts, Samoëns and Flaine.

The **Bornes** Massif, flanked by the **Chaîne des Aravis** in the east, is drained by several rivers including the Fier and extends from the valley of the Arve to the blue waters of Lac d'Annecy.

Further south, the **Bauges** Massif, extending to the Cluse de Chambéry, offers pleasant pastoral landscapes.

The **Chartreuse** Massif, with the Cluse d'Isère to the south, stands like an imposing limestone fortress; features include high cliffs, deep gorges, valleys with pastures and magnificent dense forests on the well-watered slopes.

The **Vercors** is the largest of the Préalpes massifs; within its impressive outer ramparts, this natural citadel offers beautiful forest and pastoral landscapes, as well as striking gorges and popular resorts such as Villard-de-Lans.

The southern Préalpes spread over a vast area along a curved line in a northwest–southeast direction. The Durance Valley divides them into two groups.

West of the river, on the Dauphiné side, is the wild and austere **Dévoluy**, with its cliffs and bare summits below which sheep and cattle graze. The wooded **Bochaine** marks the transition between north and south whereas the **Diois** and **Baronnies** already offer typical

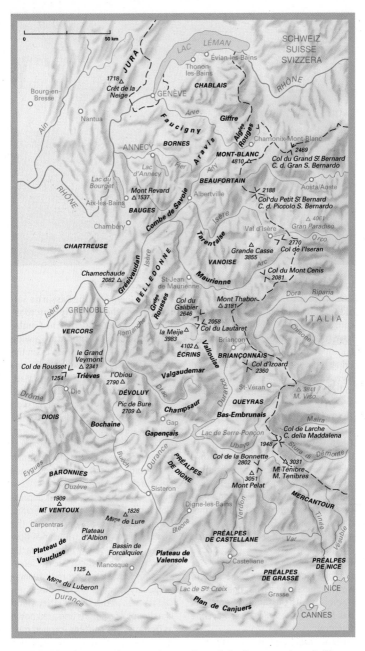

southern landscapes where soaring limestone peaks collapse into waves of rock set in conflicting directions.
To the south, the limestone massif of **Mont Ventoux** stands alone, towering 1 909m/6 263ft above the Avignon basin.

East of the Durance, the relief becomes more intricate, without any apparent plan; the mountain ranges of the **Préalpes de Digne** and **Préalpes de Castellane** are cut crosswise by deep wild gorges guarded by picturesque

Demoiselles Coiffées de Pontis

S. Sauvignier/MICHELIN

towns like Sisteron, Digne and Castel-lane. These areas are the least populated of the alpine region. Because of strict conservation regulations, the slopes have retained their varied vegetation, but the summits are mostly bare.

Lying between the River Verdon and River Var, the **Préalpes de Grasse** rise to an altitude varying between 1 100m/ 3 609ft and 1 600m/5 249ft.

The **Préalpes de Nice** are deeply cut in a north–south direction by rivers (Var, Tinée, Vésubie) which make their way to the sea through impressive gorges overlooked by villages perched high above the river beds.

Lying between the Préalpes, the **Plateau de Valensole** occupies the former delta of the River Durance filled in by an accumulation of rocks from nearby mountains.

These rocks and pebbles, bound together by a kind of natural cement, form a conglomerate which has been carved by erosion into the famous **Pénitents des Mées** (*see Vallée de la Moyenne Durance*).

Further east, there are several lime-stone plateaux through which streams penetrate and disappear into sink-holes. Spectacular gorges have been carved out by the River Verdon and River Artuby.

Alpine Trench

In the northern Alps, the **Bassin de Sallanches** and the **Val d'Arly** form, together with the depression of the **Combe de Savoie** and **Grésivaudan**, a wide longitudinal plain into which open the upper valley of the River Isère (Tarentaise) and the valleys of the Arc (Maurienne) and of the Romanche (Oisans). Owing to the means of communication provided by this internal plain, to the fertile soil which favours rich crops (maize, tobacco, vines) and to the availability of hydroelectric power, the alpine trench has become one of the most prosperous areas of the region.

In the southern Alps, a similar depression runs along the foot of the Écrins, Briançonnais and Queyras massifs; the River Durance and its tributaries flow through this relatively flat area partly flooded by the artificial Lac de Serre-Ponçon. Some strange rock formations, carved out of ancient moraines, can be seen in this region. They stand like groups of columns and are known as **Demoiselles coiffées** (capped maidens) because they are crowned by a piece of hard rock (*see Barrage et Lac de Serre-Ponçon*). Between Sisteron and Manosque, the fertile Durance Valley brings the typical vegetation and orchards of Provence into the heart of the southern Alps.

Central Massifs

This central mountain range includes **Mont Blanc**, the **Aiguilles Rouges**, the **Beaufortain**, the **Belledonne**, the **Grandes Rousses**, the **Écrins-Pelvoux** and, in the south, the **Mercantour**. Together, these massifs, rising to over 4 000m/13 123ft, form the high Alps, consisting of hard crystalline rocks, which were uplifted during the Tertiary Era while their sedimentary cover was removed. The lower-altitude Beaufortain is the only massif to have retained its layers of schist; it offers pleasant pastoral landscapes scattered with wooden chalets. Beautiful lakes have filled in the basins left by the glaciers.

Intra-Alpine Zone

Situated between the central massifs and the Italian border, the **Vanoise** Massif and the **Briançonnais-Queyras Massif** also belong to the high Alps, but they consist of a mixture of schist and metamorphic crystalline rocks. Valleys are deep and slopes are turned to pasture. Thanks to its mild, sunny climate and snow-covered slopes, the Vanoise (which has the Tarentaise and Maurienne as natural boundaries and includes the Parc national de la Vanoise) has the highest concentration of winter resorts in the French Alps, embracing Val d'Isère, Tignes, Courchevel, Méribel, Val Thorens, La Plagne and Les Arcs.

Due to the diversity of its rock structure, the Briançonnais-Queyras Massif has a more complicated relief: sandstone, limestone and schist carried over from the Italian side as a result of overthrust. Its characteristic southern light, blue skies and generous sun make this area one of the healthiest in Europe, which explains the rapid development of summer and winter tourism centred round high villages such as St-Véran (2 040m/6 693ft).

The **Gap**, **Embrun** and **Ubaye** districts, lying between the high Alps and the Préalpes, offer a mosaic of heights, small basins and wide valleys carved out of layers of "black soil", or flysch in the case of the Ubaye.

ALPINE RELIEF

The slow but irresistible action of glaciers, rivers, rain and frost has completely remodelled the Alps over thousands of years into today's mountain range.

The action of the glaciers – Around 10 000 years ago, glaciers covered the whole alpine range and spread over the adjacent flat areas as far as Lyon. Some of these "solid rivers" were huge, reaching thicknesses of 1 100m/3 609ft in the Grésivaudan, for instance. They scooped out cirques with steep back walls and dug U-shaped valleys characterised by successive narrowings and widenings and a series of steps, with tributary valleys "hanging" over the main ones.

Alpine glaciers today – Since the start of the 20C, Alpine glaciers have been

Parc national de la Vanoise

©Marco Maccarini/iStockphoto.com

Mer de Glace, Chamonix

© mcech/iStockphoto.com

consistently receding because they are not being sufficiently renewed, and today they cover an area of only 400sq km/154sq mi; four-fifths of them are in Savoie (Mont Blanc and Vanoise), the remainder being in the Écrins Massif. Research in the 21C indicates glaciers are being reduced at an even faster rate than before, an indicator of climate change.

The Mer de Glace is a very good example of a "valley glacier". Moving downstream, we find in succession a **névé**, an expanse of snow not yet turned into ice, and a **glacial "tongue"** cut by deep crevasses. Level changes are marked by jumbled piles known as **séracs**; accumulations of debris carried down by the glacier are called **lateral moraine** when deposited on the edges, **terminal moraine** when deposited at the end and **medial moraine** when deposited between two joining glaciers.

Erosion by water – When the ice mantle disappeared, mountain streams and rivers began to smooth out the relief. Connecting gorges opened up the "bolts" and joined the floor of a "hanging" valley to that of the main valley. These valleys, wide but often closed off, like that of Chamonix, for example, would be completely isolated but for audacious road construction. There are gorges of another kind, mainly in the Préalpes, which cut across the axis of the

folds: they are called **cluses** (transverse valleys). They are often the only means of communication between the mountain and the lower areas.

The most active mountain streams deposit debris they have been carrying when they reach the bottom of the main valley and their accumulation at the foot of the slopes forms alluvial cones which obstruct the valleys.

STREAMS AND RIVERS

The southern Alps have three distinct river networks: in the centre the Durance and its tributaries, in the east the Var, which gathers water streaming down the Alpes Maritimes, and in the west the tributaries of the Rhône.

Mediterranean rivers are particularly interesting because they behave like real mountain streams. During the summer, they are reduced to a trickle owing to the absence of rain and intensive evaporation, but in spring and autumn, violent rainstorms or sudden thaws fill up the river beds so suddenly that the flow of foaming water tumbles down at the speed of a galloping horse. The rate of flow of the River Var, for instance, varies from 17cu m/600cu ft per second to 5 000cu m/176 580cu ft per second. The Durance, Verdon, Aigues and Ouvèze rivers are much the same. However, the Durance and Verdon have been harnessed by dams (Serre-Ponçon across the

Durance, Castillon and Ste-Croix across the Verdon) and canals. The impressive gorges dug by these rivers (Grand Canyon du Verdon, Gorges du Cians) are one of the main attractions of Haute-Provence.

Underground streams forming mysterious hydrographic networks sometimes reappear further on; streams from the Montagne de Lure, for instance, feed the spectacular resurgent Fontaine-de-Vaucluse (👁 see THE GREEN GUIDE PROVENCE: Fontaine-de-Vaucluse).

ALPINE CLIMATE

The Alpine range is divided into two distinct climatic regions: the northern Alps, which are subject to west winds originating from the Atlantic, and the southern Alps, which enjoy a Mediterranean climate. The separation between these two regions follows a line drawn between high mountain passes from west to east: Col de Rousset, Col de la Croix Haute, Col du Lautaret and Col du Galibier.

Rainfall over the **northern Alps** is abundant all year round and temperatures are low. The Préalpes and central massifs get the brunt of the rainy weather. The intra-alpine zone, protected by these barriers, is drier and sunnier; snow remains on the slopes longer. However, many factors such as altitude, aspect and the general direction of the various ranges and valleys, contribute to create a great variety of microclimates.

Altitude – Temperatures fall rapidly as the altitude increases (roughly 1°C/2°F every 100m/328ft); interestingly, this phenomenon can be reversed in winter, during periods of settled weather, as cold, heavier air slips down the slopes and accumulates in the valleys and the warm air rises.

Relief – It has an influence on rainfall and wind direction; rain and snow fall more generously on the first heights in their path and on slopes exposed to the wind. Winds generally blow along wide valleys, particularly during the warm season when, towards midday, warm air rises from the valleys and causes clouds to form round the summits. This

is a sign of continuing fine weather. Later on in the day, the process is reversed and a cold mountain breeze blows down into the valleys. Heights usually attract storms which are often violent and spectacular.

The climate enjoyed by the **southern Alps** displays typical Mediterranean features: a good deal of sunshine, dry weather, clear skies, the absence of mist or fog, rare yet abundant precipitation and the famous mistral wind. In winter there is a fair amount of snow and plenty of fine weather in which to enjoy it. Spring is characterised by a short rainy spell while the mistral blows hard from the southwest. Summer is hot and dry over the whole of Haute-Provence and the air filled with the delicate scent of lavender and thyme.

Nearer the summits, temperatures are more moderate. In the autumn violent storms are succeeded by sunny spells, the air is pure and the light ideal for discovering the beauty of nature.

FLORA

In mountain areas the pattern of vegetation is influenced not only by the climate and the type of soil, but also by aspect and altitude, which define a succession of vertical stages. This staging is modified by humans, who have done much to alter landscapes. South-facing slopes, which offer the best conditions for settlement and agriculture, have been subject to deforestation, while northern slopes, often uninhabited, have retained their trees; a pattern seen at its best in valleys running from east to west.

Slopes are usually farmed up to an altitude of about 1 500m/4 921ft; above this there is a belt of conifer forest. From around 2 200m/7 218ft upwards, the trees give way to alpine pastures with their rich mixture of wild grasses and alpine flora. Above 3 000m/9 843ft, bare rock prevails, with mosses and lichens clinging to it in places.

TREES IN NORTHERN ALPS

The Alps are famous for their forests of conifers. Old **fir trees** have broad crowns with flattened points looking

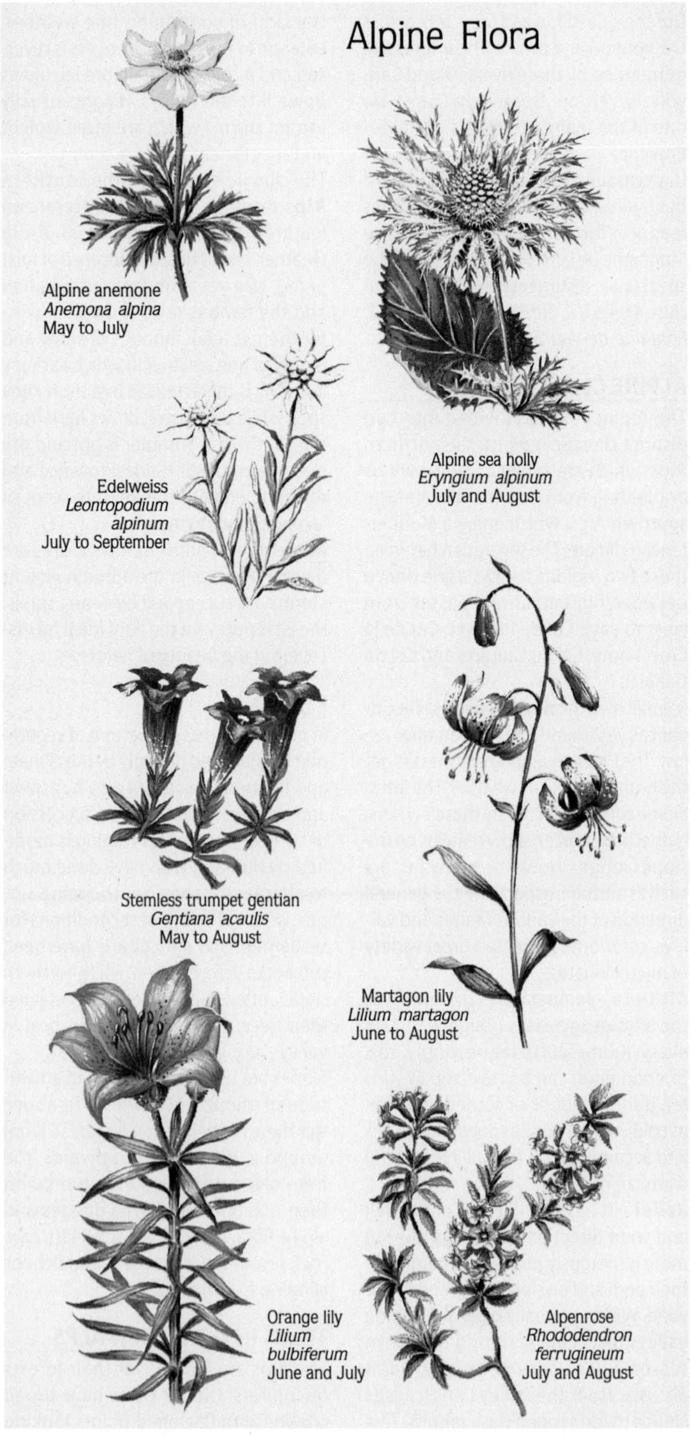

Alpine Flora

Alpine anemone
Anemona alpina
May to July

Alpine sea holly
Eryngium alpinum
July and August

Edelweiss
*Leontopodium
alpinum*
July to September

Stemless trumpet gentian
Gentiana acaulis
May to August

Martagon lily
Lilium martagon
June to August

Orange lily
*Lilium
bulbiferum*
June and July

Alpenrose
*Rhododendron
ferrugineum*
July and August

M. Janvier/MICHELIN

like storks' nests. The bark is greyish; the cones, standing up like candles, break up when ripe and shed their scales. The soft needles are lined up like the teeth of a comb and have a double white line on their inner surface. The **spruce** is the most common tree on north-facing slopes. It has a pointed, spindle-shaped crest and drooping branches, and its reddish bark becomes deeply fissured with age. It has sharp needles and its hanging cones fall to the ground in one piece when ripe. The only conifer in the French Alps to shed its leaves in winter, the **larch** is commonly found growing on south-facing slopes, particularly in the *Alpes sèches* (dry Alps). The cones are quite small. The delicate, light green foliage casts relatively little shade, thus favouring the growth of grass, one of the attractive features of larch woods, while the dropped needles create an acidic soil that favours wild rhododendrons and bushes such as blueberries. The many species of **pine** all have needles growing in tufts of two to five encased in scaly sheaths. The forest pine, with its tall slender trunk, grows in considerable numbers in the southern Alps, usually on the sunny slopes.

Deciduous Trees

The beech prevails in the Préalpes taking over from oak above an altitude of about 1 000m/3 281ft. With its thick boughs beech trees may provide shade for many rare plants, including Turk's-cap lily, belladonna or deadly nightshade and speedwell. Among other deciduous trees, there are alders, maples, birches, service trees, willows and laburnums with their lovely clusters of yellow flowers.

MEDITERRANEAN VEGETATION

Trees – Several varieties of oaks and pines, as well as almond trees and the typically Provençal cypress and olive, grow in the southern Alps, either in cultivated areas or scattered on dry, rocky moors known as *garrigue* (see below). Such landscapes can be seen in the Durance Valley, on the southern slopes of Mont Ventoux or the Montagne de Lure and in the Baronnies and Diois areas. Further north, above 600m–800m/1 969ft–2 625ft, forests of white oaks, forest pines and beeches prevail, particularly on north-facing slopes. Such forests often alternate with heaths where gorse, box and lavender grow.

The evergreen **holm oak** has a short, thick-set trunk with a wide-spreading dome and fine, dark green leaves. It grows on calcareous soil at less than 328m/1 076ft; in stunted form, it is a characteristic element of the *garrigue*. The deciduous **downy** or **white oak**, so-called because the undersides of the leaves are covered with dense short white hairs, requires more water than the evergreen oak. It is found in valleys and on the more humid mountain slopes.

The **aleppo pine**, one of the Mediterranean species of pine trees, has a light, graceful foliage and a trunk covered with grey bark, which twists as it grows.

The outline of the dark **cypress**, a coniferous evergreen, marks the Mediterranean landscape with its tapered form pointing towards the sky, while the common **almond tree** delights the eye with its lovely early spring pink blossoms.

Garrigue – This word is used to describe vast expanses of rocky limestone moors. Vegetation is sparse, consisting mostly of holm oaks, stunted downy oaks, thistles, gorse and cistus as well as wild lavender, thyme and rosemary interspersed with short dry grass which provides pasture for flocks of sheep. The scent of the *garrigue* is renowned.

ALPINE FLORA

The name "alpine" is normally used to describe those plants which grow above the tree line. Because of the short growing season (July and August), these hardy species flower early, while the disproportionate development and colouring of the flowers is the result of exposure to intense ultraviolet light. Their resistance to drought is often their main characteristic; many have woolly leaf surfaces and thick, water-retaining leaves.

Black grouse

Chamois

Bouquetin
(ibex)

Salamander

Tengmalm's owl

Mouflon

Bearded vulture

M. Guillou/MICHELIN

FAUNA

Above the tree line, at high altitudes, animals have learned how to adapt to the harsh environment, where it is possible to survive only by building up one's defences against the cold and the lack of food. Some animals are protected against the cold by their thick coats or plumage; others such as the marmot hibernate below ground, so solving the problem of food shortage. The mountain hare, stoat and the snow-partridge, which are the favourite game of foxes and birds of prey, make themselves inconspicuous by changing colour with the seasons. In winter large herbivores like bouquetin (ibex) and chamois make their way down to the forests in search of food and shelter. Human's expansion into their habitat threatens animals' survival: many seem doomed to extinction except in conservation areas.

Mammals – The **bouquetin** (ibex) is a stocky wild goat with curved, ridged horns which can be more than a metre long; this peaceful animal enjoys basking in the sun. When winter arrives, the males join up with the females, who are smaller and shyer. The males then fight for the females and the clatter of their horns echoes through the mountains.

The **chamois**, the "alpine antelope", has a reddish-brown coat, thicker and darker in winter, with a black line on its back. Its small head is surmounted by curved slender dark horns. This strong animal jumps from one rock to the next and climbs the steepest passages; its thin, strong legs and its special hooves explain its extraordinary agility. A chamois can weigh as much as 50kg/110pounds. In summer it feeds on grass; in winter it goes down to the forest and nibbles at the bark of trees.

The reddish-brown summer coat of the **stoat** becomes white in winter apart from a thin tuft of black hair at the end of its tail. This small carnivorous mammal lives among stones or near chalets.

The **marmot** is well suited to the vast parks of the area. Skiers cause it no anxiety at all, since it passes the winter season hibernating under the snow in warm tunnels. From April to September, it enlivens alpine pastures with its whistling call.

You may need a stroke of luck to catch a glimpse of a **lynx** stalking the slopes at sunset in search of birds, marmots, chamois and small deer. Virtually extinct in the region by the beginning of the 20C, this wild cat has returned to the woods of Savoie from Switzerland.

The **mouflon** is a large wild sheep, living in flocks led by the older males. Originally from Asia, but well adapted to the Mediterranean climate and vegetation, it has been introduced into the Mercantour and Queyras nature parks.

Butterflies and moths – There are more than 1 300 different species of butterflies and moths in the Alpes-de-Haute-Provence *département* alone and more than 600 species in the area around Digne (there is an exceptionally fine collection of lepidoptera in the local museum), among them some 180 butterflies which represent three-quarters of the total butterfly population of France. Among the most remarkable species are the Swallowtail butterfly, the Parnassius and, smaller but rarer, the Diana and the Proserpina, the Jason, the Vanessas and the Érèbiae (including the almost extinct Scipio), which hover over lavender fields. The destruction of the traditional environment and the development of industries are responsible for numerous species becoming extinct.

Birds of prey – **golden eagles** can often be seen throughout the Alps, circling above their territory, which might cover most of a valley. Breeding pairs remain together for life, rearing their young in eyries on the side of inaccessible cliff-faces. Eagles prey on marmots in summer and feed off carcasses when food becomes short in winter.

In winter and spring, you may hear, but probably not see, the **Tengmalm owl**, whose call is long and piercing. It is well adapted to cold and mountain forests. The reintroduction of the **bearded vulture**, which soars on wings 2.8m/9ft wide from tip to tip, has been a great success story, and you can see these magnificent birds both in the Verdon and in the Aravis mountains.

Lac d'Annecy - a view of Duingt and the Massif des Bauges
© Pierre Jacques/hemis.fr

DISCOVERING THE FRENCH ALPS

North
French Alps

Mention Annecy to anyone who has visited and a wistful sigh usually escapes them; its extraordinary setting – the colourful old town clustered around little canals that reach out to the idyllic lake is picture-postcard perfect. Lake Annecy itself, almost completely surrounded by mountains standing at a respectful distance, is equally enchanting and inviting, even if the surrounds are entirely built up. The nearby Aravis mountain resorts are renowned for their ability to sustain farming traditions at the same time as welcoming tourists.

Picture-postcard Old Town

The distinctive triangular shape of the old prison in Annecy's Palais de l'Île is said to be one of the most photographed views in France, and few can resist taking the definitive snap from the bridge over the Thiou. Walking along the flower-lined canals and peering into shops under the arches can while away a happy hour or two, before you are inevitably drawn back to the gorgeously clear lake.

Annecy is Haute-Savoie's departmental capital, and recent renovations on the new side of town have improved the somewhat awkward transition between the pretty old town, and the new part, developed to sustain the growing population. A big advantage of the influx of newcomers to the town is the proliferation of cultural events, as well as a better choice of restaurants, shops and wine bars.

Traditions and Tourism

For the visitor to the Aravis Massif, less than an hour up the road from Annecy, the sense that these mountains are not

Highlights

1 Walk on the lakeshore, or better still, take a boat trip on the lake from **Annecy** (p108)

2 On a drive around Lake Annecy, make a stop to see the exceptional bay at **Talloires** (p111)

3 A walk in the **Semnoz**, taking in the views of the lake (p113)

4 The drive from Annecy to La Clusaz via the pretty **Manigod Valley** (p119)

5 The view from the **Col des Aravis** to Mont Blanc is inspiring, especially at dusk (p125)

just for tourists is palpable, with people going about their lives in unspoiled, authentic villages.

Ever-improving ski areas are a great attraction for day trippers and holiday makers alike. In addition to a range of sporting activities, La Clusaz, Le Grand-Bornand, Manigod and Thônes offer numerous events throughout the

Talloires

© Pierre Jacques/hemis.fr

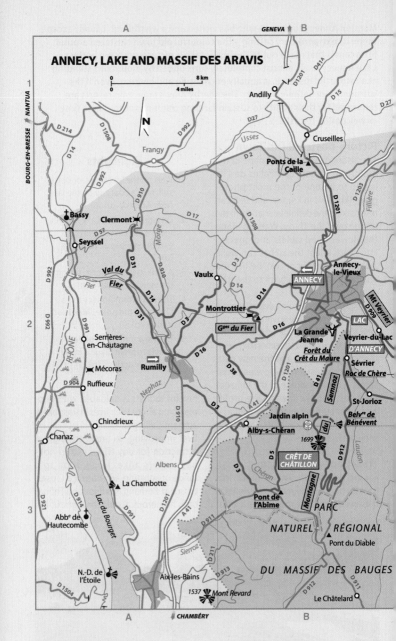

ANNECY, LAKE AND MASSIF DES ARAVIS

year; at summer festivals the russet-coloured Abondance cows, famed for the reblochon cheese made from their milk, take pride of place.

Be warned, the roads are busy on fine winter weekends when locals head up to enjoy the mountains, and it is a very popular area during the French February school holidays. At other times, there is a happy compromise between traditional farming communities, vibrant businesses and visitors enjoying the relative peace and clean air above the busy valley.

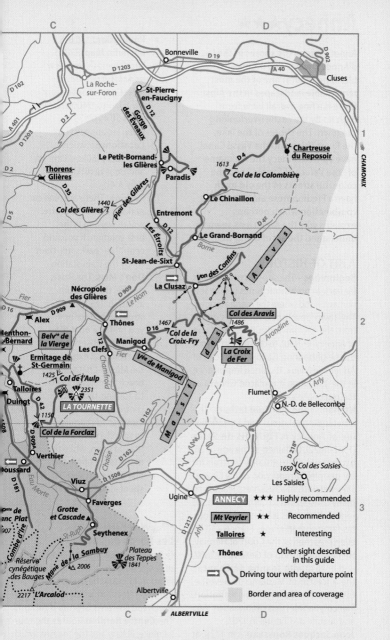

ANNECY	★★★ Highly recommended
Mt Veyrier	★★ Recommended
Talloires	★ Interesting
Thônes	Other sight described in this guide
⇨ ⭕	Driving tour with departure point
	Border and area of coverage

Winter Olympics Contender

The Aravis ski resorts welcome an unprecedented number of top-level winter-sports athletes, who formed an important part of the French team at the Vancouver Winter Olympics in 2010. The region is very experienced in hosting top-level winter-sports events, with Annecy being one of the three contenders to host the 2018 Winter Olympics, and the Aravis resorts of La Clusaz and Le Grand-Bornand ideally situated to hold the cross-country and nordic events.

Annecy★★★

Annecy lies on the shores of the Lac d'Annecy, water and mountains blending to form one of the most remarkable landscapes in the Alps: there is a fine overall view from high up by the castle overlooking the town. The shores of the lake, the River Thiou and the Vassé Canal have earned Annecy the nickname of "the Venice of Savoie", and the colourful streets of the old town have a Piedmontese air, a charming combination which perhaps explains why the Annéciens seem to understand the art of living well.

A BIT OF HISTORY

Beginnings – The site was occupied as far back as prehistoric times (a lake settlement stood where the marina is now). The town developed round its castle from the 12C onwards under the name of Annecy-le-Neuf, to distinguish it from the neighbouring Gallo-Roman city of Annecy-le-Vieux. It gained importance in the 13C when it replaced Geneva as the regional capital.

Humanist and spiritual father – The outstanding religious and literary figure of Annecy is **François de Sales** (1567–1622). Ordained at the age of 26, his manual of spirituality written for lay people, *Introduction to the Devout Life*, met with much success leading to many conversions to Catholicism in the region. Known as a friend of the poor, his fame spread across France and he even preached at the Court of Henri IV. He became Bishop of Geneva in 1602, and in 1610 with **Jeanne de Chantal**, the ancestor of Madame de Sévigné, founded the Order of the Visitation. François de Sales was canonised in 1665 and Jeanne de Chantal in 1767.

Jean-Jacques Rousseau – In 1728, at the age of 16, **Rousseau**, ill-treated by his employer, fled from his home town, Geneva, to Annecy; there he was dazzled and disarmed by **Madame de Warens**, who had been asked to convert him to Catholicism. It was the start of a lifelong love of the city for the philosopher.

▶ **Population:** 136 815.
Michelin Map: 328 J5. Local maps *see below and Massif des Aravis.*

Info: Centre Bonlieu, 1 r. J. Jaurès, 74000 Annecy. ☎04 50 45 00 33. www.lac-annecy.com.

Location: Between Chambéry (50km/31mi SW) and Geneva (61km/38mi N by A 41).

Parking: There are nine car parks in the town centre, where walking is the best solution. If you find central car parks full, then try by the train station.

Don't Miss: The Palais de L'Île, the museum at the château, and a stroll by the lake or if you prefer, a boat trip.

Kids: The Observatory, an ecological exhibit at the Musée-Château; the beach at Albigny; and La Turbine, the science centre at Cran Gevrier.

Timing: You should try to spend a morning in the old town, while the markets are open; the rest of the day can be spent around the lake.

WALKING TOURS
Les Bords du Lac★★

See map II. Allow 2hrs. Leave the car at Centre Bonlieu, or the l'Hôtel-de-Ville. From quai Eustache-Chappuis on the Canal du Vassé or place de la Libération head towards avenue d'Albigny. The **Centre Bonlieu** houses the tourist office, library and the theatre, which most notably hosts the International Film Festival of Animation as well as the Annecy Festival of Italian Film. Built by local architects Maurice Novarina and Jacques Lévy, you will see the reflection of the green lawns of the Champ de Mars in the large windows.

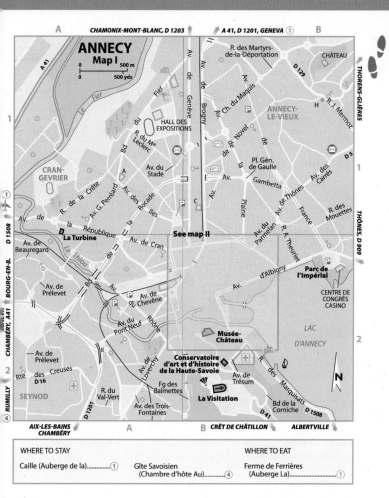

ANNECY
Map I

WHERE TO STAY		WHERE TO EAT
Caille (Auberge de la)..............①	Gîte Savoisien (Chambre d'hôte Au)............④	Ferme de Ferrières (Auberge La)..............①

Avenue d'Albigny
This royal avenue, lined with ancient plane trees, crosses the Champ de Mars where the locals used to watch military manoeuvres. On the left, the enormous **Préfecture** building, constructed after the Savoie region was annexed to France (1860), is in Louis XIII Revival style.

◉ *Walk to the viewing table by the lake.*

Parc de l'Impérial
Shaded by beautiful trees, this pleasant park at the east end of avenue d'Albigny takes its name from a luxury hotel, built in Belle Époque style, which today incorporates a conference centre and a casino. The park includes the main lakeside beach.

◉ *Return to the town along the lake.*

Pont des Amours
The bridge spans the Canal du Vassé, offering lovely views of the canal one way, with its small wooden boats, and of the wooded Île des Cygnes the other.

Jardins de l'Europe★
At the time of the annexation of Savoie to France, these gardens were laid out as an arboretum with species from Europe, America and Asia.
You can admire several huge **sequoias** and a ginkgo biloba, also called "maidenhair tree". From the banks of the Thiou, the embarkation point for the lake cruisers, you can look up to the massive castle buildings.

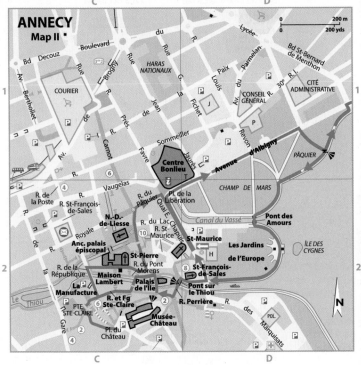

WHERE TO STAY	WHERE TO EAT	
Jardin du Château		
(Chambre d'hôte Le)..............②	Bilboquet (Le).............................②	Savoie (Auberge de)...............⑧
Kyriad Centre (Hôtel)....................④	Contresens.....................................④	St-Maurice (Brasserie La)......⑩
Nord (Hôtel du)................................⑥	Fréti (Le)..⑥	

▶ *Walk to pl. de l'Hôtel-de-Ville and continue through Old Annecy.*

Old Annecy★★
Allow 1hr 30min. Start from pl. de l'Hôtel-de-Ville and walk across quai E. Chappuis.

The waterways of the Thiou and the Vassé wind through the colourful old part of town, which is now largely pedestrianised. The sizeable churches of St-Maurice and St-François-de-Sales mark the transition between the Sardinian architecture of the 19C old town and the commercial town of the first part of the 20C.

Église St-Maurice
The church was built in the 15C with a large overhanging roof in typical

regional style. Inside, the vast Gothic nave is flanked with side chapels built by aristocratic families or guilds, whose arms and emblems are displayed.

▶ *Walk towards the river.*

Église St-François-de-Sales
St François de Sales and St Jeanne de Chantal were originally buried in this Baroque-fronted 17C church, which once belonged to the order they founded.

▶ *Cross the bridge over the River Thiou, the natural outlet of the lake.*

Pont sur le Thiou
The oddly shaped **Palais de l'Île**★★ in the middle of the river offers the most famous **view**★★ of Old Annecy.

▶ *Follow r. Perrière with its arcaded houses and turn right into r. de l'Île. Alongside the old prison, turn right into a passage. Turn right twice more to cross back over the Thiou. From the bridge over the southern arm of the Thiou, take in the pretty view of the houses along the quai de l'Île. On the right is the entrance for the Palais de l'Île.*

Palais de l'Île★★

🕐 *Open same hours as Musée-Château.*
🎫 *3.60€ (combined ticket 6.40€).*
Free first Sun of month.
📞 *04 50 65 08 14.*

This monument is so photographed, it has become a local symbol. Built on an island in the 12C, when Annecy was little more than a small fisherman's town, the palace was used in turn as the Count of Geneva's residence, the mint, the law courts and a fearsome prison, which it remained until 1870, resuming that grim role for a time during World War II.

It now houses a **centre for urban and local patrimony**, with displays of the town at different periods.

▶ *Turn right out of the passage, then left on the quai de l'Île and walk past the Morens Bridge. Next, turn left into r. de l'Île to go up the hill to the château or continue to the right and reach it climbing up from r. Ste-Claire.*

Musée-Château d'Annecy★

🕐 *Open Jun–Sept daily 10.30am–6pm; Oct–May Wed–Mon 10am–noon, 2–5pm.* 🕐 *Closed public holidays.*
🎫 *4.90€.* 📞 *04 50 33 87 34.*

This handsomely restored former residence of the lords of Geneva, from a junior branch of the House of Savoie, dates from the 12C to the 16C. The castle was damaged by fire several times, abandoned in the 17C, then used as a garrison before being restored with the help of public funds.

To the right of the entrance stands the massive 12C Tour de la Reine, with 4m/13ft-thick walls; this is the oldest part of the castle. From the centre of the courtyard, you face the austere living quarters of the Logis Vieux (14C–15C), with its stair turret and deep well; to the left is the early Renaissance façade of the Logis Nemours (16C) and to the right the late-16C **Logis Neuf**, which housed the garrison of the castle. At the end of the courtyard are the 15C Logis and **Tour Perrière**, which house the 🔵 **Observatoire régional des lacs alpins**, illustrating the various aspects of mountain lakes including the effects of pollution on the fauna and displaying archaeological finds.

The Logis Vieux and the Logis Nemours house an interesting **museum of regional art** on three floors linked by

Palais de l'Île

103

a spiral staircase. Note the remarkable fireplaces facing each other in the vast kitchen, the splendid guardroom with its rows of columns and the great hall. There are collections of art, carved glass and popular art including pottery, earthenware, glassware and furniture.

▷ *Leave the château turning right on r. Ste-Claire and down the steps; or you can turn left at côte St-Maurice or take the passage Nemours. From the Ste-Claire gate, do an about-turn and via r. de la République, reach r. J.-J.-Rousseau. On both sides of the pretty bridge the sluice-gates of the Thiou, designed by the engineer Sadi Carnot in 1874, regulate the water and the level of the lake.*

Rue Ste-Claire★

The high street of Old Annecy is lined with arcaded houses. The 16C mansion at **no. 18** has a particular link to the bishopric of St François de Sales. Thirty years before Richelieu's Académie Française was inaugurated, de Sales became the co-founder of the Académie Florimontane, a literary institution intended to promote the public good, influence opinion and spread the cult of beauty. On the corner of rue de la République stands a former convent of St Claire which became known as the "**Factory**" when it was turned into a spinning mill in 1805. The whole area has been tastefully renovated and pedestrianised.

▷ *Climb up la côte St-Maurice to the left before the Ste-Claire gate or continue to the passage Nemours alongside the ruins of the old ramparts which lead to the château and the Visitation Church.*

Ancien Palais Épiscopal
10 r. J.-J.-Rousseau.
The old episcopal palace was built in 1784, at which time the house belonging to Madame de Warens was demolished. In memory of their special encounter, in the courtyard a bust of Jean-Jacques Rousseau was placed, surrounded by his famous "gold balustrade".
The ceiling of the entrance porch reveals a contemporary painting by Claude Viallat *(Suites ovales).*
At 15 rue Jean-Jacques-Rousseau is the elegant 16C **maison Lambert**, where St François de Sales wrote his most famous treatise, l'*Introduction à la vie dévote.*

Cathédrale St-Pierre
Built in the 16C with a Renaissance façade and a Gothic interior, it became the episcopal seat of Bishop François de Sales when he was evicted from Geneva by the Calvinists; however, it was elevated officially to a cathedral only in 1822. Jean-Jacques Rousseau sang in the choir and played the flute in the cathedral.

▷ *Turn left into r. Filaterie, with its grand arcades, and arrive at pl. Notre-Dame.*

Place Notre-Dame
Enlarged in 1793 at the expense of the 14C church chevet, on one side of the square is the old **hôtel de ville** with its elegant 18C façade. Notice the beautiful forged-iron staircase on which the trout of Annecy's coat of arms forms the central point.
Église Notre-Dame-de-Liesse – The church was completely reconstructed between 1794 and 1851, retaining from the original building its bell tower along with a south-facing window built in the Flamboyant Gothic style. Dedicated to the Mother of God since the 12C, in 1338 anti-pope Clément VII of Avignon founded a seven-year jubilee here known as the **grand Annecy pardon**.

▷ *Take the r. Notre-Dame to rejoin the r. du Pâquier, bordered by arcades; at no.12, the 17C Hôtel de Sales is decorated with sculptures representing the seasons. Take the quai E.Chappuis right to get back to the pl. de l'Hôtel-de-Ville.*

ADDITIONAL SIGHTS
Conservatoire d'Art et d'Histoire de la Haute-Savoie
🕐*Open Jun–Sept daily 10am–6pm; Oct–May Mon–Fri 10am–noon, 2–5pm.* 🕐*Closed public holidays.* ⚹*Free.* 📞*04 50 51 02 33.*

This art and history museum, situated just south of the castle, is housed in a fine 17C building, extended in the 19C. The collections include numerous paintings and engravings depicting landscapes of Haute-Savoie, as well as 18C and 19C paintings.

In the chapel, the Cité de l'image en mouvement (CITIA) has an **exhibit of animated films**; for more than 20 years Annecy has hosted an annual festival of animation (🕐*open Jun–Sept daily 10.30am–6pm, Oct–May Wed–Mon 10am–noon, 2–5pm).*

Basilique de la Visitation
🕐*Open daily 7am–noon, 2–6pm.* 👣*Guided tours by appointment.* 📞*04 50 45 22 76.*

Situated high above the town, with a wide panorama, the rich interior of this 1930 building with its sturdy grey-marble pillars attracts many pilgrims to view the relics of St François de Sales and St Jeanne de Chantal; the stained-glass windows illustrate the lives of the patron saints of Annecy as does the small **museum** adjoining the church on the right.

👥 La Turbine
SW of Annecy, pl. Chorus, Cran Gevrier. 🕐*Open Tue 2–6pm, Wed–Thu and Sun 10am–noon, 2–6pm, Fri 2–7pm.* ⚹*4€.* ♿ 📞*04 50 08 17 00.* *www.ccsti74-crangevrier.com.*

This is an educational centre for scientific, technical and industrial subjects relevant to Haute-Savoie, aimed at the public, with workshops for children.

EXCURSION
Les Ponts de la Caille
▶*4km/2.5mi S of Cruseilles. Take D 1201 from Annecy towards Cruseilles.*

With Medieval Revival towers at each end, the **Charles-Albert Bridge** was inaugurated in 1839 by the king whose name it takes. Since 1939 it has been restricted to pedestrians (🚶*not advised for anyone suffering from vertigo).*

With a single fine arch spanning 138m/453ft over the ravine, the **modern bridge** was opened in 1928. At the time it was one of the largest concrete spans in the longitudinal sense. Very different in style but lying side by side 150m/492ft above the gorge formed by the Usses torrent, these two daring bridges provide a very popular local **attraction**★.

🚗 DRIVING TOUR

Gorges du Fier and Château de Montrottier
20km/12.4mi. Allow 2hrs 30min.
▶ *Leave Annecy by D 1508; 3km/1.8mi further on, beyond the motorway underpass, turn left on D 16. Turn right on D 64, follow the gorges road, then turn right onto the Liasses Bridge.*

The spectacular Fier gorges provide a fascinating outing for all ages, while you will enjoy fine mountain views at the isolated Montrottier Castle.

Gorges du Fier★★
🕐*Open daily mid-Jun–mid-Sept 9.30am–7.15pm; mid-Mar–mid-Jun and mid-Sept–mid-Oct 9.30am–6.15pm (last entry 1hr before closing).*

Gorges du Fier

© L.Bouvier/Fotolia.com

5€ (children 7–16 2.70€). ℘04 50 46 23 07. www.gorgesdufier.com.

Visitors can walk along galleries clinging to the sheer walls of the gorge; foliage forms an arched roof over the narrow defile. Beyond the exit, there is a belvedere on a rocky promontory which affords a good view of the "Mer de Rochers", an impressive cluster of boulders.

▷ *Follow D 116 and turn left into the driveway to the Château de Montrottier.*

Château de Montrottier★

Open Jun–Aug daily 2–7pm; mid-Mar–May and Sept–mid-Oct Wed–Mon 2–6pm. Guided visit 1 hr 30min. 7€ (children 5€). ℘04 50 46 23 02. www.chateaudemontrottier.com.

The castle is situated on an isolated butt between the course of the Fier and an ancient river bed left by the "Grand Fosse". Built between the 13C and the 16C, the castle is a fine specimen of Savoyard military architecture; a 36m/118ft-tall round keep towers over it. The western section was reconstructed in the 19C. Note in particular the suspended 15C **spiral staircase**★. The castle houses **collections**★ bequeathed in 1916 by the former owner to the Académie Florimontane: weaponry, earthenware, porcelain, ceramics, ivory from the Far East, antique furniture, statuettes and four 16C **bronze reliefs** by Peter and Hans Vischer of Nuremberg.

If you go up the round tower (86 steps) on a clear day, you will see the Parmelan, Mont Veyrier (behind which you can just peer at Mont Blanc), the Dents de Lanfon and the Tournette mountains.

▷ *Follow D 64 to Lovagny then right towards Poisy to return to Annecy.*

ADDRESSES

See also addresses in Lac d'Annecy.

STAY

⊝ **Chambre d'hôte Au Gite Savoisien** – 98 rte de Corbier, 74650 Chavanod. 6km/3.7mi SW of Annecy by

D 16, towards Rumilly, in the village of Corbier. ℘04 50 69 02 95. www.gite-savoisien.com. ☐. 4 rooms.

This old farm on the slopes above Annecy in the heart of a small village offers simple and comfortable rooms, three of them air-conditioned. In summer, guests can relax in the garden with a view of the mountains, or play a game of pétanque. A gîte is also offered. Evening meal available on request on Monday, Wednesday and Friday.

⊝⊝ **Auberge de la Caille** – 18 chemin de la Caille, 74330 La Balme-de-Sillingy. 12km/7.4mi NW of Annecy by D 1508 and D 3. ℘04 50 68 85 21. www.auberge delacaille.com. Closed 25 Dec–1 Jan, Sun eve and Sept–Jun Wed. ☐. 7 rooms, restaurant⊝⊝. The auberge is set in a 4ha/10-acre park with lawns, a pool and tennis courts. There is a choice of accommodation between 7 comfortable rooms, 10 brand new chalets with kitchens, 2 gîtes and a small campsite. Tasty regional cooking is served in a wood-panelled dining room or on the terrace.

⊝⊝ **Chambre d'hôte Le Jardin du Château** – 1 pl. du Château. Exit Annecy Sud, follow Albertville, then Château. ℘04 50 45 72 28. http://annecy-chambre-dhote.monsite-orange.fr. Open all year for rental of studios (non-serviced), weekly only in Jul–Aug, breakfast provided May–Jun and Sept. 5 rooms. This friendly accommodation is well located in the heart of the old town. All rooms have a kitchenette and several have balconies. Terrace with a view of Annecy, pretty garden and small snackbar.

⊝⊝ **Hôtel du Nord** – 24 r. Sommeiller. ℘04 50 45 08 78. www.annecy-hotel-du-nord.com. Wifi. 30 rooms. An unpretentious little hotel in the centre of town, ideally situated for a short visit. The rooms are functional and you should receive a friendly welcome.

⊝⊝ **Hôtel Kyriad Centre** – 1 fg Balmettes. ℘04 50 45 04 12. www.kyriad -annecy-centre.fr. Wifi. 24 rooms. This modern hotel at the entrance to the pedestrian district occupies a 16C building. The rooms, decorated in blue and yellow, are pleasant. Good service.

⛟ EAT

Auberge La Ferme de Ferrières – *800 rte des Burnets, 74370 Ferrières. 7km/4.3mi NW of Annecy by D 1201 and D 172, towards Les Burnets.* ℘*04 50 22 04 00. www.aubergelaferme deferrieres.com. Closed Feb–Mar and Wed. Reservations essential Sun–Tue eve.* The family farm provides pigeons, chickens, ducks, rabbits, fruit and vegetables for your meal. The kitchen can also offer several cheese-based Savoyard specialities. Rustic dining room, terrace with view. There are also eight bed-and-breakfast rooms.

Auberge de Savoie – *1 pl. St-François.* ℘*04 50 45 03 05. www. aubergedesavoie.fr. Closed 3–13 Jan, 24 Oct–10 Nov, Wed and Sept–Jun Tue.* Right next to the St-François church, this contemporary and warm restaurant is most professionally run. The terrace on a little square looks towards the Thiou and the castle.

Contresens – *10 r. de la Poste.* ℘*04 50 51 22 10. www.closdessens.com. Closed 28 Dec–10 Jan and Sun–Mon.* Be prepared to eat at this popular restaurant side by side with the "whole of Annecy". In the style of a modern bistro, the menu is adventurous and tasty. Terrace on the pavement.

La Brasserie St-Maurice – *7 r. Collège-Chapuisien.* ℘*04 50 51 24 49. www.stmau.com. Closed Sun–Mon.* This building dates from 1675. The attractively decorated dining room includes original wooden columns. Traditional cuisine is offered, and there is a terrace for summer.

Le Bilboquet – *14 fg Ste-Claire.* ℘*04 50 45 21 68. www.restaurant-le bilboquet.fr. Closed 15 Feb–10 Mar, Mon and Sept–Jun Sun except eves.* Adjoining the Ste-Claire gateway, the thick old walls of this restaurant keep it delightfully cool. Traditional cooking according to seasonal availability.

Le Fréti – *12 r. Ste-Claire.* ℘*04 50 51 29 52. http://le-freti.com. Closed Mon–Sat lunch and public holidays. Reservations recommended.* This establishment at the heart of the old town is above the arcades and the family-run cheese-making business, from which issue mouth-watering specialities and the scent of raclettes, fondues and tartiflettes to tempt food lovers. Simple décor. Summer terrace.

⛒ SHOPPING

Specialist shops – Several shops, particularly in the rues Ste-Claire and Royale, sell evocatively named sweets such as the "Roseau du Lac" (the "lake reed"), a coffee-filled chocolate; the "Cloche d'Annecy" (the "bell of Annecy") and the "Savoyarde", chocolate filled with nuts. For other Savoyard food specialities, simply wander the streets of the old town where you will find a wide choice. On the rue Ste-Claire, try **Le Fréti**, no. 12, for local cheese.

Market – *Open Tue, Fri and Sun 6am–1pm.* The colourful stalls of this fine food market line the rue de la République and the rue Ste-Claire.

🏃 ACTIVITIES

Annecy Croisières-Compagnie des bateaux du lac d'Annecy (Lake Cruise Company) – *2 pl. aux Bois.* ℘*04 50 51 08 40. www.annecy-croisieres. com. Closed late Dec–Jan.* Take a boat from the port of Annecy close to the Hôtel de Ville for a cruise around the lake. As well as regular lake boat trips visiting the nearby villages *(early Feb– mid-Dec: 1hr commented cruises ☜12.40€, end Apr–end Sept: taxi boat stopping at each port (2hrs)☜15.80€)* you could take a restaurant cruise (lunch or dinner prepared by an on-ship chef) and enjoy some dancing to combat any sea sickness.

♥ EVENTS

Fête du lac – Held on the first Saturday of August. The lake is lit up with an enormous fireworks display.

Noctibules – *www.bonlieu-annecy.com. Mid-Jul.* This young street-art festival sees around a hundred joyous street performers across the town.

Lac d'Annecy★★★

Lake Annecy is the jewel of the Savoie region. The dominating Tournette mountain and the pointed needles of the Dents de Lanfon tower above its deep blue waters forming one of the most attractive alpine landscapes, discovered by artists and a very few travellers in the early 19C. It was not until the later half of the end of that century that this magnificent, romantic setting became a tourist destination. Smaller and shallower than Lac de Bourget, but some 15km/9.3mi long, you can explore Lac d'Annecy by car or by bike on the road and cycle path that hug the shore. The lake view opens slowly if you approach from Albertville on D 1508 through Faverges. There are more spectacular views from Col de Bluffy (D 909) to the southeast and Col de Leschaux (D 912) to the south.

THE LAKE

Of glacial origin, the Lac d'Annecy consists of two quite different basins. Between Duingt and the Roc de Chère, the straits overlooked by Duingt Castle link them together to form one water mass, with the Grand Lac to the north and the Petit Lac to the south. The lake is fed by several streams and at its far north, by a powerful underwater spring, the Boubioz bubbling up from a depth of 82m/269ft. The main outlet of the lake is the Thiou, which flows through old Annecy and into the Fier.

The steep wooded slopes of the Petit Lac in the south offer a more austere aspect than the more accessible shores

- **Michelin Map:** 328 J6.
- **Info:** Sévrier Tourist Office, rte d'Albertville, 74320 Sévrier. &04 50 52 40 56. www.visit-lacannecy.fr. Talloires Tourist office, r. A.-Theuriet 74290 Talloires. &04 50 60 70 64. www.rivepleinsoleil.com.
- **Don't Miss:** The superb panorama of the lake from the Col de la Forclaz, where the paragliders take off.

of the Grand Lac in the north, dotted with pretty villages and even some occasional rows of vines, which were once widely planted here.

HIKES

1 BELVÉDÈRE DE LA TOURNETTE ★★★

🚶 *Walking tour from Chalet d'Aulp (circuit leaving Annecy – 35km/21.7mi). Allow a day including the climb to the Refuge de la Tournette.*

▷ *Leave Annecy by D 909 to Écharvines then D 42 towards Col de la Forclaz.*

Route du Col de l'Aulp

🚶 *3.5km/2.2mi from Le Villard.*

This forest road goes past Le Villard then climbs between steep wooded slopes, revealing the chalk cliffs of the Tournette on the right. The road gives way to a track leading to the **Chalet-Buvette de l'Aulp** at the foot of the Tournette.

Preserving One of the Purest Lakes in Europe

In the late 1950s it was realised that the water in Lake Annecy was suffering from bad pollution, and that the ecosystem had been damaged leading to the disappearance of most of the wildlife. A programme of improvement was put in place by the local municipalities and today the lake was one of the purest waters in Europe, with the return of bird-life and fish such as alpine char and *féra* (a type of trout). Today, with the high level of tourism and housing, it is deemed essential to preserve the wetlands and nesting areas around the lake.

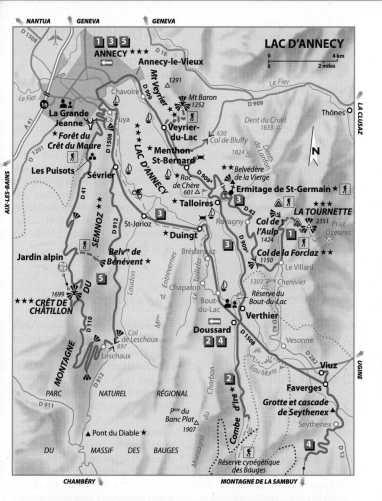

LAC D'ANNECY

NANTUA   GENEVA   GENEVA

D 1506

1 3 5
ANNECY ★★★

Annecy-le-Vieux

D 16

Le Fier

A 41

16

La Grande
Jeanne

★ Forêt du
Crêt du Maure

Les Puisots

Chavoire

Mt Veyrier

La Puya

1291

Mt Baron
1252

D 909

D 909

Dent du Cruet
1833 △

Thônes

LA CLUSAZ

Veyrier-
du-Lac

630
Col de Bluffy

Menthon-
St-Bernard

1824 △

★★ Belvédère
de la Vierge

LAC D'ANNECY

★★★

Sévrier

Roc
de Chère
601 △

D 909

Ermitage de St-Germain ★

LA TOURNETTE
★★★

SEMNOZ

D 41

D 912

St-Jorioz

3

★ Talloires

3

Duingt

Rovagny

D 42

2351

Col de
l'Aulp
1424

Praz
Dzeures

1

Jardin alpin

Belv⁺ de
Bénévent ★

3

Brédannaz

Col de la Forclaz ★★
1150

Le Villard

1303 Pⁿᵗᵉ Chenivier

★★★ CRÊT DE
CHÂTILLON

1699

5

DU

Chaparon

Réserve du
Bout-du-Lac

D 110

Col
de Leschaux
897

Leschaux

D 912

MONTAGNE

Bout-
du-Lac

Verthier

Vesonne

D 42

Doussard

2 4

D 1508

PARC

NATUREL

RÉGIONAL

D 911

2

Viuz

UGINE

D 282

Favergés

Grotte et cascade
de Seythenex

★ Pont du Diable ★

Combe d'Ire ★

Pⁿᵗᵉ du
Banc Plat
1907

Seythenex

4

D 12

DU   MASSIF   DES   BAUGES

Réserve cynégétique
des Bauges

CHAMBÉRY   MONTAGNE DE LA SAMBUY

La Tournette

© Pierre Jacques/hemis.fr

▷ *A stony, badly maintained road provides car access as far as the Chalet d'Aulp, where you can park.*

Chalet de l'Aulp to the Refuge de la Tournette

🔼 *2hrs return on foot. Vertical rise of 350m/1 148ft. Climbing to the summit of the Tournette requires good experience of hiking through rocky terrain; however, no special equipment is necessary as there are handrails and ladders along the way.*

A marked path rises to the east of the pass then skirts the limestone cliffs overlooking the Cirque du Casset. From the viewing table near the Refuge de la Tournette (1 774m/5 820ft), there is a splendid **panorama**★★ of the western shore of the lake.

For those with the equipment and stamina for a tougher climb, one of the finest **panoramas**★★★ of the northern Alps unfolds from the Tournette summit (alt. 2 351m/7 713ft).

② COMBE D'IRE★

▷ *Start from Doussard (D 281), then Chevaline (D 181), to join the Combe d'Ire forest road. Follow for 6km/3.7mi.*

This deep wooded furrow overlooked by the Montagne de Charbon, through which runs a rushing stream, used to be one of the wildest and most mysterious alpine valleys; the last bear was killed in 1893. It is now part of the Réserve cyné gétique des Bauges (Les Bauges Game Reserve).

Point du Banc Plat (1 907m/6 257ft)

🔼 *5hrs 30min return on foot – uneven ground. At the end of the forest road follow the path marked circuit du Charbon.* The footpath through the forest leads to the grassy valley of the Planay chalet. Climbing through the alpine fields, the path rejoins the trail along the crest which leads to the Refuge de la Combe (at the end of the valley).

🚗 DRIVING TOURS

③ LE TOUR DU LAC★★
See the local map (📖 p109).
Allow 1–1 1/2 days.

You can follow this superb drive around the lake in either direction, taking a day or longer to complete it.

Mainly following the edge of the lake, now and again you will glimpse lovely views of the Tournette escarpments and the rocky towers of the Dents de Lanfon. The route passes below the Bauges Massif, through Sévrier and then Duingt. Before you reach Doussard, take the Talloires direction on D 909A.

▷ *Leave Annecy by D 1508. The route passes through several villages and can be very busy, so drive slowly.*

The route skirts the promontory of La Puya, the extreme northernmost point of the Semnoz. Driving along the water's edge, from here you can see Mont Veyrier, and behind it the rocky outcrops of the Parmelan, Dents de Lanfon and finally the Tournette mountain.

Sévrier
Protected from above by the wooded slopes of the Semnoz, there are several parts of this village right on the lake. Parallel to the lake's edge, the church is particularly well sited at the top of a gentle ridge of land. You will find a fine old priory on the main square along with the public gardens.

Écomusée du Costume Savoyard
🕐*Open mid-Jun–Sept Mon–Fri 10am–noon, 2.30–6pm, Sun and public holidays 2.30–6pm; May–mid-Jun Sun–Fri 2.30–6pm.* 💶4€. 🅿 04 50 52 41 05. *www.ecomusee-lacannecy.com.*

This museum houses a lovely collection of costumes, lace, embroidery and shawls from the 19C and early 20C. There are also displays of old everyday items and of Savoie crosses, whose design is unique to each village. A short film shows a local marriage that took place in 1850.

👤👤 Musée Paccard★

🕐 Open Jun–Sept Mon–Sat 10am–12.30pm, 2.30–6.30pm, Sun and public holidays 2.30–6.30pm; Oct–May Mon–Sat 10am–noon, 2.30–5.30pm, Sun and public holidays 2.30–5.30pm. 5€ (children 6–18 3.50€). 𝄐 𝒫04 50 52 47 11. www.paccard.com.

This museum was created by the **Paccard bell foundry**, who has made bells for almost two centuries. It explains the manufacturing process and traces the history of this ancient craft through a collection of bells dating from the 14C to the 19C.

You can also learn about the history of two very large bells that were made in Annecy: the Savoyarde in Montmartre's Sacré-Cœur in Paris (1891) and the Jeanne d'Arc in Rouen Cathedral.

Between Sévrier and Duingt the road turns away inland at **St-Jorioz**. Along the beach there is a path where there is a prehistoric lake dwelling. Further on you will see the privately owned **Château de Duingt** on a wooded peninsula.

Duingt★

Situated at the narrowest part of the lake, which marks the separation between the Grand Lac and the Petit Lac, this pleasant summer resort has retained its rustic Savoyard character. In the well-preserved, rustic old village centre you will find little houses with exterior staircases, draped with creepers.

Following on from Duingt towards the Bout-du-Lac (the village name meaning the end of the lake), as far as Brédannaz, the route runs very close to the steep sides of the Petit Lac or "Lac de Talloires" framed by the rocky slopes of the Taillefer.

👤👤 Doussard

In this village you will find the **Réserve naturelle du Bout-du-Lac** (🕐 open all year, information at Réserve office at Le Grimpillon, Talloires; 𝒫04 50 64 44 03; www.asters.asso.fr) including a nature trail which leads into the rushes and a 15C tower from which you can observe birds and a beaver colony.

▷ *Take D 909A, which skirts the lake towards Annecy.*

Verthier

A charming village with a well-preserved character.

Talloires★

One of the area's best-loved resorts, with a beach and watersports centre, Talloires lies in fine **surroundings**★★, with the harbour nestling inside a rounded bay, sheltered by the cliffs of the Roc de Chère opposite the wooded promontory of Duingt Castle.

Ermitage de St-Germain★

🔼 *From D 42, 15min there and back up a steep footpath.*

This chapel (1829), in a fine **position** overlooking the Talloires bay, the Duingt strait and the Bauges mountains, is a place of local pilgrimage, particularly on Whit Monday; otherwise, the place is a charming retreat.

There is a wider **panorama** of the Grand Lac and the surrounding mountains from the **Belvédère de la Vierge**★★ (🔼 15min there and back along a steep footpath skirting the cemetery).

▷ *Continue on D 42.*

Col de la Forclaz★★

From the viewpoint of the hotel-restaurant at the pass there is a bird's-eye **view** of Lac d'Annecy; note the shallow bank just off Duingt, occupied by lake dwellings in prehistoric times.

▷ *Follow a path which goes up to the hotel-restaurant and after 100m/110yds turn left to reach the belvedere (15min there and back).*

Fine panoramic view of the summits of the Bauges Massif, including the Dents de Lanfon, Tournette and the highest peak of the Arcalod.

▷ *Take the road back towards Talloires.*

Heading to Rovagny and Menthon, the Hermitage St-Germain reigns over the

Lac d'Annecy viewed from the Col de la Forclaz

© Bertrand Rieger/hemis.fr

forested gorge of the "Saut du Moine" ("monks' leap").

On exiting the tunnel, the Grand Lac and Annecy suddenly appear, with immediately below the celebrated strait of Duingt. After rejoining D909A to Annecy, you will see up on the right the proud silhouette of the Château de Menthon.

Chateau de Menthon-St-Bernard★

🕐 *Open Jul–Aug daily noon–6pm; May–Jun and Sept Fri–Sun and public holidays 2–6pm.* ⊚*7.50€ (children 6–15 4€).* 📞*04 50 60 12 05. www.chateau-de-menthon.com.*

The château was the birthplace of St Bernard de Menthon, who founded the famous hospices of the Grand- and Petit-St-Bernard. Built in the 11C and 15C, then modified in the 19C, the château is still owned by the de Menthon family. Crowned with turrets, it has the picture-perfect look of a fairy-tale castle. From the terrace, there is a beautiful **view**★ over the lake.

▶ *Leave Menthon in the direction of Talloires and at Choseaux, turn right on the road towards Bains and then towards Roc de Chère.*

Roc de Chère★

🚶 *2hrs on foot there and back. Information at the nature reserve office, Le*

Grimpillon, Talloires. 📞*06 17 54 21 68. Open any time with guided visits Jun–Sept and boat excursions (*📞*04 50 51 08 40), reservation essential.*

Below the road, in the grounds of a mansion is the funeral chapel of the historian **Hippolyte Taine** (1828–93). The Roc de Chère forms a limestone knoll between Menthon-St-Bernard and Talloires, overlooking Lake Annecy. There are 69ha/171 acres out of the total 200ha/494 acres of forest that have been registered as a **nature reserve** since 1977.

Mediterranean vegetation coexists with northern coniferous vegetation, rich in amphibians, reptiles and butterflies. There are clear traces of the old sandstone quarries and forestry works carried out by the monks of Talloires.

Veyrier-du-Lac

There is a lovely view of the Grand Lac from the garden behind the town hall (opposite the church).

Mont Veyrier★★

🚶 *1km/0.6mi by car, then 5hrs there and back on foot. Leave Veyrier by the Rte du Mont Veyrier, turn left into the Rte de la Combe. Leave the car and follow the Sentier du Col des Contrebandiers to the summit of Mont Baron.*

From the top, there is a bird's-eye **view** of Annecy and the Grand Lac, framed by mountains on all sides. In clear weather, the view stretches from the glaciers of the Vanoise in the southeast to the peaks of the Salève and Voirons in the northeast with Lac Léman in between. From Chavoire onwards, the road opens up, affording a good overall view of Annecy overlooked by the Basilique de la Visitation and the castle.

Annecy-le-Vieux

The entry of Annecy-le-Vieux is marked by an enormous detached menhir. On the hill, close to the town hall, a beautiful Romance-period bell tower is separated from the Neoclassical church. The Dunand villa, opposite, is where the musician Gabriel Fauré lived (1919–24).

4 FAVERGES AND ENVIRONS

Start at Doussard as shown on the local map (see p109). Allow half a day.

In the plain of the Eau Morte river you can identify each of the Bauges peaks: **Arcalod**, the highest of the range (alt. 2 217m/7 274ft), is recognised by its abrupt ridges, Sambuy by its pyramidical shape, and finally, Belle Étoile and the Dent de Cons by their furrowed sides.

Viuz

Next to the church and its 12C Romanesque apse, a small **Musée archéologique** (open Jul–Aug daily 2.30–6.30pm, Sept–Jun Mon–Fri 2.30–6.30pm; closed public holidays except 14 Jul and 15 Aug; 1hr guided tours on request; 3€, children 1.75€; 04 50 32 45 99; http://viuz.sav.org) houses a collection of Gallo-Roman objects found locally, including a cauldron of the 3C, an amber necklace and numerous Roman coins.

Faverges

Situated at an important crossroads, between the Chaîne des Aravis and the Massif des Bauges, this Gallo-Roman town is overlooked by the 13C round keep of its castle. Traditional industries here include prefabricated wooden chalets, machine tooling, household appliances and the well-known pens and cigarette lighters of Tissot-Dupont.

Turn right 2km/1.2mi S of Faverges, following the path marked Grotte de Seythenex.

Grotte and Cascade de Seythenex

Open daily Jul–Aug 9.30am–6pm; May–Jun and early–mid-Sept 10am–5.30pm. 7€ (children 5€). 04 50 44 55 97. www.cascade.fr.
Several footbridges lead to the top of the waterfall, which drops 30m/98ft through a narrow crack into a picturesque wooded vale. It is possible to walk along the former underground river bed, which testifies to the power of water erosion.

Turn right at Seythenex and follow the road to Vargnoz.

Montagne de la Sambuy★

The **Seythenex chairlift** (open end Jun–end Aug daily 10am–6pm; check for rates; 04 50 44 44 45) takes you up from Vargnoz to the Favre refuge (alt. 1 820m/5 971ft) affording a fine **view** of the Belledonne range, the Aravis Massif and Lac d'Annecy to the north, the Mont Blanc Massif to the northeast and the Vanoise glaciers to the southeast.

5 THE SEMNOZ★★

Route of 52km/32.3mi shown on the local map (see p109). Allow half a day.

The Semnoz is a picturesque wooded ridge stretching from the Crêt du Maure, a forested area ideal for walking, to the Crêt de Châtillon, its highest peak.

Leave Annecy by D 41, which rises quickly towards the Crêt de Châtillon.

Forêt du Crêt du Maure★

This vast wooded area is to a large extent the result of 19C reforestation, and is criss-crossed by footpaths leading to numerous viewpoints.

From the Semnoz road, follow a steep path for 500m/546yds beginning at the second hairpin bend at the start of the forest, at the reservoir.

The Chalet Super-Panorama offers one of the loveliest **views**★★ of the lake. A bit further on D 41, the pens of the **animal park of la Grande Jeanne** house marmot, deer and reindeer.

Belvédère de Bénévent★

View of the Tournette mountain and the Duingt strait. The peaks of Le Beaufortain are visible on the horizon between the Tournette and the Dent de Cons.

Return to D 41.

The landscape changes to stony pastures dotted with blue gentians in early

summer. The climb becomes more pro-nounced and, after a right bend, a vast mountain panorama opens out.
At the cross-country skiing area is an **alpine garden** you can tour *(FRAPNA ✆04 50 67 37 34).*

Crêt de Châtillon★★★

15min return on foot.
Leave the car at the end of the road and walk up through pastureland to the summit, where a tall cross and a viewing table stand.
The **panoramic view** embraces some of the most famous mountain ranges of the western Alps: Haut-Faucigny, Mont Blanc, Vanoise, Écrins, Aiguilles d'Arves and Viso with the mountains that circle Lake Annecy in the foreground.
On the way down, you will find fine views to the Tournette and the Parmelan and southeast to the Bauges.

○ *From Col de Leschaux, return to Annecy by D 912 and Sévrier.*

ADDRESSES

🏠STAY

○ **Chambre d'hôte de la Maison de Marie** – *100 chemin des Charbonnières, 74210 Doussard. On D 1508 towards Albertville, on the left before the discothèque. ✆04 50 32 97 43. www.maison-de-marie.com.* 🅿🗷. *5 rooms* 🛏, *half-board possible.*
This fine old village house offers simple rooms including some antique furniture. There is a large dining room, a lounge with fireplace, and a pretty, shady terrace.

○ **Hôtel Les Grillons** – *74290 Veyrier-du-Lac. ✆04 50 60 70 31. www.hotel-grillons.com. Closed 16 Oct–21 Apr.* 🅿. *Wifi. 30 rooms, half-board only, restaurant* ○○○. The large swimming pool at this old-style pension makes it great for summer. The rooms were decorated in 2009 and most enjoy a lake view. The red-and-white-toned, modern dining room features exposed beams.

○○○ **Arcalod** – *74210 Doussard. ✆04 50 44 30 22. www.hotelarcalod.fr. Closed 1 Oct–15 May. Wifi. 33 rooms, half-board possible, restaurant* ○○○.
This chalet-hotel is ideal for families with plenty of free activities. The small rooms are nicely kept, and there is a shady garden with a pool. Meals for residents have a Savoyard accent served in the light and spacious restaurant.

○○○ **Hôtel Résidel** – *20 chemin des Aires, 74320 Sévrier. ✆04 50 52 67 50. www.hotel-residel.com.* 🅿. *22 rooms.*
These two chalet-style buildings have undergone extensive renovation. All the rooms have a terrace or a balcony and face the lake. Studios and apartments all have kitchenettes.

🍴EAT

○ **Bistrot du Port** – *Au port, 74320 Sévrier. ✆04 50 52 45 00. www.bistrot-du-port.com. Closed Dec–Jan.* A special holiday feeling imbues this pleasant restaurant decorated with a nautical theme. Sit in the heated veranda in winter or on the terrace in summer to admire the view while enjoying lake fish and grilled meats.

○○ **Le Poisson Rouge** – *20 prom. des Seines, les Avollions, 74320 Sévrier. By the lake, rte d'Albertville. ✆04 50 52 40 48. www.lepoissonrouge-annecy.com.*
On the shores of the lake, a restaurant accessible on foot, on roller-blades (along the bicycle path), by boat (private pontoon), or by car. The terrace has a great view of the Dents de Lanfon.

🏃ACTIVITIES

○ **Good to know** – Most of the supervised beaches around the lake offer watersports facilities with sailing, kayaking, canoeing or scuba diving.

Cercle de voile de Sévrier – *134 rte du Port, 74320 Sévrier. ✆04 50 52 40 04. www.cvsevrier.com. Apr–Oct, contact for more details and reservations.* Take a delightful trip on the lake and observe the surrounding mountains on board a sailing boat, accompanied by a skipper well versed in the region.

Rumilly

Situated at the heart of an economically successful region, Rumilly, the capital of the Albanais, nestles in the midst of green hills, with the mountains of the limestone Préalpes and the Bauges natural park not far away. Also nearby are the three principal Haute-Savoie lakes, and you can discover this charming countryside with a walk along the many pathways or on the banks of the numerous streams, much appreciated by fishermen.

▶ **Population:** 13 434.
◔ **Michelin Map:** 328 I5.
▯ **Info:** Office du tourisme de l'Albanais, 4 pl. de l'Hôtel-de-Ville, 74150 Rumilly. ℘04 50 64 58 32. www.albanais74-tourisme.com.
▶ **Location:** From Chambéry, Exit Alby-sur-Chéran (22km/13.7mi), then D 3 (8.5km/5.3mi). From Annecy, 17km/10.6mi by D 16.
◉ **Don't Miss:** The view from the Édouard-André Bridge. A look at the workings of the Rhône river at Seyssel. A walk in Alby-sur-Chéran. The secret gardens at Lagnat-Vaulx.
👪 **Kids:** The Rumilly outdoor leisure centre.
🕓 **Timing:** Half a day to explore Rumilly and Seyssel. At least half a day for the driving tour of the Albanais.

SIGHTS
Old Quarter
👣*Circuit from the old centre.*
Geographic chance placed Rumilly in the path of several nations at war. Over the years, the French, Spanish and Austrians have left their battle scars on the town and torn down its fortress.
However, the old centre of town around the corn market – the current building dates from 1869 – boasts a certain aristocratic feel to it: you can see several residences from the 16C *(14 r. d'Hauteville)* and the 17C *(8 pl. de l'Hôtel-de-Ville or 18 r. Filaterie).*
The town hall is surrounded by arcaded houses and known for its pretty fountain adorned with swans' necks.

Pont Édouard-André
Leaving Rumilly over this bridge, you will see a group of charming old houses stuck like limpets or barnacles to the bed of the River Néphaz.

Église Ste-Agathe
The Church of Ste-Agathe was built in 1837 by the Sardinian architect Melano, who restored the abbey of Hautecombe. It has an interesting façade in Tuscan style flanked by a 12C bell tower.

Chapelle Notre-Dame-de-l'Aumône
At the end of av. de l'Aumône, on the banks of the Chéran. 🕓*Open daily 2–6pm.* ℘04 50 64 58 32.
This 13C chapel was largely rebuilt and expanded in the early 19C.

Musée Municipal de Rumilly
🕓*Currently closed for renovation – re-opening forecast 2011–12, information from the town hall* ℘04 50 64 69 20.
The little town museum is housed in an old tobacco factory. It covers the history of the town as well as its links with the Albanais region.

▷ *Leave Rumilly NW by D 31 towards Lornay.*

EXCURSIONS
Château de Clermont
🕓*Open Jul–Aug daily 2–7pm; May–Jun and Sept Sat–Sun and public holidays 2–7pm.* 👣*Guided visit (45min).* ⊕5€ *(12–25s 3.50€).* ℘04 50 69 63 15.
The Renaissance castle was once a private farm estate, but has been owned by the department of Haute-Savoie for several decades. A paved, narrow driveway leads to the buildings. Built up against

the rock face between 1575 and 1577 by a rich prelate, Gallois de Regard, the main decorative feature of the palace are the **two-storey arched galleries**★ on three sides, best viewed from the main courtyard.

The southern wing has a majestic gateway built into it, flanked by two square towers. From the upper gallery, the only one not enclosed, there is a **view** over the Albanais countryside, with Rumilly remaining hidden behind a fold in the hillside.

Inside the castle you can visit several nicely furnished rooms, and also the cellars (one vaulted). Temporary exhibitions are regularly organised here.

Jardins Secrets à Lagnat-Vaulx

At Vaulx, a hamlet of Lagnat 11km/ 6.8mi NE of Rumilly by D 3. Guided visit (1hr 30min) early Apr–mid-Oct Mon–Fri 2–5pm, Sat–Sun and public holidays 1.30–6.30pm. 6.50€ (6–16s 4€). 04 50 60 53 18. www.jardins-secrets.com.

You could almost be in the gardens of a medieval palace here. The fountains, patios and pergolas in these secret gardens might even make you imagine you were in Andalusia, especially if a southerly breeze is blowing across when you visit. The environment here is constantly

evolving and every year there is something new to discover.

Seyssel

17km/10.6mi NE of Rumilly on D 14. 2 chemin de la Fontaine, 74910 Seyssel. 04 50 59 26 56. www.ot-pays-de-seyssel.fr.

The little area around Seyssel is not well enough known, and offers a range of attractions and activities: you can explore the Rhône river and its installations, walk on the Grand Colombier or the Montagne des Princes, visit the vineyard and more …

Maison du Haut Rhône

10 rte d'Aix-les-Bains. Open Jul–Aug Mon–Wed and Fri–Sat 9am–noon, 2–6pm, Thu 9am–noon, 2–8pm; Sept–Jun Mon–Sat 8.30am–noon, 1.30–5pm. Closed public holidays. Free. 04 50 56 77 04. www.maison-du-haut-rhone.org.

This modern information centre close to the Rhône and to the Gallatin port indicates the importance of the river to the town of Seyssel and the surrounding area. Various exhibits illustrate the workings of the river, the inland water transport and the history of Seyssel.

Barrage de Seyssel

1.5km/1mi above Seyssel.

This balancing dam regularises the flow of the Rhône exiting the Génissiat dam upstream. The installation has created a new reservoir at the foot of the spur on which sits the **Bassy** church.

DRIVING TOUR

L'ALBANAIS (CHÉRAN VALLEY)★

Drive of 40km/24.8mi shown on the regional map (see p98). Allow half a day leaving Rumilly to the S by D 3.

Alby-sur-Chéran★

Seven castles once encircled this picturesque town including the privately owned Château Montpon just above the town. A major centre for making shoes,

Jardins Secrets à Lagnat-Vaulx

F. Isler/MICHELIN

Alby-sur-Chéran

© ColsTravel France/Alamy

back in 1880, Alby had some 300 cobblers. An early generator installed on the Chéran river brought the town electricity as early as 1888. While the shoe-making industry was in decline, the Fonderie des Alpes (foundry) opened in 1915, remaining in operation until 1984.

In the old quarter, all around the triangular-shaped **place du Trophée**★, the old houses beneath covered arcades were once cobblers' workshops.

The stonework forming the **church** of Notre-Dame-de-Plainpalais, designed by M. Novarina (1960), was all cut by hand. Inside is a remarkable stained-glass window (1978) along one wall created by Alfred Manessier.

The **Musée de la Cordonnerie** is dedicated to the memory of the shoe-making industry here. Notably it includes a collection of tools no longer in existence today. ○*Open Jul–Aug Tue–Sat 10am–noon, 2.30–6.30pm; Jun and early–mid–Sept Tue–Sat 10am–noon, 2–6pm.* ✆*Free.* ℘*04 50 68 39 44. www.alby-sur-cheran.fr.* From the bridges straddling the Chéran, there are pretty **views**★ over the town.

▷ *Leave Alby to the S by D 3 in the direction of Héry-sur-Alby.*

The route follows the ridge of hills, with vistas over the course of the Chéran appearing from time to time. After Cusy, turn left on D 911, then D 31 towards the **Pont de l'Abîme bridge**★.

You can choose to follow D 5 south, towards the valley of Bellevaux, via Le Châtelard (○*see the Bauges p202*).

▷ *After crossing the Chéran, take D 5 left towards Gruffy.*

Musée d'Histoire Naturelle de Gruffy

On the edge of the village as you arrive, in the hamlet les Choseaux. ○*Open Jul–Aug daily 2–6.30pm; 15 Mar–end Jun and early Sept–15 Nov Tue–Fri and Sun 2–6pm.* ○*Closed 1 Jan, 1 May, 8 May, 25 Dec.* ✆*4.80€ (children under 16 3.50€).* ℘*04 50 77 58 60. www.musee-nature.com.*

This natural history museum is a re-creation of a 19C farm, where you can discover the traditional Savoyard life-

---

L'Albanais

Situated in a depression formed by Lac du Bourget and Lac d'Annecy, this rich agricultural district was once known for growing tobacco. Its varied landscape provides a wide choice of leisure activities: canoeing down the Chéran gorges; clambering up the cliffs at the La Chambotte climbing centre; taking off from the Col du Sapenay by hang glider; or exploring the Val du Fier on foot or mountain bike.

style. There are also displays of stuffed animals in both farmland and wild settings.

Follow the road via Viuz-la-Chiésaz that overlooks the long wooded ridge of the **Crêt de Châtillon** (alt. 1 699m/5 574ft), the highest point of the Semnoz mountains. It is possible to climb up to the peak *(described in the Semnoz Driving Tour in the Lake Annecy section)* by taking D 141 to Quintal, then D 241 right, and right again on D 41.

◗ *After passing under the motorway, return to Rumilly on D 31.*

ADDRESSES

⌂ STAY

Chambre d'hôte Les Bruyères – *359 rte de Mercy, 74540 St-Félix. ℘04 50 60 96 53. www.les-bruyeres.fr. 4 rooms ⌧.* You won't want to leave the comfort and calm of this gorgeous farmhouse, renovated in the colours of the south. The hosts offer a warm welcome, large individually decorated rooms and a pretty view of the valley from the terrace and garden, that beckons you out for a walk.

Chambre d'hôte La Ferme sur les Bois – *Le Biolley, 74150 Vaulx. 12km/7.4mi N of Annecy by D 1508, then D 17 and D 3. ℘04 50 60 54 50. www.annecy-attelage.fr. 🅿. 4 rooms ⌧.* This isolated, but welcoming bed and breakfast in a farm located in the mountain foothills offers four peaceful rooms. When the weather permits it, carriage drives may be arranged on reservation.

❡/EAT

Auberge de la Cave de la Ferme – *R. du Grand-Pont, 74270 Frangy. A 40, Exit 11 direction Frangy. ℘04 50 44 75 04. Closed 25 Jun–15 Jul and Sun–Mon.* The Lupin family have produced Savoie wines (Roussette and Mondeuse) along with marc since 1957. In their rustic, cosy restaurant Côté cuisine, they serve good regional food including the classic cheese specialities and charcuterie.

Boîte à Sel – *27 r. Pont-Neuf. ℘04 50 01 02 52. Closed 1–15 Jan, 1–15 Aug, Thu eve and Sun eve–Mon.* This modest restaurant located in one of the shopping streets offers bistrot-style traditional cooking. It offers a pleasant welcome with a *trompe-l'œil* countryside décor.

L'Arcadie – *8 pl. du Trophée, 74540 Alby-sur-Chéran. ℘04 50 68 15 78. www.restaurantlarcadie.com. Closed Mon eve, Sat lunch and Sun.* ♿. Traditional cooking using only fresh ingredients is presented artistically in a tastefully renovated restaurant. With efficient service too, it's not surprisingly very popular.

⛒ SHOPPING

Vins de Seyssel – Seyssel produces white wines and sparkling wines, classified as AOC since 1942. Two grape varieties are grown here – Altesse, to make Roussette dry white and Molette for the sparkling wines.

⚐⚑ ACTIVITIES

Outdoor leisure centre – *℘04 50 01 05 89. Closed Oct–Apr.* Set around a reservoir, this leisure and activity centre provides activities and relaxation for all the family. There are big green spaces, supervised swimming and games for the children. For the sportier there is mountain biking, hiking, plus canoes and kayaks are available on the spot or nearby.

Takamaka Sports-Nature – *23 fg Ste-Claire, 74000 Annecy. ℘04 50 45 60 61. www.takamaka.fr. Open Jul–Aug daily 9am–7pm; Sept–Jun Mon–Fri 9am–noon, 2–6pm.* This company arranges all sorts of outdoor mountain and sports activities by reservation.

☺ EVENT

Fête des vieux métiers – *1st Sat in Oct.* This festival celebrates the traditional crafts carried out in the region long ago. Demonstrations and activities.

Massif des Aravis★★

Balanced between Lac d'Annecy and the valley of the Arve, the Massif des Aravis stands apart from busy highways, industrial centres and the major international alpine resorts. The area does, however, attract winter-sports fans to its two popular ski villages, La Clusaz and Le Grand-Bornand, and at the same time preserves its traditional atmosphere remarkably well.

A BIT OF HISTORY
Survival
Like the other massifs of the Préalpes, the Chartreuse, Bauges and Vercors, the Massif des Aravis is surrounded by high limestone peaks. Two powerful streams, the Fier and the Borne, cut through the massif by way of long and narrow gorges. In this harsh mountain environment, settled for centuries, agriculture has never been sufficient to keep the population alive. Before the advent of tourism, using the resources of the forest was fundamental, and in the 19C there were numerous sawmills.

Reblochon country
The Thônes Valley is known as the **pays du reblochon** and the cheese produced since the 13C has been designated AOC since 1958.
Produced under strict conditions only from the unpasteurised milk of Abondance, Tarine and Montbéliard cows, this strong creamy cheese is largely responsible for the preservation of the agricultural traditions in the villages of Thônes and Le Grand-Bornand.

🚗 DRIVING TOURS

1 ROUTE DE LA CLUSAZ
Drive of 31km/19.3mi shown on the local map (see p122). Allow about 1hr.

▶ *Leave Annecy by D 909 towards Menthon-St-Bernard.*

- 📍 **Michelin Map:** 333 L/M 2/3.
- 🏠 **Info:** 74450 Le Grand-Bornand. ☎04 50 02 78 00. www.legrandbornand.com.
- ▶ **Location:** From Annecy 28km/17.4mi by D 16, then D 909, or from Menthon-St-Bernard along a superb road (D 909). Or from Geneva and Bonneville via A 40, Exit 16, then D 12.
- 👁 **Don't Miss:** Driving over the Col de la Colombière to see the Chartreuse du Reposoir. The view to Mont Blanc from the Col des Aravis is spectacular at the end of the afternoon.
- 🕐 **Timing:** Spend a week in winter or summer.

Until you reach Chavoire, the D 909 is a wide tree-lined avenue on the edge of the lake. From it you can view the long hilltop of the Semnoz, then the depression of the Col de Leschaux. This is followed by the peak of the Dent de Rossanaz overlooking Le Châtelard, in the heart of the Bauges, and then the d'Entrevernes mountain.

Veyrier-du-Lac
See p112, 3.
Between Veyrier and Bluffy stop in a lay-by to admire the view of the Château de Menthon with the landscape of the Bauges forming a backdrop. From the Col de Bluffy, the road leads down into the Fier Valley. Upstream, you can see the **Cascade de Morette**.

Alex
The Château d'Arenthon in Alex overlooks the Fier Valley. This old 13C strong house, rebuilt in the 16C, has since 1999 housed the Fondation Salomon pour l'art contemporain. The complete renovation of the château has combined certain vestiges from Renaissance time with a resolutely modern architecture of concrete and glass. The twice-yearly exhibitions at this contemporary art

centre display works from world-renowned artists. The gardens show sculptures. ⏰*Open Jul–Nov Wed–Sun 2–7pm; Mar–May Thu–Sun 2–7pm.* ⏰*Closed Easter Mon, Whit Mon, 15 Aug, 11 Nov, 25 Dec.* 👁*Free guided visits Sat–Sun 4pm.* 👁*6€ (children under 10 free)* 📞*04 50 02 87 52. www.fondation-salomon.com..*

Nécropole nationale des Glières

At this necropolis are 105 tombs of members of the Resistance, mainly forces on the Glières plateau. The **Musée de la Résistance en Haute-Savoie (Morette)** is housed in a mountain chalet dating from 1794, rebuilt here and typical of the chalets where the Resistance forces were housed.

The Resistance museum relates the stages of the battles on the plateau. ⏰*Open Jul–Sept daily 10am–12.30pm, 2–6pm; Feb–Jun and Oct–Nov Sun–Fri and public holidays 9.30am–12.30pm, 1.30–5pm.* 👁*Guided tours possible (2hrs).* 👁*Free.* 📞*04 50 51 87 00.*

Thônes

Church – The church dates from 1697. It has a bell tower with a balcony, bulb and steeple on top (42m/138ft). The decoration inside is in a typical Savoyard Baroque style. Of note especially are the massive **retable** on the high altar (1721) from the Italian sculptor Jacquetti, the carved 17C figurines on the altar left of the choir and the woodwork.

Musée du Pays de Thônes★ – ⏰*Open Jul–Aug daily 9am–noon, 1.30–5pm; Sept–Jun Sat 1.30–5pm, Sun–Fri 9am–noon, 1.30–5pm.* 👁*Guided tours possible (1hr 15min).* 👁*2.80€ (12–18s 1€).* 📞*04 50 02 97 76.* Take a journey into the history and life of the Thônes region as envisioned by Jean-Jacques Rousseau in his *Confessions* in 1793. One room is devoted to the archaeological finds made in the nearby site of La Balme-de-Thuy. There is also a beautiful 15C pietà.

Les Amis du val de Thônes – *1 r. Blanche.* ⏰*Open Jul–Aug Mon–Thu 3.30–6.30pm; mid-Jun–end Jun and mid-Sept–end Sept Tue 3.30–6.30pm.* 👁*Free.* 📞*04 50 63 11 83.* This very good complement to the museum above displays 300 photographs and old documents about the heritage and countryside around Thônes. It is particularly worth a visit to see the impressive model (1/13) of the village of Thônes and the tramway which used to link the village with Annecy (1898–1930).

Écomusée du Bois et de la Forêt – *3km/1.8mi from Thônes on the rte de Montremont.* ⏰*Open Jul–Aug Sun–Fri 10am–noon, 2.30–5.30pm; Apr–Jun and Sept–Oct Wed and Sun 2.30–5.30pm.* ⏰*Closed*

Manigod Valley

© Gsell Gerard/World Pictures/Photoshot

14 Jul, 15 Aug. Guided visit possible
(1hr). 3.50€ (6–18s 2.30€). 04 50 32
18 10. www.ecomuseedubois.com.
Until the early 20C the Malnant stream
in the Montremont Valley fed numerous
sawmills. This eco-museum, dedicated
to the history of the forests and wood
industry in the Thônes Valley, has put
the restored hydraulic sawmill at Étou-
vières to good use.

*From the centre of Thônes,
turn right on D 12 towards Serraval,
and then left on D 16 to Manigod and
Col de Croix Fry.*

Manigod Valley★★

The Fier river runs through this charming valley, enclosed by the ridges of the
Étale mountain. Old chalets are scattered across the slopes interspersed
with pine tree plantations and orchards.
Manigod – The birthplace of the
famous chef **Marc Veyrat** has maintained its traditional style with chalets
that have wooden shingles on the roofs
and basements made from local stone.
Manigod is known for reviving the
paret, a type of wooden sledge that
children still used in the 1950s to get to
school. Today, you can test one out or
attend the annual races.

From Manigod follow D 16 to the col.

Col de la Croix-Fry

At the pass is a fine little family ski
resort with ski lifts that link into the **La
Clusaz** lift system. Seen through the
forests, the vast **panorama**★ takes in
the whole Aravis range. On the way
down, the transverse valleys of La Clusaz
(River Nom) and Les Étroits (River Borne)
appear successively.

Follow D 16 towards La Clusaz.

2 ROUTE DE LA COLOMBIÈRE FROM LA CLUSAZ TO CLUSES

*Drive of 30km/18.6mi shown on the
local map (see p123). Allow 1hr 30min.
The Col de la Colombière pass is
closed from November to late May.*

Linking the Thônes and Arve valleys, this
route offers a succession of contrasting
landscapes from the austere valley
above Le Chinaillon to the delightful Reposoir Valley beyond the pass.
North of La Clusaz, the road follows the
wooded valley of the River Nom.

St-Jean-de-Sixt

This peaceful resort lies on the edge of
the Nom and Borne valleys, at the heart
of the massif.

Follow D 4 towards Le Grand-Bornand.

Le Grand-Bornand

© L.Bouvier/Fotolia.com

🎿 Le Grand-Bornand✳

The pleasant, sunny village is known as both a ski resort (with an annexe at Le Chinaillon 6km/3.7mi further up) and a summer holiday centre especially prized by families. Home to reblochon cheese, in summer its pastures are full of cows.

Around 400 old chalets scattered across the whole village are faithfully preserved and the **Maison du Patrimoine** (⏰*open mid-Jun–mid-Sept Mon–Fri 10am–noon, 3–5pm, mid-Dec–Apr Sun–Fri 2–6pm; ✺2.50€; ✆04 50 02 79 18*) has been created to show the way the local Bornandins used to live. The valley du Bouchet, reached from the village centre, is a place to start excursions to Pointe Percée. The road continues up to Pont de Venay, through Le Chinaillon, in a series of hairpin bends offering **views** of the Tournette and the Aravis range.

Col de la Colombière
Alt. 1 613m/5 292ft.

The view extends to the northeast towards the Faucigny, Les Dents Blanches and Les Avoudrues. On the way down to Le Reposoir, the peaks of the Chaîne du Reposoir come into view and the roofs of the Chartreuse du Reposoir can be seen below the village.

▶ *From Le Reposoir, take a narrow road right to the Chartreuse.*

Chartreuse du Reposoir★

This Carthusian monastery (or *chartreuse*) was founded in 1151 and restored in the 17C. Abandoned by the order of St Bruno in 1904, it is now home to a community of Carmelite nuns.

③ VALLÉE DU BORNE

Drive of 30km/18.6mi shown on the local map. Allow 1hr 15min.

▶ *Leave La Clusaz by D 12.*

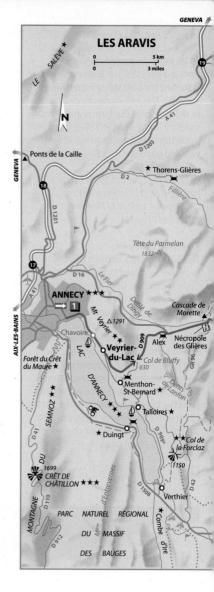

This pleasant itinerary follows the Borne Valley through two narrow and very picturesque gorges.

St-Jean-de-Sixt
🕪*See p121, ②.*

Défilé des Étroits★

The River Borne cuts crosswise through the limestone range to form this narrow gorge, which the road follows beneath

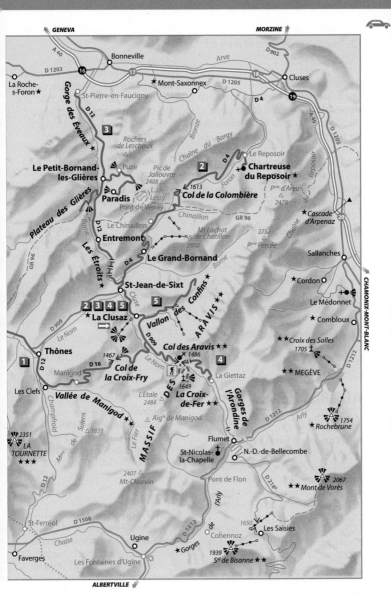

impressive cliffs. As the valley widens, the village of Entremont comes into view amid lush meadows.

Entremont
The little village has a charming **abbey church**, rebuilt several times, and the only remains of the original abbey that was founded in 1150 by the canons of Abondance. A **treasury** includes a gilt wood reliquary dating from the 12C.

The road continues through a pleasant pastoral landscape with the Jallouvre Massif looming in the distance (highest peak 2 408m/7 900ft).

Le Petit-Bornand-les-Glières
This small summer resort, set in restful surroundings, is the ideal starting point for a walk to the Plateau des Glières (2km/1.2mi S of the village, at Essert, a forest road leads to the plateau).

▷ *Take the signposted road to the left of the town hall.*

Route de Paradis

The breathtaking climb up the steep slopes of the Jallouvre offers views of the lower and upper Borne Valley *(for the best views, stop at Puze and again at a crossroads, 2.5km/1.5mi further on).* 🐾The road ends at the chalets of the tiny Paradis ski centre with stunning views of the Rochers de Leschaux and the funnel-shaped chasm below.

▷ *Return to Le Petit-Bornand.*

Gorge des Éveaux★

The road follows the Borne through another transverse valley which narrows considerably, the stream running below at the bottom of the gorge.

▷ *The road crosses the Borne at St-Pierre-en-Faucigny.*

ADDRESSES

🛏 STAY

⊜⊜ **Chambre d'hôte La Passerelle** – *Derrière l'Église 74450 St-Jean-de-Sixt. ℰ04 50 02 24 33. www.gites-chaletla passerelle.com.* 🅿 🗐. *5 rooms ⬜.* A good base to access the ski pistes of La Clusaz and Le Grand-Bornand, this new chalet opens onto a view of the Étale mountain. Rooms are comfortable, well lit with wood panelling.

⊜⊜ **Chambre d'hôte Les Lupins** – *La Clossette, 74230 Thônes. Leaving town on the right after Carrefour, towards Glapigny then La Clossette. ℰ04 50 63 19 96. www.francealpes.com. 3 rooms ⬜.* A steep little road leads to this fine 1854 chalet, lost in the middle of alpine pastures at an altitude of 1 200m/3 937ft and a perfect spot for relaxation. With their own access, the rooms are decorated in typical mountain style.

🍽 EAT

⊜ **Croix St-Maurice** – *Pl. de l'église, 74450 Le Grand-Bornand. ℰ04 50 02 20 05. www.hotel-lacroixstmaurice.com. Closed 25 Sept–21 Oct.* 🅿. Traditional chalet in the heart of the capital of reblochon cheese. Panoramic view of the church with the Aravis mountains in the background. You can choose to eat out on the terrace. Recently renovated bedrooms, most with a balcony.

⊜⊜ **Au Bon Vieux Temps** – *74450 Le Grand-Bornand. ℰ04 50 02 32 38. www.au-bon-vieux-temps.fr. Closed 2 weeks in Jun and Oct–Nov and Mon–Tue and Thu lunch out of season.* This old 1834 farm epitomises the atmosphere of "au bon vieux temps" – the "good old days". Walls are decorated with tools and the food specialities are thoroughly tempting.

🛒 SHOPPING

Reblochon Market – *74450 Le Grand-Bornand. Open Wed 8am–12.30pm.* This market has been held every Wednesday since 1795. Wholesalers purchase here direct from the farmers.

Coopérative agricole des Producteurs de Reblochon – *Rte d'Annecy, 74230 Thônes. ℰ04 50 02 05 60. www.reblochon-thones.com. Retail sales Mon–Sat.* Visit the production centre Monday–Friday from 9.30am.

🎉 EVENT

Festival Au bonheur des mômes – *74450 Le Grand-Bornand. ℰ04 50 02 78 00. www.aubonheurdesmomes.com.* Taking place over a week in August, this festival for children plays host to dozens of children's theatre companies.

La Clusaz★

To the east of Annecy, the rugged wall of the Aravis mountain range rises up dramatically. The peaks emerge relentlessly towards Pointe Percée (alt. 2 752m/9 029ft) and the ridges appear jagged above the village. This makes the gentle hillsides nearby even more of a surprise. Both lively and welcoming, the village of La Clusaz is a tourist centre of the Préalpes.

🚗 DRIVING TOURS

4 COL DES ARAVIS★★

Drive of 8km/5mi shown on the local map (⏱ see p123) leaving from La Clusaz.

The road winds up towards the Aravis pass along a valley at the foot of the strangely shaped escarpments of the Étale mountain. At the end of May mountain violets and gentians carpet the nearby slopes; by early summer they are covered in wild rhododendrons.

5 VALLON DES CONFINS★

Drive of 5.5km/3.4mi shown on the local map (⏱ see p123).

The road runs along the bottom of the valley then climbs up to the hamlet of Les Confins. Continue along this road to get a view of the Vallon du Bouchet.

Col des Aravis★★

Alt. 1 498m/4 915ft.
The chapel of Ste Anne stands amid pastures overlooked by the impressive cliffs of the Étale, with the Porte des Aravis on the opposite side. The **view** extends over the whole Massif du Mont-Blanc, from Aiguille Verte on the left to Mont Tondu on the right, with the Tête du Torraz in the foreground.

La Croix de Fer★★

🚶 *2hrs there and back on foot. Follow the path (chemin du Chalet du Curé) starting from the restaurant Rhododendrons and leading to the Croix de Fer.*

🛈 **Info:** 161 pl. de l'Église, 74220 La Clusaz. ℘04 50 32 65 00. www.laclusaz.com.

▶ **Location:** 28km/17.4mi E of Annecy on D 909.

👁 **Don't miss:** Vallon des Confins.

The **panorama** is even more impressive here than from the pass, extending from Mont Blanc southeast to the Vanoise glaciers.

ADDRESSES

🏨 STAY / 🍴 EAT

🛏 **Les Sapins** – 105 chemin des Riffroids. ℘04 50 63 33 33. www.clusaz.com. Closed 10 Apr–16 Jun, 6 Sept–15 Dec. 🅿. Wifi. 4 rooms, half-board possible, restaurant 🛏🛏.
With direct access to the pistes and facing the Aravis mountain chain, this chalet has alpine-style rooms, with pale wood balconies. In the restaurant, taste local cheese dishes, fondue and tartiflette with a mountainous backdrop.

🛏🛏 **Alp'Hôtel** – 192 rte du Col-des-Aravis. ℘04 50 02 40 06. www.clusaz.com. Closed 24 Apr–29 May, 25 Sept–30 Nov. Smart chalet situated at the centre of Clusaz, with a spacious restaurant. Traditional menu and tea room. The rooms, in cherrywood, pine or wicker, all have balconies.

🚶 ACTIVITIES

Ski area – Since the sport was first practised here in 1920, the La Clusaz ski area has grown into four linked sections, which attract ski and boarding fans. The Aravis ski pass gives access to the skiing in neighbouring Le Grand-Bornand, linked by ski bus. The areas of Manigod and l'Étale provide plenty of choice for intermediates, whereas Aiguille and Balme (alt. 2 600m/8 530ft) provide experienced skiers with black runs.

Thorens-Glières★

This small town lies on the banks of the River Fillière, a tributary of the Fier, at the point where the narrow valley opens out. It is the birthplace of St François de Sales, who was christened and later ordained as a bishop in the parish church. Nothing remains of the castle where François de Sales was born, but the Chapelle de Sales stands on the same site, along the Usillon road. Above Thorens-Glières is the Plateau des Glières, enjoyed for cross-country skiing in winter and hiking in summer. A monument on the plateau recalls its importance in the history of the Resistance movement during World War II.

CHÂTEAU DE THORENS★

Guided tours (1hr) Jul–Aug daily 2–7pm. ⊛7€. ఈ𝒫04 50 22 42 02.
The castle stands in an attractive setting, within sight of the Vallon de la Fillière and the Parmelan mountain. The foundations date from the 11C, the round keep from the 13C, and the whole edifice was remodelled in the 19C.

The vaulted basement was a guardroom and prison cells. The ground-floor rooms contain mementos of St François de Sales, 16C tapestries from Brussels, a wealth of furniture and a collection of paintings.

Two rooms are devoted to the architect of Italian unification, Count Cavour, including portraits and letters, and the desk on which the treaty uniting Savoie with France was signed.

PLATEAU DES GLIÈRES

14km/8.7mi E along a forest road.
During World War II the high-pasture area of the Plateau des Glières was chosen by Resistance leaders as a fortified camp. It was unsuccessfully attacked in February 1944 by Vichy security forces. A second attempt in March also failed. The Germans then amassed more than 10 000 soldiers, and the 465 besieged

▶ **Population:** 2 996.
ఈ **Michelin Map:** 328 K5.
▤ **Info:** 22 pl. de la Mairie, 74570 Thorens-Glières. 𝒫04 50 22 40 31. www.paysdefilliere.com.
◖ **Location:** 20km/12.4mi NE of Annecy on D 1203, towards Roche-sur-Foron.
◉ **Don't Miss:** The tapestries at the Château of Thorens. The Maquis trail at the Plateau des Glières.

men were forced to retreat, putting up a fierce resistance. There were heavy losses and surrounding villages suffered fierce reprisals.

However, the local Resistance group became gradually stronger and eventually liberated the *département* with the help of other Resistance groups in the area; Haute-Savoie became the first French territory to be liberated without the help of the Allied forces.

Where the paved road ends at the **Col des Glières**, a commemorative **monument** stands below on the right, in the form of a V for Victory incorporating a symbol of renewed hope and life.

The Resistance fighters killed in 1944 are buried in the Nécropole nationale des Glières (ఈ*see p120*).

A trail called Maquis des Glières offers a marked pathway *(2hrs)*.

ADDRESSES

♈ CAFÉ

Chez Constance – *Plateau des Glières. 1.5km/1mi from the Glières car park on the edge of GR 96.* 𝒫04 50 22 45 61. *www.les-glieres.fr.* Filling mountain food is served in this traditional chalet.

♡ EVENT

In Thorens on the Sunday following 15 August, a **pilgrim's mass** is celebrated at the Chapelle de Sales, and the town welcomes a **parade of floats**, along with folkloric dancing and songs.

ÉVIAN AND LE CHABLAIS

Its mineral water may be a household name, but Évian-les-Bains and its surroundings really are as gorgeous as the advertisements show. This fine spa town still attracts the wealthy to its grand hillside hotels, even if they probably no longer take the waters as they did a century ago. The French side of Lac Léman (known also as Lake Geneva) offers many activities for summer visitors, but do not miss the gorges, forests and villages of the Chablais mountains behind, home in winter to both traditional and modern ski resorts.

The Savoyard Riviera

Almost as far from the sea as is possible in France, sometimes when the winds pick up, the waves on huge Lac Léman make the lake seem almost like an ocean, so it is hardly surprising that over time its shores have developed a Riviera-like atmosphere, with some very desirable property on the heights above Évian and Thonon.

At peak summer holiday times, the main road running from Geneva to Évian and beyond to the Swiss border becomes extremely busy, so whenever possible plan your journeys for the first half of the morning, or the evening. Once you escape up into the Chablais – as locals try to do – you will immediately find a calmer mountain atmosphere, far from the bustle of the lakeside.

Do Drink the Water

The stories they tell are true. The world's best-selling mineral water – Évian – really does start life as rain and snow-melt from the nearby mountains,

Highlights

1 A walk along the lakeside at **Évian-les-Bains** (p130)

2 The Gorges of the Dranse at the natural "devil's bridge" **Pont du Diable** (p138)

3 **Domaine de Ripaille**, including the magnificent kitchens and the arboretum (p139)

4 The beautiful car-free village of **Yvoire** on Lac Léman (p140)

5 The panoramic view from **Mont Chéry**, reached by gondola and chairlift from Les Gets (p146)

naturally filtered through a bed of glacial sand to emerge, as it has done for more than two centuries, from the Source Cachat. After rigorous testing it is bottled in an ultra-modern bottling centre at source, as decreed by French law for mineral waters. Technically unique, each one with a different chemical

Yvoire by Lac Léman

© Gérard Labriet/Photononstop

ÉVIAN AND LE CHABLAIS

ÉVIAN AND LE CHABLAIS

LAUSANNE

LAC LÉMAN

Nyon

Yvoire

Nernier

Excenevex

Divonne-les-Bains

Messery

Chens-s-Léman

Gex

Douvaine

Bons-en-Chab

Ferney-Voltaire

SWITZERLAND

Col de Saxel 994

Grand Signal
1 480

Les Voirons

GENEVA

Rhône

Annemasse

Viuz-en-Sallaz

Arve

St-Julien-en-Genevois

Les Treize Arbres

Faucigny

NANTUA

Collonges-s/s-Salève

La Croisette

Le Salève

Grand Piton

Bonneville

Andilly

La Roche-s-Foron

Cruseilles

ANNECY

A   B

composition, there are of course many other mineral waters in the Alps. You can try the less exported Thonon water from the neighbouring spa town, which emerges from the Source de la Versoie, discovered

in spring to drink from is even more thrilling.

Maurice Novarina

The architect and town planner Maurice Novarina (1907–2002) was born in

LAC LÉMAN ★★★ Highly recommended
Yvoire ★★ Recommended
Châtel ★ Interesting
Bernex Other sight described in this guide
⇨ Driving tour with departure point
Border and area of coverage

Thonon-les-Bains and was responsible for many of the 20C urban improvements in both Thonon and Évian. As well as building 32 churches and chapels, his prolific work included numerous housing projects and civil buildings across the French Alps and Franche Comté. Many of his buildings now have protected status.

His most famous church is the Église Notre-Dame-de-Toute-Grâce at Plateau d'Assy (☞see p167).

Évian-les-Bains★★

Poetically known as the "pearl of Lake Geneva", Évian is remarkably well situated between the lake and the foothills of the Préalpes du Chablais. The resort town, renowned for its old palaces and thermal spas, climbs up from the flat lake area like an amphitheatre, with steep little roads parting in every direction. You can enjoy splendid architecture, walks or simply lazy evenings by the lake, and the town makes a fine base to explore the Chablais.

▶ **Population:** 8 137.
👍 **Michelin Map:** 328 M2.
🖼 **Info:** Pl. de la Porte d'Allinges, 74500 Évian-les-Bains. ℘04 50 75 04 26 www.ville-evian.fr.
▶ **Location:** Évian-les-Bains is about 45min from Exit 15 of A 40, or 10km/6.2mi from Thonon-les-Bains.
❀ **Don't Miss:** A boat ride on Lake Geneva is a delightful experience. The amazing panorama from the Pic de Mémise.
👪 **Kids:** The Pré Curieux is both fun and educational.
🕐 **Timing:** You can spend quite a few hours strolling along the waterfront. Spend half a day or more exploring the area.

➤ WALKING TOUR
The Lakeside★
Route shown on the town map (👍see p132).
Simply the most enjoyable walk in Évian. Firstly, because of the rare trees that border the lake, along with lawns and pretty flowerbeds. Next, because it is here that you will find the important buildings of the **Palais Lumière**, the **Villa Lumière**, today's town hall, and the **casino**.

▶ *Depart from the tourist office.*

All along the promenade up to the pleasure port Les Mouettes, the water in **musical fountains** plays in time to the music. Behind you, appearing through the chestnut groves of Neuvecelles, are the grand hotels, stacked up on the lower slopes of the Gavot.

Église Notre-Dame-de-l'Assomption – *Pl. des Anciens-Combattants.* Typical of early Gothic art in Savoie (end of 13C), the church has been rebuilt and restored frequently. To the right of the chancel in the Rosaire Chapel is a Burgundian painted wooden bas-relief of the Virgin Mary. The stalls are a masterpiece of Flamboyant Gothic art from the mid-15C, partly rebuilt in the 19C.
Villa Lumière (hôtel de ville) – 🕐*Open Mon–Fri 9–11.30am, 1.30–5pm. ℘0450 83 10 00.* Once owned by Antoine Lumière,

Lac Léman★★★ (Lake Geneva)

Lac Léman, which covers 580sq km/224sq mi and reaches depths of 310m/1 017ft, is 13 times larger than the Lac du Bourget; it is France's largest lake, even though shared with Switzerland. Shaped like a crescent, it is 72km/44.7mi long and 13km/8mi wide at its widest point between Morges and Amphion; the narrower part between Geneva and Yvoire is known as the Petit Lac, the more open part towards Montreux and St-Gingolph as the Grand Lac. The lake resembles a small sea, dotted with numerous fishing boats and crossed by the elegant boats of the Compagnie générale de la navigation, some of them restored paddle steamers. There are several lighthouses along the lake edge that are useful when the wind gets up; it is not unknown for storms to cause waves that are several meters high. Numerous yachting races take place on the lake.

Aerial view of Évian-les-Bains

Pierre Thiriet/Ville d'Évian

father of the cinema pioneer, this grand 1896 villa now houses the town hall; the ground-floor rooms and the **grand staircase**★ are especially elegant, while the next-door **theatre** is a splendid relic of 19C excess.

Also on the lakeside, on the same site as the Château de Blonay, willed to the town in 1877, are the **casino**, built in 1911 by the same architect as for the **Buvette Cachat**, and the **Palais Lumière**, a thermal spa until 1984 when it was converted to a cultural centre.

Buvette Cachat (Information Centre about Évian water) – 19 r. Nationale. ◷ Open mid-Jun–mid-Sept daily 10.30am–12.30pm, 3–7pm; mid-May–mid-Jun and end Sept Mon–Sat 2.30–6.30pm. ⊛Free. ♿ ℘04 50 26 80 29.

The centre is housed in the former pump room (1905) of the **Cachat spring**, an Art Nouveau building surmounted by a cupola. The spring is named after its owner, who improved the installations in 1824.

Parc thermal – The new baths are situated here. The pump room, designed by Maurice Novarina, was erected in 1956 and the Espace Thermal in 1983. This is partly built below ground in order to preserve the appearance of the park.

Jardin anglais – Beyond the harbour where yachts find a mooring and where the lake's pleasure boats come alongside, the Jardin anglais offers a view of the Swiss shore.

Le Pré Curieux Water Gardens★

Guided tour (2hrs, by reservation 4 days ahead; leaves from pontoon opposite the casino) Jul–Aug daily 10am, 1.45pm, 3.30pm; May–Jun and 1st 2 weeks Sept Wed–Sun 10am, 1.45pm, 3.30pm. ⊛11€ (children 6.50€). ♿ ℘04 50 70 15 44. www.precurieux.com.

This pretty garden demonstrates the rich variety of marshland ecosystems. You reach the elegant, Colonial-style villa on a solar-powered boat.

EXCURSION

The nearby town of **Amphion-les-Bains** (4km/2.5mi W) was the first spa resort of the Chablais region, which became fashionable as early as the 17C, when the Dukes of Savoie regularly took the waters. The medicinal properties of Évian water were discovered in 1789, when a gentleman realised it was dissolving his kidney stones.

The water, filtered by sand of glacial origin, is cold (11.6°C/52.9°F) and low in minerals. As well as for drinking it is prized for its beneficial effects on kidney disorders and rheumatism.

You can visit the very modern **bottling factory** (◷open Jan–mid-Dec Mon–Fri 9–10.30am, 2–3.30pm; ◷closed public holidays; *guided tour (1hr 30min) by appointment at the Évian information centre; ⊛free; ♿ ℘04 50 84 86 54), which produces an average of 5 million litres

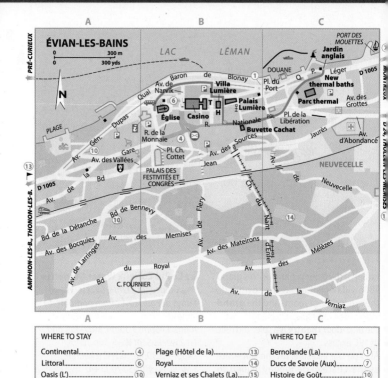

ÉVIAN-LES-BAINS

of water per day, the highest output of any producer.

🚗 DRIVING TOURS

FALAISES DE MEILLERIE★★
Drive of 23km/14.3mi shown on the regional map (👉 see p128). Allow 1hr. The route crosses the border into Switzerland.

▶ *Leave Évian E by the lake.*

The road is lined with imposing properties and passes beneath a gallery linking the Château de Blonay (16C–19C) to the shore. Beyond Lugrin, the road skirts the foot of the Meillerie cliffs opposite the town of Montreux on the Swiss shore of the lake, overlooked by the Rochers de Naye.

Meillerie★
This fishing village, where Rousseau set part of his *Nouvelle Héloïse* (1764), surrounds its squat church (13C steeple) in a charming **setting★** backed by the

From the Rhône to the Lake

An unusual phenomenon can be observed from Meillerie on the French side of the lake: the muddy mountain waters of the River Rhône flowing into the lake from the Swiss canton of Valais seem to be completely absorbed by the lake. In fact, part of the river flow remains at a depth of 20m/66ft until the temperature drops in autumn and the undercurrent of the river water blends into the cooling lake. These heat exchanges between the air and the water mean that the areas bordering the lake enjoy a pleasantly benign microclimate: even with frequent mists, the autumn can be really glorious.

most impressive cliffs. At the east end of the village, take the road down off the main national road to drive down to the quayside.

St-Gingolph

In the 18C, St-Gingolph was held to be one of the largest Swiss towns as the young Savoyards wishing to enrol in the regiments of Louis XV's royal guard all claimed to be from the Swiss part of the town because the pay in Swiss francs was better than in French francs.

Musée des Traditions et des Barques du Léman –
*Open Jul-Aug daily 2–5pm; Apr–Jun and Sept–Oct Sat 2–5.30pm. 3,50€ (children under 16 free). 0041 24 482 70 22.*The museum in is housed in the magnificent larch-wood eves (1752) of the castle. Through its displays of 33 model crafts of all styles, it traces the development of the shipping trade on Lac Léman. Splendid **views** over the lake from Novel at the foot of the Dent d'Oche *(take the steep D 30 road up from St-Gingolph).*

PAYS GAVOT★

Drive shown on the regional map (see p129). Allow 1hr.
The **Pays Gavot**, situated inland from Évian, is a plateau bounded to the south by the Dranse d'Abondance Valley and in the east by the cliffs of the Pic de Mémise. This countryside is popular with hikers. It was once known for peat production, and today there are moves to protect the remaining peat bogs.

Pic de Mémise★★

Alt. 1 677m/5 502ft. 30min return on foot.
The gondola from Thollon-les-Mémises brings visitors up to the top of the Mémise cliffs. From there it is possible to reach the highest point and enjoy the **panorama** of the lake and of the Swiss shore from Nyon to Montreux.

LA DRANSE D'ABONDANCE

Drive of 47km/29.2mi shown on the regional map (see p128). Allow 2hrs.

 Leave Évian by D 21 towards Thollon.

Bernex

This holiday resort and small mountain-eering centre is the starting point of the ascent of the **Dent d'Oche**.
From Vacheresse, D 22 follows the deep wooded valley of the Dranse d'Abondance, which opens up beyond Abondance (*see p143*). The traditional chalets have large grey-slated roofs, gables marked with a cross and balconies with wooden balustrades.

ADDRESSES

STAY

Continental – *65 r. Nationale. 04 50 75 37 54. www.hotel-continental-evian.com. Wifi. 32 rooms.* Family-owned hotel, from 1868, rooms include attractive old furniture collected by the proprietor. Pedestrian street.

Hôtel de la Plage – *431 r. de la plage, 74500 Amphion-les-Bains. On D 1005. 04 50 70 00 06. www.hotelplage74.com. Closed Nov–Apr. 39 rooms, restaurant .* You could not stay closer to the lake. Bright, quiet rooms have all been renovated. Eating in the restaurant on stilts is adorable.

Littoral – *Av. de Narvik. 04 50 75 64 00. www.hotel-evian-littoral.com. Closed 29 Oct–14 Nov. Wifi. 30 rooms.* A 1990s hotel built next to the casino. Rooms in regional style, with lake views (most have balconies).

L'Oasis – *11 bd Bennevy. 04 50 75 13 38. www.oasis-hotel.com. Closed Oct–Mar. Wifi. 17 rooms.* On the heights of Évian, a charming hotel with pretty rooms. Some face the lake; others are in small houses nestled in the pretty shaded garden.

La Verniaz et ses Chalets – *Rte d'Abondance. 04 50 75 04 90. www.verniaz.com. Closed 12 Nov–11 Feb. 22 rooms, restaurant .* This lovely hotel has several buildings set in a beautiful garden. Large bedrooms have a view over the lake.

Royal – *04 50 26 85 00. www.evianroyalresort.com. Wifi.140 rooms.* Built in Art Nouveau style in 1907, this luxurious hotel is set in a park. Well-equipped wellness centre and spacious, stylish rooms. You can enjoy gastronomic cuisine in the Édouard VII restaurant, or on the terrace with a lake view. Other choices are buffet or barbecue at La Véranda, or special diet dishes at the Jardin des Lys.

℘/EAT

🍽 **La Bernolande** – *1 pl. du Port.* *℘04 50 70 72 60. Closed Jan, Wed and Sept– Apr Thu.* On a fine day, the terrace of this little restaurant is the perfect spot to sit back and enjoy homestyle cooking whilst watching ferry boats crossing the lake.

🍽🍽 **Aux Ducs de Savoie** – *R. 23 juillet 44, 74500 St-Gingolph. ℘04 50 76 73 09. www.ducsdesavoie.net. Closed 4-26 Jan, Mon and Sept–Jun Tue.* Pleasant chalet in the middle of the village. Tasty, classic recipes are served in a bourgeois setting inside or on the shady terrace with lake view.

🍽🍽 **Histoire de Goût** – *1 av. Gén. Dupas. ℘04 50 70 09 98. www.restaurant -histoiredegout.com. Closed 3–18 Jan and Mon.* Named the "story of taste", the choice here is to eat in a room with a wooden/zinc bar and décor of wine boxes, or another vaulted room with ironwork décor.

🏃‍♂️ACTIVITIES

🚣 **Good to know** – The **sailing centre** offers courses and races for all levels. The **Évian-Plage** swimming centre has two heated pools. At Cité de l'Eau in Amphion-les-Bains you will find an indoor pool, wave pool, diving pool sauna and jacuzzi.

🎭 EVENT

Escales musicale d'Évian – *La Grange au lac. ℘ 04 50 26 85 00. www.evianroyalresort.com. 2nd and 3rd weeks of May.* Évian hosts a renowned festival of classical music.

Thonon-les-Bains★

The second-biggest town in Haute-Savoie, and a well-known spa town, Thonon has suffered a little from its rapid expansion. However, it is worth having a stroll in the town centre, where you will find 19C architecture side by side with more contemporary styles. When you view the huge lake from the terrace of the Musée du Chablais or visit the pretty port of Rives you do indeed discover a town of contrasts. Thonon is an excellent base for touring the Chablais district.

🐾WALKING TOUR

The lakeshore★

At the well-preserved port of **Rives**, there are still some professional fisher-men who sell their catch daily at 9.30am. Towards Ripaille you will find a **beach**. From Rives, the best way up to Thonon is by an attractive **funicular** (built in 1888)

▶ **Population:** 31 562.
👤 **Michelin Map:** 328 L2.
ℹ **Info:** Château de Sonnaz, r. Michaud, 74200 Thonon-les-Bains. ℘04 50 71 55 55. www.thononlesbains.com.
▶ **Location:** The French side of Lake Geneva is urbanised with dense traffic on D 1206. Either take A 40, Exit 15, then D 1005 and D 1206; or you can drive from Cluses, 60km/37.3mi to the S on D 902.
👁 **Don't Miss:** Take the funicular between Thonon and the port of Rives; stop to visit the château at the Domaine de Ripaille.
🕐 **Timing:** Allow minimum one day to explore both the town of Thonon and the lakeshore sights. At least a further day for the Chablais region.

with excellent views (○*open Jul–Aug daily 8am–11pm, mid-Apr–Jun and Sept 8am–9pm, Oct–Apr 8am–12.30pm, 1.30–6.30pm, Sun 1.30–6pm [every 2–4min]; ○1.80€ return; ℘04 50 71 21 54).*

▲▲ Écomusée de la Pêche et du Lac (Port of Rives)

○*Open Jul–Aug daily 10.30am–12.30pm, 3–6pm; Jun and Sept Wed–Sun 2.30–8pm. ℘04 50 70 26 96.*
Occupying three former fishing huts, this little museum describes the resources, fishing, history, water quality and other facts about Europe's most celebrated lake. The aquariums hold some fine specimens of lake fish.

Place du Château
The castle of the Dukes of Savoie which once stood on this site was destroyed by the French in 1589. In the centre of the square stands the statue of **Général Dessaix** (1764–1834), a native of Thonon, who joined French revolutionary forces when they occupied the Savoie and who was made a general by Napoleon. From the terraces, there is an open **view**★ of the Swiss side of Lake Geneva from Nyon to Lausanne. Below, the Rives district clusters round the brownish roofs of Rives-Montjoux Castle and Ripaille Castle can be seen to the right. The Vaudois Alps and Jura mountains form the panoramic background.

Jardin du Château de Sonnaz
A pleasant place to relax; situated at the end of the vast open space of the Jardin Paul-Jacquier, the ancient Chapelle St-Bon, adjacent to a 13C tower (part of the town's fortifications), attracts many painters.

Musée du Chablais
○*Open Jul–Aug daily 10.30am–12.30pm, 3–6pm; mid-May–Jun and Sept–mid-Nov Wed–Sun 2–6pm. ○2.05€ (ticket combined with Écomusée de la Pêche et du Lac). ℘04 50 70 69 49.*
Housed in the cellars of the 17C Château de Sonnaz, this museum was renovated in 2009. One room illustrates the history

Savoie Wines
Benefiting from the benign climate around Lake Geneva, the vineyards of Ripaille, as well as Marin, Marignan and Crépy, are all designated AOC Savoie. These dry white wines are all made from the Chasselas grape, almost exclusively grown in this part of France and across the lake in Switzerland.

of the smuggling in this border region; another has models and the history of the majestic traditional sailing crafts of Lake Geneva; a room is devoted to sculptor Marguerite Peltzer, who lived in Thonon. Various temporary art exhibitions are held.

Église St-Hippolyte
⊶*Closed for restoration.*
Inspired by the preachings of François de Sales and the return to Catholicism of the Chablaisiens, inside this fine church is decorated in 17C style.

Basilique St-François-de-Sales
Connected with the St-Hippolyte church, and built in the 20C in a Gothic Revival style, the transept of this pilgrims' sanctuary includes the last works by Maurice Denis of the Nabis school, a movement close to the Pont-Aven school.
Two paintings illustrate the 14 stations in the Way of the Cross (1943), to which are added two large frescoes, the one on the left representing the dying Christ and the one on the right transept, His appearance to the Holy Women after the Resurrection. There are also baptism fonts (13C) and a 14C statue of the Virgin and Child.

Monastère de la Visitation
This monastery (17C) has recently been restored. According to tradition, the chapel was built to the plans of Ste Jeanne de Chantal including arches with diagonal ribs. A rare vestige of Gothic architecture, it is situated in the heart of the Visitandines quarter renovated by Maurice Novarina in the 1960s.

Hôtel-Dieu

In the old Convent of the Minimes, founded in 1636, the Hôtel-Dieu is built around a Classic, elegant cloister, of Baroque style.

Foyer Don-Bosco

The modern chapel of this organisation is decorated inside with ceramics: a panel and tabernacle from Marie Arbel, stations of the cross from Paul Bony.

Viewpoints★★

Along the boulevard de la Corniche to the Jardin anglais you can stop at several fine viewpoints.

⚑ HIKES

Grand Signal des Voirons★

Route shown on the regional map (see p129). Take D 903 to Annemasse as far as Bons-en-Chablais, then head S on D 20 towards Boëge.

The road rises gently through the woods, offering glimpses of the Bas-Chablais and Lake Geneva. From the Col de Saxel, D 50 follows the line of the ridge to the right through a small wood; the view gradually extends to the east beyond the Chaîne du Reposoir to the Dents du Midi, Mont Buet and the snow-capped peaks of the Mont Blanc Massif. The wooded slopes of the Voirons mountain are very popular with walkers.

⚑ *Allow 1hr there and back. Leave the car at the end of the road, near the monastery. From there take the path marked voie sans issue and head uphill through the wood. At the edge of the wood, follow a path on the left marked Les Crêtes. After this path joins the chemin des Crêtes, turn right. The path divides in front of the monastery building; take the left fork to the ridge and follow it to the right to the cross that marks the summit of the Grand Signal.*

Le Tour du Char des Quais

⚑ *Allow 2hrs there and back.*
From Col de l'Encrenaz (D 328 from Morzine) to Côte-d'Arbroz.
This easy circular walk climbs up to the Col de Basse from where there is a superb view to Mont Blanc. It then goes alongside the pastures of Les Praz returning to the starting point.

🚗 DRIVING TOURS

🚗 *See also tours from Évian-les-Bains.*

The **Chablais★★**, extending between Lake Geneva and the Giffre Valley, is the largest massif in the Préalpes with the twin summits of Dent d'Oche and Château d'Oche. The geological structure comprises three distinct areas. The **Bas-Chablais** is a relatively low, hilly area bordering the southern shores of Lake Geneva (Lac Léman), with lively summer activities along the Savoyard Riviera between Yvoire and Évian-les-Bains.
Pays Gavot is the countryside above Évian (see p133). The **Haut-Chablais**, centred round Morzine, is an area of pastures and forests. Three rivers cut their way through it: the Dranse d'Abondance, Dranse de Morzine and Brevon; all are tributaries of the Dranse de Savoie, flowing into Lake Geneva.

ROUTE DES TROIS COLS★

Drive of 54km/33.6mi shown on the regional map (see p129). Allow 3hrs 30min.
▶ *Leave Thonon-les-Bains south, towards Bellevaux.*
The D 26 runs above the Gorges de la Dranse and the valley of Bellevaux. There are views to the Dent d'Oche escarpments in the distance.

Bellevaux

🛈 *Bâtiment Les Contamines, 74470 Bellevaux. ℘04 50 73 71 53. www.bellevaux.com.*
The **situation★** of this charming village at the foot of the Roc d'Enfer, on the left bank of the Brevon, is charming nestled below the pretty green slopes of the valley of the same name. The church, with an unusual onion dome bell tower in copper, has fine sculpted wood pieces inside and retains a 14C chapel, a vestige from the old church. An 18C covered bridge at the edge of the village sits on a large block of misshaped granite.

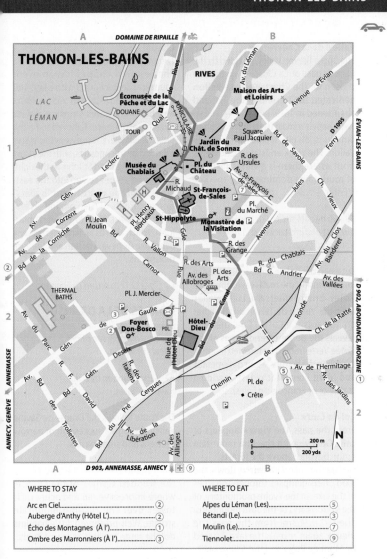

THONON-LES-BAINS

DOMAINE DE RIPAILLE

RIVES

LAC LÉMAN

Écomusée de la Pêche et du Lac
DOUANE
TOUR
Maison des Arts et Loisirs
Square Paul Jacquier
Jardin du Chât. de Sonnaz
Musée du Chablais
Pl. du Château
R. des Ursules
R. Michaud
St-François-de-Sales
Pl. du Marché
St-Hippolyte
Monastère de la Visitation
R. des Grange
Pl. Jean Moulin
Pl. Henry Bordeaux
R. Vallon
Carnot
R. des Arts
Pl. des Arts
Av. des Allobroges
R. du Chablais
G. Andrier
Av. des Vallées
THERMAL BATHS
Pl. J. Mercier
Gaulle
Foyer Don-Bosco
Hôtel-Dieu
POL
Desaix
Rue de l'Hôtel Dieu
Av. de l'Hermitage
Av. des Jardins
Pl. de Crête
Cergues
Av. de la Libération
Av. des Allinges

D 903, ANNEMASSE, ANCY
ANNECY, GENÈVE, ANNEMASSE
ÉVIAN-LES-BAINS
D 902, ABONDANCE, MORZINE

0   200 m
0   200 yds
N

WHERE TO STAY		WHERE TO EAT	
Arc en Ciel	②	Alpes du Léman (Les)	⑤
Auberge d'Anthy (Hôtel L')	②	Bétandi (Le)	③
Écho des Montagnes (À l')	①	Moulin (Le)	⑦
Ombre des Marronniers (À l')	③	Tiennolet	⑨

Musée de l'Histoire et des Traditions
(&04 50 73 71 53) – This museum of local history and traditions includes a re-creation of the main room of a typical 19C Savoyard house.

Musée de la Faune alpine – &⊙Open Mid-Dec–end Sept Wed–Thu 3–4pm. ≈3€ (children 2€).
The museum includes 140 stuffed alpine animals, displayed in their typical habitat. This educational visit can be complemented with a look at the **alpine garden** (200 species).

◯ *After Bellevaux cemetery, turn right over the Brevon, then left on a forestry track.*

Overlooking the Bellevaux Valley, the road climbs up relentlessly until you reach the Buchille chalets, where there is a pretty **view** over the Mont d'Hermone, to the northwest.

◯ *Return to Bellevaux and continue towards the hamlet of Jambaz, then take the chemin de la Chèvrerie.*

Vallon de la Chèvrerie★

The upper Brevon Valley, guarded by the narrow pass of La Clusaz, was the site chosen for the **Chartreuse de Vallon** dedicated to St Bruno in the 12C and abandoned in 1619.

Two chapels remain from the monastery buildings, on either side of the Lac de Vallon. The track ends at La Chèvrerie, from where there is a view to a circle of mountains dominated by the Roc d'Enfer.

> *Go back to the Col de Jambaz, turn left and almost immediately right onto D 32.*

Between the Col de Jambaz and the Col de Terramont, the road leaves the Risse Valley, briefly enters the Lullin Valley then the Vallon de Terramont. Further on, towards the Col du Cou, the road reveals the peaceful landscapes of the Vallée Verte framed by forested heights, including the Voirons, Mont d'Hirmentaz and Mont Forchat (the last bearing a statue of St François de Sales).

Col de Cou★

From the pass, the **view**★ appears of Lake Geneva with the Jura mountain range beyond, above the forests.

During the 16km/10mi drive down, the road offers glimpses through the trees of the lake, of the Yvoire promontory, of the Voirons and of the Jura mountains. Then 7km/4.3mi from the pass the **view**★ again reveals the lake, framed by Mont de Boisy and the Allinges hill.

> *As you enter Mâcheron, take the first right turn. Leave the car at the top of the ascent on the flat area on the right, then walk up towards the first gateway.*

Château des Allinges

The hilltop was originally crowned by two castles belonging to rival feudal lords until 1355 when both came into the possession of the Count of Savoie. Walk through the fortified gates to the east platform offering a **view** of the Bas-Chablais region and the Dent d'Oche.

Chapel – *Switch on the left of the entrance for lighting the fresco.*

The restored **chapel** has an oven-vaulted apse decorated with a late-10C Romanesque fresco, its rich colours and hieratic figures showing a clear Byzantine influence. Believed to be the oldest in Savoie, it represents Christ surrounded by the Apostles, with the Virgin Mary on the left and St John on the right. The round stones sealed into the eastern wall of the château are "bullets" from catapults of the Carolingian era. Before leaving, walk to the west platform, which affords an extended **view**★ over Lake Geneva, Thonon and the Jura mountains.

> *Take D 12 to return to Thonon.*

GORGES DE LA DRANSE

Drive of 33km/20.5mi shown on the regional map (see p129). Allow 1hr 45min.

> *Leave Thonon by D 902 towards Cluses.*

The route follows the Dranse de Savoie Valley through a succession of narrow sections and small basins.

From Thonon to Bioge, the road follows the wooded Gorges of the Dranse, where impressive red and ochre cliffs tower over the rushing mountain stream. Well-preserved, little hamlets dot the route towards St-Jean d'Aulps.

Gorges du Pont du Diable★★

Guided visits (45min) May–Sept daily 9am–6pm. 5.30€ (children 3.20€). 04 50 72 10 39. www.lepontdudiable.com.

Enormous rocks, coloured in ochre, grey, green and blue by various deposits and eroded into all kinds of shapes, luxuriant vegetation and smooth vertical cliffs up to 60m/197ft high all contribute to make this visit fascinating; landslides have occurred in places, forming huge piles of boulders and a spectacular natural bridge known as the Pont du Diable.

Abbaye Notre-Dame-d'Aulps

🕐 *Open Jul–Aug daily 10am–7pm; April–Jun and Sept Sun–Fri 2–6.30pm; mid–Dec–Mar Sun–Fri 10am–6pm.*

👣 *Guided visits of the ruins Jul–Aug daily 4pm.* 🎫 *6€ (children 3€).* 📞 *04 50 04 52 63. www.valleedaulps.com.*

The atmospheric ruins of the 12C–13C church are the only remaining part of this Cistercian abbey; however, this fascinating site has been converted into an educational centre explaining the fascinating history of the abbey. Temporary exhibitions and events are also held. From here there is a view to the Morzine Valley and its main summits.

▷ *Return by the same route or via Taninges and St-Jeoire.*

EXCURSIONS
Domaine de Ripaille★

▷ *Go down to Rives and follow quai de Ripaille to the end, then turn left into the avenue leading to Château de Ripaille.*

This monastery and castle comprises a group of imposing buildings in typical Savoyard style, set in the midst of fine vineyards. It was originally a hunting estate for the Counts of Savoie. When purchased in the 15C by Amédé VII, who became Pope in 1449 under the name of Félix V, it became a meeting place for the European intellectual elite.

Château

👣 *Guided tours (1hr) Jul–Aug daily 11am, 2.30, 3.30, 4.15pm; Feb–Jun and Sept–Nov times vary. Self-guided tours also possible.* 🎫 *6€.* 📞 *04 50 26 64 44. www.ripaille.fr.*

The castle has, since 1976, been the headquarters of the Fondation Ripaille, which promotes research into ecology, geography and the development of natural resources.

The monastery buildings, between 1619 and the Revolution, were occupied by Carthusian monks. The visit includes a courtyard of mulberry trees, the old wine press and the huge kitchens (17C) used by the monks.

Forest and Arboretum

🕐 *Open daily May–Sept 10am–7pm; Jan–Apr and Oct–Nov 10am–4.30pm.* 📞 *04 50 26 28 22.*

Marked paths lead to the arboretum, whose trees, including firs, red oaks from America and black walnuts, were planted between 1930 and 1934.

Vongy

▷ *E Thonon, adjoining Ripaille.*

The **Église Notre-Dame-du-Léman** is a graceful modern building (1935) by the architect Maurice Novarina.

Topped with a high steeple, this highly original building takes the form of an upturned boat and the façade features a large triangular stone claustra.

ADDRESSES

🛏 STAY

🍽 **À l'Écho des Montagnes** – *74200 Armoy.* 📞 *04 50 73 94 55. www.echo-des-montagnes.com. Closed 1 Jan–7 Feb, 4–8 Oct, Sun eve and Sept–May Mon.* 🅿. *47 rooms, half-board possible, restaurant* 🍽. This imposing 19C house offers simple but practical rooms; larger ones are available in an annexe. The friendly restaurant serves generous portions of regional cuisine incorporating vegetables from the garden.

🍽 **À l'Ombre des Marronniers** – *17 pl. Crête.* 📞 *04 50 71 26 18. www.hotelles marronniers.com. Closed 25 Apr–6 May, 20 Dec–5 Jan. Wifi. 17 rooms, half-board possible, restaurant* 🍽. Rooms in this chalet-style hotel are old-fashioned, but functional. Traditional cuisine and mountain specialities are served in the conservatory dining-room or on the terrace beneath the chestnut trees.

🍽 **Arc en Ciel** – *18 pl. Crête.* 📞 *04 50 71 90 63. www.hotelarcencielthonon.com. Closed 25 Apr–6 May, 19 Dec–4 Jan. Wifi. 40 rooms.* Close to the town centre, this is a modern hotel with a nice garden and pool. Guest rooms with a balcony or terrace are spacious and well equipped, some with a kitchenette.

🍽 **Hôtel L'Auberge d'Anthy** – *2 r. des Écoles, 74200 Anthy-sur-Léman.* 📞 *04 50 70 35 00. www.auberge-anthy.com.*

Wifi. 16 rooms, restaurant⊖⊖. This unpretentious village inn offers small, simple rooms and straightforward bistro-style food with regional accents.

⊝/ EAT

⊖ **Le Bétandi** – *2 r. des Italiens.* ✆*04 50 71 37 71. www.fermedesalpes.com.* Although close to the town centre, this little restaurant resembles an old Savoyard farmhouse. Typical local fare with the inevitable fondue, tartiflette and reblochonade, as well as pizzas baked in a wood oven.

⊖ **Le Moulin** – *13 av. St-François-de-Sales.* ✆*04 50 26 29 43. www.lemoulin-thonon.com Closed mid–Jun–mid-Jul and Sun–Mon.* This pizzeria occupies an old mill made of stone on a little canal. There are two terraces, one on the street and one in a garden shaded by acacia trees. Simple décor inside.

⊖⊖ **Les Alpes du Léman** – *3 bis r. des Italiens.* ✆*04 50 26 51 24. Closed 15 Jul–13 Aug, Sun eve and Wed.* Situated in a shopping street, there is trendy new beige and chocolate décor at this friendly, family restaurant. Nicely prepared, seasonal food is offered.

⊖⊖ **Tiennolet** – *74420 Habère-Poche.* ✆*04 50 39 51 01. Closed 2–28 Jun, 13 Oct–14 Nov, Tue eve, Sun eve, and Wed except school holidays.* 🅿. In the centre of the village, this welcoming mountain restaurant has a fully south-facing terrace. Traditional, local cuisine.

🏃 ACTIVITIES

Circuit des Chapelles et les Lavoirs – A guided visit in a little train touring what were once hamlets that have since been incorporated into the town of Thonon. *Information from the Thonon tourist office.* ✆*04 50 71 55 55. Open end Apr–early Sept Thu–Tue 2.30–5pm, Wed 9.30am–5pm.*

Réserve naturelle du delta de la Dranse – The natural reserve of the Dranse Delta beyond Ripaille covers 53ha/131 acres and is a good place for walks and to observe birds and flowers.

🎉 EVENT

A **street festival** takes place on the first Thursday of September each year, with entertainers and food stalls.

Yvoire★★

The charming medieval village of Yvoire occupies a splendid position on the shores of Lake Geneva. With cars forbidden, you can wander freely up and down the flower-filled streets, taking in the lake views before settling down in one of the restaurants, renowned for their lake fish specialities.

THE MEDIEVAL VILLAGE★★

Yvoire has retained part of its 14C fortifications, including two gateways, the **castle** (⊶ *closed to the public*) with its massive square keep flanked by turrets, and a few old houses. The fine silver onion-domed **Église St-Pancrace** (14C–19C) completes the picture.

The lively streets are lined with artists' workshops; now and then a lovely square decorated with flowers offers views of the lake. From the end of the

▶ **Population:** 811.
⚫ **Michelin Map:** 328 K2.
🚩 **Info:** Pl. de la Mairie, 74140 Yvoire. ✆04 50 72 80 21. www.yvoire tourism.com.
▶ **Location:** 16.2km/10.1mi W of Thonon-les-Bains via D 25 and Excenevex. Cars must be left outside the medieval village.

pier (*cruise boats to Thonon, Geneva and other Swiss ports* ✆*+41 (0) 848 811 848*), there are views across to the city of Nyon on the Swiss shore, with the Jura mountains above.

Jardin des Cinq Sens★ – *R. du Lac, Yvoire.* 🕐*Open daily Apr–May 11am–6pm; Jun–mid-Oct 10am–7pm.* ⊕*10€.* ♿✆*04 50 72 88 80. www.jardin5sens.net.* The former kitchen garden of the castle has been turned into a reconstruction of a medieval enclosed garden with vegetables and herbs.

ADDRESSES

🛏 STAY

◻◻◻ **Le Pré de la Cure** – *Pl. de la Mairie.* ℘*04 50 72 83 58. www.pre-delacure.com. Closed 12 Nov–26 Feb.* ♿ 🅿. *Wifi. 25 rooms, restaurant*◻◻◻. On the edge of the medieval village, this hotel offers large modernised rooms with lake or garden views. Local perch fillets served in view of the lake.

🍴 EAT

◻ **Le Denieu** – *300 av. Bonnatrait, 74140 Sciez-sur-Léman. 6km/3.7mi SE of Yvoire by D 25 and D 1005.* ℘*04 50 72 35 06. www.fermedesalpes.com.* ♿🅿. Do not be put off by the fact that this large restaurant is on the side of the main road. Once an old farm, lovely old wood and farm objects feature in the dining room serving Savoie specialities.

◻◻ **Du Port** – *R. du Port.* ℘*04 50 72 80 17. www.hotelrestaurantduport-yvoire.com. Closed 4 Nov–25 Feb. 7 rooms*◻◻◻. This is an ideal site on the marina next to the lake, and the terrace and flower-decked façade make the most of it. Fish dishes are a speciality. Nice rooms.

🚣 ACTIVITIES

Messery – The beach stretches over 3km/1.8mi with public access at "Sous les Prés" and "La Pointe". Plenty of watersports activities available.

Sailing – Several sailing schools offer beginners and other courses *(details from Yvoire tourist office)*.

Le Salève★

The limestone cliffs of Mont Salève tower above Geneva on the French side of the border reaching 1 380m/ 4 528ft, and from the end of the 19C were used as a training ground for climbers. With numerous shelters carved into the rocks in the neolithic period, as early as the 18C the cliffs became a rare hunting ground for geologists and botanists. Being so close to Geneva, the Salève can get very busy, but it continues to be recognised as a particularly interesting environmental site.

🥾 HIKES
Climbing Salève and Le Circuit géologique★

🚶 *From Collonges-sous-Salève. Leave the car at the Coin car park (alt. 666m/ 2 185ft), 4hrs. For fit hikers only.* Follow the Circuit Géologique et Botanique. Start on the path created in 1905 by the Geneva section of the Swiss Alpine Club (CAS) that leads to the Corraterie *(2hrs).* After a stroll along the ridge, you reach the Grande-Gorge route.

- ⏱ **Michelin Map:** 328 K4.
- ℹ **Info:** Office de Tourisme d'Annemasse-Agglo, pl. de la Gare, 74100 Annemasse. ℘04 50 95 07 10. www.annemasse-aglo-tourisme.com.
- ▷ **Location:** Off D 15 from Cruseilles or A 40, Exit 14.
- ⏰ **Timing:** Avoid belvederes in the mornings, when fog may obscure the views.

Salève Cable Car★ (1 100m/3 609ft)

🚶 *From D 1206, Exit Pas de l'Échelle-Étrembières; or by A 40 towards Annemasse-St-Julien, leave the car at the rest stop, which gives direct access to the cable-car station. Opening depends on weather conditions. Apr Tue–Wed and Sun 9.30am–6pm, Thu–Sat 9.30am–9pm; May–Sept Thu–Sat 9.30am–11pm, Sun–Wed 9.30am–7pm. Contact for rest of year and ticket prices.* ℘*04 50 39 86 86. www.telepheriquedusaleve.com.*

Opened in 1932 the cable car whisks you up to the ridge in four minutes. From there is a glorious **view**★★ over Geneva (and its famous Jet d'Eau), to the Jura, Lake Geneva, the Dents du Midi and right over to the Mont Blanc Massif and beyond to the Préalpes and la Meije en Oisans.

 ## DRIVING TOUR

LA ROUTE DES CRÊTES

Drive shown on the regional map (◐ see p128). Allow 1 day. In snowy conditions the road may be closed between les Avenières and the Col de la Croisette.

Cruseilles

The Maison de Fésigny, 50m/55yds from the church, is all that remains of the wealthy 14C–15C mansions in this little Genevois town, now under constant threat of modern urbanisation.

Continuing up from Cruseilles, the view reveals the Bornes Massif, with behind the Haut Faucigny, the Bargy and Mont Blanc. From Petit Pommier to Col de la Croisette, a corniche offers good overhead views of Geneva and the Jura.

▷ *Head N to St-Blaise and Andilly.*

👤👤Le Petit Pays★

◐*Open Jul–Aug and mid-Oct–Mar.* ✆*6.70€ (children 4.70€). ✆04 50 32 73 64. www.lepetitpays.com.*

This imaginary country is home to the **Hameau du Père Noël** lived in by Father Christmas and a forest full of elves. In July–August, you can see even more elves and magicians at the **Parc des Légendes**.

Cure d'Andilly

◐*Open Jul–Aug daily 2–6pm. ✆3€ (children 1.50€).*

This old **presbytery** stages temporary exhibitions and around it are medieval gardens including herbs along with old vegetable species.

▷ *Return to D 1201 heading N, then follow left on D 18 then D 218.*

Maison du Salève at Présilly

Rte de Mikerne. ◐*Open Jul–Aug Tue–Sun 10am–6pm; Sept–Jun Wed–Sun 2–6pm. ✆6€ (children 3€). Guided visits, workshops and excursions. ✆04 50 95 92 16. www.maisondusaleve.com.*

A successful fusion of an 18C farm with contemporary architecture houses the Salève Information Centre.

🚶*45min easy walk.* The discovery trail Sur les Pas des Chartreux ("following the steps of the monks") provides a history of the mountain landscape.

▷ *Return to St-Blaise and follow D 41A towards Annemasse. The old road passes farms and former quarries.*

Les Treize Arbres Viewpoint★★

🚶*From D 41, 15min on foot there and back.*

Splendid **view** of the peaks. Very popular with paragliders.

Annemasse

On the Swiss border, close to Geneva, Annemasse has many parks and several concert halls and theatres.

Villa du Parc – *12 r. de Genève.* ◐*Open Tue–Sat 2–6.30pm.* ✆*Free (guided visit 4€).* ♿ *✆04 50 38 84 61. www.villaduparc.com.*

Temporary contemporary art exhibitions are held in this villa.

ADDRESSES

🛏 STAY

🍽🛏 **Rey** – *131 rte d'Annecy, 74350 St-Blaise, at the Col du Mont Sion. ✆04 50 44 13 29.* 🅿. *Wifi. 30 rooms.* With just a garden between it and the road, you might want to choose a quieter room at the rear. Breakfast is served on the veranda.

🍴/EAT

🍽🛏 **L'Angélick** – *74560 La Muraz. ✆04 50 94 51 97. www.angelick.fr. Closed 9–23 Aug, 21–30 Dec, Sun eve–Tue and lunch Wed–Fri.* 🅿. A cosy and warm interior with ironwork or leather chairs, the table settings here are modern and the food inventive.

Abondance★

The upper Chablais is framed by mountains that provide a beautiful luminosity to the rich landscape of the Abondance Valley below. Located at the intersection of the Dranse and Malève rivers, the village of Abondance has long been famous and lives up to its name for the great abundance of its position. Today, the village is known as a family-friendly holiday resort, and for its cheese.

SIGHTS
Abbey★

During the Middle Ages, the **Abbaye d'Abondance** had a major influence on the whole valley.

Cloisters – ⏰*Open Apr–Sept Wed–Mon 9.30am–noon, 2–5pm; 21 Dec–Mar, Mon –Fri 9.30am–noon, 2–5pm.* ☛*Guided tours (1hr) 10am–3pm.* ⏰*Closed 1 Jan, 25 Dec.* ⊛2€. ♿ ✆*04 50 81 60 54. www.abbaye-abondance.org.*

There are two 14C galleries left, and beautiful **frescoes**★★ painted in around 1430 and attributed to the Piemontese Giacomo Jacquerio.The Porte de la Vierge, which gives access to the **church**, is richly decorated, although badly damaged.

At the abbey is also the **Exposition du Patrimoine Religieux** displaying a large collection of liturgical ornaments, paintings, statues and old manuscripts.

▶ **Population:** 1 351.
♿ **Michelin Map:** 328 N3.
🛈 **Info:** 74360 Abondance. ✆04 50 73 02 90. www.valdabondance.com.
▶ **Location:** Abondance is 30km/18.6mi S of Évian between Morzine and Lake Geneva (Lac Léman). The easiest route is by D 22 towards Châtel.
👁 **Don't miss:** The abbey's 15C frescoes; trying the local abondance cheese.
🕐 **Timing:** Allow at least a couple of hours to visit the abbey, and then a half-day or more for excursions and walks in the area.

Maison du Val

Plaine d'Offaz. ⏰*Open Dec–Oct Mon–Sat 9.30am–noon, 2–6pm.* ⏰*Closed public holidays.* ⊛3–4.60€. ✆*04 50 73 06 34.*

This exhibit demonstrates how history, geography and pastoral traditions are all reflected in the making of the celebrated cheese. Taste the cheese at the end of the visit with a glass of Savoie wine or local apple juice, with sales too.

☛WALKING TOURS

From La Chapelle-d'Abondance the two peaks provide wonderful routes

15C frescoes depicting The Wedding at Cana, Abbaye d'Abondance

© Fred de Noyelle/Godong/Photononstop

for experienced hikers. Be aware of prevailing weather conditions.

Les Cornettes de Bises

Allow 4hrs. Take a passport.
From the village centre, walk N to the Chalets de Chevenne, then continue to climb alongside the stream to the Col de Vernaz on the Swiss border.

The splendid **panorama**★★★ at the summit (alt. 2 433m/7 982ft) extends over Lake Geneva, and the Alps from Mont Blanc to the Bernese Oberland.

Mont de Grange

Allow 3hrs 30min. Cross the Dranse and walk S along the path leading to the Chalets du Follière.

The ascent starts at the Chemine Valley; from the summit (alt. 2 433m/7 982ft) there is a striking **view**★★ of the Val d'Abondance, the shores of Lake Geneva and the vast Châtel Basin.

Nature Trail "On the Trail of the Chamois"

Allow 3hrs climbing with 380m/ 1 247ft vertical rise. Leave from the Plan des Feux at La Chapelle-d'Abondance, route of Crêt Bénit.

Signposts guide you along the easy path up to the chalets of Pertuis in the hunting reserve of Mont de Grange.

Pic de Morclan★★

*Access by **Super-Châtel gondola** (Jul–Aug; ℰ04 50 73 34 24) to an altitude of 1 650m/5 413ft. The summit is reached by chairlift or on foot; allow 1hr 30min there and back on foot.*

From the summit (alt. 1 970m/6 463ft) the **panorama** includes the Cornettes de Bises and Mont de Grange to the west and the Diablerets and jagged Dents du Midi on the Swiss side. It is possible to walk along the ridge to the Pointe des Ombrieux or to the Swiss **Lac du Goleit** *(from the La Conche mid-station).*

Tête du Linga★★

Alt. 2 127m/6 978ft. Skiers have access by the Linga 1 cable car and Linga 2 chairlift. On arrival, go to the top of the Combes chairlift and climb to the ridge

in a few minutes.
Splendid panorama of Morgins below.

Lac du Pas de Morgins★

Alt. 1 371m/4 498ft.
The lake lying at the heart of this forested area forms a picturesque scene with the Dents du Midi in the background.

EXCURSIONS
Les Plagnes

5.5km/3.4mi SE. Cross the Dranse d'Abondance. Turn left before a sawmill towards Charmy and Les Plagnes.

The road reveals the bottom of the valley dominated by the Pic de la Corne and the Roc de Tavaneuse. Beyond Sur-la-Ravine, it dips into the forested upper Malève Valley and reaches Les Plagnes de Charmy.

La Chapelle-d'Abondance

6km/3.7mi E on D 22.

At the foot of the Mont de Grange and the Cornettes de Bises, this is a charming family resort where the typical regional houses are reminiscent of Swiss chalets across the border. The **Maison des Soeurs** houses the tourist office and temporary exhibits.

There are fine cross-country tracks towards Châtel and Abondance.

Châtel ❋

11km/6.8mi E from Abondance.
ℰ04 50 73 22 44. www.chatel.com.

Châtel is both a tourist village and a farming community. On the south-facing slopes, vast farms remind us of times gone by. Yet this is a modern popular summer and ski resort, and at 1 235m/ 4 052ft also the highest in the Chablais. The **ski area** of Super-Chatel extends over the Morclan and Linga massifs, which are linked by bus and form part of the Franco-Swiss **Portes du Soleil**, an area boasting over 650km/404mi of pistes. Torgon and Morgins are accessible from Morclan; more experienced skiers may prefer the Massif de Linga with the Les Renards black run and easy connections to the slopes of Avoriaz by the Col de Bassachaux. Cross-country skiers are also well catered for.

Morzine★

The towns of Morzine and Montriond lie at an altitude of 980m/3 215ft, in a vast alpine combe flanked by the Pointe de Ressachaux and the Pointe de Nyon. Owing to its prime position at the intersection of six attractive roads, Morzine has been the main tourist centre and base of the Haut-Chablais region.

THE RESORT
Capital of Haut-Chablais
Morzine became a tourist destination in 1880 with the opening of the route des Grandes Alpes. The farming village then developed on the hillsides with chalets and hotels spreading out over the various plateaux.

Summer Activities
Lively and charming, Morzine is an ideal family resort. Free car parks and shuttle buses keep the centre for pedestrians only. The mid-altitude mountains of the Chablais with their gentle slopes are ideal for hikers of a modest standard, but above all the mountain bikers will find the challenges here. The Portes du Soleil area offers them 380km/236mi of marked routes, with a permanent downhill piste at Pléney.

Ski Area 🎿🏂
The resort's gentle slopes and beautiful landscapes make Morzine the ideal ski area for those who prefer a more relaxed style of skiing. Itineraries leading from Super-Morzine to Avoriaz are particularly enjoyable. Beginners can have a go down the "Choucas" green run (from the summit of the Ranfolly).
Experienced skiers are mainly drawn to the Creux and Aigle runs or to Avoriaz at the heart of the **Portes du Soleil** ski area (*see Avoriaz*). For cross-country skiers, there are 90km/56mi of tracks.

THREE VIEWPOINTS★★
Pointe de Nyon★
Access by cable car and chairlift.
04 50 74 72 72.

- **Population:** 2 937.
- **Michelin Map:** 328 N3.
- **Info:** Pl. de l'Office du Tourisme, 74110 Morzine. *04 50 74 72 72.* www.morzine-avoriaz.com.
- **Location:** Morzine is 30km/18.6mi SE of Thonon-les-Bains by D 902.
- **Don't Miss:** An afternoon on the shores of Lac de Montriond is very pleasant.
- **Kids:** Children will love a ride on the summer luges.
- **Timing:** Half a day is enough to explore Morzine, but it is an ideal resort to spend longer relaxing or indeed indulging in winter or summer mountain activities.

Impressive view of the rocky barrier of the Dents Blanches and of Mont Blanc on one side, of Lake Geneva and of the Morzine Valley on the other.

Le Pléney★
🥾 *1hr there and back. Access by cable car then on foot. 04 50 79 00 38.*
From the upper cable-car station, walk alongside the Belvédère chairlift to a small mound crowned by a viewing table offering a **panoramic view** of Avoriaz and the Dents Blanches to the east, of the Mont Blanc Massif to the southeast, of the Aravis range to the south and of the Pointe de Marcelly, Mont Chéry and Roc d'Enfer to the west.

Chamoissière★★
In winter, access is by chairlift, for skiers only; in summer, the climb is on foot.
From the viewing table, splendid **panorama**★★ of the Dents du Midi, Dents Blanches, Buet, Aiguille du Midi, Mont Blanc and the Aravis range.

Musée de la Musique Mécanique
294 rte des Grandes-Alpes. Open mid-Dec–Oct. Closed 1 May. Guided

tour (1hr) daily 2.15–7.15pm. 7€ (children 4€). 04 50 79 85 75.

The 16C former "Maison des Sœurs" is now devoted to all forms of mechanical music; an interesting collection includes barrel organs, music boxes, player pianos, gramophones and orchestrions, as well as animated scenes.

HIKE
Mont Chéry★★

10min gondola and chairlift ride from Les Gets, or 2.5km/1.5mi by road to the Col de l'Encrenaz then 1hr 30min there and back on foot.

From the cross at the summit (alt. 1 827m /5 994ft is a vast **panorama**★★ of Faucigny; the peaks are, from left to right, the Pointe de Nantaux, the Hautforts, at 2 464m/8 084ft the highest point in the Chablais, the Dents du Midi, Haut-Faucigny, Ruan, Buet, the Points de Sales with Mont Blanc, the Désert de Plate, Pointe Percée and the Pic de Marcelly.

DRIVING TOURS

LAC DE MONTRIOND AND COL DE LA JOUX VERTE★★

Drive of 20km/12.4mi shown on the regional map (see p129). Allow 2hrs.

▶ *Leave Morzine NW towards Montriond along the right bank of the Dranse. Just after the Montriond church turn right to the lake.*

At 1 049m/3 442ft altitude, **Montriond lake**★, the third largest in Haute-Savoie, is surrounded by steep pine-covered escarpments. Shady paths lead around the lake. Stop at a viewpoint on the right-hand side of the D228. You can view the **Cascade d'Ardent** below.

The road then climbs up in a series of hairpin bends to a ledge gullied by a succession of waterfalls; there is a good view of the Roc d'Enfer downstream. Beyond the village of Les Lindarets, the road rises along the wooded slopes of the Joux Verte, within sight of the Mont de Grange to the north.

A road leaves the **Col de la Joux Verte** on the left towards Avoriaz.

▶ *During summer, you can take a left on D 338 (often snow-bound in winter).*

On the left-hand side of the road is the isolated **Avoriaz chapel** built by Maurice Novarina in 1960 in the form of the prow of a boat. There is a pleasing view of the Lac d'Avoriaz. The road continues above the Vallon des Ardoisières with, opposite, the snow-capped Hautforts summit (2 466m/8 090ft) and the Pointe de Ressachaux.

Avoriaz★★

Also accessible by cable car from a station 4.5km/2.8mi from Morzine.
Pl. Centrale, 74110 Avoriaz. 04 50 74 02 11. www.avoriaz.com.

Private motor vehicles are banned from the centre and replaced by sleighs. In the evening, little electric taxi vehicles may be booked in advance.

Created out of alpine pastures in 1966, Avoriaz is a modern resort situated at an altitude of 1 800m/5 906ft. Its original and uniform architectural style – buildings clad with wood, looking like huge rocks and with roofs covered in red cedarwood shingles – blends well with the surroundings.

Summer activities – Avoriaz has developed a range of summer activities, notably a golf course with gorgeous surroundings, mountain-biking trails accessible by the ski lifts, and well-being spas.

Ski area – Avoriaz enjoys excellent snow conditions and a favourable position at the heart of the vast **Portes du Soleil** ski area, which includes 12 French and Swiss winter resorts between Lake Geneva and Mont Blanc with an impressive total of 650km/404mi of ski runs. However, in order to take full advantage of the area, visit when the snow is plentiful at low altitudes (all the resorts, with the exception of Avoriaz, barely exceed 1 000m/3 281ft).

The Avoriaz ski slopes are ideal for intermediate skiing; the ski runs leading to Les Lindarets offer pleasant skiing through the forest.

Architectural drawing of Hôtel des Dromonts

R.Corbel/Michelin

The "Brasilia of the Alps"

The striking modern architecture of Avoriaz couldn't fail to catch the imagination of the public and the press, who soon dubbed the new town "Brasilia des Neiges", drawing a parallel with Brazil's state-of-the-art capital. The irregular contours of the first hotel, Les Dromonts, were designed to blend in with the rugged landscape, and subsequent developers followed architect Jaques Labro's lead with jutting façades overlaid with sequoia. Even if the look isn't to everyone's taste, the resort's facilities have made it a firm favourite with skiers.

Advanced skiers can take the Combe chairlift, which gives access to four black runs, including the Combe-du-Machon. There are also links to the Châtel and Morzine areas and, in Switzerland, to the resorts of Champéry and Les Crosets. For cross-country skiers there are lovely trails in the forest.

ROUTE DU COL DE JOUX-PLANE★★

Drive of 20km/12.4mi shown on the regional map (see p133). Allow 30min. The narrow road *(D 354)*, which is passable only in summer, rises very quickly above the Morzine Valley, winding across high pastures and some lovely wooded sections.

It goes right round the Ran Folly in a wide loop and over the pass of the same name (where the Les Gets ski runs culminate) before reaching the Plateau de Joux-Plane.

Col de Joux Plane★★
Alt. 1 712m/5 617ft.

The road runs between a small lake and a restaurant. From the restaurant, there is a remarkable **view** of Mont Blanc to the southeast, extending south to the Platé Massif and the distinctive buildings of Flaine.

The road continues beyond the path on the left, which ends at the Col de Joux-Plane, and runs down towards Samoëns offering **views** of the Eméru Combe and the Giffre Valley.

EXCURSIONS
Les Gets★

 Leave Morzine by D 28 W towards Les Gets, then take D 902.

Since 2003, Les Gets has adopted an environmentally sustainable approach including installing a communal wood stove, helping the locals remain in the area, and in particular, limiting car use in the resort by providing car parks, shuttle buses and a little train.

The well-equipped, family-friendly **ski area** is linked to **Les Portes du Soleil**; cross-country skiers can choose from six loops covering 20km/12.4mi in total. *BP 27, Maison des Gets, 74260 Les Gets. 04 50 75 80 80. www.lesgets.com.*

ADDRESSES

STAY

Les Marmottes – *Essert-Romand, 3.7km/2.3mi NW by D 902 towards Thonon and then left on D 329. 04 50 75 74 44. www.campinglesmarmottes.com. Closed Apr–end Jun and mid-Sept–mid-Dec. 26 sites.* This modest campsite, surrounded by greenery, is well kept, with impeccable, modern sanitary facilities.

L'Hermine Blanche – *414 chemin du Mas Metout. 04 50 75 76 55. www.hermine blanche.com. Closed 18 April–2 Jul, 6 Sept–18 Dec. Wifi. 25 rooms.* This chalet-hotel offers nice, comfortable rooms with a balcony. There is also a pleasant, partially covered swimming pool and jacuzzi. Traditional cuisine served for residents.

Hôtel Florimontane – *Av. de Joux-Plane. 04 50 79 03 87. www.renouveau-vacances.fr. Closed mid-Apr–early Jun and Oct–mid-Dec. 41 rooms, half-board only.* Three chalets linked by an underground passage offer wood-panelled rooms and 20 holiday studio-flats that are very practical for families. Traditional and local cuisine. Gym, entertainment and guided hikes.

Les Dromonts – *74110 Avoriaz. 04 50 74 08 11. www.christophe-leroy.com Closed 29 Apr–14 Dec.* Contemporary and cosy rooms, an intimate lounge-bar and designer fireplace. The mythical (1965) hotel known as the "Brasilia of the Alps" remains a desirable address!

EAT

There are around a dozen restaurants close to the main Avoriaz centre. Recommended are Le Crépy and Chez l'Envers, for their speciality cuisine. For more refined eating, try La Réserve, which has a good wine list, or La Table du Marché, with inventive cuisine.

L'Auberge du Verdoyant – *By the lake, 74110 Lac-de-Montriond. Follow in direction of Montriond and Lac de Montriond. 04 50 79 21 96. Closed Oct–Jan.* Very close to a beach, the pretty terrace overlooking Lac de Montriond is this restaurant's big plus point. On the menu you will find mainly local specialities. At teatime, you can try their selection of crêpes.

Le Bistro – *Close to the tourist office, 74110 Avoriaz. 04 50 74 14 08. Closed May–Jun and Sept–mid-Nov.* Depending on where and when you are staying in Avoriaz, sleigh might well be the best way to get here. Seated around a large friendly table, or in a more peaceful corner, guests can sample specialities such as fondue or stone-grilled meats.

ACTIVITIES

Aventure Parc – *74260 Les Gets. 04 50 75 84 65. www.aventure-parc. fr. Open Jul–Aug daily 10am–7pm; early Jun and Sept–early Oct Wed and Sat–Sun 1–6pm. Closed early Oct–early Jun. 21€.* This adventure park in the woods is accessible to adults and children from eight years old upwards. There are 4 different levels of courses with 86 different activities.

École de parapente des Portes du Soleil – *04 50 75 76 39. www.morzine parapente.com. Open 9am–7pm depending on the weather. 70€ experience flight.* This paragliding school offers a wide range of tailor-made experiences and courses for both beginners and experienced pilots.

École de ski internationale – *Pl. des Rûches, - 74110 Avoriaz. 04 50 74 02 18. www.ecoledeglisse.com. Open 9am–noon, 1.30–6.30pm. Closed May–Nov.* This school offers lessons and guiding for skiers and boarders as well as high-mountain excursions, biking, rafting and paragliding. Reserve at the Centre de réservation des activités de montagne.

Mountain biking – Experienced mountain-bike riders can undertake the **Tour Franco-Suisse** of the Portes du Soleil, which takes a full day. Those addicted to speed can tackle the nine permanent **downhill cycle pistes** *(suitable for all levels).*

Multi Pass Portes du Soleil – *04 50 73 32 54. www.portesdusoleil.com. 1€ per day.* A discount card which gives access to numerous sporting and cultural activities taking place over the area.

MONT-BLANC AND LE FAUCIGNY

Mont-Blanc is the highest peak in the Alps, with the entire massif easily accessible from Geneva, making Chamonix appear on almost every tourist's essential list. Do not be put off, as although the town is busy, it retains an alpine charm alongside the buzz from lovers of the great outoors planning another day of daring mountain feats. Once you reach one of the amazing viewpoints, not only the altitude, but the ensemble of high mountains, glaciers – and in summer, the deep green pastures below – will leave you breathless.

The "Accursed Mountain"

Until the 18C, Mont-Blanc was known as "La Montagne Maudite", and the massif still has a peak named Mont Maudit. The word *maudit* ("accursed") expressed the fear the mountain engendered, in particular for those approaching from Geneva, who had heard only bad stories about it. Today, one only has to drive there on the main road along the narrow, cliff-enclosed valley, to imagine how terrifying it once was.

Once the successful ascension of the mountain was achieved in 1786 it heralded the start of a new era in mountaineering, yet even today the more challenging summits in the massif encourage daredevils, vying with each other to set new, ever more ambitious records. Whether skiing on the Grands-Montets glacier area of Argentière or the legendary Vallée Blanche, or undertaking any serious hike, this high-mountain area requires fitness, a cautious approach and plenty of preparation. Local guides are second to none and should always be consulted.

The Original French Alps Tourist Villages

Megève may have become the first fashionable French ski resort, as far back as the 1920s, aiming to emulate St Moritz in Switzerland, but other villages in the Mont-Blanc and Faucigny areas retain much of their original charm. Ski addicts may insist on a holiday in one of the big-name linked resorts, but summer or winter, families in particular will love the welcoming, quieter and less developed mountain villages such as Les Houches, Les Contamines-Montjoie, Combloux, Les Carroz-d'Arâches or Samoëns, which all offer good sporting facilities with fantastic mountain backdrops.

Highlights

1   The spectacular ride up to the **Aiguille du Midi** for a close view of Mont-Blanc (p153)

2   See deer, mouflons and ibex running wild at **Merlet Animal Parc** (p164)

3   The contemporary church at **Plateau d'Assy**, with works from Chagall, Léger and Matisse (p167)

4   Visit one of the first fashionable ski resorts, the still charming **Megève** (p170)

5   The Jaÿsinia botanical alpine gardens at **Samoëns** (p178)

Mont-Blanc

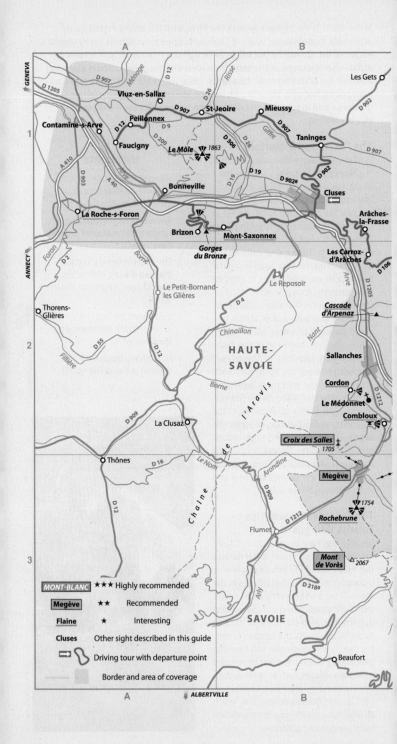

GENEVA

Les Gets

D 1205

D 907

Ménoge

D 12

Risse

D 902

Viuz-en-Sallaz

D 26

St-Jeoire

Mieussy

D 907

D 907

Peillonnex

D 9

Giffe

Taninges

Contamine-s-Arve

D 12

D 200

D 305

D 907

Faucigny

Le Môle ✻ 1863

D 26

D 902

A 410

Arve

D 19

D 902B

A 40

D 19

Cluses

Bonneville

D 903

Arâches-la-Frasse

La Roche-s-Foron

Brizon ▲

Mont-Saxonnex

Les Carroz-d'Arâches

D 106

Foron

D 2

Gorges du Bronze

Arve

ANNECY

Borne

Le Reposoir

D 1205

Le Petit-Bornand-les-Glières

Cascade d'Arpenaz ▲

Thorens-Glières

D 4

Nant

D 55

Chinaillon

HAUTE-SAVOIE

Sallanches

Filière

D 12

Borne

Cordon

Le Médonnet

D 1212

La Clusaz

l'Aravis

Combloux

D 909

Croix des Salles ‡
1705

Thônes

D 16

Le Nom

Chaîne

Megève

D 12

de

Arondine

✻ 1754

D 909

Rochebrune

D 1212

Flumet

Mont de Vorès
△ 2067

SAVOIE

Arly

D 218B

Beaufort

MONT-BLANC ★★★ Highly recommended

Megève ★★ Recommended

Flaine ★ Interesting

Cluses Other sight described in this guide

↪ Driving tour with departure point

  Border and area of coverage

↑ ALBERTVILLE

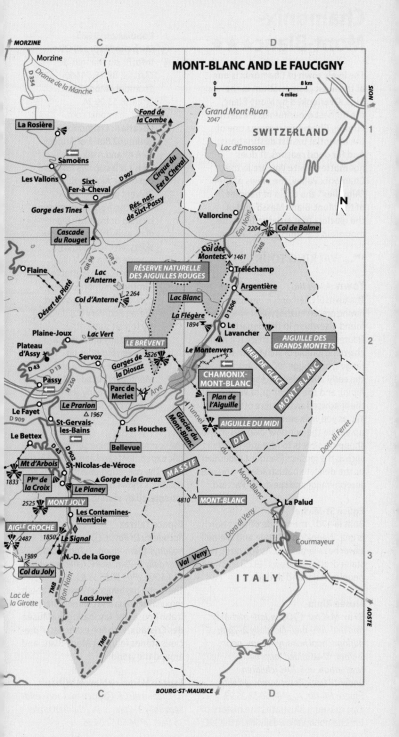

MONT-BLANC AND LE FAUCIGNY

MORZINE

Morzine

Dranse de la Manche

D 354

SION

C

D

0 _____ 8 km
0 _____ 4 miles

Grand Mont Ruan
2047

SWITZERLAND

N

1

Fond de
la Combe

Lac d'Emosson

La Rosière

Samoëns

Les Vallons

Sixt-
Fer-à-Cheval

D 907

Cirque du
Fer à Cheval

Vallorcine

Eau Noire

Col de Balme
2204

TMB

Gorge des Tines

Rés. nat.
de Sixt-Passy

Cascade
du Rouget

Col des
Montets

1461

Tréléchamp

Flaine

GR 96

GR 5

Lac
d'Anterne

RÉSERVE NATURELLE
DES AIGUILLES ROUGES

Argentière

D 1506

Désert de Platé

Col d'Anterne

2264

Lac Blanc

La Flégère
1894

Le Lavancher

Plaine-Joux

Lac Vert

LE BRÉVENT

Le Montenvers

AIGUILLE DES
GRANDS MONTETS

Plateau
d'Assy

Servoz

Gorges de
la Diosaz

2526

MER DE GLACE

2

D 43

D 13

N 250

Parc de
Merlet

Arve

CHAMONIX-
MONT-BLANC

MASSIF

MONT-BLANC

Passy

Le Fayet

D 909

Le Prarion
1967

St-Gervais-
les-Bains

Les Houches

Plan de
l'Aiguille

Tunnel du Mont-Blanc

AIGUILLE DU MIDI

DU

Dora di Ferret

Le Bettex

D 43

Bellevue

Glacier du
Mont-Blanc

Mont-Blanc

Mt d'Arbois
1833

St-Nicolas-de-Véroce

Gorge de la Gruvaz

MASSIF

Plᵘ de
la Croix

Le Planey

4810

MONT-BLANC

La Palud

2525

MONT JOLY

Les Contamines-
Montjoie

Courmayeur

3

AIGLE CROCHE

2487

1850

Le Signal

N.-D. de la Gorge

Val Veny

Dora di Veny

1989

Col du Joly

Bon Nant

TMB

ITALY

Lac de
la Girotte

Lacs Jovet

TMB

AOSTE

C

BOURG-ST-MAURICE

D

151

Chamonix-Mont-Blanc★★★

The lively town of Chamonix is one of the most cosmopolitan in the Alps. Overlooked by Mont-Blanc, the highest mountain in Western Europe, Chamonix remains one of the essential tourist destinations. And for good reasons. It does not matter where you are in the Chamonix Valley, the views of the "Aiguilles", the chain of needles of the Mont-Blanc Massif and of the glaciers that emerge from the mountain are simply spectacular.

▸☙WALKING TOUR

Town *Allow 1hr.*

The town of Chamonix is unusual for not having preserved the typical village style found elsewhere in the department of Haute-Savoie. Instead, there is a rather charming jumble of architectural styles, ranging from huge 19C constructions, to the early 20C palaces (⟳*see the Musée Alpin*), and the rather grim vestiges of the ill-advised architecture of the 1970s. Yet, as you walk around the centre, look up above the window displays in the shopping streets to find subtle details, such as the mosaics (Banque Laydernier) or the delicate balustrades in the rue Joseph-Vallot and rue du Dr Paccard.

Église St-Michel

Built in 1707, the façade of the church is in a "Napoléon III" style and the bell tower has a large bulb. As you go in, two stained-glass windows (1925) illustrate people on skis and sledges.

Musée Alpin

89 av. M.-Croz. ⟳*Open Jan–mid-May and mid-Jun–mid–Oct daily 2–7pm; during school holidays 10am–noon, 2–7pm;* ▸☙*Guided tours by reservation.* ☙*5.70€ (children under 18 free). Ticket combined with Espace Tairraz.* ♿ ☏*04 50 53 25 93.*
This museum illustrates the history of the Chamonix Valley, daily life in the 19C,

▸ **Population:** 9 086.
♿ **Michelin Map:** 328 O5.
☰ **Info:** Pl. du Triangle-de-l'Amitié, BP 25, 74400 Chamonix-Mont-Blanc. ☏04 50 53 00 24. www.chamonix.com.
▸ **Location:** Chamonix is 101km/62.8mi E of Annecy by A 41 and A 40.
☙ **Don't Miss:** Views from the top of the Aiguille du Midi, Brévent and Flégère by cable car; from Montenvers by train or from Lac Blanc via a walk. For experienced skiers, an excursion with a guide down the Vallée Blanche is unforgettable.
⏱ **Timing:** Chamonix is very crowded July–August and during February holidays; try to visit some other time. At any time of year, reserve your rides up the Aiguille du Midi and Montenvers in advance and plan an early start. Be sure to check the weather.

the conquest of alpine summits, scientific experiments and early skiing in the area. The collection of engravings and paintings shows how the area has been intrepreted by visiting artists.

Espace Tairraz

Rocade du Dr Payot. ⟳*Open school holidays 10am–noon, 2–7pm; rest of year daily 2–7pm.* ☙*4€ (children under 12 1.50€).* ☏*04 50 55 53 93.*
The centre has temporary exhibits about regional heritage and contemporary life. It also houses the fascinating ▸▴**Musée des Cristaux**, with fine examples of precious stones found at Mont-Blanc and around the world.

Espace Mémoire Marcel Wibault

62 chemin du Cé. ⟳*Open mid-Jun–mid-Sept daily 3–7pm.* ☙*3€ (children under 16 free).* ☏*04 50 53 04 35.*

A Spectacular Climb to Fame

Chamonix entered the history books in 1091 thanks to a donation from the Benedictine abbey of St-Michel-de-la-Cluse, in Piedmont. However, it was to be another 650 years before the first tourists arrived in the valley in 1741. When Englishmen William Windham and Richard Pocock arrived at Montenvers they named the glacier "Mer de Glace" or the "sea of ice". From then on, this forbidding mountain region became an important attraction for European aristocrats exploring the unknown world. The first ascension of Mont-Blanc in 1786 is seen as the birth of mountaineering and established Chamonix as a tourist centre. In the 19C its fame reached a peak, with the mountains featuring in the passionate and thrilling romantic prose of the age from Victor Hugo, George Sand, Alphonse de Lamartine, Shelley and George Byron. In 1821 after a series of accidents the Compagnie des guides was founded, the first official mountaineers organisation. All over the valley massive hotels were built, radically transforming this little farming village. With the opening of the Montenvers railway in 1908, and as host for the first Winter Olympics in 1924, Chamonix entered into the modern era of tourism. Thanks to the opening of the Mont-Blanc Tunnel in 1965, it became the first ski resort with motorway connections and for half a century, it has seen a huge property boom that has continued to expand into the early 21C.

The artist Marcel Wibault (1904–98) was devoted to painting mountain scenes and to architectural drawings. His chalet, beautifully painted by the artist, now holds temporary exhibitions of his art, each with a different theme.

ADDITIONAL SIGHTS
Le Bois-Prin
(1hr) Follow the mainly steep route du Brévent on the left side of the church, continuing up to the lower station of the cable cars, then turn left on the route des Moussoux. From there the Mont-Blanc chain appears in all its glory. Keep following straight until you reach the edge of the forest, starting point for several walks.

Le Lac des Gaillands
(1hr) South of Chamonix, on a continuation of the rue du Dr Paccard, follow rue Ravanel-le-Rouge and turn left at the roundabout on the route des Pècles. You will reach the climbing cliff named Gaillands and two charming little lakes.

EXCURSIONS
There are several cable cars spread across the valley that give access to the different peaks above Chamonix.

Do read the practical information given for each different mountain. In peak season, it is essential to reserve tickets for the cable cars. The Mont-Blanc multi-pass for 1–14 days covers all the cable cars run by La Compagnie du Mont-Blanc.
Timetables indicate the first ascent and the last descent of the cable cars. The last ascent is usually 1hr–1hr 30min before the last descent.

Aiguille du Midi★★★
Minimum 2hrs return by cable car. Av. de l'Aiguille-du-Midi. ◯*Mid-May–mid-Jun 8.10am–5.30pm; mid-Jun–early Jul and 23 Aug–mid-Sept 7.10am–5.30pm; early Jul–mid-Aug 6.30am–6pm; end Sept–early Nov 8.30am–4.30pm; rest of year: check. Departures every 10–30 min, takes 20 min.* ◯*Early Nov–mid-Dec.* ✉*Check. It is possible to book tickets online.* ✆*04 50 53 22 75. www.compagniedumontblanc.com.*
In just a few minutes you are whisked up into the grandiose environment of the high mountain. Sufferers from vertigo should avoid this excursion.
A mid-station, **Plan de l'Aiguille**★★ (alt. 2 317m/7 602ft), already provides fine views over the upper areas of Mont-

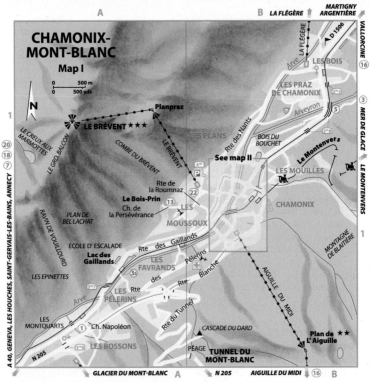

CHAMONIX-
MONT-BLANC
Map I

0   500 m
0   500 yds

N

A   B   LA FLÉGÈRE   MARTIGNY
                                                                  ARGENTIÈRE

LE BRÉVENT ★★★   Planpraz   VALLORCINE
                                              LES BOIS
LE CREUX-AUX
MARMOTTES   LES PRAZ
                                         DE CHAMONIX
                    COMBE DU BRÉVENT   MER DE GLACE
LE GRD BALCON   LE BRÉVENT   LES PLANS   Rte des Nants
                                                  BOIS DU   Le Montenvers
                                     See map II   BOUCHET   LE MONTENVERS
                                                                 LES MOUILLES
                          Rte de
                          la Roumnaz
Le Bois-Prin   ⑬   CHAMONIX
PLAN DE   Ch. de
BEL LACHAT   la Persévérance   LES
                                 MOUSSOUX
RAVIN DE VOUILLOURD
               ÉCOLE D'ESCALADE   Rte des Gaillands   MONTAGNE
               Lac des   LES   Pèlerins   DE BLAITIÈRE
               Gaillands   FAVRANDS   Blanche
LES EPINETTES   des   Rte
               LES   Rte
               PÈLERINS
Arve   AIGUILLE DU MIDI
LES   Ch. Napoléon
MONTQUARTS   CASCADE DU DARD
               LES BOSSONS   Plan de
                                                      L'Aiguille ★★
N 205   PÉAGE   TUNNEL DU
                                        MONT-BLANC
        GLACIER DU MONT-BLANC   A   N 205   AIGUILLE DU MIDI   B

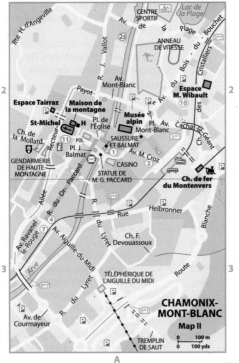

Rte H. d'Angeville   CENTRE   Lac de
                            SPORTIF   la Plage
                            de
                                 ANNEAU
                                 DE VITESSE
         Av. Mont-Blanc
Espace Tairraz   Maison de   Espace
                 la montagne   M. Wibault
St-Michel   Musée
Ch. de   alpin   Pl. de
la Mollard   l'Église   Pl. Av.
                POL   SAUSSURE   Mont-Blanc
GENDARMERIE   Pl. J. ET BALMAT   Av. M. Croz
DE HAUTE   Balmat
MONTAGNE   CASINO
                        STATUE DE   Ch. de fer
                        M. G. PACCARD   du Montenvers
Av. Ravanel
le-Rougi   Rue   Helbronner
Arve
                         Ch. F.
                         Devouassoux   Route
                TÉLÉPHÉRIQUE DE
                L'AIGUILLE DU MIDI
                                   CHAMONIX-
Av. de   MONT-BLANC
Courmayeur   Map II

0   100 m
0   100 yds
                TREMPLIN
                DE SAUT
            A

WHERE TO STAY

Aiguille du Midi.....................①

Anatase
(Chambre d'hôte L').............③

Arveyron.................................⑤

Beau Site (Auberge)..............⑦

Faucigny (Hôtel)....................⑪

Girandole
(Chambre d'hôte La)........⑬

Mer de Glace
(Camping La)....................⑯

Montagny (Auberge Le).......⑱

Prarion (Hôtel Le).................⑳

Savoyarde (La).......................㉒

WHERE TO EAT

Atmosphère.............................①

Bergerie (La)............................②

Calèche (La)..............................④

Dru (Le)....................................⑦

Maison Carrier (La)................⑩

3842 (Le)..................................⑯

Aiguille du Midi

© Neil Harrison/Dreamstime.com

Before you go back down on the cable car, make sure you explore the tunnels dug from the Piton Nord. One leads to a terrace right opposite Mont-Blanc, the other goes to the Vallée Blanche cable car that connects the Aiguille du Midi with Pointe Helbronner (🔆 *see p161*).

Mer de Glace via Montenvers Railway★★★
Minimum 2hrs return. ⏲*Hours vary depending on season and weather.* ⏲*Closed 2 weeks in Oct.* 🎫*24€ (children 19.20€).* 📞*04 50 53 22 75. www.compagniedumontblanc.com.*
This picturesque train enables non-climbers to experience the high mountains and the glaciers.

🔼 From the upper station at **Montenvers** (alt. 1 935m/6 348ft) there is the fine **panorama★★★**, a natural wonder comprising the **Mer de Glace** and two impressive "needles" **Aiguille du Dru** and **Aiguille Verte** with the **Grandes Jorasses** in the background.

At the summit, you can visit the **Galerie des Cristaux**, **Le Musée de la Faune Alpine** and the **Grand Hôtel-Restaurant du Montenvers**, which has a museum with exhibits explaining the history of the site.

It is possible to visit an **ice cave** (🔒 *closed autumn and winter 2012 for renovations*) freshly dug every year into the living Mer de Glace. A **gondola** descends to it from the Montenvers

Blanc. From here are relatively easy hikes *(with good boots)*, especially one to Montenvers at the foot of the jagged peaks of the Aiguilles de Chamonix.

The upper station, **Piton Nord** (alt. 3 800m/12 467ft), is separated from the highest point, **Piton Central** (alt. 3 842m/12 605ft, *accessible by lift, check for opening hours*), by an abyss over which there is a walkway.

From the panoramic terrace the **view** sweeps down over the Chamonix Valley 2 800m/9 186ft below. Above the snowline you will see the peaks of L'Aiguille Verte, Grandes Jorasses and the Aiguille du Géant.

Mer de Glace and the Montenvers Railway

© Pierre Jacques/hemis.fr

upper station. In summer, you can descend (and return) by a footpath *(15min)* to the right of the station.

For hikers experienced in high-mountain walking, it is possible to go up the Mer de Glace taking the via ferrata **balcon de la mer de Glace** *(check in advance with the Office de Haute Montagne).*

Le Brévent★★★

Alt. 2 525 m/8 284ft. 1hr 30min return by gondola to Planpraz (20min) then cable car. Rte du Brévent. ⊙*Open Jun–Sept and end Dec–end Apr: check for timetable.* ∞*24€ (children 9–15 19.20€) return for the 2 sections.* ℘*04 50 53 22 75. www.compagnie dumontblanc.com.*

Planpraz★★ – *(alt. 2 062 m/6 765ft)*
From this mid-station there is a perfect view of the Aiguilles de Chamonix. From here are several moderate hikes, such as across to Flégère (returning by the Flégère cable car) or to **Lac Blanc**★★. Once you reach the Brévent summit *(orientation table),* you are high up enough to appreciate the whole **panorama**: the French side of the Mont-Blanc Massif, along with the Chamonix Valley from the village of La Praz *(on the left)* to Les Bossons *(on the right).*

In the other direction you will see the high peaks of first the Haut Faucigny (Buet, Avoudrues, Pointe de Salles), then the Fiz (Aiguille de Varan) and finally the Aravis (Pointe Percée, Charvin).

La Flégère★

Alt. 1 894m/6 214ft. Reached by cable car. 2km/1.2mi N of Chamonix – Les Praz. Les Praz–La Flégère cable car (15min) then the Index chairlift (20min). Jul–Aug 7.40am–5.45pm; Jun and Sept 8.30am–4.30pm; check for rest of year. ∞*22€ (children 4–15 17.60€) Combined return ticket.* ℘*04 50 53 22 75. www.compagniedumont blanc.com.*

From Flégère there is an impressive **view** (⊙*see orientation table)* of the Aiguille Verte and the Grandes Jorasses peaks enclosing the Mer de Glace

depression. Do not skip taking the chairlift from Flégère up to the **Index**★★ (alt. 2 385m/7 825ft).

From there is a **view** right over the Mont-Blanc Massif, from the Aiguille du Tour over to the Aiguille du Goûter.

Glacier du Mont-Blanc★★

▶ *2km/1.2mi S of Chamonix. Les Bossons. Contact for prices and timetable.* ℘*04 50 53 22 75. www.compagniedumontblanc.com.*
On a 15-minute ride the chairlift takes you up to a café in a chalet (1 425m/4 675ft) from where you can admire the glacier that emerges from the snows of Mont-Blanc.

Note the grim sight of a wheel from the Air India plane that crashed here in 1950, killing more than 140 passengers.

🏔 Higher up at 1 900m/6 234ft *(1hr 15min),* you can cool off in front of the ice pyramids as high as 40m/131ft (⊙*do not get too close to these seracs as they can come crashing down at any time)* to reach the Balmat bivouac (1786) *(3hrs 30min).* Add another 30 minutes to admire the meeting point of the Bossons and Taconnaz glaciers.

Servoz

▶ *11km/6.8mi SW of Chamonix. After Les Houches, follow D 13.* ⊶*Guided visits available in season, contact tourist office at the Maison d'Alpage (℘04 50 47 21 68; www.servoz.com), which is in an old farmhouse transformed into an information centre about agricultural life in the mountains.*
Charming little village at the start of the Chamonix Valley. Old Servoz has preserved its traditional farms with stone bases and huge grain stores above.

Gorges de la Diosaz★ – Take the car to the kiosk at the start of the gorges *(Jul–Aug 9am–6pm, Jun and Sept 9.30am–5pm;* ∞*5€ (children 4€);* ℘*04 50 47 21 13; www.gorgesdeladiosaz.com).*
🏔 The walk begins with a path and suspended walkways. Further up, you reach successive waterfalls. From the Soufflet Bridge, you can admire the three stages

of the highest and most dramatic Aigle waterfall. Overhead walkways continue until the "Pont Naturel", a block of rock squeezed into a crack in the mountain from where the **Soufflet waterfall** emerges.

Montagne de Pormenaz★★ – *(alt. 1 945m/6 381ft)* 🥾 *6hrs return. Follow D 143 to Le Mont and park at Souay Bridge. Information from the Maison d'Alpage.* The narrow, windy path can appear endless due to its impressive vertical rise (1 000m/3 281ft), but the varied landcape and the panorama at the top make it worth the effort. From the Pormenaz mountain you can see the Aiguilles Rouges and the limestone layers of the Fiz mountains. From June to October you can see sheep and cows in the pastures. From the chalets there is a magnificent view of Mont-Blanc and the Aiguillette des Houches. To reach the lake needs another 30 minutes.

Vallorcine
🔘 *16km/10mi N of Chamonix.*
🏛 *74660 Vallorcine.* 📞*04 50 54 60 71. www.vallorcine.com.*
Thanks to its isolated position in a preserved environment, Vallorcine seems almost from another age. Protected from avalanches by the dignified mountain face of the Vauban, the church stands out from the sheer slopes of the Aiguille de Mesure (at the extreme north of the Aiguilles Rouges and the Mont-Blanc massifs).
🥾 From Vallorcine you can take two heritage walks (to the Bérard waterfall and the chemin des Diligences) or wander along some of the 80km/50mi of marked paths.

Musée "La maison de Barberine" –
🔘*2km/1.2mi from Vallorcine towards Le Châtelard.* 🕐*Open Jul–Aug daily 2.30– 5.30pm.* 💰*2.50€.* 📞*04 50 54 63 19.* In an early 18C building, hidden in a secret valley, is a little ecological museum devoted to the history of the area.

Lac Blanc★★
🥾 *Alt. 2 352m/7 712ft. At Les Praz take the Flégère cable car and then the Index chairlift. 1hr 15min walk to the lake. 1hr walk directly down to the Flégère cable car.* ⊙*Good walking boots are essential (the route crosses frozen glacier snow and the path is very rocky).*
The view from here is extensive, from left to right, over the Tour glacier, Aiguille du Chardonnet, Aiguille d'Argentière and the glacier, Grands-Montets, Aiguille Verte, Drus, the Mer de Glace, Grandes Jorasses, Aiguille du Géant, Aiguille du Midi and Mont-Blanc…Even if it is at a busy tourist period, the best time of year to enjoy the beautiful reflections in the lake is at the end of July.

🚶 HIKES
Walk from Flégère to Planpraz★★
Take the bus to Les Praz and then the Flégère cable car. Return down to Chamonix by Planpraz cable car.
🚶 *2hrs 30min walk.*
This pleasant and easy hike crosses the central part of the Grand Balcon Sud that connects the Col des Montets to Les Houches. Views to the Mont-Blanc chain reward you all along this pretty path, bordered by wild rhododendrons.

Plan de l'Aiguille to Montenvers★
🥾 *2hrs 15min walk. Views across the whole valley from Les Houches to Argentière and especially over to the Aiguilles Rouges Massif. At the end, take the left path to return to Mer de Glace.*

ADDRESSES

🛏 STAY
⊙ To make a selection from all there is on offer in Chamonix, consult the reservation centre at the tourist office.

🏕 **Camping La Mer de Glace** –
200 chemin de la Bagna, at Bois, 80m/ 88yds from l'Arveyron. 📞*04 50 53 44 03. www.chamonix-camping.com. Closed early*

Oct–mid-Apr. ♿ 🚭. *150 pitches.* This is the best campsite in the valley. The various buildings, designed as chalets, blend harmoniously into the natural setting. There is no entertainment, so as not to disturb the tranquillity. Simple and clean.

🛏🍴 **Chambre d'hôte La Girandole** – *46 chemin de la Persévérance. 1.5km/1mi NW of the town centre towards the Brévent cable car and rte des Moussoux.* 📞*04 50 53 37 58. www.la-girandole-chamonix.fr.* 🅿 🚭. *3 rooms* 🛏. A typical Savoyard chalet located in a very chic residential area above the town. The attractive lounge overlooks Mont-Blanc, the Aiguille du Midi and the Aiguille Verte. Simple, welcoming rooms.

🛏🍴 **Chambre d'hôte L'Anatase** – *Les Plans, 74660 Vallorcine. At the north end of the village, 3km/1.8mi from the Swiss border .* 📞*04 50 54 64 06. www.lanatase.com Closed 15 Nov–15 Dec.* 🅿 🚭. *5 rooms* 🛏. A charming welcome is offered in this house, one of the last before you enter Switzerland. Behind its wooden shutters, you will find delightful rooms with wood, antique furniture, carefully chosen fabrics and more. There is a fitted kitchen at your disposal. An ideal place for a family.

🛏🛏🍴 **Auberge Beau Site** – *74310 Les Houches.* 📞*04 50 55 51 16. www.hotel-beausite.com. Closed 21 Apr–31 May, 27 Sept –19 Dec.* 🅿. *18 rooms.* In the resort made famous by Lord Kandahar's ski races, this family hotel is at the foot of the bell tower. The rooms are of a good size, functional and brightened up with blue and green fabrics.

🛏🛏🍴 **Auberge Le Montagny** – *490 rte du Pont, 74310 Les Houches.* 📞*04 50 54 57 37. www.chamonix-hotel.com. Closed 7 Apr–18 Jun, 27 Sept–20 Dec.* 🅿. *8 rooms.* All that remains from the original 1876 farm is the main door and some beams. However, this friendly little chalet offers neat little rooms in mountain style.

🛏🛏🍴 **Hôtel Aiguille du Midi** – *479 chemin Napoléon, 74400 Les Bossons.* 📞*04 50 53 00 65. www.hotel-aiguille dumidi.com. Closed 7 Apr–11 May, 20 Sept– 17 Dec.* 🅿. *Wifi. 4 rooms, half board possible, restaurant* 🛏🛏🍴. In this 1908 hotel, it is best to choose rooms that have been recently refurbished in a modern alpine style. A panoramic lounge looks out onto the Bossons Glacier. There is a massage room, and a round restaurant with a pretty terrace on the garden side serving traditional and Savoyard meals.

🛏🛏🍴 **Hôtel Arveyron** – *1650 rte du Bouchet, 2km/1.2mi.* 📞*04 50 53 18 29. www.hotel-arveyron.com. Closed mid-Apr –mid-Jun and 23 Sept–Christmas run-up.* 🅿. *30 rooms, half-board possible, restaurant* 🛏🍴. Inside this agreeable family hotel are typical mountain-style rooms, with the quieter ones on the forest side. Facilities include a lounge-bar, billiard table and the garden under the Aiguilles de Chamonix. Local cuisine is served in a wood-panelled dining room or on the terrace.

🛏🛏🍴 **Hôtel Faucigny** – *118 pl. de l'Église, opposite the tourist office.* 📞*04 50 53 01 17. www.hotelfaucigny-chamonix.com. Closed mid-Apr–mid-May, early Jun, end Sept–end Dec except 1 week end Oct, early Nov.* 🅿. *20 rooms.* The central location and fair prices are the advantages of this renovated hotel. Some first-floor rooms have a view of Mont-Blanc; those on the second floor are under the mansard roof.

🛏🛏🍴 **Hôtel Le Prarion** – *Alt. 1 860m/ 6 102ft, 74170 St-Gervais-les-Bains.* 📞*04 50 54 40 07. www.prarion.com. Closed end Mar–19 Jun, 14 Sept–17 Dec. Wifi. 12 rooms, half-board only, restaurant* 🛏🛏🍴. At the summit of Prarion, the calmest night you will ever spend. The panoramic view is astonishing, from the Aravis to the snowy peaks of Mont-Blanc. The restaurant offers traditional cooking and the small rooms are simple alpine style.

🛏🛏🍴 **La Savoyarde** – *28 rte Moussoux.* 📞*04 50 53 00 77. www.lasavoyarde.com. Closed May–Jun and Oct–Nov.* 🅿. *Wifi. 14 rooms.* In an ideal position just 50m/55yds from the Brévent cable car this neat Chamoniard house from the 19C provides simple rooms, some wood panelled, some in the eves or extended with a mezzanine.

🍴/EAT

🛏 **La Bergerie** – *232 av. M.-Croz.* 📞*04 50 53 45 04. www.labergerie chamonix.com. Closed 2 weeks in May.* The décor features traditional local farming implements. Hearty grills prepared over an open wood fire. Regional dishes are also on offer, and there is a peaceful shady terrace for summer days.

Atmosphère – *123 pl. Balmat.* ☎*04 50 55 97 97. www.restaurant-atmosphere.com.* Plenty of atmosphere here with contemporary décor and a few tables with views over the Arve river. Traditional cuisine is served and there is a good wine list.

La Calèche – *18 r. du Dr Paccard.* ☎*04 50 55 94 68. www.restaurant-caleche.com.* This restaurant at the heart of the resort resembles a bric-à-brac fair, with a variety of antique copper pots, bells and old skis displayed. Waiting staff wear traditional costume. A folk group performs weekly.

La Maison Carrier – *44 rte du Bouchet.* ☎*04 50 53 00 03. www.hameaualbert.fr. Closed 30 May–17 Jun, 14 Nov–14 Dec, public holidays and Sept–Jun Mon.* Treat yourself in this good-value restaurant on the premises of Hameau Albert I. The salle des Guides has been built with wood from an old local farmhouse, and has a fireplace with charcuterie smoking above. The cooking is typical of the rural mountain region, and there is an excellent list of local wines.

Le Dru – *25 r. Ravenel-le-Rouge.* ☎*04 50 53 33 06.* The painted façade of this mid-town chalet draws the eye. Comfortable décor including wood, old peasant tools and a collection of oil lamps. Try the cheese fondue or the "Trio du Dru" with three local meat and cheese dishes.

Le 3842 – *At the top of the Aiguille du Midi by cable car.* ☎*04 50 55 82 23. Closed 3 weeks in Nov.* Travel up in the cable car and negotiate a series of walkways and footbridges to reach this high-altitude restaurant. In these extreme conditions, the dining room necessarily has narrow windows, but you are eating more or less on the rooftop of Europe!

🛒 SHOPPING

Aux Petits Gourmands – *168 r. du Dr Paccard.* ☎*04 50 53 01 59. Open 7am–7.45pm.* Children, tourists and locals all love this place that is a pastry shop, chocolate shop and tea room, all rolled into one. Served with a smile, the almond–blueberry confection, fruit tarts and the home-made chocolate will make it hard for you to leave.

L'Alpage des Aiguilles – *91 r. J.-Vallot.* ☎*04 50 53 14 21. Open 9am–8pm. Closed 2 May–15 Jun, 1 Oct–15 Dec.* This boutique is a marvel, bursting with regional produce: sausages, hams, remarkable cheese.

🍷 NIGHTLIFE

L'M – *81 r. J.-Vallot.* ☎*04 50 53 00 11. www.chamonixhotels.com. Open 9am–11pm.* One of Chamonix's finest terraces with picture-postcard views. Glass in hand, admire the Aiguilles, de Charmoz, de Blaitière, du Plan and du Midi.

🎿 ACTIVITIES

A wide variety of leisure pursuits – In summer there are swimming pools, tennis courts, golf courses and other outdoor activities available around the resort. At the top of the cable cars you have access to walking paths that will lead you to spectacular panoramas.

The ski area – In a high mountain setting and with some of the finest downhill runs, the Chamonix Valley ski area is without doubt the best that the Haute-Savoie can offer. The whole ski region is spread across several mountains, connected to each other by ski bus: Brévent and Les Planards at Chamonix, Flégère at Les Praz, Grands-Montets at Argentière and La Balme at Le Tour. Snow cover is, in most seasons, excellent above 1 900m/6 234ft (equivalent of the upper section of each mountain), but it is often not sufficient to ski down to the bottom of the pistes *(the alternative is by cable car)*.

For expert skiers, the classic runs are the Charles-Bozon piste, the Combe de la Charlanon and the Col Cornu (at Brévent), Les Pylônes and Le Pic Janvier (at Flégère), and above all the top section of **Grands-Montets**★★★ (🕐*see Argentière p161*). Off-piste itinerary runs are exceptional (though best undertaken with a guide), the most notable being the famous **Vallée Blanche**★★★ (20km/12.4mi with an impressive drop of 2 800m/9 186ft leaving from the top of the Aiguille du Midi cable car).

Massif du Mont-Blanc★★★

With its year-round mantle of snow at an altitude of 4 810m/15 781ft, Mont-Blanc reigns supreme as the highest mountain in the Alps. Yet, the massif owes it fame essentially to the wonderful variety of scenery offered by its peaks, domes, needles and glaciers. The Mont-Blanc range is 50km/31mi long, its foothills reaching as far as the Tarentaise in the south, and the Swiss Valais and Italy's Aosta Valley in the northeast. With its succession of valleys it is impossible to view the range in its entirety, but its majesty may still be appreciated from the many viewpoints reached from the valley by cable cars or on serious hikes.

- **Michelin Map:** C/D 2/3.
- *See Chamonix.*
- **Don't Miss:** The cable-car ride and view from the top of the Grands-Montets. Keen and fit hikers should plan to undertake the short round tour of Mont-Blanc.
- **Kids:** Merlet animal park, Indiana'Ventures adventure park.
- **Timing:** Plan according to weather conditions.

A BIT OF HISTORY
The First Ascent of Mont-Blanc
In 1760 a young scientist from Geneva, **Horace Benedict de Saussure**, offered a reward to the first person to reach the summit of Mont-Blanc. In 1776, **Jacques Balmat**, caught out by nightfall while looking for crystals in the mountains, showed that you could survive a night at high altitude. **Michel-Gabriel Paccard**, a doctor from Chamonix, found Balmat's experience interesting. He had often surveyed Mont-Blanc with his telescope, trying to plot a path to the summit and the two of them took up Saussure's challenge; they left on 7 August 1786 and reached the summit the following evening, completely exhausted.

It has taken another two centuries to explore the whole massif. Some routes like the Directissime des Drus or the north face of the Grandes Jorasses are considered by top alpinists among the most mythical climbs. More anecdotal stories tell of descents by motorbike, bicycle or even on a paella dish!

Mont-Blanc ... Like the rest of the alpine range, Mont-Blanc has two different aspects. On the French side, it looks like a "gentle giant", impressively flanked by snowy domes underlined by a few rocky escarpments, while the view from the Italian side is of a grim, dark wall bristling with rock pinnacles or needles. The ascent from this side requires a lot of mountaineering skill, but endurance is more important if you want to climb from Chamonix or St-Gervais.

... and its satellites – The Chamonix Valley owes its fame to the **"needles"** (aiguilles) formed from greenish coarse granite. The most famous peaks are the Grépon, the Aiguille de Blaitière and the Aiguille du Dru. Three huge **glaciers** are sought by summer visitors: the **Mer de Glace**, the longest (14km/8.7mi from the head of the Géant Glacier) and most popular, owing to the famous Montenvers scenery; the **Glacier des Bossons** (7km/4.3mi), the most picturesque, thrusting through the forest; the **Glacier d'Argentière** (11km/6.8mi), the most impressive.

The Mont-Blanc Tunnel – It was Saussure once again who in the 18C imagined the possibility of digging a tunnel through the mountain linking France with Italy. The feat was finally accomplished in 1965 when the 11.6km/7.2mi road tunnel opened linking Chamonix with Courmayeur in Italy. In 1999 a fire broke out in the tunnel causing the tragic death of 41 people, leading to a review of the tunnel's security systems and those in all alpine tunnels.

CROSSING MONT-BLANC
By cable car and gondola, you can cross the Mont-Blanc chain into Italy.

Before setting off, do check the local mountain weather forecast and allow sufficient time for this excursion. Note that rapid changes in altitude may cause tiredness and sickness.

Stages, leaving from Chamonix:

Chamonix★★★ – Plan de l'Aiguille★★ – Rise: 1 300m/4 265ft. 9min by cable car.

Plan de l'Aiguille – Piton Nord de l'aiguille du Midi – Rise: 1 500m/4 921ft. 8min by cable car.

Ascent to the Piton Central de l'aiguille du Midi – Rise: 65m/213ft. 35secs by lift. Panoramic terrace.

Aiguille du Midi★★★ – Pointe Helbronner★★★ – Descent: 380m/1 247ft. 35min by gondola. One of the finest views in the Alps, sweeping over the Géant Glacier and the Vallée Blanche, panoramic terrace at Helbronner.

Pointe Helbronner – Refuge Torino – Descent: 100m/328ft. 5min walk. From the Torino mountain hut there is a beautiful view over the Val Ferret, as well as a view to the Val Veny and the back of Mont-Blanc.

Refuge Torino – La Palud – Descent: 2 000m/6 562ft (descent). 15min by cable car (2 sections).

▶ *Return via Entrèves and then bus to Chamonix through the Mont-Blanc Tunnel, or you can go back using the same route you arrived via the lifts.*

EXCURSIONS FROM ARGENTIÈRE

Argentière✻

▶ *8km/5mi NE of Chamonix.*
24 rte du Village, 74400 Argentière.
℘04 50 54 02 14. www.chamonix.com.
A paradise for expert skiers, the pistes of the Grands-Montets above Argentière, mainly not-machined, are famous for their length, snow quality, vertical drop and the fabulous setting. The village at the foot of the glacier consists of a collection of old houses around a typical Savoyard church. Following the hairpin bends above the village, take a right to Le Tour, where the landscape is wilder and the Tour Glacier appears with a view behind it stretching to Mont-Blanc.

Aiguille des Grands Montets★★★ 🎿

About 2hrs 30min return. Access by the Lognan and Grands-Montets cable cars. ℘04 50 54 00 71. www.compagniedumontblanc.com.
At 3 297m/10 817ft, the **panorama★★★** is breathtaking. The view extends to the Argentière Glacier over which tower the Aiguille du Chardonnet and Aiguille d'Argentière to the north, Mont Dolent to the east, Aiguille Verte and Les Drus to the south, with the Aiguille du Midi and Dôme du Goûter further away.

Trélechamp

On D 1506 amid pretty alpine pastures, these hamlets are famed for the fine **vista★★** of the Mont-Blanc Massif.

Réserve Naturelle des Aiguilles-Rouges★★★

▶ *3km/1.8mi N of Argentière by D 1506 to Col des Montets.*
This nature reserve covering 3 300ha/8 154 acres, between Argentière and Vallorcine at an altitude of 1 200m/3 937ft to 2 965m/9 728ft, lies within sight of the magnificent Massif du Mont-Blanc. An **ecological discovery trail** (2km/1.2mi) which follows the old stagecoach route from Chamonix to Martigny, shows you the remarkable diversity of high-altitude flora and fauna. The **chalet d'accueil** (*℘04 50 54 02 24; www.rnaiguillesrouges.org*), situated on the Col des Montets, presents exhibits about the area's fauna, flora and geology.

Col de Balme★★ 🎿

▶ *From Le Tour 3km/1.8mi NE of Argentière. Access all year round by 2 gondolas then 10min walk. ℘04 50 54 00 58 for timetable and tarifs.*
The **view★★** extends northeast to the Swiss Alps and southwest to the Chamonix Valley surrounded by the Aiguille Verte, Mont-Blanc and the Aiguilles Rouges Massif.

🐾The **Charamillon pastures★★** used to be grazed by the famous Hérens cattle. You can see the old cowherd chalets in the valleys of the Col de Balme, from where there are easy walks

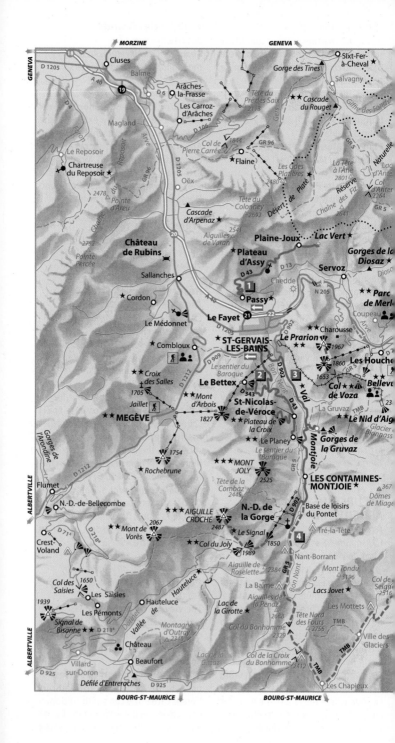

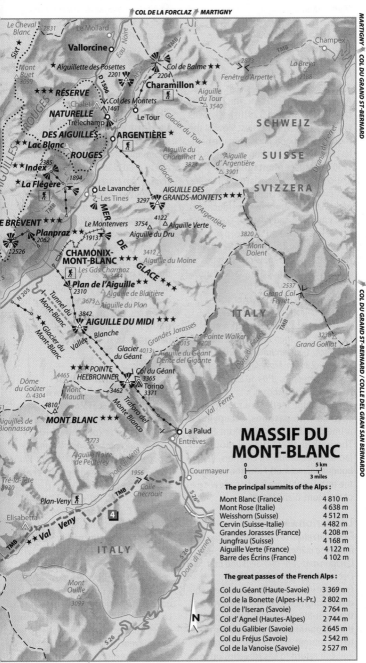

COL DE LA FORCLAZ ⟩ MARTIGNY

Le Cheval Blanc △2831
Le Mollard
Champex
Vallorcine
★ Aiguillette des Posettes ★ 2201
Col de Balme ★★
220A
La Breya 2188
Mont Buet △3099
Charamillon ★★
Fenêtre d'Arpette △2823
★★★ RÉSERVE
Chalet
Col des Montets 1461
Aiguille du Tour △3540
SCHWEIZ
NATURELLE
Trélechamp
Le Tour
DES AIGUILLES
ARGENTIÈRE ★
Glacier du Tour
SUISSE
Lac Blanc
ROUGES
Aiguille du Charmnet 3824
Aiguille d'Argentière △3901
SVIZZERA
★ Index △2385
★ La Flégère △1894
Le Lavancher
Les Tines
AIGUILLE DES GRANDS-MONTETS ★★★ △3297
LE BRÉVENT ★★★
Le Montenvers
△4122
3820
Planpraz △2062
△1913
△3754 △Aiguille Verte
Mont Dolent
△2526
Aiguille du Dru
△2537
CHAMONIX-MONT-BLANC ★★★
△3412 Aiguille du Moine
Grand Col Ferret
Les Gds Charmoz △3444
MER
Plan de l'Aiguille △2310
Aiguille de Blaitière
DE
GLACE
ITALY
△3673 △Aiguille du Plan
△3842
AIGUILLE DU MIDI ★★★
Grandes Jorasses
△3238
Grand Golliat
Blanche
△4015 △4208
Pointe Walker
Vallée
Glacier du Géant
Dôme du Goûter △4304
△4465
★★★ POINTE HELBRONNER
Col du Géant 3365
Aiguille du Géant
Dente del Gigante
△4013
Tunnel du Mont-Blanc
Glacier du Mont-Blanc
△3462 △Torino 3371
Testa del Monte Bianco
△4810
MONT BLANC ★★★
Mont Maudit
La Palud
Entrèves
Aiguilles de Bionnassay
△3773
Aiguille Noire de Peuterey
Courmayeur
Tré-la-Tête △3930
△1956
Plan-Veny
Colle Checrouit
Val Ferret
Dora di Veny
Elisabetta
★★ Val Veny
4
ITALY
Mont Ouille △3099
Dora di Verney

MASSIF DU MONT-BLANC

0 ——— 5 km
0 ——— 3 miles

The principal summits of the Alps :

Mont Blanc (France)	4 810 m
Mont Rose (Italie)	4 638 m
Weisshorn (Suisse)	4 512 m
Cervin (Suisse-Italie)	4 482 m
Grandes Jorasses (France)	4 208 m
Jungfrau (Suisse)	4 168 m
Aiguille Verte (France)	4 122 m
Barre des Écrins (France)	4 102 m

The great passes of the French Alps :

Col du Géant (Haute-Savoie)	3 369 m
Col de la Bonette (Alpes-H.-Pr.)	2 802 m
Col de l'Iseran (Savoie)	2 764 m
Col d'Agnel (Hautes-Alpes)	2 744 m
Col du Galibier (Savoie)	2 645 m
Col du Fréjus (Savoie)	2 542 m
Col de la Vanoise (Savoie)	2 527 m

N

and lovely picnic spots with a view to Mont-Blanc.

EXCURSIONS FROM LES HOUCHES

Les Houches

▶ *6km/3.7mi SW of Chamonix.* ✆*04 50 55 50 62. www.leshouches.com.*

At the foot of Mont-Blanc, this pleasant family resort (1 000m/3 281ft) has kept its village charm. The prettiest view of the Aiguilles de Chamonix is from the hamlet Les Chavants. In a house dating from 1750, the **Musée Montagnard** presents a re-creation of traditional mountain life.

Even if the setting is not on a par with that of Chamonix, Les Houches is well equipped and ideal for skiers who prefer not to take on the steeper, high-altitude slopes. The resort offers a wide range of runs and snow cannons are on standby to make good any lack of snow. The famous "la verte" piste (black in fact!) requires a high level of skill.

Animal Parc, Merlet★★

▶ *6km/3.7mi, then 10min walk there and back.* ◷*Open Jul–Aug daily 9.30am–7.30pm; May–Jun and Sept Tue–Sun 10am–6pm.* ✆*04 50 53 47 89. www.parcdemerlet.com.*

The Balcon de Merlet is a promontory covered with pastures, occupying a prime position opposite Mont-Blanc. The park shelters typical mountain fauna (deer, mouflon, chamois, llama, bouquetin, marmot). From the terrace of the restaurant there is a fine **view**★★★ of the Mont-Blanc Massif.

Le Prarion★★

30min return to the viewing table including a 20min gondola ride. ◷*Open mid-Jun–mid-Sept and mid-Dec–mid-Apr.* ✆*04 50 54 42 65.*

From the viewing table next to the Hôtel du Prarion, there is an extended **view** of the Mont-Blanc Massif. In order to enjoy the **full panorama**★★★, climb the ridge to the summit of Le Prarion *(1hr return)*. You can return to Les Houches on foot via the Col de la Forclaz and the pastures of **Charousse**★★, known for its pretty traditional chalets.

Bellevue★★

Alt. 1 812m/5 945ft. 1hr there and back including a 15min cable-car ride.

It is possible to combine this excursion with a climb up to the Nid d'Aigle and then to go back down via St-Gervais on Tramway du Mont-Blanc.

EXCURSION FROM THE ITALIAN SIDE

Le Haut Val Veny★★

Alt. 1 535m/5 036ft – 1 942 m/6 371ft. Information from Courmayeur tourist office: ✆*0039 165 84 20 60. 2hrs easy climb. From Entrèves (at exit of Mont-Blanc Tunnel), towards Val Veny to Plan-Veny. Walking paths marked "Aosta" district and "Espace Mont-Blanc".*

The path runs next to the Miage Glacier, one of the largest on Mont-Blanc. It leads to the Miage lake, which is fed by the blocks of ice breaking off from the glacier. It is not recommended to sit too close to the water. All around are huge rock faces. You can extend the walk into the heart of the massif by following the path up to Lac Combal.

HIKE

A Short Round Tour of Mont Blanc on Foot★★★

A complete circuit of Mont-Blanc on foot requires 10–12 days and is only suitable for very fit and experienced hikers.

Essential to take a passport and the topoguide of the GR Tour du Mont-Blanc path. An early start is necessary for all stages of the walk.

Marked on map p162–163 (route 4).

From Les Contamines, follow D 902 for 2km/1.2mi, then paths marked GR 5 and TMB. Then follow the path from La Saxe to Palud. Return by cable car. *Reservations are essential for mountain huts.*

This slightly less strenuous four-day walking tour is ideal for fit tourists. It goes from Les Contamines in France to La Palud in Italy, with overnight stops in Les Chapieux, refuge Elisabetta and Courmayeur. Walking gear and protection for all weathers is essential.

ADDRESSES

See also addresses in Chamonix, Megève, St-Gervais.

⍩/EAT

Le Pèle – *Near the church, 74310 Les Houches. ✆04 50 55 51 16. www.hotel-beausite.com. Closed lunchtimes except 2 weeks over Christmas, Wed out of season and public holidays. 18 rooms.*
You will love the charm and tasteful décor of this rustic and cosy restaurant. Not only this but there are delicious local dishes served here too. For summer, there is a shady and pretty terrace.

ACTIVITIES

HIKES
Advice Before Leaving:
Equip yourself with warm clothes, hiking boots and sunglasses. Check the weather forecast carefully. Bulletins are posted at the tourist offices and at the *Maison de la montagne de Chamonix (forecast for the whole of the Alps).*

To check snow and ice conditions: *Office de haute-montagne de Chamonix. ✆04 50 53 22 08. www.ohm-chamonix.com. Open: Mon–Sat 9am–noon, 3–6pm.*

♦ If you are planning a stay in a mountain hut over a busy period, remember to make a reservation.
♦ Equip yourself with topographical maps and guidebooks to the many walks in the Chamonix Valley, available in local bookshops.

La Compagnie des guides – This professional guides organisation offers numerous mountain and other outdoor activities in the Chamonix Valley with something for all ages. Choose from rock-climbing, glacier walking, hiking excursions, mountain climbs, rafting, canyoning, paragliding or other adventures. There are specialised guides that you can hire for a day for excursions at mid-altitude (up to 2 500m/8 202ft) or in the high mountain above that altitude.
Information from the guides offices in Chamonix (open daily except Mon, Sun out of season 9am–noon, 3–7pm; ✆04 50 53 00 88; www.chamonix-guides.com), in Argentière (✆04 50 54 17 94) or at Les Houches (✆04 50 54 50 76).

Le sentier du Baroque – *✆04 50 58 60 49 or 04 50 47 01 58. May–Oct – information from tourist offices. 7–8hrs on foot.* A chance to explore the valley's many Baroque churches, chapels and oratories along this 20km/12.4mi waymarked walk. Start at the church at Combloux, finish at Notre-Dame de la Gorge at Contamines-Montjoie.

Tour du Mont-Blanc – The long (320km/199mi) Tour du Mont-Blanc (TMB) circuit, via the Grand and Petit St-Bernard passes, is particularly recommended, but recommended only to experienced hikers.

Indiana'Ventures – la forêt du Mont-Blanc – *2185 rte de Coupeau, 74310 Les Houches. ✆06 62 67 28 51. www.indian aventures.com. Open 9am–7pm.*
This adventure park will appeal to young *(min height of 1.35m/4ft 6in)* and old alike. Defy the laws of gravity with a wide choice of safe adventure circuits through the trees, including rope bridges, ladders and skywalks.

La Compagnie des Ânes – *55 chemin du Vieux-Four, 74310 Les Houches. ✆04 50 47 26 18. Jul–Aug by reservation (children 11€ per hour).* Donkey rides. Possibility of doing a round tour of Mont-Blanc.

Natural Skating Rink – *Av. des Alpages, 74310 Les Houches. ✆04 50 54 52 99. www.leshouches.com. School holidays daily; rest of year Wed and Sat–Sun 3–6pm, 8–11pm, weather dependent. 2.85€ (children 1.70€).* Skate on a frozen lake with a view to Mont-Blanc.

🎉 EVENT

Le combat des reines – For decades the cowherds of the Aosta Valley (Italy), the Valais (Switzerland) and the Mont-Blanc Valley have organised "cow fights" to elect the leader of the herd of black Hérens cows, known for their large horns. A wonderful traditional event held at the end of September in a Mont-Blanc village. *✆04 50 55 50 62.*

St-Gervais-les-Bains★

St-Gervais-les-Bains was established as a successful spa town in the early 19C. The town occupies one of the most open sites in the Alps, and is renowned for its benign climate. It is the starting point for many drives and cable-car rides offering outstanding views. Mountaineers traditionally start the ascent of Mont-Blanc from St-Gervais, via the Tramway du Mont-Blanc. Linked together with its higher satellite resorts, Bettex, "Voza-Prarion" and St-Nicolas-de-Véroce, and in an ideal position between Megève and Chamonix, St-Gervais has developed into an important ski resort.

VISIT

The town (850m/2 789ft) fans out from its typical Savoyard Baroque-style church (1697), on the last gentle slopes of the Val Montjoie above the wooded gorge through which flows the River Bon Nant, spanned here by the **Pont du Diable**. Looking up the valley from the bridge, there is a clear view of Mont Joly, Mont Tondu and the Dômes de Miage framing the Val Montjoie. The **thermal spas** are located at **Le Fayet** at Bon Nant Gorge, inside a park with a lovely waterfall.

🏃 HIKES

From Contamines-Montjoie

The resort of Contamines-Montjoie is a **hiking centre and departure point for mountain races**. The best starting point for big climbs is from the hotel Tré-la-Tête. Casual walkers will find some of the most beautiful paths in the Alps here. Nature lovers should visit the Contamines-Montjoie Nature Reserve to admire the peat bogs of the Rosière plateau (information from the Les Contamines tourist office).

👫The **Pontet leisure centre** is set around a little lake and is recommended to take children at the end of the day. The **Tour du Mont-Blanc** (TMB) passes

through the Nature Reserve of Les Contamines. From **Notre-Dame-de-la-Gorge** join it for a hike (5hrs return) up to the magical spot of the **Jovet lakes★** surrounded by mountains.

An easy walk (30min climb) from the top of **Le Signal★** gondola takes you to the **Col du Joly★★** (1 989m/6 526ft) from where there is a splendid panorama over the Mont-Blanc Massif, the Hauteluce Valley and the Lac de la Girotte with the Aravis beyond. In the distance is Mont Granier in the Chartreuse. Note that from the top of the gondola there is also a marvellous view over the Dômes de Nuage, the Tré-la-Tête Massif and beyond (Gorge and Signal gondolas: Jul–Aug; ◎11€ (children 8.20€); ℘04 50 47 02 05; www.lescontamines.net).

From Col du Joly strong hikers can climb up (1hr 30min return) to the **Aiguille Croche★★★** (2 487m/8 159ft) to reach one of the most extensive and beautiful **panoramas★★★** in the Alps, from the Mont-Blanc Massif over to the Aravis. From there you can continue up to Mont Joly for more amazing **views★★★**.

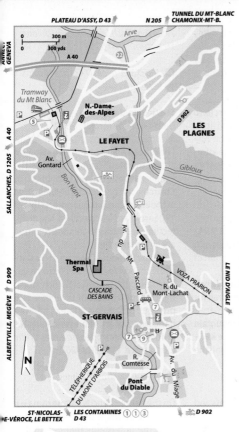

The D 43 climbs up through areas of increasingly dense forest, facing south, with views eventually opening up to the peaks above the Chamonix Valley, which appear on the left of the wooded hillside of the Tête Noire.

On arrival at Plateau d'Assy, the Aiguille Verte can be seen peeping up behind Brévent.

Plateau d'Assy – Église Notre-Dame-de-Toute-Grâce★

🕐 Open 9am–noon, 2–6pm. 🗣️ Guided visits possible. 💶5€. 📞04 50 58 80 61.

Few visitors are left indifferent after seeing this 1937–1945 church, a fine example of the contemporary revival of religious art. It was built by Maurice Novarina.

Canon Devémy called upon the great contemporary artists of the day to provide both the interior and exterior **decoration**★★. The dazzling mosaics on the façade are by **Fernand Léger**; the chancel features a huge, colourful tapestry by **Jean Lurçat**. **Bazaine** conceived the stained-glass windows of the gallery and **Georges Roualt** those opening up behind the façade.

In front of the main altar is a bronze statue of Christ by Germaine **Richier**, controversial in its day, and there are also works to be seen by **Bonnard**, **Matisse**, **Braque**, **Chagall** and **Lipchitz**.

Jardin des Cimes★

224 rte du Dr-Davy. 🕐 Open Jun–mid-Oct, times vary. 💶6€ (children 3€). ♿ 📞04 50 53 44 74. www.jardin descimes.com.

A sublime **panorama** of Mont-Blanc can be seen from these interesting gardens, which have two parts. A delightful walk through the first hilly garden takes you through a simulation of what might be

🚗 DRIVING TOURS

1 ROUTE DU PLATEAU D'ASSY★★

Drive of 12km/7.4mi shown on the local map (👤see p162). From Passy to Plaine-Joux, allow 1hr 30min.

Passy★

ℹ️ 35 pl. du Dr-Joly, 74190 Passy. 📞04 50 58 80 52.

A pleasant family resort, appreciated long ago by the Romans, Passy provides lovely views over the massif. The "**Contemporary Sculpture Route**", which runs up to Plateau d'Assy presents large pieces from 24 sculptors The sanatoriums dating from the 1930s and situated at Plateau d'Assy are mostly built in an avant-garde style by famous architects such as Pol Abraham and Henri-Jacques Le Même.

grown on a mountain, from the valley to the glaciers, with works of art in line with the Plateau d'Assy's contemporary art theme, scattered along the route.

Plaine-Joux

In the centre of this little ski resort (also used for paragliding), you can visit an interactive exhibition about the history of the local landscape at the information centre chalet of the **Réserve Naturelle de Passy** (⏱*open holidays daily 10.30am–5.30pm, rest of year Sat–Sun 1.30–5.30pm; ₰04 50 78 00 03*). In the meeting place between the massifs, this nature reserve covers 2 000ha/4 942 acres. It includes 530 plant species and recently has seen the reintroduction of bearded vultures.

👫Near the chalet, the path **Grand-Père Nature** is an ideal nature trail for families with young children.

Beyond Plaine-Joux are high mountain pastures and opposite the **view**★★ reveals the cliffs of the Fiz range and the scree-covered Pas du Dérochoir.

Lac Vert★

Overlooked by the Fiz escarpments and surrounded by pine trees, the lake has deep green reflections. You can walk around it *(15min)* but it gets very busy.

② LE BETTEX AND CORNICHE DU VAL MONTJOIE★★

Drive of 20km/12.4mi shown on the Massif du Mont-Blanc map (♿see p162). Allow 45min.

▶ *Take D 909 (towards Megève), then D 43 left towards Le Bettex. You can also reach Bettex by cable car from St-Gervais.*

Le Bettex

Very varied views over the Mont-Blanc, Fiz and Aravis mountain ranges.

This excursion can be extended by going up the cable car from Bettex to **Mont d'Arbois**★★ (alt. 1 827m/5 994ft – ♿*see map*). Magnificent view over the Aravis, the Fiz and Mont-Blanc.

End Jun–early Sept. St-Gervais–Le Bettex: 9am–12.30pm, 2–6pm. Le Bettex–Mt d'Arbois: 9.15am–12.45pm,

2–5.45pm. Each section ⊷9€ (children 7€) return. ₰04 50 93 11 87.

▶ *Via D 343, rejoin D 43 to St-Nicolas-de-Véroce.*

St-Nicolas-de-Véroce

🏠*4054 rte de St-Nicolas, 74190 St-Nicolas-de-Véroce. ₰04 50 93 20 63.*

The village enjoys a fine **situation**★★ facing the Mont-Blanc chain. See the chapels at Les Plans and Les Chattrix.

Church – Its style wavers between that of the end of the Baroque era and that of 19C Sardinian Neoclassicism. The architecture, decorative motifs and furniture are all remarkable.

The huge Baroque altarpiece at the back of the chancel reveals a painted archway illustrating the legend of St Nicholas. In the **treasury**, pieces of silverware and precious ornaments sit next to more basic works of art, expressing religious ardour. ⏱*Check opening times at the tourist office. ₰04 50 93 20 63.*

▶ *Follow towards Le Planey.*

On the hairpin bend is a **panorama**★★ showing the whole of the Val Montjoie, with the mountains that overlook it (Mont Tondu, Aiguilles de la Pennaz and de Roselette).

▶ *Return to St-Nicolas and take the road to the Plateau de la Croix.*

Plateau de la Croix★★

Leave your car near the chalet "L'Étape" and walk to the foot of the cross. The **panorama**★★ encompasses, apart from Mont-Blanc, the Aiguilles du Bionnassay, the Miage Massif, the Fiz chain (Aiguille de Varan) and the Aiguilles de Chamonix.

③ LE VAL MONTJOIE★

Drive of 16km/10mi shown on the Massif du Mont-Blanc map (♿see p162). Allow 45min.

▶ *Leave St-Gervais by D 902 (towards Les Contamines).*

Just as in the Maurienne and Tarentaise valleys, the Montjoie Valley includes a fine collection of churches and chapels with typically Baroque interiors contrasting with the simple style of their façades. After Bionnay, a narrow wooded stretch then opens out into the Contamines dip where the attractive mountain scenery begins: to the right of the Col du Bonhomme depression the Aiguille de la Penaz peeps out and then, closer, the Aiguille de Roselette.

Gorges de la Gruvaz

At hamlet La Gruvaz. 1.5km/1mi from St-Gervais towards the chalets de Miage on the left off D 902.
Take care! There are footbridges to cross in the first half of the walk, then a steep and slippery path in the second half. Jul–Aug. ℘04 50 47 01 58.

You will end up at a **belvedere**★ from where you can view the crack above that forms a perfect V. From the gorge carved out of the schist rock you will really see the falls of the mountain torrent that comes down from the Miage Glacier.

Les Contamines-Montjoie★

Located at an altitude of 1 164m/3 819ft, at the foot of Mont Joly and the snow-capped Dômes de Miage, Les Contamines is one of the most pleasant and restful holiday resorts in the Mont-Blanc Massif (*8 r. Notre-Dame-de-la-Gorge, 74170 Les Contamines-Montjoie; ℘04 50 47 01 58; www.lescontamines.com*). You can read the construction date (1759) of the **Église de la Ste-Trinité** on the four forged iron tie beams on the corners of the walls.

▶ *Follow D 902 for 4km/2.5mi until the end of the road.*

Notre-Dame-de-la-Gorge

With venerable origins, this place of pilgrimage (*15 Aug and 1st week Sept*) is built at the end of a wooded valley. Alongside the alleyway leading to the church are 15 oratories reserved for the marian sect (1728). The very homogenous interior of the chapel is one of the best examples of Baroque art in Haute-Savoie. The **retable** of the main altar (1707) with its twisted columns is the most important piece.

EXCURSION

Col de Voza and Le Nid d'Aigle (Glacier de Bionnassay)★★

Alt. 2 386m/7 828ft. 3hrs there and back aboard the **Tramway du Mont-Blanc**. *10 May–30 Nov, weather dependent. 26.50€ (children 17.60€). ℘04 50 47 51 83. www.compagniedu montblanc.com.*

The electric tram on its way to the Nid d'Aigle stops first at the Col de Voza; halfway up the mountainside, above the Bionnassay Valley, where there are fine **views**★★ of Mont-Blanc Massif.

The surroundings provide a good introduction to high-altitude mountain landscapes in the wild setting of the Bionnassay Glacier (*walk to the glacier moraine, 1hr there and back*) stretched out at the foot of the Aiguilles de Bionnassay (*spectacular avalanches*) and of the Aiguille du Goûter.

ADDRESSES

🏠 STAY

⊖⊖🖥 **Arbois-Bettex** – ℘04 50 93 12 22. www.hotel-arboisbettex.com. Closed 20 Apr–27 May, 27 Sept–19 Dec. 🅿. Wifi. 33 rooms, restaurant⊖⊖🖥. Sited next to the gondola, this chalet-hotel has a superb view of the Mont-Blanc Massif. Indoor pool, spa and massage.

🍴 EAT

⊖⊖ **Auberge de Bionnassay** – 3084 rte de Bionnassay, 3.5km/2.2mi S of St-Gervais-les-Bains towards Les Contamines then Bionnay. ℘04 50 93 45 23. Closed Oct–May and Mon in Jun and Sept. This inn and farm dating from 1810 stands at where several walking paths meet and is an ideal stopping place for hikers. The cosy interior reflects the charm of life in the mountains in years gone by.

🥾 ACTIVITIES

Les Thermes de St-Gervais – 74170 St-Gervais-les-Bains. ℘04 50 47 54 57. www.thermes-saint-gervais.com. This celebrated spa offers traditional treatments as well as mountain balneotherapy and beauty therapy.

Megève★★

A village with a long history, in 1790 Megève had 2 400 inhabitants. Tourists were welcomed early in the 20C, and in 1916 Baronne Noémie de Rothschild envisaged making the village into a chic mountain resort, in the style of St Moritz in Switzerland. The first luxury hotel opened on Mont d'Arbois in 1921, and Megève has not looked back. The landscape around the village is simply charming with the dark greens of the spruce forests below the rounded peaks of La Giettaz, Rochebrune and Mont d'Arbois contrasting with the white snow-capped Mont Joly. Its position at the junction of the Sallanches basin and the Val d'Arly brings spectacular views, easily accessible from the ski-lift network.

▶ **Population:** 3 878.
◔ **Michelin Map:** 328 M5.
▯ **Info:** R. Monseigneur-Conseil, BP 24, 74120 Megève. ℘04 50 21 27 28. www.megeve.com.
◖ **Location:** Megève is 13km/8mi from Sallanches by D 1212.
◶ **Don't Miss:** The view at Mont d'Arbois, reached by gondola, and if you are a keen hiker, the panorama from Mont Joly.
▴▪ **Kids:** The Megève swimming pool.
◔ **Timing:** Sunny Megève is ideal for skiing early in the season. Or enjoy hiking from spring onwards.

A YEAR-ROUND RESORT

Megève's slopes appeal more to exponents of "relaxed skiing" than to experts, although the resort has a good reputation for well-maintained ski runs (with snow cannons to ensure good snow cover at this relatively low altitude), and for its ski school. Its mountain restaurants are renowned. The ski area is linked by gondola or shuttle to the other resorts of the Mont-Blanc Massif.

In summer the area is popular for its bracing climate, nearby forest, opportunities for mountain walking and drives, and wide choice of sporting activities (tennis, swimming, skating).

The historic part of Megève is around the tourist office. Some massive old stone houses surround the old priory and the church.

Église St-Jean-Baptiste

The church was founded in 1085 by the Benedictines and has an interesting interior and an onion dome bell tower (1754). Dating back to the 14C Flamboyant period, the chancel is the most ancient part. The nave was rebuilt in 1692, and has arches decorated with paintings by the Italian Mucengo (1830).

The 18C **altar** by a sculptor working for Emperor Ferdinand VI of Austria was commissioned by Megèvan J.-B. Perinet, who had made his fortune in Vienna.

Musée du Haut Val d'Arly

88 ruelle du Vieux-Marché. ◔*Open mid-Jun–mid-Apr daily 2.30–6.30pm.* ◔*Closed public holidays.* ⊜*3.50€.* ℘*04 50 91 81 00.*
The museum, housed in the Ferme de Marius built in the 1850s, displays collections of traditional objects in reconstructed authentic settings: domestic life, agricultural tools, milk processing and textiles. A room is devoted to the history of winter sports.

Le Calvaire

This Way of the Cross, set in a wooded area, was built 1844–63, encouraged by Reverend Martin, then the vicar of Megève, who wanted it modelled on the one at Jerusalem. The 15 oratories and chapels have paintings or small sculptures, sadly badly deteriorated, that were all the work of local people.

From outside the lowest chapel is a pleasant view over the upper Val d'Arly and stretching to the distinct pyramid form of Mont Charvin.

EXCURSIONS
Combloux★
▶ 5km/3mi N by D 1212.
Tourist Office, 49 chemin des Passerands, 74920 Combloux. ℘04 50 57 60 49. www.combloux.com.

In a fine south-facing position above the Sallanches plain, this summer and winter family resort has retained its traditional farms and old-world charm. Yet, it also boasts the first biotope natural swimming pool at altitude in France (℘*see Activities*). The 18C **church** is of typical alpine style with a sumptuous altar.

🎿 🎿 The **Combloux-le Jaillet ski resort** specialises in family entertainment and skiing without risk. There are 100km/62km of pistes, and cross-country skiing in a beautiful setting. Experienced skiers seeking greater challenges should head to **Évasion Mont-Blanc**.

For a magnificent **panorama**★★★ over the Mont-Blanc, Fiz and Aravis massifs, take the route du Haut-Combloux from the centre of the resort to La Cry *(bus possible and return on foot by small footpaths).*

Sallanches
▶ 13km/8.1mi N of Combloux by D 1212.
🚹 31 quai de l'Hôtel-de-Ville, 74700 Sallanches. ℘04 50 58 04 25. www.sallanches.com.

At the top of the Arve Valley, Sallanches is located on the route through to the majestic Mont-Blanc region. The large commercial town was rebuilt in the 19C on a grid system.

On the place Charles-Albert an orientation table indicates the important points in the Mont-Blanc Massif. The large **Église St-Jacques** has an interior in Neoclassical style, typical of sacred art in Savoie in the 19C.

Château des Rubins
👥 **Centre de la Nature Montagnard**
🕐Open Jul–Aug Mon–Fri 10am–6.30pm; Sept–Jun Mon–Fri 9am–noon, 2–6pm; Jan–Aug Sat–Sun and public holidays 2–6pm. 🕐Closed 1 Jan, 1 May, 25 Dec. ⊛5.80€ (children 3.50€). ℘04 50 58 32 13.

Instructive presentations of ecosystems in mountainous areas involving flora, fauna, geology, climate, etc. Contemporary problems are addressed such as climate change, species dying out, etc.

Cascade d'Arpenaz★
▶ From Sallanches take D 1205 towards Cluses as far as Luzier. Turn left towards Oëx; the waterfall is on the right. *This impressive 200m/656ft-high waterfall gushes from a curiously stratified channel in the rock.*

It has been a subject for artists since the 18C and was studied by 18C Swiss geologist Horace-Bénédict de Saussure, who found in its folds and stratifications evidence that the Earth's surface has undergone massive transformation over the eons; this was some of the earliest geological fieldwork.

Cordon★
▶ 4km/2.5m from Sallanches by D 113.
🚹 74700 Cordon. ℘04 50 58 01 57. www.cordon.fr.

This charming village ("cordon" means a "steep-sided torrent" in Franco-Provençal) lies in the upper Arve Valley against the Aravis chain, in a fine **position**★ facing the majestic Mont-Blanc Massif. 🎿🎿In winter, the resort offers possibilities of alpine and cross-country skiing.

Église Notre-Dame-de-l'Assomption – 🔊*Guided visits possible.* ℘04 50 58 01 57. Built in 1781, this church is a masterpiece of Savoie **Baroque** art. The interior was painted by the Swiss Léonard Isler in 1787 and there is a lavish **retable** with cable columns.

Chapelle du Médonnet – *From Cordon, take the road to Combloux, then left to Nant Cruy. Cross the hamlet. Follow the road down for 2km/1.2mi to a fork; turn right on the old Combloux road and follow for about 1km/0.6mi to the hamlet of Médonnet. Follow the track to find the chapel 600m/660yds on your right.* The chevet of this humble sanctuary faces a superb **panorama**★★ revealing from left to right, the Pointe d'Areu, the imposing mountains of the Fiz range (Aiguilles de Varan, Pointe de Platé,

Pointe d'Anterne), the Aiguilles-Rouges (Brévent), and finally, the Mont-Blanc Massif stretching from the Aiguille Verte to the Bérangère.

HIKES
Viewpoints by Gondola
Sentier du Tétras-Lyre au Jaillet

🚶 *Alt. 1 763m/5 784ft. 1hr 30min there and back on an easy round walk. From Megève, follow to the Jaillet gondola (40min), then the Frasses car park, waymarked Espace Mont-Blanc.*

The pretty forested path links old mountain pastures along the ridge. Where the path ends is a unique viewpoint of the Aravis and Mont-Blanc massifs. Signboards describe the different ecological zones that you pass through in this land of the *tétras-lyre* (black grouse).

Mont d'Arbois★★

Alt. 1 833m/6 014ft. Access by gondola (10min). Jul–Aug 9am–1pm, 2–6pm. ℘04 50 21 22 07. ⊚10.60€ return.

Splendid **panoramic view** of the Aravis and Fiz mountains as well as Mont-Blanc.

🚶 *You can walk in 20min to the upper station of the cable car which goes back down to St-Gervais.*

Croix des Salles★★

🚶*About 1hr 30min return, including 12min ride in the Jaillet gondola and 45min on foot. End Jun–early Sept and mid-Dec–end Mar. ℘04 50 21 27 28. ⊚9.70€ (children 8.40€) return.*

Having reached the upper station, continue on foot to the cross through pastures and woodland. View of the Fiz range and Mont-Blanc Massif.

Rochebrune★

🚶 *About 1hr return, including an 8min cable-car ride. ℹ️ ℘04 50 21 01 51.*
View of the Val d'Arly, the Aravis mountains and Mont-Blanc.

For Experienced Walkers
Mont Joly★★★

4hrs 30min return on foot from the Mont d'Arbois via a well-marked path.
🚶 The exceptional **panorama**★★★ from the summit (alt. 2 525m/8 284ft)

includes the Mont-Blanc Massif and Vanoise, Beaufortain, Écrins ranges.

Mont de Vorès★★

🚶 *5hrs 30min on foot. Allow a day. 800m/2 625ft vertical rise. Not technical, but requires a good level of fitness. If the cable car isn't working, you can make an almost identical round trip from Leutaz.*

The path rises to L'Alpette and the Col de Véry on the way to the Mont de Vorès (alt. 2 067m/6 781ft). Splendid **view** of the Mont-Blanc Massif to the east, with the Col du Joly and Lac de la Girotte in the foreground, and the Aravis mountains to the west.

The path then follows the mountain ridge to the Crêt du Midi, which offers a remarkable **view** of Megève on the right and Le Planay on the left. Walk down to Les Fontanettes then up again to Rochebrune (☺*hard-going walk for about 1hr*) along a fairly steep path.

ADDRESSES

🛏️ STAY

⊖ **Chambre d'hôte L'Alpe** – *Chemin du rucher, 74310 Servoz. ℘04 50 47 22 66. www.chez.com/lalpe. Closed 2 weeks in May, Oct and Nov. ♿🅿️. 5 rooms ⊑.*
A recent business that is ever improving. The rooms are decorated tastefully with a good mix of wooden furniture and old Provençal tiles. Guests have the use of a kitchen, and an area is provided to relax. Depending on the season, there are walks, or ski touring.

⊖⊖💲 **La Chaumine** – *36 chemin des Bouleaux, via Chemin du Maz. ℘04 50 21 37 05. www.hotel-lachaumine-megeve.com. Closed 1 Apr–25 Jun, 6 Sept–17 Dec. 🅿️. 11 rooms.* A pretty chalet with a friendly, home-like atmosphere at the end of a quiet track a few minutes away from the centre and well placed for the ski slopes. There are cosy rooms and light evening meals with local products are provided.

⊖⊖💲💲 **Lodge Park** – *100 r. Arly. ℘04 50 93 05 03. www.lodgepark.com. Closed 1 Apr–17 Dec. 🅿️. Wifi. 49 rooms.*
Hunting trophies, stone fireplaces and comfortable furnishings re-create the atmosphere of a Canadian hunting cabin.

But don't be fooled, this is one of the best hotels in Megève, and the "natural" atmosphere in no way compromises the sophisticated luxury and high standard of service. International cuisine is served in the restaurant.

⍭/EAT

◉ **Les Marronniers chez Maria** – *18 imp. le Chamas.* ✆*04 50 21 22 01. Closed May–mid-Jun, 3 weeks in Oct and Tue out of season.* This rustic chalet at the heart of the resort is a crêperie with a bit more on the menu. Besides the usual crêpes made with wheat or rye flour, there are salads and omelettes. The house speciality, that must be ordered in advance, is a surprise casserole dish.

◉◉ **La Grange d'Arly** – *10 r. Allobroges.* ✆*04 50 58 77 88. www.grange-darly.com. Closed end Mar–end Jun and mid-Sept–mid-Dec.* 🅿. *22 rooms* ◉◉◉⊡. An impeccably run family-owned establishment, the restaurant serves traditional cuisine in warm surroundings with tones of yellow and blue. All in wood, the guest rooms are spacious and functional, with some in the eves or arranged as a duplex.

◉◉ **Le Crystobald** – *489 rte Nationale.* ✆*04 50 21 26 82. Closed 21 Jun–8 Jul, 15 Nov–9 Dec, Mon, Tue out of season, Sun eve.* You will find a friendly ambience and charming service at this family-owned chalet, with well-cooked contemporary food. The décor in the dining room has been refreshed in tones of deep red and beige.

◉◉ **Le Refuge** – *2615 rte du Leutaz.* ✆*04 50 21 23 04. www.refuge-megeve.com. Closed 10 Jun–10 Jul, 15 Oct–15 Nov, Tue out of season, Mon and Wed.* 🅿. A really charming refuge or mountain hut perched high up above the resort. A simple alpine style shows through in both the décor and the tasty and simple cuisine. Large terrace with a view.

◉◉◉ **Flocons de Sel** – *1775 rte du Leutaz, 4km/2.5mi SW by the rte du Bouchet – ZA.* ✆*04 50 21 49 99. www.floconsdesel.com. Closed Jun and 4 Nov–10 Dec.* ♿🅿. In a collection of chalets on their own in the middle of the countryside, Emmanuel Renaut serves creative food, focused on the top ingredients. The well-lit dining room is in contemporary alpine style.

◉◉◉ **La Sauvageonne** – ✆*04 50 91 90 81. www.sauvageonne-megeve.com. Closed May–Jun, Oct–Nov, Mon and Tue lunchtimes outside school holidays.* Sought after by show business types, inside this restored farm (1907) you will find an amazing dining room with exposed beams, crystal chandeliers and a fine open fireplace. Traditional cuisine is served in a relaxed atmosphere.

🚶‍♂️ACTIVITIES

Summer activities – Megève offers a wide range of sports facilities including an excellent **swimming pool complex** (*r. du Palais-des-Sports;* ✆*04 50 21 59 11; closed May–Jun and 10 Sept–15 Oct*) with Olympic-sized pool, slide, covered children's pool, saunas, hammam and trampoline. There is also an open-air **ice-rink** (*35 r. Oberstdorf;* ✆*04 50 21 23 77; open 2–6pm*). The mountains of Megève provide an ideal environment to introduce children to hiking. For those who enjoy flying, paragliding, ballooning or helicopter trips are available in the village or environs; courses of instruction also available.

🗺 The tourist office provides detailed topographical maps for walks and mountain-biking routes.

Plan d'eau biotope – *Plan-Perret, 74920 Combloux.* ✆*04 50 91 21 62. www.combloux. com. Open Jul–Aug daily 11am–7pm; mid-Jun Wed and Fri–Mon 11am–7pm.* ◉*4.50€ (children* ◉*4€).* The pride of Combloux, this biotope lake open for swimming is the first of its type in France. Aquatic plants keep the water alive. Fabulous view to Mont-Blanc and fitness equipment available.

Ski area – At the foot of Mont-Blanc, this huge area covers 325km/202mi of pistes over an area of attractive bowls and wooded areas. The Evasion Mont-Blanc ski pass gives access to 127 ski lifts in Megève, La Giettaz, St-Gervais, St-Nicolas-de-Véroce, Combloux, Les Contamines and Cordon, linked together by lifts or shuttle buses.

Cluses

Known today as the world capital for machine tooling, Cluses has hardly developed into a tourist town. However, it is worth stopping here to see the fascinating clock-making museum, and also to look at the recent renovations of its historic town centre, especially the broad avenues, with arcades in the style of Turin. Drive through Cluses to reach the nearby ski resorts of Les Carroz and Flaine, and close by, you can seek out the hidden Giffre Valley.

▶ **Population:** 17 880.

▯ **Info:** 100 pl. du 11 Novembre, 74300 Cluses. ℘04 50 98 31 79. www.cluses.fr/.

◐ **Location:** 62km/39mi from Annecy on A 41, then A 40; centre of a cluster of small towns and industrial zones.

◉ **Don't Miss:** The drive through the Giffre Valley and the Faucigny.

👪 **Kids:** The Musée paysan at Viuz-en-Sallaz.

◷ **Timing:** Winding route de Giffre demands patience.

A BIT OF HISTORY

An important watchmaking centre – The painstaking craft of watch- and clock-making has been a skill practised by the town and the Faucigny region since the 18C, when Clusiens returning from Germany offered their new-found skills to the watchmakers of Geneva. The town's reputation grew, and in 1848, a school of watchmaking, the École nationale d'horlogerie, was founded in Cluses, today a Lycée. These skills have transferred over the years to machine tooling, and today the Cluses Valley is known as the "Technical Valley."

VISIT

Musée de l'Horlogerie et du Décolletage (Espace Carpano et Pons)

100 pl. du 11 Novembre. ◐*Open Jul–Aug Mon–Sat 10am–noon, 1.30–6pm, Sun and public holidays 10am–noon, 1.30–5.30pm; Sept–Jun Mon–Fri except public holidays 1.30–6pm, Sat 1.30–5.30pm.* ⌨*5.50€.* ℘*04 50 96 43 00.*
This museum illustrates the technical evolution of time-measuring instruments and includes exhibits such as Louis XIV's one-handed watch, one of Voltaire's desk clocks, marine chronometers and watchmaking tools.

Vieux Pont – The old bridge built in 1674 spans the Arve with a single arch. The best view is from the tourist office.

Church – ◕◕*Guided visits by appointment (15min).* ⌨*3€ (children 1.50€).* ℘*04 50 32 65 00.* Old chapel (15C–17C) of

a Cordeliers Convent. Seek out the huge **font**★ (16C), decorated with the coat of arms from the family who donated it, surmounted by a stone cross at the foot of which is a statue of Madeleine crying on her knees. Note also the 18C Calvary at the back of the chancel and from the same era, in the nave are a few amusing painted statues.

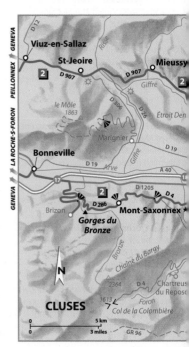

🚗 DRIVING TOURS

1 LA CLUSE DE L'ARVE

Drive of 28km/17.4mi shown on the Cluses map (🕐 see below). Allow 1hr.

▶ *Leave Cluses to the S by D 1205 towards Chamonix.*

The road follows the narrow passage between the Chaîne du Reposoir (Pointe d'Areu on the west bank) and the Chaîne des Fiz (Croix de Fer, Tête du Colonney and Aiguilles de Varan on the east bank) through which the Arve flows; the narrowest part lies between Cluses and Magland, where the A 40 motorway and D 1205 run alongside the railway line.

▶ *From Balme-Arâches take D 6.*

The Arâches road breaks through the escarpments that perforate the "balme" (cave), which gave its name to the hamlet. Where the road enters the ravine, it widens allowing you to stop on the side to take some time to observe the

Cluses–Sallanches cutting more closely. Do watch out, as there is a risk of rockfalls from the cliffs above.

Arâches – A little winter-sports village in a pleasant forested setting.

Les Carroz-d'Arâches

Founded in 1936 and built along the edge of a plateau above the Arve Valley, the resort of Les Carroz links into the Grand Massif ski area (Flaine, Samoëns, Sixt, Morillon). A range of leisure activities are offered throughout the year. Leaving Les Carroz towards Flaine, after 2km/1.2mi the peaks of the Croix-de-Fer and Grandes Platières appear. The road climbs to 1 844m/6 050ft, then down towards Flaine, which you will see about 3km/1.86mi before you get there.

Flaine★

Built in Bauhaus style, the architecture of this modern resort in a secluded valley (1 600m/5 249ft) might shock at first. In summer and winter, life in the car-free resort concentrates round the Forum, decorated with a polychrome geometric

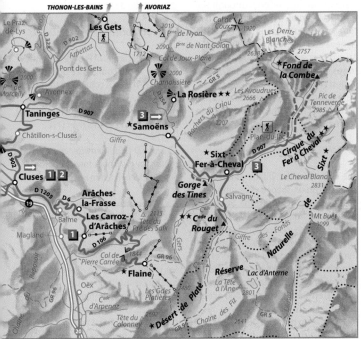

sculpture by Vasarely. Close by stands a sculpture entitled *Woman's Head*, which is the monumental version (12m/39ft) of a model made by Picasso in 1957.

☞ The resort makes use of a vast area, known as "Le Grand Massif", linking the resorts of Les Carroz, Morillon, Samoëns and Sixt *(area pass)*. In addition, a remarkable 13km/8mi run links Flaine to Sixt.

Désert de Platé★

The **Téléphérique des Grandes Platières** *(○open mid-Jul–Aug daily 9am–12.30pm, 2–5pm; ◎11.90€ (children 8.90€) return; ℘04 50 90 40 00)* gives access to the **Désert de Plat**é with views over the Mont-Blanc Massif, from the Aiguille Verte to the Aiguille de Bionnassay.

② LA VALLÉE DU GIFFRE ET LE FAUCIGNY★

Drive of 80km/50mi shown on the local map (℅ see p174). Allow a day.

▷ *Leave Cluses to the N by D 902.*

This tour takes you through the pretty Giffre Valley and returns through the historically important Faucigny district, today a busy thoroughfare between Geneva and the Mont-Blanc Tunnel. An excellent summer-walking base, **Taninges** is proud of its **church** (1825), the largest Neoclassical example in Savoie. Here you can also visit the **Chartreuse de Mélan** (13C), which today puts on contemporary art exhibitions.

▷ *Take D 907 towards Annemasse.*

The **church** at the village of **Mieussy** boasts an onion-shaped spire, enhanced by the green of its landscape. **St-Jeoire** is a pleasant holiday resort in a wooded valley. Here the road overlooks the confluence of the rivers Giffre and Risse and through the gap appear the peaks of the Reposoir and the rocky Bargy range. An interesting stop is the **Musée Paysan** at **Viuz-en-Sallaz**, where 2 500 everyday objects used in Savoie from 1860 to 1950 are on display. *○Open Jul–Aug Sun–Fri, 2–6pm; Sept–Jun Mon–Sat,*

1.30–5pm. ○Closed public holidays. ◎5€. ♿ ℘04 50 36 89 18.

▷ *S of Viuz take D 12.*

Peillonnex has an interesting 12C **priory**, where *son et lumière* shows are held *(Jul–Aug; ℘04 50 36 89 18)*. Just 2km/1.2mi before you reach the beautiful old village of **Contamine-sur-Arve**, you can stop at **Faucigny** to visit the **Musée des Ornaments de la Femme**, a museum in an old farm devoted to women's clothing and accessories.

▷ *Continue to Roche-sur-Foron by D 1205, D 2503 and D 903.*

The town of **Roche-sur-Foron** belonged to the Genevois nobility in the 11C and came to be as important as Geneva or Annecy in the 14C, becoming a Savoyard possession 100 years later. A walk through the charming **old town**★ leads past many houses with ogee-arched mullioned windows and old tiled roofs, being carefully restored. The **tour des Comtes de Genève** is the last vestige of the château destroyed in 1590.

▷ *Leave Roche-sur-Foron by D 1203.*

The former capital of Faucigny, **Bonneville** lies at the confluence of the Borne and Arve rivers. A column by the bridge across the Arve commemorates the king of Sardinia Charles-Félix who ordered the harnessing of this river (19C).

▷ *Take D 1205, then after crossing the motorway, turn right towards Mont-Saxonnex, then left to Brizon.*

A **viewpoint**★ at Brizon sweeps down over the Bronze Gorges with the Môle and Marcelly summits in the distance. The attractive summer resort of **Mont-Saxonnex**★, overlooking the Arve Valley, includes two main villages, **Le Bourgeal** nestling below the church and **Pincru** at the beginning of the Gorges du Bronze. There are many easy hikes in the area, including a two-hour walk to **Lac Bénit**. Leave the car by the church for a plunging **panorama**★★ down to the Arve plain and the Giffre Valley.

ADDRESSES

🛏 *See also addresses in Samoëns.*

🏠 STAY

⊜ **Chambre d'hôte La Ferme de Béatrix** – *100 r. É. Devant, 74300 Châtillon-sur-Cluses. A 40, Exit Cluses-Scionnier then CD 902 rte des Grandes-Alpes.* ✆*04 50 89 43 97.* 🅿🍴. *3 rooms* 🍽. You will receive a pleasant welcome at this old farm that has been converted into a guesthouse.

⊜⊜⊜ **Le Foron** – *Imp. de l'Étang, 74800 La Roche-sur-Foron, D 1203.* ✆*04 50 25 82 76. www.hotel-le-foron.com. Closed 26 Dec–3 Jan and Sun.* 🅿. *Wifi. 26 rooms.* Practical, well-maintained and sound-proofed rooms are available at this hotel by the industrial estate. Terrace and pool.

🍴 EAT

⊜ **Restaurant Alpage de l'Airon** – *Rte de Flaine, 74300 Araches la Frasse. 7km/4.3mi*

from Flaine, rte de Cluses. ✆*04 50 90 33 84.* ♿🍴. After driving 500m/547yds down a bumpy track (cars permitted after 5pm), walk the remaining distance to this chalet perched at an altitude of 1 700m/5 577ft. In an informal setting you can enjoy omelettes, salads, farm cheeses and water pumped from the spring in front of your eyes.

⊜⊜ **La Croix de Savoie** – *768 rte du Pernand, 74300 Les Carroz-d'Arâches.* ✆*04 50 90 00 26. www.lacroixdesavoie.fr.* 🅿. This restaurant is justly popular for the tasty regional recipes reinvented by the owner and served on her terrace with a splendid view to the mountains and the valley below.

🏃 ACTIVITIES

🚠 **Les Carroz** is part of the Grand Massif ski area with 145km/90mi of pistes and a natural ice rink. In summer there is a pool, canyoning, a rock-climbing area plus hikes.

Flaine ski area – Part of the Grand Massif, Flaine's own ski area has more than 50 pistes and a snowpark for boarders, accessed by 29 lifts.

Samoëns★

In the upper Giffre Valley at the heart of limestone-rich Faucigny region, Samoëns was known for its stonecutters (known as "frahans") from the 16C. Indeed, their reputation extended throughout Europe with their skills being used for many significant constructions by Vauban, for example. The stonemasons here also created a famous philanthropic brotherhood. Evidence of their skills can be seen in the stone houses of the charming village centre and in its church. Beyond Samoëns, the beautiful landscape of the Sixt Nature Reserve provides a huge attraction for lovers of both nature and mountain sports.

🐾 WALKING TOUR

Place du Gros-Tilleul★
Located at the centre of the village, the square owes its name to the lime tree

- ▶ **Population:** 2 368.
- 🛏 **Michelin Map:** 328 N4.
- ℹ **Info:** BP 42, 74340 Samoëns. ✆04 50 34 40 28. www.samoens.com. Guided tours (2hrs) of the town (Mon) and surrounding hamlets (Thu) Jul–Aug and mid-Dec–Apr. For times, contact the tourist office.
- ◐ **Location:** Samoëns is 21km/13mi from Cluses on D 902, then on D 907 until Taninges.
- ◉ **Don't Miss:** A walk through the Jaÿsinia gardens; a visit to view the spectacular landscape of the Cirque du Fer-à-Cheval.
- ◷ **Timing:** Allow plenty of time for outdoor activities and reserve guides when required.

planted here in 1438. The **Grenette**, a 16C covered market restored in the 18C, stands on the south side; note the strange bulges on the central pillars: the arms of Samoëns were to be carved on these pillars, but the mason did not complete his work following a disagreement with the municipality over his contract. A lovely fountain stands in the centre of the square, with the church and the Château de la Tour on the north side. In front is a remarkable war memorial with a soldier who carries no weapons as a symbol of peace.

Église Notre-Dame-de-l'Assomption

Rebuilt at the end of the 16C and the 17C, at the base of the 12C bell tower, the church still retains a graceful porch roof covered in copper tiles. From the doorway rebuilt in the 16C one can still see part of the original doorway with two crouching lions supporting the cable columns. Gruesome faces and heads of angels sculpted on the tops of the columns attest to the great workmanship of the celebrated local stonemasons.

Samoëns' great benefactor Madame Marie-Louise Cognacq-Jaÿ (a local girl, whose fortune came via her husband, the founder of "La Samaritaine", the department store in Paris) provided staff in 1917 to decorate the church interior in a Gothic Revival style.

The interior was renovated in 1978 and in 1982, resulting in new stained-glass windows and a contemporary look to the nave, within which is a magnificent pulpit, sculpted in 1699.

Left of the porch, the St-Claude Chapel is a fine example of the Flamboyant Gothic style and includes a font (1717) made by a Samoëns' stonemason from a single block of marble. A sundial on the front of the **presbytery** indicates the time in 12 large cities of the world.

Jardin Botanique Alpin Jaÿsinia★

🕐 *Open daily May–Oct 8am–noon, 1–7pm; Nov–Apr 8am–noon, 1–4.30pm (possible closure if snow).* ✆*Free.*
℘*04 50 34 11 93.*

These botanical gardens are on sloping ground overlooking the village, covering an area of 3ha/7.4 acres, with a zigzag path running through them. They were created in 1906 by Madame Cognacq-Jaÿ under supervision from the Natural History Museum in Paris, and contain more than 5 000 species of mountain plants from the main temperate areas of the world.

Beyond the **Chapelle de la Jaÿsinia**, one of nine chapels in Samoëns, is a terrace, with the ruins of a foedal castle (12C), from which extends a view over the village in its mountain setting.

Chapelle de la Jaÿsinia, Jardin Botanique Alpin Jaÿsinia

F. Isler/MICHELIN

EXCURSIONS
Ferme-écomusée Le Clos Parchet
Cessenex, about 5km/3mi from Samoëns, towards Col de Joux Plane.
Open Jul–Aug Tue and Thu–Fri 2.30–4.30pm; mid-Jan–Jun and Sept–15 Nov Thu 2.30–4.30pm. Guided visits by appointment (2hrs). 6.50€ (children under 12 free), includes tasting of cider and cakes. 04 50 34 46 69. *www.le-clos-parchet.com.*

At this farm-museum, Simone and Pierre Déchavassine give a passionate insight into daily life for the 19C peasants of the region. You can combine a visit here with one to the hamlet of Mathonex.

Point de vue de La Rosière★★
6km/3.7mi. Leave Samoëns by D 907 towards Sixt-Fer-à-Cheval, then immediately left on chemin des Allamands. In 750m/820yds, turn left. 1km/0.6mi after, turn sharply right.

From the chalets at La Rosière, Mont-Blanc appears beautifully framed, from the left in the foreground by the wooded slope of the Criou, and on the right by the formidable, sheer Pointe de Sales. Very close by towards the east is the wild-looking Avoudrues range.

Lac and Col d'Anterne
Alt. 2 264m/7 428ft. 3hrs to the lake, 4hrs to the pass. This route for strong hikers follows GR 5 from the Chalets du Lignon.

A splendid liaison between the Sixt Valley and the Sallanches basin or Chamonix Valley, across the Chaîne des Fiz.

🚗 DRIVING TOUR

3 CIRQUE DU FER-À-CHEVAL★
13km/8mi from Samoëns shown on the Cluses map (see p175). Allow 45min.

Leave Samoëns SE by D 907.

The single street of **Les Vallons** has some fine fountains and a chapel. To explore the narrow **Gorges de Tines**, the gap through which the Giffre bub-

bles, park the car just before the quarry and head right towards the footbridge. Once back at the car, you will enter into the Sixt basin.

Sixt-Fer-à-Cheval★
Like many other communities in Savoie, this traditional village at the top of the Giffre Valley has successfully reinvented itself as an attractive centre for walking and skiing holidays. Its great attraction, however, remains the **Cirque du Fer-à-Cheval** from which it takes its name. Hollowed out by an Ice Age glacier, this horseshoe-shaped ridge is celebrated for the waterfalls which splash down its steep, rocky face and wooded slopes.

Maison de la Réserve Naturelle
Open daily 9am–12.30pm, 2.30–7pm. Free. 04 50 34 91 90.

Three-quarters of the Sixt area has been designated as a nature reserve. This visitor centre in the middle of Sixt village presents a history of the area and an introduction to its flora, fauna and geology.

Cascade du Rouget★★
5km/3mi S from Sixt. Cross the Giffre in Sixt and follow the small road to Salvagny.

Beyond Salvagny, the road runs down to the foot of this double waterfall, the largest in a whole chain of cascades which continues downstream.

Return to D 907, which leads to the famous Cirque du Fer-à-Cheval.

Réserve Naturelle de Sixt★
Created in 1977, this nature reserve was one of the first environmental initiatives put in place by the department of Haute-Savoie. The reserve extends over the whole limestone massif of the Haut-Giffre, whose foothills are next to the Passy Nature Reserve to the south and the Mont Ruan in Switzerland to the north. It covers an area of 9 200ha/ 22 733 acres. With altitudes from 900m/2 953ft to 3 096m/10 157ft, different alpine environments follow, each one rich in a variety of fauna and flora.

The cliffs of the Cirque du Fer-à-Cheval, lakes, the alpine meadows of Praz de Commune and Salvadon, the lapiaz (limestone pavements) of the Grandes Platières, mixed forests and wetlands all create an ever-changing landscape. Heritage is protected in this sanctuary in the Alps, which continue to be exploited.

Cirque du Fer-à-Cheval★★
🅿 *Fee in Jul–Aug.*
The most spectacular sight in the nature reserve. On leaving Sixt, there is a fine view of the pyramid-shaped peak of the Tenneverge (2 985m/9 793ft), and its Corne du Chamois, the "chamois horn", at the end of the basin.
From the lake the road loops to give you an amazing view of the cirque and its waterfalls. In June, as many as 30 stream down the thick limestone walls (500m–700m/1 640ft–2 297ft) and add to the magical attraction of the place. The cirque forms a near-perfect ring, broken only at its north end, where the Giffre has cut a path through the rock.

Fond de la Combe★
🚶 *1hr 30min on foot there and back.*
A marked path branches off at the end of the road, 50m/55yds beyond the kiosk, and leads to the Bout du Monde, the "end of the world", where the Giffre rises at the foot of the Ruan and Prazon glaciers.

ADDRESSES

🛏STAY

😐😐 **Gai Soleil** – ✆04 50 34 40 74. *www.hotel-samoens.com. Closed 21 Apr–4 Jun, 19 Sept–17 Dec.* 🅿. *Wifi. 22 rooms, half-board possible, restaurant*😐😐. At the entrance to the village, this chalet-hotel has dark rooms decorated in Savoyard style, all with a large balcony. A lounge-bar has a fireplace; children's play area in the garden. The restaurant serves local specialities.

😐😐😐 **Edelweiss** – *La Piaz, 1.5km/1mi NW via rte de Plampraz.* ✆04 50 34 41 32. *www.edelweiss-samoens.com. Closed*

10–26 Apr, 23 Jun–10 Jul, 22 Oct–18 Nov. 🅿. *Wifi. 20 rooms, half-board possible, restaurant*😐😐😐. Edelweiss is among the flowers grown in the Jaÿsinia gardens close to this simple, family-owned chalet-hotel. There are panoramic views over the village and the valley. Traditional cuisine is served in the south-facing dining room or on the terrace.

😐😐😐 **Hôtel Le Moulin du Bathieu** – *2km/1.2mi SW of Samoëns towards Vercland (follow Samoëns 1600).* ✆04 50 34 48 07. *www.bathieu.com. Closed Jun–10 Jul and 4 Nov–mid-Dec.* 🅿. *5 rooms.* This old walnut oil mill has a splendid view to the Dents Blanches mountains. Snug rooms sometimes include a mezzanine. Traditional, regional cooking is served in a dining room with wooden beams. Take a look at the perfectly preserved, 100-year-old *grenier* (traditional Savoyard chalet away from the house).

🍴/EAT

😐😐 **Auberge de La Feuille d'Érable** – *In the main village, 74740 Sixt-Fer-à-Cheval.* ✆04 50 34 44 47. *Closed 15 May–15 Jun, 1–26 Oct, 7 Nov–16 Dec. and Mon, Tue lunchtimes.* Exit the village towards the Rouget Waterfall to find this huge Savoyarde house dating from the early 20C. In a rustic little dining room, full of advertising mirrors, you can feast on carefully prepared local dishes.

😐😐 **Le Monde à L'Envers** – *Pl. Criou.* ✆04 50 34 19 36. *Closed 29 May–2 Jul, 24 Oct–14 Dec, Tue, Sept–Jun Wed and winter school holidays.* A very warm atmosphere imbues this restaurant. Tastefully decorated with objects from around the whole world.

🏃ACTIVITIES

This area is very popular in summer, prized for its varied **mountain activities**, **canoeing**, **kayaking** and **rafting** on the Giffre, **paragliding** and **hang gliding** in Samoëns.

In winter, the resort has a large ski area (60km/37.2mi of pistes) reached by the Saix gondola and also linking into the lifts of the Grand Massif area. There are also 90km/56mi of cross-country tracks.

CHAMBÉRY, *Aix-Les-Bains, Bauges, Beaufortain*

Once the capital of the duchy and today the departmental capital of Savoie, it is well worth allocating a few hours to explore Chambéry's old centre. The temptations of spending the rest of your time in the surrounding Savoie heartland are many: from the huge expanse of the Lac du Bourget, through the pretty wine villages of the Combe de Savoie, to the green pastures of the Bauges and the Beaufortain, this is gorgeous countryside to explore in the warm summers, when Savoie's ski slopes seem a distant memory.

France's Largest Inland Lake

On warm weekends and holiday times, a beach-like atmosphere pervades on Aix-les-Bains' waterfront, with its colourful marinas and inviting restaurant terraces. The Lac du Bourget, both the largest and the deepest of inland lakes entirely in France, has been a source of inspiration and contemplation for writers, nobility and religious orders. Hautecombe Abbey is best reached by a delightful cruise across the deep blue waters from the port of Aix. Benedictine, and later Cistercian, monks settled at Hautecombe, also chosen by the Savoie nobility as their burial ground.

Cleaned up in the 1970s, the lake remains ecologically important in part due to its benign, almost Mediterranean climate, which encourages a range of vegetation to grow on its borders, including an expanse of reed beds. Certain areas are almost wild, encouraging a great variety of birds to settle, including raptors, which enjoy the proximity of massive limestone cliffs.

A number of different lake fish are present in the Lac du Bourget, including perch, carp, lake trout, catfish and three typical alpine freshwater fish: *omble chevalier* (a type of char), *féra* and *lavaret*.

Although there are fishing restrictions on some of these, the fish are much prized by the large number of gastronomic, Michelin-starred restaurants in and around the lake.

Highlights

1. Amazing *trompe-l'œil* paintings in **Chambéry**'s cathedral (p185)
2. Take a boat across the Lac du Bourget to visit the **Abbaye de Hautecombe** (p199)
3. The dramatic **Château de Miolans** looming over the Combe de Savoie (p205)
4. In summer enjoy the flower-decked, car-free streets of the medieval town of **Conflans** (p208)
5. A fascinating half-day drive from Beaufort on the **Route du Cormet de Roselend** (p211)

Abbaye de Hautecombe by the Lac du Bourget

© Cinzia8/Dreamstime.com

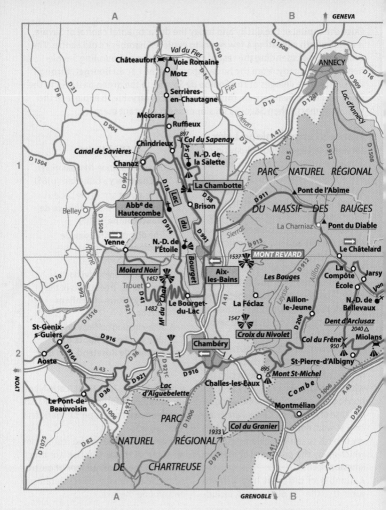

The Prince of Gruyères

In the 19C Brillat-Savarin gave beaufort cheese the nickname "le prince des Gruyères", and today it is considered France's most famous and tastiest hard cheese. It is part of the gruyère family and production is strictly controlled, being AOC since 1968. Beaufort is made from unpasteurised milk from the Tarine and Abondance breeds of cow in a delimited area of the Beaufortain and Tarentaise. Each wheel of cheese weighs 20–70kg/44–154lbs and is aged for six months to a year; the best is labelled "beaufort d'été" (summer beaufort), made when the cows are grazing between June and October.

Mountain Wines

Today, the wines of Savoie are no longer considered only as tipples for skiers. Some serious producers have emerged and are being encouraged by sommeliers in the region's top restaurants. With the biggest concentration of vineyards near Chambéry at the foot of Mont Granier and along the Combe de Savoie towards Albertville, you can taste the wines where they are made and learn about a range of unusual grape varieties. The wine museum at Montmélian is a good place to start.

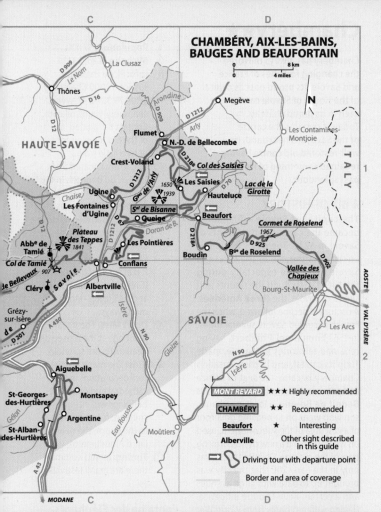

CHAMBÉRY, AIX-LES-BAINS, BAUGES AND BEAUFORTAIN

8 km
4 miles

N

HAUTE-SAVOIE

Le Nom
La Clusaz
D 909
Thônes
D 16
D 12
D 909
Arondine
Megève
D 1212
Les Contamines-Montjoie
Flumet
Arly
N.-D. de Bellecombe
Crest-Voland
D 218a
Col des Saisies
D 1212
Les Saisies
Gce de l'Arly
1650
1939
Ugine
Chaise
Hauteluce
D 70
Lac de la Girotte
Les Fontaines d'Ugine
Sal de Bisanne
Queige
Beaufort
ITALY
Plateau des Teppes
D 1212
Doron de B.
D 218a
Cormet de Roselend
1967
Abbe de Tamié
1841
Les Pointières
Boudin
Bge de Roselend
D 925
D 12
Col de Tamié
907
Conflans
Savoie
D 902
Vallée des Chapieux
de Bellevaux
Cléry
Bourg-St-Maurice
AOSTE
VAL D'ISÈRE
Albertville
Grézy-sur-Isère
A 43
Isère
SAVOIE
Les Arcs
D 201
Glaize
N 90
Isère
N 90
Aiguebelle
Eau Rousse
Moûtiers
St-Georges-des-Hurtières
Montsapey
Gélon
Argentine
A 43
St-Alban-des-Hurtières

MODANE

MONT REVARD ★★★ Highly recommended

CHAMBÉRY ★★ Recommended

Beaufort ★ Interesting

Alberville Other sight described in this guide

Driving tour with departure point

Border and area of coverage

Village of Conflans, near Albertville

P. Huchette/MICHELIN

Chambéry★★

Chambéry has always mirrored the changing fortunes of France and Savoie. Its proud past as capital of the House of Savoie can be seen in its proud château. Today, it remains the centre of the Savoyard heartland, its well-restored old centre having regained something of its past splendour.

A BIT OF HISTORY

The capital of Savoie – Chambéry became the capital of the Counts of Savoie in 1232. The city's fortune is linked with the rise of the House of Savoie and came especially during the 14C–15C through the Counts and Dukes of Savoie, the **three Amédées**. A century of decline followed, when the French occupied Savoie several times. In 1562 **Emmanuel-Philibert**, having regained territories for Savoie, made Turin its capital, and in compensation Chambéry became the seat of justice and administrative centre. In the 1830s **Benoît de Boigne**, a local merchant's son who went on to become governor of a vast area of the subcontinent, used his wealth to build a new city, destroying part of the old one. Despite this, it was only in the early 20C that the city was brought up to date with large avenues and a certain Belle Époque influence. Having suffered badly from World War II bombardments, in the past 20 years the town has seen considerable renovations of its historic quarters such as the Carré Curial.

☛WALKING TOUR

Old Town★★

When you walk through the town, you can see many walls decorated with impressive *trompe-l'œil* paintings such as at the covered market and the Théâtre Charles-Dullin.

▶ *Route shown on the town map (☞see p186). Allow 4hrs to include a visit to the château.*

▶ **Population:** 57 420.
☉ **Michelin Map:** 333 I4.
▣ **Info:** Pl. du Palais-de-Justice, 73000 Chambéry. ✆04 79 33 42 47. www.chambéry-tourisme.com. Contact for guided tours of the old town on foot or by a little train.
▷ **Location:** Located S of the Lac du Bourget, in the depression between the Bauges and Chartreuse massifs, Chambéry is close to the three principal alpine parks of Vanoise, Chartreuse and the Bauges. It is at the junction of A 41 (Grenoble–Annemasse) and A43 (Lyon–Modane) motorways.
☙ **Don't Miss:** The Italian paintings at the Musée des Beaux-Arts are splendid.
👪 **Kids:** The many *trompe-l'œil* decorations in the cathedral and on public buildings will intrigue children; for an outing to the beach, the nearby Lac d'Aiguebelette.
⏱ **Timing:** In mid-summer there are many festivals.

Fontaine des Éléphants

Chambéry's famous monument was erected in 1838 to celebrate **Général Comte de Boigne** (1751–1830), a great benefactor of the town, as a reminder of the time he spent in India.

▶ *Follow bd du Théâtre.*

Théâtre Charles-Dullin

The theatre is named after the actor-director from Savoie. It has retained the original stage curtain painted by Louis Vacca in 1824, depicting *Orpheus' Visit to the Underworld*.

▶ *Continue along bd du Théâtre, which becomes r. Ducis. In the r. de la Croix d'Or, turn right again down passage Métropole.*

Musée Savoisien★

🕐*Open 2nd half Jan–Dec Wed–Mon 10am–noon, 2–6pm.* 🕐*Closed public holidays.* ⌗*3€ (children free).* 📞*04 79 33 44 48.*

The museum is housed in a former Franciscan monastery; the 13C, 15C and 17C buildings, surrounding vast cloisters, contain a large collection of prehistoric and Gallo-Roman exhibits from finds made near the Bourget lake. Primitive art is represented on the first floor by a series of 15C Savoyard paintings on wood. There is also a fine collection of medieval murals painted in the 13C and showing daily life in Savoie.

Cathédrale Métropolitaine St-François-de-Sales★

Known as "Métropole", this was the former church (13C) of a Franciscan monastery. The existing, huge cathedral building dates from the 15C and the 16C, when the Franciscan order was at its height. Saved from ruin in 1810, the interior features an unusually large expanse of amazingly lifelike *trompe-l'œil* decoration by three Italian painters. The lower room of the bell tower is all that remains of the 13C church and includes in the **treasury** a fine Venetian ivory **diptych**★.

▶ *Walk back to r. de la Croix d'Or.*

Rue de la Croix d'Or

This street, lined with old mansions, was the most aristocratic avenue in Chambéry. The **Hôtel de Châteauneuf** at no. 18 was built by an ironmaster in the 17C (remarkable **wrought-iron work**★ in the courtyard). The **Hôtel des Marches et de Bellegarde** at no. 13 opposite has a lovely façade dating from 1788. Napoleon stayed here in 1805; Pope Pius VII had been imprisoned here on the emperor's orders the year before. The restored **place St-Léger**★, paved with pink porphyry and adorned with fountains, is a very pleasant place to sit down for a drink.

Rue Basse-du-Château★

Picturesque footbridge-gallery and old workshops; note in particular the 15C shop at no. 56 and the little 16C tower on the Hôtel du Chabod *(no. 76)*. The street leads to the castle.

Place du Château

Overlooked by the castle, the square is framed by the fine 18C **Hôtel de Montfalcon**, an Italian-style palace, and the 17C **Hôtel Favre de Marnix**. A statue of the brothers **Joseph** and **Xavier Maistre** stands in the centre.

Château★

🗨*The château can be visited only on a guided tour; contact the Bureau du Patrimoine, opposite the Maistre brothers statue.* ⌗*4€.* 📞*04 79 33 42 47.*

Château des ducs de Savoie

© Bertrand Rieger/hemis.fr

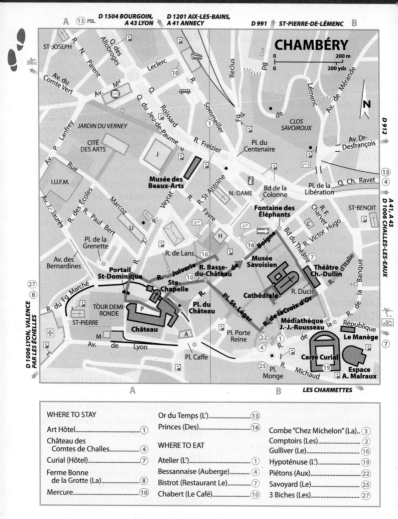

This former residence of the Counts and Dukes of Savoie and occasional home to the Kings of Sardinia was rebuilt in the 14C–15C and partly destroyed by two fires in the 18C.

◗ *Follow the ramp leading to the courtyard surrounded by the Ste-Chapelle and the préfecture buildings.*

The 14C **Tour Trésorie** includes historical documents of Chambéry. The vaulted 14C **Salles Basses** probably served as a chapel and a crypt before the Ste-Chapelle was built.

Ste-Chapelle★

The building was named Ste-Chapelle when the Holy Shroud was deposited inside in 1502 (a replica is displayed). The large tapestry showing the arms of Savoyard towns was made in just two weeks to celebrate the union of Savoie and France. Numerous historic weddings were celebrated inside, including that of Charlotte of Savoie and Louis XI (1423–83) and Alphonse de Lamartine (1790–1869) and his English wife, Marianne-Elisa Birch.

A **carillon of 70 bells** (1993) installed in the Yolande tower and made by a local foundry, is considered to be one of the finest in Europe.

▷ *Near the Tour Demi-Ronde, go down the steps leading to pl. Maché.*

Go through the 15C Flamboyant archway of the **Portail St-Dominique**, part of a Dominican monastery re-erected here in 1892.

▷ *From pl. Maché, start back towards the castle and turn left onto r. Juiverie.*

Rue Juiverie
Bankers and money changers used to live in this pedestrianised street.

▷ *Continue along the narrow r. de Lans leading to pl. de l'Hotel-de-Ville.*

Walk along the covered passage on the right *(nos. 5 and 6 pl. de l'Hôtel-de-Ville)*, one of the many "**allées**" in the old town. Designed by Général de Boigne and lined with arcades as is customary across the Alps, **rue de Boigne**'s orderly yet lively atmosphere makes this one of the town's most characteristic streets. It leads back to the Fontaine des Éléphants.

QUARTIER CURIAL
Most of the buildings in this important military district, dating from the napoleonic period, were restored when the army left in the 1970s.

Carré Curial – ⊙ *The courtyard is open to the public.* These former barracks, built in 1802 and modelled on the Hôtel des Invalides in Paris, have retained their original plan and have been refitted to house shops and offices.

Centre de congrès "Le Manège" – Today a conference centre, this was once the stables for the Sardinian cavalry forces. The modern architecture incorporates a traditional military look.

Jean-Jacques-Rousseau Library – In the form of a vast curve and with a panoramic glass upper level, this was built by the architect Aurelio Galfetti in 1993.

ADDITIONAL SIGHTS
Musée des Beaux-Arts★
⚬▬ *Closed for renovations. Check for opening times and charges.*
𝄢 04 79 33 75 03.

In this fine arts museum, the vaulted room on the ground floor is where the people of Chambéry voted for union with France. There is a large collection of Italian painting: works by Primitive Sienese artists (altarpiece by Bartolo di Fredi), Renaissance paintings, and works from the 17C and the 18C. The 19C is represented by two major trends, Neoclassicism and Realism.

Église St-Pierre-de-Lémenc
⊙ *Open Sat 5–6pm, Sun 9.30–10.30am.* 𝄢 04 79 33 35 53.
On the Lémenc hill, where the original Roman settlement was based, during the height of the Middle Ages this priory was one of the most active Christian centres in Savoie. Thought to have been a Carolingian baptistery, it would have been a reliquary in the 11C. Below the little rotunda, the 15C **crypt**★ in Gothic style was built to support the church above. It houses a 15C *Entombment*, damaged during the Revolution.

AROUND CHAMBÉRY
Les Charmettes
▷ *2km/1.2mi SE. Leave Chambéry on r. Michaud. At the first roundabout out of the town, follow D 4 then drive straight on along the narrow lane to Les Charmettes.* ⊙*Open Apr–Sept Wed–Mon 10am–noon, 2–6pm; Oct–Mar 10am–noon, 2–4.30pm.* ⊙*Closed public holidays.* ⊜*Free.* 𝄢 04 79 33 39 44.
The country house of Madame de Warens, who converted the Calvinist Jean-Jacques Rousseau to Catholicism and which he immortalised in his *Confessions*. Careful restoration has preserved the 18C furnishings; on the ground floor, the dining room has *trompe-l'œil* decoration and the music room recalls Rousseau's musical career.

Challes-les-Eaux
▷ *6km/3.7mi SE by D 1006. From Chambéry, drive E along av. Dr-Desfrançois, N 512, which veers SE and joins N 6.*
This little spa town specialises in the treatment of gynaecological and respiratory diseases.

187

The spring waters contain a high concentration of sulphur. The casino and the baths, in mid-19C style, are situated in a park.

Lac d'Aiguebelette★

 9km/5.6mi W by A 43, see map opposite.
This emerald lake is in a beautiful setting, and has deep, clean waters. The steep and forested eastern shore contrasts with the more accessible western and southern shores where leisure activities are concentrated: walking, fishing, swimming, boating and pedalo rides.

St-Christophe-la-Grotte

Park at the exit of Échelles tunnel. Entrance at the Auberge du Tunnel on D 1006, east exit (Chambéry side) of the tunnel. Guided visits (1hr 15min) Apr–Oct. 6.80€ (children 4.80€). 04 79 65 75 08. www.animgrotte.com.
The two caves at St-Christophe owe much of their reputation to the historical significance as a thousand-year-old thoroughfare. The gorge that separates the caves is a natural tunnel, used since Roman times, and for many years was the only passageway between the Couz Valley and the Échelles basin. The tunnel that exists today was dug on the orders of Napoleon in 1816.
You can visit both caves, the **grotte supérieure** (upper cave) and the lower cave, the **Grand Goulet**★.
From the southern exit there is a pretty **view**★ over the Chartreuse range. If the caves are closed, you can still walk along the interesting **Sardinian way** (1720) to learn about its importance.

DRIVING TOURS

ROUTE DE L'ÉPINE★

Drive of 85km/52.8mi shown on the map opposite. Allow one day.
 Roads between Chambéry and the Lac d'Aiguebelette are busy in season. The Col de l'Épine is closed in winter.

 Leave Chambéry S by D 1006 then turn right on D 916.

Between St-Sulpice and the pass, the road offers a **panorama**★★ of Mont Revard with its cable-car station, and of the huge cross on the Dent du Nivolet; beneath them lie Aix-les-Bains, its lake and the city of Chambéry.

Col de l'Épine

The pass may take its name from a thorn believed to be from Christ's crown of thorns. Beyond the pass, the cliff road offers views of the Lac d'Aiguebelette overlooked by the sparsely forested escarpments of Mont Grelle, with the Chartreuse summits in the background and the Vercors cliffs still further away. D 916 follows the line of the massif to Col de la Crusille, then runs parallel to a small tributary of the Rhône.

St-Genix-sur-Guiers

Close to a bend in the Rhône around the lower Bugey, this old town was once the border between Savoie and France.
Today it remains a link between the departments of Ain, Savoie and Isère and with its proximity to the motorway, has also become a busy tourist centre.

Repaire Louis Mandrin

R. du Faubourg. Open Jul–Aug: 10am–noon, 2–6pm; Sept–Jun Tue–Sun 2–5.30pm. 4€. 04 76 31 63 16. http://repaire-mandrin.com.
An interesting exhibition in the gloomy light of the St-Genix-sur-Guiers tourist office basement, describes the life and times of the famous smuggler Louis Mandrin (1724–55).

 Follow D 1516 SW for 3km/1.8mi.

Aoste

This busy market town once controlled, in Roman times, the traffic between the main city of Vienne (south of Lyon) to Italy via the Petit-St-Bernard Pass. Aoste, named after Emperor Augustus, was a leading producer of pottery and ceramics; the well-displayed exhibits of the **Musée gallo-romain** (open Feb–Nov Wed–Mon 2–6pm; closed public holidays; 4.60€; 04 76 32 58 27)

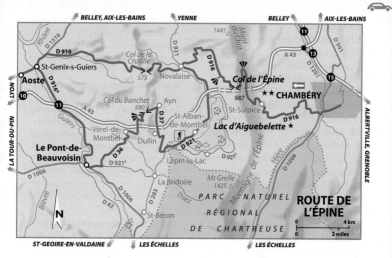

illustrate Roman life and include a fine collection of **ceramics**★.

▷ *Return to D 916A.*

Le Pont-de-Beauvoisin

This was the most vibrant of the old Franco-Savoyard border towns, known for furniture making since the 16C. From the **bridge** spanning the Guiers, there is a pleasant view of the river lined with fine old houses over which towers the steeple of the Église des Carmes.

A reconstruction of an early 20C wood-working workshop can be seen in the **Musée de la Machine à bois** (pl. Trillat; ⊙ open May–Sept Wed–Mon 2–6.30pm Mar–Apr and Oct–mid-Dec Sat–Sun and public holidays 2–6.30pm; ⊙ closed 1 May, 1 Nov; ℘04 76 37 27 90; ⊜4€). On the first floor is a **Resistance museum**.

Leave Le Pont-de-Beauvoisin by D 36 towards Dullin with glimpses over the Montbel countryside, and a good **view**★ on the left before the Col du Blanchet.

▷ *At Ayn take D37 S towards Lac d'Aiguebelette. Follow the road to Novalaise and then back to Chambéry.*

ROUTE DES TROIS COLS★★

Drive ③ of 54km/33.6mi shown on the Chartreuse map (⌂ see p287). Allow 2hrs.

▷ *Leave Chambéry by D 1006 to Col de Couz through the Chartreuse regional park. At Col de Couz, turn right to cross St-Jean-de-Couz; follow D 45.*

Beyond **Col des Égaux** the road runs above Les Échelles basin, then above the Gorges du Guiers Vif. Excellent **view**★ of the Pas du Frou. Corbel stands at the entrance to another valley, out of which D 45 climbs steeply.

Entremont-le-Vieux
♟♟ Musée de l'ours des cavernes

⊙Open mid-Dec–Oct, times vary. ⊜4.40€ (children 2.50€). ⴺ ℘04 79 26 29 87. www.musée-ours-cavernes.com.
The discovery in 1998 of remains of *Ursus spelaeus*, or cave bears, in the Grotte de Balme at Collomb launched intense research into this Ice Age beast.
The narrow route follows the Gorges d'Entremont and the Cozon stream, then climbs to the Mont Granier pass.

Col du Granier★★

This pass opens the way to the Chartreuse Massif from Chambéry. In 1248 a massive landslide buried many villages, forming a huge pile of rocks at the foot of the mountain. Today, the **Abymes de Myans** is covered with vineyards and dotted with lakes.

EXCURSION
Croix du Nivolet★★

Allow 2hrs. ▶ *48km/29.8mi. Leave Chambéry by D 912 heading E, then follow signs to Massif des Bauges.*

Between Villaret and St-Jean-d'Arvey the road rises steeply beneath the cliffs of Mont Peney and the Dent de Nivolet. After a glimpse of the Château de la Bâthie and, on the other side, the wooded gorges of the Bout-du-Monde, literally the "end of the world", a series of tight bends leads to an impressive view of the Chambéry Valley and Mont Granier.

From St-Jean-d'Arvey to Plainpalais, the road runs along the top of the Leysse Valley, until the river vanishes into a fissure in the rock after Les Déserts.

🎿**La Féclaz** –This cross-country ski area is part of the Savoie Grand Revard region. In summer it is a vast walking and mountain-biking area (🚶*2hrs there and back*).

Follow the yellow-marked footpath (*no. 2*) to the Chalet du Sire and continue through the woods.

Go along the Nivolet ridge to reach the **Croix du Nivolet** from where there is a **view**★★ of the Lac du Bourget and the mountains including Mont Blanc.

ADDRESSES

🏠STAY

🛏🍽 **Art Hôtel** – *154 r. Sommeiller.* 𝄢*04 79 62 37 26. www.arthotel-chambery.com.* 🅿. *36 rooms.* This hotel is a stone's throw from the old town and its shopping districts. It offers contemporary comfort and is fully soundproofed. Buffet breakfast.

🛏🍽 **Hôtel Curial** – *371 r. de la République.* 𝄢*04 79 60 26 00.* 🅿. *149 rooms.* A very practical location close to the town centre and the Curial quarter. Rooms, furnished in beech, sleep from one to six people, and kitchenettes are available.

🛏🍽 **L'Or du Temps** – *814 rte de Plainpalais, 73230 St-Alban-Leysse.* 𝄢*04 79 85 51 28. www.or-du-temps.com. Closed 1–10 Jan.* 🅿. *Wifi. 18 rooms, restaurant*🍽🛏.

A nicely restored house, typical of the region and with a splendid view to the Bauges mountains. Bright and modern rooms, and a welcoming restaurant serving modern dishes. Shady terrace.

🛏🍽 **Château des Comtes de Challes** – *247 montée du Château, 73190 Challes-les-Eaux.* 𝄢*04 79 72 72 72. www.chateaudescomtesdechalles.com. Closed 25 Oct–15 Nov. Wifi. 50 rooms, restaurant*🍽🛏. Surrounded by a park with century-old trees, this pretty 15C castle has mainly renovated rooms, some with antiques, other more modern. Inventive cuisine is served in the rustic restaurant in front of a large 1650 fireplace.

🛏🍽 **La Ferme Bonne de la Grotte** – *73360 St-Christophe-la-Grotte.* 𝄢*04 79 36 59 05. www.gites-savoie.com. Wifi. 5 rooms*🛏. Next to the cliffs and the caves, this old farm has cosy and warm rooms. You can also dine here in a charming, authentically Savoyard setting with food to match.

🛏🍽🍽 **Des Princes** – *4 r. Boigne.* 𝄢*04 79 33 45 36. www.hoteldesprinces.eu. Wifi. 45 rooms.* Close to the Elephant statue, this hotel is beautifully decorated with portraits of the "royalty" of Savoie, and themed rooms.

🛏🍽🍽 **Mercure** – *183 pl. de la Gare.* 𝄢*04 79 62 10 11. www.mercure.com.* ♿. *Wifi. 81 rooms.* This hotel opposite the station is easy to get to and functional. Its rooms are spacious and fitted with soundproofing and air-conditioning.

🍷/EAT

🍽 **Aux Piétons** – *30 pl. Monge.* 𝄢*04 79 85 03 81.* At the gates of the old town, several small rooms have been done up to look like old streets with paving on the floor, a pavement and guardrails. Terrace. Friendly atmosphere.

🍽 **Le Café Chabert** – *41 r. Basse-du-Château.* 𝄢*04 79 33 20 35. Closed 1–20 Aug, 20 Dec–2 Jan, Sun and Sat–Thu eves.* This friendly café offers good-value meals in a 14C street below the château.

🍽 **Le Gulliver** – *4 r. de Lans.* 𝄢*04 79 33 36 50. Closed Sun–Mon.* A good place to stop for lunch with a set dish and a menu of savoury crêpes and generous salads. Bistro-style décor.

Le Savoyard – *35 pl. Monge.* *℘04 79 33 36 55.* In a lively part of town is this well-kept restaurant with a pretty terrace. Practical, soundproofed rooms are also available. Car park.

Restaurant Le Bistrot – *6 r. du Théâtre.* *℘04 79 75 10 78. www.restaurant-lebistrot. com. Closed 2 weeks in Aug.* &. Behind the rather austere front is a comfortable bistro with menus on a blackboard and an original take on classic dishes.

Les 3 Biches – *38380 Miribel-les-Échelles.* *℘04 76 55 28 02. Closed 2 weeks Jan, 1 week Jun, 1 week Sept and Sept–Jun Wed.* Generous portions of traditional meals are cooked by the owner in this pleasant family inn at the heart of the village of Miribel.

Auberge Bessannaise – *28 pl. Monge.* *℘04 79 33 40 37. Closed Mon–Tue.* Easily recognised by its terrace and flower boxes outside a traditional building, traditional dishes such as fondue, foie gras, steak, and fish from Lac du Bourget are all well prepared.

L'Hypoténuse – *141 carré Curial.* *℘04 79 85 80 15. www.restaurant-hypotenuse.com. Closed 2 weeks April, 17 Jul–16 Aug and Sun–Mon.* Contemporary décor in keeping with the area, together with stylish furniture and paintings, and traditional cuisine.

L'Atelier – *59 r. de la République.* *℘04 79 70 62 39. www.atelier-chambery.com. Closed 19 Jul–2 Aug and Sun–Mon.* Modern cooking is served here without being too fancy. The atmosphere is bistrot style, trying to be fashionable.

Les Comptoirs – *183 pl. de la Gare.* *℘04 79 96 97 27. www.homtel.fr. Closed Sat lunch and Sun.* A glass pyramid reveals a contemporary dining rooom. Fusion cuisine with Asian influences and a relaxed atmosphere to match.

La Combe "Chez Michelon" – *73610 La Combe.* *℘04 79 36 05 02. www.chez-michelon.fr. Closed mid-Nov– mid-Dec, Mon except lunchtime Apr–Sept and Tue.* 🅿. *5 rooms*. In a wonderful setting above Lac d'Aiguebelette, this restaurant offers lake fish as well as traditional dishes. A superb list of regional wines.

℉ CAFÉS

La Régence – *20 r. d'Italie.* *℘04 79 33 36 77. Open Tue–Sat 8am–12.30pm, 2.30–7pm, Sun 8am–12.30pm.* This chocolate and cake shop with a tea room is renowned for its specialities.

Le Fidèle Berger – *15 r. de Boigne.* *℘04 79 33 06 37. Open Tue–Sat 8am–7pm, Sun 8am–noon. Closed 3 weeks in Aug.* Since 1832, the years have hardly altered this shop: the luxurious décor, magnificent counter, old furniture, wood panelling… In the tea room, you will enjoy delicious pastries and cakes.

⛒ SHOPPING

Confiserie Mazet – *2 pl. Porte-Reine.* *℘04 79 33 07 35. Open Mon 2–6.30pm, Tue–Sat 8.30am–12.30pm, 2–7pm. Closed holidays.* This shop is over 180 years old, as is its most renowned speciality, the *mazet*, a fruit-flavoured acid drop. The ducs de Savoie and the tomme de Savoie with bilberries are among the 70 kinds of chocolate and sweets.

Local tipples – Chambéryzette, a dry vermouth, is flavoured with wild strawberries, while "vermouth de Chambéry", created by the Maison Dolin in 1821, is made by steeping a mixture of herbs in dry white wine.

🏃 ACTIVITIES

Beaches and watersports – Lac d'Aiguebelette has a beach, as well as several pretty areas to bathe. Motorboats are banned on the lake so it is an ideal spot for windsurfers too.

Velostation – *217 r. de la Gare.* *℘04 79 96 34 13. Open Mon–Fri 7am–7pm, Sat–Sun 9am–7pm. Closed Sun and public holidays in winter.* ☜*1€ per hour, 5€ 1 day.* Bicycle rental near the station.

♖ EVENTS

Festival mondial de folklore – *℘04 79 33 42 47. 1st week Jul.* Folk festival.

Les Estivales du château – *℘04 79 70 63 93. Open mid-Jun–end Aug.* In the lower courtyard of the castle a festival of music, dance and theatre.

Aix-les-Bains★★

With a glorious past as a fashionable spa town, Aix is once again emerging as a fine place to visit, not only for the thermal baths, but also for the town itself and, down the hill, its pretty waterside on Lac de Bourget. Over recent years, the fine Belle Époque buildings, notably the baths, the casinos and the splendid palace hotels, have gradually been reopened to welcome visitors.

A BIT OF HISTORY

Taking the waters – Aix's health-giving waters, rich in sulphur and calcium, have been famous for almost 2 000 years. The Romans, who conquered the area, were the first to build spas for medical use; and the name of the town comes from *Aquae Gratianae*, "the waters of Emperor Gratianus".

After a period of neglect, in 1775 Victor-Amédée III, the King of Sardinia, decided to build the new spas, but initially they were only equipped with showers of such very hot water, that those taking the cure often fainted or emerged scarlet in the face, eyes popping out. The treatment offered improved in the 19C with the introduction of the steam bath and shower-massage.

The splendour of Aix-les-Bains – The expansion of the spa town, which began in 1860, reached its peak during the Belle Époque. Luxury hotels were built in order to attract the aristocracy and monarchs of Europe: the "Victoria", for instance, welcomed Queen Victoria on three occasions, whereas the Splendide and the Excelsior counted among their guests a maharajah from India, the Emperor of Brazil and Empress Elizabeth ("Sissi") of Austria-Hungary.

Most of the buildings were designed by an architect from Lyon, **Jules Pin the Elder** (1850–1934), whose masterpiece was the Château de la Roche du Roi. After World War II, most of these magnificent hotels closed down for economic reasons. Today, the life of the spa town is concentrated round the baths, the municipal park with its vast open-air

- ▶ **Population:** 27 267.
- ⊙ **Michelin Map:** 333 I3.
- ℹ **Info:** Pl. Maurice-Mollard, 73100 Aix-les-Bains. ℘04 79 88 68 00. www.aixlesbains.com. The tourist office organises various guided tours.
- ▶ **Location:** Aix-les-Bains lies at the foot of Mont Revard, on the eastern shore of Lac du Bourget. Follow A 41 and A 43, 10km/6.2mi from Chambéry.
- 🅿 **Parking:** The town hall car park is located at the heart of the town, near spas, gardens and pedestrian malls.
- ⊙ **Don't Miss:** The Faure museum for the bronze sculptures by Rodin.
- 🕐 **Timing:** Try to spend an evening in town, strolling along the lakeside.

theatre, the Palais de Savoie and the new casino, as well as along the lake with its beach and marinas.

The two main spas, **thermes Pellegrini** (1832) and **thermes Chevalley** (2000), are open year-round, fed by two springs, the sulphur spring and the alum spring.

🐾 WALKING TOURS

The Roman Town★

▶ *Begin at tourist information.*

Thermes Nationaux and Caves

For visits, contact the tourist office.

Inaugurated in 1783, renovated and enlarged during the 19C, the baths were completed by the Nouveaux Thermes in 1934, and modernised in 1972.

The **caves**, reached from outside along a 98m/107yd gallery, include one of the sources of Aix's sulphurous waters. There are **roman remains** of a caldron and a round pool in the Anciens Thermes.

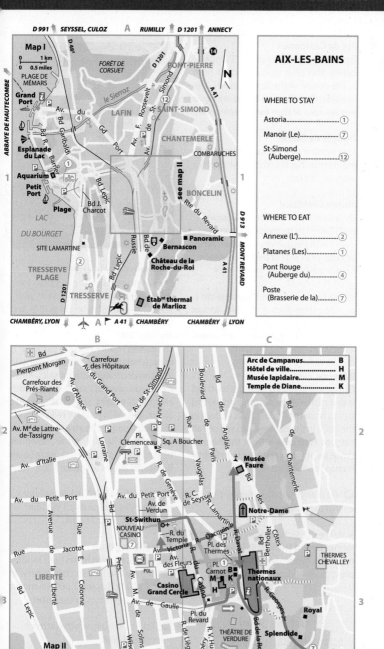

Map I

0 — 1 km
0 — 0.5 miles

A — D 991 — SEYSSEL, CULOZ — RUMILLY — D 1201 — ANNECY

FORÊT DE CORSUET

D 48ᵉ
D 1201

PONT-PIERRE

N

PLAGE DE MÉMARS

Grand Port

Av. du Gd Port

Av. F. Roosevelt

le Sierroz

LAFIN

SAINT-SIMOND

⑫

A 41

ABBAYE DE HAUTECOMBE

Bd Garibaldi
R. Barbier

Esplanade du Lac

Aquarium

Petit Port

Plage

Bd Lepic

Bd J. Charcot

CHANTEMERLE

COMBARUCHES

see map II

BONCELIN

Rte du Revard

LAC DU BOURGET

SITE LAMARTINE

②

Bd de Russie

Bernascon

Panoramic

Château de la Roche-du-Roi

TRESSERVE PLAGE

D 1201

Bd Lepic

TRESSERVE

D 913 — MONT REVARD

A 41

Étabᵗ thermal de Marlioz

CHAMBÉRY, LYON — A 41 — CHAMBÉRY — CHAMBÉRY — LYON

AIX-LES-BAINS

WHERE TO STAY

Astoria.................... ①
Manoir (Le)................ ⑦
St-Simond (Auberge)............... ⑫

WHERE TO EAT

Annexe (L')................. ②
Platanes (Les)............. ①
Pont Rouge (Auberge du)............ ④
Poste (Brasserie de la)........... ⑦

Arc de Campanus................ B
Hôtel de ville................ H
Musée lapidaire................ M
Temple de Diane................ K

Map II

0 — 200 m
0 — 200 yds

Bd Pierpont Morgan

Carrefour des Hôpitaux

Av. du Grand Port

Carrefour des Prés-Riants

Av. d'Alsace

Av. Mᵈ de Lattre-de-Tassigny

Av. d'Italie

Av. du Petit Port

Pl. Clemenceau

Sq. A Boucher

Bd des Anglais

Bd de Paris

Rue de Genève

Av. du Petit Port

Av. de Verdun

R. C. de Seyssel

R. Lamartine

Boulevard des Côtes

Bd de Chantemerle

Musée Faure

Notre-Dame

St-Swithun

NOUVEAU CASINO

R. du Temple

Av. Victoria

Av. des Fleurs

R. Dacquin

Pl. des Thermes

R. Davat

Bd Berthollet

THERMES CHEVALLEY

LIBERTÉ

Bd Lepic

Rue de Jacotot

Av. de la Liberté

Colonne

Casino Grand Cercle

Pl. ①

Carnot

M B K

H

Thermes nationaux

R. Georges 1ᵉʳ

Royal

Av. de Gaulle

Pl. du Revard

R. de Liège

R. V. Hugo

R. de Chambéry

R. S. Monard

THÉÂTRE DE VERDURE

Bd de la Roche-du-Roi

Splendide

⑦

Map II

D 50

Av. de

Tresserve

CENTRE DES CONGRÈS

LE BOIS VIDAL

Arc de Campanus

Erected by a member of the "Pompeia" family, this arch stood 9m/30ft high in the centre of the Roman town. The remains of the **Roman baths** only give a rough idea of their former splendour.

Temple de Diane

This remarkable rectangular Roman monument has its stones set in place without mortar.

Musée Lapidaire

Entry by the tourist office. ☎☎*Guided visit (45min) by reservation 1 month ahead with the guides association Au fil de l'eau, or as part of the Gallo-Roman tours organised by the tourist office.* ℘*04 79 61 06 57.*

In the Diana room of this museum is an interesting display of Gallo-Roman remains including fragments of precious stones, ceramics, glass and coins as well as an impressive marble bath.

Hôtel de Ville

Of a typical Savoyard style, the town hall is in a castle of the Marquis de Seyssel dating from the Middle Ages (rebuilt in the 16C). In the hallway, you will see an elegant **staircase**★ from the Renaissance, incorporating stones from nearby Roman monuments.

▷ *Go along the r. du Casino, to the west of the Hôtel de Ville.*

Note the Classic Italianate façade on the former **Grand Hôtel** (1853) on the corner of the casino, once one of the most prestigious addresses in town.

A Love Story

In 1816 Aix-les-Bains was the setting of one of the most famous love stories in French literature, between the Romantic poet Alphonse de Lamartine and Julie Charles, who died a year later and inspired the lines of "Le Lac".

Le Casino Grand Cercle

© Franck Guiziou/hemis.fr

Le Casino Grand Cercle★

The casino remains the symbol of the splendour of the spa town at its peak. The building itself dates from 1849, but the rooms, which are well worth visiting, are from 1883.

The **games room**★ (1883) in particular is impressively spacious and colourful with a ceiling decorated with mosaics. Antonio Salviati covered the five cupolas with allegorical figures, signs of the zodiac and genies, all in tones of red and gold. The Belle Époque **theatre** seems somehow to have kept alive the memories of actors who played there, from Sarah Bernhardt to Luis Mariano.

▷ *Turn left on r. du Casino until you reach av. Victoria, go down this road and then take r. du Temple.*

Église St-Swithun

This Anglican church was built in 1869, funded by the British community. In 1884 3 000 British and 2 000 Americans were regular visitors to the resort.

▷ *Take r. Dacquin, which you reach from r. de Genève.*

Église Notre-Dame

The church was inaugurated in 1900 when the resort was at its peak. It is based on a mixture of Byzantine and Roman styles. The chancel has 12 paintings (17C) representing the Apostles.

Musée Faure★
🕐*Open March–Oct Wed–Mon 10am–noon, 1.30–6pm; rest of year Wed–Sun 10am–noon, 1.30–6pm* 🕐*Closed 20 Dec–5 Jan and public holidays.* 📷*Guided visits on request.* ⊖*4.70€ (children free).* ♿ 📞*04 79 61 06 57.*

In 1942 Dr Faure bequeathed to the town a rare collection of paintings and sculptures including a large number of **works by the Impressionists** and their lesser-known predecessors. Sculptures include the powerful *l'Homme qui marche* by **Rodin**.

▶ *Return to the thermal baths and go up the r. Georges 1er at the back.*

La Corniche des Palaces
This quarter of Aix, on the edge of the cliff, enjoys a fine view over the resort and in the Belle Époque era became the prime building area. Here you can admire the façades of some of the smart hotels such as the **Royal**, **Splendide** and the **Panoramic**, and returning to the Congress centre the **Bernascon**. Their lavishly worked conservatories are examples of an eclectic mix of building styles using modern materials such as cast iron, metalwork and glass.

From there, along the cliff road you will reach the fairy-tale **Château de la Roche-du-Roi**. You can also see the shady park with the **thermes de Marlioz**, famous for its respiratory cures.

Lakeshore
The rue de Genève *(partly pedestrianised)*, rue du Casino and adjacent streets together form the main Aix shopping area. During the summer season, the lakeside becomes the other main point of attraction for the town with two marinas and a beach.

Esplanade★ – This vast open space (10ha/25 acres) is equipped with children's games and picnic tables. A shaded alleyway along the Lac du Bourget calls for pleasant walks with views across the lake to the Hautecombe Abbey and the steep slopes of the Dent du Chat.

Petit Port – This is a fishing port and a marina with a beach at the end. An aquarium at 🎣**La Maison du lac du Bourget** (🕐*open Jul–Aug daily 10am–7pm, Feb–Apr and Oct–Nov 2–6pm, May–Jun and Sept 10am–12.30pm, 2–7pm;* ⊖*6.50€ (children 4–12 5.30€);* 📞 *04 79 61 08 22; www.aquarium-lacdubourget.com),* containing around 50 freshwater species in their natural environment, with educational displays of plankton, stuffed lake birds and more, provides an educational experience to learn about the life of the lake.

EXCURSION
Mont Revard★★★
Alt. 1 537m/5 043ft.

▶ *21km/13mi E by D 913.*

Towards Trévignon are views back to Aix-les-Bains, initially seeming cut off by the lake and the Tresserve hill. Continue towards Mont Revard driving along the cliff. Le Revard is geographically the last peak of the Bauges to the east. The **panorama★★★** is splendid: to the west, there is an aerial view of the Lac du Bourget, the Dent du Chat, the Rhône like a shiny ribbon in the distance and Aix-les-Bains in the foreground; to the east, there is a fine vista of Mont Blanc behind a series of forested heights.

Le Revard is well known as a cross-country ski area (🌊*see La Féclaz p190).*

ADDRESSES

🏨STAY
🍴 **Auberge St-Simond** – *130 av. St-Simond.* 📞*04 79 88 35 02. www.saintsimond.com. Closed 15 Dec–25 Jan, Sun eve and Oct–Apr Mon lunch.* ♿ 🅿. *Wifi. 24 rooms, restaurant*🍴🍴.

A popular hotel known for its pleasant atmosphere, well-kept individual rooms and a pretty garden with pool. Well-prepared, simple traditional food is offered. There is a terrace.

🍴🍴 **Le Manoir** – *37 r. Georges 1er.* 📞*04 79 61 44 00. www.hotel-lemanoir.com. Closed 19 Dec–9 Jan.* 🅿. *Wifi. 73 rooms, restaurant*🍴🍴. In buildings in the grounds of the old Splendide and Royal palaces, the most refined rooms here are to be found in the Villa Grimotière from 1900. There is a very pleasant indoor pool and spa in the main building. The traditional dining room extends into a veranda and terrace overlooking the pretty floral, well-kept garden.

😊😊🛏🛏 **Astoria** – *Pl. des Thermes. ✆04 79 35 12 28. www.hotelastoria.fr. Closed 1 Dec–31 Mar. Wifi. 94 rooms, restaurant😊😊.* A relic of Aix's famous past, this old palace-hotel (1906) is opposite the baths. The Belle Époque décor has been restored; rooms are comfortable and modern. The Art Nouveau style has been preserved in the elegant, large dining room.

⚥ EAT

😊 **Brasserie de la Poste** – *32 av. Victoria. ✆04 79 35 00 65. Closed Sun eve–Mon.* This family-run establishment has won a loyal local clientele. The terrace opens on the street and the principal dining room is enlivened by models of boats. Daily menu written on a slate in traditional style.

😊 **L'Annexe** – *205 bord du Lac, 73100 Tresserve. ✆04 79 35 25 64. www.restaurant-lannexe.com. Closed 15 Feb–1 Mar, 19 Dec–3 Jan and Sun–Mon.* Overlooking the lake, this modern pavilion serves meals in a tidy, contemporary dining room or on its panoramic terrace. Fusion cuisine.

😊😊 **Auberge du Pont Rouge** – *151 av. du Grand-Port. ✆04 79 63 43 90. Closed Sun eve–Mon, Tue eve and Wed eve.* In a prettily renovated dining room in contemporary style or on the terrace you can enjoy daily menus from the blackboard or indulge in their specialities from southwest France and lake fish.

😊😊 **Les Platanes** – *Petit Port. ✆04 79 61 40 54. www.lesplatanes-aix-les-bains.com. Closed Nov–Jan. 14 rooms😊😊.* Near the lake, a paradise for jazz lovers. Patrons can dine to the rhythm of mini-concerts on Fridays and Saturdays, enjoying lake fish and fresh frogs' legs. There is a pleasant terrace in the shade of plane trees.

🛒 SHOPPING

La Royale – *2 r. Albert 1er. ✆04 79 35 08 84. Open Mon–Sat 9am–noon, 2.30–7pm, Sun 10am–12.30pm. Closed 1–15 Feb, 1–15 Jul.* Chocolate is the speciality here. The variety is dazzling and their house specialities delicious.

Les Artisanales – *Quai J.-Baptiste-Charcot. ✆04 79 88 68 00. Open mid-May–mid-Sept Wed 2–7pm.* Find local crafts and farm products at this weekly afternoon market: charcuterie, cheese, leather goods and wooden objects.

🍸 NIGHTLIFE

Casino Grand Cercle – *200 r. du Casino. ✆04 79 35 16 16. www.casinograndcercle. com. Open Fri–Sat and public holidays 11am–4am, Sun–Thu 11am–3am.* This 19C thermal spa architecture has preserved its opulent interior design, including the Italian theatre and the Salviati room with its magnificent mosaic ceilings. Roulette, blackjack, stud poker, boule and 175 slot machines. Irish pub, piano-bar, restaurants, discothèque and tea-dancing outside.

Colisée – *200 r. du Casino. ✆04 79 35 16 16. www.casinograndcercle.com. Open Mon–Sat 7pm–2am, Sun 4pm–1am.* In a stylish setting with décor inspired by the 1930s, relax in the piano-bar inside the casino.

🚴 ACTIVITIES

Beaches – Aix-les-Bains has three beaches where you can swim, one of which is managed by the city and has a nautical sports centre with a range of activities. The two other beaches, Aix-Mémars and Aix-Rowing, have lifeguards in season as well as restaurants nearby, or bring a picnic.

Croisières sur le lac – *Compagnie des bateaux du lac du Bourget et du haut. ✆04 79 88 92 09. www.gwel.com.* You can enjoy a one-hour cruise or the entire day on Lac du Bourget, the canal of Savières and the Haut-Rhône, with or without meals on board. Also, they can organise party or conference cruises with cocktails or tastings.

🍷 EVENTS

Lac en fête – A big festival at the Petit Port on the last Sunday in July *(shuttle bus to the town centre).* You can spend the whole day by the lake, where activities start with a Mass followed by free entertainments and mini-cruises.

Lac du Bourget★★

With its clear, deep waters and its impressive mountain setting, the Lac du Bourget has attracted visitors ever since the Romantic poet Lamartine celebrated the changing colour of its waters and the wild beauty of its steep shores. Today, hikers, cyclists and sailors all enjoy its mild climate and the gentle landscape of its surroundings.

A BIT OF HISTORY

This is the largest natural lake in France (4 500ha/11 120 acres), and the deepest (145m/476ft).

Unlike Lac d'Annecy, it has never been known to freeze in winter. Windstorms can be extremely violent. Part of an ongoing clean-up project in recent years, its waters abound in fish.

🚗 DRIVING TOURS

The most impressive view of the lake is from La Chambotte (see p200).

1 LAKE TOUR★★
Drive of 58km/36mi shown on the Lac du Bourget map (see p198). Allow 3hrs from Aix-les-Bains.

- ⚲ **Michelin Map:** 333 H/I 3/4.
- 🅸 **Info:** Pl. du Gén-Sevez, 73370 Le Bourget-du-Lac. ☎04 79 25 01 99. www.bourgetdulac.com.
- **Location:** The lake is 13km/8.1mi N of Chambéry.
- **Don't Miss:** One of the many panoramic viewpoints of the lake; a stroll in the village of Chanaz by the Savières Canal; a drive through the amazing Val du Fier.
- **Timing:** Ferries cross the lake daily, between Aix-les-Bains and the abbey of Hautecombe.

The road overlooking the western shore of the lake clings to the steep slopes of the Mont du Chat and the Mont de la Charvaz, offering superb vistas.
On the east side, the road runs close to the lake at the foot of the cliffs of the Mont de Corsuet, revealing the changing moods and colours of the lake.

▷ *Leave Aix by D 1201 towards Chambéry.*

The road, skirting the foot of Tresserve hill, follows the low-lying shore opposite the Dent du Chat.

Lac du Bourget from La Chambotte

© Franck Guiziou/hemis.fr

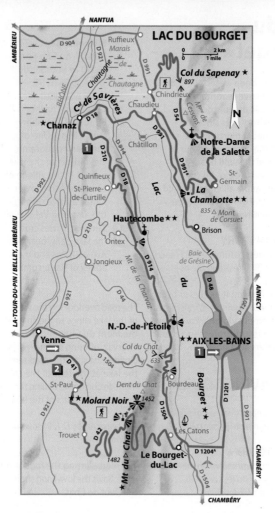

Le Bourget-du-Lac

This lakeside town, once linked by steamers to Lyon via the Canal de Savières and the Rhône, is now a holiday resort with a harbour and a beach. Built on an ancient religious site, the **church** (⊙ *all year; for guided tours contact the tourist office*) was rebuilt in the 13C and remodelled in the 15C and 19C. Don't miss the **frieze**★ on the choir screen around the altar, considered to be a masterpiece of 13C Savoie sculpture.

The **priory** (👣 *guided tours Jul–Aug Tue and Sat 3.30pm, Thu 4pm*) is adjacent to the church, and was built in the 11C by St Odilon, Abbot of Cluny, then remodelled in the 13C and 15C. Attractive gardens are planted with different shrubs, trimmed to look like chess pieces.

Château Thomas II – *Near the mouth of the Leysse.* 👣 *Guided tours Jul–Aug Tue and Sat 4–5pm, Wed 10am–noon.*

The hunting lodge of the Dukes of Savoie was the scene of intrigue until the 15C. The nearby marshland has been turned into a reserve.

▶ *Continue along D 1504; at the second intersection signposted Bourdeau, turn left onto D 914 for Abbaye de Hautecombe.*

The road rises above the lake towards the Col du Chat; from the second hairpin bend, there is a fine **panorama**★ of the Chambéry Valley.

The indented Massif d'Allevard appears in the distance, and the Grand Som above the Grande Chartreuse monastery appears at the end of the Hières Valley.

Chapelle Notre-Dame de l'Étoile

15min return on foot. The path leads off a wide bend of D 914.

From the platform in front, there is a fine **view**★★ of the lake and its frame of mountains including the Grand Colombier, the Semnoz and Mont Revard.

After crossing a plain, just beyond Petit-Villard, the road dips into a valley.

After the fork in the road at Ontex, with the Jura in the distance, you swing into the valley of St-Pierre-de-Curtille. The road descends towards the north end of the lake and the Château de Châtillon.

▷ *Turn right onto D 18 to the Abbaye royale de Hautecombe.*

Abbaye de Hautecombe★★

You can visit the abbey by taking a boat cruise, from Aix-les-Bains, with a stop at the abbey. Audio-guides are included. 7 Feb–11 Nov 9am–noon, 2–6pm. ⊚13€. ℘04 79 88 92 09. www.gwel.com.

In a magnificent setting, Hautecombe was the chosen burial place of 42 members of the House of Savoie, including **Béatrix de Savoie** (1198–1266), whose ambitions for her beautiful four daughters were more than fulfilled when three of them became queens (of England, France and the Two Sicilies) and the fourth, Empress of Germany.

During the 19C, the **church** (⊙open Wed–Mon spring–autumn 10–11.15am, 2–5pm; winter 10–11.15am, 2.30–5pm; *guided visits possible (30min)*) was entirely restored in Gothic Revival style by artists from Piedmont, which explains the profusion of ornamentation, including **300 statues**★★ in marble, stone or gilded wood.

Near the landing stage, the **grange batelière** (water barn), built by Cister-

cian monks in the 12C, was designed to store goods reaching the abbey by boat; the barrel-vaulted lower part comprises a wet dock and a dry dock.

▷ *Return to D 914 and follow to Quinfieux; then take D 210 to Chanaz.*

Chanaz★

Situated on the banks of the Canal de Savières, this lively old border town found a new purpose when the canal was opened to pleasure boats. There is an oil mill still producing walnut oil.

Maison de Boigne (today, the town hall) – Dating from the 17C, is notable for having two entrance main doors. General de Boigne bought it in 1831 (*see Chambéry*).

Musée Gallo-Romain – *In the Chapelle Notre-Dame-de-la-Miséricorde. ⊙Open Jul–Aug daily 2.30–6.30pm; Apr–Jun and Sept–Oct Fri–Mon 2.30–6.30pm. ℘04 79 52 11 84. ⊚3€ (children 2.30€).* A 5C pottery workshop, once one of the most important in the Rhône-Alpes region, was excavated at Portout (1976–87). On display is a rich collection of glazed ceramics, articles of daily use, money and jewellery.

▷ *From Chanaz, drive along D 18 towards Aix-les-Bains.*

Canal de Savières

This canal connects the Lac du Bourget to the Rhône and acts as a "safety valve" when, after the spring thaw or heavy autumn rains, the flow is reversed and the river overflows into the lake.

▷ *At Chaudieu, turn right on D 991 to return to Aix-les-Bains.*

From here the route runs almost all alongside the lake with glimpses to the Dent du Chat and the Hautecombe Abbey.

As the road narrows, you will pass **Brison-les-Oliviers**, a sunny village (hence the evocation of "oliviers" or olive trees) of fishermen and winegrowers, and then reach the lovely Grésine Bay, before reaching Aix-les-Bains.

LA CHAUTAGNE

Drive of 50km/31mi shown on the
Lac du Bourget map (see p198).
Allow 3hrs from Chindrieux.

This small area of Savoie runs along the east side of the upper Rhône, and is a country of vineyards, marshes and poplars, with the Savières Canal and the Lac du Bourget adding to its charm. Its mild climate explains its varied agriculture and nickname "Provence de Savoie".

In Roman times, the admiral of the boatmen of the upper Rhône used the strategic position of today's 13C **Château de Châtillon** (⊶ *closed to the public*) in **Chindrieux** to control one of the most important lines of communication in Gaul. The village is notable for its stone walls and staircases supporting the vineyards. The pebbled Châtillon beach has a lovely view of the lake.

▷ *Take D 56, then D 991B along the side of the Cessens mountain up towards Chambotte. Turn right just before the chapel.*

View from the Restaurant de la Chambotte★★

Splendid **view** over the Lac du Bourget and the mountains lining its shores; in the distance are the Allevard, Grande-Chartreuse and southern Jura massifs.

▷ *Return to La Chambotte and turn right on D 991B. At St-Germain, take D 58 N towards the Col du Sapenay.*

Chapelle Notre-Dame de la Salette

This chapel was where the monks of Hautecombe first settled; the **view**★ extends over agricultural valleys.

In a more mountainous setting of pine trees and woods, **Col du Sapenay**★ pass (alt. 897m/2 943ft) is a popular launching place for paragliders and hang gliders.

The road winds down to the Chautagne plain, with views to the lake, the abbey, the Rhône and the mountains.

▷ *Turn right on D 991 following through vineyards and villages to Motz. Take D 14 (towards Rumilly) to St-André.*

Val du Fier★

The subject of many local legends, this impressive route was cut through a narrow gorge by the Romans, then later abandoned until 1855 when it began to be restored. Just before the second tunnel, on the left a short path leads to a gate protecting the entry of the **voie romaine du val du Fier**, the remaining section of the original 1C road dug 75m/246ft into the rock and linking the Albainais with the Rhône Valley.

2 ROUTE DU MONT DU CHAT

Drive of 34km/21.1mi shown on the
Lac du Bourget map (see p198).
Allow 2hrs.

Yenne

▯ *50 r. A.-Laurent, 73170 Yenne. ☎04 79 36 71 54. www.yenne-tourisme.fr.*

The small capital of the Bugey Savoyard region is at the entrance of the Défilé de Pierre-Châtel, through which the Rhône forces its way out of the Alps. The town centre offers pleasant walks through streets lined with old houses. The **church** (12C–15C) includes finely sculpted wooden **pews**★ (15C) from the Chartreuse de Pierre-Châtel.

▷ *From Yenne take D 41; from St-Paul continue S on D 41 past Trouet, then left onto D 42 towards Lac du Bourget.*

Mont du Chat★

A pylon stands south of the pass. Fine **view** from the platform below.

Molard Noir★★ ▯*1hr return on foot from Mont du Chat.* Follow the ridge to the north, through the woods; from the clifftop on the west side, a fine stretch of the Rhône Valley can be seen from the Défilé de Pierre-Châtel north to the Grand Colombier.

The top of Molard Noir offers a **panorama** of Mont Revard and of Aiguilles de Chamonix, Mont Blanc, the Vanoise Massif, the Belledonne and Mont Granier.

ADDRESSES

See also addresses in Aix-les-Bains.

STAY

Hôtel Le Clos du Lac – *85 rte du Bourget-du-Lac, 73420 Viviers-du-Lac. 04 79 54 40 07. www.monalisahotels.com. 40 rooms.* A chain hotel managed by friendly, competent staff. In the back, a garden with a large green lawn is perfect for relaxation.

Ombremont – *73370 Le Bourget-du-Lac, 2km/1.2mi N on D 1504. 04 79 25 00 23. www.hotel-ombremont. com. Closed 3–23 Jan, 15 Nov–4 Dec and Dec–Apr Mon–Tue. Wifi. 17 rooms.* Set in a wooded park with flower beds. Most of the pretty, individually decorated rooms have idyllic views over the lake. Lovely swimming pool.

EAT

Auberge de Savières – *73310 Chanaz. 04 79 54 56 16. Closed Jan–Feb, Tue and Wed eve in Mar and Dec.* Some people moor their boats opposite this inn after a trip along the Savières canal. Or you might like to cruise in one of the restaurant's own boats, before sitting down to family recipes by the side of the canal.

Beaurivage – *1171 bd du Lac, 73370 Le Bourget-du-Lac. 04 79 25 00 38. www. beaurivage-bourget-du-lac.com. Closed 18 Oct–20 Nov, Sun eve, Thu and Sept–Jun Wed. 4 rooms.* A large and inventive menu based on regional products including lake fish can be served on the shady terrace. The comfortable rooms enjoy a lake view.

Les Oliviers – *212 rte de Paris, 73100 Brison-St-Innocent. 6km/3.7mi N of Aix-les-Bains by D 48 and D 991. 04 79 54 21 81. http://restaurant-les-oliviers.com. Closed 21–28 Jun, 25 Oct–2 Nov and Sun eve–Mon.* Facing the lake, the smart dining room has a fireplace. The chef offers contemporary cuisine and some regional dishes using fresh local products, according to the season. Shaded terrace in summer.

Atmosphères – *618 rte des Tournelles, 73370 Les Catons. 04 79 25 01 29. www.atmospheres-hotel.com. Closed 18 Oct–11 Nov and Tue–Wed. 4 rooms.* Modern décor with a view to the lake provides a fine backdrop for this excellent, creative chef who serves up very tasty, but delicate and balanced dishes. Modern-style, comfortable rooms.

Auberge Lamartine – *73370 Le Bourget-du-Lac. 3.5km/2.2mi N on D 1504. 04 79 25 01 03. www.lamartine-marin. com. Closed 20 Dec–20 Jan, Sun eve, Mon except public holidays and Sept–May Tue lunch.* Time stands still at this restaurant above the lake. Elegant cuisine is served attentively with fine wines, either in the warm dining room or on the gorgeous terrace.

La Grange à Sel – *73370 Le Bourget -du-Lac. 04 79 25 02 66. www.lagrange asel.com. Closed 2 Jan–12 Feb, Sun eve and Wed.* This old salt storage barn has an interior with old stonework and beams, and a lovely, shady garden. The chef will delight you with his carefully chosen specialities.

SHOPPING

Caves de Chautagne – *73310 Ruffieux. 04 79 54 27 12. www.cave-de-chautagne.com. Open daily 9am–noon, 2–6pm.* Large choice of wines to taste and buy.

ACTIVITIES

A **brochure** is available from tourist offices in **Aix-les-Bains, Chanaz** and Le Bourget-du-Lac/Bourdeau detailing the **watersports** facilities provided on the lake such as windsurfing, scuba diving and waterskiing.

EVENTS

Fête médiévale – *3rd week in Jul in Le-Bourget-du-Lac.* Medieval festival with costume parades and fireworks over the lake.

VISITS

Moulin à huile (1868) – *Chanaz. 04 79 54 56 32. Open Mar–Sept daily 10.30am– noon, 2.30–6pm.* Free visit of the mill with a demonstration of how walnut and hazelnut oil are made.

Les Bauges★

The Bauges mountain range stands tall with its high limestone cliffs looming above the valley. Protected by its status as a regional park, you will discover a relaxing landscape of high alpine pastures, woods and traditional villages, criss-crossed by the Chéran river. This is a friendly mountain area, and the walking paths will occupy you for some time.

BAUGES REGIONAL PARK

Maison du Parc, 73630 Le Châtelard.
Open Mon–Fri 8am–noon, 1.30–5.30pm. Closed 2 weeks at Christmas and public holidays. 04 79 54 86 40. www.parcdesbauges.com.

The **Réserve nationale des Bauges**, created in 1950 and home to 600 chamois and 300 mouflons, stretches across 5 500ha/13 590 acres.

Since 1995, the **Parc naturel régional du massif des Bauges** has been responsible for conservation and development of facilities within an area covering over 81 000ha/200 148 acres including 58 towns and villages over the Bauges Préalpes ranging from 270m/886ft to 2 217m/7 274ft in altitude. The village of Châtelard marks the boundary between the "Bauges Derrière" with its broad, grassy plateaux and the rockier "Bauges Devant" with the highest summits. Until the end of the 19C, villages rang with the sound of nails being formed on anvils, metalwork being once an important economic activity.

The **Réserve cynégétique des Bauges** (National Game and Wildlife Preserve of the Bauges) contains more than 1 000 chamois as well as numerous mouflons, roe deer and black grouse. Fifteen nature trails *(3–7hrs)* bring you closer to the wildlife *(04 50 52 22 56 or 04 79 54 84 28).*

🚗 DRIVING TOURS

1 LA TRAVERSEE DES BAUGES
Drive of 60km/37.3mi shown on the Bauges map opposite. Allow 3hrs.

Michelin Map: 333 J/K 4.

Info: Pl. Grenette, 73630 Le Châtelard. 04 79 54 84 28. www.lesbauges.com.

Location: In a triangle formed by Chambéry, Annecy and Albertville. Whichever town you choose to leave from, you will have to follow winding mountain roads across imposing natural barriers: the Croix du Nivolet, Mont Revard or the Montagne du Charbon.

Kids: Consider renting a donkey for the day to trek across the Bauges.

Timing: Allow time for double-tracking when you drive through the Bauges.

▷ *Leave Chambéry on D 1006 towards Albertville, take D 11 at the crossroads, and follow towards Curienne.*

Beyond Leysse, there is a clear view of the Chambéry Valley, with Mont Granier towering above, and of the junction of the Chambéry, Combe de Savoie and Grésivaudan valleys, with the Allevard Massif in the background.

▷ *From Le Boyat, follow the lane to Montmerlet. Continue on foot .*

Mont St-Michel★

Head uphill on the path to the right. Always follow the most obvious route and as you enter the woods, turn right to arrive at the Chapelle du Mont St-Michel. Notice the huge diversity of the forest with the rocky hillsides attracting young oaks, boxwood and a group of Montpellier maples.

From the top, there is a bird's-eye **view** of the Chambéry Valley, with the snow-capped peaks of the Belledonne range in the distance. The Lac du Bourget is partly visible to the northwest, with the Mont du Chat towering above.

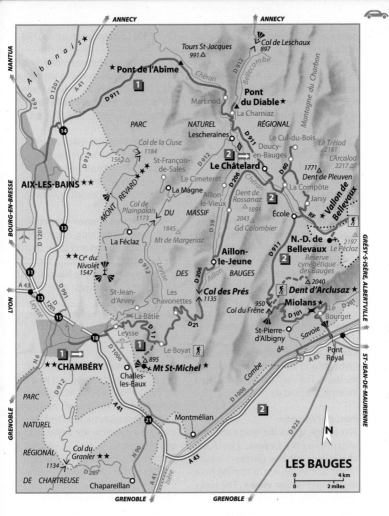

LES BAUGES

0 2 miles
0 4 km

N

◐ *Return to D21.*

From Boyat to Chavonettes, you can see the Col de Plainpalais with the cliffs of the Margeriaz above, then on the left, Mont Peney and the Croix du Nivolet. Between Chavonettes and the Col des Prés, the panorama widens to the Chambéry basin with Mont Granier above. At the Col des Prés (alt. 1 135m/3 724ft) above the pastures is the Grand Colombier, the highest point.

◐ *Take D 206 to Aillon-le-Jeune.*

Aillon-le-Jeune 🐾
There are still some traces of the Chartreux monks who settled here in the 12C including the Chapelle de la Correrire, the monastery *(Maison de Patrimoine;* ◔ *open Jul–Aug;* 📞 *04 79 34 03 09)* and the barns in the hamlet of Pénon. Situated at 1 000m/3 281ft, the winter-sports resort, established 1964, forms a group of chalets in the base of the valley. The valley's cheese farm was established in 1880. You can enjoy an educational visit at **Fromagerie du Val d'Aillon** *(*◔ *open daily 9am–noon, 3–7.30pm;* 📞 *04 79 54 60 28; www.fromagerieaillon. com)* to learn about the local cheeses, in particular the tome des Bauges (with

only one "m"), a recently designated AOC cheese.

Towards Le Châtelard, the road then follows the Aillon Valley with angled sides of the Grand Colombier (2 043m/ 6 703ft) and the rocky Dent de Rossanaz (1 891m/6 204ft) on the right.

▷ *After crossing the Chéran, go through Le Châtelard and continue on D 911 N to Charniaz.*

Pont du Diable★

Follow the road to the Col de Leschaux for 600m/656yds; leave the car near two chalets facing each other and follow the marked path on the right; it goes round a private house to reach the wood and the bridge *(15min there and back on foot)*. 🚶A small bridge spans the foaming Bellecombe mountain stream. This place is the main starting point of hikes included in the Tour des Bauges. To go to the Lac d'Annecy, follow D 912 from here to the **Col de Leschaux**. Otherwise, return to Charniaz and take D 911 towards Aix-les-Bains. The road follows the Chéran Valley to the Pont de l'Abîme.

Pont de l'Abîme★

The bridge spans the gorge through which flows the Chéran, 94m/308ft above the river bed ("abîme" means "abyss"). It's well worth coming here for the spectacular **view**★. The rocky needles of the **Tours St-Jacques** look up above the slopes of the Semnoz.

② THE HEART OF BAUGES
Drive of 40km/24.8mi shown on the Bauges map (♨ see p203). Allow 3hrs.

Le Châtelard

The village, its central street lined by old houses with wooden shutters, lies on either side of a wooded ridge once crowned by a castle, which separates the wide and open Lescheraines basin from the mountainous upper Chéran Valley. The 19C church has some charm, with huge frescoes of stars in the sky painted under the arches. Opposite the Maison du Parc des Beauges, follow a grassy path behind the church.

▷ *Past Le Châtelard, turn left on D 60.*

The road crosses a pastoral valley dotted with small wooden barns. In the village of **La Compôte**, the farms have distinctive balconies supported and extended by *tavalans*, curved trunks of wood.

▷ *After La Compôte, follow towards Doucy-Dessus from where there is a pretty view over the meadows and numerous barns scattered below the Grand Colombier. Turn left to Jarsy.*

This little road crosses hamlets and fields before reaching Jarsy, whose sturdy stone houses and large church are indications of its status as the most populous village in the Bauges, with more than 250 residents.

▷ *Before the bridge over the Chéran, turn left along the forestry road of the Vallon de Bellevaux.*

Vallon de Bellevaux★

Emerging from this wild and wooded valley, the road passes alongside the bottom of the ravines of the Pécloz and finishes about 1.5km/1mi after a roundabout, below the alpine meadows of Orgeval.
🚶 An interesting nature path with exhibits borders the Chéran.

Chapelle Notre-Dame de Bellevaux
🚶*35min there and back.*

Leave the car in the car park of the Office National des Forêts then follow the narrow path up for around 600m/660yds. At a clearing, follow the path that climbs up to a spring on the left to reach the Chapelle Notre-Dame de Bellevaux, known as the Ste Fontaine (1859), an old place of popular pilgrimage on Whit (Pentecost) Monday.

▷ *Return to the Chéran bridge and follow D 60 to École.*

École

In the **church**, a painting on the ceiling of the chancel represents the oratory of Ste Fontaine, in the Vallon de Bellevaux.

The church also has the 11C statue of the Virgin and Child that was found in the oratory. The **Maison Faune-Flore** (⊙open 22 Jun–end Aug Tue–Sun 10am–12.30pm, 1.30–6.30pm; ⊛2.50€; ♿ ℘04 79 52 22 56) gives a good interactive introduction to the animals and plants in the Bauges Massif.

▷ Follow to Col du Frêne on D 911.

Col du Frêne

Hike to Dent d'Arclusaz★ – 🄷 Allow a day including breaks (2hrs 30min there, 3hrs back). Recommended in fine weather conditions. Remember to take sufficient water, as there are no sources of drinking water along the route. From the **Col du Frêne** and on the way down to St-Pierre-d'Albigny there are splendid **vistas**★ of the Combe de Savoie with the canalised Isère below.

▷ Follow D 911, then D 101 to Château de Miolans, passing through some traditional hamlets.

Château de Miolans★

Leave the car at the car park in Miolans, 100m/109yds away. ⊙Open Apr–Oct, check for times. ⊛6€ (children 3€). ℘04 79 28 57 04.

The castle, one of the finest examples of Medieval military architecture in the Savoie region, occupies a commanding **position**★★ on an isolated rocky spur 200m/656ft above the Combe de Savoie. This enabled an observation of roads leading from the Bauges, Tarentaise and the Maurienne. The **view**★ from the upper courtyard looks over the Combe de Savoie (Isère Valley) and the mouth of the Maurienne (Arc Valley). There is a medieval garden with medicinal herbs. The square **keep** is the most characteristic part of the castle.

From the top of the **Tour St-Pierre** there is an even more breathtaking **view**★★. Reached from the garden, narrow steps lead down to the secret dungeons known as **oubliettes**; equally interesting is the **Galerie souterrain**, an underground watch-path with loopholes covering the access ramp to the castle.

▷ Follow D 101 then D 201.

EXCURSION
St-Pierre-d'Albigny

▷ Between Albertville and Montmélian by A 43, Exit 23. 🄸**Info:** Pl. de l'Europe, 73250 St-Pierre-d'Albigny. ℘04 79 25 19 38 (Jul–Aug) or 04 79 28 50 23 (town hall). www.saintpierredalbigny.fr.

This town is the historic gateway to the Bauges mountains, today the regional park. With several village houses and even fortified houses, its position owes much to being not far from the fortress **Château de Miolans**.

On the southern side of the Bauges Massif, St-Pierre-d'Albigny enjoys a view stretching from Mont Aiguille to Mont Blanc. The town reveals a few fine entrance doors at the start of rue Jean-Louis-Bouvet. On rue Louis-Blanc-Pinget is a fountain decorated with the emblem of the Papal Tiara and the keys of St Peter.

Caveau des Augustins – ⊙Only open for cultural events. The Augustine convent was founded in 1380. Until the Revolution the church held the tombs of several families of the region.

Écomusée de la Combe de Savoie et Musée du Sapeur-pompier

▷ Grésy-sur-Isère, 8km/5mi E of St-Pierre-d'Albigny by D 201. From the church at Grésy, follow the steep road signposted Écomusée Coteaux du Salin. ⊙Open Jul–Aug 10am–6pm; rest of year 2–5pm. ⊛8€ (children free). ♿ ℘04 79 37 94 36.

This eco-museum has created a walking circuit of 350m/383yds located above the village. It displays a **rich collection**★ of more than 7 000 objects in everyday use or related to rural activities.

Roman Church at Cléry

▷ From Grésy, follow to Frontenex, then turn left towards Cléry.

The village overlooks the Combe de Savoie, with a fine view from the church. Occupied since Neolithic times, the village expanded with the establishment of an Augustine priory in the 12C.

ADDRESSES

🏠STAY / 🍴EAT

🛏🛏 **Chambre d'hôte La Grangerie** – *Les Ginets. 73340 Aillon-le-Jeune, 2km/ 1.2mi from the resort towards Les Ginets.* 📞*04 79 54 64 71. www.lagrangerie.com.* 🅿🚲. *4 rooms, half-board only.*
On a winding road above the village, this converted old farm has views of the Bauges Massif. The proprietor is a mountain guide who can take you on walks. In winter, you can ski directly to the pistes.

🛏 **Christin** – *73390 Chamousset, near St-Pierre-d'Albigny.* 📞*04 79 36 42 06.* 🅿. *16 rooms*🛏🍴. In a rustic dining room, this family hotel offers authentic cooking with vegetables from the garden, and a good list of local wines.

🤸ACTIVITIES

🚶👥 **Ânes et compagnie** – *Les Dalphins, 73340 La Motte en Bauges.* 📞*04 79 63 80 01. www.anes-et-compagnie.info. May–Oct by reservation.* 🎫*50€ per day.* Donkey tours.

Montmélian

This ancient little town surrounds its rocky knoll, on which one of the most powerful strongholds in Europe once stood. After the fort was dismantled in 1706 by Louis XIV the town, with no military vocation, turned to farming, in particular vines. Today it is at the centre of the Savoie wine-producing region.

🌿WALKING TOUR

To appreciate the town's position in relation with the valley, drive up to the viewpoint from the fortress.
Montmélian has retained the **pont Cuénot**, whose ten arches have spanned the Isère since the 17C, and was for years the only way to travel between Chambéry and the Maurienne.
Musée d'Histoire – 🕐*Open Wed, May– Oct 5–6.30pm; Nov–Apr 3–4.30pm.* 🎫*Free.* 📞*04 79 84 42 23. www.montme lian.com.* In this fine Renaissance residence is a copy of a relief map of the fortifications, a collection of Gallo-Roman objects and a craftsman's workshop. Nearby, the governor's house, also from Renaissance times, has retained its character despite restoration in the 18C.
Musée régional de la Vigne et du Vin – 🕐*Open Jun–Sept Tue–Sat except public holidays 10am–noon, 2–6.30pm; Oct– May Wed 10am–noon, 2–5.30pm, Thu–Fri 2–5.30pm, Sat 10am–12.30pm.* 🕐*Closed*

- ▶ **Population:** 3 933.
- 🧭 **Michelin Map:** 333 J4.
- ℹ **Info:** 46 r. du Dr-Veyrat, 73800 Montmélian. 📞04 79 84 42 23. www.montmelian.com.
- ◗ **Location:** The rock overlooks D 1006, the Isère and A43 motorway on the opposite bank.
- ◉ **Don't miss:** A visit to the wine museum.
- 🕐 **Timing:** Allow a day to explore the town and the Combe de Savoie.

23 Dec–3 Jan. 🎫*4€.* 📞*04 79 84 42 23. www.montmelian.com.* The very steep vineyard slopes in this region require particular techniques. Vineyard and winemaking tools are displayed here, along with an explanation about the local wines.
Le Rocher – *Follow the road signposted* Le fort. The top of the rock is now occupied by a platform which offers a **panorama**★★ of the Isère Valley and of the Alps as far as Mont Blanc.

Combe de Savoie

Combe de Savoie is the name given to the Isère Valley between Albertville and the junction of the Chambéry Valley. Villages, occupying sunny positions at the foot of the Bauges mountains between

Montmélian and Grésy-sur-Isère, are either lost among orchards or surrounded by fields of maize and tobacco, or by vineyards. The roads from the fort at Mont, or the Cols du Frêne and Col de Tamié, give the best views of the valley.

ADDRESSES

☺ EVENT
La Foire de Qu'ara Bara – Held on the first Sunday of September, this fair dates from the Middle Ages and is one of the oldest in Savoie.

Aiguebelle

On the edge of the Maurienne, the valley around Aiguebelle makes a pleasant summer stop. The valley's historic significance can be seen through the remains of its past as an important mining centre. Today, the town retains its tradition as a trading centre and thoroughfare.

> ► **Population:** 1 080.
> ◔ **Michelin Map:** 333 K4.
> 🛈 **Info:** Grande-Rue, 73220 Aiguebelle. ℘04 79 36 29 24.
> ◑ **Location:** Near the meeting of the Isère and the Arc rivers, 29km/18mi SW of Albertville. Take A 43 and D 1006.
> ☺ **Don't Miss:** The green valley of Hurtières.
> ◷ **Timing:** Aiguebelle hosts a music festival in July.

SIGHTS
The town stretches out along a long shopping street. The **church** retains a 14C chancel and bell tower, and it is worth going inside to see the decoration, in particular the remarkable *Merciful Christ* in polychrome wood.

Rocher de Charbonnière – *Allow 1hr. From the main road, follow signs to Lac du Vivier, and then the Sentier du Rocher de Charbonnière.*
A path takes you through woodland up to a rock above the town, with the ruins of the Château de la Charbonnière. There is a fine panorama over the Bauges mountains and the Arc Valley.

EXCURSIONS
St-Georges-des-Hurtières
◑ *Take the road towards St-Jean-de-Maurienne, then right on D 73 for 6km/3.7mi.*
Not far from the major thoroughfares of the region, the Hurtières Massif is worth discovering. The village of St-Georges-des-Hurtières is a good base to explore traditional local industries.
Le Grand Filon★ – *La Minière. 4km/2.5mi S of the village.* ◷*Times vary, see website.* ☞*6.40€.* ℘*04 79 36 11 05. www.grandfilon.net.* An educational centre that retraces more than seven centuries of

the history of mining in these mountains, including interactive displays and visits to mining relics.
1hr 30min. A path from the chapel indicates many vestiges of the mines.
Musée des Quatre Saisons – *Le Reposet.* ◷*Open Jun–Oct.* ℘*04 79 44 39 89.* This museum is notable especially for its collection of herbs, fruits and flowers.

Argentine
◑ *6.5km/4mi S by D 72.*
On the other side of the Arc, facing the Hurtières plateau, this little village lived from metalwork and agricultural pursuits. The iron industry was brought here in the 16C. Reconstructions of this past can be seen at the **Musée du Félicien** (℘*04 79 44 33 67; www.museedufilicien.com*).

Montsapey
◑ *10km/6.2mi SE of Aiguebelle.*
The church is in troubadour style, with 19C mural *trompes-l'œil* paintings. An arts festival takes place here in July.

Albertville

At the intersection of three important and scenic alpine valleys, the Tarentaise, Beaufortain and the Arly, the Winter Olympic town of Albertville seals off the basin of the Combe de Savoie.

Stretched out along the foothills of the Bauges mountains to the west, the new town lies next to the Olympic park, while the 18C quarter, with its pretty Sardinian colours, aligns its streets around the church. Look up and across the other side of the Isère river to see the fine medieval city of Conflans.

▶ **Population:** 17 814.
◉ **Michelin Map:** 333 L3.
▤ **Info:** Pl. de l'Europe, 73204 Albertville. ℰ 04 79 32 04 22. www.albertville.com.
◉ **Location:** 50km/31.1mi from Chambéry on A 430, Albertville is on the route to the mountain resorts of Mont Blanc and the Tarentaise.
◉ **Don't Miss:** A walk around the medieval city of Conflans; the views from above the Fort du Mont.

THE OLYMPIC CITY

The town of Albertville will never forget its role as host of the 16th Winter Olympic Games in 1992, and indeed the Olympic flame is lit each time an important sporting event is held.

The town's position at the crossroads of the routes leading to the main ski resorts hosting the key events in the games was the reason for choosing it as host for the opening and closing ceremonies.

The **Halle olympique** (Olympic stadium) is a training centre for the French ice-hockey team, as well as a public ice-skating rink and a venue for the European Ice-Skating Championship.

The artificial climbing wall, open to the public, is one of the biggest in Europe.

The **Maison des 16es Jeux olympiques** (ⓒopen Jul–Aug Mon–Sat 10am–noon, 2–7pm, Sun and public holidays 2–7pm, Sept–Jun Mon–Sat and public holidays 10am–noon, 2–6pm; ⓢ3€; ⬥ ℰ04 79 37 75 71) houses an exhibition devoted not only to the Games with the original costumes for the ceremony and videos, but also exhibits in memory of the Olympics in general.

Le Dôme – Place de l'Europe

Designed by Jean-Jacques Moisseau, this new cultural centre stands on place de l'Europe and comprises a theatre, a multimedia reference library and a cinema with a panoramic screen.

EXCURSIONS
Conflans★

▶ Drive N across the pont des Adoubes and up to the montée A. Hugues; leave the car in the car park on the right. Continue on foot. Visit 45min.

Perched on a rocky spur overlooking the confluence of the River Isère and River Arly, the old town is well worth visiting. Visit in the evening, when the medieval atmosphere is strongest.

Château Manuel de Locatel – ⊶ Closed for renovations (check with tourist office). Dating from the 16C, this castle was built on the side of the hill that looks over the town of Albertville.

Porte de Savoie – Before going through the gate, admire the lovely **view**★ of the building dominated by the slender Tour Ramus and of the charming 18C fountain.

Rue Gabriel-Pérouse – This is the former "Grande-Rue" (High Street), lined with workshops still occupied by craftsmen whose shops are advertised by signs in wrought iron.

Church – Built in a harmonious 18C style, of note is the very beautiful **pulpit** made in 1718 by Jacques Clérant.

Grande-Place★ – A lovely 18C fountain decorates the centre of this picturesque floral square. On one side is the 14C Maison Rouge, and an art gallery.

Maison Rouge – ⓒOpen daily Jun–Sept 10am–noon, 2–7pm; Oct–May 2–6pm. ⓒClosed 1 Jan, 1 May, 24 Dec, 25 Dec,

31 Dec. 👁3€ *(children free).* 📞*04 79 37 86 86.* This striking brick building (14C) has sheltered both monks and soldiers, and now houses the **Musée d'Art et d'Histoire**. Exhibits include archaeological finds from Gilly-sur-Isère, reconstructions of Savoyard homes, regional furniture, traditional tools and utensils; the clothes and old skis complete an excellent ethnographic collection illustrating Savoyard life.

La Grande Roche – This terraced area, under the Sarrasine tower (12C) shaded by lime trees, overlooks the confluence of the River Isère and River Arly, offering fine views of the Combe de Savoie depression, with the rocky Alpette and Mont Granier mountains of the Chartreuse Massif in the distance.

🚗 DRIVING TOURS

ROUTE DU FORT DU MONT★★
29km/18mi shown on the regional map (♿see p183). Allow 1hr 30min.

▷ *From the Porte de Savoie in Conflans, drive along D 105. (Snow may block this steeply rising road between December and April.)*

With a series of hairpin bends, the road climbs continuously, offering a panoramic view of the Doron de Beaufort and Arly valleys. Through the Arly gap the Ugine basin appears below the pyramid-like Mont Charvin. Further up, at a wide left-hand bend, is a **vista** over the lower Tarentaise and the Feissons and Aigueblanche mountains.

Continue past the Fort du Mont to the second hairpin bend overlooking the pretty meadows of Mont.

From a grassy plateau at Les Croix, there is a fine **panorama**★★ over the whole of the Mont Blanc Massif, extending to the Combe de Savoie, through which flows the River Isère. To the southwest, you can see the Chartreuse Massif, and then to the right of the Dent de Cons, cut off between the Ugine basin and the Col du Tamié depression, you can make out the ridges of the Tournette mountain.

▷ *Return by a forestry road on the left towards Molliessoulaz. Then take direction Marolland and then Pointières.*

🐾 A little way before reaching **Pointières** there is an interesting and very easy **nature trail** *(1hr 30min)* which illustrates how people lived in the mountains before they started leaving for the towns. It makes an ideal family outing.

▷ *Take D 105 to return to Albertville.*

ROUTE DU COL DE TAMIÉ
Drive of 30km/18.6mi shown on the regional map (♿see p183). Allow 2hrs.

▷ *Take D 104 W towards Faverges.*

The road climbs up to the Col de Ramaz, affording pretty views. Take the first right turn after the pass.

Plateau des Teppes★
The road climbs, passing the hamlet of La Ramaz on the left, and then soon offering a nice view of Tamié Abbey.

▷ *Leave the car at the second hairpin bend and take a path on the right.*

As you leave the wood, follow the verge on the right from where is a good **view**★ over the Albertville basin.

▷ *Return to the Col de Ramaz and follow towards the Col de Tamié.*

The **Fort de Tamié** was built in 1876 by the French army and lies just before you reach the pass.

From here there is an extended **view**★ over the Albertville basin. There is a nature path as well as an orientation table within the fortifications. 🕐*Open mid-May–mid-Sept 10am–7pm.* 🐾*Guided tours on request (1hr).* 👁*2.90€.* 📞*04 79 32 30 17.*

The **Abbaye de Tamié** was founded in 1132 by St Pierre de Tarentaise. The beautifully simple church is entirely built in grey stone. Inside dark stained-glass windows, a fine organ and the pews are all resolutely modern.

Beaufortain★★

The Beaufortain offers a spectacular landscape, full of character, with an unbroken belt of forest (lower Doron Valley) and pastoral landscapes likely to appeal to those who prefer a gentle mountain scenery that rarely scales the heights you might find in the Mont Blanc Massif.
The smooth contours of the hills have proved ideal for long-distance ski races and several ski resorts have emerged.

SIGHTS
Beaufort★
◗ *19km/11.8mi E of Albertville by D 925.*
The village of Beaufort is set in pleasant meadows which provide rich grazing for the Tarine and Abondance cows that produce milk for the famous unpasteurised cheese of the same name.

Village walk – Beaufort lies at the meeting of the Roselend and Arêches valleys with its old quarter on the left bank of the Doron river. Wander along the windy little roads to discover finely decorated and sculpted balconies on almost every corner.
There are remains of a 15C castle with a tower adjoining the town hall. The Baroque **church** is built in Savoyard style, with large beams and altars of gilded and sculpted wood. The sculpted pulpit (1772) by Jacques Clérant is extraordinarily fine.
The ruined **château de Beaufort** emerges from among the pine trees, between Villard and Beaufort at the foot of the Outray Massif, whereas the characteristic V profile of the **Entreroches Gorge** *(1km/0.6mi SE on D 925)* stands out behind the village.

Les Saisies
◗ *14km/8.7mi from Flumet by D 218.*
Check the state of the roads in winter as the Gorges d'Arly road is often closed.
This mountain resort lies near the **Col des Saisies** (alt. 1 650m/5 413ft) on typical alpine pastureland. From here, you can see the distinctive Mont Blanc range on the horizon. The villages of Crest-

Voland, Cohennoz and Hauteluce count among the most beautiful in the Alps.
The resort – In 1963 the villages of Crest-Voland, Cohennoz, Hauteluce and Villard-sur-Doron decided to combine their land to create a ski resort around the Col des Saisies.
The good snow conditions and attractive position ensured the venture succeeded in becoming an important cross-country ski resort.
All the cross-country skiing of the 1992 Winter Olympics took place in Les Saisies. Downhill ski pistes are also available, today known as **L'Espace Cristal**. In summer, there is a large choice of hikes and activities.
At the **Col des Saisies** pass itself, from the unusual semicircular, modern **Notre-Dame-de-Haute-Lumière chapel**, is an extended **view★** of the Beaufortain mountains, from east to west: l'Aiguille du Grand-Fond, Pierra Menta, Crêt du Rey and Grand Mont.

Signal de Bisanne★★
◗ *Follow signs up from the centre of Les Saisies, or drive 13km/8.1mi from Villard-sur-Doron.*
Part of the Les Saisies downhill ski area. From Villard-sur-Doron, the road climbs along a cliff overlooking the Doron de Beaufort Valley. Once at Signal (alt. 1 939m/6 362ft), there is a **circular panorama** over the Combe de Savoie, the Aravis, Beaufortain and Mont Blanc massifs, and on the right, the characteristic "tooth" of Pierra Menta (at alt. 2 714m/8 904ft the highest mountain in the Beaufortain).
According to local legend, the shape of the Pierra Menta is due to a kick to the Aravis chain by Gargantua, disappointed

Ⓘ **Info:** Grande-Rue, 73270 Beaufort. ℰ04 79 38 37 57 www.areches-beaufort.com.
◗ **Location:** Bounded by the Val d'Arly, Val Montjoie and Tarentaise, the Beaufortain is only accessible by tortuous roads.

at not being able to reach Mont Blanc. The sky above here is often filled with distinctive, multicoloured paragliders and hang gliders.

🚗 DRIVING TOURS

VALLEY OF HAUTELUCE
Drive of 15km/9.3mi shown on the regional map (& see p183). Allow 2hrs.

▷ *Leave Les Saisies by D 218B.*

The summer and winter resort of Hauteluce offers a view of **Église St-Jacques-d'Assyrie** (1558) in the foreground and Mont Blanc in the distance, across the Col du Joly.
With a graceful onion-shaped tower (55m/180ft high), the church is decorated with Baroque (17C–18C) retables and 19C painted murals. In the village centre the **écomusée** shows the old way of life in the region (⏲ *open in winter and summer seasons;* 📞*04 79 38 80 31 or 04 79 38 21 64).*
Its sunny position attracts skiers taking advantage of the good reputation for late-season snow enjoyed by the resorts of Les Saisies and Val Joly.
Between Hauteluce and D 925 notice the tower of the Château de Beaufort on an entirely wooded hillock.

Lac de la Girotte★
2hrs 30min there and back from the power station at Belleville, about 5km/3mi before the Col du Joly, at the end of the Hauteluce Valley road.
The excavation of the Girotte mountain lake was first begun in 1923 to control seven power stations along the Dorinet and Doron rivers.
In 1946 and 1948 capacity was doubled and a dam built. Later a glacial spring needed to be used to add to supply during the busy winter tourist season, and this provided an interesting challenge, because the lake at 1 775m/5 823ft altitude was higher than the base of the glacier.
A tunnel beneath the glacier solved the problem, the first of its kind in the world.

ROUTE DU CORMET DE ROSELEND★★
Drive of 45km/28mi shown on the regional map (& see p183). Allow about 3hrs.

▷ *Leave Beaufort by D 218A S towards Arêches.*

Arêches 🎿
Surrounded by gentle slopes ideal for skiing, Arêches is one of prettiest winter resorts of the Beaufortain region.

Boudin★
The hamlet of Boudin is remarkably preserved and typically alpine. With its large chalets rising in tiers, its little church and its communal bread oven, it came under heritage protection in 1943.

Barrage de Roselend★
The buttressed dam rests against a natural arch blocking the gorge of the River Doron. The **artificial lake**★ comes into view on the way down from the Col du Pré. At the far end of the lake a Roman **chapel** (⟊ *closed*), in the foreground of a superb **panorama**★, is a copy of the Roselend village church that was flooded by the lake. Past a belvedere, the road follows the top of the dam, skirts the lake, then begins its final climb.

Cormet de Roselend★
This long depression links the Roselend and Chapieux valleys, in a landscape of remote pastures dotted with rocks. For the most extended **view**★ of the peaks above Chapieux Valley, climb the hillock with a cross on top, on the right.
The drive down from Cormet offers a glimpse of the Aiguille des Glaciers, the most southern peak of the Mont Blanc Massif. D 902 continues above Les Chapieux, partly destroyed in 1944, before entering the valley.

Vallée des Chapieux★
This valley, at the confluence of the Glaciers and Versoyen torrents, looks rather bleak, hardly softened by the dark stone ruins of the old Auberge des Mottets. This is a departure point for many hikes

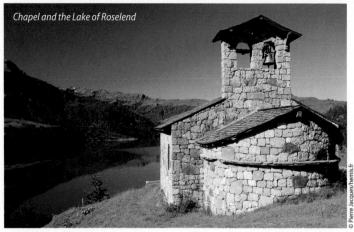

Chapel and the Lake of Roselend

© Pierre Jacques/hemis.fr

towards the Col de la Seigne, the Tour du Mont Blanc and the Aosta Valley. The road levels off, crossing a marshy area in a deserted valley, before descending in a series of hairpin bends. In the distance twinkle the Mont Pourri glaciers.

ADDRESSES

STAY

 Hôtel Grand Mont – *Pl. de l'Église, 73270 Beaufort.* 04 79 38 33 36. *Closed 25 Apr–7 May, 1 Oct–8 Nov and Fri eve out of holidays. Restaurant* . In the same family for four generations, this village house offers simple and rustic, small or family rooms. Regional cuisine includes cheese specialities based on beaufort.

 Auberge du Poncellamont – *L'Ilaz.* 04 79 38 10 23. *Closed 16 April–14 Jun, 16 Sept–21 Dec, Sun eve, Mon lunch and Wed out of season. Restaurant* . In a village, this Savoyard chalet overflows with flower boxes in summer. Simple and practical rooms, some with terrace. Pleasant country dining room or eat on the terrace to the sound of a fountain.

 Hôtel Le Météor – *1440 rte de Bisanne, 2.4km/1.5mi SW of Les Saisies by rte du Mont-Bisanne 1500.* 04 79 38 90 79. *www.lemeteor.com. Closed May–Jun and Sept–Nov.* . *15 rooms.* Renovated in 1978, this pretty chalet dates from the beginning of the 20C. Right by the pistes, yet the cosy rooms are far removed from the usual ski resort hotel room. Typical Savoyard meals.

 Les Campanules – *Chemin de la Grange, 73590 Crest-Voland.* 04 79 31 81 43. *www.lescampanules.com.* . *Wifi. 3 rooms* . With a view to the Aravis and Mont Charvin, this chalet will appeal to those seeking a quiet stay in the countryside. Nicely kept comfortable rooms, a lounge with fireplace and copious breakfasts are offered. You can eat a communal meal in the evening with Savoyard dishes.

 Le Calgary – *73 r. des Periots, Les Saisies.* 04 79 38 98 38. *www.hotel calgary.com. Closed 26 Apr–18 Jun, 6 Sept– 10 Dec.* . *Wifi. 39 rooms.* Named after local champion Frank Piccard, who won at the Calgary Olympics in 1988, this typical Austrian-style chalet-hotel offers spacious, renovated rooms. Sauna, hammam. Classic and Savoyard dishes offered in a large dining room.

EAT

 La Pierra Menta – *Col du Pré, 15km/ 9.3mi from Beaufort towards Barrage de Roselend.* 04 79 38 70 74. *http://lapierra menta.free.fr. Closed end Oct–end May.* From this chalet perched high up in the middle of the fields, it would be hard to find a better view to the Roselend Dam and Mont Blanc. Lovely terrace and simple, local food.

 La Ferme de Victorine – *Le Planay, 73590 Notre-Dame-de-Bellecombe.* 04 79 31 63 46. *Closed 16 Jun–4 Jul, 11 Nov–19 Dec, Sun eve and Mon 15 Apr–15 Jun and Sept– Nov.* A perfect replica of a traditional mountain house with attractive rustic décor. Tasty seasonal cooking includes fish in summer and game in autumn.

LA TARENTAISE AND LA VANOISE

Tignes, Val d'Isère, Courchevel, Méribel, Val Thorens, La Plagne, Les Arcs, La Rosière … the Tarentaise has a greater roll call of world-class ski resorts than anywhere in the world. In winter the only routes to the resorts are from Moûtiers, Aime or Bourg-St-Maurice off the main highway running east from Albertville; in summer you can reach the valley over a number of spectacular mountain passes. Thanks to the protected Vanoise National Park, summer visitors can admire an array of flora, fauna and wild mountain scenery.

The White Gold of the Alps

If ever there was a valley that has prospered thanks to the natural abundance of "white gold" (snow), it must surely be the Tarentaise, an area which equates to the upper valley of the Isère river. Courchevel 1850 was the first purpose-built ski resort, developed soon after World War II and is part of the Three Valleys, today the largest linked ski area in the world.

As with the nearby Espace Killy, which connects the Val d'Isère and Tignes ski areas, the Three Valley resorts have learned to cater to all skiers, ranging from affectionately known "ski bums" through families on a budget to an extremely wealthy crowd.

Highlights

1 See the distinctive ibex close up in the **Vanoise National Park** (p216)

2 Admire the panorama at **Cime de Caron** above Europe's highest resort, Val Thorens (p222)

3 The preserved hamlets of **Champagny-le-Haut**, ideal for a skiing or walking holiday (p227)

4 The **Glacier de la Grande Motte**, reached by funicular railway (p239)

5 Race on the **Face de Bellevarde** downhill piste in Val d'Isère (p242)

Cows, Gentians and Chamois

The abundance of winter snow turns into an abundance of an altogether different kind in summer. Whereas in Tignes and Val Thorens there are still high glaciers with perennial snow to ski on, on the slopes below, the pistes turn green and are home to cows, sheep and goats; the forests and rocky outcrops give shelter to chamois, ibexes and marmots; and if you come in May or June, you should spot the distinctive blue spring gentian. France's oldest national park, the Vanoise National Park, has successfully restricted further expansion of the ski areas to protect this fragile alpine environment, and as well as reintroducing the ibex it preserves more than 1 000 flower species.

Hiking in the Vanoise National Park with a view to the Grand Pic de la Lauzière

© Pierre Jacques/hemis.fr

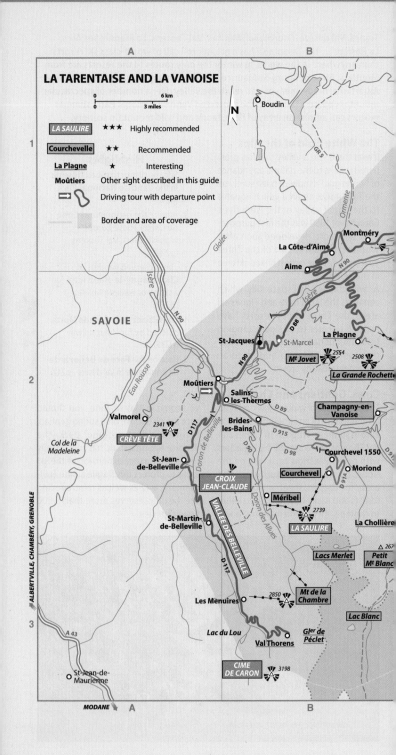

LA TARENTAISE AND LA VANOISE

0 — 6 km	
0 — 3 miles	

LA SAULIRE	★★★	Highly recommended
Courchevelle	★★	Recommended
La Plagne	★	Interesting
Moûtiers		Other sight described in this guide
⟶		Driving tour with departure point
		Border and area of coverage

N

Boudin

Montméry

La Côte-d'Aime

Aime

SAVOIE

St-Jacques

St-Marcel

La Plagne

Mt Jovet 2554

2508

La Grande Rochette

Moûtiers

Salins-les-Thermes

Champagny-en-Vanoise

Valmorel

2341

Brides-les-Bains

CRÈVE TÊTE

Courchevel 1550

Courchevel

Moriond

St-Jean-de-Belleville

CROIX JEAN-CLAUDE

Méribel

2739

La Chollière

St-Martin-de-Belleville

VALLÉE DES BELLEVILLE

LA SAULIRE

Lacs Merlet

Petit Mt Blanc 267

Les Menuires

2850

Mt de la Chambre

Lac Blanc

Lac du Lou

Gler de Péclet

ALBERTVILLE, CHAMBÉRY, GRENOBLE

A 43

Col de la Madeleine

Eau Rousse

Isère

Glaize

Ormente

GR 5

N 90

D 88

D 89

D 915

D 90

D 98

D 117

D 91A

Doron de Belleville

Doron des Allues

Val Thorens

CIME DE CARON 3198

St-Jean-de-Maurienne

MODANE

A

B

Massif de la Vanoise★★★

From the gentlest walks to the most vertiginous climbs, the huge Vanoise National Park offers hikers and climbers a vast choice. And, on the edge of the park, extensive ski pistes are available to winter-sports lovers. Yet in this magnificent mountain landscape, with its fragile ecosystems, the park is also home to more than a thousand flower species and a dazzling array of wild animals including ibexes and marmots.

VANOISE NATIONAL PARK

The Vanoise was the first national park in France, created in 1963 almost a century after the first American national park. Its 53 000ha/130 961 acres includes the whole of the Vanoise mountain range between the upper Isère Valley on the Tarentaise side and the upper Arc Valley on the Maurienne side (♨ *see La Haute Maurienne p256*), and adjoining the Italian Grand Paradis park for 14km/8.7mi. Twined since 1972, together these parks comprise 1 250sq km/483sq mi, the largest protected space in Western Europe. Extending from 1 200m/3 937ft to 3 855m/12 648ft (the height of the Grande Casse) and made up of very diverse geological formations (especially limestone and schist), the park is rich in fauna and flora. The latter, in particular, with more than 1 000 species, is quite exceptional including arctic species such as the glacier buttercup and moss campion.

Fauna and flora – The original aim of the park was to protect the last alpine ibex, an objective fully achieved with numbers rising from only 40 in 1963 to more than 2 000 today. The ibex, seemingly very at home here, was chosen as the park's emblem. As for the chamois population, it has raced ahead, rising from 400 animals to more than 5 500.

The glorious **native flora** include the rare columbine or androsace (rock jasmine). Among protected species are several types of sedge, the *cortuse de*

- **Michelin Map:** 333 M/N/O 4/5/6.
- **Info:** Maison de la Vanoise, 73500 Termignon. ♨04 79 20 51 67. www.3petitvillages.com or www.savoie-mont-blanc.com.
- **Location:** The Vanoise Massif occupies nearly a third of the Savoie. It extends from the Isère Valley in the north to the Arc Valley in the south. To the E, it adjoins the Italian national park of Grand Paradis.
- **Don't Miss:** All the main viewpoints are spectacular.
- **Timing:** When on a hike, plan carefully for changes in weather.

Matthiole, globe thistle and various saxifrages. The only example of twinflower (*Linnaea borealis*) is found in and around the Vanoise National Park, in particular the Plan de Tueda Nature Reserve.

Protected zones – The park is made up of a central zone, specifically protected, and a peripheral zone including 28 villages or towns. In the latter are five nature reserves, adjacent to the central zone: Tignes-Champagny in Tignes and Champagny-en-Vanoise; La Bailletaz in Val d'Isère; Grande Sassière in Tignes; Plan de Tueda in Les Allues (Méribel).

The **peripheral zone** (1 450sq km/ 560sq mi) includes picturesque villages and hamlets with lovely architecture on both the Tarentaise side and the side of the upper Maurienne (♨*see p256*).

It also includes the most prestigious Tarentaise ski resorts.

The **heart of the park** (530sq km/250sq mi) is essentially a high-mountain area, with 107 summits above 3 000m/9 843ft and glaciers covering an area of 88sq km/34sq mi. The highest Vanoise peak is the Grande Casse (3 855m/12 648ft).

Evidence of Ancient Human Habitation

Numerous **Neolithic stone monuments** show that the Vanoise has been a centre of human activity for thousands of years. Cut into with little cavities, no one knows what these rocks were used for. The **Pierre aux Pieds**, the best-known megalith in Savoie, was found at an altitude of 2 750m/9 022ft.

On its sides are engraved 82 feet *(pieds)*, the significance of which has not been discovered. The sheer wealth of archaeological finds in such a wild mountain environment, including paved roads, cairns, crosses, and even a network of paths between passes, illustrates that the Vanoise must have been a through-route.

Before designating the mountain range, the name **Vanoise** referred to the pass and route connecting the Pralognan and Termignon valleys, in particular the huge ice cap stretching from the Col de la Vanoise to the Col d'Aussois. Its medieval name, vallis noxia (dangerous valley), referred to the difficulties travellers would have met in the high mountains between the Arc and Isère valleys, and the many crosses and chapels were built as protection.

A mountain area, rich in minerals, copper mining began in the Bronze Age, iron was first mined in the 15C, galena (lead ore) in the 17C and then cobalt just before the industrial era. Limestone rocks and schist were used for building.

Below 2 000m/6 562ft, there are some beautiful forests with a variety of species including spruce, larch and arolla pine, notably at Méribel and Peisey-Nancroix. As well as the very rare species walkers will see the familiar gentians, rhododendrons and anemones, sprouting freely along the footpaths, and occasionally edelweiss.

Marmots or ibexes are quite frequently encountered, but to spot the ptarmigan, rock partridge, black grouse and golden eagle, requires a great deal of patience and a fair knowledge of animal habits in mountain areas.

SKI AREA

The peripheral zone of the Vanoise Massif includes an exceptionally fine skiing area with three major assets: its size, the quality of its facilities and its dependable snow cover.

The Maurienne Valley, to the south of the park, specialises in charming family resorts, while the Tarentaise, arching over the north and Bourg-St-Maurice towards the east, has, since the 1930s, developed an impressive number of winter-sports resorts.

The **Espace Killy** linking **Tignes**★ and **Val d'Isère**★★ and the Three Valleys including **Courchevel**★★, **Méribel**★★,

Les Menuires and **Val Thorens**★ count among the Alp's most popular ski areas.

ADDRESSES

ACTIVITIES

HIKING

The Vanoise park has more than 500km/310mi of hiking routes (GR 5, GR 55 plus the park's network of paths) and 35 refuges, 19 within the park.

Five refuges act also as information points: Portes du Parc at l'Orgère (above Modane); Fort Marie-Christine (Aussois) at Plan du Lac (above Termignon); Rosuel (Peisey-Nancroix) and Le Bois (Champagny-le-Haut).

All summer they provide nature walks, educational events and films. You can also arrange a half- or one-day excursion with a park guide. Walking maps and guides for the park, as well as the main GR 5 and GR 55 paths, can be purchased.

SKI AREA

The Espace Olympique Pass gives access to the following areas: the Trois Vallées, the Espace Killy, the Espace La Plagne-les-Arcs, Pralognan, Ste-Foy-Tarentaise, La Rosière, Valmorel and Les Saisies *(6-day pass with one day in each)*.

A Selection of Hikes in the Vanoise National Park

It would take a lifetime to exhaust all the walking possibilities in the Vanoise. Make your base in the small villages of Pralognan, Champagny or Peisey-Nancroix, or stay in one of the big ski resorts that also make excellent hiking centres: **Tignes, Les Menuires, Méribel** or **Courchevel** (*see also the Haute Maurienne p256*).

Main Viewpoints Accessible by Lift

★★★ Aiguille Rouge – *see p232*

★★★ Bellevarde – *see p243*

★★★ Cime de Caron – *see p222*

★★★ La Grande Motte – *see p239*

★★★ La Saulire – *see p225*

★★ Bellecôte – *see p236*

Family Walks *(short, easy routes)*

Lac de la Sassière★★ – 1hr 45mins – *See p239*

Le Monal★★ – 2hrs – *See p232*

Refuge de Prariond★★ – 5hrs – *See p242*

Plan de Tueda★ – time varies – *See p224*

Hikes
(no technical difficulties, but need a good level of fitness)

Crève-Tête★★★ – 2hrs 15min – *See p220 (Moûtiers)*

Col du Palet and Col de la Tourne★★★ – 1 day – *See p239*

Col de la Vanoise★★★ – 5hrs 30min – *See p228*

Col des Fours★★ – 4hrs 30min – *See p242*

Lacs Merlet★★ – 3hrs – *See p226*

Lac de la Plagne★★ – 4hrs 15min – *See p232*

Three-day Round Tour of the Vanoise Glaciers
(for experienced walkers in good training)

Before leaving, it is essential to book overnight stays in refuges *(ask at the Pralognan tourist office, see p228)* and to check the weather forecast over several days.

Day 1: Pralognan – **Mont Bochor**★ (by cable car) – **Col de la Vanoise**★★★ – **Refuge de l'Arpont**.

Day 2: Refuge de l'Arpont – La Loza – La Turra – **Refuge du Fond d'Aussois**★★.

Day 3: Refuge du Fond d'Aussois – **Col d'Aus**.

Moûtiers

Moûtiers lies deep inside a basin, at the confluence of the Tarentaise valleys of the Doron and Isère. To the east, the distinctive Roc du Diable (devil's rock) creates a magnificent setting for the town. The town grew in the 16C when the salt works were established. Today it is known by winter-sports enthusiasts as the base town for the roads up to the Three Valley ski resorts.

- ▶ **Population:** 3 893.
- ⚲ **Michelin Map:** 333 M5.
- ⓘ **Info:** Pl. St-Pierre, 73600 Moûtiers. ℘04 79 24 04 23. www.ot-moutiers.com.
- ▷ **Location:** 26km/16.2mi S of Albertville.
- 👥 **Kids:** A swim at the Morel leisure centre; a forest walk by the Torrent du Morel.
- ◷ **Timing:** The main N 90 road near Moûtiers is very busy on winter weekends.

☞ WALKING TOUR
Cathédrale St-Pierre

The entrance porch and the overall building date from the 15C, but the Roman foundations of this cathedral are still visible in the apse and the chancel. It was partly destroyed by revolutionaries in 1793, then restored in the 19C in a Neoclassical style. Of note are the wooden episcopal seat (15C) and the statue of a Roman Virgin Mary, comparable to the 13C Burgundy style.

In the archbishop's palace in place St-Pierre is the **Musée d'histoire et d'archéologie** (◷ open Mon–Sat 9am–noon, 2–6pm; ◷ closed public holidays; ∞2€, children free). The history of the Tarentaise is explored from prehistoric times to the 19C through Bronze Age jewellery, Roman pottery and documents. Also for viewing are the episcopal room with 17C paintings and the 18C chapel.

The **Musée des Traditions populaires de Tarentaise** (pl. St-Pierre; ◷ open Mon–Sat 9am–noon, 2–6pm; ◷ closed public holidays; ∞2.50€ ♿) presents forgotten rural professions and traditional ways of life with Tarentaise costumes.

EXCURSIONS
Les Stations Thermales (Spa Resorts)

Two spas in the lower Doron de Bozel Valley are within easy reach of Moûtiers: **Brides-les-Bains** (5km/3mi SE by D 915; ⓘ ℘04 79 55 20 64; www.brides-les-bains.com) specialises in obesity and circulatory complaints, and is also a well-equipped mountain holiday resort, linked with Méribel by gondola; and **Salins-les-Thermes** (on the southern edge of Moûtiers) offers stimulating salty waters, recommended in the treatment of gynaecological problems and complaints affecting the lymph glands. A third, more recent spa **La Léchère-les-Bains** (7.5km/4.7mi NW of Moûtiers by N 90; ℘04 79 22 51 60), at the bottom of the lower Tarentaise Valley, was originally discovered in 1869 after a landslide. It specialises in treatments for circulation and gynaecological problems, as well as rheumatism.

Valmorel

ⓘ 73260 Valmorel. ℘04 79 09 85 55. www.valmorel.com.

At times it seems as if Valmorel, built in 1976, has been part of the landscape for centuries. It is one of the most attractive modern resorts in the Alps, at the upper end of the verdant Morel Valley and surrounded by mountains. Trompe-l'œil façades in the Savoyard tradition brighten a traffic-free centre, which resembles an old alpine village. Fine old hamlets (Doucy, Les Avanchers) are dotted along the valley, which is renowned for its beaufort cheese.

☞ **Ski area** – Part of the Grand Domaine (Valmorel, François-Long-champ, Doucy-Combelouvière), there is a wide choice of runs for all abilities. Experienced skiers will prefer the area around St-François de la Lauzière via the Madeleine chairlift and the runs on the Massif de la Lauzière. The Morel ski lift makes it possible to avoid the centre and go straight to the Gollet and Mottet ski areas. There are good snow-making facilities, and night skiing is offered on Planchamp and in the snowpark.

In summer there are plenty of opportunities for serious climbers, as well as more recreational hikers. Some lifts are open for paragliders, or simply for those wanting to admire the view.

⚡ HIKE

Crève-Tête ★★★

⚡ *Alt. 2 341m/7 680ft. Take the Pierrafort gondola at Valmorel.*

From the arrival station of the gondola, you soon arrive at the **Col du Gollet**, which already offers a lovely view. From here, the path to the summit is steeper but you are rewarded with a splendid **panorama** of the Valmorel Valley framed by the Cheval Noir, Grand Pic de la Lauzière and the Belledonne range in the distance. On the other side you can see the Belleville Valley with the resorts of St-Martin and Les Menuires as well as the peaks of Caron and the Aiguille de Péclet. Further to the left, you will see in turn the summit of Bellecôte, Mont Pourri, the resort of Les Arcs, then Mont-Blanc and finally the Isère Valley.

ADDRESSES

🏠 STAY

⊖ **Chambre d'hôte Chalet Les Pierrets** – *73600 La Perrière. 6km/3.7mi S of Moûtiers by D 915 towards Courchevel. ℘04 79 55 26 95. 🍴 5 rooms ⌑.* Next to the church this B&B offers functional rooms, some with balconies. Breakfast includes farm products. A kitchenette is available for guests.

⊖⊖ **Chambre d'hôte Le Manoir de Bellecombe** – *25 rte de St-Oyen, 73260 Aigueblanche. 4km/2.5mi N of Moûtiers by N 90. ℘04 79 24 31 95. www.manoir-de-bellecombe.com. Closed Nov. 🅿 🍴. 5 rooms ⌑.* A warm welcome awaits you in this old 17C manor house, restored using old materials. Rooms are quite dark, but sleep 1–4 people. Residents may eat in an arched dining room. Pretty garden.

⊖⊖ **Le Belvédère** – *R. É.-Machet, Quartier des Sources, 73570 Brides-les-Bains. ℘04 79 55 23 41. www.hotel-73-belvedere.com. Closed end Oct–mid-Dec. 🅿. Wifi. 28 rooms.* Hotel in a fine bourgeois house facing the Vanoise mountains. Chalet-style rooms are comfortable and charming. Jacuzzi, hammam and heated pool in summer.

🍴 EAT

⊖ **Le Grenier** – *Hameau de Mottet, 73260 Valmorel. ℘04 79 09 82 52. www.legrenier-valmorel.com. Closed May–Jun and Sept–mid-Dec.* A huge restaurant at the heart of the ski resort with a terrace at the base of the pistes. Good-quality, well-presented country cooking with Savoyard and Corsican specialities.

⊖⊖ **La Voûte** – *172 Grande Rue. ℘04 79 24 23 23. www.restaurantlavoute.com. Closed 4–11 Jan, 26 Apr–10 May, 20 Sept–4 Oct, Sun eve, Wed eve and Mon.* In a pedestrian street near the cathedral, this friendly restaurant offers contemporary cooking in a mountain-style dining room.

⊖⊖⊖ **Le Coq Rouge** – *115 pl. A. Briand. ℘04 79 24 11 33. www.lecoqrouge.com. Closed 27 Jun–20 Jul and Sun–Mon.* Lots of chicken ornaments as well as paintings by the owner-chef decorate the dining room in this charming house dating 1735. Creative seasonal cuisine.

🏃 ACTIVITIES

👥 **Leisure Centre at Morel** – *Bellecombe, 73260 Aigueblanche. 3km/1.8mi N of Moûtiers by N 90. ℘04 79 24 05 25. www.morel-loisirs.com.* In a relaxed, wooded location, this leisure centre offers indoor swimming pools and sauna (all year), and outside pools, slides, etc. in summer.

VISIT

Coopérative laitière de la région de Moûtiers – *Av. des XVIe-Jeux-Olympiques, 73600 Moûtiers. ℘04 79 24 03 65. www.beaufortdesmontagnes.com. Guided visits Mon–Fri 9am–noon.* Visit the production and ageing cellars for beaufort cheese.

Vallée des Belleville★★★

On the edge of the Vanoise Massif, the Belleville Valley is best known for its winter-sports resorts within the Three Valleys area: St-Martin-de-Belleville, Les Menuires and Val Thorens. In summer this pretty valley offers visitors a wonderful landscape, perfect for walkers.

> ⚐ **Michelin Map:** 333 M5.
> ℹ **Info:** 93440 St-Martin-de-Belleville. ℘04 79 00 20 00. www.st-martin-belleville.com.
> ◑ **Location:** S of Moûtiers, this huge area lies between the Tarentaise and the Maurienne.
> ◉ **Don't Miss:** The panoramic view from Cime de Caron.

VILLAGES

St-Jean-de-Belleville

Rebuilt in 1928 after a major fire, the village has retained a richly decorated **church** with two fine altarpieces: one by Todesco and another over the high altar in early Empire style (early 19C). From St-Jean, you can explore the pretty **Nant Brun Valley**, start of many walks.

St-Martin-de-Belleville 🎿

This charming old village has gentle sunny slopes linked by chairlift to those of Méribel and Les Menuires.

The stocky **Église St-Martin**, surmounted by a Lombard-style steeple, is characteristic of 17C–18C hall-churches and contains an **altarpiece** in fine red colours. The **Chapelle Notre-Dame-de-Vie** presents an unusual silhouette on the side of the road to Les Menuires (1km/0.6mi) and is an important place of pilgrimage. The 17C **altarpiece** by Molino is particularly admirable, with a hundred chubby-cheeked cherubs. On dry summer days, the drive down to **Salins-les-Thermes via St-Laurent-de-la-Côte** on the way to Moûtiers offers exceptional village views.

LES MENUIRES

ℹ *Belledonne, 73440 Les Menuires. ℘04 79 00 73 00. www.lesmenuires.com.*

The town-like architecture that Les Menuires was known for has been improved in recent years, with wood cladding for many buildings, and construction of some classy, beautiful chalets. The resort extends over 2km/1.2mi between 1 780m/5 840ft and 1 950m/6 398ft within the convenient areas of La Croisette and Les Bruyères.

🎿🎿 **Ski area** – Les Menuires is a top-class ski resort for all levels, with

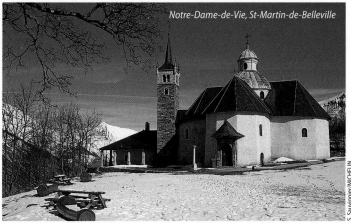

Notre-Dame-de-Vie, St-Martin-de-Belleville

S. Sauvignier/MICHELIN

expert skiers enjoying black runs like the Pylônes, Léo Lacrois and Le Rocher Noir. Cross-country skiers have 30km/18.6mi of runs and enjoy the Doron piste linking the villages of Beattaix and Châtelard.

Mont de la Chambre★★

🏔 Alt. 2 850m/9 350ft.

Take the Croisette gondola. The fine panorama includes Mont-Blanc, the Méribel Valley, the Val Thorens and Vanoise glaciers and the Belledonne. It is possible to walk to Les Menuires (2hrs).

VAL THORENS★

🏠 Maison de Val Thorens, 73440 Val Thorens. ✆04 79 00 08 08. www.valthorens.com.

The highest ski resort in Europe (2 300m/7 546ft) and car-free, Val Thorens is set in magnificent surroundings, overlooked by the Aiguille de Péclet (3 561m/11 683ft) and bounded by three glaciers marking the limits of the Parc national de la Vanoise. In summer the landscape attracts rock-climbers.

🎿 Ski area – Val Thorens is a skiers' paradise: two funitels take you up to the high mountain with breathtaking views of the Mont-Blanc, Vanoise and Écrins massifs, famous runs and access (20min) to the ski areas of Mont de la Chambre and Méribel's Mont Vallon.

Cime de Caron★★★

🏔 Access by Caïrn and Caron gondolas then Caron cable car (🕐 open Jul–Aug and winter season; ≋12.50€ return; minimum 2hrs up and down).

The summit is reached from the arrival point in five minutes. The extraordinary panorama★★★ embraces much of the French Alps, in particular the imposing summits of the Mont-Blanc, Vanoise, Queyras, Thabor and Écrins massifs.

Glacier de Péclet★

Access by funitel (🕐 open Dec–May daily; ≋12.50€; ✆04 79 00 08 08).

Close-up view of the glacier and the Cime de Caron. Advanced skiers can take the chairlift to the summit from which there is a splendid panorama★★★.

🚶 HIKES

Inexperienced hikers should enjoy the walks to the Lac du Lou (2hrs 30min there and back from Les Bruyères) and Hameau de la Gitte★ (1hr 45min there and back from Villaranger). The following are suitable for experienced hikers.

Croix Jean-Claude★★★

🚶 4hrs 30min. Vertical rise 600m/ 1 968ft. Just before Béranger, take a path right to Les Dogettes; turn right towards the 2 small Fleurettes mountains; continue to the spring and to the ridge at Col de Jean; turn left to Croix Jean-Claude.

Magnificent view★★ of the villages. The path reaches the Roc de la Lune (incorrectly signed "Col de la Lune").

Pointe de la Masse and Tour of the Lakes★★

Take the gondolas to La Masse. From the first section, allow five hours for the whole itinerary. 🚶 Inexperienced hikers are advised to skip the ascent of the Masse (allow 3hrs 30min). From the viewing table at the top of La Masse, there is a splendid panorama★★.

Vallée des Encombres

The village of Le Châtelard, near St-Martin, lies at the start of this secluded 14km/8.7mi-long valley. To preserve the alpine fauna tourist facilities are limited and you should stay on marked paths. There are guided hikes (Menuires guides office ✆04 79 01 04 15; www.guides-belleville.com) to the Petit Col des Encombres★★ and the Grand Perron des Encombres★★★ offering views of the Maurienne Valley and Écrins Massif.

ADDRESSES

🏃 ACTIVITIES

😊 Good to know – The large sports centre at Val Thorens offers a range of activities including pools, a spa and gym with children's areas. The mountain guides at Les Menuires also offer climbing courses for children.

Méribel★★

Méribel lies at the heart of the Three Valleys, the largest linked ski area in the world. It was a British ski lover, Lord Lindsay, who in 1938 discovered the hidden Allues Valley with its 13 hamlets and founded the resort, naming it Méribel after one of the pretty hamlets. After the war, regulations concerning architectural styles were laid down to ensure residential buildings were chalets with ridged roofs and wood or stone façades. This architectural unity, with its picturesque villages along with extensive walking and mountain-biking tracks, has made Méribel a popular resort year-round.

THE RESORTS

Méribel

Chalets are dispersed through the forest between 1 450m/4 757ft and 1 800m/5 906ft and a drawback is that the resort does not really have a proper centre, except perhaps Chaudanne. The road winds up to the altiport, where you can play golf in summer. In any season you can book a range of flights over the Three Valleys or towards Mont-Blanc. The church at St-Martin-des-Allues contains a Baroque altarpiece, which is a major work of Jacques Todesco.

Méribel-Mottaret

Set at the foot of the Vanoise park, in the heart of the Three Valleys ski area, at altitude 1 800m/5 906ft at its highest point, the resort of Méribel-Mottaret offers a compromise between traditional architecture and modern facilities.

Summer

Méribel makes an excellent **hiking base** with almost a quarter of the valley situated within the Vanoise National Park. Ideal for hikers of all abilities, Méribel offers walkers 20 maintained and sign-posted circuits through forests or pastures *(walking guide on sale in the tourist offices)*.
From the ridges of Tougnète, La Saulire and Le Mont-Vallon there are lovely

- ⏱ **Michelin Map:** 333 M5.
- **Info:** BP 1, 73551 Méribel. ℰ04 79 08 60 01. www.meribel.net.
- ▶ **Location:** Méribel is 30min S of Moûtiers. Take D 915 in the direction of Brides-les-Bains, then take D 90, a pretty drive on a scenic ridge.
- **Don't Miss:** Winter-sports fans should not fail to pause for some of the amazing panoramas. In summer, take an excursion to the Lac de Tueda.
- **Kids:** If you are hiking with young children, there are several walks along easy forest trails.
- 🕑 **Timing:** Winter or summer, always check opening and closing times of the lifts.

Méribel-Mottaret

©Julian Withers/World Pictures/Photoshot

views over the Mont-Blanc, Beaufortain and Vanoise mountain ranges.

Ski Area

A network of gondolas from Méribel provides fast and comfortable links with Courchevel, La Tania, Les Menuires and Val Thorens. The areas of Mont Vallon, Mont de la Chambre, Roc des Trois

Marches and Roc de Fer offer some of the finest ski slopes in Europe, ideal for competent skiers. As one of the main sites in the 1992 Winter Olympics Méribel hosted all the women's ski races on the difficult Roc de Fer pistes.

The cross-country ski area is not very extensive, but delightful: from the altiport and Plan de Tueda are around 30km/20mi of circuits with good snow cover in a beautiful woodland area.

Non-skiers can enjoy the superb landscapes of the Trois Vallées area. Various paths criss-cross the forest or skirt the ski runs, and a special **pedestrian pass**, known as a *forfait piéton*, gives hikers access to gondolas and chairlifts.

EXCURSIONS TO THE PEAKS
La Saulire★★★
◗ *Access from Méribel by the Burgin Saulire gondola or from Mottaret by the Pas du Lac gondola.* ◷*Open Jul–Aug.* ☏*04 79 00 43 44. www.s3v.com.* Splendid **panorama** (◷*see p225*).

Mont Vallon★★
Alt. 2 952m/9 685ft. ◗ *From Mottaret, walk to the Plan des Mains. Allow 1hr 15min in summer. In winter, access for skiers only by the Plattières gondola. Continue to the summit by the Mont Vallon gondola.*
On arrival, go to the panel Réserve de Tueda: superb **view★★★** of the Allues Valley. Turn back and take the path on the left to Lacs du Borgne for a fine view of the Belleville Valley with the Aiguille d'Arves and Grandes Rousses beyond.

Roc des Trois Marches★★
◗ *In winter, access from Mottaret by the Plattières gondola (three sections).* Beautiful **circular view**, including the Vanoise glaciers and the Meije.

Tougnète★★
◗ *Access from Méribel by gondola; if possible, sit facing backwards rather than in the direction of travel.* ◷*Jul–Aug Sun–Fri.* ⊛*10€.* ☏*04 79 08 65 32.* On the way up, there is a view of Méribel and the villages dotted around the valley, with Mont-Blanc and the Beau-

fortain in the background. From the upper station (2 410m/7 907ft), the view extends over the whole Vallée des Belleville. Skiers can also enjoy panoramas of **Roc de Fer★★**, **Pas de Cherferie★★**, **Mont de la Challe★**, **Mont de la Chambre★★** and **Col de la Loze★★**.

⚑ HIKES
Plan de Tueda★
◗ *At Mottaret, follow signs for Le Chatelet and park your car at the end of the road.*
The **Réserve naturelle de Tueda** (*information and café at Maison de la Réserve at Lac de Tueda; ☏04 79 01 04 75; www. vanoise.com*) was created in 1990 to preserve one of the last large forests of arolla pines in Savoie. The Tueda Forest surrounds a lovely lake overlooked by the silhouette of the Aiguille du Fruit and Mont Vallon. A **nature trail** leads hikers through this fragile environment.

Col de Chanrouge★★
Alt. 2 531m/8 304ft. ◗ *Start from the Plan de Tueda. On the way up, allow 2hrs to the Refuge du Saut then 1hr 15min to the pass. On the way down, allow 2hrs.*
From the pass, there is a fine **view** of the Courchevel Valley, of the ski area of La Plagne and of the Mont-Blanc Massif.

ADDRESSES

⌂ STAY
☺ **Good to know** – Méribel is less jet-set than Courchevel, but the price shoots up in winter.

⊟⊟⊟⊟ **Adray Télébar** – *On the pistes (with pedestrian access)* ☏*04 79 08 60 26. www.telebar-hotel.com. Closed mid-Apr–mid-Dec. 24 rooms, half-board only.*
The friendly welcome to this unique location, where you will be collected by snowmobile, more than makes up for the simple interior.

☯/EAT
⊟ **Le Martagon** – *Rte des Allues.* ☏*04 79 00 56 29. www.restaurant-martagon.com.* This chalet at the foot of the gondola is a spot to relax after the slopes. A large fireplace stands in the pine-panelled dining room. In summer there is a pleasant terrace.

Courchevel★★

Courchevel is undoubtedly one of the major and most prestigious winter-sports resorts in the world. Founded in 1946 by the Conseil général de la Savoie (regional council), it was the first in Savoie to introduce the ski-in ski-out concept and played a leading role in the development of the **Three Valleys ski area**. However, Courchevel also owes its reputation to the high quality of its hotels and gastronomic restaurants, unrivalled in mountain areas. In summer, the proximity to the Vanoise National Park allows visitors to discover a wilder mountain landscape.

- ⚓ **Michelin Map:** 333 M5.
- 🗐 **Info:** Le Cœur de Courchevel, BP 37, 73120 Courchevel. ℘04 79 08 00 29. www.courchevel.com.
- ▷ **Location:** The drive up is 50km/31.1mi from Albertville to Courchevel, the last part on D 91 with its spectacular panoramic views.
- 🕮 **Don't Miss:** The cable-car trip up the Saulire is a high point of any visit.
- 🕙 **Timing:** If you spend a few days in summer, the "Forfait de loisir" gives access to many activities.

THE RESORTS

The Three Valleys comprising Courchevel, Méribel, Les Menuires, Val Thorens and several smaller resorts is the largest linked ski resort in the world, having 200 lifts on a single pass and 600km/373mi of ski runs.

Courchevel, built like a huge circular arc opening up onto the ski pistes, is opposite the mountains of l'Aiguille du Fruit, Saulire and Croix des Verdons. Among pastures and wooded areas, in a vast open landscape framed by impressive mountains, the area includes four resorts on the slopes of the Vallée de St-Bon. Between 1 300m/4 265ft and 1 850m/6 070ft, luxury hotels and chic chalets line the rue de Bellecôte, le Jardin Alpin and the road to the altiport.

There are excellent runs for beginners along the lower sections of the Courchevel 1850 ski lifts. Advanced skiers prefer the great Saulire corridor and the Courchevel 1350 area. Cross-country skiers can explore the network of 130km/80.8mi of trails linked across the Trois Vallées area. Snow cover is guaranteed in Courchevel from December to April, owing to the north-facing aspect of the slopes.

Le Praz 1300 – The impressive ski jumps used during the 1992 Olympic Games are close to the old village. A picturesque 7km/4.3mi-long forest road leads to the resort of **La Tania**, and on to Méribel.

Courchevel 1550 – Family resort situated on a promontory near woodlands.

Moriond-Courchevel 1650 – Sunny resort where urban architecture contrasts with traditional chalets. There is an interesting semicircular chalet.

Courchevel 1850 – Courchevel 1850 is the main resort of the complex as well as the liveliest and most popular. There is an impressive **panorama**★ of Mont Jovet, the Sommet de Bellecôte and the Grand Bec peaks.

VIEWPOINTS ACCESSIBLE BY GONDOLA

La Saulire★★★

From Courchevel 1850 by the Verdons gondola (6min) and the Saulire cable car (3min). 🕙Open Jul–Aug Sun–Fri 9.30am–4.40pm. ⚲10.20€ return, both sections; 6.20€ return for one section.

The summit links the Courchevel and Méribel valleys and is the starting point of several well-known ski runs.

From the top platform (2 690m/8 825ft), the view embraces the Aiguille du Fruit in the foreground, the Vanoise Massif and glaciers further away, the Péclet-Polset Massif to the south, and to the north the snow-covered Mont-Blanc towering above the ridges of Mont Jovet. The terrace of the Pierres Plates restaurant offers a view of the Allues Valley with an orientation table available.

Sommet de la Saulire (TV Mast)

🚶 *Alt. 2 739m/8 986ft. 1hr return.*
This excursion is recommended in summer to tourists familiar with mountain conditions and not prone to vertigo. The summit can be reached from the cable car, along a wide track and then a shorter steep, narrow path on the right. Splendid panorama including the Meije, and the Écrins and Vanoise massifs.

Télécabine des Chenus★★

Access from Courchevel 1850. Check times and prices with the tourist office.
From the upper gondola station, you can view the Rocher de la Loze and, further away, the Croix de Verdon, the Saulire, Aiguille du Fruit, the Vanoise and Mont-Blanc. Skiers can go to the **Col de la Loze**★★ for a fine view over the Allues Valley and the altiport.

🚶 HIKES

A map of the area's network of footpaths is available from the tourist office.

Petit Mont-Blanc★★

🚶 *Allow 3hrs 30min on the way up and 2hrs 15min on the way down. Start from Le Belvédère (Courchevel 1650) or from the top of Mont Bel-Air.*
Walk across the lovely Vallée des Avals, free of all ski lifts, then up to the summit via the Col de Saulces. Very fine **panorama** of the Pralognan Valley below the Grande Casse, the Vanoise glaciers and the Pointe de l'Échelle.

Lacs Merlet★★

🚶 *Ascent: 2hrs; start from Mont Bel-Air.*
The position of the lakes at the foot of the Aiguille du Fruit forms a splendid **setting**★★. Go to the upper lake, the deepest of the Vanoise lakes, and walk along the right-hand shore to the end.

Walk to La Rosière

🚶 *Access by car along an unsurfaced forest road starting between Courchevel 1650 and Le Belvédère.*
Lovely lake overlooked by the Dent de Villard. Nature trail introducing a few rare species including columbine and lady's slipper. Continue along the waterfall path.

ADDRESSES

🛏 STAY

🈁 **Good to know** – In this ultra-fashionable resort, the tourist office reservation centre can help you find lodgings that provide a compromise between value and comfort.

🍴🍴🍴 **Les Peupliers** – *73120 Le Praz.* 🖀*04 79 08 41 47. www.lespeupliers.com. Closed May–Jun and Sept–Oct Sat–Sun.* 🅿. *Wifi. 35 rooms.* This family hotel close to a little lake gives a warm welcome with renovated wood-panelled rooms with south-facing balconies.

🍴 EAT

🍴🍴 **La Cloche** – *Pl. du Rocher, 73120 Courchevel 1850.* 🖀*04 79 08 31 30. Closed May–Jun Sat–Sun and Sept–Nov.* There is a warm atmosphere in this dining room in which tradition is revived. The décor is typical of mountain establishments, with pastel colours combined with rough wooden floorboards and chairs covered with embroidered fabric.

🍴🍴🍴 **La Fromagerie** – *La Porte de Courchevel, 73120 Courchevel 1850.* 🖀*04 79 08 27 47. Closed May–Nov.* Not surprisingly from the name, cheese specialities provide the theme, but other traditional dishes are also offered. Objects picked up in antique shops adorn the restaurant.

🍷 BARS

🈁 **Good to know** – If you are getting bored of the well-known, chic bars like the Byblos, the Grange, the Milk or others, then drop into **"Prends ta luge et tire-toi"** ("grab your sledge and pull yourself"), both a snowboard store and a trendy bar.

Champagny-en-Vanoise★★

A lively village, linked to La Plagne's ski area, Champagny-le-Bas is divided from Champagny-le-Haut by a deep gorge. The latter, with two preserved hamlets, lies in a deep valley enclosed by the Grande Casse mountain. Its magnificent alpine grazing pastures were once the most prized grazing of the region, said to give beaufort cheese its distinct hazelnut character. One of the five gateways to the Vanoise National Park, it is excellent hiking country.

▶ **Population:** 664.
⚲ **Michelin Map:** 333 N5.
▮ **Info:** Le Centre, 73350 Champagny-en-Vanoise. ℘04 79 55 06 55. www.champagny.com.
⟁ **Location:** Take A 430 to Albertville, then by N 90 towards Courchevel.
⚘ **Don't Miss:** Exploring the hamlets of Champagny-le-Haut, including a walk along the easy nature trail and a visit to the glacier centre at Le Bois.

THE RESORT

The 17C **Baroque church** of Champagny-le-Bas (🕐open Jul–Aug Tue–Sun 3–6pm) sits at the top of a hillock. It includes a marvellously sculpted **altarpiece** (1710) dedicated to the Virgin Mary, covered with cherubs.

🎿 **Ski area** – Pleasant and sunny and linked to **La Plagne** and Paradiski by gondola and chairlift, it offers pistes for skiers of all levels. The **Mont de la Guerre red run** has views of the Courchevel and Pralognan ski areas. Champagny-le-Haut has very pretty cross-country skiing trails.

Télécabine de Champagny★ – Alt. 1 968m/6 457ft. 🕐Open Jul–Aug and winter season, times vary. ◉4€.
From the top of the gondola you can see the Péclet- Polset, the Vanoise glaciers and the Grand Bec. Skiers in winter and walkers in summer can go up to the top of the Borseliers chairlift for the **view★** from the terrace of the restaurant (🕐closed in summer).
It extends to the Grande Casse, Aiguille de l'Épena, Grande Glière, Pointe de Méribel and the Three Valleys.

⚑ HIKING

Champagny provides an exceptional **base for hikes** (walking map available from the tourist office). The best hikes start at **Champagny-le-Haut★★**.
⚑The following walks require good fitness levels. They are long, but not technical.

Begin early at Laisonnay-d'en-Bas (alt. 1 559m/5 115ft); from there, trails lead to the **Col du Palet★★** (7hrs 30min return), **Col de la Grassaz** (7hrs return) and **Col du Plan Séry** (5hrs 30min return).
Walkers are rewarded with views of the Grand Bec, Grande Motte and Grande Casse summits.

ADDRESSES

🛏 STAY

◉◉ **L'Ancolie** – Les Hauts du Crey. ℘04 79 55 05 00. www.hotel-ancolie.com. Closed 19 Apr–17 Jun, 6 Sept–19 Dec. Wifi. 31 rooms, restaurant◉◉. Named for the wild columbine, this hotel at the top of the village has small, south-facing practical rooms.

◉◉ **Les Glières** – ℘04 79 55 05 52. www.hotel-glieres.com. Closed 19 Apr–2 Jul, 23 Aug–17 Dec. 20 rooms, restaurant ◉◉. A family hotel in a quiet hamlet. Sauna and lounge with fireplace leading to a pretty terrace.

🍽/EAT

◉◉ **Chalet Refuge du Bois** – R. M. Ruffier-Lanche. ℘04 79 55 05 79. www.gitedubois.com. Closed May and Oct–20 Dec. 🅿▨. Even though modern, this chalet fits in perfectly with its superb surroundings in the Champagny-le-Haut Valley. The food is Savoyard and copious.

Pralognan-la-Vanoise★

In a protected area prized by ibex, Pralognan is the capital of the Vanoise National Park, reached by crossing vast forests along the Doron river. Tucked into the bottom of a dramatic glacial valley, this scenic mountain village makes a perfect hiking base.

> ▶ **Population:** 735.
> ◔ **Michelin Map:** 333 N5.
> ▤ **Info:** 73710 Pralognan-la-Vanoise. ℘04 79 08 70 08. www.pralognan.com.
> ◖ **Location:** Located 27km/16.8mi SE of Moûtiers on D 915.
> ◈ **Don't Miss:** Walk to hamlet of Les Prioux.
> ♟♟ **Kids:** The Ouistiti forest trail includes a via ferrata for six–eight-year-olds. The bureau des guides also organises excursions.

THE RESORT

The village has preserved its mountain charm with characteristic houses of stone and wood.

Summer activities – Attracting thousands of hikers and climbers, Pralognan is one of the most dynamic resorts in Savoie, providing a programme of activities and entertainments.

Ski area – Pralognan has some fine snow conditions to offer on the shady slopes. Ski possibilities are exceptional.

EXCURSION

The Alpine Pastures of Prioux

▶ *From the rte du Plateau, drive into the Chavière Valley.*

⛰This valley extends into the Vanoise Massif and can be reached by car or on foot *(1hr 10 min).* In spring you will often come across ibex. In the small hamlet of Prioux some craft workshops and restaurants are open in summer. Fishing enthusiasts will find a section along the Doron de Chavière for "no kill" fishing. If you feel energetic, continue the walk up to the Roc de la Pêche mountain hut. From Prioux a hike *(3hrs 30min ascent via the Col du Mône)* takes you to the **Petit Mont-Blanc** with a superb **panorama**★★ over the Pralognan Valley.

⛰ HIKES

La Chollière★

⛰*1.5km/1mi along a mountain track, then about 30min on foot. Start from the Hôtel La Vanoise, cross the Doron and follow the road up to La Chollière. Leave the car above the chalets.*

A handsome group of mountains can be seen behind the hamlet: the Pointes de la Glière and the Grande Casse (alt. 3 855m/12 648ft, the highest peak of the Vanoise Massif). The surrounding pastures are famous for their wild flora, including narcissi and edelweiss in June and alpine and globe thistle, known as the "Queen of the Alps", in August.

Mont Bochor★

⛰ *About 3hrs there and back on foot or 6min by cable car.* ◔*Open mid-Jun–early Sept.* ℘04 79 08 70 07.

From the upper station, walk up to the summit (2 023m/6 637ft) to an orientation table. The view looks down on the Pralognan basin and the Doran of Chavière Valley, closed off by the Péclet-Polset Massif.

On the left is part of the huge Vanoise Glacier and the highest Vanoise summit the **Grande Casse**.

A nature trail *(1.4km/0.9mi)* explains this mountain environment.

Col de la Vanoise★★★

⛰ *Alt. 2 517m/8 258ft. Start from Mont Bochor. Climb 3hrs; descent to Pralognan 2hrs 30min.*

Walk along the mountain's edge to the Barmettes refuge, then the path rises steeply to the Lac des Vaches before reaching the pass; view of the Grande Casse Glacier and Pointe de la Réchasse. Inexperienced hikers can come down via the Barmettes refuge and Fontanettes car park. More experienced hikers can in fine weather conditions enjoy a splendid hike via the Arcellin cirque and ravine.

Lac Blanc★★

🥾 *Start from the Pont de la Pêche. A long and arduous climb; 3hrs 15min up, 2hrs 30min down.*

Situated below the **Péclet-Polset refuge**, the Lac Blanc is one of the loveliest lakes in the Vanoise Massif. Walk along the right side of it and climb towards the Col du Soufre. View of the Aiguille de Polset, the Gébroulaz Glacier, the Col de Chavière, the Pointe de l'Échelle and the Génépy Glacier

ADDRESSES

🏨 STAY

🛏 **Hôtel A +** – *R. de l'Arbellaz.* 🕿*04 79 08 87 00. http://hotelaplus.site.voila.fr.* ♿🅿. *25 rooms.* This unmistakable chalet with its square tower functions like a budget hotel.

🛏🍽 **Du Grand Bec** – 🕿*04 79 08 71 10. www.hoteldugrandbec.fr. Closed 14 Apr–31 May, 19 Sept–18 Dec. 39 rooms, restaurant*🍽🛏. At the entrance to the village, below the ridge of the Grand Bec, this hotel offers mountain-style rooms and suites with balconies.Traditional and Savoyard dishes in the warm restaurant or terrace with a view.

🛏🍽 **Les Airelles** – *Les Darbelays, 1km/0.6mi N.* 🕿*04 79 08 70 32. www.hotel-les-airelles.fr. Closed 16 Apr–4 Jun, 18 Sept–17 Dec.* 🅿. *21 rooms, restaurant*🍽🛏. At the edge of the Granges forest, this pleasant 1980s hotel has a fine view to the mountains. The restaurant offers regional food, in particular cheese specialities.

🍴 EAT

🍽 **Le Régal Savoyard** – *Opposite the tourist office.* 🕿*04 79 08 74 76. Closed end Sept–15 Dec.* In the middle of the resort, this little stone-and-wood chalet is popular with locals. Enjoy Savoyard food in a mountain-style dining room or on the shady terrace.

Bourg-St-Maurice

Bourg-St-Maurice is at the foot of the Col du Petit St-Bernard, once a strategic route between Savoie and the Aosta Valley in Italy. In the heart of the Haute Tarentaise, Bourg is today a busy commercial centre.

> ▶ **Population:** 7 681.
> 🗺 **Michelin Map:** 333 N4.
> 🛈 **Info:** Pl. de la Gare, 73700 Bourg-St-Maurice. 🕿04 79 07 12 57. www.lesarcs.com.
> ◉ **Location:** 55km/34.2mi SE of Albertville.

Musée des Minéraux et Faune de l'Alpe

82 av. du Mar.-Leclerc. 🕙*Open Jul–Aug, Mon 10am–noon Tue–Sat 10am–noon, 3–7pm.* 🕿*04 79 07 12 74.*
Fine crystals, with an exhibit showing where they are found and how they are cut, and an exhibit of alpine animals.

EXCURSIONS
Chapelle St-Grat at Vulmix

▶*4km/2.5mi S on D 86.*
This simple chapel, restored in 1995, contains splendid 15C **frescoes**★ depicting the life of St-Grat, known as

the protector of crops, in 18 panels. The village of Vulmix was once known for its rock-salt mines.

Hauteville-Gondon

▶*4km/2.5mi from Bourg, by D 90 towards Aime then follow D 220.*

Église St-Martin-de-Tours – 👣

Guided tours on request at the tourist office. 🕿*04 79 07 04 92.*
This 17C church is decorated in Baroque style.

Séez

▶ *3.5km/2.2mi from Bourg-St-Maurice, take N 90 towards Val d'Isère and Italy.*

This ancient village, situated on the old Roman road, was named Séez because it stood close to the sixth milestone between Lyon and Milan.

Église St-Pierre – ⏰*Open daily 3–6pm except Sat mid-Jun–mid-Sept.* In this 17C Baroque church is a superb altarpiece by Fodéré, as well as a beautiful 15C statue on the left of the entrance.

Espace baroque Tarentaise – *R. St-Pierre.* 🏛 ℘*04 79 40 10 38.* This museum offers a working forge, a collection of Savoie jewellery and an educational exhibit on Baroque art in the region.

🚗 DRIVING TOUR

ROUTE DU PETIT ST-BERNARD★
32km/19.9mi shown on the regional map (⏱see p215). Allow 1hr. ⚠ *The pass is usually closed mid-Nov–May.*
🗂 *La Rosière tourist office* ℘*04 79 06 80 51).*

▶ *Leave Bourg-St-Maurice on N 90 towards La Rosière.*

After La Rosière, this delightful road, built during the reign of Napoleon III, climbs steadily over a five percent gradient, rising from 904m/2 966ft at Séez up to 2 188m/7 178ft at the pass.

Col du Petit St-Bernard★
Supposedly founded by **St Bernard de Menthon** (923–1008), the hospice provided shelter for travellers from bad snowstorms. The building was greatly damaged during World War II. Further on, just before the border post with Italy, stands the Colonne de Joux, surmounted in Roman times by a statue of Jupiter (Jovis). From the pass to the right of the Hotel de Lancebranlette, is a beautiful **view**★ of the steep Italian side of Mont-Blanc, above the Aiguille Noire de Peuterey.
La Chanousia (⏰*open Jul–Aug, and Sept depending on snowfall 9am–1pm, 2–7pm;* ℘*04 79 07 43 32)* is a late-19C **botanical garden** founded by the Canon Chanoux to preserve alpine natural surroundings. Neglected after

World War II, it has been replanted and now contains about 1 000 species of alpine plants.

Lancebranlette★★★
🥾 *Leave from the Col du Petit St-Bernard. 4hrs there and back on foot by a mountain path, often in poor condition in early summer. Information available at the Chalet de Lancebranlette.* From the chalet, climb the northwest slope of the pass towards an indented crest on the left.
An isolated building halfway up is a useful landmark to aim for. Once you reach a vast cirque in a landscape of screes and pastures, keep going left to join the path which zigzags up to the summit at 2 928m/9 606ft.

ADDRESSES

🛏 STAY

⌂ **L'Autantic** – *69 rte Hauteville.* ℘*04 79 07 01 70. www.hotel-autantic.fr.* ♿🅿. *Wifi. 29 rooms.* Rooms are a little dark, although some have balconies. Pleasant indoor pool.

⌂⌂ **Hôtel Le Relais des Villards** – *2376 rte du Petit-St-Bernard, 73700 Séez.* ℘*04 79 41 00 66. www.relais-des-villards.com. Closed 25 Apr–May and 26 Sept–23 Dec.* 🅿. *10 rooms, restaurant* ⌂⌂. Well-run hotel in a traditional chalet; the 10 wood-panelled rooms are very sweet. Good-value restaurant.

🍽 EAT

⌂⌂ **Le Montagnole** – *26 av. du Stade.* ℘*04 79 07 11 52. Closed 10–27 May, 15 Nov–8 Dec and Tue.* Owned by artists whose works adorn the rooms; they also cook up really original dishes.

⌂⌂⌂ **L'Arssiban** – *253 av. A.-Borrel.* ℘*04 79 07 77 35. Closed 3–7 Jan, 20 Jun–10 Jul, 24 Oct–4 Nov, Wed and Sept–Jun Sun.* Stone archways, old tiles and wooden tables provide the setting for generous, contemporary food.

🎉 EVENT

Fêtes de l'edelweiss – *Mid-Jul.* ℘*04 79 07 12 57. www.lesarcs.com.* International folklore gathering.

La Tarentaise★★

With the Maurienne Valley, the Tarentaise is one of the two important Savoyard valleys that lead up to the famous passes used by travellers for centuries to cross into Italy. Formed by glaciers long ago, these beautiful valleys are wide, sometimes cut through by narrow gorges stretching up to the ridges dividing the two countries. The sinuous course of the upper Isère Valley is the main geographical feature of the Tarentaise region. The long and narrow defiles of the Haute and Basse Tarentaise provide a contrast with the more open Moyenne Tarentaise stretching from Moûtiers to Bourg-St-Maurice. This pastoral and wooded middle Tarentaise is the natural habitat of the fawn-coloured **Tarine cows**, one of the most carefully preserved mountain breeds in France.

🚶 HIKES

FROM STE-FOY-TARENTAISE
La Sassière★★
🚶 *10km/6.2mi then 2hrs there and back on foot.*

▶ *Take the first left out of Ste-Foy, D 84 towards l'Iseran.*

- 🚲 **Michelin Map:** 333 L/M/ N 4/5.
- ▶ **Location:** Different sections of the Tarentaise valley fan out from Bourg-St-Maurice. You can reach Les Arcs by road or by cable car directly from the town. La Plagne is reached via Aime. The road up to Tignes and Val d'Isère passes through St-Foy-Tarentaise, with La Rosière reached on the road to the Col du Petit-St-Bernard. The Ponturin valley leads up to Peisey-Nancroix.
- 😍 **Don't Miss:** Exploring the countryside beyond the major ski resorts.

After driving for 4km/2.5mi, you come within sight of **Le Miroir**, with the large balconies of its chalets facing the south. The road continues to rise, eventually reaching the high-pasture area with its typical stone houses from long ago.

▶ *Leave the car at the end of the road and continue on foot.*

🚶 The path rises among clusters of rhododendrons. As you approach the

Le Monal with a view to Mont Pourri and its glaciers

© Pierre Jacques/hemis.fr

Chapelle de la Sassière, the Ruitor Glacier suddenly comes into **view**★★.

Le Monal★★
🥾 *8km/5mi then 1hr return trip on foot.*

▷ *Drive S along D 902 then before the 3rd tunnel turn left to Chenal along a very narrow, bendy road. Leave the car there and continue on foot.*

🥾 From the very pretty hamlet of Le Monal, there is a **view**★★ of Mont Pourri and its glaciers, in particular the waterfalls issuing from the Glaciers de la Gurra and the village of La Gurraz below. You can continue to the summit *(15 min)* or to Bonconseil *(a further 1hr 30min)*.

FROM LES ARCS★
Aiguille Rouge★★★
🥾 *Alt. 3 227m/10 587ft. From the main square in Arc 2000, take the path up (15min) to the base of the Varet gondola. Take the chairlift, followed by the Aiguille Rouge cable car. Orientation at the top. Good walking boots and sunglasses are necessary, as the summit is always snow covered.* ◷*Open Jul–Aug.* ◉*10€ return.* ✆*04 79 07 12 57.*
Enjoy the stunning close-up view of Mont Pourri and, further away, of the Sommet de Bellecôte and Les Trois Vallées. You can spot in the distance the Belledonne and Lauzière ranges as well as the Aravis Massif to the west, the Mont-Blanc Massif to the north and the summits marking the Italian and Swiss borders to the east.

▷ *Take the cable car back and either go down by chairlift, or head downhill on foot to the lovely Lac Marlou (check about the risk of avalanches).*

Télécabine Transarc★★
🚡 *Access from Arc 1800.* ◷*Open Jul–Aug, check times.* ◉*10€ return.* ✆*04 79 04 24 00.*
The gondola passes over the Col du Grand Renard and reaches the foot of the Aiguille Grive at an altitude of 2 600m/ 8 530ft. There are good views of the Aiguille Rouge, Mont Pourri, Grande Motte de Tignes and the impressive ridge of Bellecôte, as well as the Mont-Blanc and Beaufortain massifs to the north. There are numerous possibilities of hikes of varying levels of difficulty.

Aiguille Grive★★★
🥾 *Alt. 2 732m/8 963ft. Experienced walkers, who do not suffer from vertigo, can reach the summit in about 30min up very steep slopes. The ascent should only be attempted in dry weather.*
From the viewing table, there is a stunning **view**★★★ of the Vanoise Massif.

Refuge du Mont Pourri★★
🥾 *3hrs via Col de la Chal, Mont Pourri mountain hut and the Lac des Moutons.*

Peisey-Nancroix with a view of Mont Pourri and Aiguille Rouge

© Pierre Jacques/hemis.fr

A relatively untaxing round tour on the edge of the Parc de la Vanoise.

It is also possible to take a trip to the Aiguille Rouge from the highest point reached by the Transarc gondola. The walk by the Col de Chal to the Aiguille Rouge cable car takes under an hour; take the cable car up and down the Aiguille Rouge, then continue on foot to Lac Marlou and return to the arrival platform of the Transarc gondola.

Télésiège de la Cachette★
Alt. 2 160m/7 087ft. Access from Arc 1600 (Arc Pierre Blanche). Open Jul–Aug. 10€ return. 04 79 07 12 57.
From the top of this chairlift are fine views of the Isère Valley, Bourg-St-Maurice and Mont-Blanc.

Walk to L'Arpette★★
From the top of the La Cachette chairlift, go right to join a path which climbs alongside the Arpette chairlift and leads to the Col des Frettes. Once there, take a path to the left which leads to L'Arpette (alt. 2 413m/7 917ft), a hang-gliding and paragliding take-off point.
Splendid **views**★★ of La Plagne, Les Arcs and the main peaks of the Haute Tarentaise.

FROM PEISEY-NANCROIX
Lac de la Plagne★★
Start from Rosuel – 2hrs 30min ascent. Vertical rise 650m/2 133ft.
Follow footpath GR 5 as far as the bridge over the Ponturin, then continue along the left side of the river. A path on the right bank leads down to the lake in 1 hour 45 minutes. From the lake, it is possible to rejoin GR 5, which leads to the Col du Palet *(about 4hrs return)*.

Notre-Dame-des-Vernettes
Access from Plan Peisey. 45min by an easy forest path. You can take the car and park at Vieux Plan (take the "no through road" at Plan Peisey).
This walk leads you to the chapel of Notre-Dame-des-Vernettes (*guided visits Sat 11am – check with tourist office 04 79 07 94 28*) built in 1727 near a miraculous spring. From there, follow

a path shown by 12 wooden crosses to arrive at the Chapelle de la Fontaine, built a few years before.
Both chapels are colourfully decorated in Baroque style. There is an annual pilgrimage on 16 July and a weekly Mass on Friday morning.

DRIVING TOURS

MOYENNE TARENTAISE★
45km/28mi shown on the regional map (see p214). Allow 2hrs.

▷ *Leave Moûtiers N on N 90.*

To make the most of the richness of the landscape in the middle section of the Tarentaise Valley, this tour takes you up above Aime on a series of small routes on the valley's sunny side, where there are crops and orchards; opposite are woodlands, with Mont Pourri (alt. 3 779m/12 398ft) behind.
Just before entering the gorge, below you is the **Chapelle St-Jacques**, perched on a steep spur – the site of an old episcopal castle – the other side of which is the village of St-Marcel.

Étroit du Siaix
Stop 50m/55yds before the tunnel (*beware of falling rocks*) in order to appreciate the depth of this gorge, which is the narrowest passage of the whole Isère Valley. On the way to Aime, the valley is blocked by two glacial obstructions. Beyond the first of these, within sight of the Mont Pourri summit and glaciers, lies the small **Centron basin**, which takes its name from the Celtic tribe who settled in the area.

FROM MOÛTIERS TO MONTALEMBERT
An alternative route from Moûtiers to Aime is by D 88. You pass through Notre-Dame-des-Prés, overlooking the Moûtiers basin, and the authentic, pretty village of Montalembert.
The road crosses a forest and then a vast green plateau. There are some interesting trees on the route down to Aime.

Aime

🏛 *Av. de Tarentaise, 73210 Aime.* ℘*04 79 55 67 00. www.aimesavoie.com.*

Under the name Axima, the town was once the capital of the Roman province of Alpes Graies. In the Middle Ages it became the home of the Viscounts of Tarentaise, the nobility of Montmayeur. The town's architecture has preserved its very regional character.

Ancienne basilique St-Martin★★ – 🕐*Open Jul–Aug Mon–Sat 9am–12.30pm, 2–7pm, Sun 9am–12.30pm; Sept–Jun Mon–Sat except public holidays 9am–noon, 2–6pm.* ∞*2€.* This 11C basilica with its massive bell tower is a fine example of early Romanesque architecture. The buildings were repaired to some extent in 1875, but it was in 1958 that what were then ruins were recovered. Inside one can appreciate the age of the building, and excavations have shown the existence of two previous religious buildings constructed on top of each other. In the chancel and apse are fragments of 13C **frescoes**★ representing New Testament scenes.

Housed in a former 14C chapel, the small **Musée Pierre-Borrione** (🕐*times same as for the basilica)* displays Gallo-Roman and Merovingian local finds. A 5C tomb is made from tiles. Fine collection of minerals and fossils.

The **Tour Montmayeur** (🕐*open Jul–Aug 10am–noon, 2–6pm;* ∞*3€)* was built in 1221 by the sires of Montmayeur. It has been restored to house a museum of local Tarentaise life. There is a fine view of the town and surroundings.

FROM AIME TO GRANIER

▶ *Leave N 90 onto D 218 (route de Tessens) to the left.*

The road continues up through hairpin bends with Mont Pourri in view, and far below you can see the narrow Isère Valley (Siaix straits) and the Aime basin.

▶ *At Granier, follow D 88 then D 86.*

FROM LA CÔTE-D'AIME TO BOURG-ST-MAURICE

La Côte-d'Aime lies on the southern side of the Beaufortain mountains in the Tarentaise Valley. Its pretty Savoyard villages stretch between 800m/2 625ft and 1 300m/4 265ft. **Montméry** is the most delightful with its elegant chapel of St-Jacques looking over the Isère Valley. Further up the mountain you can discover the *montagnettes*, mountain farmhouse chalets, in the pretty Foron Valley *(GR 5 trail).*

The peaks you will see pointing up into the sky are: the famous Pierra Menta, the Roignais, Aiguille de la Nova, Aiguille du Grand Fond, Pointe de Portette. After Valezan, at the point where you see a cross, the view takes in the Vallée du Ponturin, enclosed by the Bellecôte Massif, with its highest point at 3 416m/11 207ft.

Beyond Montgirod, Bourg-St-Maurice comes into view, with the silhouette of Roc du Belleface appearing behind the Petit St-Bernard depression.

LA HAUTE TARENTAISE

Drive of 12km/7.4mi shown on the regional map (🕐see p215). Allow 30min. From Bourg-St-Maurice D 902 leaves the broad valley where you can see the Malgovert electricity station fed by the Tignes Dam (🕐see p238).

Ste-Foy-Tarentaise

🏛 *73640 Ste-Foy-Tarentaise.* ℘*04 79 06 95 19. www.sainte foy.net.*

With stone houses, their roofs covered in *lauze* (slate-like stone tiles), and narrow windows framing the pastures, this authentic village seems from another age. The nearby hamlets of Ste-Foy are also beautiful, especially the protected site of **Le Miroir**, known for its distinctive houses with roofs extended by the support of pillars imported from the Aosta Valley. This allowed for extra aeration, providing space to dry hay.

Above Ste-Foy, the valley opens up, and you can make out the Mont Pourri glaciers, with its streams forming a series of pretty waterfalls, which depending on the time of day, can look lovely in between the rays of sunshine. The distinctive curve of the Tignes Dam lies at the end of the valley.

ADDRESSES

🏠 STAY

🛏 **Good to know** – **Les Arcs** (1600, 1800, 1950 and 2000) as well as **Bourg-St-Maurice** and the surrounding villages offer a wide choice of accommodation options. Contact the central reservation service of the tourist office, which is open all year.

🛏 **Chambre d'hôte Malezan** – *Rte de la Plagne, 73210 Macot-la-Plagne. 16km/10mi N of La Plagne on D 221. ☎04 79 55 69 90. www.malezan.com. 🛏. 2 rooms ⊡.* A warm welcome is offered here to skiers or walkers. Even though it is by the road, it is a haven of peace and quiet. A gîte is also available.

🛏 **Gîte du Chenal** – *73640 Ste-Foy-Tarentaise. 10km/6.2mi SE of Ste-Foy by D 902, rte de Val-d'Isère and a small road to the right. ☎04 79 06 93 63. Closed Nov–Apr. 🛏. 5 rooms.* At the start of many hikes, this mountain chalet offers simple but practical rooms on three floors. Traditional Savoyard food with garden vegetables served in a rustic dining room.

🛏 **La Forêt** – *73700 La Rosière 1850. 2km/1.2mi S by N 90, rte de Bourg-St-Maurice. Walk to village. ☎04 79 06 86 21. www.campinglaforet.free.fr. Closed mid-Sept–mid-Jun. ♿. 67 sites.* A very pleasantly situated camping and caravan site (for winter) in the heart of a spruce forest, close to La Rosière's ski pistes, or hikes in summer. Mobile homes rented.

🛏🍽 **Chambre d'hôte Chalet Le Paradou** – *Pré Bérard, 73210 La Côte d'Aime. ☎04 79 55 67 79. www.chaletleparadou.com. 🅿. 5 rooms ⊡.* Overlooking the Tarentaise Valley, this magnificent wooden chalet offers beautifully kept, comfortable rooms, a pretty lounge with fireplace and a piano, a pleasant garden, plus sauna and jacuzzi. They also arrange snow-shoeing or walking holidays.

🛏🍽 **Chambre d'hôte Les Carlines** – *Pré Bérard, 73210 La Côte d'Aime. ☎04 79 55 52 07. http://carlines.free.fr. 🅿🛏. 5 rooms ⊡.* A recently built chalet, this B&B is run by a family from Alsace. The dining

room and a relaxing lounge are on the ground floor with non-smoking rooms furnished with pine upstairs. Home-made jams for breakfast; Savoyard, Italian or eastern France specialities for dinner.

🛏🍽 **Hôtel Relais du Petit St-Bernard** – *73700 La Rosière. ☎04 79 06 80 48. www.petit-saint-bernard.com. Closed 26 Apr–26 Jun, 7 Sept–11 Dec. Wifi. 20 rooms, restaurant🍽🍽.* Right by the pistes, this big chalet also includes a restaurant and a souvenir shop. Meals are brasserie style, with a backdrop to the snowy mountains.

🛏🍽 **La Vanoise** – *Plan Peisey, 73210 Peisey-Nancroix. ☎04 79 07 92 19. www.hotel-la-vanoise.com. Closed 25 Apr–Jun and Sept–17 Dec. 🅿. Wifi. 33 rooms ⊡, restaurant🍽🍽.* There is a pretty view to the Dôme de Bellecôte from this typical mountain hotel, which has nice alpine-style rooms, some south facing with balcony, a wellness area, and the expected Savoyard dishes on the menu.

🍴 EAT

🍽 **Le Matafan** – *Shopping centre at the foot of the pistes, 73210 La Plagne. ☎04 79 09 09 19.* You may well work up an appetite to reach this restaurant in Belle Plagne. And hearty menus are available here in the museum-piece dining rooms or on the vast terrace.

🚶 ACTIVITIES

Cycle route – From **Aime** to **Séez**, this cycle route of about 20km/12mi goes alongside the Isère. You can also walk it or use rollerblades.

Mountain biking – The "spot" for mountain bikers in the **Haute Tarentaise** is certainly **Ste-Foy**, with a variety of half- to full-day itineraries, from 15km/9mi to 40km/25mi, reaching up to 1 000m/3 280ft vertical descent.

🎉 EVENTS

Festival de Tarentaise – A festival of music and Baroque art that takes place in the various Tarentaise resorts mid-July to mid-August. *Programme and ticket reservation at the tourist offices.*

Belle Plagne, La Plagne

© Basilisk/ Dreamstime.com

Ski Resorts of the Tarentaise Valley

La Plagne★

La Plagne is 20km/12.4mi S of Aime, in the Bellecôte Massif. *Le Chalet, 73210 La Plagne.* ✆04 79 09 79 79. www.la-plagne.com. The **Grande Plagne**★★, covering an area of 10 000ha/ 24 711 acres, is one of the most extended ski areas in France. Gentle slopes and beautiful views embracing the Mont-Blanc, Beaufortain and Vanoise massifs lend a particular magic to its mountain landscapes, which can be explored on foot in summer and using snowshoes in winter. A superb variety of sports and activities detracts little from the unspoiled character of the village.

Ski area and summer activities – Created in 1961, La Plagne comprises six high villages and four lower ones. An intermediate skier's paradise, the high villages enjoy good snow cover above 2 000m/6 562ft; being centrally located, they offer easy access to the whole ski area. Since 2003 La Plagne has been part of the **Paradski** area, which includes Peisey-Vallandry and Les Arcs. Plagne Bellecôte, **Plagne Centre** and Aime 2000 have a more urban atmosphere, while Plagne 1800, Plagne Villages and above all **Belle Plagne** blend harmoniously with the landscape.

The lower villages of **Champagny-en-Vanoise**★★ (*see p227*) and, to a lesser extent, Montchavin offer superb views of the Vanoise Massif. Hikers can climb up to **Mont Jovet**★★, which offers a beautiful view of the Alps. *As well as a gym and watersports facilities, La Plagne offers fun activities, such as a circus school, an "urban park" and various mechanical rides.*

Viewpoints accessible by gondola

La Grande Rochette★★ – *Alt. 2 508m/8 228ft. Access by Funiplagne gondola from Plagne Centre. Mid-Dec–end Apr.* ✆04 79 09 67 00. From the upper station the splendid **panorama** includes the main summits of the Vanoise Massif and the Oisans.

Télécabine de Bellecôte★★ – *Access from Plagne Bellecôte. Jul–Aug.* 12€ return. ✆04 79 09 67 00. The long gondola ride leads to Belle Plagne and then to the **Roche de Mio**. Climb to the summit (viewing table) *(5min)* to enjoy the splendid **panorama**★★. The Sommet de Bellecôte and its glaciers can be seen in the foreground, with the Grande Motte, the Grande Casse, Péclet-Polset and the Three Valleys further away to the south. Next, take the gondola to the pass, then on to the **Glacier de la Chiaupe** (alt. 2 994m/9 823ft) for a very fine **view** over the Vanoise. In summer and autumn, skiers can enjoy an even wider panorama by taking the Col ski lift. In winter, expert skiers should take the Traversée chairlift for the most interesting slopes. A fantastic off-piste route down to Montchavin gives a 2 000m/6 562ft vertical descent *(take a guide)*.

Les Arcs★

▶ *Take N 90 NE of Bourg-St-Maurice and turn right onto D 119. Arc 1600: 12km/ 7.4mi (or funicular), Arc 1800: 15km/9.3mi, Arc 2000: 26km/16.2mi.*

🅑 *73700 Bourg-St-Maurice.* ✆*04 79 41 55 55. www.lesarcs.com.*

This ski centre, one of the most important in the Alps, was created by a team of Modernist architects in the 1960s, and includes the pedestrian-only resorts of Arc 1600, Arc 1800 connected to Vallandry and Villaroger, on the edge of the Vanoise National Park, Arc 1950 and Arc 2000. Arc 2000 is famous for its **Kilomètre lancé** (speed-skiing) track, which has a 77 percent gradient with a record speed being reached of 251.4km/h/156.2mph.

The resort as a whole is modern and functional, its architectural style blending in reasonably well with the landscape owing to the extensive use of wood. The lines of the buildings are such that each apartment faces the sun, with a view to the mountain. The four levels are linked by a free shuttle service.

Arc 1600 – *Access is by the* **Arc-en-ciel** *funicular from behind the Bourg-St-Maurice train station. 7.30am–9pm.* 🔁*10€ return.* ✆*04 79 07 12 57.*

This resort is known for its traditional family atmosphere and forests. There is a lovely **view**★ of Bourg-St-Maurice, the Beaufortain and Mont-Blanc.

Arc 1800 – South of Arc 1600, the most compact resort occupies a fine position overlooking the Isère Valley with **panoramic views**★ of the Beaufortain, Mont-Blanc and Bellecôte massifs, and the Haute Tarentaise Valley.

Arc 1950 – This small village, opened in 2003, is a direct contrast to the others; abandoning the austere style of the 1970s, the architects chose wood, slate and bright colours in a modern interpretation of traditional style. Relaxation and comfort were the priorities.

Arc 2000 – More remote than the other Arcs, this high-mountain resort, just beneath the Aiguille Rouge with a remarkable **view**★ of La Rosière and Mont-Blanc, attracts advanced skiers. It is on the edge of the Vanoise park.

Ski area and summer activities – The **Paradiski** region, linking Les Arcs with La Plagne and Peisey-Vallandry, is accessible by the Vanoise Express. In summer, there is a huge range of sporting and leisure activities, and is particularly prized by paragliding enthusiasts.

Peisey-Nancroix

▶ *Take N 90 from Bourg-St-Maurice, and then left up the Vallée du Ponturin.*

🅑 *73210 Peisey-Nancroix.* ✆*04 79 07 94 28. www.peisey-vallandry.com.*

This popular family resort is made up of three villages: Nancroix, known for cross-country skiing, the more alpine, Plan Peisey, and the most recent, Vallandry. They are linked to the **Paradiski** area of La Plagne and Les Arcs via the **Vanoise Express**.

La Rosière-Montvalezan

▶ *20km/12.4mi from Bourg-St-Maurice by N 90, towards the Col du Petit St-Bernard, or by D 84 past picturesque villages. Montvalezan is 11km/6.8mi S.*

🅑 *73700 La Rosière-Montvalezan.* ✆*04 79 06 80 51. www.larosiere.fr.*

In a wonderful high setting, the ski area of the traditional village of La Rosière is part of the **Espace San Bernardo**. It offers good snow coverage and plenty of sunshine within a vast international skiing area linked to the Italian resort of La Thuile. The Roc Noir, Traversette and Belvédère summits, the San Bernardo and La Tour pistes, afford superb **views**★ of Mont-Blanc.

Tignes★

In its high mountain lake setting, Tignes counts among the most important ski resorts of France. Not everyone likes the manner in which the town's buildings at 2 100m/6 890ft, and the pylons of its extensive ski lifts, have spoiled the wild and beautiful mountain landscape. However, for several years efforts made to improve the integration of the resort into its environment have paid off.

THE RESORT

It is hard to imagine now that back in 1952, the construction of the dam, flooding the old village of Tignes, forced the exile of large numbers of locals to Paris or the south of France. Shortly after, the handful who remained contributed to the birth of a new resort, built from nothing and dubbed Super-Tignes. This later developed into several areas around the lake: Tignes-le-Lac, Le Lavachet and Val-Claret. To that must be added the two traditional villages remaining below the dam, Les Boisses and Les Brévières.

Ski area – Tignes is linked with Val d'Isère to form the fabulous **Espace Killy**, one of the most extensive and most beautiful ski areas in the world, in a totally barren high-mountain setting. Snow cover is excellent, allowing good spring skiing (and on the Grand Motte in summer). Due to recent climatic conditions, the resort has invested in around 200 snow cannons for skiing down the resort October to May. There are runs for all standards but **expert skiers** are drawn especially to the Vallon de la Sache, Les Pâquerettes and La Ves. Tignes attracts lovers of freestyle skiing in particular, and the resort hosts the freestyle skiing **world championships** every year.

Lac de Tignes

This small natural lake lies at the centre of a treeless high-pasture basin backed by the long snow-covered slopes of the **Grande Motte** above the rocky cirque

- ▶ **Population:** 2 169.
- **Michelin Map:** 333 O5, p215:C2.
- **Info:** BP 51, 73321 Tignes Cedex. ℘04 79 40 04 40. www.tignes.net.
- **Location:** You can reach Tignes from N 90 to Bourg-St-Maurice then D 902; in summer only you can drive from Bonneval-sur-Arc over the Col de l'Iseran, but it is a difficult drive.
- **P Parking:** After you unload your luggage you are required to park in one of the four covered parking areas. Free shuttles connect Tignes-les-Boisses with Val-Claret and Tignes-le-Lac.
- **Don't Miss:** Go up to the glacier of the Grande Motte on the funicular.
- **Kids:** Teenagers should enjoy the snowboarding scene in winter or the skatepark in summer.

of La Balme. The setting of the **Grande Sassière** across the river is very similar. The Tovière summit to the east, facing Val d'Isère, is accessible by gondola. The Col du Palet and Col de la Tourne to the west give access to the Vanoise National Park. In summer, the lake offers a variety of watersports and there is an 18-hole golf course nearby.

Summer – Tignes makes a superb base for hiking in the Vanoise Massif.

Espace Patrimoine

🕔Check for times. ℘04 79 40 04 40. Through photographs, objects and recordings, displays recall the memory of the old Tignes village.

Barrage de Tignes★

The reservoir, known as the **Lac du Chevril**★, is held back by a wall which is 180m/591ft high (including its foundations). The massive downstream side of this arch dam, inaugurated in 1953, was decorated with a huge fresco depicting **Le Géant** (the giant), but since the storms of 1989, the details are hardly visible. A commemorative **statue** (2003) by Livio Benedetti represents a young, graceful and proud Tarentaise woman. The height of the total fall of water at this **hydroelectric complex** is 1 000m/ 3 281ft. The water first supplies the **Brévières** power station, before travelling along a 15km/9.5mi tunnel to the **Malgovert** power station near Bourg-St-Maurice. Via the Isère river, it also supplies the power station of **Randens** downstream of Moûtiers.

A **viewpoint** on the roof of the Chevril power station, just off D 902, offers an overall **view**★ of the dam, its reservoir and the mountains encircling Tignes.

Glacier de la Grande Motte★★★

Last week Jun 7.15am–1pm; Jul–Aug 7.15am–4pm (6min ride every 30min). ⚲15€ return. ✆04 79 06 60 12.

You can reach one of the most famous glaciers in the Vanoise by way of an impressive underground **funicular** from Val-Claret. On arrival is the huge terrace of the popular Panoramic bar and restaurant, where skiers, hikers and tourists alike all arrive with cameras around their necks. The view is of the whole of the glacier, with La Grande Casse and the Aiguille de l'Épena on the right. From here a giant cable car (125 people) takes skiers up to an altitude of 3 456m/ 11 3 39ft, by the Grand Motte summit.

La Tovière★★

🚶*Alt. 2 695m/8 842ft. ⚲Access from Tignes-le-Lac by gondola in summer and by Aéro-Ski in winter.*

Panorama over the Espace Killy ski area, the Grande Motte, Dôme de la Sache, Mont-Blanc and the Grande Sassière.

EXCURSIONS
Réserve Naturelle de la Grande Sassière★★

▶ *From the Tignes Dam, take the road to Val d'Isère. Just beyond the Giettaz Tunnel, turn left up a narrow road (6km/3.7mi) and park at the Saut Dam.*

The nature reserve was created in 1973, and the beauty of the environment has been totally preserved. Overlooked by the **Grande Sassière** and **Tsanteleina** summits, it extends to the Glacier du Rhêmes-Golette on the Italian border.

Lac de la Sassière★★ – 🚶*1hr 45min there and back on foot from Le Saut. Follow a path along the stream on the opposite bank from the EDF road.*

This easy walk leads to a pleasant lake with the Aiguille de Dôme towering above it.

Glacier de Rhême-Golette★★ – 🚶 *Alt. 3 000m/9 843ft. 1hr 30min steep climb from the Lac de la Sassière. Do not venture onto the glacier.*

Magnificent setting backed by La Grande Casse and the Grande Motte.

🚶 HIKES
Col du Palet and Col de la Tourne★★★

🚶 *Allow 1 day. Minimum 750m/2 461ft vertical rise. Experienced walkers can extend the itinerary to the Col de la Grassaz or Lac de la Plagne.*

From Tignes-le-Lac, 90 minutes to the Col du Palet with interesting flora; from the pass, a further, vertiginous 30 minutes to the **Pointe du Chardonnet**★★★: exceptional panoramic view of the Tarentaise region. Less adventurous walkers can aim for the **Col de la Croix des Frêtes**★★, 10 minutes from the Col du Palet. Walk down to the Lac du Grataleu then up again to the **Col de la Tourne**★★, offering splendid views of the Espace Killy. En route down to Tignes, admire the **Aiguille Percée**.

Refuge de la Martin★★

🚶 *Alt. 2 154m/7 067ft. 5hrs there and back from Tignes-le-Lac or Les Boisses.* This undemanding walk offers lovely views of the Lac du Chevril, the surrounding summits and Mont-Blanc in the distance. Walkers can continue as far as the edge of the glacier and admire the view. (☞*Remember that it is highly dangerous for untrained walkers to venture onto a glacier.*) 🚶*1hr 30min steep climb*

Skiing by the Aiguille Percée

© Don Fuchs/Look/Photononstop

from the Lac de la Sassière; it is dangerous to go onto the glacier. Beautiful scenery with the Grande Casse and Grande Motte in the distance.

ADDRESSES

🏠 STAY

🏠 **Good to know** – The Tignes reservation service at the tourist office, offers a wide range of lodgings.

🍽️🍽️ **Hôtel Gentiana** – *Montée du Rosset.* 🕿 *04 79 06 52 46. www.hotelgentiana.com. Closed 3 May–30 Jun, 24 Aug–30 Nov. Wifi. 40 rooms, half-board only.* Rooms in this hotel have been gradually renovated and are of a warm chalet style, some with balconies. A large fitness area includes hammam and sauna. The restaurant serves both traditional and more exotic dishes.

🍽️🍽️🍽️ **Le Paquis** – *Le Rosset.* 🕿 *04 79 06 37 33. www.hotel-lepaquis.fr. Closed May–Jun. Wifi. 33 rooms, restaurant* 🍽️🍽️*.* At the top end of Tignes, this 1960s hotel offers functional rooms; choose the most recently renovated that are in chalet style. Traditional food served in a dining room, decorated mountain style.

🍴 EAT

🍴 **Tignes** and its surrounding villages offer a vast array of restaurants: crêperies, saladeries, pizzerias, pubs, even tex-mex and Chinese food.

🍽️🍽️ **La Chaumière** – *Les Almes.* 🕿 *04 79 40 01 44. www.vmontana.com. Closed May–mid-Dec.* Within the Villa Montana complex by the pistes, La Chaumière offers authentic, regional cuisine, served in lovely Savoyard décor of wood and stone, or on the terrace.

🍽️🍽️ **La Ferme des 3 Capucines** – *Le Lavachet.* 🕿 *04 79 06 35 10. Closed 6 May–14 Dec.* 🅿. An unusual but special place to eat at a cheese farm, with the cows in a stable next to you. Filling family cuisine and local dishes.

🍷 BAR

Grizzly's Bar – *Pl. des Curlings.* 🕿 *04 79 06 34 17. Open Nov–Apr 9am–2am.* Beneath the benevolent gaze of two bears carved from wood, skiers and hikers can enjoy a mulled wine by the fire. Fashion boutique and gift shop.

🏃 ACTIVITIES

Espace aquatique Le Lagon – *BP 51.* 🕿 *04 79 40 29 95. www.tignes.net. Open Sun–Fri 11am–9pm, Sat 2–7.30pm. Closed 9 May–17 Jun, 29 Aug–23 Sept.* 💰*5€.* Swimming pool complex by the lake.

📅 EVENTS

Fête du lac – 🕿 *04 79 40 04 40. 2nd fortnight Aug.* Summer festival including fireworks and a ball.

Val d'Isère★★

Once you have gone beyond the narrow part of the road from the Tignes Dam to Val d'Isère, what surprises is the vast size of the resort. The valley is very open and spread out, with the Bellevarde rock face blocking it in on the right. The centre was transformed for the 1992 Albertville Olympic Games and is full of stone chalets, two or three storeys high, with charming balconies protected by Aosta-style overhanging roofs. This leading Savoie resort shares the icy, bleak, but splendid southern slopes of the Vanoise.

THE RESORT

At an altitude of 1 850m/6 070ft Val d'Isère was developed in the 1930s, at the base of the imposing Bellevarde rock face, the Tête de Solaise and the high peaks of the Grande Sassière Nature Reserve. Besides the resort centre, Val d'Isère includes the old hamlet of Le Fornet higher towards the Col de l'Iseran, and below, the modern annexe, named La Daille. The 16C church contains a fine Baroque altarpiece.

Summer activities – For those visitors immune to the call of the mountains and all the opportunities they present for sports, Val d'Isère has even more to offer. With aerobic steps, tennis and football facilities this is not a resort that takes fitness lightly. Lessons, courses and trainers can be booked for an hour or a week.

Ski area – After installing its first ski lift in 1934 and the École nationale du ski français (French National Ski School or ESF) being formed by Émile Allais in 1935, Val d'Isère gained in particular from the construction of the **route de l'Iseran★★★**. In 1942 the resort inaugurated the Solaise and Bellevarde cable cars. Replacing the latter at La Daille, the funicular dubbed the "Funival" was completely overhauled in 2003 *(end Nov –early May; ☃9.50€ (children under 13 7.50€); ✆04 79 06 00 35).*

Val d'Isère has produced numerous ski champions, starting with **Henri**

- ▶ **Population:** 1 691.
- **Michelin Map:** 333 O5, p215:D2.
- **Info:** BP 228, 73150 Val d'Isère. ✆04 79 06 06 60. www.valdisere.com.
- **Location:** Val d'Isère is 32km/19.9mi SE of Bourg-St-Maurice by D 902, a good road, but with heavy traffic during school holidays. In summer, you can reach it over the Col de l'Iseran.
- **Don't Miss:** Take the cable car up to the Rocher de Bellevarde. Skiers should try the famous Bellevarde downhill race piste.
- **Kids:** The adventure park in the Forêt de Rogoney.
- **Timing:** In summer, to drive over the Col de l'Iseran, start early before the traffic becomes heavy.

Oreiller, who in 1948 became the first French Olympic gold medallist. The 1960s were France's heyday for competitive skiing with the most important champion being Val d'Isère's own **Jean-Claude Killy**, who in the 1968 Olympic Games won a gold for the three alpine ski disciplines: downhill, giant slalom

Val d'Isère

©Robert Maxwell/iStockphoto.com

and special slalom. Today, there are snowboard champions from the resort. In 2009 Val d'Isère hosted the Alpine skiing world championships.

The **Critérium de la Première Neige** has been held on the Oreiller-Killy run in early December every year since 1955 and each year, this downhill race marks the opening of the international ski season. The men's alpine events of the 1992 Olympic Games were held on the spectacular **Face de Bellevarde** piste. Today, Val d'Isère owes its international reputation as a resort both for families and for high-level skiers to its abundant snow cover and extensive pistes, linked with the Tignes area to form the **Espace Killy**; the Face de Bellevarde, "S" de Solaise, the Épaule du Charvet and Tunnel runs are all impressive tests of skill. Summer skiing is possible high on the Pissaillas Glacier, reached from Le Fornet, with artificial snow-cover on some runs. Amazing views are available.

Some 30 passes and summits soaring to 3 000m/9 843ft, within a 10km/6.2mi radius of the resort in the Vanoise Massif, ensure plenty of choice for **cross-country ski** enthusiasts.

Sentier du Fornet – The hamlet of Le Fornet, on the north side of the resort, and surrounded by dense forests, lives in shadow for several months of the year. Only on the avalanche-prone slopes on the other side of the Isère can fields by cultivated. This path has informative panels along it explaining an alpine way of life that goes back for centuries.

MOUNTAIN HIKES

There is little to inspire walkers in the ski area itself, but some excellent itineraries begin in the Parc national de la Vanoise, a few kilometres from Val d'Isère.

Refuge de Prariond and Col de la Galise★★

Park the car by the pont St-Charles on the way to the Col de l'Iseran. 1hr on foot up to the refuge (hut) then 2hrs to the pass. Vertical rise: 900m/2 953ft. 2hrs descent.

The steep path goes through the Gorges du Malpasset, where ibexes roam freely,

to the foot of the Glacier des Sources de l'Isère. Beyond the hut it becomes steeper until it reaches the Col de la Galise (alt. 2 990m/9 810ft), complete with cairns and a view over to the Grand Paradis peaks.

Col des Fours★★

Taxing walk requiring stamina. From the centre of Val d'Isère, drive 3km/1.8mi S to Le Manchet. 1hr 30min up to the Fonds des Fours refuge (vertical rise: 1 000m/3 281ft) then 1hr to the pass. 2hrs descent.

At the refuge, pause to take in the **view**★ of the Grande Sassière, the Mont-Blanc Massif, the Dôme de la Sache and Bellevarde. The path then veers to the left and climbs steeply to the pass: splendid **view**★★ of a lake surrounded by the Glacier de la Jave and of the Maurienne and Tarentaise mountains. You can often see chamois here.

DRIVING TOUR

ROUTE DE L'ISERAN★★★

Drive of 16km/10mi shown on the Route de l'Iseran map (see p265). Allow 1hr. Note the pass is usually closed for snow early Nov–early Jul.

From Val d'Isère to the pont St-Charles, the road follows the bottom of the Isère Valley, becoming more desolate as it climbs. At Le Fornet, you can see the Tsanteleina peak and its glacier, and further on in the heart of the Vanoise Massif the dazzling dome of the Grande Motte appears. At the edge of the Vanoise National Park, there is a car park just before the St-Charles bridge.

The road climbs along the southern side of the valley with a view to the Val d'Isère basin, and the snow-capped La Sache and the rocky Mont Pourri behind. The Tignes Dam appears below.

The **Tête de Solaise**★★ *(above)* can be reached from the road in a pleasant mountain walk *(1hr 30min return)*.

After a long stretch on the edge of the mountain, the road enters the start of the real pass.

Rocher de Bellevarde and Funival

© Pierre Jacques/hemis.fr/Photoshot

Belvédère de la Tarentaise★★

15min there and back on foot. Park the car at the exit of the hairpin bend.
From the orientation table at 2 528m/ 8 294ft altitude, the **panorama** is of the Vanoise (Grand Motte), Mont Pourri and Grande Sassière massifs. Closer you can see Val d'Isère, the Tignes lake and behind the Pointe des Lessières.

Col de l'Iseran★

Reached in winter by cable car and gondola from Le Fornet. The restaurant at the col is also open in summer.
Above the pass (2 764m/9 068ft) on the Tarentaise side, the snow remains all year. The site is incredibly bleak, with only the Chapelle de Notre-Dame de l'Iseran (1939) offering shelter from the regular north winds. There are limited views from the pass.

EXCURSIONS
Viewpoints Accessible by Cable Car
Rocher de Bellevarde★★★

Alt. 2 826m/9 272ft. ⏱*Open Jul–Aug Sun–Fri 9.30am–12.30pm, 1.30–4.30pm.* 🚠*7€ return. 1hr there and back, including 5min on the Olympic cable car. In winter (end Nov–mid-May) access from La Daille by* **Funival** *(4min 30secs).*
From the top station, steep flights of steps lead to the viewing table in five minutes. The splendid **panoramic view**★★★ includes Val d'Isère 1 000m/ 3 281ft below, with its peaks and glaciers all around. To the north is the Lac du Chevril (the Tignes Dam) and Mont-Blanc behind. In the opposite direction are the main peaks of the Vanoise.

Tête de Solaise★★

Alt. 2 551m/8 369ft. ⏱*Open Jul–Aug. Also open in winter (end Nov–mid-May).* 🚠*6.50€. 45min there and back, including 6min cable-car ride.*
The **panorama** includes a fine view of the Isère Gorge below Val d'Isère and the Tignes Dam, as well as the Vanoise, Mont Pourri and Grande Sassière peaks.

ADDRESSES

🛏STAY

🏷**Good to know** – It may not be as fashionable as Courchevel, but it remains hard to find inexpensive lodgings in **Val d'Isère**. The central reservation office gives details of self-catering options, while the tourist office caters more for B&Bs and campsites.

🍽🍽**Chambre d'hôte du Chalet Colinn** – *Le Franchet, 73320 Tignes. 7.5km/ 4.7mi NW, by rte de Tignes and road on right.* 📞*04 79 06 26 99. www.chaletcolinn.com. Closed May–15 Jun. 5 rooms, half-board only.* Lovingly renovated, this chalet has a spacious lounge with a bay window offering a magnificent mountain view. The rooms are superb, all at ground level, opening onto a terrace with a hot tub.

🛏🍽🏨**Hôtel Le Kern** – *La Grange.* 📞*04 79 06 06 06. www.le-kern.valdisere.com. Closed May–Nov. 18 rooms* 🛏. Set back from the main road, this unobtrusive hotel offers the comfort of an old beamed house, with polished wood and antiques. Although not luxurious, the rooms are impeccable, and unusually for a hotel, the price includes breakfast.

🍽 EAT

🎿 Whether on the piste or right in the middle of the resort, you are bound to find a restaurant to your taste. Savoyard classics abound, but there are also many restaurants offering pizzas, crêpes, Asian food, tex-mex or even Alsace or Mediterranean specialities.

🍽 **Le Samovar** – *La Daille.* 📞*04 79 06 13 51. www.lesamovar.com. Closed 21 Apr–9 Dec.* 🅿. Close to the Funival, this big chalet-hotel offers simple food in its brasserie-pizzeria.

🍽🍷 **L'Arolay** – *Le Fornet. 2.5km/1.5mi E of Val d'Isère by D 902.* 📞*04 79 06 11 68. www.arolay.com. Closed Sun eve–Mon.* You might well meet a celebrity at this restaurant, on the edge of a mountain hamlet. In very rustic, attractive surroundings, there is a room especially for grills with each table having its own copper extraction hood. Also served are potato dishes and bilberry tarts. The terrace is on the edge of the Isère.

🍽🍷🏨 **La Fruitière** – *Mid-station of La Daille gondola.* 📞*04 79 06 07 17. www.lafoliedouce.com. Closed May–Nov.* In a room faithfully replicating a cheese-producer, there are old milk churns, wheels of cheese and other paraphernalia in this restaurant, where the cooking is traditional with no frills. The terrace receives the first rays of sun.

🛍 SHOPPING

La Fermette de Claudine – *Val-Village.* 📞*04 79 06 13 89. www.lafermettede claudine.com. Open daily 8am–7pm. Closed May–Jun and Sept–Nov.* In the old village of Val, this shop sells farm produce from the Ferme de l'Adroit, owned by the same family for three generations.

A big range of traditional local cheese is available, along with smoked and dried meats and specialities like Génépi Noir.

🍷 BAR

Bananas – *Immeuble La Bergerie.* 📞*04 79 06 04 23. Open 9am–1.30am. Closed May–Jun and Sept–Nov.* With its pastel tones, this bar is one of the resort favourites. Every day there is a backgammon tournament here, often going on long into the night. Happy hour 7–8pm; French, Indian or tex-mex food.

🏃 ACTIVITIES

🎿 **Good to know** – After the snow has melted, there are walking and mountain-bike tracks, or for the more adventurous, climbing cliffs, via ferrata or summer skiing on the glacier. There is also golfing, or fishing, or simply relaxation by the Lac de l'Ouillette.

👫 **Adventure course** – *Forêt de Rogoney, Savonnette ski lift.* 📞*04 79 06 05 90.* 💶*22€. From 6 years old (min height of 1.45m/4ft 9in with arms raised).* On the parcours du Lémurien adventure course in the forest, there are 75 obstacles to test out your balance and rhythm.

🎭 EVENTS

Le festival Grandeur Nature – Festival of documentary films on animals, flowers and environmental issues in July.

Le Festival international du film aventure et découverte – International adventure film festival in April.

Le Salon international du 4x4 et du tout-terrain – This 4x4 all-terrain vehicle show takes place the last week of July.

TRANSPORT

A free shuttle bus is available between the different parts of the resort and the ski lifts.

Contrasting aspects mark the Maurienne Valley: 80 percent of the freight traffic between France and Italy speeds along it, and in future a high-speed railway is planned from Lyon to Turin; its importance both as birthplace of the House of Savoie and as a cross-border transit route means there is a wealth of fascinating historical markers, from fine Savoie Baroque churches to World War II fortifications; and off the main road, you will find gorgeous alpine countryside, unspoiled villages and magnificent mountains.

Historical Border Country

In 1034, Humbert "White Hands", already the first Count of Maurienne, became the first Count of Savoie, and thus the founder of the House of Savoie; his descendents ruled the area, together with lands as far away as Nice, Turin and Sardinia for many centuries. Even after the annexation of Savoie by France in 1860, the family provided the Kings of Italy until 1946.

The role of the Maurienne was to guard and keep the peace of the important alpine passageways, hence the region was known as the "gatekeeper to the Alps". One of Savoie's most important cities, St-Jean-de-Maurienne was, until 1966, the capital of the diocese.

Tunnel Vision

The road up to the Mont Cenis pass was built on the orders of Napoleon and completed in 1811. Sixty years later and the Fréjus Rail Tunnel (known also as the Mont Cenis Tunnel), the first of the big alpine rail tunnel projects, was completed ahead of schedule. At 12.8km/8mi in length, it is more than

Highlights

1 The Opinel knife museum in **St-Jean-de-Maurienne** (p248)

2 A drive up to the **Col de la Croix de Fer** (p249)

3 Drive along the **Baroque trail** in the upper Maurienne, with a special stop for the chapel at Lanslevillard (p256)

4 The **Esseillon forts** near Aussois (p259)

5 Visit the preserved village of **Bonneval-sur-Arc** and walk on to nearby l'Écot (p264)

twice as long as previous tunnels. Today the tunnel stillcarries trains between Paris and Rome via Turin and Chambéry. The tunnel was always seen as a possible invasion route, giving rise to the construction of major fortifications around Modane on the French side of the tunnel.

Inaugurated in 1980 after six years of construction work, the Fréjus

Fortifications de l'Esseillon

© Alessandro Catzolaro/Fotolia.com

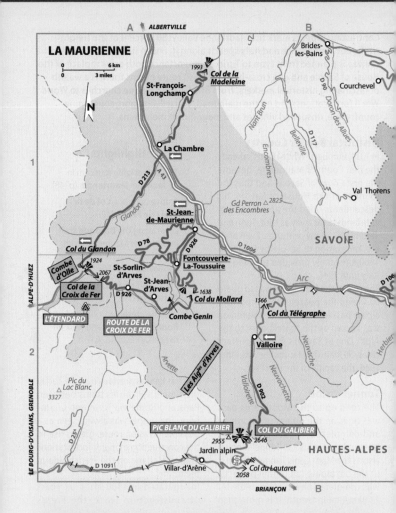

LA MAURIENNE

0 ——— 6 km
0 ——— 3 miles

N

ALBERTVILLE

A

B

Brides-les-Bains

Courchevel

St-François-Longchamp

1993
Col de la Madeleine

D 90

Mont Brun

Doron des Allues

D 117

La Chambre

Belleville

Encombres

D 213

A 43

Val Thorens

Glandon

St-Jean-de-Maurienne

Gd Perron des Encombres △ 2825

SAVOIE

1

Col du Glandon

D 78

D 926

Fontcouverte-La-Toussuire

D 1006

Arc

D 106

Combe d'Olle

1924
2067

St-Sorlin-d'Arves

ALPE-D'HUEZ

Col de la Croix de Fer

D 926

St-Jean-d'Arves

1638
Col du Mollard

L'ÉTENDARD

1566
Col du Télégraphe

ROUTE DE LA CROIX DE FER

Combe Genin

Valloire

Neuvache

Herbier

2

Arnette

Les Alg Jes d'Arves

Valloirette

Neuvachette

Pic du Lac Blanc
3327

D 902

LE BOURG-D'OISANS, GRENOBLE

D 254

PIC BLANC DU GALIBIER

2955 △ ✸ 2646

COL DU GALIBIER

HAUTES-ALPES

Jardin alpin

D 1091

Villar-d'Arène

Col du Lautaret
2058

BRIANÇON

A

B

View from the Pointe de Lessières, Route de l'Iseran

F. Isler/MICHELIN

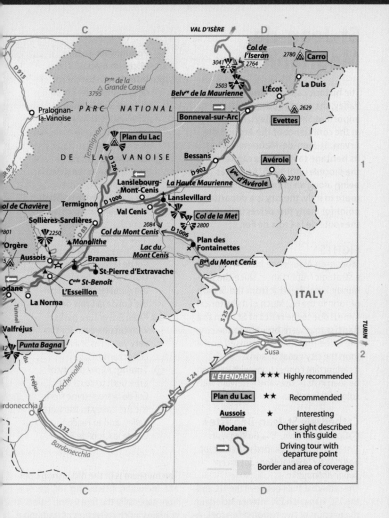

Map legend:

L'ÉTENDARD	★★★	Highly recommended
Plan du Lac	★★	Recommended
Aussois	★	Interesting
Modane		Other sight described in this guide
⇨		Driving tour with departure point
		Border and area of coverage

Road Tunnel is shorter than the Arlberg Tunnel (Austria) and the St-Gothard Tunnel (Switzerland), but longer than the Tunnel du Mont-Blanc.

The Franco-Italian project was designed to ease road traffic when the Col du Mont Cenis is blocked by snow. When the Tunnel du Mont-Blanc was closed after a tragic accident in 1999, the Fréjus Tunnel had to absorb the extra traffic; safety features in the tunnel were improved soon afterwards.

In 2013 the much-disputed Lyon Turin Ferroviaire project to allow high-speed trains to travel between the cities is expected to start, with the excavation of a new 50km/31mi "base" tunnel from St-Jean-de-Maurienne to Chiusa San Michele in Italy.

Rambles and Serious Treks

Bonneval, Bessans and Val Cenis in the Upper Maurienne Valley are all excellent bases for hikes of all levels of difficulty. Relatively easy walks to admire the scenery include that from Bonneval to the Chalets de la Duis, to the Refuge d'Avérole from Bessans or to Plan du Lac from Termignon; for those with sufficient fitness, steeper hikes from Bonneval to the Refuge du Carro or the Refuge des Évettes reward with fantastic mountain panoramas.

St-Jean-de-Maurienne★

The historic capital of the Maurienne Valley, the most southern of the important Savoie valleys, is situated at the confluence of the Arc and the Arvan. St-Jean-de-Maurienne owes its heritage to its role as capital of the diocese until 1966. As well as being along an important through-route to Italy, the city is a departure point for many fine drives including the route de la Croix de Fer.

SIGHTS

St-Jean-de-Maurienne has always held a strategic importance, since the Burgundy kings freed it from the Bishop of Turin in the 6C. Much of its historical fame is due to the **relics of St John the Baptist** that were brought to the city; the three fingers that baptised Christ form the city's coat of arms.

Its important connections with Italy can be seen in its houses and gateways with colourful façades.

Cathédrale St-Jean-Baptiste★

Open 9am–7pm. Guided visits (1hr 30min) 3€. Guided visits of crypt and cloister (45min) Mon–Sat except public holidays.

The cathedral, built between the 11C and the 15C, has a rich 15C interior including the remains of two restored frescoes. A delicately carved alabaster **ciborium**★ is on the left of the apse. The magnificent 43 upper and 39 lower wooden **stalls**★★ (1498) took Pierre Mochet, a sculptor from Geneva, 15 years to carve. The Roman **crypt**★ contains parts of the original 11C church. On the north side of the church, the well-preserved 15C **cloister** has retained its original alabaster arches.

Musée des Traditions et Costumes Mauriennais

Open Jun–mid-Sept Mon–Sat 10am–noon, 2–6pm; 2 weeks Feb 2.30–5.30pm.
Closed public holidays.
04 79 83 51 51.

- **Population:** 8 633.
- **Michelin Map:** 333 L6.
- **Info:** Ancien Évêché, pl. de la Cathédrale, 73300 St-Jean-de-Maurienne. 04 79 83 51 51. www.saintjeande maurienne.com.
- **Location:** A 43 takes you directly to the town. In summer, it is more pleasant to arrive through the St-Jean Valley, either from the south by the Col de la Croix de Fer or from Moûtiers in the N by the Col de la Madeleine.
- **Don't Miss:** The view of the Aiguilles d'Arves from the Col de la Croix de Fer.
- **Kids:** Adventure parks with circuits even for the very young at St-François-Longchamp.
- **Timing:** Allow plenty of time both to cross the Col de la Madeleine from the Arc Valley to the Isere Valley, and to reach the Col de la Croix de Fer.

The museum is in the old bishop's palace, including interesting 18C decoration, especially the fine Grand Salon. It contains a rich collection of traditional costumes worn by the village women of the Maurienne.

Musée Opinel

Open Mon–Sat 9am–noon, 2–7pm.
Closed public holidays. 04 79 64 04 78. www.opinel-musee.com.

The museum illustrates the history of the famous knives from Savoie produced by local company Opinel. A film is shown of the production of the steel knives with their distinctive beechwood handles.

HIKE
Refuge de l'Étendard★★★

Allow 3hrs 15min return on foot from the Col de la Croix de Fer.

After climbing *(1hr 50min)*, you suddenly glimpse the refuge lower down on the shores of Lake Bramant, overlooked by the Pic de l'Étendard (3 464m/11 365ft). The Belledonne range, stretching across the horizon to the west, is spectacular. To the northwest are the Aiguilles d'Argentière and to the northeast there is a magnificent **view**★★ revealing Mont-Blanc, Grandes Jorasses, Grand Combin, Grand Bec and Grande Casse. For those wanting a one-day hike, you can continue along the lakes of Bramant, Blanc and Tournant to reach the foot of the **St-Sorlin** Glacier.

DRIVING TOURS

ROUTE DE LA TOUSSUIRE★

Drive of 36km/22.4mi shown on the regional map (see p246). Allow 2hrs.

▷ *From St-Jean, drive along D 926 then turn right towards La Toussuire.*

During the drive, the **Aiguilles d'Arves**★★ stand out from a broad horizon of mountains. Higher up the road overlooks the St-Jean-de-Maurienne basin.

The ancient hilltop village of **Font-couverte-la-Toussuire**★ commands a panoramic view of the surrounding area. Continue to the resorts of La Toussuire and Le Corbier.

The ski areas of **Le Corbier** and **La Toussuire** are linked together with St-Sorlin d'Arves and other villages within the ski area of **Les Sybelles**. (*04 79 59 88 00; www.les-sybelles.com*).

ROUTE DE LA CROIX DE FER★★★

Drive of 32km/19.9mi shown on the regional map (see p246).
Allow 1hr 30min.

▷ *Leave St-Jean-de-maurienne on D 80 towards Albiez-Montrond.*

The road ascends steeply with stretches along the edge of the cliff, offering views down to the Arvan gorges.

Col du Mollard★

From the highest point of the road are very attractive **views**★ of the Aiguilles d'Arves behind the first peaks of the Vanoise and the Maurienne massifs. As you come into the hamlet of Mollard, the scree-covered **Combe Genin** is visible. From the Col du Mollard, with the majestic Aiguilles d'Arves above, the road drops down across meadows, crosses the Arvan and enters the **gorges**★.

▷ *Turn right on D 926 (rte de St-Jean-de-Maurienne), then where the Combe Genin ends, just before a tunnel turn left on the scenic route D 80 to reach the hamlets of St-Jean-d'Arves.*

Aiguilles d'Arves from the Col de la Croix de Fer

© Valeriya Silanteva/Dreamstime.com

St-Jean-d'Arves

🛈 ℰ04 79 59 73 30. www.sja73.com.

Quite high up on the opposite slope the **picture**★ of the hamlet and church of Montrond is visible in front of the Aiguilles d'Arves. After the exit of the tunnel the road goes round a bend avoiding the ravines of the Clietaz stream.

At the beginning of a turn, 2km/1.2mi further, the narrow strait of the Entraigues Valley appears. After the hamlet of Le Villard, cross the Combe de La Tour to arrive at the church of St-Jean-d'Arves overlooking the upper Arvan Valley. From this **site**★ is a view of the snowy peaks of the Grandes Rousses.

▶ *Return to D 80 towards St-Sorlind'Arves. At Malcrozet, turn right on D 926.*

St-Sorlin-d'Arves

🛈 ℰ04 79 59 71 77.
www.saintsorlindarves.com.

New buildings connected with the nearby ski area somewhat spoil the traditional character of this village, despite its attractive surroundings.

Walking path – *Leave from the La Balme car park after the hairpin bend; follow the signs Vieux village des Prés Plans.*

Along a path overlooking the Arvan Valley, this easy family walk *(1hr 30min)* takes you to the village of Prés Plans, with its 1630 chapel and several fine alpine chalets. The views on the drive from St-Sorlin to the Col de la Croix de Fer are mainly of the Aiguilles d'Arves and the pretty Arvan Valley with its hamlets in the midst of the meadows. Now and again you can see the peak of the Grand Sauvage and the Pic de l'Étendard, with its glacier reaching down one slope (the St-Sorlin Glacier).

Col de la Croix de Fer★★

Alt. 2 068m/6 785ft. 15min return on foot.

Climb onto the rocky knoll bearing a commemorative pyramid south of the pass, and turn towards the east for a fine **view** of the Aiguilles d'Arves.

ROUTE DU GLANDON

Drive of 22km/13.7mi shown on the regional map (see p246). Allow 1hr 30min. The road is closed above St-Colomban-des-Villards Nov– early Jun.

This is the most direct route from Le Bourg-d'Oisans or Vizille to the Arc Valley and it also connects Grenoble with Moûtiers via the Col de la Madeleine. The relaxing D 927 road runs through the Glandon Valley, known also as the Vallée des Villards, with views to Mont-Blanc along the route.

Col du Glandon★

Alt. 1 924m/6 312ft. 250m/273yds from the Chalet-Hôtel du Glandon.

The pass, with the colourful rock formations of the Aiguilles d'Argentière above, offers a splendid **vista** of Mont-Blanc far in the distance. Between the col and Léchet, the upper Glandon Valley affords austere landscapes of meagre pastures and rocky slopes, brightened by a carpet of red rhododendrons in summer.

ROUTE DE LA MADELEINE★

Drive of 25km/15.5mi shown on the regional map (see p246). Allow 1hr.

Opened in 1969, linking the Maurienne and Tarentaise valleys, this is a lovely route to take from the Arc Valley to the Tarentaise resorts.

Across moderately high mountains, you will drive through an area of beautiful landscapes and charming hillside villages. D 213 from La Chambre *(11km/6.8mi NW of St-Jean-de-Maurienne)* climbs up in a series of hairpins with views to the Belledonne and Grandes Rousses chains through the Glandon gap.

St-François-Longchamp

🛈 ℰ04 79 49 10 56. www.otsfl.com.

This resort spreads out between St-François and Longchamp on the east side of the Bugeon Valley, beneath Cheval Noir summit.

Linked with Valmorel (see p219) it is one of the biggest ski resorts in the Maurienne. In summer it becomes a busy hiking centre.

Col de la Madeleine★

Covered with pastures, this wide gap between the Gros Villan (Lauzières chain) and Cheval Noir summits offers a remarkable **view** of the Mont-Blanc Massif to the northeast, and beyond the Glandin Valley, the Grandes Rousses and Écrins massifs *(orientation table)*.

EXCURSION
Vaujany

◯ *27km/16.8mi SW of Col du Glandon (♨ see p250) towards Bourg-d'Oisans and then left on D 43A.*

This south-facing village lies in a lovely **setting★** on the slopes of the Rissiou, facing the Grandes Rousses. From the end of the village, there is a splendid view of the **Cascade de la Fare★** and its spectacular 1 000m/3 281ft drop from the point of the Étendard peak.

The **Maison de la Faune** (♨ *open Jul–Aug and Jan–Apr Sun–Thu 10am–noon, 2–7pm; ℘04 76 79 87 07) museum* offers free guides who explain the habits of alpine animals.

Vaujany is linked by cable car to the Dôme des Rousses (2 805m/9 203ft) via the Alpettes station. From Alpette you can reach the ski area of Alpe-d'Huez (♨ *see p303).* A road starting near the Vaujany cemetery leads to the **Collet de Vau-jany★★.** An extended view of the west side of the Grandes Rousses, with the Pic de l'Étendard and Lac Blanc.

ADDRESSES

🛏 STAY

☞ **Les Airelles** – *73300 La Toussuire. ℘04 79 56 75 88. www.hotel-les-airelles.com. Closed 21 Apr–14 Dec. 🅿. Wifi. 31 rooms.* At the bottom of the ski lifts, this large family hotel has both traditional and contemporary décor. Simple meals available at the bar at lunchtime; in the evening, residents are offered traditional meals.

☞☞ **Beausoleil** – *Le Pré 73530, St-Sorlin-d'Arves. ℘04 79 59 71 42. www.hotel-beausoleil.com. Closed 19 Apr–Jun and Sept–19 Dec. 🅿. Wifi. 21 rooms, restaurant☞☞.* A hotel in the middle of the resort, at the bottom of the pistes, which offers small or family rooms, all well kept and with balconies. Wellness area with hammam, sauna and gym. A brasserie-style menu at lunch at the bar or on the terrace, Savoyard dishes served in the modern dining room.

☞☞🍴 **Les Soldanelles** – *R. des Chasseurs Alpins, 73300 La Toussuire. ℘04 79 56 75 29. www.hotelsoldanelles.com. Closed 20 Apr–27 Jun, 1 Sept–20 Dec. 🅿. Wifi. 38 rooms, restaurant☞☞.* A family hotel at the top of the resort, where you will receive a warm welcome and spacious rooms with balconies (south facing give the best view). Pool, hammam. Traditional recipes and cheese specialities served in an elegant panoramic restaurant.

🍽/EAT

☞ **Auberge Passoud** – *Enversin d'Oz, 38114 Oz. Rte de Vaujany. ℘04 76 80 73 18 www.gite-passoud.com. Closed 1 Dec–25 May. ♿ 🅿. 5 rooms☞☞ 🍴.* A country inn tucked away in a hamlet overlooking the Verney Dam. Vegetables are mainly from the garden and accompany magical recipes concocted by the chef (or wizard of Oz…). The old barn has practical rooms, and there are also two small, basic gîtes to let.

☞☞ **La Remise** – *Shopping area, 38114 Vaujany. ℘04 76 80 77 11. www.restaurant-laremise.com. Closed 15 Apr–Jun and Sept–15 Dec.* Decorated in mountain style, the restaurant offers a menu including a new take on traditional dishes, as well as pizzas and some more complicated dishes.

🤸🏃 ACTIVITIES

🧗🧗 **Les Aventures du Nant Burian** – *73130 St-François-Longchamp. ℘04 79 59 13 80. www.parcoursaventure.fr. Jul–Aug 9.30am–5pm; Jun and Sept Sat–Sun 1.30–5pm. ☞20€.* Three different adventure circuits for adults, children and toddlers (two–four years old).

Valloire★

At the foot of the Rocher St-Pierre, Valloire is the most important tourist centre in the Maurienne. Its hamlets stretch across a plateau enclosed by the Col du Lautaret. On fine days, hundreds of cyclists are seen in the area, because, despite its quite high altitude (2 058m/6 752ft), this pass is one of the busiest in the Alpes du Dauphiné. To reach the pass, one climbs up an increasingly austere mountain, with rock ridges either side. Once reached, the pass offers a view over the nearby mountains that is almost mysterious in its beauty.

SIGHTS

Valloire includes 17 hamlets stretched along a valley below the famous Col du Galibier, and conveniently situated on the edge of the Vanoise and Écrins national parks.

Church★ – ○*Open Jul–Aug Mon–Sat 10am–noon, 2–5pm; Sept–Jun Mon–Fri 4–7pm.* Most of the church dates from the 17C, and is one of the most lavishly decorated in Savoie.

The gilt-wood Baroque **altarpiece**★★ includes a statue of St Peter on the right and to the left, Ste Thècle (a local girl who, in the 6C, brought back St John the Baptist's relics to St-Jean-de- Maurienne). The cross above the door to the sacristy is believed to be a copy of Albrecht Dürer's *Christ* (1609).

Summer activities – The 17 hamlets of Valloire offer a range of activities. Keen cyclists in particular have a wealth of choice with two prestigious passes nearby and 150km/93.2mi of marked mountain-bike routes.

The ski area – Valloire is a well-equipped ski resort with a choice of red and black runs for experienced skiers in the Colérieux, and the Sétaz (with the Olympic black run). An impressive number of snow cannon ensure adequate snow cover all winter and the ski area is linked to that of Valmenier (shared ski pass).

▶ **Population:** 1 293.
◉ **Michelin Map:** 333/334 G2.
▯ **Info:** 73450 Valloire.
  𝒞04 79 59 03 96.
  www.valloire.net.
◉ **Location:** The gateway from the south to the Alps, Valloire lies 27km/16.8mi from Briançon off D 1091, then D 902 takes you over the Col du Galibier.
◉ **Timing:** Every Sunday in summer there is a festival. The traditional Ascension Day procession on 15 August is very colourful.

EXCURSION
Col du Télégraphe★

Alt. 1 566m/5 138ft. ▶*5km/3mi N.*
Climb to the top of the rocky knoll, on the north side, to get a bird's-eye **view** of the Arc Valley. Between the pass and Valloire, the road overlooks the Valloirette rushing through steep gorges towards the River Arc.

🚗 DRIVING TOUR

ROUTE DU GALIBIER★★★

Drive of 19km/11.8mi shown on the regional map (©see p246). Allow 30min ⊙The Col du Galibier is closed end Oct– end May (sometimes to Jul).

This road, one of the most famous in the French Alps, linking the Maurienne and the Briançonnais (©see p340), takes you through an austere and totally unspoiled mountain area. The panorama unfolding from the Col du Galibier is one of the finest in France, particularly in the early morning or late afternoon. The itinerary starts with a steep climb from the Arc Valley to the wooded "hanging" valley of the Valloirette, a tributary of the Arc. As the road continues to rise in a series of dizzying curves, the landscape begins to look bleak, then utterly grim with the crest of the Galibier being a steep, rocky and barren slope. The impressive Écrins Massif comes into view beyond the Col du Galibier. The route du Galibier is well known to cyclists as one of the most challenging stages of the Tour de France.

Col du Galibier★★★

The road goes through a tunnel, or over the pass itself (alt. 2 646m/8 681ft), which is the highest point of the **route des Grandes Alpes** after the Col de l'Iseran (alt. 2 770m/9 088ft).

Leave the car and walk up *(15min there and back)* to the viewing table (alt. 2 704m/8 871ft); nearby is an old boundary stone marking the border between France and Savoie. The splendid circular **panoramic view** includes the Aiguilles d'Arves and Mont Thabor to the north and the glaciers and snow-capped peaks of the Écrins Massif to the south.

At the southern exit of the tunnel stands a monument to **Henri Desgrange**, editor of the newspaper *L'Auto* who organised the first Tour de France in 1903, covering 2 500km/1 554mi in six stages.

HIKE
Pic Blanc du Galibier★★★

Alt. 2 955m/9 695ft. This 3hr hike is only suitable for experienced hikers.
Leave the car by the Henri Desgrange monument and follow the marked path across the fields, aiming for a round summit on the left which it is advisable to climb on its left side *(steep climb)*: remarkable **panorama**★★ of the Meije and Mont Thabor. *People inclined to vertigo are advised to turn back here.*
The itinerary continues along a path following the narrow mountain ridge (*dangerous if wet*). The ascent to the summit of the Pic Blanc du Galibier is very steep but well worth it for the exceptional **panorama**★★★: Pic des Trois Évêchés and Aiguilles d'Arves in the foreground, Mont Thabor and to the north the snow-capped peaks of the Vanoise, Mont-Blanc and the Grandes Jorasses.

▶ *On the way back, follow a narrow path on the left leading to the viewing table near the pass, then bear right to return to the car park.*

ADDRESSES

🛏 STAY

🍽 **Christiania** – *Av. de la Vallée d'Or.* ℰ*04 79 59 00 57. www.christiania-hotel.com. Closed 16 Apr–14 Jun, 16 Sept–14 Dec. Wifi. 24 rooms, restaurant🍽.* In summer covered in flowers, and in January, the perfect place to view the unusual ice-sculpture competition. Well-kept rooms have been brought up to date in mountain style. The friendly establishment offers brasserie food at lunchtime, more serious later.

🍽 **Relais du Galibier** – *Les Verneys.* ℰ*04 79 59 00 45. www.relais-galibier.com. Closed 6 Apr–11 Jun, 6 Sept–17 Dec.* 🅿. *Wifi. 26 rooms, restaurant🍽.* Pleasant family hotel near the ski slopes. Some of the simple, clean rooms have a view to the Grand Galibier. Generous portions of regional food, made with quality ingredients served in a dining room with large bay windows.

🍴 EAT

🍽 **La Ferme du Poingt Ravier** – *Hameau du Poingt-Ravier, 5km/3mi past the campsite.* ℰ*04 79 59 07 78.* ♿🅿🚭. It is well worth a stop at this old farm (1898), which became a restaurant 20 years ago. Perched at an altitude of 1 670m/5 479ft, it has a magnificent view over the Alps, and a lovely interior with old furniture and decorations. On the grass of the summer terrace, chickens and peacocks roam. Traditional cuisine.

🚶 ACTIVITIES

🎫 **Good to know** – The **Multipass** gives access to the pool, ice rink and gondola, as well as certain reductions on other activities.

Bureau des guides et accompagnateurs de la compagnie Savoie-Maurienne – *3 La Place.* ℰ*04 79 83 35 03. www.guides-savoie.com.* The professional local guides can lead you on easy glacier walks, wildlife walks, or accompany keen climbers to the most challenging peaks.

Modane

Near the entrance of the important Fréjus Tunnel linking France and Italy, the border town of Modane is nearly overwhelmed by the dense traffic passing through the narrow valley of the Arc. However, the town centre retains a real Savoyard character. A short distance away, the resorts of La Norma and Valfréjus are set in pleasant landscapes.

▶ **Population:** 3 754.
◉ **Michelin map:** 333 N6.
▤ **Info:** R. des Bettets, 73500 Valfréjus. ℘04 79 05 33 83.
◖ **Location:** Directly accessible from A 43, 30min from Italy via the Fréjus Tunnel.
◈ **Don't miss:** Fort St-Gobain.

SIGHTS

The oldest quarter of Modane is **Pâquier**, whose streets fan out from the church, but the most interesting historic quarter is **Loutraz**, on the right bank of the Arc river. In rue de Chavière are several houses with outside spiral staircases. An old Greek temple, the **Rizierie des Alpes**, houses an exhibition devoted to the much-fought-over, planned construction of the cross-border Lyon–Turin railway link, which includes the building of a 50km/31mi tunnel near Modane.

Fort St-Gobain

🕐*Open 10am–noon, 2–6.30pm Jul–Aug daily; May Wed–Sun; Jun and Sept Wed–Mon.* ◌8€. ℘04 79 05 01 50.
Uniquely preserved part of the Alpine Maginot Line, this fortification museum includes a huge underground area with arsenal and prison zones.

Muséobar

42 r. de la République. 🕐*Open Jul–Aug Tue–Wed and Sun 3–7pm, Thur–Sat 10am–noon, 3–7pm; Sept–Jun Tue–Wed 3–7pm, Thu–Sat 10am–noon, 3–7pm.* ◌4.50€. ℘04 79 59 64 23.
www.museobar.com.
This museum presents a delightful voyage back in time to the birth of this alpine border town at the end of the 19C, at the time of the annexation of Savoie to France and the building of the first railway tunnel under a mountain.

👥 The Underground Laboratory

Carré Sciences LSM, 1125 rte de Bardonnèche. 🕐*Open Mon–Fri 2–5pm.*
◌*Free.* ♿ ℘*04 79 05 22 57.*
www.lsm.in2p3.fr.
Entry for children from nine years old, this is a permanent exhibition at Modane's unusual national science laboratory, 1 700m/5 577ft below ground in the Fréjus Tunnel.

🚶 HIKES

Sentier Nature de l'Orgère★

🚶 *From Modane, take D 1006 at Freney; turn right onto D 106, which rises steeply to the Orgère refuge (parking) over a distance of 13km/8.1mi.*
This nature trail (2km/1.2mi) is an easy, pleasant walk that winds through the Orgère Valley across meadows, woodland and pastures. It starts just below the porte de l'Orgère.

Hike to Col de Chavière★★

🚶 *Departure from the Orgère refuge: 3hrs up (including 2hrs to the Lac de Partie); 2hrs down. Vertical rise: approx. 900m/2 953ft. Climbing boots are recommended and binoculars.*
The path, with a view of the Râteau d'Aussois and the Aiguille Doran, climbs to the ruins of the Chalets de l'Estiva: **view**★★ *(left to right)* of Longe Côte, La Norma, Modane, Valfréjus. When the path starts going down, after a further hour's walking, the Col de Chavière comes into view flanked by the snow-capped **Péclet-Polset** and high cliffs. Chamois and ibexes roam the area. The path then continues through a rocky area until the Lac de la Partie. It then becomes steeper, climbing up to the pass (2 801m/9 190ft) from where there is a fine view over the Prolagnan Valley, and beyond to Mont-Blanc.

EXCURSION
La Norma
▶ *6km/3.7mi from Modane by D 1006.*
🏠 *℘04 79 20 31 46. www.lanorma.com.*
This quiet, car-free and picturesque little resort, founded in 1971, occupies a favourable position on a plateau overlooking the upper Maurienne Valley.

Summer activities – There is a huge leisure area at Avenières next to a fishing lake. The nearby Vanoise park is a dream for hikers, and other activities are available like all-terrain skateboarding or for a novice climbing experience, the **Via Ferrata du Diable**★.

🎿 **Ski area** – The resort's northwest orientation guarantees good snow cover, and a good number of lifts serve 65km/40.4mi of pistes between 1 350m/4 429ft and 2 750m/9 022ft. Expert skiers will find some steeper slopes at the highest part of the area.

Valfréjus✳ 🎿
8km/5mi S of Modane by D 1 006.
The main attractions of this small ski resort, created in 1983, below Mont Thabor and the Vanoise Massif, are its tasteful architecture, which fits in well with the landscape, and the nearby forest planted with spruces and larches.

Ski area – The north-facing slopes enjoy good snow cover particularly on higher sections; there are 12 ski lifts and some 20 pistes.
The Arrondaz gondola and the Punta Bagna chairlift above bring you to a splendid **panorama**★★: slightly to the left is the Pointe du Fréjus, in the middle the pointed peak of Rochebrunne and the Italian Alps through the Col du Fréjus. On the right is the rocky mass of the Grand Argentier.
Behind the restaurant terrace you can admire the Meije, the Rateau and the Thabor as well as two of the three Aiguilles d'Arves.
Finally, to the north, you will see the Valfréjus ski area and the Vanoise mountains and glaciers beyond.

ADDRESSES

🛏 STAY
😋😋 **Chambre d'hôte Ché Catrine** – *88 r. St-Antoine, 73500 Villarodin-Bourget. A 43, Exit 30, 3km/1.8mi on D 1006. ℘04 79 20 49 32. www.che-catrine.com. Closed 15 Oct–mid-Apr. 🅿 🍽. 5 rooms⛄.* This old village house (1524) is a little jewel, meticulously restored in Savoyard style. The rooms are exquisite and the dining room in an old vaulted stable is superb. Jacuzzi and sauna available.

😋😋 **Hôtel Le Perce-Neige** – *14 av. J.-Jaurès. ℘04 79 05 00 50. www.hotel-leperceneige.com. Closed 1st half May, 2nd half Oct and Sun. Wifi. 18 rooms, restaurant😋😋.* This slightly old-fashioned hotel is near the railway, but the simple, practical rooms are well sound-insulated. Choose one looking over the river. Traditional cooking.

🏃 ACTIVITIES
Dog-sledging outings – *73500 La Norma. ℘04 79 20 31 46. ⊜38€.* These unforgettable excursions take place twice a week, and give you the chance to really appreciate these special nordic breeds of dogs.
Le Centre d'activités Montagne – *73500 Valfréjus. ℘04 79 05 32 58. www.esi-valfrejus.com.* This centre provides guides for walks and snow shoeing outings in winter, around the resort or into the Vanoise park.
👪 **Water leisure park** – *73500 La Norma, A 43, Exit 30. ℘04 79 20 31 46. Open Jul–Aug, 11am–6pm. ⊜3€.* Supervised swimming, fishing and picnics.

VISITS
Entrée monumentale du tunnel ferroviaire – Off the road from **Modane** to **Valfréjus**, a small exhibit and steam train at the entrance to the first **alpine railway tunnel**, built 1857–71.

Les moulins de St-André – These **mills** with horizontal wheels are a rarity. One of them has been converted into a museum. Details from the **La Norma tourist office**.

Sculpture paths, La Norma – These paths have huge sculptures with mountain themes by international artists along the way. Map available at the La Norma tourist office.

La Haute Maurienne★

An important thoroughfare to
Italy, the Maurienne Valley (the
course of the Arc river) runs along
the edge of the Vanoise Massif.
There is a striking contrast between
the industrial landscape between
Modane and Bramans and the
magnificent rocky and wooded
mountain scenes that appear
beyond the Esseillon fort, on the
climb from Bramans to Lanslebourg.

Info: Maison de la Vanoise,
Termignon. ℘04 79 20
51 67. www.3petits
villages.com.

Location: This region
stretches from the Col de
l'Iseran above Val d'Isère,
SW towards Modane on
the Italian border along
D 902 and D1006.

Don't Miss:
The paintings in the
Chapelle St-Sébastien.

Kids: The educational
nature trail at Termignon.

🚗 DRIVING TOUR

THE TRAIL OF THE BAROQUE
*Drive of 29km/18mi shown on the
Haute Maurienne map (☞see right).
Allow time to visit the chapels.*
☞*D 902 between Bonneval and
Bessans may be closed Dec–Mar.*
From the plain exteriors of the chapels
and churches, you can hardly imag-
ine the richness of colours, and detail
that decorate the Baroque altarpieces
inside, created as part of the 16C–17C
Counter-Reformation movement. The
surrounding countryside, placed under
the protection of the Parc national de la
Vanoise, reveals the rugged beauty of
this alpine massif.

Bessans and the Avérole Valley★
☞*See p263.*

▷ *Take D 902 towards Lanslevillard.*

The **Col de la Madeleine** between
Bessans and Lanslevillard, with its
piles of rocks scattered among larches,
marks a transition in the landscape:
downstream, the slopes appear more
rounded, the vegetation is darker and
the view extends further towards the
Dent Parrachée, behind which rises the
jagged ridge of the Rateau d'Aussois.

Lanslevillard★
The village lies on a promontory overlooked by the church and high tower.

Chapelle St-Sébastien★ – *Leave the car near the village church and walk to the school.* ⏱*Open mid-Jun–mid-Sept and Jan–Apr, check for times.* ☎*04 79 05 93 78.*

The chapel was built in the 15C by a local man following a vow made after he survived an epidemic of the plague. The **paintings**★★, which cover all the walls, were realised in the distemper technique, an early form of whitewashing. With impressively bright colours and very expressive, they represent scenes of the martyrdom of St Sébastien and the life of Christ. The clothes and decorations correspond to the era of Louis XI.

▷ *Take D 1006 towards Termignon for 6km/3.7mi.*

Termignon
The *commune* of Termignon covers nearly one-third of the Vanoise park. A wide range of activities is offered, with information and exhibitions at the **Maison de la Vanoise**. The 17C church includes an arolla pine **retable**★.

🏔 At Termignon, three marked **nature trails** 🚶 *(sentiers de la découverte – 2hrs, half-day and full day)* take you into the Suffet forest and explain the history, climate and vegetation.

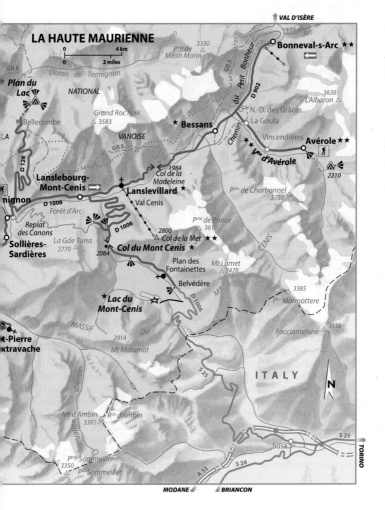

LA HAUTE MAURIENNE

VAL D'ISÈRE

Bonneval-s-Arc ★★

Plan du Lac ★

NATIONAL

P^{nte} de Méan Marin 3330

Doron de Termignon

Bellecombe

Grand Roc Noir △ 3583

VANOISE

GR 5

Lanslebourg-Mont-Cenis

Lanslevillard ★

Val Cenis

★ Bessans

Col de la Madeleine 1984

D 902

N.-D. des Grâces

La Goula

Vincendières

V^{on} d'Avérole ★★

Avérole ★★

L'Albaron △ 3638

P^{nte} de Charbonnel 3750

2210

nignon

D 1006

Forêt d'Arc

Replat des Canons

Sollières-Sardières

La Gde Turra 2770 △

Col du Mont Cenis ★

2084

Col de la Met ★★ 2800

P^{nte} de Ronce 3610

Plan des Fontainettes

Belvédère

Mt Lamet △ 3478

CENIS

3385

P^{ca} Marmottere

★ Lac du Mont-Cenis

t-Pierre xtravache

MASSIF

DU

2914 Mt Malamot

Rocciamelone △ 3538

ITALY

N

Mt d'Ambin △ 3381

R^{ca} d'Ambin

S 25

TORINO

P^{nte} Sommeiller 3350 △

P^{ta} Sommeiller

Susa

S 25

S 24

A 32

MODANE

BRIANÇON

15C paintings, Chapelle St-Sébastien, Lanslevillard

© Nicolas Thibaut/Photononstop

Refuge du Plan du Lac★★

🚶 *2hrs return. Leave Termignon by D 126 and stop at the car park in Bellecombe.* From the refuge viewing table, there is a splendid **panorama**★★ of the Dent Parrachée, Dôme de Chasseforêt, the Vanoise glaciers and beyond.

▶ *Go back to D 1006 and follow for 8km/5mi, towards Modane.*

South of Termignon in **Sollières-Sardières**, an **archaeological museum** (🕐*open mid-Jun–mid-Sept; ℰ04 79 20 59 33*) presents displays of local daily life as it might have been 3 000 years ago. Finds made in 1970 in the Grotte des Balmes form the basis for the displays. The **church** at **Bramans**, rebuilt many times, includes an interesting altarpiece with twisted columns engraved by village sculptors.

Turn left on D 100 to Le Planay, then follow signposts to the charming isolated 10C church at **St-Pierre d'Extravache**. This is one of the earliest religious buildings in Savoie. Remarkably preserved, it retains its chancel and bell tower.

▶ *Return to D 1006 for 6.5km/4mi, then turn right for 2km/1.2mi to Avrieux.*

Avrieux

The 17C church (👟*guided tours Jul–Aug; ℰ04 79 20 33 16*) founded by two English families is dedicated to Thomas Becket, and is notable for its remarkable interior with Baroque **decoration**★. The odd shapes of huge metal you will see are the **Modane-Avrieux turbines**, the largest in Europe.

An Industrial Valley between France and Italy

The valley of the Arc, known as La Maurienne, is one of the longest intra-alpine valleys (118km/73.3mi). For many years a quiet valley, it was opened up dramatically in the 20C with the building of the important through-routes between France and Italy (the Col du Mont Cenis and, particularly from 1980, the Fréjus Road Tunnel). Using the resources from around 20 power stations, there are a dozen aluminium, steel and chemical manufacturers in the lower valley. The two Aussois dams, which feed the large turbines at Avrieux, and the underground power station of Randens, both built in the 1950s, are the largest hydroelectric installations. Paradoxically, to compensate for this industrial activity, a generation of engineers and craftsmen emerged willing and able to preserve the heritage of the valley's traditional little villages.

Aussois★

In a fine position, high above the Arc Valley at an altitude of 1 500m/ 4 921ft, Aussois faces the Long-Côte and the Pointe de La Norma. One of the gateways to the Vanoise National Park, the village nestles on a sunny slope at the foot of the Rateau d'Aussois and the Dent Parrachée. The narrow lanes around its 17C church are lined with old stone houses. The resort offers full winter-sports facilities.

▶ **Population:** 663.

Michelin Map: 333 N6.

Info: Maison d'Aussois, rte des Barrages, 73500 Aussois. ℰ04 79 20 30 80. www.aussois.com.

Location: 7.5km/4.7mi E of Modane in the Haute Maurienne. From Modane take D 215.

Don't Miss: The impressive Esseillon forts, perched at staggered levels on the mountain.

Kids: Tackle the via ferrata provided especially for kids.

Timing: In the summer holidays (July–August) the tourist office lays on a free welcome walk for visitors.

SIGHTS
Église Notre-Dame-de-l'Assomption

Dating from the 17C the façade of the church includes a door dating back to the 13C. This example of Savoie Baroque art includes one of the most beautiful rood screens in the department.

Maison du Patrimoine – L'Arche d'Oé

⏱*Open mid-Dec–end Apr Mon and Thu 3–7pm; check for rest of the year.* ☞*Guided visits (2hrs) on reservation 1 week ahead.* ☞3.60€. ℰ04 79 20 49 57. In one of the oldest houses here, this small museum dedicated to the history of the village is unusual in encouraging visitors to meet the village residents.

Parc Archéologique des Lozes

⏱*Open Jul–Aug Thu afternoon.* ☞*Guided visit.* ☞3€. ℰ04 79 20 30 80. This is a region rich in archaeological evidence of life since Neolithic times. The early inhabitants engraved scenes of everyday life on glacial rocks. At this park, there are two circuits that explain their significance.

Fortifications de l'Esseillon★

⏱*Open Jul–Aug Tue afternoon.* ☞*Guided visits by request.* ☞5.50€. ℰ04 79 20 30 80. Between Aussois and Avrieux the Esseillon is a rocky knoll crowned by impressive fortifications built by the Sardinian monarchy between 1817 and 1834 to

y defend the Mont Cenis pass. The forts were built along the principles of Montalembert: a defensive line perpendicular to the line of attack, and fire power by *tour à canon* (artillery towers), predating the **Séré de Rivières** system. This meant that, lying at different altitudes, the forts could protect each other. Esseillon groups five forts. The highest fortification, **Fort Marie-Christine**, has been restored and now serves as a gateway into the Parc national de la Vanoise. ⏱*Open mid-May–mid-Nov and mid-Dec–mid-Apr 8am–11pm.* ☞*Guided visits (1hr) Jul–Aug Tue afternoon.* ☞*Free.* ℰ04 79 20 36 44.

The largest is the **Fort Victor-Emmanuel**, which is being restored and can be reached from the road.

Opposite, on the south bank of the Arc, the **Redoute Marie-Thérèse** (🅱ℰ04 79 20 33 16; www.avrieux.com) is linked to the complex by the impressive **Pont du Diable** (⏱*open Jul–Aug daily 10am–7pm, Jun and Sept Wed–Sun 10am–noon, 2–6pm;* ☞*guided visits (1hr);* ☞2€; ♿ ℰ04 79 20 33 16; www.redoute marietherese.fr). The site is a good base for embarking on numerous walks such as the **Sentier des Bâtisseurs** (*7.4km/4.6mi – 4hrs*) between the

Charles-Albert Fort and Fort Victor-Emmanuel, the nature trail **Sur les traces du marabout** and the **Sentier découverte du plateau d'Aussois**.

The ski area – Downhill enthusiasts are offered a good selection of lifts and pistes rising to 2 750m/9 022ft, with snow remaining decent until April, despite being mainly south facing. Cross-country skiers have 35km/21.8mi of tracks running to Sollières-Sardières.

Summer activities – A large number of walks, suitable for all standards, begin close to Aussois. On the surrounding cliffs in a 10km/6.2mi radius there are more than 500 climbing routes for novice climbers and experienced alike. Considered one of the finest in France, the **Via Ferrata du Diable**★ in La Norma (⌚ see p255) is also close by.

EXCURSIONS
Le Grand Jeu Chairlift★
⏱ *Open Jul–Aug and the winter ski season.*
From the summit (alt. 2 150m/7 054ft) is a good view over the Longe-Côte, l'Aiguille de Scolette, the Pointe de La Norma and at the bottom of the valley, the Thabor Massif. Climb alongside the Éterlou chairlift from where there is a view to the Rateau d'Aussois, the lakes, Plan d'Amont and Plan d'Aval.
In summer, you can continue to the Refuge du Plan Sec. In winter, from the Bellecôte ski lift you can reach the foot of the Dent Parrachée, giving a **view**★★ over to the south side of the upper Maurienne, and in the southwest the Meije.

Walk to the Fond d'Aussois★★
▷ *6km/3.7mi drive from Maison d'Aussois.*
The drive goes first to the dam of the Plan d'Aval *(stop at the first car park to admire the lake)*. No longer paved, but still graded, the road leads to a little bridge and a final hairpin to the bottom of the dam of the Plan d'Amont.
🚶 *3hrs 30min there and back. Vertical rise: about 250m/820ft. Leave the car*

at the extreme left of the dam and continue on foot.
The path goes along the left bank of the lake and then reaches the Refuge du Fond d'Aussois.

Walk to the Col d'Aussois★★★
🚶 *4hrs there and back. Vertical rise: about 700m/2 297ft. Access from the Refuge du Fond d'Aussois.*
⚠ *Should only be undertaken when dry and when snow has melted (end Jul). Mountain boots essential.*
From the pass experienced hikers can climb left up to the **Pointe de l'Observatoire** (3 015m/9 892ft). Amazing circular view.

Monolithe de Sardières★
From Aussois, the road goes up through fields and pine woods. Once it levels up the Ambin and Thabor massifs appear.

▷ *Enter the village of Sardières and take the chemin du Monolithe.*

Much prized by rock-climbers, in the midst of a pine wood, this distinctive rock point is 93m/305ft high.

Cascade de St-Benoît
From Aussois, turn left in front of the church.
You can stop to admire the **St-Benoît waterfall** *(opposite the chapel of the same name)*. The road follows down into the Avrieux basin.

ADDRESSES

🚶 ACTIVITIES
Fishing – ☎04 79 20 30 80. *Check with the Maison d'Aussois.* Both the lakes and the rivers offer various possibilities for fishing.

👥 **Mountain biking in Haute Maurienne–Vanoise d'Aussois to Bonneval-sur-Arc** – ☎04 79 20 30 80. Around 200km/124mi of marked tracks with a wide range of itineraries for all the family are on offer for mountain bikers. Detailed maps are on sale at the Maison d'Aussois.

Val Cenis

On the itinerary of the route des Grandes Alpes, Val Cenis cannot exactly be described as a resort, but instead is an amalgamation of two villages, Lanslevillard and Lanslebourg. On the slopes of Mont Cenis, the huge, north-facing ski area attracts beginners and good skiers to enjoy the pistes in between the arollo pines and the larch trees. In summer, these same slopes, part of the Vanoise National Park, become an excellent starting point for hikes.

- **Michelin Map:** 333 O6.
- **Info:** La Maison de Val Cenis, Grande-Rue, 73480 Lanslebourg-Mont-Cenis. ℘04 79 05 23 66. www.valcenis.com.
- **Location:** The resort is located 10km/6.2mi from Lanslebourg, towards the Col du Mont Cenis.
- **Don't Miss:** The Mont Cenis lake, at an altitude of 2 000m/6 562ft.
- **Timing:** To learn about the planets and the stars, visit in July for the astrology festival.

THE RESORT

Ski area – The largest ski area in the Arc Valley, the Val Cenis ski area covers an area of 500ha/1 236 acres between 1 400m/4 593ft and 2 800m/9 186ft. It includes an unusually long (10km/6.2mi down from Col du Mont Cenis) green run, named the **Escargot** (snail), as well as some more technical runs (Jacquot, Le Lac and Arcelle). A pass is available to include all the Maurienne resorts.
Summer activities – The two villages are in a fine position at the crossroads of the roads to the Iseran and Mont Cenis passes, meaning easy access to the beautiful valleys of the Maurienne and the Tarentaise.

EXCURSIONS
Lanslebourg-Mont-Cenis

At the junction with the route du Mont-Cenis, Lanslebourg is a village marked by its border position. Its houses spread out on the hillsides.
Lanslebourg has a monument dedicated to **Flambeau**, the army dog who, between 1928 and 1938, helped to carry the mail from the barracks to the Sollières Fort.

Espace Baroque Maurienne★

Montée du Canton. Open mid-Dec–Apr Mon–Wed 9.30am–noon, Thu–Fri 9.30–noon, 3–7.15pm; rest of year check. 2.50€. ℘04 79 05 90 42.
In the old church is the start of the **chemins du Baroque** (Baroque pathways), a permanent exhibition of Baroque art. There are also temporary exhibitions about local history.

Les Chemins de l'Histoire

Open mid-Jun–mid-Sept and Jan–Apr, times vary. Visit on foot, or in winter on skis or snowshoes. 5€ and 30€ deposit. ℘04 79 05 93 78.
Start with the Chapelle St-Roch, where you will receive a large key and tokens to open the doors to 10 restored chapels to learn about the history of the village.

VIEWPOINTS
Télécabine du Vieux Moulin★

Alt. 2 100m/6 890ft. Open Jul–Aug and winter. Details from tourist office.
From the top of this gondola is a view of the Dent Parrachée, the Vanoise glaciers and the Arc Valley.

Col de la Met★★

Alt. 2 800m/9 186ft. Reached by chairlift, open for walkers in Jul–Aug and for skiers in winter.
Magnificent view to the south over the Italian Alps, to the southwest to the dam and lake of Mont Cenis (with Mont Malamot above), with the Aiguille de Scolette and the Meije behind, and to the Vanoise in the north.

The Opening Up of a Region

Val Cenis is overlooked to the northwest by the Dent Parrachée (alt. 3 684m/12 087ft), to the north by the Grand Roc Noir, and to the south by the Pointe de Ronce (alt. 3 583m/11 755ft) and the Col du Mont Cenis. The area was closed off, only accessible by challenging paths, until Napoleon ordered the construction of the road, still used today. Built from 1803 to 1811, and meticulously planned, the road has an average gradient of eight percent, with views to the Vanoise Massif.

🚗 DRIVING TOUR

ROUTE FROM LANSLEBOURG-MONT-CENIS TO LAC DU MONT CENIS★

Drive of 16km/10.2mi shown on the Haute Maurienne map (see p257). Allow 45min. The Col du Mont Cenis is usually closed from Dec–Apr.

From Lanslebourg-Mont-Cenis, drive south along D 1006 towards Italy. The road rises through a conifer forest, including fine larches, then continues beyond the treeline. Leave the car in a bend to the left *(8km/5mi from Lanslebourg, at the top of a ski lift).*

There is a beautiful **view**★ of the Vanoise glaciers reclining against the Dent Parrachée and of the whole of the Haute Maurienne from Lanslebourg to Bessans through the narrow opening of the **Col de la Madeleine**, where the Arc river has carved a passage.

Stop just before the pass near a small monument; walk along the road leading to the **Replat des Canons**; 1km/0.6mi further on, there is a striking **view**★★ of the Dent Parrachée taking in the village of Bessans.

Col du Mont Cenis★

Between the summits of the Grande Turra and La Tomba, the Col du Mont Cenis pass used to mark the border between France and Italy, now a few kilometres further south. The view encompasses the lake and the immense, green Mont Cenis bowl framed by Mont Lamet and the Pointe de Clairy. To the south are the high summits of the Aiguille de Scolette and Pointe Sommeiller. Below the restaurant **Plan des Fontainettes** is the pyramid-shaped priory chapel. The **Musée de la Pyramide** (open mid-Jun–mid-Sept 10am–12.30pm, 1.30–6pm; 3€; 04 79 64 08 08) is housed below the chapel and traces the history of the pass, daily life in the area and the building of the dam. Also at the pass is an educational alpine garden (*open for the period the pass is open*) created in the 1970s.

Lac du Mont Cenis★

From the EDF viewpoint *(car park)*, there is a **view**★ of the whole lake and the **dam** to the south. The latter is longer at its top, but not as high, and also thinner at the base, than the Serre-Ponçon Dam in the southern Alps.

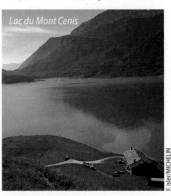
Lac du Mont Cenis

F. Isler/MICHELIN

ADDRESSES

🏃 ACTIVITIES

👥 In summer the **Mont Cenis reservoir** turns into a pleasure lake, with **sailing** lessons for children.

🎭 EVENTS

Astronomy festival – Held in the last week of July with workshops, entertainment and lots of star-gazing.

Bessans★

Bessans lies on a mountain plateau enclosed by the high peaks of the Vanoise. The old village was largely destroyed by fire in 1944; however, there remains a strong sense of tradition in this village. The devil, who has become an emblem of the village, is not the only example of decorative woodcarving, which is a local speciality. Look out for fine sculpted crosses, beams and more.

▶ **Population:** 337.
⊙ **Michelin Map:** 333 O6.
🔲 **Info:** R. Maison-Morte, 73480 Bessans. ℘04 79 05 96 52. www.bessans.com.
▶ **Location:** 36km/22.4mi from Modane by D 1006, then D 902.
◉ **Don't Miss:** The paintings in the St-Antoine Chapel.

RESORT

Ski area – The resort has a large cross-country ski area with over 80km/50mi of groomed tracks. With excellent snow conditions at an average altitude of 1 700m/5 577ft, ski touring can be enjoyed for a large part of the season.

SIGHTS

Église St-Jean-Baptiste – The church contains numerous 17C statues and a **Rosary altar**, by Clappier, one of a local dynasty of sculptors who made the village famous for its art. Frescoes include a magnificent **Ecce Homo**★.

Chapelle St-Antoine★★ – *Enter by the cemetery opposite the side door of church.* 🔊*Guided visits (1hr 15min, reservation 1 day ahead).* ⊛*5€ (children free).* ℘*04 79 05 96 52.* The exterior decoration of this 14C chapel is somewhat damaged, but inside is much better conserved. Inspired by the local landscape the **frescoes**★★ cover the walls on two levels, illustrating the life of Christ.

Of the same era, but more naive than those at Lanslevillard, the clothes enable the frescoes to be dated to the 15C. The Renaissance **ceiling**★, decorated with stars, dates from 1526.

🏃 HIKES

Vallée d'Avérole★★

Typical of the Haute Maurienne, the pastoral villages of La Goula, Vincendières and Avérole are remarkably preserved. 🔊*Leave your car in the car park 0.5km/ 0.3mi before Vincendières*

and continue on foot to Avérole *(45min return).*

Refuge d'Avérole★★

🏃 *Alt. 2 210m/7 251ft. Easy hike from Avérole, the only steep climb coming at the very end (2hrs 15min return).*
Beautiful mountain setting with glaciers, waterfalls and the Bessanese summit (3 592m/11 785ft) before you.

From Bessans to Bonneval★★

🏃 *2hrs 30min there and back. Guide available from the tourist office.*
The **Petit Bonheur** path runs along the bottom of the valley, parallel to the road, passing the 17C Villaron chapel and then the Rocher du Château, where if you look very carefully, you can make out the Neolithic rock paintings of deer.

ADDRESSES

🛏 STAY

◍◍ **Le Mont-Iseran** – *Pl. de la Mairie.* ℘*04 79 05 95 97. www.montiseran.com. Closed 11 Apr–19 Jun, 26 Sept–14 Dec. Wifi. 18 rooms, restaurant* ◍◍*.* Close to the ski tracks at the heart of the village, this family pension has small rooms with balconies. Local dishes served in a rustic restaurant, complete with devil!

🛍 SHOPPING

Take home a devil – *R. St-Esprit.* ℘*04 79 05 95 49. www.chapoteur.com. Open 10am–noon, 3–7pm.* The Personnaz family carve an astonishing range of objects, based on the inspiration of the village's emblematic devil, carved in anger by a spurned parishioner in 1857.

Bonneval-sur-Arc★★

The last village of the Haute Maurienne, Bonneval nestles in a high valley surrounded by peaks above 3 000m/9 843ft. The old village is charming with stone buildings a feature everywhere, blending in superbly with the surroundings of pastures dotted with rocks. Isolated from the modern world, this village offers the visitor a little slice of mountain life.

▶ **Population:** 244.
◔ **Michelin Map:** 333 P5.
▯ **Info:** 73480 Bonneval-sur-Arc. ℘04 79 05 95 95. www.bonneval-sur-arc.com.
◖ **Location:** Situated below the Col de l'Iseran, in the imposing cirque where the River Arc begins, Bonneval is the highest municipality in the Maurienne region.
◉ **Don't Miss:** Be sure to visit the hamlet of L'Écot, and drive up to the pass.

THE VILLAGE
Old Village★★

Bonneval has preserved the character of its old streets and houses by burying electric and telephone cables and banning individual television aerials and satellite dishes, as well as cars.

You can walk undisturbed through the narrow streets lined with stone houses, covered with rust-coloured *lauzes* and adorned with wooden balconies where dried cow-dung, still used as fuel because wood is scarce, is sometimes stored.

You can visit the **Grande Maison**, and admire the carved beams of this old house once owned by a rich Piedmont family, exiled in 1860, when Savoie was annexed by France.

L'Écot

It is recommended that you leave your car at the edge of Bonneval-sur-Arc and continue on foot. 1hr there and back.

This hamlet, which lies in imposing and austere surroundings at an altitude of more than 2 000m/6 562ft, has retained its old stone houses and 12C Chapelle Ste-Marguerite. Once extremely remote, it is today a favourite excursion, and the start of many walks.

Ski area – The 10 Bonneval ski lifts serve an area which though not large is of high quality. From December to May, intermediate skiers will enjoy the Moulinet ski lift on the edge of the Vallonet glacier; good skiers can take the Télésiège des 3000 (Chairlift 3000) to

Bonneval-sur-Arc and the Arc Valley

F. Isler/MICHELIN

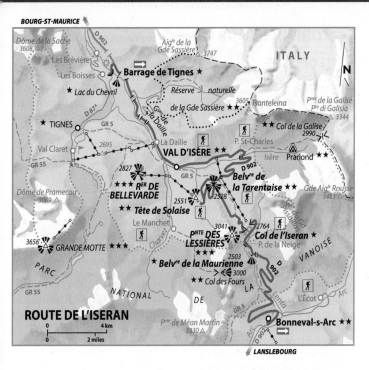

ROUTE DE L'ISERAN

reach the foot of the Pointe d'Andagne. For there is a magnificent **view**★★ over the Haute Maurienne. In summer, you can ski on the Grand Pissaillas Glacier, reached from the Col de l'Iseran (part of the Val d'Isère ski area, ⏱see p241).

🚶 HIKES

Bonneval is the ideal **base for walks** through the Vanoise park and the conservation area of **Les Évettes** with a huge network of paths (120km/74.6mi). It is also a climbing centre with some very interesting expeditions on the frontier mountains of La Levanna, La Ciamarella and the Albaron.

Refuge du Criou★

Alt. 2 050m/6 726ft. In winter, access by the Vallonet chairlift and in summer 30min walk.

View of the Vallonet and Sources de l'Arc glaciers and the route du Col de l'Iseran.

Refuge du Carro★★

🚶 *Alt. 2 780m/9 121ft.*
From l'Écot, steep climb 3hrs 15min, descent 2hrs. It is also possible to

take the path along the edge of the mountain from the Pont de l'Oulietta (alt. 2 480m/8 136ft), on the rte du Col de l'Iseran: this splendid tour is long (4hrs), but not technical.

Views★★ over the Sources de l'Arc glaciers, the Évettes, Albaron and the Vallonet peaks. At the refuge, you can see the Lac Noir and the Lac Blanc.

Refuge des Évettes★★

🚶 *Alt. 2 629m/8 625ft. From l'Écot, climb 1hr 45min, descent 1hr.*

The climb is steep, but the view to L'Écot, Bonneval and the **panorama**★★ to the Évettes Glacier, the Albaron, Narcisse and the Lacs de Pareis when you arrive is worth the effort.

Those who do not suffer from vertigo can continue with a detour to the lovely **Cascade de la Reculaz**★ *(1hr return from refuge).*

Walk to Chalets de la Duis★

From l'Écot, 2hrs there and back.
The wide track provides an easy family walk. The landscape is over green pastures overlooked by the glaciers.

🚗 DRIVING TOUR

ROUTE DE L'ISERAN★★★

Drive of 14km/8.7mi shown on the Route de l'Iseran map (p265). Allow 30min. The Col de l'Iseran is usually closed early Nov–early Jul.

This road, which goes over the Col de l'Iseran, was opened in 1937 to link the Tarentaise and Maurienne valleys and reaches the highest point (2 770m/ 9 088ft) of the route des Grandes Alpes. Many cyclists struggle with this route, which, with an impressive vertical rise, is usually one of the high points of the Tour de France.

Bonneval

Driving up above Bonneval, there is a view down to the village. To the east the sides of the upper Arc Valley are quite bare, with little grass, contrasting with the hay fields and larches on the west. The road continues into the Vanoise park and the Lenta Valley, where there are a few high alpine chalets in the pastures, and marmots on the sides of the road.

Belvédère de la Maurienne★

View of the Haute Maurienne, including the Ciamarella and anvil-shaped Albaron summits and the Pointe de Charbonnel. Beyond the Pont de la Neige is the "hanging" Lenta Valley below the Grand Pissaillas Glacier, from which melt-water runs like a waterfall onto a rocky terrace. The landscape becomes one of the high mountain, with glaciers and scree close by and grassy areas becoming rarer.

Col de l'Iseran★

Alt. 2 764m/9 068ft.

This pass is incredibly austere and **views** are limited to the Albaron summit on the Maurienne side, and the Grande Sassière and the Tsanteleina on the Tarentaise side (see also Driving Tour in Val d'Isère p242).

Pointe des Lessières★★★

🚶 *2hrs 30min there and back.*

This steep mountain path requires caution and should only be attempted by well-equipped experienced hikers in clear weather only. Depart from behind the restaurant at the Col de l'Iseran.

The **panorama** from the summit is ample reward for the effort of climbing up here: the Vanoise Massif, Mont Pourri, the Italian side of Mont-Blanc and the border range between the Grande Sassière and Albaron.

ADDRESSES

🛏 STAY

🍽🍽 **À la Pastourelle** – 📞04 79 05 81 56. *www.pastourelle.com. Closed 1 week in Jun and end Oct. Wifi. 12 rooms, restaurant*🍽🍽. There is a warm welcome in this typical mountain hotel, with cosy, well-kept rooms. The rustic restaurant serves Savoyard specialities including *diot* sausages.

🍽 **La Bergerie** – 📞04 79 05 94 97. *Closed 24 Apr–13 Jun, 27 Sept–17 Dec.* 🅿. *Wifi. 22 rooms, restaurant*🍽🍽. This peaceful hotel offers rooms full of light with lovely views to the Évettes mountains. Simple brasserie food at lunchtime; traditional or Savoyard meals in the evening.

🍴 EAT

🍴 There are at least a dozen restaurants and snack bars offering a range of cuisines in the three zones of the resort, **Vieux Village, Pré Catin, Tralenta** and on the **pistes**.

🍽 **Le Col de l'Iseran** – *At the pass, 73150 Val d'Isère.* 📞04 79 06 00 05. *Closed mid-Sept–mid-Jun.* 🅿. This restaurant-bar on the pass, next to the chapel, has a view to both the Tarentaise and the Maurienne. A daily menu is offered on the blackboard, plus snacks and traditional bilberry tarts and *potée Savoyard* (casserole). Souvenir shop.

🍽🍽 **Le Glacier des Evettes** – *Vieux village.* 📞04 79 05 94 06. *www.evettes.fr.st. 19 rooms*🍽🍽. A hotel, bar and newsagent combined, this establishment in the old village offers contemporary rooms, some with south-facing balconies. In the restaurant, to the inevitable local specialities is added a salad menu.

GRENOBLE, *Chamrousse and La Chartreuse*

Surrounded by the spectacular mountain scenery of the Chartreuse, Belledonne and Vercors massifs, it would be easy to simply ignore the city of Grenoble as a transit place. Yet, this vibrant metropolis of the Alps, a centre for technological advance, has plenty to offer the visitor in terms of historical interest, culture and entertainment. Just to the north, the Isère river gives rise to farmlands, and a countryside so gentle that it almost mocks the dramatic limestone cliffs of the Chartreuse above.

A Dynamic City at the Cutting Edge of Technology

It is over 40 years since Grenoble hosted the 1968 Winter Olympics. At that time, not only were world-class sporting facilities built, but also new civic buildings such as the town hall by the fashionable architect of the time, Novarina. Today Grenoble remains the largest manufacturer of ski lifts in the world.

In recent years this university town and base for several important technological companies has reviewed its urban development programme, particularly in the light of environmental concerns. Its new sports stadium Stade des Alpes inaugurated in 2008 uses power from a huge expanse of solar panels, and at the end of 2009 the new Bonne quarter of town, a 21C symbol for modern urban habitation, won the town a national award.

The Sounds of Silence

The Chartreuse is home to the Motherhouse of the silent order of Carthusian monks, and also to a wonderful array of flora and fauna protected by the large Parc Naturel Régional de Chartreuse. The symbol of the nature park is the large, powerful eagle owl that particularly enjoys the rocky cliffs so close to woodlands.

The silent, but industrious monks drew on the park's natural resources to live, being among the first to exploit the iron mines, as well as to create their famously secret recipe for Chartreuse liqueur.

Highlights

1   Take the cable car up to the **Fort de la Bastille** above Grenoble (p271)
2   Visit the **Musée de Grenoble** for the best fine arts in the Alps (p274)
3   Admire the stunning panorama from the **Bec du Margain** (p279)
4   A short walk to view the **Grande Chartreuse Monastery** from Charmant Som (p289)
5   Get bogged down in ecology at **Lac Luitel** (p292)

Monastère de la Grande Chartreuse

F. Isler/MICHELIN

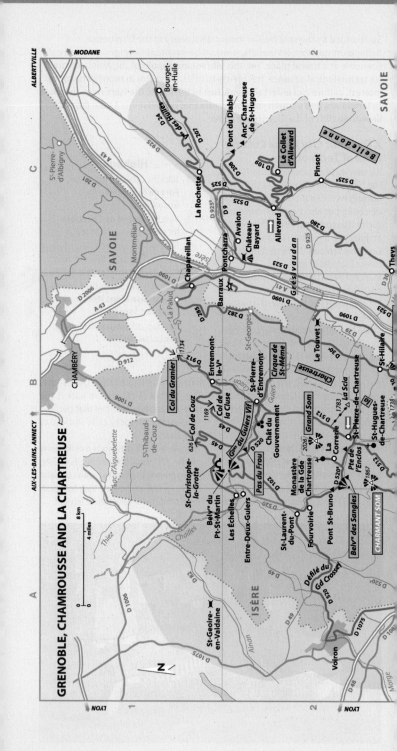

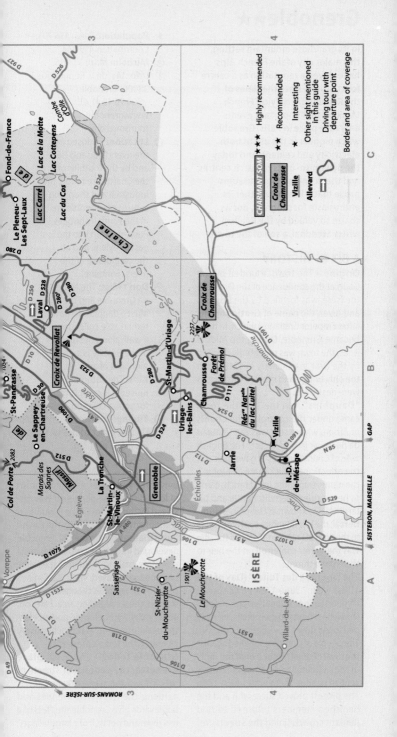

Highly recommended ★★★
Recommended ★★
Interesting ★
Other sight mentioned ○
in this guide
Driving tour with
departure point
Border and area of coverage

CHARMANT SOM

Croix de
Chamrousse

Vizille

Allevard

Fond-de-France
Le Pleneu- ○
Les Sept-Laux
Lac Carré
Lac Cottepens
Lac de la Motte
Combe
d'Olle
Lac du Cos
D 526
D 526
Chaîne
D 280
Laval
D 250
D 528
D 280
D 280
Croix de Revollat
D 10
D 523
D 523
St-Pancrasse
D 30
St-Sappey-
en-Chartreuse
D 1034
Marais des
Sagnes
Col de Porte
2082
Massif
D 512
St-égrève
La Tronche
St-Martin-
le-Vinoux
D 1075
Voreppe
D 1532
D 3
D 49
Sassenage
D 531
St-Nizier-
du-Moucherotte
D 218
Le Moucherotte
1901
ISÈRE
Villard-de-Lans
D 531
D 106

Grenoble
D 524
D 41
Isère
D 1090
D 280
St-Martin-d'Uriage
Uriage-
les-Bains
Chamrousse
Forêt
de Prémol
Croix de
Chamrousse
2257
Rés⁰ⁿ Natⁱˡ
du lac Luitel
D 111
D 524
Vizille
D 5
D 1091
Romanche
D 111
Jarrie
Échirolles
N.-D.-
de-Mésage
Drac
N 85
D 529
A 51
D 1075
D 106

SISTERON, MARSEILLE

GAP

ROMANS-SUR-ISÈRE

269

Grenoble★★

In its grandiose mountain setting, this major city of the French Alps has enjoyed a reputation as a centre for creativity since the times of the Revolution, defying French thinking that important events only take place in Paris. Grenoble was a pioneer in the use of both electricity and cement, and today the dynamism of its research centres and the richness of its museums prove that it has lost neither its enthusiasm for progress, nor its charm so valued by the Realism writer Stendhal, a son of the town.

A BIT OF HISTORY

Origins – The town, founded by the Gauls at the confluence of the Drac and the Isère, was fortified by the Romans and given the name of **Gratianopolis** (after Emperor Gratianus) which, in time, became Grenoble. During the Middle Ages, the town was repeatedly flooded by the Drac, particularly in 1219 when the only bridge and most of the houses were destroyed.

"Dauphins" – In the 12C, the town came under the control of the Counts of Albon, whose seat was the Château de Beauvoir in the Vercors. The English wife of Count Guigues III gave their son the affectionate nickname "Dolphin"; the name, translated into French, came to be the ruler's hereditary title and his territory was known as Dauphiné. **Humbert II**, the last dauphin, sold his estates to the King of France in 1349 and the title was thereafter conferred on the heir to the French throne.

The "Journée des Tuiles" (Day of the Tiles) – On 7 June 1788 news spread through Grenoble that the regional *parlements*, or high judicial courts, were to be closed down by order of Louis XVI. The people of Grenoble rebelled against the royal decree, climbed onto the roofs of the buildings and pelted the troops sent to subdue them with heavy tiles. The protest proved successful and the banished members returned to find jubilant crowds lining the streets, yet

▶ **Population:** Town 156 793; Conurbation 419 334.

🜁 **Michelin Map:** 333 H6.

ℹ **Info:** 14 r. de la République, 38000, Grenoble. ℘04 76 42 41 41. www.grenoble-tourisme.com.

◖ **Location:** Enclosed by the rivers Drac and Isère and by the foothills of the Chartreuse range, the industrial and shopping centres of Grenoble are in the south (Échirolles, Point-de-Claix), to the east (Meylan), and at the confluence of the rivers (Fontaine).

◉ **Don't Miss:** The Musée de Grenoble and the Musée dauphinois have remarkable collections; a walk along the heights of the Bastille is a highlight of any trip.

👪 **Kids:** The autumata museum is great fun for young children.

◷ **Timing:** The Notre-Dame district comes to life in the evening.

only three years later, in an ironic turn of local history, the *parlement* was dissolved by the leaders of the Revolution without any resistance from the town.

Industrialisation – In the 19C, Grenoble developed into a prosperous industrial city. Glove-making, the town's speciality, became mechanised, while coal mines and cement factories changed the landscape of the surrounding area. Later on, paper mills, hydroelectric power, electrometallurgy and electrochemistry increased the town's prosperity.

Grenoble today – The lively **place Grenette**, the pedestrian streets of the old town, the many parks and flower gardens, the tree-lined avenues and boulevards give Grenoble the "feel of a real town and not that of a large village", as Stendhal once said. The **university**, founded in 1339 by Humbert II, includes highly specialised institutes of alpine geography and geology and a centre of nuclear studies. The Winter Olympics of 1968 brought changes to the town's infrastructure and facilities, including a sports hall and a speed-skating rink, but also encouraged new trends in civic architecture.

Maison de la Culture – Known locally as "MC2", this imaginatively designed cultural centre stands on elegant narrow columns. Black and white surfaces, cylinders and cubes contrast to make a striking modern structure.

An open-air museum – Grenoble's enthusiasm for modern civic art is on permanent view, as works by contemporary sculptors enliven urban spaces around the town, from the station square and the Quartier Alpin to the Olympic village.

THE SETTING

The town of Grenoble lies in a deep valley surrounded by spectacular mountain ranges: the mighty escarpments of the Vercors dominate the skyline to the west, the sheer faces of the Néron and the St-Eynard rise up in the north, with the Chartreuse Massif behind, and to the east stand the dark, often snow-capped peaks of the Belledonne range.

Panorama from the Fort de la Bastille★★

The fort is accessible by cable car (6min), by car or on foot. Car park next to the lower station. Cable car ℘04 76 44 33 65. www.bastille-grenoble.com.

From the rocky promontory situated on the left as you exit the upper station, the **view★★** takes in the town, the confluence of the Isère and Drac and the Isère Valley framed by the Casque de Néron on the right and, in the Vercors, the Moucherotte summit on the left.

Information panels identify the **panorama★★** of mountains: Belledonne, Taillefer, Obiou, Vercors (Grand Veymont and Moucherotte) and even Mont Blanc. There is a fine view of Grenoble, the old town and the 19C districts to the south and west, all overlooked by the high-rise tower blocks of the **Île Verte**.

From the Haxo fortifications below the top cable-car station, two marked paths lead back to town: one through the **Parc Guy-Pape** and Jardin des Dauphins *(1hr 30min)* the other follows the **Circuit Léon-Moret** *(1hr. If you dislike heights or have trouble walking then avoid the 380-step stairway),* crossing the fortifications and ends at porte St-Laurent.

Other marked walks cross the Bastille area including the Grande Traversée des Alpes 2. The **Mont Jalla** *(1hr)* takes

Saint-Laurent district and the Fort de la Bastille with the cable cars

© Ludovic Maisant/hemis.fr

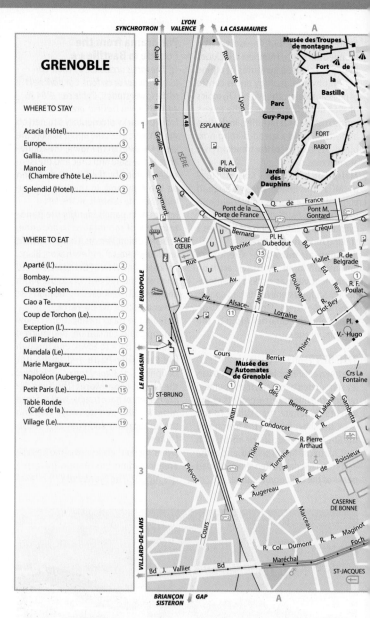

GRENOBLE

you up to an extended panorama of La Bastille and the Chartreuse park.

🔍 WALKING TOUR

Walking route shown on the town plan above. Allow 1hr. ▶ *Leave from pl.Grenette.*

From the place Grenette to the rue Chenoise spreads a maze of streets dating from the Middle Ages to the 19C. Try to peer into some of the many courtyards (🛈*information from the tourist office*).

Place Grenette

The old cornmarket and animal market, this lively square lined with shops and cafés is a favourite haunt of locals. This is also the spot where, on 19 June 1889, six lamps provided the first electric street lighting in the city.

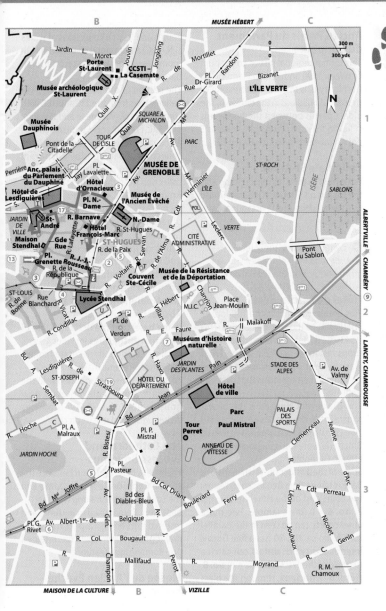

The Grande Rue leads off from the square, to the right of the fountain.

Grande Rue

This former Roman road is lined with fine old houses; no. 20, facing a Renaissance mansion, is the **Maison Stendhal**, where the novelist spent part of his childhood. Two courtyards date from the 15C and 18C (○━ *closed to the public).*

Rue Jean-Jacques-Rousseau starts almost opposite; no. 14 was Stendhal's birthplace.

Place St-André

In the centre stands a statue of the knight Bayard. The appropriately chivalric-sounding Café de la Table Ronde (1739) is one of the oldest in France.

Ancien Palais du Parlement du Dauphiné

This former regional justice court, built between 1490 and 1510 in Flamboyant Gothic style, is the most interesting of the official buildings in the old town. The oldest part is between the two wings (*guided visits (1hr 30min), reserved 3 days in advance through tourist office*).

Collégiale St-André

Brick-built in the 13C, this building was the Dauphin's Chapel. It is surmounted by a tower with a pretty octagonal limestone spire.

> *Continue behind the church of St-André and from pl. d'Agier, you can go into the park named Jardin de Ville.*

Hôtel de Lesdiguières

This house was built in the 16C for the military hero the Duc de Lesdiguières (1543–1626), but he preferred his sumptuous residence in Vizille. In the 17C it was the seat of government for the Dauphiné, then served as the town hall until 1967.

The **place aux Herbes** is the oldest square in the city and has a lively market (*Tue–Sun*). The streets around nearby rue Brocherie were once the most sought-after in Grenoble.

Some of the aristocratic town mansions have retained their Renaissance design; the courtyard of the Hôtel de Chasnel at **no. 6** is a fine example. Two more inner courts can be seen in the parallel rue Chenoise. **No. 10** has a fine Gothic interior courtyard; visitors can catch a glimpse of the 17C **staircase**★ at **no. 8**, **Hôtel d'Ornacieux**, through the glass panel of the front door.

Musée de Grenoble★★★

Open Wed–Mon 10am–6.30pm. Closed 1 Jan, 1 May, 25 Dec. 5€ (children free). 04 76 63 44 44. www.museedegrenoble.fr.

A model of restrained modern architecture, the Museum of Fine Arts, inaugurated in 1994, is located along the Isère, at the heart of the old town. This is one of the most prestigious museums in France and its rich collections of works (13C–19C) are arranged on one floor with rooms on either side of a corridor, with bare white walls.

The section of **old paintings** includes Italian works from the 13C and 18C with some works by Veronese and Pérugin. The 17C French and Spanish schools are well represented including a large collection of paintings by **Zurbarán**. Rubens is also represented among a collection from the north.

Among the **19C works** are paintings by Ingres, Corot and Gauguin among others, with a section of artists from Grenoble.

Paintings from Matisse feature in the **20C modern art** collection with both **Cubist** and **Dadaism** represented, along with important works from Chagall, **Modigliani**, **Picasso** and **Léger**. **Abstract** art is also featured.

In the basement the rich collection of **Egyptian antiquities** includes several royal stelaes, brightly decorated coffins and refined funeral masks.

Tour de l'Isle – Incorporated into the museum, this medieval tower now houses more than 3 000 drawings including several masterpieces.

The Cathedral and Diocese Buildings

There have been two churches since the 4C: the **Cathédrale Notre-Dame** and the Église St-Hugues, along with the 11C baptistery. Remodelled many times and restored to its original aspect, the cathedral (*open 10am–6pm*) has retained pre-Romanesque features.

Musée de l'Ancien Évêché – Patrimoines de l'Isère★★

Open Mon and Wed–Sat 9am–6pm, Tue 1–6pm, Sun 10am–7pm. Closed 1 Jan, 1 May, 25 Dec. 04 76 03 15 25. www.ancien-eveche-isere.fr.

Situated at the heart of the town's historic centre, this interactive museum is housed in the former bishops' palace; it offers an account of the regional heritage. In the basement, visitors can see in situ a palaeo-Christian **baptistery**★, one of the oldest of its kind (4C).

Place Notre-Dame

Excavations under the cathedral square have revealed the foundations of the **Gallo-Roman walls** surrounding Gratianopolis and palaeo-Christian remains. The **Tour Clérieux** is all that remains of the episcopal buildings which stood here during the Middle Ages.

The elegant fountain, known as the **Fontaine des Trois-Ordres**, in the centre of place Notre-Dame takes its name from its three figures who represent the traditional classes of society: the clergy, the nobility and the third estate.

Off the square to the right of the fountain **rue Barnave** includes at no. 22 the Gothic **Hôtel François Marc**, which dates from 1490; the archway bears a winged lion emblem, the symbol of St Mark the Evangelist. Beyond the door is a courtyard with an elegant spiral staircase typical of the Grenoble bourgeoisie in the Renaissance period.

▷ *Via r. P.-Duclot, continue along the extension of Pl. Notre-Dame, r. R.-Blanchard.*

The former Jesuit college is now the **Lycée Stendhal**. The walls and ceiling of the staircase were designed to work as a **sundial**, which has operated perfectly since the 17C. On it are marked the solar and lunar calendars, religious festivals and feast days, as well as the time in 24 cities of the world.

▷ *Return to pl. Grenette via r. de la République.*

MUSEUMS IN STE-MARIE-D'EN-HAUT AND ST-LAURENT

After the Pont de la Citadelle, go up the steps to the left leading to the Musée Dauphinois. By car, access is via quai Perrière and the narrow, steep r. M.-Gignoux.

Musée Dauphinois★

🕐*Open Wed–Mon Jul–Aug 10am–7pm; Sept–Jun 10am–6pm.* 🕐*Closed 1 Jan, 1 May, 25 Dec.* ♿*℘04 57 58 89 01. www.musee-dauphinois.fr.*

This museum of regional art and traditions is housed in a former 17C convent. The tour takes you round the cloister, the chapter house and the Baroque chapel. The main rooms display a collection of furniture and traditional tools typically used in the Alps. There is also a detailed **history of skiing** illustrating the impact of the sport on daily life in the mountains. Extremely well-presented long-term themed **exhibitions**★★ make this museum one of the main ethnographical centres of the region. The early 17C Baroque **chapel**★★ is the highlight and a popular venue for concerts.

▷ *Go back down the steps into the St-Laurent quarter.*

St-Laurent District

On the right bank of the River Isère this old district, flanked by the porte de France and the porte St-Laurent, takes the form of a single village street, lined with houses that have brightly coloured façades. In the 19C it was the centre of the glove industry. From the 1920s to the 1950s, many families moved to St-Laurent from Corato (Puglia, Italy) and it became Grenoble's Italian quarter.

Musée Archéologique, Église St-Laurent★★

🕐*Open May–Sept Mon and Wed–Sat 10am–7pm; Oct–Apr Mon and Wed–Sat 10am–6pm, Sun 10am–7pm.* 🕐*Closed public holidays.* 👥*Guided visits possible.* 🎫*Free.* ℘*04 76 44 78 68.*

The church of St-Laurent is one of the few in France dating from the High Middle Ages, and is particularly interesting owing to extensive excavations over a 30-year period, revealing numerous phases up to the 18C. Beneath the current 12C Roman church, the **St-Oyand Crypt**★★ was built in the early 6C on the site of a pagan cemetery. This early Medieval oratory is adorned with Roman and Merovingian decorative motifs blended with Carolingian elements.

The museum has recently been transformed with a brand new design, including a 3D reconstruction of the different architectural phases, allowing the visitor

275

to understand better the various developments through the centuries.
Beyond the St-Laurent Church, tower the 17C **porte St-Laurent** and the 19C bunkers and defensive walls of Haxo.

CCSTI Grenoble – La Casemate

Pl. St-Laurent. Open Jul–Aug, check for times; Sept–Jun Mon–Fri 9am–noon, 1.30–5.30pm, Sat–Sun and public holidays 2–6pm. 5€ (children free). 04 76 44 88 80. www.ccsti-grenoble.org.
This bunker houses Grenoble's **Centre de culture scientifique, technique et industrielle** since 1979. The scientific, technical and industrial centre holds temporary interactive exhibitions, often linked to current affairs.

ADDITIONAL SIGHTS

Musée de la Résistance et de la Déportation★

Open Jul–Aug Wed–Mon 10am–7pm, Tue 1.30–7pm; Sept–Jun Mon and Wed–Fri 9am–6pm, Tue 1.30–6pm, Sat–Sun 10am–6pm. Closed 1 Jan, 1 May, 25 Dec. 04 76 42 38 53. www.resistance-en-isere.fr.
This museum re-creates settings and sounds, and explains the motives of members of the Resistance and the sacrifices entailed by their actions.
The intense activity of the local Resistance movements is illustrated by several reconstructions. Note the three doors of the former Gestapo prison in Grenoble, covered with graffiti drawn by members of the Resistance.

Musée des Automates de Grenoble

1hr Guided tours 2–6.30pm (last entry 5.45pm). 5€. 04 76 43 33 33.
Hidden at the end of a narrow street, this museum houses a rich collection of automata and music boxes. The visit includes live shows by enthusiasts.

Muséum d'Histoire Naturelle

1 r. Dolomieu. Open Mon–Fri 9.30am –noon, 1.30–5.30pm, Sat–Sun and public holidays 2–6pm. Closed 1 Jan, 1 May, 25 Dec. 2.20€. 04 76 44 05 35. www.museum-grenoble.fr.

Established early in the 19C, this museum reflects that period's passion for nature studies. The Salle des Eaux Vives on the ground floor contains several aquariums.

Le Magasin – Centre National d'Art Contemporain

155 cours Berriat. Open according to the exhibition programme Tue–Sun 2–7pm. 3.50€. 04 76 21 95 84. www.magasin-cnac.org.
Original exhibitions of contemporary art held under an immense glass roof inside a former industrial building, known as **Le Magasin**, designed in 1900 by the Eiffel Group.

Musée des Troupes de Montagne

Fort de la Bastille. Open Tue–Sun 11am–6pm. Free. 04 76 00 92 25.
This army museum shows the visitor both the history of the troops based in the mountains and the techniques used by these men, trained to survive in extreme conditions.

EXCURSIONS
St Martin-le-Vinoux – La Casamaures

8 bis av. du Gén.-Leclerc (off A 48), 38950 St-Martin-le-Vinoux (2.5km/1.5mi NW of Grenoble towards Voiron).
Guided tour (1hr 15min) Wed and 1st Sat of month at 2pm; check for entry fees. 04 76 47 13 50. www.casamaures.org.
This 1855 Moorish Revival villa from the heyday of cement construction offers a profusion of Moorish arches and moucharabies (window grills) based on designs from a palace in Istanbul.

La Tronche – Musée Hébert

2.5km/1.5mi N of Grenoble towards St-Pierre-de-Chartreuse. Entrance in chemin Hébert. Open summer Mon and Wed–Sat 10am–6pm, Sun 10am–7pm; rest of year except Jan Wed–Mon 10am–6pm. Closed 1 May, 25 Dec. Free. 04 76 42 97 35.
Very beautiful gardens including a rose garden surround the charming former country house of the painter **Ernest**

Hébert (1817–1908), a native of Dauphiné. The house allows an intimate portrait of the artist and the museum includes various examples of his work.

Lancey

⊙ *16km/10mi NE of Grenoble. Take D 523 towards Domène. In Lancey turn right at the traffic lights, up towards La Combe-de-Lancey and av. des Papeteries.* **P** *Car park.*

Maison Bergès-Musée de la Houille blanche – *40 av. des Papeteries.* ⊙*Open Wed–Sun Apr–Oct 1–6pm; Nov–Mar 1–5pm.* ⊙*Closed 1 Jan, 1 May, 25 Dec.* ℘*04 38 92 19 60. www.musee-houille-blanche.fr.* This new museum opened in 2011 in the family home of Aristide Bergès, a 19C industrial pioneer in hydroelectricity (who also coined the phrase "houille blanche" or "white oil"). The house itself has Art Nouveau features and displays industrial machinery, documents and photographs.

ADDRESSES

🏠 STAY

⊜ **Europe** – *22 pl. Grenette.* ℘*04 76 46 16 94. www.hoteleurope.fr. Wifi. 45 rooms.* Located at the heart of Grenoble's historic quarter, the Europe was the first hotel to be built in the city. Refurbished guest rooms in a contemporary, but sensible style.

⊜⊜ **Gallia** – *7 bd Mar. Joffre.* ℘*04 76 87 39 21. www.hotel-gallia.com. Closed 24 Jul–23 Aug. Wifi. 35 rooms.* Most of the rooms in this family-run hotel have been brought up to date in bright colours, with a hint of the south. It has a smart, well-lit sitting room.

⊜⊜ **Hôtel Acacia** – *13 r. de Belgrade.* ℘*04 76 87 29 90. www.hotelacaciagrenoble.com.* **P**. *20 rooms.* This hotel, located close to the cable car of la Bastille, was recently renovated. The guest rooms are modern; the reception area and breakfast room are decorated in Provençal colours.

⊜⊜⊜ **Chambre d'hôte Le Manoir** – *636 chemin du Berlioz, 38190 Villard-Bonnot. 5km/3mi from Grenoble towards Villard-Bonnot.* ℘*04 76 71 40 00. http://domaineduberlioz.pagesperso-orange.fr. Closed Nov–Feb.* ♿ **P**. *Wifi. 3 rooms* ⊇.

Today this 12C residence is an equestrian centre and includes two spacious rooms and one suite, with fine furniture. They look out to the vegetable garden or the horses. Meals available for residents. Warm welcome.

🍽 EAT

⊜ **Bombay** – *60 cours J. Jaurès.* ℘*04 76 87 71 80. Reservations essential Sat–Sun. Closed Aug and Mon.* ♿. You will leave the Alps behind once across the threshold of this restaurant and be transported to distant climes by the tempting smell of Indian spices and the exotic flavours of the food.

⊜ **Café de la Table Ronde** – *7 pl. St-André.* ℘*04 76 44 51 41. www.restaurant-table ronde-grenoble.com.* ♿. Huge mirrors on the walls reflect the regulars in lively discussion at the bar as well as photographs signed by Sarah Bernhardt, Raymond Devos and many other stars. Brasserie-style local cooking.

⊜ **L'Aparté** – *5 r. A. Gaché.* ℘*04 76 59 12 85. www.laparte38.fr. Closed eve and Sun.* Savoury tarts, vegetable terrines and bright salads vary according to the seasons and the whim of the chef-owner. Eat inside or outside on the terrace.

⊜ **Le Coup de Torchon** – *8 r. D.Villars.* ℘*04 76 63 20 58. Closed Wed eve and Sun–Mon.* Close to an area of antique shops, this friendly restaurant offers modern, creative cooking according to what's at market. Bright and cosy setting with keen pricing too.

⊜ **L'Exception** – *4 cours J. Jaurès.* ℘*04 76 47 03 12. www.restaurant-lexception.com. Closed Sat–Sun.* A restaurant that's always full probably due to sensible pricing for good portions of creative, locally inspired food. Modern décor.

⊜ **Marie Margaux** – *12 r. M. Porte.* ℘*04 76 46 46 46. www.lemariemargaux.com. Closed 28 Jun–13 Jul, Sun eve, Mon eve and Tue eve.* Named after the first names of the owner's two grandmothers, this attractive restaurant serves good, down-to-earth fish dishes in a warm Provençal décor.

⊜⊜ **Chasse-Spleen** – *6 pl. Lavalette.* ℘*04 38 37 03 52. Closed Mon lunch, Sat lunch and Sun.* Named after a famous Médoc wine from Bordeaux, which itself was named by Charles Baudelaire, his poems grace the walls, while local dishes grace the tables.

⊜⊜ **Ciao a Te** – *2 r. de la Paix. ℘04 76 42 54 41. Closed 2 weeks in Feb, 1st week Aug and Sun–Mon.* This Italian restaurant in an old part of the city is near the Musée de Grenoble. Behind its timber front and hand-painted sign, it serves "fast" cuisine and of course pasta.

⊜⊜ **Grill Parisien** – *34 bd Alsace-Lorraine. ℘04 76 46 10 16. Closed 13–17 May, 1–23 Aug, Sat–Sun and public holidays.* Regulars and newcomers to this restaurant all sit together at tables in the kitchen or under the beams of the dining room to enjoy traditional food, with a slight southern accent.

⊜⊜⊜ **Auberge Napoléon** – *7 r. Montorge. ℘04 76 87 53 64. www.auberge-napoleon.fr. Closed 1–10 May, 9–14 Jul, 16–30 Aug and Sun.* Named after Napoleon Bonaparte, its most famous habitué, the Empire dining room serves as a theatre for original cuisine.

⊜⊜⊜ **Le Mandala** – *7 r. R. Blanchard. ℘04 76 44 49 80. Closed Sun–Mon, reservations advised.* The reputation of this very pleasant restaurant has spread through word of mouth. High-quality fresh and seasonal ingredients form the owners' motto.

🍴 TAKING A BREAK

La Soupe aux Choux – *7 rte de Lyon. ℘04 76 87 05 67. www.jazzalasoupe.free.fr. Open 6pm–1am. Closed Jul–Aug and Sun–Mon. ⊜12€.* This jazz club is a local institution. Well-known international musicians appear here often; the rest of the time local groups perform the standards.

Salon de thé Pignol – *18 r. de l'Alma. ℘04 76 24 85 85. www.pignol.fr. Open 8am–7.30pm. Closed Sun–Mon.* By the cloister of Ste-Cécile convent, this little haven of peace offers cakes from the famous Lyon pâtissier and caterer Pignol.

🛒 SHOPPING

À l'Abeille d'Or – *3 r. de Strasbourg. ℘04 76 43 04 03. Open 9.30am–12.30pm, 2.30–7.30pm. Closed 1 week in Feb and Sun–Mon.* The interior of this shop is exactly as the grandparents of the present owners left it. You will find 14 sorts of honey, pollen, royal jelly, spice cake, barley sugar, licorice, many sorts of tea, preserves, and interesting condiments.

🏃 ACTIVITIES

Walks in the local mountains are good in spring or summer. In winter you can head for Chamrousse for skiing – the very first French alpine ski club was formed in Grenoble in 1896!

Parks and gardens – You can escape the summer in several parks: **Parc Paul Mistral** near the town hall, **Parc de l'Île d'Amour** including a fitness route, and on the foothills of the Bastille the **Jardin des Dauphins**.

Grenoble beach – *2 r. G. Flaubert (tramway stop MC2). ℘04 76 23 57 16. www.plagedegrenoble.com. Tue–Fri 6–9pm, Sat 10am–2pm. Closed 6 Nov–11 Apr. 6€ session (children 3€).* Half an acre of sandy beach open for a whole range of beach activities. Shady areas, palm trees, terrace and showers.

🎭 EVENTS

Cabaret frappé – *℘04 76 42 41 41. www.cabaret-frappe.com.* This festival gathers together jazz and world musicians to perform in the towns, green space, the elegant Jardin de Ville.

TRANSPORT

The Visitag is a one- or five-day pass for unlimited tram or bus journeys in the town and local area (*℘04 76 20 66 11*), available at TAG agencies, the railway station, tourist office, Grand-Place shopping centre and at automatic machines at the tramway stops. Trams run 5am–1am; buses 5.30am–9.40pm except 1 May.

Le Grésivaudan★

Abutting the Chartreuse Massif to the west and the slopes of the Belledonne to the east, this sheltered depression, deeply eroded by Ice Age glaciers, has been a rich agricultural area for many centuries.

🚗 DRIVING TOURS

1 THE VALLEY OF A HUNDRED CHÂTEAUX★
Drive of 95km/59mi shown on the local map (⌖ see p280). Allow 2hrs 30min.

▷ *From Grenoble, drive along D 1090 towards Chambéry; at Eymes take D 30.*

The road climbs up to the Plateau des Petites Roches, a wide terrace beneath the escarpments of the Chartreuse.

▷ *Turn left off D 30, before St-Pancrasse, towards the Col du Coq.*

Col du Coq
The road winds along the slopes of the Dent de Crolles offering lovely views of the Isère Valley before reaching the pass. From the pass itself (1 434m/4 705ft) the panorama extends to Chamechaude in the Belledonne.

▷ *Return to D 30 passing through St-Pancrasse on the edge of the plateau, at the base of the Dent de Crolles.*

Bec du Margain★★
🚶 *30min from D 30. Leave the car by the tennis courts and follow the path to the right through a pine wood.*
Walk along the edge of the escarpment to the viewing table above the Isère Valley, with another fantastic **view**.

St-Hilaire
This health and ski resort is a favourite with paragliding and hang-gliding enthusiasts. Since 1924 it has been linked to Montfort on N 90 by the steepest **funicular**★ *(end May–early Sept; ☏04 76 08 00 02; www.funiculaire.fr)* in Europe,

- 🧭 **Michelin Map:** 333 J5/6.
- ▷ **Location:** The Grésivaudan is partly E of the Isère river, where D 523 goes N from Grenoble along the line of the Belledonne mountain chain; on the W, A 41 and N 90 lead up to St-Hilaire and Le Touvet.
- 🚗 **Don't Miss:** The road up to the Croix de Revollet.
- 👪 **Kids:** Taking the St-Hilaire funicular.
- 🕐 **Timing:** Visit the northeast section in the evening for the fabulous sunset.

which carries 40 people over a distance of 1.5km/1mi with a rise of 720m/2 362ft. From the upper station, there is a striking **view**★ across the valley. The road continues along the edge of the Chartreuse and descends to St-Gorges. From there D 285 winds down to Petit-St-Marcel, where the Combe de Savoie and the peaks of the Bauges appear.

▷ *In La Palud, D 285 turns to the right towards Chapareillan, the last Dauphiné village in the Grésivaudan just S of the former border between Dauphiné and Savoie at the "Pont-Royal". Take D 1090 towards Grenoble.*

At Pontcharra, D 9 leads to **Fort Barraux**, built by the Duc de Savoie in 1597 on French territory.

Chateau du Touvet★
🚶 *Guided tour (45min) Jul–Aug Sun–Fri 2–6pm; Apr–Jun and Sept–Oct Sun and public holidays 2–6pm. ⊗7€. ♿☏04 76 08 42 27. www.touvet.com.*
The castle on the slopes of the Chartreuse Massif began as a simple 13C fort; two round towers marking the entrance remain, but most of the building dates from the 15C.
The castle was remodelled in the 18C: the courtyard was enclosed, a main staircase built inside and the **gardens**★ adorned with a **water stairway**★.

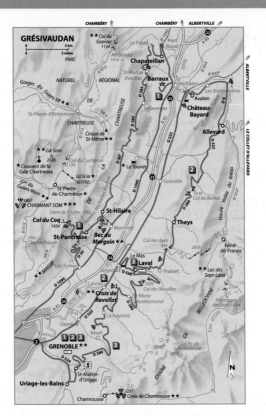

The **interior** is richly decorated. The gallery houses letters signed by Henry VIII of England and François I of France.

▶ *Return to Grenoble by D1090.*

2 FROM GRENOBLE TO PONTCHARRA★

Drive of 100km/62.2mi shown on the local map (above). Allow 3hrs.

▶ *Leave Grenoble by D 523 towards Domène. From Brignoud drive up to Laval, going around Château du Mas.*

Laval

Pretty village with overhanging roofs and a charming manor, the Château de la Martellière. Between Prabert and the Col des Ayes, there is a fine view of the Chartreuse Massif.

Theys

Nestling in a valley, this little town has retained several old houses built with the local violet-tinted stone. The 14C **château** (⚬— *closed to the public*) has walls painted with murals.

The spa and town centre of **Allevard** (🜂 *opposite*) and the **panorama**★★ from the Collet d'Allevard are worth a short detour. Between Allevard and Pontcharra, D 9 goes round the heights of Brame Farine and gives a fine **view**★ of the lower Gelon Valley.

▶ *From Pontcharra, follow a small road on the right to Château-Bayard.*

Château-Bayard

The road climbs from a square and passes Pontcharra's schools; at the top, turn right then immediately left. Car park 🕐*Open Jul–Aug Wed–Mon 2–6pm; mid -May–Sept Sat–Sun and public holidays 2–6pm.* ◉*Free.* 📞*04 76 97 11 65.*
The doorway situated between the farm buildings and the former gatehouse gives access to the terrace and the **museum**, housed in a 15C square

building with mullioned windows. The **panorama**★ over the Chartreuse, Belledonne and Bauges massifs is majestic. Close by, you can see an isolated 12C tower in the village of **Avalon**. From there you can look over to the vineyards of the Combe de Savoie.

▶ *From Pontcharra, return to Grenoble by D 523.*

③ CROIX DE REVOLLAT★
Drive of 79km/49.1mi shown on the local map (☙opposite). Allow 2hrs 30min.

▶ *Leave Laval S on D 280.*

After the Col des Mouilles D 280 descends to the St-Mury Valley. The Cirque du Boulon, with waterfalls streaming from the glacier, towers above the road and Les Trois Pics de Belledonne stand out sharply against the sky.

Croix de Revollat★★
50m/55yds to the right of D 280.
The main interest lies in the **view** over the Grésivaudan below and, across the river, the Plateau des Petites Roches overlooked by the Chartreuse; the Vercors Massif to the left and the Bauges Massif to the right. At another cross 1.5km/1mi further on the road crosses

the ravine of the Lancey stream. After Le Naysord, the road climbs the terraced slope offering sweeping views of the Chartreuse. Running above the Revel Valley, D 280 heads out of the trees to the very populated Uriage Valley.

Uriage-les-Bains
☙*See Chamrousse p292.*

▶ *At Uriage, turn right on D 524 to Grenoble.*

ADDRESSES

🛏 STAY
Auberge Au Pas de l'Alpette – Bellecombe, 38530 Chapareillan. ℘04 76 45 22 65. www.alpette.com. Closed 10 Oct–10 Nov and Sun eve. Wifi. 13 rooms, restaurant. A quiet mountain inn with an exceptional view to Mont Blanc. The simple garret rooms are all different. Seasonal country food with a local accent. Pool terrace.

🍴 EAT
Auberge des Paletières – Mont-Farcy, 38570 Theys. ℘04 76 71 17 07. www.les-paletieres.fr. Closed autumn. Wifi. 2 rooms. A relaxing place to come and eat with rustic décor and traditional, fine home cooking.

Allevard

Lying in the green Bréda Valley, Allevard established itself as an iron smelting centre as early as the 13C, and remains of the smelting-houses are reminders of the town's past. In 1791 an earthquake revealed the "black water" of Allevard, whose therapeutic qualities were quickly recognised leading to its establishment as an important spa and cure centre. The town is the starting point for numerous excursions towards the Allevard Massif (highest peak: Puy Gris, 2 908m/9 541ft), the northern extension of the Belledonne chain.

▶ **Population:** 3 824.
🧭 **Michelin Map:** 333 J5.
ℹ **Info:** Pl. de la Résistance, 38580 Allevard. ℘04 76 45 10 11. www.allevard-les-bains.com.
▶ **Location:** At an altitude of 475m/1 558ft Allevard is midway between Grenoble and Chambéry. Leave A 41 at Exit 23, follow D 29, then D 525 to the resort.
👁 **Don't miss:** The walks in the upper Bréda Valley.

SIGHTS
Église St-Marcel
In this 19C Gothic church, the altar dedicated to St Éloi was made in 1865 at the Allevard forge and is decorated with representations of the local metalwork and mining industries.

Musée Jadis Allevard
◷*Open mid-May–mid-Oct 2–6pm; Christmas and Feb holidays 2–5pm.*
•*Guided visits possible (1hr 30min).*
◷*Closed 1 Jan, 14 Jul, 15 Aug, 25 Dec.*
2€ (children free). ✆*04 76 45 16 40.*
www.musee-jadis-allevard.fr.
Housed in the old village forge, this museum retraces the history of Allevard through its development of iron mines, and then the establishment of its thermal spas and ski facilities.

Spa Resort
Allevard is not only an excellent base for hikes, it has also been a popular thermal spa and cure resort since 1836. Its sulphurous waters, high in volatile carbonic acid, are inhaled to treat respiratory disorders. The baths are a striking architectural mix of the Classical and the Oriental.

➤The winter-sports resort **Collet d'Allevard**★★ (✆*04 76 45 01 88*) offers downhill ski pistes and snowshoe tracks.

🚗 DRIVING TOURS

1 ROUTE DU COLLET D'ALLEVARD★★
Drive of 11km/6.8mi shown on the local map (opposite).
Allow 30min.

▷ *Leave Allevard by D 525A to Fond-de-France. Turn left after 1.4km/0.9mi onto D 109.*

Hairpin bends afford glimpses of Allevard, the Veyton and Gleyzin valleys and the upper Bréda Valley.
As the road reaches the winter-sports resort of ➤ **Le Collet d'Allevard**★★ (alt. 1 450m–2 100m/4 757ft–6 890ft), it reveals a vast panoramic view.

🔭 For an even better view drive 4km/2.5mi further to the **Super Collet** area with an orientation table at the summit.
◷*Les Plagnes chairlift open Jul–Aug and in winter.*

2 CHARTREUSE DE ST-HUGON
Drive of 8.5km/5.3mi shown on the local map (opposite), then 1hr return.

▷ *Leave Allevard by D 525 N, turn right onto D 209 then right again after the bridge across the Buisson. After 6.5km/4mi, ignore D 109A on your right and park the car near the St-Hugon forest lodge.*

🚶*1hr there and back. Continue on foot along the forest track for 1.5km/1mi then, near a corrugated iron hut, turn left onto a path leading down to Pont Sarret (boots may be needed after a thaw or heavy rain). Cross the bridge and take the path down below the right bank of the Bens.*

Chartreuse de St-Hugon
A *chartreuse* is a Carthusian monastery in an isolated spot; little remains of this one founded in the 12C except a 17C building with a fine, large door. Since 1982 it has been occupied by **Karma Ling**, one of the most important Buddhist centres in Europe.

▷ *Continue along the path, bear left at the fork.*

Pont du Diable
Three hundred years old, this bridge spans the Bens and used to mark the France–Savoie border.

▷ *Cross the bridge to rejoin the road and the forest lodge on the right.*

3 VALLÉE DES HUILES★
Drive of 50km/31.1mi round tour shown on the local map (opposite).
Allow 2hrs 30min.

▷ *Leave Allevard by D 525 N then right on D 925 towards Albertville. Turn right to La Rochette.*

La Rochette

The cardboard factories of this industrial town and tourist centre are among the largest in Europe.

▷ *Drive E towards Étable for 1km/0.6mi and turn right.*

The road climbs through the upper Gelon Valley, known as the Vallée des Huiles, which contrasts with the forested slope opposite.
Upstream from Étable stands the solitary Pic de l'Huile, which gave its name to the whole valley.

▷ *Continue on D 24 towards Bourget-en-Huile and turn left along D 207 towards Allevard.*

After crossing the Gelon, the road winds along the forested slope of the valley. Beyond Villard there is a fine view of the basin of La Rochette and the lower Bréda Valley leading to the Grésivaudan.

▷ *Return to Allevard along D 209.*

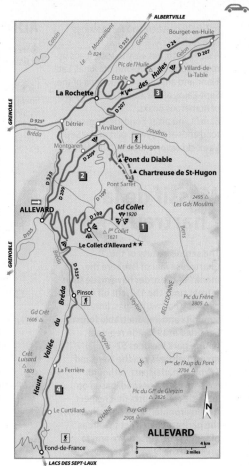

4 **HAUTE VALLÉE DU BRÉDA**

Drive of 17km/10.6mi shown on the local map (above).
Allow 30min.

▷ *Follow D 525A to Fond-de-France.*

Pinsot

The **Maison des forges et moulins** is a reconstruction of a tool-making establishment in an 18C mill.
There is an exhibition and **demonstrations** of the metalwork hammers, forge and metal press (*guided tour Jul–Aug 10.30am–2pm, 3–5pm, May–Jun and Sept Wed–Sun except public holidays 2–4.30pm; 5€; ℰ04 76 13 53 59).*
The visit concludes with the **sentier du Fer** (2hrs).

▷ *Continue on the main road to Fond-de-France (alt. 1 100m/3 609ft).*

Lacs des Sept-Laux★★

Leave the car in Fond-de-France in front of the Sept-Laux hotel. This hike is suitable for experienced walkers: 3hrs 45min climb; 1 150m/3 773ft vertical rise; mountain boots recommended.
Most of the walk is through woodland (follow markings).
At the halfway mark, take the sentier des deux Ruisseaux track to the left. Beyond the Lac Noir (2hrs 30min walk) the walk is easier as the path skirts several superb **glacial lakes: Lac Carré★★, Lac de la Motte, Lac Cottepens, Lac du Cos.**
Walk along the Lac Cottepens towards the Col des Sept-Laux; bear left

283

to Lac Blanc where you see markings
on a rock.

A steep path, not easy to spot, leads up
to a mound overlooking the small Lac
Blanc and affording a panorama of the
Sept-Laux, of the Eau d'Olle Valley and
of numerous peaks.

6km/3.7mi after Fond-de-France, the
road ends at **Pleynet**, part of the **Sept-
Laux ski resort** (120km/75mi pistes).

Massif de la Chartreuse★★

The serene beauty of the
Chartreuse Massif is where the
monks of the order have made their
retreat since the 11C, cut off from the
world by narrow gorges, limestone
summits and impenetrable forests.
Founded in 1995, the regional
nature park includes 52
municipalities from the Isère and
Savoie *départements*. Although
tourism is encouraged, based on
activities and sports that respect
the environment, the objectives of
the park are to protect the areas
of biological importance and to
preserve the high plateaus.

🚗 DRIVING TOURS

1 COL DE PORTE AND ROUTE DU DÉSERT★★

*Drive of 79km/49.1mi shown on the local
map (⊙see p287). Allow 4hrs.*

⊙ *Leave Grenoble via La Tronche
and D 512.*

The road from La Tronche to the Col de
Vence climbs in hairpin bends along
the slopes of Mont St-Eynard, offering
bird's-eye views of the Grésivaudan
depression and Grenoble with remarkable **vistas**★★ of the Belledonne range,
the Taillefer, Thabor and Obiou summits
as well as part of the Vercors. On clear
days, you can see Mont Blanc.

ADDRESSES

⊙*See also addresses in Grenoble,
Le Grésivaudan.*

🏃ACTIVITIES

There are numerous **walks** from Allevard,
including the six-day Tour du Pays
d'Allevard. Ask at the tourist office.
The Lac de la Mirande, N of Allevard
(D 525), is good for swimming.

⊙ **Michelin Map:** 333 H5.

ℹ **Info:** Relais du Parc, 73670
St-Pierre-d'Entremont.
📞04 79 65 81 90.
www.chartreuse-
tourisme.com.

▷ **Location:** The Chartreuse is
easily accessible from either
Grenoble or Chambéry.
You will enjoy a splendid
view of the massif driving
from Grenoble towards
St-Pierre-de-Chartreuse.

⊛ **Don't Miss:** The viewpoint
of Charmant Som.

⊙ **Timing:** May–June is ideal
to appreciate the profusion
of colourful wild flowers.

Le Sappey-en-Chartreuse

This mountain resort nestles in a
basin with forested slopes, below the
imposing Chamechaude peak. The little **church** has been restored and has
eight stained-glass windows by **Arcabas** (2002) on the theme of the Resurrection, with the colours moving from
dark to flamboyant.

Le Marais des Sagnes – The most
extensive high-altitude marshlands in
the park. Signboards create a relaxed
and interesting visit *(details from Sappey
tourist office 📞04 76 88 84 05).*

The road follows the Sappey basin and
then the Sarcenas Valley with the jagged Casque de Néron at its southern
end. At **Col de Porte**, the tilted limestone shelf of Chamechaude looks like
a huge lectern.

▶ *From Col de Porte take D 57D left towards Charmant Som.*

Charmant Som★★★
The road rises steeply through a forest scarred with rocky ridges, which gradually gives way to pastures. The Plateau du Som is viewed on the way up.
🚶 *1hr return. Park at les Bergeries.*
Walk to the edge of the escarpment to get an overall view of the **setting**★ of the Grande Chartreuse Monastery.

▶ *Return to the Col de Porte. Continue with particular care as this route is often used by timber trucks. The road offers closer views of the Chamechaude shelf.*

St-Pierre-de-Chartreuse★
♿*See St-Pierre-de-Chartreuse (p290).*

▶ *Turn back to follow the "Route du Désert" (D 520B, to St-Laurent-du-Pont).*

Belvédère des Sangles★★
4km/2.5mi on foot from Valombré bridge (♿see St-Pierre-de-Chartreuse p290).

Porte de l'Enclos
The valley seems completely enclosed by high cliffs. The very wooded **Gorges du Guiers Mort**★★ is overlooked by limestone ridges on which perch pine trees. This is the famous "**Route du Désert**", which in the 16C marked the boundary of the Chartreuse monastery.

▶ *At the St-Pierre bridge, take the road on the right to La Correrie (one way).*

La Correrie
♿*See Monastère de la Grande Chartreuse (p288).*

▶ *Return to the Route du Désert.*

The road goes downhill through three successive tunnels; note the strange limestone needle, known as the **Pic de l'Œillette**, standing at the roadside.

Pont St-Bruno
Leave the car on the left bank and walk down to the old bridge (15min return).

This single-arched bridge is an important work of art in the Chartreuse. The stream disappears into sinkholes and flows under a boulder forming a natural bridge (👁*viewpoint; keep a close watch on children*).

Fourvoirie
This place name *(forata via)* is a reminder that, at the beginning of the 16C, the Carthusian monks originally hewed this passage through the rock. It marked one of the entrances of the Grande Chartreuse site, beyond which only unarmed men were allowed.

St-Laurent-du-Pont
This lively tourist centre lies at the foot of the Grande Sure. From the 13C Notre-Dame-du-Château Chapel is a vast panorama over the valley.
From the tourist office is a pleasant two-hour historic circuit. Between St-Joseph-la-Rivière and St-Laurent the peatbogs of the **Tourbière de l'Herrentang** are able to be visited with a marked discovery path.

Défilé du Grand Crossey
The eastern entrance of this deep gorge is particularly impressive at sunset. The wooded valley with high limestone cliffs is typical of the Chartreuse.

▶ *At St-Etienne-de-Crossey, turn left towards La Croix-Bayard.*

Voiron
This busy trading centre, situated on the edge of the Chartreuse Massif, is known for its high-technology industry and makes the famous Rossignol skis. It is also the centre for production of herb-based liqueurs such as Chartreuse.
Caves de la Chartreuse★ – *10 bd E.-Kofler.* ⏰*Open Apr–Oct daily 9–11.30am, 2–6.30pm; Nov–Mar Mon–Fri except public holidays 9–11.30am, 2–5.30pm.* ⊜*Free.* ☎*04 76 05 81 77. www.chartreuse.fr.*
The formula of the elixir of life was given to the Carthusian monks in 1605 but it was brother **Jérôme Maubec** in 1737 who first actually created the herbal 70 percent alcohol that still forms the basis

of the **Chartreuse** liqueurs; even today, only two monks know the secret recipe. Until 1935 the liqueur was still produced at the Chartreuse Monastery. This interesting visit starts in the cellars and ends with a tasting.

② THE HEART OF THE CHARTREUSE★★

Drive of 50km/31.1mi shown on the local map (opposite). Allow 4hrs.

▶ *St-Pierre-de-Chartreuse to St-Laurent is described in ① above. Leave St-Laurent towards Révol, then follow D 102. The road rises to Berland. Here take a small road N.*

Belvédère du Pont St-Martin

Beyond St-Christophe-sur-Guiers, just before the bridge over road D 46, a path on the right follows the left bank of the Guiers Vif gorge to a viewpoint. Towards St-Pierre-d'Entremont, the road follows the impressive **Gorges du Guiers Vif★★**, including the **Pas du Frou★★**. This overhang, is the most spectacular section of road.

St-Pierre-d'Entremont

The Guiers river used to mark the border between France and Savoie. The village is still divided into two administrative parts: 478 villagers live in the Isère *département* and 372 in Savoie.

Cirque de St-Même★★

The Guiers Vif springs out of a cave and forms two waterfalls.

▶ *Return to St-Pierre-d'Entremont and drive S on D 102B.*

Château du Gouvernement★

A fine **view★** over the basin with Mont Granier and Alpette to the east.

ADDRESSES

STAY

🛏 **Chambre d'hôte de Montbel** – *73670 St-Pierre-d'Entremont.* ☏ *04 79 65 81 65. Closed 1 Nov–26 Dec, Sun eve and Mon out of*

season. Wifi. 5 rooms. Roger Vincent, formerly owner of a hotel-restaurant, today welcomes guests to the warm atmosphere of his own home. He serves tasty dishes, introducing guests to local specialities.

🛏🛏 **Beau Site** – *38380 St-Pierre-de-Chartreuse.* ☏ *04 76 88 61 34. www.hotel*

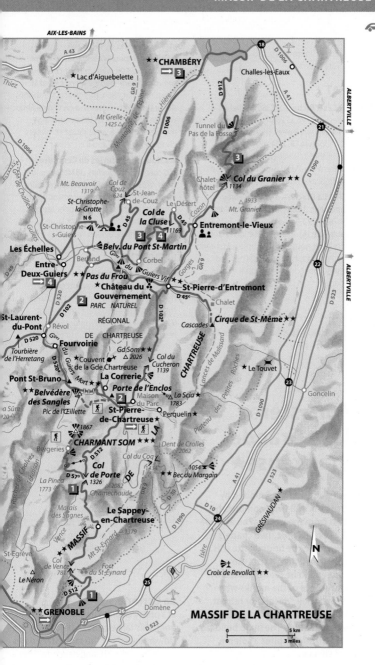

beausite.com. Closed 2 Apr–2 May, 15 Oct–26 Dec. Wifi. 26 rooms, restaurant ⊜ ⊜.
A collection of paintings from local artist Peter Rahmsdorf decorate this large hundred-year-old house. Plain, but comfortable rooms and a pool with a view over the valley.

⊜⊜⊜ **Hôtel Les Skieurs** – Giroudon, 38700 Le Sappey-en-Chartreuse. ☏ 04 76 88 82 76. www.lesskieurs.com. Closed for spring holiday, mid-Dec–mid-Jan and Sun eve–Mon. 🅿. 18 rooms. From here you can go on a ramble, sightsee or stretch out by the pool. Small, recently decorated rooms, some with balconies. Attractive dining room and a newly renovated terrace.

EAT

Les 3 Biches – *38380 Miribel-les-Échelles.* *04 76 55 28 02. Closed 2 weeks Jan, 1 week Jun, 1 week Sept and Sept–Jun Wed. 7 rooms*. A family inn at the heart of the little village of Miribel near St-Laurent-du-Pont. Generous portions of traditional dishes.

La Blache – *2 pl. du 10éme Groupement, 38380 St-Laurent-du-Pont.* *04 76 55 29 57. Closed 4–26 Jan, 1–15 Sept, Sun eve–Tue.* In an old station near the Guiers Mort gorges, this simple restaurant features wooden armchairs. The food is freshly cooked from seasonal market produce.

TAKING A BREAK

Bonnat – *8 cours Sénozan, 38500 Voiron.* *04 76 05 28 09. www.bonnat-chocolatier. com. Open 9am–noon, 2–7pm. Closed Mon.* Established in 1884, this chocolate shop is decorated with mosaics, a carved ceiling, wooden features, old lamps and big mirrors. It offers a wide range of sweets, chocolates, cakes and ice creams.

Nouvelles Écuries du Centaure – *100 chemin des Agnelets, 38140 Réaumont.* *04 76 35 44 70. www.ecuriesducentaure. com. Open all year by appointment.* Near Voiron these horse stables offer lessons and rides out for everyone. A large range of events and activities.

EVENTS

Festival des Nuits d'été – A series of classical music concerts is offered throughout summer in the churches of the Chartreuse and the Aiguebelette Valley, near Chambéry. *Information and reservations at the local tourist office.*

Monastère de la Grande Chartreuse★

The first hermitage founded by St Bruno in 1084 was completely cut off from the world at an altitude of 1 190 m/3 904ft. Two chapels show where the original site was. Until the 18C the Chartreuse Massif would be really marked by the presence of the monks who guarded their "desert" or retreat jealously to keep it as a haven of peace and quiet. The huge building at La Correrie inspires a solemn air of silence.

VISIT

It is not possible to visit the monastery; however, the museum at La Correrie provides an insight into the history and life of the monks. The distillery is at **Voiron** (*see p285*).

- **Michelin Map:** 333 H5.
- **Location:** 4km/2.5mi W of St-Pierre-de-Chartreuse by D 520 or "route du Désert".
- **Don't Miss:** The Grande Chartreuse museum.
- **Timing:** Allow 1 hour 30 minutes for the walk to the monastery.

La Correrie

In a pretty clearing below the Charmant Som, this large annexe (known as the "lower house") of the monastery dates partly from the 11C and has certain Renaissance features.

The lay brothers of the order used to live here and in the last century, the old or sick monks were looked after here, probably because its position is somewhat more comfortable than in the "upper house".

The Carthusian Order

The Grande Chartreuse is so named because it is the motherhouse of the Carthusian order. In 1084 Hugues, the Bishop of Grenoble, dreamed of seven stars, warning him of the arrival of seven travellers, who under Bruno's leadership, had decided to live in a retreat. Hugues led them into the "desert" of Chartreuse that subsequently gave its name to both the monastery and the order. The founder, St Bruno died in Italy in 1101. A successor, Father Guigues, rewrote the Carthusian rites, which have since been reformed, notably in 1981. The order has expanded, notably in the Renaissance period when there were 200 foundations; today 24 Carthusian monasteries exist around the world.

The Daily Life of a Carthusian Monk

The monk or hermit leads an essentially solitary life of prayer, intellectual work and manual work. Each lives in a cell surrounding the cloister. Meals are left in a "turn" or cubby-hole. The monks do meet for Vespers and to celebrate Mass, and on Sundays for a communal meal and walk in the surrounding woods.

The Grande Chartreuse

In 1132 an avalanche destroyed the monastery. Father Guigues rebuilt it, and through the ages, the buildings have been damaged by fire eight times. Today's buildings date from 1676. As well as the church, the cells, the library and other communal rooms, it includes the general chapter room and lodgings for visitors.

The monks have been exiled several times: during the Revolution, and in 1903 when the law expelled them from France. They returned in 1941.

Musée de la Grande Chartreuse★

🕐 *Open May-Sept daily 10am-6.30pm; Oct–Nov Mon–Fri 1.30–6pm, Sat–Sun and public holidays 10am–6.30pm.* ⊙6€ *(children 2.50€).* ♿ ✆*04 76 88 60 45. www.musee-grande-chartreuse.fr.*
According to the monks' wishes, the complete renovation of this museum (2010–11) has returned the building to its original composition: a monastery made up of cells – lodgings where the monks, in solitary confinement, lead their lives of prayer and contemplation. Through 18 rooms, the visitor learns about the history of the monks and their daily lives through numerous documents, objects used in daily life as well as films and commentary from monks or their relatives.
The reconstructions of the cloister and of a new hermitage with its bedroom, office and workshop are among the most evocative of the displays. The new areas allow the visitor to see some of the treasures of the Carthusian order, as well as a model of the Grande Chartreuse, created by a brother, showing the different buildings of this vast monastery. Overall this attractive and modern museum pays tribute to a long tradition and helps us to understand what the sons of St Bruno look for and find in this place.
There is also an alpine garden here.

🚶 HIKE

Grande Chartreuse Monastery★

🐾 *Short, easy walk. 1hr 30min.*
From the car park at La Correrie, go back on yourself for 150m/165yds, then turn right on the tarmac road forbidden to cars; the monastery is 2km/1.2mi along this road. Keep dogs on a lead.
Even though it is impossible to visit the monastery, this circuit allows you to admire it from the outside... stay quiet, because you are in the monks territory! Once you arrive at the **viewpoint**★ you can return to La Correrie through the forest.
Go up to the calvary that you can see from the monastery and follow the signs indicating Correrie (40min).

St-Pierre-de-Chartreuse★

This charming resort sits in a peaceful valley surrounded by the soaring peaks of the Chartreuse Massif. In winter, there is fine skiing on the Scia, and in summer, 270km/168mi of marked paths lead out into forested landscapes.

- **Population:** 901.
- **Michelin Map:** 333 H5.
- **Info:** Pl. de la Marie, 38380 St-Pierre-de-Chartreuse. 04 76 88 62 08. www.st-pierre-chartreuse.com.
- **Location:** The village is easily accessible from either Voiron or Grenoble.
- **Don't Miss:** The interior of St-Hughes Church.

THE RESORT

The slopes of the Scia offer 35km/21.8mi of ski runs at all levels of difficulty, plus 80km/49.7mi of cross-country tracks in St-Hugues.

In summer, St-Pierre-de-Chartreuse is a popular base for excursions by car across the beautiful landscape of the Chartreuse Massif between Grenoble and Chambéry. Keen hikers will enjoy the climb to the **Dent de Crolles** or **Mont Granier**.

HIKES
Le Grand Som★★

Alt. 2 026m/6 647ft. 4hr ascent for fit hikers. Vertical rise: 1 175m/3 855ft. From St-Pierre, drive west along D 520B for 3km/1.8mi; car park reserved for walkers.

Walk back and take the road on the right leading to la Grande Chartreuse. Walk alongside it and turn right past a house on the left. The path leads to a calvary; climb to the top of the meadow on the edge of the forest for a fine **view**.

Return to the road and continue in the direction of the Grand Som via the Col de la Ruchère.

After walking for 30 minutes and reaching two chapels, take the steep path right *(marked in orange)*; 15 minutes later, turn right again and shortly after, left onto a steep path leading to the Habert de Bovinan refuge *(45min)*. Continue until you reach the foot of the Grand Som, then take the marked path on the right. At the next intersection, take the stony sheep path. From the cross at the summit, there is a **panorama★★★** of the whole Chartreuse Massif and of the monastery.

Belvédère des Sangles★★

2km/1.2mi then 2hrs 30min return on foot. Drive to La Diat and follow D 520B to St-Laurent-du-Pont. Leave the car beyond the bridge over the Guiers Mort, then cross back and take the Valombré Forest road.

It leads to the **Prairie de Valombré**, which offers one of the best **views★** of the Grande Chartreuse Monastery.

Perquelin★

3km/1.8mi E of St-Pierre.

The path ends in the upper valley of the River Guiers Mort, beneath the escarpments of the Dent de Crolles.

La Scia★

1hr 30mins return including 45min ride on the Essarts gondola and then the Scia chairlift (or Combe de l'Ours in summer). 04 76 88 62 08.

From the top of the second section of the gondola, is an easy climb to the top of the Scia for a lovely **panorama** over the Chartreuse summits. Through the Col des Ayes you can see to the Vercors and to the north is the Grand Colombier of the southern Jura.

EXCURSION
Église St-Hugues-de-Chartreuse

4km/2.5mi S of St-Pierre. Open Wed–Mon 10am–6pm. 04 76 88 65 01.

This 19C church may be plain on the outside, but inside contains a **monumental example of sacred art★** created 1953–86 by **Arcabas** (Jean-Marie Pirot), a famous sacred artist living locally.

Vizille★

This small industrial town has retained a major historic building of the Dauphiné region, the château of François de Bonne de **Lesdiguières** (1543–1627). Until 1972, it was one of the national estates at the disposal of the French president.

Château★

🕐*Open Wed–Mon Apr–Oct 10am–12.30pm, 1.30–6pm Nov–Mar, 10am–12.30pm, 1.30–5pm.* 🕐*Closed 25 Dec–1 Jan.* *Guided tour (1hr 30min).* *Free.* *04 76 68 07 35.*

The original building burned down in 1825. It was rebuilt, but another fire in 1865 destroyed its two wings and resulted in its present asymmetric silhouette.

One of the entrances is decorated with a bronze low relief (1616) by Jacob Richier, depicting Lesdiguières on horseback. The main austere façade gives onto the place de Vizille; the park side is more elegant, in Renaissance style with a 1676 monumental staircase.

Interior – The **Musée de la Révolution française**★ is arranged in a modern style on four levels. It offers a vision of the tumultuous period that inspired artists over a half-century to produce work both supporting and opposing the revolutionary spirit. The historic part of the old château on the top floor comprises reception rooms including the Grand Salon des Tapisseries and the Salon Lesdiguières (Louis XIII furniture), the terrace (lovely view of the park with Le Thabor in the distance) and the library (walnut panelling from 1880).

Park★ – 🕐*Open Jun–Aug daily 9am–8pm; Sept–Oct and Mar–May Wed–Mon 9am–7pm; Nov–Feb Wed–Mon 9am–5pm.* 🕐*Closed 1 May. Cyclists and dogs not allowed. Commentated tour of gardens in little train (35min).* This large, elegant park extends south of the castle with water features, deer and a lake with big trout and carp. Children will love the maze, while adults will appreciate the charming flowers and trees.

▶ **Population:** 7 714.
⚲ **Michelin Map:** 333 H7.
🅸 **Info:** Pl. du Château, 38220 Vizille. *04 76 68 15 16.* www.sudgrenoblois-tourisme.com.
▶ **Location:** Vizille is 15km/9.3mi S of Grenoble.

EXCURSIONS
Jarrie

▶ *7km/4.3mi N of Vizille.*

The 19C Maison Jouvin, set in a vast park, houses the **Musée de la Chimie** (🕐*open Mon–Wed and Fri–Sat 2.30–5.30pm;* *3€;* *04 76 68 62 18).*

The museum is a tribute to the chemical industries of Grenoble. The four round towers of the 15C **Château de Bon Repos** can be seen from Jarrie. This castle, with its elegant façade, was rescued from certain ruin in 1976.

Notre-Dame-de-Mésage

▶ *2.6km/1.6mi S of Vizille on Route Napoléon. Key at the town hall* *04 76 68 07 33.*

Below the main road, the village church of Notre-Dame-de-Mésage has an old Romanesque bell tower above its Carolingian nave. Beyond the road on top of a hillock is the old 13C **church**★ of the Hospitaliers de Jérusalem.

Panorama de Montrochat

Leave from church at St-Pierre-de-Mésage (S of Vizille by D 1091 and D 101A). 3hrs. 300m/984ft vertical rise.

The path takes the old Roman road following the side of the Connex. At the end of this circular route is a superb view over the Romanche Valley.

ADDRESSES

🏠 STAY

⌂ **Hôtel Sandra** – *46 r. des Docteurs-Bonnardon.* *04 76 68 10 01. www.hotelsandra.fr. Closed 1 weekend Aug.* 🅿 *18 rooms.* A family hotel, close to the castle. Rooms are simply decorated and regularly renovated.

Chamrousse

The summits of the Chamrousse Massif, which are the last important heights at the southwest tip of the Belledonne range, are the favourite haunt of skiers from Grenoble. A sought-after tourist centre in summer as well as in winter, the cable car whisks you up to the Croix de Chamrousse for a superb view over the Belledonne Massif. In the valley below, the spa town of Uriage and the nearby village of St-Martin are pleasant holiday resorts.

- **Michelin Map:** 333 I7.
- **Info:** 42 pl. de Belledonne, 38410 Chamrousse. ℘04 76 89 92 65. www.chamrousse.com.
- **Location:** The resort is 30km/18.6mi from Grenoble via Uriage.
- **Don't Miss:** The Croix de Chamrousse.

THE RESORT

This large winter complex above the Grenoble plain is actually made up of two resorts, **Recoin** (1 650m/5 413ft) and **Roche-Béranger** 100m/328ft higher. In summer, there are numerous hiking possibilities. There are also two via ferrata (℘04 76 59 04 96; www.maisonmontagnechamrousse.com).

HIKE
The Heights of St-Martin-d'Uriage★
600m/1 969ft. 6hrs there and back from the centre of St-Martin-d'Uriage.
From the village, head towards St-Nizier passing through Le Rossin, Les Vignasses and Champ Ruti. Go along Champ de l'Église and the chemin Bonafond to the top of Pinet. Return by Les Quatre Chemins, Les Seiglières, Le Marai, La Carrière, Champogne and Le Meffrey. Well worth the length for the fantastic views.

DRIVING TOUR

ROUND CHAMROUSSE★
Drive of 39km/24.2mi shown on the regional map (see p269). Allow 2hrs.

D 111 climbs steeply into the **Forêt de Prémol**★, where there are pretty glimpses to the Vercors and the Chartreuse. The only remaining building of **Ancienne Chartreuse de Prémol**

has been turned into a forest lodge. Beyond the Col Luitel, the road continues to climb.

Réserve Naturelle du Lac Luitel★
Car park near the information centre. Welcome centre open Jul–Aug Tue–Sun 1.30–6pm. Nature reserve open all year. Guided tours (2hrs) available. 4€. ℘04 76 86 39 76. Dogs forbidden.
This nature reserve, the oldest in France, covers 18ha/44 acres of **peat moss**, a unique ecosystem which developed in a depression of glacial origin.

Croix de Chamrousse★★
1hr return including a cable-car ride. Open end Jun–early Sept 9.15am–5pm. 7€ return. ℘04 76 59 09 09.
The upper cable-car station is only a few steps from the base of the cross, a splendid viewpoint affording a vast **panorama**★★.
Road D 111 continues beyond Chamrousse on its way down through the St-Martin forest, offering **glimpses**★ of Uriage, the Vercors Massif and Grenoble. Just as the road leaves the forest, there is a fine **view**★ of the Uriage Valley.
The road then goes down into the valley past the 13C–14C castle, just before arriving at **Uriage**.

Uriage-les-Bains
Uriage has been famous for its waters since antiquity, but their healing properties were only recognised in the 19C. The isotonic waters containing chloride, sulphur and sodium are used to treat medical conditions such as rheumatism.

L'OISANS AND LES ÉCRINS

Less than an hour's drive southeast of Grenoble, the wild and relatively unspoiled Oisans Massif lies within the Parc national des Écrins, with the small town of Bourg d'Oisans at its western edge. As well as mountaineering, every summer the region attracts large numbers of cycling enthusiasts, aiming to emulate their Tour de France heroes on some of the gruelling road climbs. With an experienced driver to cope with quite vertiginous drives, those with less endurance can explore verdant valleys and authentic mountain villages.

The Challenge of the Tour de France

As the 110th anniversary of the Tour de France approaches, as often in modern times, the ski resort of L'Alpe-d'Huez is in contention to be a stage finish. It was first included as part of the legendary cycling competition in 1952, being the first mountaintop finish of the race; each of the 21 hairpins on the 13.8km/8.6mi climb is named after one or more of the winners of this particular stage.

Be warned, if you plan a visit to the region in late June or July, check the exact dates and the route of the Tour in advance, as you will need to make a choice: either stake your place on the roadside well in advance to be among the thousands of spectators, or steer well clear of the area on the day the race comes through, as road closures last several hours. The Tour is a fantastically popular free spectator sport in France and the L'Alpe-d'Huez stage is one of the most popular. If you pick a good spot, it is a wonderful experience to be part of the crowds, even if you know little or nothing about the race.

Highlights

1 Take a thrilling cliff-edge drive to a **terraced village** (p298)

2 Take the gondolas up to **Pic Blanc** for the panorama (p304)

3 Experience the glaciers and high mountains via the **Jandri Express** (p306)

4 The legendary off-piste runs at **La Grave** are a joy for keen, expert skiers (p306)

5 Put aside half a day for a walk along the high valley of the **Bonne** (p308)

Precious Metals

In 1767 a shepherd from Allemont found a vein of silver, the beginning of a rush to mine this metal in the local valleys that continued for 30 years. Today, around 60 different minerals have been identified in the Oisans Massif.

The museum at Bourg d'Oisans has the largest collection of alpine minerals in the French Alps.

Terraced village of the Oisans

© Franck Guiziou/hemis.fr

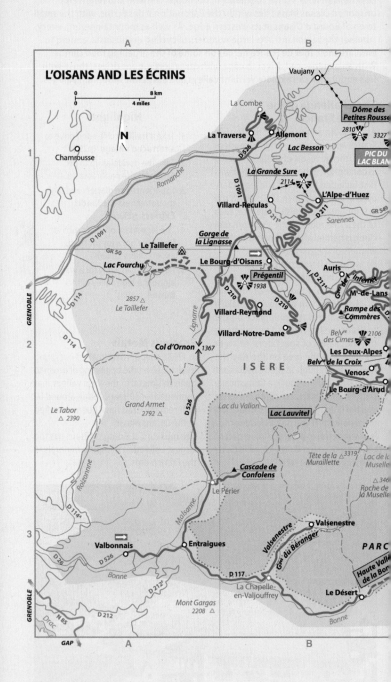

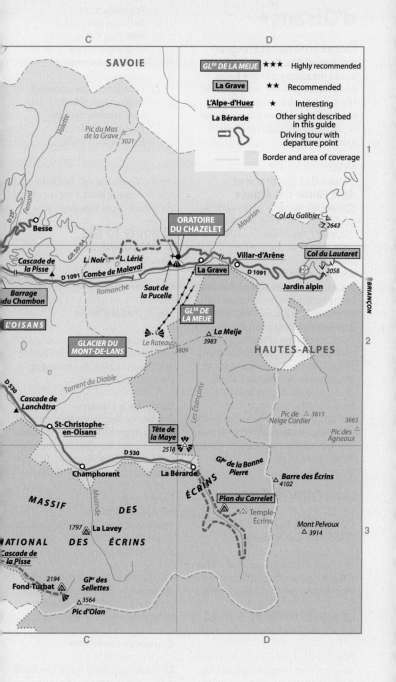

SAVOIE

GL^{ER} DE LA MEIJE ★★★ Highly recommended

La Grave ★★ Recommended

L'Alpe-d'Huez ★ Interesting

La Bérarde Other sight described in this guide

Driving tour with departure point

Border and area of coverage

Pic du Mas de la Grave *3021*

Col du Galibier *2643*

Besse

ORATOIRE DU CHAZELET

Villar-d'Arène

Col du Lautaret *2058*

Cascade de la Pisse

L. Noir   L. Lérié

La Grave

D 1091   Combe de Malaval   D 1091

BRIANÇON

Barrage du Chambon

Romanche

Saut de la Pucelle

Jardin alpin

L'OISANS

GL^{ER} DE LA MEIJE

GLACIER DU MONT-DE-LANS

Le Rateau *3809*

La Meije *3983*

HAUTES-ALPES

Torrent du Diable

Les Étançons

Pic de Neige Cordier *3613*

3663

Cascade de Lanchâtra

Pic des Agneaux

St-Christophe-en-Oisans

Tête de la Maye *2518*

Gl^{er} de la Bonne Pierre

D 530

D 530

Champhorent   La Bérarde

ÉCRINS

Barre des Écrins *4102*

MASSIF   DES

Plan du Carrelet

Muande

1797 La Lavey

Temple-Écrins

Mont Pelvoux *3914*

NATIONAL   DES   ÉCRINS

Cascade de la Pisse

2194   Gl^{er} des Sellettes

Fond-Turbat

3564

Pic d'Olan

Le Bourg-d'Oisans★

Located at the foot of a range of impressive cliffs, Bourg d'Oisans marks the entrance to the Écrins park, the largest and the highest of the national parks. The capital of the Oisans area, Bourg, is a popular departure point both for climbers and for cyclists.

▸ **Population:** 3 012.
⚬ **Michelin Map:** 333 J7.
▯ **Info:** Quai Girard, 38520 Le Bourg-d'Oisans. ✆04 76 80 03 25. www.bourg doisans.com.
▸ **Location:** At the crossroads of six valleys, 52km/32.3mi E of Grenoble through the Gorges de la Romanche (D 1091).

VISIT

Musée des Minéraux et de la Faune des Alpes★

🕑Open Jul–Aug daily 10am–6pm; Sept –Oct and Dec–Jun Wed–Mon 2–6pm. 🕑Closed 1 Jan, 25 Dec. ⊛4.60€. ✆04 76 80 27 54. www.musee-bourgdoisans.com.

Housed in a part of the attractive church, this museum serves as the information centre for the Parc national des Écrins. Exhibits include a rich selection of alpine minerals, including a variety of quartz. There are displays of stuffed animals in their environment, and a palaeontology section includes locally found fossils.

☛Continue along the path by the church to reach a terrace at the highest point.

There is a wide view over the Bourg-d'Oisans basin, the peaks of the Grandes Rousses and the range south of Vénéon (45min return on foot).

🚗 DRIVING TOURS

CORNICHES DU BASSIN D'OISANS★★

The dramatic narrow road to **L'Alpe-d'Huez** cut into the cliff face is one of the most impressive drives in the Alps.

1 ROUTE TO L'ALPE-D'HUEZ
13km/8.1mi. About 30min.

From Le Bourg-d'Oisans, follow the Briançon road then turn left to L'Alpe-d'Huez. The road climbs in hairpin bends, affording vistas of the Roman-che and Vénéon valleys. Just before the hillside village of **Huez** there is a view of the remote upper Sarennes Valley.

2 ROUTE TO THE VALBONNAIS
29km/18mi. About 1hr.

This interesting itinerary links the Bourg-d'Oisans basin and the Valbon-nais via the Col d'Ornon.

▷ From Le Bourg-d'Oisans take D 1091 towards Grenoble. Turn left at La Paute onto towards La Maure, climbing up the Lignarre Valley.

Gorges de la Lignarre★
The river has dug its way through schist. As you approach Le Rivier-d'Ornon, there is a fine view behind you of the Belledonne and Grandes Rousses ranges.

Col d'Ornon
Alt. 1 367m/4 485ft.
The pass crosses a barren stony land-scape. The road follows the narrow val-ley of the Malsanne.

▷ At Le Périer, turn left towards the Cascade de Confolens. Leave the car at the entrance to the Parc national des Écrins and continue on foot.

Cascade de Confolens★
2hrs there and back.
🚶 The left path leads to the 70m/230ft-high waterfall. At **Entraigues** there are **views**★ of Mont Aiguille, southwest.

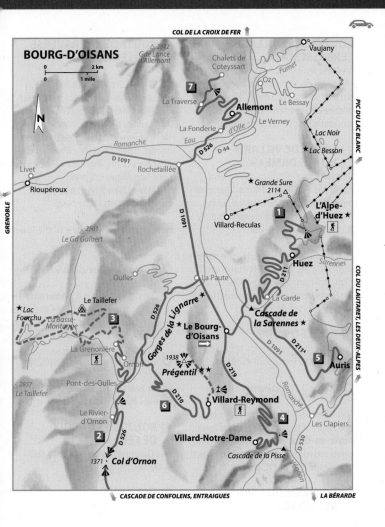

3 ROUTE TO TAILLEFER REFUGE AND LAC FOURCHU★

14km/8.7mi drive then 3hrs on foot – vertical rise 800m/2 625ft.

◐ *Follow drive 2 above. At La Paute turn left, then right at Pont-des-Oulles towards Ornon and La Grenonière.*

🚶 Beyond the Parc des Écrins information panel *(on a bend)* the road is unsurfaced. Park and continue on foot for 200m/219yds, then take a path on the right which leads to La Basse-Montagne *(20 min)*.

◐ *From La Basse-Montagne, allow 2hrs for experienced hikers. Leave the stream on your left and follow the path (red markings) through the woods. After 1hr the path, meandering through pastures, reaches the Taillefer refuge.*

From the refuge (2 050m/6 726ft) there is a fine view of the Taillefer Massif and the Lignarre Valley. An easier path west *(45min)* takes you to Lac Fourchu surrounded by wild flowers and overlooked by the steep Taillefer.

◐ *You can return to La Basse-Montagne via the Lac de la Vache.*

ROUTES DES "VILLAGES-TERRASSES"★★

These itineraries follow very narrow cliff roads and tunnels, with designated passing points. With the exception of drive 7 experience of driving on mountain roads is recommended.

4 ROUTE DE VILLARD-NOTRE-DAME★★

From Le Bourg-d'Oisans, 9km/5.6mi – about 1hr. The road has a 10 percent gradient and must be avoided during or after a rainy period; dangerous gully across the road at the start.

This road ends at a picturesque mountain village. On a left-hand bend, 8km/5mi from Le Bourg-d'Oisans, view the lower Vénéon Valley enclosed by the Aiguille du Plat-de-la-Selle.

5 ROUTE D'AURIS

From La Garde (on the way to L'Alpe-d'Huez), 8km/5mi. About 45min.

▷ *Follow D 211A towards Le Freney.*

This itinerary is interesting for its bird's-eye views of the Bourg-d'Oisans basin. **Auris-en-Oisans** – In a sunny position, surrounded by a pretty spruce forest, this village has an 11C church.

6 ROUTE DE VILLARD-REYMOND★

▷ *From Bourg-d'Oisans, take D 1091 towards Grenoble, then left on D 526 to Col d'Ornon and La Pallud. Then turn left on D 210 to Villard-Reymond.*

From the village of Villard-Reymond, walk to the cross of the Col de Saulude *(15min return)* to admire the **view**★ of Grandes Rousses, the plateau of Emparis, the Meije, the Rateau, the Aiguilles d'Arves and the Girose Glacier.

Prégentil – 1hr 30min return on foot from Villard-Reymond (NW). From the summit (alt. 1 938m/6 358ft) is a **sweeping view**★★ of the mountains surrounding the Bourg-d'Oisans basin.

7 ROUTE DE LA TRAVERSE D'ALLEMONT★

▷ *10km/6.2mi. From Le Bourg-d'Oisans, drive towards Grenoble, then turn right onto D 526 and D 43 towards Allemont. At the village, turn left onto rte de la Traverse; shortly before this hamlet, turn right onto a forest road; after 6km/ 3.7mi, leave the car beyond a right-hand bend (car park).*
Walk 100m/109yds along the path which starts at the bend.

Here is a splendid **view**★ of the lower Bourg-d'Oisans basin.

▷ *Drive for another 200m/219yds.*

On the right, there is a **panorama**★★ of Le Bessay village and the Dôme des Petites Rousses as well as the Col de la Croix-de-Fer and **Lac Noir**★★★.

▷ *Drive on for another 300m/328yds.*

There is a clear view of the Grandes Rousses Massif and the Combe d'Olle.

8 ROUTE DE LA CROIX DE FER★★★

From Bourg-d'Oisans, 38km/23.6mi – see Maurienne (p249).

EXCURSIONS
Cascade de la Sarennes★

1km/0.6mi NE, then 15min there and back on foot. ▷ Leave Le Bourg towards Briançon. In 0.8km/0.5mi turn left on D 211 towards L'Alpe-d'Huez and leave the car just before the bridge over the Sarennes. A path leads to the right. This tributary of the Romanche forms a three-stage waterfall.

Rioupéroux

▷ *16km/10mi W by D 1091.*
Musée de la Romanche – *Livet et Gavet, 10km/6.2mi from Bourg-d'Oisans. Open Tue–Wed and Fri 3–6pm. ℘04 76 68 42 00.* In the narrow gorges of the **lower Romanche**, the museum describes how the local villages were established.

ADDRESSES

🏨 STAY

Hôtel Oberland – *R. Principale.*
*𝒫04 76 80 24 24. www.hoteloberland.com
Closed Oct–Nov.* ♿🅿. *Wifi. 26 rooms,
restaurant*🍴. One look at the front

of this hotel decorated with bicycles,
helmets and yellow jumpers, and you
can see that this is a special favourite
of cyclists and indeed, the owner offers
special deals to keen cyclists. Decent
rooms and traditional food.

L'Oisans★★★

After the Mont Blanc Massif, L'Oisans
is the second-highest mountain
range in France, with the Barre des
Écrins reaching 4 102m/13 458ft.
Compared to its brilliant rival,
l'Oisans is more unspoiled and
wilder; with fewer tourist facilities,
it tends to attract a more dedicated
type of mountain lover.

🚗 DRIVING TOURS

1 VALLÉE DU VÉNÉON★★★
LE BOURG-D'OISANS
31km/19.3mi. About 1hr 30min drive.

The road follows the deep Vénéon Valley, giving only occasional glimpses of
the high summits; we therefore strongly
advise you to go on the hikes suggested
below, according to ability.

▷ *From Le Bourg-d'Oisans, drive E
along D 1091 towards Briançon.*

The road to La Bérarde *(D 530)*, branching off from D 1091 at Les Clapiers,
enters the wide lower Vénéon Valley, which is in contrast to the narrow
Romanche. The depression of the Lac
Lauvitel is overlooked by the Tête de la
Muraillette.

Lac Lauvitel★★
▷ *2.5km/1.5mi from D 530 then
3hrs there and back on foot. At the
Les Ougiers bridge, turn right to La
Danchère and park on the roadside.
Past La Danchère, take the left fork
via Les Selles.*

- **Michelin Map:** 333 J7.
- **Info:** Quai Girard, 38520
  Le Bourg-d'Oisans. 𝒫04
  76 80 03 25. www.bourg
  doisans.com.
- **Location:** The Oisans
  region is mostly within
  the high Écrins Massif,
  bounded by the valleys of
  the River Romanche, River
  Durance and River Drac.
- **Timing:** To enjoy the thrill
  of the heights, make time
  for one of the hikes.

🚶 This trail is lined with markers providing explanations on geology, local
fauna and flora, detailed in a book sold
in information centres. The path follows
the natural dam formed by landslides,
which contains Lac Lauvitel.

▷ *Follow the La Rousse path back
to La Danchère.*

*Vallé du Vénéon and the
Grand Aiguille de la Bérarde*

J. Malburet/MICHELIN

Venosc

38520 Venosc. *℘04 76 80 06 82.*
*www.venosc.com. Turn left off D 530
to a car park.* You can also take the
gondola from Les Deux-Alpes. *Open
daily mid-Jun–Aug 8am–8pm; Dec–Apr
8am–6pm. 7€ return.*
℘04 76 79 75 01.

Walk up to the village, which is a
centre of local handicrafts. A paved
street leads to the **church** with its fine
altarpiece (17C Italian school). All around
are hamlets to explore, such as **Courtil**,
with its sundial dating from 1669.

Le Bourg-d'Arud

The steepest climb of the route avoids
the first glacial obstruction, a jumble of
huge boulders.

The road then runs through the Plan du
Lac Basin, with the Vénéon meander-
ing below, towards St-Christophe-en-
Oisans, past the **Cascade de Lanchâtra**
on the right and across the Torrent du
Diable.

St-Christophe-en-Oisans★

La Ville, 38520 St-Christophe-en-Oisans.
℘04 76 80 50 01. www.berarde.com.
Although it includes 15 hamlets, this
vast *commune*, one of the largest in
France, has barely 30 inhabitants in
winter, many of whom are professional
guides.

The **church** shows up against the Barre
des Écrins; in the cemetery, young
mountaineers who lost their lives in
the Écrins Massif are buried next to local
guide families.

A museum, **Mémoires d'alpinismes**,
describes the valley, its mountaineering heroes, and its history and culture.
*Open daily Jun–Sept 10am–noon,
2.30–7pm; other school holidays 2–5pm.
Closed 1 Jan, Easter Sun–Mon, 8 May,
25 Dec. 3.60€ ℘04 76 79 52 25.*
After Champhorent, the view takes in
the Lavey Valley, with the glacial cirque
of the Sellettes at the end.

The road passes through a tunnel, and
then the green Combe des Étages leads
to La Bérard, with the Barre des Écrins
behind.

La Bérarde

Once a sleepy hamlet, inhabited by the
local shepherds, or *bérards* in the old
dialect, La Bérarde is now a popular
starting point for challenging mountaineering expeditions in the Écrins Massif,
as well as family walks.

2 VALLÉE DE LA ROMANCHE★★★

57km/35.4mi. About 2hrs.

This itinerary, combined with those of
the Col de la Croix de Fer (*see p250*)
and of the Galibier (*see p252*), completes the unforgettable round tour of
the Alps' great passes.

*The Col du Lautaret is open in winter,
but can be closed for a few hours in the
event of heavy snowfalls or poor visibil-*

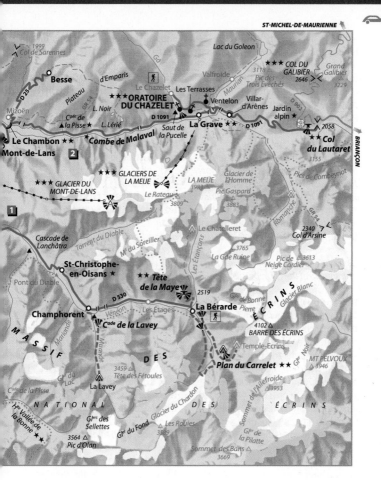

ity; watch out for information panels in Le Bourg-d'Oisans, Le Péage-de-Vizille and Champagnier or telephone for the recorded information at Lautaret.
&04 92 24 44 44.

The road leaves the Bourg-d'Oisans basin and runs to the old glacial valley of the Romanche.

◯ From Le Bourg-d'Oisans, take D 1091.

At first, the road runs along the flat Boug basin, leaving the road to L'Alpe-d'Huez to the north. The dimensions of the Vénéon Valley to the south show how big the Vénéon Glacier used to be; the Romanche Glacier is only a tributary.
Rampe des Commères – In the days of stagecoaches, tongue-wagging was the favourite pastime of travellers who had to step down and walk up this section, hence the name: "gossips' slope"!

Gorges de l'Infernet★
Fine **viewpoint**★ over this wild gorge in a tight bend, near a ruined oratory. The green Freney basin offers a pleasant contrast.

◯ At the Chambon Dam, turn right towards Les Deux-Alpes.

Mont-de-Lans &See p305.

◯ Return to D 1091 and take a left on D 25 towards L'Alpe-d'Huez.

Besse-en-Oisans
This high **mountain village** is very

authentic (alt. 1 550m/5 085ft): the houses lining its narrow twisting lanes have heavy roof structures which used to be coveredwith *lauzes* (thick slabs of schist).From the Ferrand Valley are severalwalks towards the lakes of the **Plateau d'Emparis**, with remarkable panoramas over the Meije glaciers.

At the **Maison des Alpages** *(end of the village beneath the church;* ◷*open Jul–Aug daily 10am–noon, 3–7pm, May–Jun Sept–Oct and winter school holidays 2–6pm;* ♿ ✆*04 76 80 19 09)* a modern, educational exhibition pays homage to the farming heritage of the area.

▷ *Return to D 1091, and turn left to go over the top of the Chambon Dam.*

Barrage du Chambon★★

The dam was built across a narrowing of the Romanche Valley in order to regulate the spates of summer and autumn and supply hydroelectric power stations. This gravity dam is 294m/965ft long at the top, 70m/230ft thick at the base, and 90m/295ft high (137m/449ft including the foundations). Three hamlets, Le Chambon, Le Dauphin and Le Parizet, were flooded when the dam was built.

Combe de Malaval★

The rushing waters of the Romanche are almost level with the road all the way through this long gorge, past two impressive waterfalls on the north bank, the **Cascade de la Pisse**★ and **Cascade du Saut de la Pucelle**.
The Mont-de-Lans and the Girose glaciers are visible through gaps in rock.

La Grave★★ ◷*See p306.*
Upstream from Villar-d'Arêne, the road leaves the Romanche Valley, which veers southeast along the Val d'Arsine.

🚶 HIKES

Champhorent to the Refuge de la Lavey★★

🚶*Alt. 1 797m/5 896ft. 3hrs 30min there and back on foot; a fairly easy hike (vertical rise 380m/1 247ft). Leave the car just outside Champhorent.*
The path leads rapidly down to the Vénéon. Markers signal the entrance of the Parc national des Écrins and the view extends towards the **Glacier du Fond** on the left and the **Glaciers des Sellettes** on the right. A picturesque stone bridge leads over to the left bank of the Muande *(close the gate behind you).* The view is of the **Glacier d'Entre-Pierroux**, **Glacier du Lac** and the **Pic d'Olan** filling the horizon to the south.

▷ *Return to Champhorent.*

Tête de la Maye★★

🚶*Alt. 2 517m/8 258ft. 4hrs there and back (2hr 30min ascent); suitable for hikers familiar with steep terrain and*

How the Massif des Écrins Was Conquered

The summits of the massif form a huge horseshoe round the Vénéon Valley. The **Barre des Écrins** is the highest point of the massif (alt. 4 102m/13 458ft); it is so well concealed that from the road you catch only fleeting glimpses of its peak, first reached in 1864 by the famous British mountaineer **Edward Whymper**. In fact, since Mont Blanc only became French after the annexation of Savoie in 1860, **Mont Pelvoux** at 3 932m/12 900ft altitude was long regarded as the highest point in the French Alps. It was first climbed in 1828 by the French military engineer Captain Durand.
The glorious **Meije** comprises three summits: the Meije Orientale to the east, the Meije Centrale or Doigt de Dieu ("finger of God") and finally the Meije Occidentale or Grand Pic de la Meije (alt. 3 983m/13 068ft) to the west. The last, the second-highest mountain in the Écrins, with its dramatic, craggy peak, is very distinctive when viewed from La Grave. After 17 failed attempts, the Grand Pic summit was conquered on 16 August 1877 by Boileau de Castelnau, accompanied by the father-and-son guides **Gaspard**.

not liable to vertigo. Vertical rise 800m/2 625ft.

The path starts before the bridge over the Étançons at the entrance of La Bérarde. *Bear left at the intersection with the path to Le Châtelleret;* ☝*metal steps and safety cables make difficult sections a little easier, but caution is still required.* From the orientation table at the summit, there is an overall **view**★★ of the Écrins Massif and of the peaks surrounding the Vénéon Valley: from left to right, the **Grand Pic de la Meije**, the **Glacier des Étançons**, the **Dôme des Écrins** and the **Glacier de Bonne Pierre**. The highest point is the **Barre des Écrins**.

Plan du Carrelet and Refuge★★

🚶 *Alt. 2 000m/6 562ft. S of La Bérarde. 2hrs there and back, easy hike to the Plan. Vertical rise 300m/984ft. Before Jul, the névé (granular glacial snow) on the final stretch to the refuge means that this last leg should only be attempted by experienced and fully equipped hikers.*

Take the footpath starting beyond the Maison du Parc and following the east bank of the Vénéon. From the park's information panels, turn around to see a fine view of the **Meije** and **Tête de la Maye** overlooking La Bérarde. The

U-shaped valley widens at the confluence of the Vénéon and Chardon. Retrace your steps, cross the stream and follow the path towards the Chardon Glacier. Go over two footbridges in order to come back along the left bank of the Vénéon. Cross as you reach the car park in La Bérarde.

ADDRESSES

🏠 STAY

🔸 **Good to know** – The park has five refuges open all year accessible to hikers from La Bérarde. To reach the **Promontoire**, via **ferrata** or **glacier** equipment is required; for the others good boots and fitness should suffice. Contact guides office for more details.

🍴 EAT

🔸 **La Cordée** – *38520 St-Christophe-en-Oisans.* ☎*04 76 79 52 37. www.la-cordee.com* ♿🅿. *Wifi. 7 rooms*🔸. Frequented by alpine guides since 1907, this multipurpose *commerce* offers food and lodging, loans books and organises meetings with the authors. Good local cuisine. Concerts *(Jul–Aug Thu eve)* and classical music festival *(Jul last weekend).*

L'Alpe-d'Huez★

L'Alpe-d'Huez is one of France's famous winter-sports resorts as well as an important walking and mountain-race centre in summer. It is also at the end of one of the most famously gruelling climbs of the Tour de France cycle race.

THE RESORT

🚡🎿 **Ski area** – L'Alpe-d'Huez (1 250m–3 330m/4 101ft–10 925ft) is the most important ski resort in Dauphiné and connected with Auris, Oz, Vaujany and Villard-Reculas as part of the Domaine des Grandes Rousses. Today it has 120 alpine ski pistes totalling 240km/149mi, catering for all

- 🔸 **Michelin Map:** 333 J7.
- 🔸 **Info:** Pl. Paganon, 38750 Alpe-d'Huez. ☎04 76 11 44 44. www.alpedhuez.com.
- 🔸 **Location:** 65km/40.4mi E of Grenoble, via N 85, then D 1091 and D 211. Free buses circulate the resort in winter and part of summer.
- 🔸 **Don't Miss:** The panorama from the Pic Blanc.
- 🔸 **Kids:** The ice cave enchants children.

standards.There are cross-country ski tracks, plus evening ski and sledging slopes.

Summer activities – Some ski lifts run in summer, with access to a choice of walking and mountain-bike routes. From the top of the funitel **Les Marmottes III**, is a fine **view** over the Chartreuse, Vercors, Belledonne and Écrins ranges (🕐for times and charges 📞04 76 80 30 30; www.satavtt.com).

SIGHTS
Musée d'Huez et de l'Oisans
🕐Open Jul–Aug and Dec–Apr Mon–Fri 10am–noon, 2–6pm. 🎯Guided visits (45min). ⬟2€ (children free), combined with the archaeological site ⬟3€. 📞04 76 11 21 74.

A permanent exhibition displays objects found at the Brandes archaeological site. Finds since 1977 include vestiges from a Middle Age silver-mining complex.

Notre-Dame-des-Neiges
Built as a rotunda with a spiral roof, this modern church (1969) is lit with a series of 13 stained-glass windows, which were made by a well-known local artist, Arcabas.

Ice Grotto
At the top of the Grandes Rousses cable car (2 700m/8 858ft), an ice cave includes necessarily fleeting sculptures.

Route d'Auris
🍃See Le Bourg d'Oisans p298.

🎯WALKING TOURS
Pic du Lac Blanc★★★
Alt. 3 323m/10 902ft. 🎿Access by two gondolas followed by a cable car. 🕐Jul–Aug, check for times. ⬟14.50€ (5–12s 7.50€). 📞04 76 80 30 30.

During the second gondola ride, the **Lac Blanc** appears in a rocky valley. As you come out of the top cable car go onto the terrace and onto a hillock for the viewing table. There is a sweeping **panoramic view**★★.

Dôme des Petites Rousses★★
🎯1hr return on a path to the left. The summit (2 810m/9 219ft) is reached from the Lac Blanc.

La Grande Sure★ (or Le Signal)
Alt. 2 114m/6 936ft. 🎿Access by the Le Signal chairlift in winter and on foot (🚶1hr 50min return) in summer. Extensive **views** of the Grandes Rousses range, the Oisans region, the Taillefer mountain and the Belledonne range.

Lac Besson★
6.5km/4mi by the road leading to Col de Poutran in the N.

The road winds through pastures, reaches Col de Poutran and L'Alpe-d'Huez basin and, beyond, a high plateau dotted with glacial lakes. From Lac Besson it is possible to climb on foot up to a ridge that reveals **Lac Noir**★★★ below in wild surroundings.

EXCURSION
Route de Villard-Reculas★
▶Direction Huez by D 211, then right in 4km/2.5mi by D 211B.

From this steep road are plunging views to the Bourg-d'Oisans basin. Part of the Grandes Rousses ski area, the village has kept its pretty, traditional houses of stone, with wooden attics.

ADDRESSES

🏠 STAY / 🍴 EAT
The resort has some **32 000 beds** available, with a wide range of prices. Contact the tourist office or reservation service; lodging in the valley is cheaper. You will find restaurants not only in the resort area, but also on the slopes, open even in summer. Try the alpine menu at **Le Génépi** or **Le Passe Montagne** with its family atmosphere.

🛏🛏🛏🛏 **Au Chamois d'Or** – Rd-pt des pistes. 📞04 76 80 31 32. www.chamoisdor-alpedhuez.com. Closed 21 Apr–14 Dec. 🚻🅿. Wifi. 40 rooms, restaurant🍽🍽🍽. A big chalet at the foot of the pistes with modernised interior. Big spa, children's area, south-facing terrace and cosy rooms, some with mountain views. Pretty restaurant in a chic mountain style with well-prepared classic dishes.

🤸ACTIVITIES
🎿 **Good to know – Visalp** is a pass available from three to eight days in winter and summer, that gives entry to sporting facilities and cultural events.

Les Deux-Alpes ★

The twin resorts of L'Alpe-de-Mont-de-Lans and L'Alpe-de-Venosc, known as "Les Deux-Alpes", form the highest ski resort in Isère. Skiing and snowboarding reign here both winter and summer on the largest glacier in Europe. Rising from 1 300m/4 265ft to 3 600m/11 811ft in just a few minutes, you can exchange the peaceful villages in the valley for the exceptional panoramas of the highest mountain in the Oisans Massif.

- **Michelin Map:** 333 J7.
- **Info:** Pl. Deux-Alpes, 38860 Les Deux-Alpes. ℘04 76 79 22 00. www.les2alpes.com.
- **Location:** The resort is 75km/46.6mi from Grenoble by D 213, which branches onto D 1091 just after the Lac du Chambon.
- **Don't Miss:** The Mont-de-Lans Glacier, reached by cable car, is a superb sight.
- **Kids:** Youngsters will enjoy the ice cave (Grotte de Glace) and the Maison de la Montagne.

THE RESORT

Good skiers should aim for the steep lower section and the Tête Moute summit, as well as the snowpark.

Less experienced skiers will also find plenty of gentle slopes with excellent snow. The Mont-de-Lans Glacier is the **largest European glacier suitable for skiing**, and a dozen ski lifts serve many green and blue runs between 2 800m/9 186ft and 3 568m/11 706ft, the highest altitude of any groomed ski run in France. The long run down to the resort gives a drop of 2 000m/6 562ft.

There are excellent off-piste possibilities (taking precautions and preferably a guide) in the Meije Valley, which links Les Deux-Alpes with La Grave.

Summer skiing – Glaciers form one of the largest **summer ski** areas in Europe. There are paragliding sites, a skating rink and a heated open-air pool. Walkers enjoy the La Fée refuge and Le Sapey.

Chapelle St-Benoît

Although modern, the stone walls give this chapel a traditional look.

Maison de la Montagne

Av. de la Muzelle, Deux-Alpes 1650. *Open Sun–Fri mid-Jun–Aug 10am–noon, 3–7pm; Dec–Apr 2–6pm.* ℘04 76 79 53 15.
This nature centre offers an introduction to mountain animal life using multimedia exhibits.

EXCURSIONS
Mont-de-Lans

℘04 76 80 18 85.
Just five minutes before you arrive at the resort of Les Deux-Alpes, the village of Mont-de-Lans, and the hamlets of **Le Cuculet** and **Bons** retain their traditional architecture. From the ridge leading from the church is a fine **view**★ of the Chambon Dam, Mizoën, and the Infernet Gorges.

The educational **Musée des Arts et Traditions populaires** relates daily life as it was in the Oisans a century ago and also showcases the lesser-known role of the old peddlers. *Open Sun–Fri mid-Jun–Aug 10am–noon, 3–7pm; Jan–early Apr 2–6pm.* *Free.* ℘04 76 80 23 97.

From **Chemin des Serres**, go to the viewing table that offers a unique vista of the Lac du Chambon (hydroelectric dam), the Meije Valley and the Grand Pic de la Meije (3 983m/13 068ft). The path leads to Bons, where you can see a Roman gate cut into the rock face 2 000 years ago. Continue to the verdant hamlets of **Ponteil** and **Les Travers** tucked into the side of the mountain.

VIEWPOINTS
Glacier du Mont-de-Lans★★★

2hrs there and back to the Dôme du Puy Salié and half a day to the Dôme de Lauze. Walking boots advised. Mid-Jun–Aug 7.15am–4.30pm; Dec–Apr

9.15am–4.15pm. 🚡*16.90€ return.*
📞*04 76 79 75 01.*
Access by the **Jandri Express** two-stage cable car from the resort centre up to 3 200m/10 499ft, from where there is a fine **view** over the Vercors and the Oisans. Next take a lift and funicular to the Dôme du Puy Salié (3 421m/11 224ft). Magnificent **view**★★ of the Écrins Massif. Then walk to the top of the ski lift to admire the Vercors and further right the Belledonne, Grande Rousses ski area (L'Alpe d'Huez), Mont Blanc and the Vanoise. Even Mont Ventoux is visible on a clear day.

Skiers can take the ski lift to La Lauze and walk up a little to the top of a hillock for a quite splendid **panorama**★★★.

👥▲ Dôme Express
At the top of the funicular in winter and of the Jandri Express from July, in this ice cave you will find some interesting figures among the fascinating **ice sculptures**. *Check times.* 🚡*4€* 📞*04 76 79 75 01. www.grottedeglace.com.*

Croisière Blanche★★★
🕐*Access during hours of Jandri Express. It is advisable to get bookings from the tourist office during the season.* 🚡*32€ (includes return cable car from Deux-Alpes, ride in "croisière", visit to ice cave).* 📞*04 76 79 75 01.* Walkers can reach the **Dôme de la Lauze** in a tracked minibus. This unique excursion gives you a real flavour of the high-altitude mountains.

Belvédère de la Croix★
On the way out of the resort on the Alpe-de-Venosc side, one looks down a sheer drop to the bottom of the Vénéon Valley with jackdaws whirling above.

The pointed Aiguille de Venosc stands across the river and the **Roche de la Muzelle** (alt. 3 459m/11 348ft), with its suspended glacier, towers above the landscape.

🏃ACTIVITIES
🚡 **Good to know** – In July–August a pedestrian pass *(52.50€)* gives you six days of access to all ski lifts, two pool entries, one entry to the ice rink and one to the ice cave.

Guides office – *Maison des 2 Alpes.*
📞*04 76 11 36 29. www.guides2alpes.com.* All through summer there are courses and lessons with excursions for all levels into the high mountains, an ice school, climbing wall and freshwater sports.

La Grave★★

La Grave lies deep in a valley in the shadow of the Meije, one of the most impressive summits of the Écrins Massif. For winter and summer mountaineers this area offers a large range of classic alpine itineraries, and tourists are offered spectacular high-mountain views in the most splendid setting. The village itself is one of the most beautiful in France.

THE VILLAGE
In spite of their tourist appeal, La Grave and its picturesque hamlets have avoided property developers. The main street of La Grave may be a little grim, but traditional houses remain, and the outstanding surroundings ensure this resort retains its appeal for both fami-

- 🕎 **Michelin Map:** 334 F1.
- 🔲 **Info:** 05320 La Grave.
  📞04 76 79 90 05.
  www.lagrave-lameije.com.
- ▷ **Location:** 28km/17.4mi E of Bourg-d'Oisans on D 1091, La Grave is on the way up to the Col du Lautaret (11km/6.8mi).
- 👁 **Don't Miss:** Cable-car ride to the la Meije glaciers.
- 🕐 **Timing:** Spend at least four days in La Grave to make the most of the excursions.
- 👥▲ **Kids:** Climbing schools offer lessons for children.

lies and mountain-sports enthusiasts. Beside the towering Meije peaks, La

Grave and its neighbouring village Villar d'Arène have no fewer than 50 summits reaching heights ranging from 3 000m/9 843ft to 4 000m/13 123ft. In the little cemetery surrounding the beautiful Romanesque 12C **church** are many victims of the mountains. Next to it, the 17C **Chapelle des Pénitents** has a ceiling covered in frescoes.

Ski area – In spite of having only a few ski lifts and marked pistes, the resort is famous for its off-piste possibilities and its long descent between the Dôme de Lauze and La Grave. The cable car leads to two classic powder runs (Les Vallons de la Meije and Chancel) offering splendid views and the finest snow from late January to mid-May.

Alpine skiing takes place on the slopes of the Meije and around Le Chazelet and the Col du Lautaret. This high-mountain area is only suitable for competent skiers. There are numerous possibilities for ski touring, and 30km/18.6mi of cross-country skiing tracks near Villar d'Arène, on the edge of the Parc national des Écrins, with a further 20km/12.4mi at the bottom of the quiet Arsine Valley.

HIKES

The main hikes lead to the **Plateau d'Emparis** (from Le Chazelet), the **Col d'Arsine** (from Pied du Col) and **Lac du Goléon** (from Valfroide).

Glaciers de la Meije et Grotte de Glace★★★

Allow one day in order to explore all the possibilities of the site. ◔*Open mid-Jun–mid-Sept.* ◉*22€ return.* ℘*04 76 79 91 09. www.la-grave.com.*

The ride is in two sections: first up to the Peyrou d'Amont Plateau (alt. 2 400m/7 874ft), then to the Col des Ruillans (alt. 3 200m/10 499ft) on the northwest slopes of the Rateau summit, offering on the way views of the Meije, Rateau and Girose glaciers. The view from the upper station includes the Aiguilles d'Arves due north, Mont Thabor to the northeast with the Vanoise summits in the distance and Mont Blanc further still, the Grandes Rousses and Belledonne mountains to the northwest.

At Col des Ruillans, you can visit the **Grotte de glace** (◔*open mid-Jun–mid-Jul and mid-Aug–mid-Sept 10am–3.45pm, mid-Jul–mid-Aug 8am–3.45pm;* ◉*4€ (children 3€);* ℘*04 76 79 91 09; www.grottedeglace.com)*, an ice cave decorated with many ice carvings.

From the Peyron d'Amont station lower down, it is possible to explore the area for half a day or a whole day, along marked hiking trails.

At an altitude of 3 550m/11 647ft the **Trifdes** and **Lauze** ski lifts give skiers an even more impressive **panorama**★★★.

EXCURSIONS

Oratoire du Chazelet★★★

▷ *5km/3mi along D 33A branching off from D 1091 to the Col du Lautaret at the exit of the first tunnel and then through the village of Les Terrasses.*

From the Oratoire du Chazelet, there is a splendid **view** of the Meije Massif *(viewing table higher up, alt. 1 834m/6 017ft).*

Villar-d'Arêne★

▷ *3km/1.8mi E of La Grave.*

In an amazing landscape, the stone houses with *lauze* tiled roofs are built onto the rock.

Col du Lautaret★★

▣ *An automatic answering service advises if the pass is open.* ℘*04 92 24 44 44. www.savoie-route.com. 25km/15.5mi. About 3hrs.*

The viewing table is on a hillock above the alpine garden. The **panorama**★★ provides arresting views over to the Meije Massif and its glaciers. At an altitude of 2 100m/6 890ft the 100-year-old **Jardin alpin**★ (◔*open Jun–Sept 10am–6pm;* ◉*6€;* ℘*04 92 24 41 62)* includes more than 2 000 plant species.

ADDRESSES

 STAY

Good to know – La Grave is the practical place to stay because of the cable-car station (the **Edelweiss**, booked far in advance). We prefer the authenticity of Villar-d'Arène.

Le Valbonnais★

Southwest of the Écrins Massif, the charming Valbonnais area has been shaped over centuries by agriculture and forestry.
Today visitors enjoy the diversity of this wild landscape.

🚗 DRIVING TOUR

FROM VALBONNAIS TO VALSENESTRE

Drive of 55km/34.2mi shown on the regional map (see p294).
Allow 1hr 30min.

Between La Mure and le Pont Haut, there are wide panoramic views from N 85, especially of the Obiou mountain to the south.

▷ *At Pont Haut, take D 526.*

Valbonnais

Located on a fine site on the Bonne, with Entraigues, Valbonnais is the region's commercial centre. Strong houses and finely decorated residences remind us that this was once a rich farming area.

Entraigues

One of the gateways to the Parc national des Écrins, this small village sits on a sunny ledge overlooked by the Bonne and the Malsanne.

▷ *Take D 117 towards Valjouffrey, then at the Chapelle-en-Valjouffrey Bridge turn left on D 117A for 6km/3.7mi.*

The **route de Valsenestre**★ rises above the **gorges du Béranger**★, and then follows slopes covered in pines and larches, with numerous waterfalls.
The hamlet of **Valsenestre** is at the entrance of a vast cirque enclosed by the Pic Clapier du Peyron, the Roche de la Muzelle and the Pic de Valsenestre. With typical local architecture its little streets are well preserved, and the village is a departure point for numerous hikes in the mid- and high-mountain.

- ⛰ **Michelin Map:** 333 I8.
- ℹ **Info:** Office de tourisme, 38740 Valbonnais. 𝄞04 76 30 25 26. www.ot-valbonnais.fr.
- ▷ **Location:** The lower valley of the Bonne is known as the **Valbonnais**. Above Entraigues, **Valjouffrey** corresponds to the upper Bonne Valley at the foot of the Olan summit. The Grenoble–Gap road is to the SW.
- ⊗ **Don't Miss:** The preserved village of Valsenestre.

▷ *Return on D 117.*

HIKE
Haute Vallée de la Bonne★★

🚶 *3hrs. Park outside Le Désert.*
This pretty walk follows the bottom of a glacial valley.
The farming village of **Le Désert-en-Valjouffrey** at the end of the valley, still retains some interesting old barns. After the park entrance *(read the rules carefully)*, the landscape becomes wilder and the path crosses a rockfall before arriving at the **Cascade de la Pisse**★, on the left. Once you have crossed the footbridge and a small pine wood, the majestic Pic d'Olan (3 564m/11 693ft) appears above the **Cirque de Fond-Tur-bat** and you enter a much more alpine environment with glistening minerals.

▷ *Return to Le Désert the same way.*

ADDRESSES

🍴/EAT

⊜⊜⊜ **Auberge Le Chardon Bleu** – *38740 Valbonnais. 𝄞04 76 30 83 44. www.aubergelechardonbleu.fr. Closed Mon except summer. &. 6 rooms ⊜⊜.* Completely renovated and with panoramic views, this pleasant inn provides refined food, varying with the season. The rooms are decently sized.

LE VERCORS AND LE TRIÈVES

Just southwest of the conurbation of Grenoble and within easy reach of Lyon, the Vercors is not recommended for the timid. A visit here equates to a confrontation with dramatic cliff roads, cold and dark caves, and bridges perching high above deep gorges, not to mention the very moving Resistance stories from World War II. On the other hand, go slightly east to the Trièves region, where Napoleon confronted the imperial army, and you can just relax by the Laffrey lakes.

The Réserve Naturelle des Hauts Plateaux was declared as a nature reserve in 1985. This desolate area covers almost 17 000ha/42 000 acres at altitudes of 1 000m–2 300m/3 2807ft–546ft and has neither a road going through it, nor any permanent dwellings. The reserve is bounded by deep valleys of Gresse to the east and Chapelle-en-Vercors to the west and includes the two highest peaks in the Vercors, the distinctive table-top-shaped Mont Aiguille and the Grand Veymont.

With its main aim to protect the area's biodiversity, the park is a sanctuary to numerous species of wild animals and birds including black grouse, red grouse, hares, chamois and ibexes. For this reason there are relatively few marked walking paths across the Hauts Plateaux. However, GR 91 crosses from north to south and GR 93 crosses the southern part as part of the recently created Grandes Traversées du Vercors.

With full documentation available and places to stay along the way, this latter route is possible to hike, cycle, ride, or in winter cross on skis or snowshoes.

Highlights

1 Dress up warm and delve into the **Grottes de Choranche** (p312)

2 Drive through the vertiginous **Combe Laval** (p317)

3 **Resistance memorial and museum** at Col de Lachau (p320)

4 **Pont-en-Royans** (p323)

5 A late afternoon swim at the **Lacs de Laffrey** (p327)

Raviole de Royans and Walnuts

After some exercise you might want to indulge in the two delicacies from the Royans area to the west of the mountains. The *raviole de Royans* are delicious tiny ravioli stuffed with cheese and herbs and served with a cream sauce, sometimes with the blue vercors cheese or with local walnuts. These walnuts are grown in the same area and are protected with an *appellation d'origine contrôlée*. They are also eaten fresh, and used in salads, cakes and confectionery.

Mont Aiguille viewed from Chichilianne

© Franck Guiziou/hemis.fr

LE VERCORS AND LE TRIÈVES

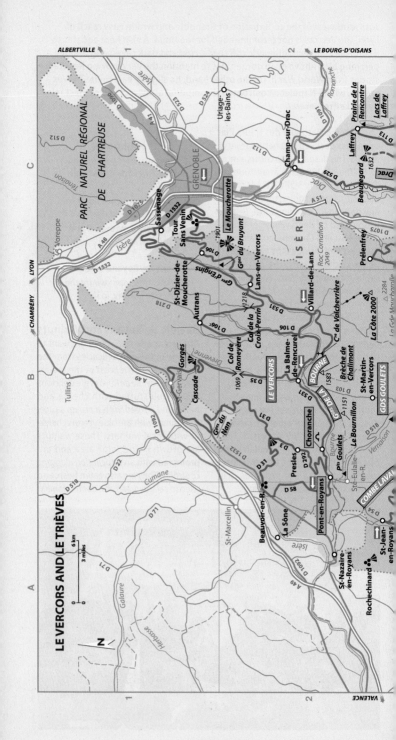

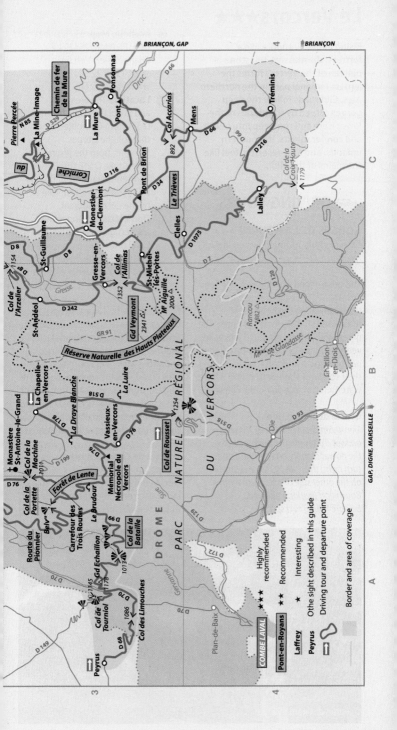

BRIANÇON, GAP

BRIANÇON

Pierre Percée

Chemin de fer de la Mure

La Mine-Image

N 85

La Mure

Ponsonnas

Pont

Col Accarias

Mens

D 66

Tréminis

D 529

Drac

892

D 66

D 216

Corniche

D 116

Pont de Brion

D 34

Le Trièves

Col de la Croix Haute

1179

Clelles

Lalley

Monastier-de-Clermont

D 1075

St-Guillaume

D 8

Gresse-en-Vercors

Col de l'Allimas

St-Michel-les-Portes

D 7

Col de l'Arzelier

1154

D 8

1352

Mt Aiguille 2006

D 120

St-Andéol

D 242

Gresse

Gd Veymont 2341

Réserve Naturelle des Hauts Plateaux

GR 91

Rancou 1882

Montagne de Glandasse

Châtillon-en-Diois

Monastère
St-Antoine-le-Grand

La Chapelle-en-Vercors

La Draye Blanche

D 518

La Luire

PARC NATUREL RÉGIONAL DU VERCORS

1254

Col de la Machine

1017

Vassieux-en-Vercors

D 76

D 518

Die

D 93

D 178

Forêt de Lente

D 199

Mémorial Nécropole du Vercors

Col de Rousset

D 76

D 729

Col de la Portette

Belvé

Le Brudour

Carrefour des Trois Routes

Gd Échaillon 1013

Col de la Bataille

D 69

D R O M E

Route du Pionnier

D 70

Col de Tourniol 1145

1178

Col des Limouches

1086

D 172

PARC

Gervanne

D 70

D 68

D 70

Peyrus

Plan-de-Baix

D 149

GAP, DIGNE, MARSEILLE

★★★ Highly recommended

★★ Recommended

★ Interesting

Othe sight described in this guide

Driving tour and departure point

Border and area of coverage

Laffrey

Peyrus

COMBE LAVAL ★★★

Pont-en-Royans

311

Le Vercors★★★

Rising above Grenoble like a fortress, the massive limestone plateau of the Vercors forms the largest regional park in the northern Alps. Cliff roads follow the deep gorges carved by tributaries of the lower Isère and run deep into beech and conifer forests. Its southern uplands, arid and deserted, feel like the plains of the Midi.

🚗DRIVING TOURS

GORGES DE LA BOURNE★★★
Drive of 49km/30.5mi shown on the regional map (⚲ see p310). Allow 2hrs.

This gorge, lined with layers of coloured limestone, gets deeper as you head upstream along the Bourne.
After Pont-en-Royans, D 531 enters the gorge and follows the river. The valley widens slightly before Choranche, then narrows again and the road leaves the river to climb the north bank, where waterfalls cascade down the cliffside.

Grotte du Bournillon
1km/0.6mi S of D 531, then 1hr return on foot. Turn onto the private road to the power station, cross its yard and turn right; the path to the cave starts on the other side of a bridge over the Bournillon (parking allowed, beware falling rocks).

- 🛈 **Michelin Map:** 332 F/G 2/3.
- 🗎 **Info:** Pl. Pietri, 26420 La Chappelle-en-Vercors. 📞04 75 48 22 54. www.vercors.com.
- ▶ **Location:** The area is W and SW of Grenoble from D 531 from Grenoble through the Gorges d'Engins; from the Rhône Valley, take D 518 through Pont-en-Royans; from the S, D 518 leads up from Die by the Col de Rousset.
- ✪ **Don't Miss:** Driving along the vertiginous Combe Laval route.
- 🕐 **Timing:** For the driving routes, allow plenty of time.

🚶 Continue left along a steep path at the base of the escarpments to reach the **entrance**★ of the cave. Walk as far as the footbridge to appreciate the size of this enormous arch. The Bournillon spring, now piped, was the continuation of the underground River Vernaison, which has its source in the Grotte de la Luire. Opposite the semicircular walls around the spring is the Cirque de Choranche.

Grottes de Choranche★★
2.5km/1.5mi from D 531.
Discovered in 1875, these extraordinary caves, each one different from the next, lurk in the tall cliffs overlooking the vil-

Grottes de Choranche

© Philippe GR/Fotolia.com

A Maze of Caves

The "crust" of the Vercors Plateau consists of a gently undulating layer of limestone, which forms impressive cliffs in the gorges and along the edge of the massif. Water flows freely through these calcareous rocks; streams disappear into sink-holes *(scialets)* and reappear as resurgent springs. The most striking example of this phenomenon is the **underground Vernaison**; identified in the depths of the Luire Cave, it reappears in the Bournillon Cave, 20km/12.4mi further on, which makes it one of the major underground rivers in France.

Parc Naturel Régional du Vercors

Maison du Parc, 225 chemin des Fusillés, 38250 Lans-en-Vercors.
℘04 76 94 38 26. www.parc-du-vercors.fr.

Created in 1970, the park includes 85 municipalities situated in 8 designated natural regions including the Réserve des Haut Plateaux.

🚶 Several long-distance footpaths go through the area, including the Grandes Traversées du Vercors, created by the park, and crossing the high plateaus.

A remarkable ecosystem – Forests cover more than half the total area of the Vercors Massif and offer great variety: beeches and firs are gradually replaced by mountain pines in the south of the region. There are over 1 800 different plant varieties including some rare protected species: martagon lily and forest tulip. The Vercors is one of the rare areas where the six species of wild hoofed animals living in France can be found: argali sheep, chamois, roe deer, wild boar, mouflon and bouquetin (ibex). Birds of prey are also well represented: golden eagle, eagle owl, Bonelli's eagle (in the south) and a few bearded vultures. Since 1994, griffon vultures have gradually been reintroduced. Wolves have made a comeback due to declining agriculture and the increase in wild prey. Wolves venturing off into valleys have developed a taste for sheep; the park is working to find a solution.

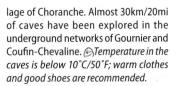

lage of Choranche. Almost 30km/20mi of caves have been explored in the underground networks of Gournier and Coufin-Chevaline. 🕐*Temperature in the caves is below 10°C/50°F; warm clothes and good shoes are recommended.*

The 🏊🏊**Grotte de Coufin**★★ (🕐open Jan–mid-Nov, check for times; 🅐9€ (children under 14 5.70€); ℘04 76 36 09 88; www.choranche.com) is the most spectacular cave in the Vercors Massif. Its name means "narrow neck" and refers to the cave entrance in contrast to the vast chamber you enter first. Thousands of delicate **stalactites**★★ are reflected in the lake. The visit continues through the caves including an aquarium of **Proteus**, the largest cave-dwelling animal in the world, a blind amphibian.

Outside, a **scientific trail** *(1km/0.6mi there and back)* runs to the tufa "waterfall" and explanation boards provide an understanding of the phenomenon.

The **Grotte du Gournier** contains a pretty lake, 50m/55yds long and 8m/26ft deep, fed by an underwater spring. This underground network, stretching over 18km/11mi, consists of a succession of big waterfalls.

The road then runs through the calm basin of La Balme at the confluence of the Rencurel and Bourne valleys (🕐see Route des Écouges, p314), then enters the precipitous Goule Noire Gorge.

La Goule Noire

This large spring is visible downstream of the Pont de la Goule Noire, level with the river bed.

After the bridge, the gorge narrows and before the tunnels on the other bank, the entrance to the Grotte de la Goule Blanche appears.

▷ *From Villard-de-Lans, you can return to Pont-en-Royans by the Grands*

Goulets tunnel, taking first D 531, then D 103 left at the pont de la Goule Noire.

The road rises above the bank of the Bourne, offering views of cliffs known as the Rochers du Rang. Before St-Martin-en-Vercors, note the impressive rock; it is known as the Vierge de Vercors.

▷ *From Les Barraques-en-Vercors turn right on D 518.*

The road passes through the Grands Goulets tunnel and then along the **Petits Goulets**★. This gorge is characterised by the high razor-like rock faces that drop almost vertically into the river. After Ste-Eulalie the landscape softens as the Royans area is reached.

ROUTE DES ÉCOUGES AND NAN★★
Drive of 81km/50.3mi shown on the regional map (●see p310). Allow 2hrs 30min.

This route opened up in 1883 includes one of the most vertiginous sections in the Vercors, but promises superb views down to the Bas-Dauphiné.

▷ *From La Balme, drive N on D 35.*

The road runs up the pleasant Rencurel Valley to the **Col de Romeyère**, where a forest road left leads to the vast Coulmes Forest. At the Chabert-d'Hières bridge the road follows a **gorge**★ briefly towards the Isère Valley with **views**★★ to the valley and the hills beyond. From the **bridge** over the Devrenne you can get out to look at the **waterfall** below.

▷ *After St-Gervais, the road joins D 1532 along the Isère to Cognin-les-Gorges. Continue on D 22 to Malleval.*

Gorges du Nan★
The Nan, a mountain stream flowing down from the western foothills of the Vercors, is followed from a great height by a picturesque cliff road.
D 22 rises in a series of hairpins along the escarpment overlooking the Nan Val-

ley. Stop between the second and third tunnels on the most impressive section of the route.
A second, less vertiginous narrow defile leads to the cool and verdant upper valley. The road continues upwards through meadows to Malleval, from where, in summer, you can continue to the Coulmes Forest and D 31 leads up to the Vercors Plateau.

▷ *At D 531 crossroads, turn left towards La Balme-de-Rencurel and Gorges de la Bourne★★★ (●see p312).*

ROUTE DU COL DE ROUSSET★★
Drive of 24km/14.9mi shown on the regional map (●see p311). Allow 1hr 30min.

La Chapelle-en-Vercors
This tourist centre was bombed and burned down in July 1944. Two plaques in a farmyard (Ferme Albert) honour the memory of 16 inhabitants of the village who were shot, and that tragic occasion is evoked in displays in the ruins.

▷ *Follow D 518 towards Grotte de la Luire and Col de Rousset.*

Grotte de la Luire
*0.5km/0.3mi off D 518 on the left and 15min return on foot; allow 30min more to see the **Decombaz Chamber**. ●Open Jul–Aug daily. ●Guided tours (30min) Jul–Aug 10.30am–6pm; rest of year times vary. ●6.70€ (children 4.50€). ●04 75 48 25 83.*
The cave is interesting from both a geological and a historical point of view. In July 1944 the Nazis killed or deported the wounded and the staff of the Resistance hospital set up inside the cave.

▷ *Continue along D 518 to the relatively new ski resort of Col de Rousset and drive through the tunnel.*

Col de Rousset★★
Leave the car at the southern exit of the tunnel and walk up to a viewpoint.
●The start of many walks into the Hauts Plateaux reserve, the Col de Rous-

set marks the climatic limit between the northern and southern Alps: the green landscapes of the Vercors to the north; and the surprise of an almost arid **landscape**★★ in the Die basin to the south. From the **viewing table**★★ at the top, stone signposts indicate the high peaks: the Grande Moucherolle to the north, the Grand Veymont to the east (in the foreground) and the heights with Mont Ventoux on the horizon to the south.

▶ *Head N and turn left onto D 76 towards Vassieux-en-Vercors.*

The road leads gradually uphill through the woods above the Vernaison. 500m/550yds before Vassieux, note the World War II debris. After the Necropolis of Vercours, take the right on the D178 towards La Chapelle-en-Vercours.

▶ *Follow the signs for Draye Blanche.*

Grotte de la Draye Blanche★
🕐*Open Apr–Sept daily 10am–5pm.*
💶*8.80€.* 📞*04 75 48 24 96.*
La Grotte de la Draye Blanche was discovered in 1918, and remained preserved until it was opened to the public in 1970. The visit takes you into the **Grande Salle**★ (100m/110yds long), where you can see a huge stalagmite, and falls of white, ochre and blue-grey crystals.

🚶 HIKE
Grand Veymont★★
Allow 1 day. Vertical rise 1 000m/ 3 281ft. No particular difficulty, suitable for hikers used to several hours' walking.

▶ *From La Chapelle-en-Vercors, drive along D 518 towards the Col de Rousset; 1km/0.6mi before Rousset, turn left along a narrow forest road marked Route Forestiere de la Coche.*

Follow it to the car park of the Maison Forestière de la Coche (9km/5.6mi) and leave the car.
This is one of many hikes in the vast **Réserve Naturelle des Hauts Plateaux**★★. Topo-guides are available from local tourist offices.

GORGES DE MÉAUDRE★
Drive of 46km/28.6mi shown on the regional map (⛟ see p310). Allow 5hrs. From Villard, drive W along D 531.

The road follows the River Bourne. At Les Jarrands, where the valley suddenly narrows, turn right onto D 106, which goes up the **Gorges de Méaudre**. Beyond Méaudre, bear left onto D 106C.

Autrans
🏠 *R. du Cinéma, 38880 Autrans.*
📞*04 76 95 38 63. www.autrans.com.*
Cross-country skiing is king here with 160km/100mi of tracks.

Col de la Croix-Perrin
The pass is a vast clearing between slopes clad with splendid firs. In Jaume, D 106 veers to the right, goes through **Lans-en-Vercors** and rises above the Furon Valley. Views of the Gorges d'Engins and Gorges du Bruyant.

Lans-en-Vercors
👥 La Magie des automates –
🕐*Open Nov–Sept Tue–Sat 2–6pm, Sun, school holidays and public holidays 10.30am–6.30pm.* 💶*7€.* 📞*04 76 95 40 14. www.magiedesautomates.com.* Mechanical toys, crafts and a Father Christmas village with 1 500 figurines.

St-Nizier-de-Moucherotte – This summer and winter resort, sited on an open plateau, was rebuilt after being burned down in a raid in June 1944.
From the **orientation table**★★ (take the path up from beside the Hôtel Bel-

---

Les Grands Goulets★★★
One of the most amazing natural phenomenons of the Vercors, this famous gorge road, built in the 19C and clinging to the rock face, has been closed since 2008, replaced by a modern tunnel. Studies are currently being undertaken by the Drôme department to see how to make this magnificent sight accessible to visitors again.

Ombrage) is an extended view of the Chartreuse, the southeast face of Mont Blanc, the Belledonne and the Écrins. The **Moucherotte summit** can be reached on foot *(3hrs return from the Olympic ski jump, then GR 91)* for a spectacularly **wide view**★★★, magical at night.

Tour sans Venin
15min there and back on foot.
One of the Seven Wonders of Dauphiné. According to legend, a crusader brought back soil from the Holy Land and, by spreading it round his castle, rid the area of venomous snakes, hence the name "tower without venom". From the foot of the tower is an extended **view**★.

GORGES D'ENGINS
Drive of 32km/19.9mi shown on the regional map (see p310). Allow 2hrs.

▷ *From Grenoble, drive NW to Sassenage along D 1532, along the Isère Valley.*

Sassenage
Close to the Grenoble ring road, Sassenage marks the start of one of the busiest roads into the Vercors.
The town's 17C **château** (*château open May–Oct, park all year; ℘04 38 02 12 04; www.chateaude-sassenage.com*) was family owned until 1971 and conserves much of its original interior decoration.
Its large **park**★, with its view over the Vercors, includes ruins of the old feudal castle on a wooded hillock.

From the banks of the Furon, walk up to **Les Cuves**, two superimposed caves connected by a waterfall, with a labyrinth of stalactites and stalagmites.

Gorges d'Engins★
The edges of this eroded rocky cutting are often smooth and polished.
From Jaume, the road follows the Lans Valley, clad with pine forests.

Gorges du Bruyant
A convenient footpath, linking D 531 and D 106, leads to the bottom of the gorge *(1hr return).*

ROUTE DU COMBE LAVAL★★★
Drive of 41km/25.5mi shown on the regional map (see p311). Allow 3hrs.

▷ *Leave the pass to the N and bear left onto D 76 to Vassieux-en-Vercors.*

The road climbs to the Col de Lachau site of the **Mémorial de la Résistance du Vercors**★ (*see Vassieux-en-Vercors*), which has plunging views of the Vassieux Valley.

Grotte du Brudour
From the bridge across the Brudour, 30min there and back on foot along a very pleasant path. Take a torch.
It leads to a cave with a resurgent spring from the nearby Urle. Follow the left-hand gallery to a chamber containing a small lake *(30min return).* The Brudour disappears into various sink-holes to reappear as the Cholet.

Combe Laval

© Jean-Paul Garcin/Photononstop/Tips Images

Forêt de Lente★★

Mainly firs and beeches. A great storm in 1982 devastated the forest, and 220 000 trees have since been replanted.

Combe Laval★★★

The journey starts from the **Col de la Machine**. The road, hewn out of the rock face, literally hangs above the gorge of the upper Cholet.

After going through several tunnels, the road suddenly overlooks the Royans region, offering **views**★★ of the Bas Dauphiné plateaux (Chambaran Forest).

COL DE LA BATAILLE★

Drive of 45km/28mi shown on the regional map (see p311). Allow 2hrs.

▶ *From Peyrus, drive along D 68.*

The road rises above a wooded vale. About half a mile before it reaches the plateau, there is a view of the Valence plain with the Cévennes in the background.

The **Col des Limouches** leads to the Léoncel Valley, with a distinctly Mediterranean landscape.

Léoncel

From its Cistercian abbey founded in 1137, the village has retained a vast Romanesque **abbey church**★ (*guided visits on request; 04 75 44 51 10*) dating from the late 12C. Built 1150–1210, the interior demonstrates the changing taste in architecture: the apse and apsidal chapels are typical of Provençal Romanesque style, whereas the nave has the mark of Gothic art.

▶ *Take D 101 to the Col de Tourniol.*

Col de Tourniol★

In front of you are the last foothills of the Vercors, above the Valence plain. Barbières with its ruined Château Pélafol is seen on the rocky cliffs.

▶ *Return to Léoncel.*

Shaded by beech trees, the D 199 runs along the eastern Léoncel Valley, pass-ing the cross-country ski resort, **Echaillon**, to reach an uneven plateau.

Col de la Bataille★★

☺ *The road is closed 15 Nov–15 May.*
A tunnel gives access to the pass overlooked by the Roc de Toulau. From the pass to Malatra, the **cliff road**★★ winds its way above the Bouvante Cirque and its small lake; there are three viewpoints along this section, before the road veers north towards the Col de la Portette.

Belvédère de la Portette★

15min on foot return from the Col de la Portette. Leave the car in the last bend and follow the stony path which starts behind a forest marker; bear right 200m/219yds further on.
The **view** looks down to the Val Ste-Marie, with the Royans region and Isère Valley beyond; note the huge modern bridge of St-Hilaire-St-Nazaire. After this pass you arrive at the Carrefour des Trois-Routes.

ADDRESSES

STAY

⊜⊜ **Le Val Fleuri** – *730 av. L. Fabre, 38250 Lans-en-Vercors. 04 76 95 41 09. www.le-val-fleuri.com. Closed 16 Mar–6 May, 20 Sep–16 Dec, Sun eve and Mon except in school holidays.* ▣. Wifi. *14 rooms, restaurant⊜⊜.* Time seems to have stood still in this pretty hotel dating from 1928. Nicely kept rooms, sometimes graced with Art Deco lamps or furniture. Food is served in the 1930s dining room or on the terrace.

⊜⊜ **Les Tilleuls** – *La Côte, 38880 Autrans. 04 76 95 32 34. www.hotel-tilleuls.com. Closed 12 Apr–6 May, 18 Oct–10 Nov, Tue eve and Wed outside peak holiday season.* ▣. *Wifi. 18 rooms, restaurant⊜⊜.* In a good location near the centre of the resort, this hotel offers a warm welcome and functional rooms, six renovated. Classic cooking is offered including game in season.

⊜⊜⊜ **La Petite Ferme des Prés Verts** – *351 chemin de Prenay, 38250 Lans-en-Vercors. 04 76 95 40 60. www.gite-presverts.com.* ♿▣✍. *7 rooms, half-board only.* Open all year this B&B consists of three wooden chalets, built in Finnish style offering comfortable accommodation. Residents' meals include locally sourced farm produce. Small heated swimming pool in summer and children's play area.

🍴 **La Poste** – *38880 Autrans. 𝄞04 76 95 31 03. www.hotel-barnier.com. Closed 19 Apr–10 May, 18 Oct–3 Dec. Wifi. 29 rooms, restaurant*🍴. The same family has run this pleasant hotel in the heart of the village since 1937. The rustic rooms are being renovated little by little. Sauna and hammam. In a welcoming dining room, tables are prettily set and local meals are served.

🍴 EAT

🍴 **Café Brochier** – *Pl. du Village, 26420 St-Julien-en-Vercors. 𝄞04 75 48 20 84. www.hotelrestaurantcafebrochier.com. Closed 15 Nov–2 Dec and Tue–Wed. 3 rooms*🍴. A young, dynamic chef has brought this old café-restaurant to life with his new take on local dishes, often using organic produce, and his pretty décor.

🍴 **Auberge Le Collet** – *26420 St-Agnan-en-Vercors. 𝄞04 75 48 13 18. www.auberge lecollet.com. Reservations advised in season. Check for closures out of season. 6 rooms*🍴. This old 19C farm provides a charming welcome with attractive rooms, and a menu that combines innovation with local dishes.

🍴 CAFÉ

🍴 **Cabane Café** – *Le Cellier, 38680 Choranche, on the road to the caves. 𝄞04 76 38 90 50. Closed end Oct–mid-Mar, and if bad weather, except mid-Jun–Aug.* You can make up your own snack here from local farm products, and then relax on a hammock or hay bale with a view of the Bournillon cliffs and the Moulin Marquis waterfall.

🏃 ACTIVITIES

🎯 **Good to know** – In **summer** you can choose from cultural activities, **caving, hiking, mountain biking, climbing, riding,** and **canyoning**. In winter, **skiing**, snow shoeing and dog-sledging are the main activities on offer.

Hiking – Tips before setting out:
◆ Water is scarce. Carry plenty.
◆ Do not leave marked hiking trails. Mountain biking is only permitted on the Grandes Traversées du Vercors. Paragliding is not allowed.
◆ Camping and fires are forbidden. Sheep huts appearing unoccupied should not be slept in unless they are obviously open to the public.

Grandes Traversées du Vercors: This marked route of 150km/93mi between Méaudre and Lente is suitable for hiking, mountain biking, riding or on skis. There are numerous gîtes but remember to book in advance.

Vassieux-en-Vercors

Lying at the bottom of a defor-ested valley, Vassieux-en-Vercors is overlooked by the Lente Forest on the ridges to the west, and by the foothills of the Hauts Plateaux du Vercors to the east. Hiking the many marked paths here, it is worth pausing a moment to recall the Resistance forces who walked those same paths over 60 years ago. The Resistance memorial and the necropolis will ensure that the memories of the painful events that took place on 21 July 1944 will never be forgotten.

SIGHTS

Vassieux was entirely rebuilt and a monument, surmounted by a recum-

▶ **Population:** 355.
🕐 **Michelin Map:** 332 F4.
🔲 **Info:** Pl. A.-Pietri, 26420 La Chapelle-en-Vercors. 𝄞04 75 48 22 54.
▶ **Location:** At the crossroads of three roads into the Vercors, Vassieux is crossed by D 76 and can be reached from Romans-sur-Isère in the W through the Forêt de Lente, from the S via the Col de Rousset, or from the N via La Chapelle-en-Vercors by D 178.
🎯 **Don't Miss:** The museum and Resistance memorial at Col de Lachau.
🕐 **Timing:** This village makes a good base for a long stay.

The Vercors, Resistance Stronghold

Background

According to historian François Marcot, the term "maquis" refers to "a gathering of men grouped together illegally in a forested area or an isolated village". In the Vercors, the groups who formed from 1943 were mainly young men avoiding enlistment into the Service du Travail Obligatoire (STO or Compulsory Work Service) joining earlier groups of "franc-tireurs" established there since 1942. Life for the maquis was both difficult and dangerous, but they were supported by most of the population on the Vercors plateau, who provided sustenance. The strategic advantage of the Vercors Massif, thinly populated and easy to defend, became apparent to the local Resistance movements who created the "**plan Montagnards**". The so called "citadelle imprenable" (impregnable fortress) of the Vercors became an allied support base.

Battles

The first big allied parachute drop of arms and food took place in November 1943. Alerted, several days later the Gestapo carried out the first of repeated raids. On 9 June, the Vercors proclaimed itself to be a free zone, leading to an increase in forces from 500 to nearly 4 000 men. Symbolically, on 3 July, their leaders proclaimed the area to be the "République du Vercors". On the 14th, the allies parachuted in light arms and equipment and the Vercors became entirely cordoned off by the Resistance. But German divisions, 15 000 men strong, began to close in, and with the young Resistance fighters lacking in food and arms, things came to a head. Vassieux was considered by the Allies and the Resistance as a perfect landing place. So, when the Germans launched the attack on **21 July 1944**, with planes dropping numerous special commandos and SS on Vassieux, Resistance fighters were taken by surprise, believing them first to be Allied planes. Without time to turn back, they were massacred by the Nazis, along with the inhabitants of the village.

After three days of hard fighting, the Resistance forces dispersed to the very dense Lente Forest. The St-Martin hospital was evacuated to the Grotte de la Luire, which was attacked on the 27th. One injured person escaped into a sink-hole of the cave; the nurses were deported to Ravensbrück. Until 19 August, terror reigned with civilians killed and villages burned down. The whole of the Vercors region was ravaged.

bent figure by Émile Gilioli, was erected to the "Martyrs of the Vercors, 1944" as well as a commemorative plaque on the place de la Mairie, with the names of the 74 civilian victims.

The **church** was built after the war and includes a fresco by Jean Aulame of the Assumption and a memorial plaque. Two of the wrecked planes remain still, one in front of the church, the other opposite the Resistance museum.

Musée de la Résistance de Vercors

Open Apr–Sept daily 10am–noon, 2–6pm; Feb–Mar and Oct–Dec Wed–Sun 2–5pm. Closed 24, 25, 31 Dec. 4€. 04 75 48 28 46. www.ladrome.fr.

The founder of this museum, a local Maquisard, has put together an amazing collection of objects connected with the battles of 1944. The educational and lively displays relate the history of the massif from the end of the 19C, and deal in detail with Resistance activity in the Vercors leading up to its tragic end.

Musée de la Préhistoire du Vercors★

3km/1.8mi S by D 615 (signposted). Open daily Jul–Aug 10am–6pm; Sept–Jun 10am–12.30pm, 2–5pm. Closed 1 Jan, 25 Dec. 5€. 04 75 48 27 81. www.prehistoire-vercors.fr.

Excavations in 1969 on this spot revealed flint shards and blades spread over a

Musée de la Résistance de Vercors

A. de Valroger/MICHELIN

large area. The specialised knife and dagger blades were cut in what must have been a 4 000-year-old workshop. The level of workmanship is remarkable and it is known that these blades were exported across Europe.

Displays, films, practical demonstrations and reconstructions of prehistoric dwellings reveal the working methods of these early craftsmen with the museum having dedicated guides, themselves experienced flint-cutters.

Nécropole du Vercors

1km/0.6mi N of Vassieux by D 76.
This necropolis contains the graves of 193 fighters and civilians, killed in the attacks of July 1944.

Mémorial de la Résistance du Vercors (Col de Lachau)★

3km/1.8mi NW of Vassieux; at the Nécropole du Vercors take a left on D 76.
🕐*Open Jul–Aug daily 10am–6pm; Apr–Jun, Sept and school holidays daily 10am–12.30pm, 2–5pm; Oct and mid-Dec–Mar Sat–Sun.* 🕐*Closed 1 Jan, 25 Dec.* ♿*6€ (children 3€).*
♿ 𝄞*04 75 48 26 00.*
www.memorial-vercors.fr.
With a particularly plain architectural design, emphasising the solemn remembrance of this place, the memo-

rial stands like the prow of a ship against the dense Forêt de Lente. Built on the north face of the site, it is covered with junipers and pines.

A very modern approach is taken in the museum, which links the Resistance activities of the Vercors with the events happening nationally during this period, favouring personal accounts.

Reconstructions and slide shows feature the important issues including interrogations and the treatment of women; the battles of July 1944 can be relived through contemporary films.

At the end of the visit, a large wall on the right incorporates 840 lead plates each inscribed with the name of one of the civilian victims of the Vercors. And a vast terrace overlooks the plateau, unchanged since the tragedy.

ADDRESSES

🎭 EVENTS

Fête de la forêt – *Pentecost weekend.*
Forest covers 50 percent of the Vercors, and until the early 20C was of fundamental economic importance. The forest plays host to three days of celebrations with demonstrations, wood sculptures, and more.

Villard-de-Lans

The tourist capital of the Vercors region, the little town of Villard-de-Lans enjoys a dry, sunny climate, clean air and a sheltered position at the foot of the Cornafion, Gerbier and Moucherotte making it an ideal resort for skiing in winter, and hiking, biking, cave exploration or canyoning in summer.

Maison du Patrimoine

1 pl. de la Libération. ⏱*Open Jul–Aug Mon and Wed–Sat 3–6pm, Sun 10am–noon; Sept–Jun Wed–Sat 3–6pm.* ⬡*3€ (children under 13 free).* ☎*04 76 95 17 31.*

Life in the Vercors long ago is evoked through a fine **collection of objects**, **written documents** and **tools**. Four large rooms in the museum are devoted to different themes including the history of the resort and the story of the villarde breed of cattle, particularly hardy and well suited to the Vercors terrain.

♟ La Tanière Enchantée

Edge of the town, rte de Corrençon. ⏱*Open Mon–Sat 2–6pm; Sun, public holidays and school holidays 10am–noon, 2–6pm.* ⬡*6.50€ (children under 13 5.50€).* ♿ ☎*04 76 94 18 40.*

This exhibition uses mechanical historical reconstructions and the display of stuffed animals to illustrate the relationship between men, bears and other animals currently living in the Vercors.

- ▶ **Population:** 4 023.
- ⬡ **Michelin Map:** 333 G7.
- ▯ **Info:** 101 pl. Mure-Ravaud, 38250 Villard-de-Lans. ☎08 11 46 00 15. www.villarddelans.com.
- ▶ **Location:** 36km/22.4mi SW of Grenoble via Sassenage and the Gorges d'Engins on D 531.
- ⬡ **Don't Miss:** A visit to the Maison du Patrimoine.
- ♟ **Kids:** The exhibition at La Tanière Enchantée.

🥾 HIKES
Cote 2000★

🚶 *4.5km/2.8mi SE. Then, 1hr there and back for gondola and walk. Take av. des Bains to the end of the valley. Turn left onto D 215B to Corrençon and then to the Cote 2000 gondola station.* ⏱*Open Jul–Aug.* ⬡*6€ return.* ☎*04 76 94 50 50.* From the top of the gondola (1 720m/5 643ft) follow signs along the ridge to the summit. The view includes the rolling plateaux of the Lans mountains to the north, the Vercors to the west with the Cévennes in the distance. Glimpses of Mont Blanc to the northeast.

Crêtes de la Molière

🚶*Leave 10km/6.2mi above Autrans, from the Molière car park. 2hrs return.* This easy, well-marked walk leads to a magical panorama over the Belledonne range, the foothills of the Chartreuse mountains and the northern Vercors.

The Resort

The villages of Villard-de-Lans and Corrençon-en-Vercors linked together at the end of the 1980s to form one big resort with quite varied mountain landscapes: the plateau is ideal for walking, steep cliff-sides are prized by mountain-climbing enthusiasts, and slopes of different gradients ideal for skiing. Cross-country skiers are particularly well-looked-after at the Site Nordique du Haut Vercors with over 160km/100mi of tracks. Several important ski champions come from the area, notably **Carole Montillet**, a gold medallist in downhill at the 2002 Salt Lake City Winter Olympics and **Raphael Poirée**, world champion in biathlon.

🚗 DRIVING TOUR

ROUTE DE VALCHEVRIÈRE★
Drive of 10km/6.2mi shown on the
regional map (see p310).

▶ *Leave Villard-de-Lans by the av. des*
Bains. At the junction at the end of the
valley, follow D 215C uphill towards
Le Bois-Barbu.

This small scenic road is lined with the
Stations of the Cross dedicated to the
victims of the fighting of 1944. There are
pretty glimpses over the Bourne gorges
and the green valley of the hamlet of
Méaudre in the middle of the forest.
The hamlet was a maquis camp before
being destroyed 22–23 July 1944. It
has been left in its existing state and is
a place of meditation.

Calvaire de Valchevrière★
On a site that was defended right to the
end of the hostilities of July 1944, this
large cross *(the 12th station)* marks the
summit of the pilgrimage. In front, the
view looks over to the hamlet of Val-
chevrière, burned to the ground, except
its chapel, today the 14th station of the
cross. Below is the Goule Noire section
of the deep Bourne gorges.

Brèche de Chalimont★
Continue the drive uphill to the chalet de
Chalimont; turn right on a stony forest
track (possible by car in dry weather or
1hr return on foot).
A narrow, rocky ridge gives a more
extended view taking in the higher
Bourne gorges, the Lans mountains, as
well as the Rencurel Valley.

ADDRESSES

🛏 STAY

🛏 **Chambre d'hôte Le Val Ste-Marie** –
Bois-Barbu, refuge de la Glisse, then 1st path
on the left. ℘04 76 95 92 80. www.leval
saintemarie.villard-de-lans.fr. 🅿. *3 rooms* ⌷
Nature lovers will enjoy this 200-year-
old renovated farm in the middle of
the countryside, and in winter by the

cross-country ski tracks. The rooms are
simple, but comfortable. Evening meals
must be reserved in advance at least the
day before.

🛏 **Le Christiania** – *Av. Prof. Nobecourt.*
℘04 76 95 12 51. www.hotel-le-christiania.fr.
Closed 18 Apr–20 May, 1 Oct–16 Dec. Wifi.
5 rooms. A family-run hotel with large,
individually decorated rooms, almost all
with a balcony and mountain view.
Indoor pool.

🍴 EAT

🍽 **Auberge de la Croix Perrin** – *38250*
Lans-en-Vercors, Col de la Croix-Perrin.
℘04 76 95 40 02. www.vercors-hotel.com.
Closed 10 Apr–15 May, 23 Oct–18 Dec. 🅿.
9 rooms 🛏. Encircled by pine trees, the
restaurant in this old forestry house enjoys
a splendid view. Local food, more original
in the evening. The rooms are charming.

🍽 **Auberge des Montauds** –
Les Montauds, Bois-Barbu. ℘04 76 95
17 25 - www.auberge-des-montauds.fr.
Closed 15 Apr–8 May, Nov–15 Dec. ♿🅿.
On the hills above Villard, the road ends
just above this quiet inn, with nothing but
countryside above. Generous portions
of traditional and mountain food are
served by the fireplace or on the terrace
in summer. There are renovated rooms
and a studio.

🍽 **Les Trente Pas** – *16 r. des Francs-*
Tireurs. ℘04 76 94 06 75. *Closed 15 Apr–*
1 May, 15 Nov–15 Dec, Thur eve and
Mon–Tue. Not far ("Trente pas" means 30
paces) from the village church, this little
restaurant is decorated with paintings
from a local artist and serves satisfying
traditional meals.

🛒 SHOPPING

Vercors lait – *Rte de Jarrands.* ℘04 76 95
00 11. www.vercorslait.com. *Open 9am–*
noon, 3–7pm. Working with modern
equipment and age-old know-how, this
successful milk cooperative also offers
regional cheeses such as the famous blue
vercors-sassenage.

🏃 ACTIVITIES

🎿 **Good to know** – Apart from **skiing**,
in season there is a **swimming** pool
complex, an ice rink and a **fitness**
centre. For **fine days** there is an outdoor pool,
riding and **tennis** courts.

Pont-en-Royans★★

The novelist Stendhal was captivated by this picturesque little village. At the exit of the long gorge of the River Bourne, the narrow streets and audacious architecture of the houses clinging to the mountain face exude a definite southern atmosphere and great charm.

SIGHTS
The Village

For Vercors residents the Pont-en-Roy-ans was once the only bridge across the Bourne leading to the Royans plain. Enjoy a short, but pleasant walk in the old medieval village. The church has a Gothic chancel and a Romanesque belfry.

The Site★★

At pont Picard, take the bridge down to the quays of the Bourne. You can then reach the medieval quarter.

Walking towards the place de la Halle from the bridge, the lovely atmosphere of the old quarter is enhanced by the whisper of little waterfalls, vestiges of an old grain mill. Life was not always so quiet here: during the 16C Ward of Religion, many houses were destroyed, but were rebuilt in an unpretentious way,

▶ **Population:** 879.
Michelin Map: 333 F7.
Info: Grande-Rue, 38680 Pont-en-Royans. ℘04 76 36 09 10. www.ot-pont-en-royans.com.
▷ **Location:** Situated between Romans-sur-Isère and Villard-de-Lans, Pont-en-Royans is a gateway to the Vercors region. Approach from the W for the best view of the pretty dam and reservoir downstream from the town.
Don't Miss: The Presles excursion offers lovely scenery.
Kids: The many interactive activities offered by the Musée de l'Eau, devoted to water, should amuse children on a rainy day.

taking nothing away from their beauty. Lopsided and clinging to the rock, the façade of the houses goes straight down to the Bourne river, with wooden balconies hang out into a void.

Panorama des Trois-Châteaux★ – *1hr on foot there and back. The paths climb steeply, with short sections across rock-falls, supported by a staircase at pl. de la Porte-de-France.* From the view-

Façade of the houses in Pont-en-Royans

© Brigitte Merle/Photononstop

point is a view over the Royans plain and the Isère Valley.

Musée de l'Eau★★ – *Open daily Jul–Aug 10am–6pm; Apr–Jun and Sept 10am–noon, 2–6pm; Oct–Mar 10am–noon, 2–5.30pm.* *6€ (children 4€).* *04 76 36 15 53. www.musee-eau.com*
In an old factory overlooking the Bourne river this hands-on interactive museum is dedicated to the understanding of water including its natural cycle, ecosystems of drought areas and scientific discoveries.

A second section is devoted to water in the Vercors. The visit is quite technical and a guided tour helps to bring the place to life. At the end of the visit, you can taste spring waters from around the world at the **bar à eau** (water bar).

🚗 DRIVING TOUR

ROUND TOUR VIA PRESLES★★
Drive of 32km/19.9mi shown on the regional map (see p310).
Allow 1hr 30min.

▷ *From Pont-en-Royans, drive along D 531 towards Villard-de-Lans and turn left onto D 292 immediately after the Pont Rouillard over the Bourne.*

The road climbs within sight of the escarpments overlooking the river. From the "Croix de Toutes Aures" on a bend (but with no cross), the view extends from the rolling hills of the Royans region to the gorge of the River Bourne overlooked by the Grand Veymont.
After a series of hairpin bends, the road finally reaches the **Presles** plateau. It continues to rise beyond Presles through the Coulmes Forest to a small hamlet called Le Fas, where the view embraces a long stretch of the lower Isère Valley, including the imposing aqueduct of St-Nazaire-en-Royans.
The road then winds steeply down to St-Pierre-de-Chérennes.

▷ *D 31 reaches D 1532. Turn left almost immediately towards Beauvoir-en-Royans.*

Beauvoir-en-Royans
Château de Beauvoir – In a pretty spot, the ruins of the 13C castle stand on top of an isolated hill overlooking the village. A square tower, a gate, a Gothic window, part of the former chapel and the old, ivy-covered walls are all that remain of the former residence of the "dauphins".
Couvent des Carmes – *Open Apr–Oct and 2 holiday weeks in Feb 10am–6pm (check on Sat).* *5€ (children 3€).* *Joint ticket available with the Musée de l'Eau.* *04 76 38 01 01. www.couventdescarmes.com.*
Next to the ruins of the Beauvoir château, the old convent founded by Humbert II in 1343 houses an educational multimedia museum on the history of the dauphins of France, as well as an exhibition of the local Vercors flora. An on-site restaurant serves regional specialities and organic raw vegetables.

▷ *Return to N 532 and, in St-Romans, take D 518 back to Pont-en-Royans.*

ADDRESSES

🛏 STAY

Chambre d'hôte Les Fauries – *Les Fauries, 38680 Presles. 10km/6.2mi NE of Pont-en-Royans by D 531, then 2km/1.2mi N of Presles.* *04 76 36 10 50. www.lesfauries.fr. Closed 14 Nov–28 Jan.* *4 rooms.* Perched at an altitude of 938m/3 077ft this old stone house has been attractively restored and is a great place to recharge one's batteries. The rooms, all quiet, have been warmly decorated and there is a bonus of an extended view over the Hauts Plateaux.

Du Musée de l'Eau – *Pl. Breuil.* *04 76 36 15 53. www.musee-eau.com. Closed 3-16 Jan.* *Wifi. 31 rooms, restaurant.* This modern hotel is part of the museum complex. Rooms are small, furnished in a modern style, and some overlook the mountain and the suspended old houses of the village. The uncluttered restaurant has a terrace with water sprays.

St-Nazaire-en-Royans

The old houses of the fortified village of St-Nazaire-en-Royans rise up like an amphitheatre from the bridge over the Bourne river up to the ruins of the Delphinale tower. Its slender aqueduct, framed by the 17 arches, straddles the turbulent waters of the Isère and the houses clustered at its base.

SIGHTS
Grotte Préhistorique de Thaïs

Open Jul–Aug daily 11am–7pm; Apr–Jun Tue–Sat 2–6pm, Sun and public holidays 11am–6pm; check for rest of year. 7€. *04 75 48 45 76. www.grotte-de-thais.com.*

Situated on the shore of the lake, beneath the aqueduct, the caves contain a labyrinth of narrow and tortuous passages resulting from the erosion of the water of one of the biggest underground rivers in the Vercors. Inhabited in prehistoric times, the cave has yielded tools and engraved bones. The aquariums include cave-dwelling animals.

Aqueduct – Maison de l'Aqueduc

Open Jul–Aug daily 10am–noon, 1–7pm; Jun and Sept Tue–Sun 10am–noon, 2–6pm; check for rest of year. 3.50€ (children 2€). *04 75 48 49 80.*

Here the saga of building the aqueduct is retraced from 1810 to engineering projects that have continued in modern times. Built in 1876, this work of art has 17 arches and irrigates the Valence plain through 118km/73.3mi of channels. The visit starts with a panoramic lift, and includes explanatory panels and audio (in English) relating the history and geography of the surrounding area. An orientation table shows the geological situation of St-Nazaire.

From here one can view the old village of Musan clinging to the mountain.

- **Population:** 703.
- **Michelin Map:** 332 E3.
- **Info:** Maison de l'Aqueduc, 26190 St-Nazaire-en-Royans. *04 75 48 49 80. www.saint-nazaire-en-royans.com.*
- **Location:** On the left bank of the Isère, at the crossroads of the Valence–Grenoble road and the important tourist routes such as Gorges de la Bourne and the Combe Laval (*see p316*).
- **Don't Miss:** Crossing the Isère on the aqueduct.
- **Kids:** There's plenty to occupy them with the aqueduct, and at Château de la Sône, the garden of the petrified springs.

EXCURSIONS
La Sône

8km/5mi by D 1532, then D 71.

Château de la Sône

Follow signs from the village.
Guided visits (1hr 10min) of the château Jul–Sept Sun–Fri 2–6pm. 7€ *château and park.* *04 76 64 41 70. www.chateaudelasone.com.*

The castle, with its foundations dating back to the 12C, is perfectly sited on a rocky platform overlooking the Isère Valley. A Historic Monument, it has been very well restored and furnished with taste, and has pleasant parkland.

Jardin des Fontaines Pétrifiantes

Next to the château de la Sône. Open Jun–Aug daily 10.30am–7pm; May and 1st 2 weeks Sept Tue–Sun 10.30am–6.30pm; end Sept–mid-Oct Sat–Sun 11am–6pm. 8.50€ (children 5€; 20€ combined ticket with paddle boat trip and the grotte de Thaïs). *04 76 64 43 42. www.jardin-des-fontaines.com.*

This pleasant garden, with 1 500 different species of plants and flowers, is laid out round petrified springs, created by water laden with limestone forming a thin layer of sparkling crystals over various objects – leaves, pebbles, seeds – and forming interesting shapes.

Rochechinard

❯ 4.5km/2.8mi S by D 209.

The village is overlooked by the ruins of an 11C–12C **castle** (o— closed to the public). Its small country **church** surrounded by a cemetery form a lovely picture with the cliffs of the Combe Laval in the background.

The **Musée de Royans** (◷open Jul–Aug 3–7pm; 🗄 📞04 75 47 74 23) relates the history of the castle and contains a collection of tools and regional costumes as well as reconstructions of traditional interiors.

St-Jean-en-Royans

❯ From Château de Rochechinard, follow D 209, 5km/3mi SE by D 209.
🗄 13 pl. de l'Église. 📞04 75 48 61 39.

Lying below the vertiginous limestone cliffs of the Vercors Plateau, this quiet town is the starting point of many breathtaking excursions on foot or by car. The town is also celebrated for its cuisine, including Royans **ravioli**, introduced by Italian colliers working in the Vercors forests.

For a view over the town, the Royans countryside, Bourne gorges and the Combe Laval go to the **orientation table of the colline du Toura** reached from chemin du Cimétiere.

Route du Pionnier★

❯ 17km/10.6mi from St-Jean-en-Royans S by D 131, then D 331.

From the Col de la Croix, the road climbs along the cliff, with views over the Lyonne Valley and the wooded cirque of the Bouvante. Next you see the Royans and the Isère Valley. After the Pas de l'Échelle (also called Pionnier) tunnel, the road climbs further to meet D 199.

❯ From there you can reach the Col de la Bataille (&see p317 for reverse direction) or return to St-Jean-en-Royans by the magnificent rte de Combe Laval (D 199 then N on D 76) to reach St-Laurent-en-Royans by D 54.

Monastère St-Antoine-le-Grand

❯ At St-Laurent-en-Royans (4km/2.5mi NE), follow signs to Col de la Machine (D 2); take the first right marked Gorge de Laval (D 239).
The monastery is 5km/3mi further on.
◷Open 11.30am–12.30pm, 2–5.30pm.
⚭3.50€ (children under 12 free).
♿ 📞04 75 47 72 02.

This monastery is located at the end of the Combe de Laval and since 1978 has been lived in by a small community of Orthodox monks from the Simonopetra Monastery on Mount Athos.

A sculpted wooden door leads into the Byzantine-style church (1988–90), beautifully integrated into the magnificent alpine surroundings, yet re-creating a small corner of Greece. The interior includes some exceptional large murals that took two Moscow artists six years to paint.

ADDRESSES

🍽 STAY

⌂ **Rome** – In the village. 📞04 75 48 40 69. www.hotelrestaurantrome.com. Closed 4–17 Jan, early Nov, Sun eve out of season and Mon. 🅿. Wifi. 10 rooms, restaurant⌂⌂. The nicest of the bright and sound-proofed rooms in this large hotel have views over the aqueduct and the Bourne lake. The local *raviole de Royans* are served among other regional specialities at this very friendly restaurant.

🏃 ACTIVITIES

Paddle boat "Royans-Vercors" – 📞04 75 48 45 76. www.bateau-a-roue.com. Cruises with commentary. Apr–mid-Oct: check for times, leaving from St-Nazaire-en-Royans and La Sône. ⚭10.50€ (children under 13 6.50€; or combined ticket with the Petrified Gardens or the Grotte). Here is the most interesting way of seeing this picturesque valley. From La Sône to St-Nazaire you will discover the variety of animals and preserved landscape at the foot of the Vercors mountains.

Lacs de Laffrey★

Carved out by glaciers between Trièves and Valbonnais, the four Laffrey lakes nestle in a gentle landscape of pastures and fields, with the mountains of Oisans and Vercors behind. Yet the history of this region was not always so peaceful with religious wars in La Mure in 1580, and a strategic turnaround when imperial forces welcomed Napoleon on his return from the island of Elba. The 19C Industrial Revolution changed the landscape too, with mines, the railway and hydroelectric plants.

- **Michelin Map:** 333 H7.
- **Info:** 43 r. du Breuil, 38350 La Mure. ℘04 76 81 05 71. www.ville-lamure.com.
- **Location:** S of Grenoble, the lakes from N to S are: Lac Mort, Lac de Laffrey (the longest at 3km/1.8mi), Lac de Petichet and Lac de Pierre-Châtel.
- **Don't Miss:** The coal-mine museum at La Mine-Image.
- **Kids:** The adventure park at the Lac Laffrey.
- **Timing:** Check to see if the famous La Mure railway is open, following a landslide.

🚗 DRIVING TOURS

1 ROUTE NAPOLÉON★
15km/9.3mi. Allow 45mins.

La Mure

This lively market town, on the southern edge of the Plateau de la Matheysine, owed its prosperity to the nearby coal mines. From its mountain railway (*see p329*) are amazing views of the Drac corniche. Near the covered market, the **Musée Matheysin** (*open May–Oct Wed–Mon 1–6.30pm; 2.30€; ℘04 76 30 98 15; www.matheysine.com*) relates local history from earliest times to 1997 when the last mine was closed.

The road to Laffrey runs along the rather austere plateau by the former mine of Le Villaret, the largest in the area, then along the lakes, with the heights of the Chartreuse Massif filling the horizon ahead. With its north–south axis the plateau is windswept and exposed, fully deserving of its nickname "the Siberia of the Dauphiné"; in spite of its relatively low altitude the lakes often freeze over during the winter months.

The drive up to the **Prairie de la Rencontre**★ is marked by two monuments bearing the imperial eagle symbol. They lead to a statue of Napoleon I on his horse, marking the exact spot where the emperor met the imperial forces sent from Grenoble to stop him.

Laffrey★

This charming holiday resort is popular for swimming and fishing.

Point de vue de Beauregard – An easy walk (*about 2hrs*) from Laffrey via the village of Notre-Dame-de-Vaulx to the **Montagne de Beauregard**. Park the car near the Chalet de l'As and continue on foot to the top of the ridge, which offers a splendid **view** of the plateau, the lakes and the Drac Valley.

Le Sapey★

The narrow road skirts Lac Mort. From the end of the road, you can climb (*15min return*) to the Chapelle du Sapey for a view to the Chamrousse, Belledonne and Taillefer massifs.

2 ROUTE DE LA MORTE★
45km/28mi. Allow 2hrs.

Towards the Col de Malissol are views to the Matheysine plateau, the Obiou and the eastern escarpments of the Vercors Massif. From the Col de Malissol to the Col de la Morte, the road runs along the narrow valley of the Roizonne.

La Morte

Lying at the foot of the Grand Serre and Taillefer summits, La Morte offers beautiful ski runs. In summer, the ascent of the Taillefer starts here. The

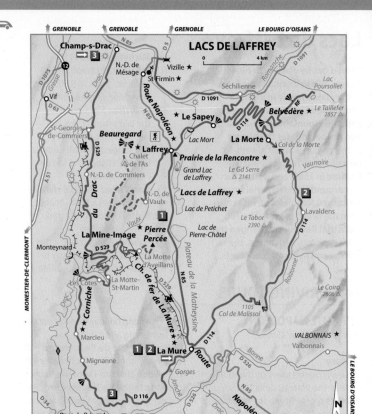

forest road leading to the Lac Poursollet affords fine views of the Romanche Valley, but is only open in summer.

From the first hairpin descending on D 114 north from the Col de la Morte the **view**★ overlooks the industrial corridor of La Romanche framed by mountains.

③ CORNICHE DU DRAC★★
45km/28mi. Allow 2hrs.

The village of Champ-sur-Drac includes **le vieux village** with its 1587 tower, but is best known as an early 20C industrial centre. Towards Monteynard, the road rises gradually and offers views of the Drac Valley and its hydroelectric installations. On leaving Monteynard, the lake of the **Barrage de Monteynard** with Mont Aiguille above is visible on the right.

▷ *Continue along D 529 to La Motte-d'Aveillans.*

▲ La Mine-Image
Les 4 Galeries, 38770 La Motte-d'Aveillans. Guided tours (1hr, reserve 1 month ahead). 6€ (children 3.20€). ℘04 76 30 68 74. www.mine-image.com.
This site of a coal mine inaugurated under Napoleon shows the evolution of coal-mining technology.

▷ *Turn left from D 529 at signpost La Pierre Percée, and leave the car.*

La Pierre Percée★
A path starting from the car park leads to the ridge *(45min)*. Legend has it that this rock, one of the "seven wonders of the Dauphiné", a 3m/10ft-high arch, represents the devil turned into stone!

▷ *Return to La Motte-d'Aveillans and turn left onto D 116.*

Beyond Les Côtes, the cliff road affords **views**★★★ of the escarpments plunging into the Drac, of the Monteynard Dam and lake and of the Vercors Massif. From Marcieu onwards there are fine mountain views before arriving at the Jonche gorges outside La Mure.

EXCURSION

La Mure Mountain Railway★

○━ *Closed at time of publication.* ℘08 92 39 14 26. www.trainlamure.com.

This railway line was opened in 1888 to transport coal from La Mure to St-Georges-de-Commiers, and from there to the national network. It has been known as a pioneering technical transport achievement, a means of transport for pilgrims to see the **Pierre Percée**★, an industrial train (1950–62) and a successful tourist train. The line suffered a landslide in October 2010 and its complete reopening is uncertain. Before the landslide, the train season ran between April and October.

ADDRESSES

🏠 STAY

⊜🍽 **Hôtel du Grand Lac** – *La plage, 38220 Laffrey, rte de Cholonge.* ℘04 76 73 12 90. 📶. *Wifi. 20 rooms, restaurant*⊜🍽.
With a great position by the beach on the lake, the comfortable rooms are in two buildings. Traditional food served in the restaurant *(Jul–Aug only)*, shady terrace.

🍷 NIGHTLIFE

Le Barrage de Monteynard – *Bateau La Mira, 38650 Treffort.* ℘04 76 34 14 56. http://bateau.la.mira.monsite.wanadoo.fr. Short excursions to see cliffs, waterfalls on the lake of the Monteynard Dam.

Le Trièves★★

The rivers Drac and Ébron have carved trenches through the verdant and undulating Trièves depression. With its colourful landscape and villages, the region offers a foretaste of Provence. On the eastern edge of the Vercors mountains, the best-known summit is **Mont Aiguille**, a table mountain with very steep sides that inspired the earliest-recorded French mountaineering feat in 1492. Three years earlier King Charles VIII had been to the region, and on admiring the mountain, he ordered Antoine de Ville to scale it.

🥾 HIKE

Tour du Mont Aiguille

🐾 *7hrs 30min for the circuit in 1 or 2 days. Overall vertical rise 1 100m/3 609ft. Leave from Chichilianne (a hamlet of La Richardière) or La Bâtie (near Gresse).* This strangely shaped mountain is easier to circle than to climb. The circular route crosses several villages, two passes and offers fine views over the unusual architecture of the region. If you want to climb the mountain, more than 30 routes up are available for all levels. *Information from the relais du PNR du Vercors at Chichilianne,* ℘04 76 34 44 95.

- **Michelin Map:** 333 H9.
- **Info:** R. du Breuil, 38710 Mens. ℘04 76 34 84 25. www.trieves-tourisme.fr.
- **Location:** S of Grenoble, on the eastern edge of the Vercors.
- **Don't Miss:** A visit to Mens.

🚗 DRIVING TOUR

① THE UPPER VALLEY OF THE GRESSE RIVER

61km/38mi. Allow 2hrs.

▷ *Leave Monestier-de-Clermont by D 1075.*

Monestier-de-Clermont

Once a thermal spa, and an early sports resort, the village has an old centre with the 17C Château de Bardonench and a quarter of fine 19C villas. The woods offer many possible walks, and 9km/5.6mi to the north, blocking the Drac, is the Monteynard Dam and its reservoir.

From Monestier the D 8 road goes through **St-Guillaume**, a typical Trièves village, with its stocky houses covered with steep, tiled roofs, in perfect harmony with the surrounding landscape.

Prélenfrey

This small summer resort lies at the heart of a **high valley**★ beneath the escarpments of the Vercors Massif (Arêtes du Gerbier). The Échaillon flows through a narrow gorge, through which there is a pleasant view of the Drac Valley.

Col de l'Arzelier

The road rises to the Col de l'Arzelier (the pass is laid out as a ski area at 1 154m/3 786ft), then runs down to Château-Bernard, offering fine views. The pastoral landscapes of the Trièves are backed by the impressive cliffs of the Vercors, including the Grand Veymont, the eastern massif's highest peak. A deep gorge appears at St-Andéol, where the Échaillon stream carves a way through to the Gresse below.

Gresse-en-Vercors

Partly within the Vercors Natural Park, this village is a base for the climb up to Grand Veymont. Note the strange form of transport here, the *trinqueballes*, designed to cope with uneven ground.

Col de l'Allimas★

From the pass there is a striking view of Mont Aiguille. Heading down to D 1075, the last village is **St-Michel-les-Portes**, a typical Trièves village.

▷ *Return to Monestier along D 1075 towards Grenoble.*

② THE HEART OF TRIÈVES★

72km/44.7mi . Allow 3hrs. D 34 runs around the Trièves basin via Col du Fau.

Pont de Brion★

This suspension bridge, looking surprisingly delicate, spans the gorge of the Ébron, 66m/217ft below. It used to be even higher over the river bed, but the building of the Monteynard Dam raised the level of the Ébron.

Mens★

The capital of the Trièves region was a stopping point on the Roman road; the old covered **market**★, the 17C town houses in the rue du Bourg, and both a temple and a church hint at the past prosperity and importance of Mens.

The **Café des Arts**, mentioned in Jean Giono's *Triomphe de la Vie*, features a mural (1896) by Gustave Riquet depicting local landscapes and farming scenes. In the historic town centre, the **Musée du Trièves**★ (○open Jul–Aug Tue–Sun 3–7pm, May–Jun and Sept Tue–Sun 3–6pm, Oct–Apr Sat–Sun and school holidays; ○Closed 1 Jan, Easter Monday, 1 May, 1 Nov, 11 Nov, 25 Dec; ∞2.30€; ☇04 76 34 88 28) relates the history and particularities of the Trièves region using interactive displays.

Terre vivante – *Domaine de Raud.* Take D526 towards Clelles for 5km/3mi, then left on D 216. ○Open daily Jul–Aug Apr–Jun and Sept–Oct Sat–Sun 11am–6pm. ☇04 76 34 80 80. www.terrevivante.org. This ecology centre provides several interesting circuits, ideal for families, that encourage you to think about day-to-day ecological issues. The **circuit sur l'eau**★ is particularly recommended.

▷ *Take D 66 and D 216 to reach Tréminis to the S.*

In the upper Ebron Valley lies **Tréminis**, covered with pine forests and overlooked by the limestone escarpments of the Dévoluy. This **setting**★ is one of the most attractive of the whole area.

In **Lalley, Espace Giono**, a permanent exposition of French author **Giono**, holds photographs, works and extracts of gionesque work related to Trièves.

▷ *Take D 1075 N to Clelles.*

At the heart of the Vercors Natural Park, **Clelles** has retained its village charm.

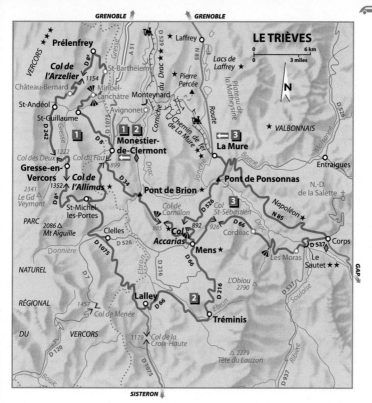

LE TRIÈVES

0   3 miles   6 km

▶ *Return to Monestier-de-Clermont on D 1075 heading N.*

3 FROM LA MURE TO THE BARRAGE DU SAUTET
70km/43.5mi. Allow 3hrs.

La Mure *See Route Napoléon (p327).*

▶ *Leave La Mure SE on N 85 then D 526 to the right. Head towards Mens over the high* **Pont de Ponsonnas**.

Col Accarias★
Alt. 892m/2 927ft.
Extended view of the Trièves enclosed by the Obiou, the Grand Ferrand and the Tête du Lauzon.

▶ *From* **Mens★**, *take D 66 in the direction of Corps.*

Barrage du Sautet★★
See p394. This impressive dam has a span with a height of 126m/413ft.

The lake is also most attractive.

Corps
The main village of the Beaumont area, Corps sits in a wonderful position above **splendid countryside★★**. It is much visited on the journey up to the cathedral of **Notre-Dame-de-la-Salette★** at 1 800m/5 906ft altitude (*see p395*).

▶ *Return to La Mure by N 85 (Route Napoléon, see p327).*

ADDRESSES

🛏 STAY

🍴 **Hôtel Au Gai Soleil du Mont Aiguille** – *La Richardière, 38930 Chichilianne, 3km NW of Chichilianne.* ℘*04 76 34 41 71. www.hotel gaisoleil.com. Closed end Oct–20 Dec.* ♿🅿. *Wifi. 20 rooms, restaurant*🍴. This family hotel occupies a site at the foot of Mont Aiguille, the start of many walks. In winter, cross-country ski to the door.

South
French Alps

BRIANÇON AND LE BRIANÇONNAIS

Once coveted by soldiers because of its strategic position, this region with its blue skies, soaring summits and sunny disposition is today a popular tourist destination. Briançon, its capital, lies at the intersection of four valleys, and just to the west is France's largest national park, Parc National des Écrins. Although it lacks the glitz of some major ski areas, skiers will not be disappointed with its top-quality resorts. In summer the verdant valleys and spectacular lakes are perfect for long walks, and even longer pauses to admire the authentic villages.

A Sentinel City

Briançon has guarded the pass into Italy since pre-Roman times. After the fire of 1692, which destroyed a large part of the town, Louis XIV commissioned Vauban to rebuild the fortifications. The great military engineer set to work reinforcing ramparts and gates, and turned the town into an impenetrable stronghold. In 1700, Vauban came to inspect the progress of the work. He was surprised at the vulnerable position of the town, and decided to extend the project to include a ring of protective forts (Têtes, Dauphin, Randouillet), whose construction was completed in 1730. These were complemented in 1875 by those of Granon, Janus and Gondran, which crown the surrounding mountains. After Waterloo, August–November 1815, an Austrian–Sardinian army tried to besiege the impregnable city. A mere 70 gunners, 500 infantry and General Eberlé successfully defended it against the attack.

The Birth of Skiing

The area has become a major ski centre. The small town of Montgenèvre is said to be the birthplace of French skiing. A young officer garrisoned at Briançon

Highlights

1 Wander around **Briançon** and its ancient fortifications, one of the 12 major Vauban sites (p336)

2 Expert skiers can practise on the black ski runs at **Serre-Chevalier** and **Montgenèvre** (p342 and p344)

3 A botanical extravaganza awaits you from June to September at the **Jardin alpin** in Villar-d'Arêne (p344)

4 Walks in the picturesque **Vallée de la Clarée** (p345)

was so convinced of the usefulness of skis that he funded the equipment for seven of his men in 1901. These alpine troops skied down the slopes in front of a panel of military experts. The demonstration was apparently conclusive, since in 1903, the War Ministry founded a ski school, and ordered all alpine troops to be equipped with skis. This followed, in 1907, with the first International Military Ski Contest, held at Montgenèvre. It consisted of two competitions: the ski jump and a ski race.

Larch forest in the Vallée de la Clarée in autumn

© Gérard Labriet/Photononstop

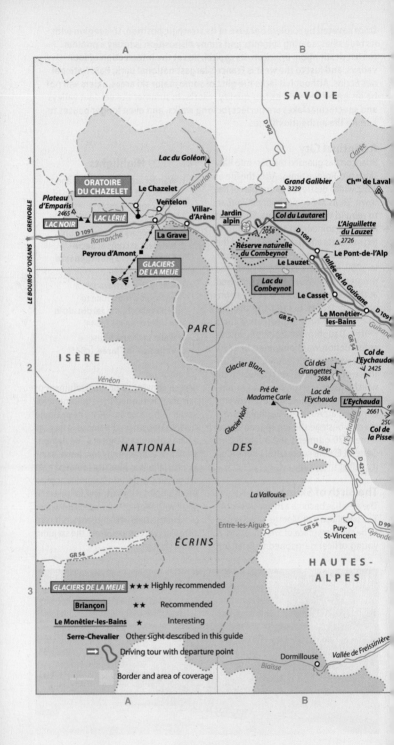

SAVOIE

A   B

Lac du Goléon

Grand Galibier
△ 3229

Ch^ets de Laval

ORATOIRE
DU CHAZELET

Le Chazelet

Ventelon

Villar-
d'Arène

Jardin
alpin

Col du Lautaret

L'Aiguillette
du Lauzet
△ 2726

*Plateau
d'Emparis*
2465

LAC LÉRIÉ

LAC NOIR

La Grave

2058

D 1091

*Réserve naturelle
du Combeynot*

Le Pont-de-l'Alp

Vallée de la Guisane

D 1091

Romanche

D 1091

Peyrou d'Amont

Le Lauzet

GLACIERS
DE LA MEIJE

Lac du
Combeynot

Le Casset

Le Monêtier-
les-Bains

GR 54

Guisane

GRENOBLE

LE BOURG-D'OISANS

D 902

Mauran

Clarée

ISÈRE

Vénéon

Glacier Blanc

Col de
l'Eychauda
↙ 2425

Col des
Grangettes
2684

Lac de
l'Eychauda

L'Eychauda

2661

250

Col de
la Pisse

Glacier Noir

Pré de
Madame Carle

PARC

NATIONAL

DES

L'Eychauda

D 994?

D 421?

ÉCRINS

La Vallouise

Entre-les-Aigues

GR 54

Puy-
St-Vincent

D 99

Gyronde

**HAUTES-
ALPES**

GR 54

GLACIERS DE LA MEIJE	★★★	Highly recommended
Briançon	★★	Recommended
Le Monêtier-les-Bains	★	Interesting
Serre-Chevalier		Other sight described in this guide
⟲		Driving tour with departure point
		Border and area of coverage

Dormillouse

Vallée de Freissinière

Biaisse

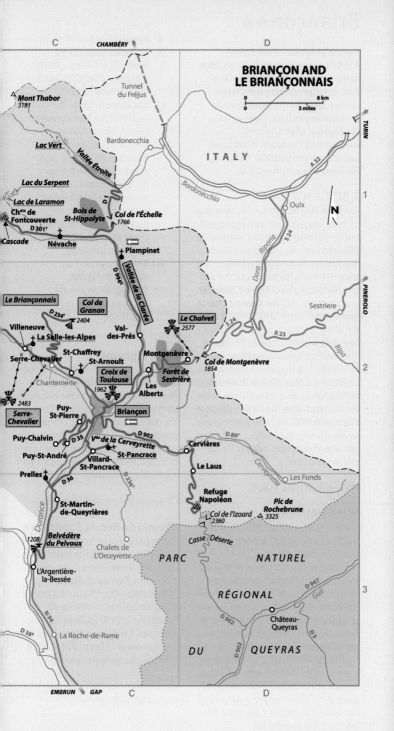

BRIANÇON AND LE BRIANÇONNAIS

0   6 km
0   3 miles

TURIN

ITALY

PINEROLO

△ *Mont Thabor*
3181

Tunnel
du Fréjus

Bardonecchia

Lac Vert

Vallée Étroite

Bardonecchia

A 32

Oulx

S 24

Riparia

N

1

Lac du Serpent

Lac de Laramon

Ch^{ets} de
Fontcouverte

D 301^T

Cascade

*Bois de
St-Hippolyte*

Col de l'Échelle
1766

Névache

D 994^a

Vallée de la Clarée

+ Plampinet

Dora

S 24

Sestriere

Le Briançonnais

*Col de
Granon*
2404

D 234^T

Villeneuve

+ La Salle-les-Alpes

Serre-Chevalier

St-Chaffrey

St-Arnoult

Chantemerle

*Croix de
Toulouse*
1962

Val-
des-Prés

Le Chalvet
2577

Montgenèvre

*Forêt de
Sestrière*

Les
Alberts

Col de Montgenèvre
1854

R 23

Ripa

2

2483

*Serre-
Chevalier*

Puy-
St-Pierre

Briançon

D 902

D 89^T

Cervières

Puy-Chalvin

D 35

V^{lle} de la Cerveyrette

St-Pancrace

Cerveyrette

Les Fonds

Puy-St-André

Villard-
St-Pancrace

Le Laus

Prelles +

D 36

D 236^T

*St-Martin-
de-Queyrières*

*Refuge
Napoléon*

*Pic de
Rochebrune*
△ 3325

1208

*Belvédère
du Pelvoux*

Col de l'Izoard
2360

*L'Argentière-
la-Bessée*

Chalets de
L'Orceyrette

Casse Déserte

PARC

NATUREL

Durance

RÉGIONAL

D 947

Guil

3

N 94

D 38^a

La Roche-de-Rame

D 902

D 902

Château-
Queyras

D 5

DU   QUEYRAS

Briançon★★

Europe's highest city (1 326m/
4 350ft) occupies a strategic position
at the intersection of the Guisane,
Durance, Cerveyrette and Clarée
valleys, close to the Montgenèvre
Pass leading to Italy. This explains
the number of strongholds
surrounding the town. It has been
included in the UNESCO World
Heritage site list since 2008.

A BIT OF HISTORY

The **Ville Haute**, surrounded by a ring
of forts, has retained its steep streets,
but the forbidding setting which once
deterred enemies now draws tourists.
Briançon has had a military skiing school
since 1904 and forms part of the winter-sports complex of **Serre-Chevalier**.
In accordance with the **Grande Charte**
granted to them in 1343, 52 municipalities of the Briançonnais region formed a
free state with Briançon as the capital.
The fortifications were strengthened
in 1590 by the Huguenot commander
Lesdiguières. After a fire destroyed most
of the town in 1692, Louis XIV rebuilt the
fortifications. After Napoleon's defeat at
Waterloo in 1815, Briançon was besieged
by allied forces, but held out until peace
was signed under the Treaty of Paris several months later.

◥◣WALKING TOUR

VILLE HAUTE★★

Allow 2hrs. Park at the Champ de Mars.
Guideposts are placed at principal
buildings and sights.
The walled city is accessible through
four gates. It is divided into four districts
by the intersection of Grand' Rue and
rue Porte-Méane: Quartier du Temple
grouped round the Collégiale Notre-
Dame, Quartier Mercerie, which was
the commercial and administrative district, the residential district of the Grand
Caire, and Quartier de Roche, which was
centred on the various monasteries. Two
steep streets running through the town,
known as *gargouilles*, have a fast-flowing stream in the middle.

▶ **Population:** 11 604.
◔ **Michelin Map:** 334 H3.
▤ **Info:** 1 pl. du Temple, 05100
  Briançon. ℘04 92 21 08 50.
  www.ot-briancon.fr.
◖ **Location:** To get to the
  capital of the Briançonnais
  region, take D 1091 from
  the Col du Lautaret, or N 94
  from Gap. Follow the road
  sign Briançon-Vauban to
  find the old town, entered
  through the Dauphine and
  Pignerol gates. You can
  park on the Champ de Mars.
◔ **Don't Miss:** The Ville Haute
  and its fortifications.
▲▲ **Kids:** Maison du Parc
  national des Écrins.
◕ **Timing:** Allow around
  two hours to visit the
  Ville Haute.

Porte Pignerol

As was usual in the 18C, the gate comprises several separate defences.
The outer gate, rebuilt in the 19C, bears
an inscription recalling the 1815 siege.
The guardhouse, known as "D'Artagnan",
stands in front of the line of defence: the
drawbridge, a gate reinforced by a port-
cullis and another gate decorated with
a splendid frontispiece.

▶ *Follow the road left of the gate.*

Chemin de Ronde Supérieur★

This upper line of defence overlooks the
roofs of the city with the towers of the
Collégiale Notre-Dame rising above.
It skirts the **Fort du Château**
(◕*open May–Oct;* ◥◣*guided tour*
(2hrs) available at the Service du
Patrimoine ℘*04 92 20 29 49, Jul–Aug,*
ask at the Club du Vieux Manoir; ◔*5.50€*
(children under 12 free); ℘*04 92 21 36*
46; www.clubduvieuxmanoir.fr).

▶ *Continue along the road which*
leads down to the town.

From the **porte de la Durance** there is a fine **view** of the river.

Pont-d'Asfeld★
This single-arched bridge spanning the Durance was built in 1729–31 to link the town with the Fort des Trois Têtes.

▷ *Turn onto the r. du Pont-d'Asfeld.*

The "religious" district. Note the restored steeple of the **Chapelle des Pénitents**, badly damaged by fire in 1988.

▷ *Left onto the Grande Gargouille.*

Grande Gargouille (Grand' Rue)★
Going down the street, note the **Fontaine des Soupirs** under an arch on your right and the doorway of no. 64, dating from 1714.
The **Fontaine François I** stands under an archway on a street corner. **Maison Payan**, at no. 37, has a fine Renaissance front decorated with masks.
The **Maison des Têtes** at no. 13 was decorated at the turn of the 20C with figures in regional costume representing the owner's family.

Place d'Armes
Brightly coloured façades and pavement cafés give this former market square, decorated with two **sundials**, a southern atmosphere.
A street to the left leads to the former Cordelier monastery (now the town hall) and to its church, the **Église des Cordeliers**.

▷ *Return to the Grande Gargouille, which leads to the pl. Médecin Gén.-Blanchard.*

👥 Maison du Parc National des Écrins
Pl. Médecin Gén.-Blanchard. ◑Open Jul –Aug daily 10am–noon, 3–7pm; Sept– Jun Mon–Fri 2–6pm. ◑Closed holidays except 14 Jul and 15 Aug. ✍Free. ♿ ✆04 92 21 42 15 or 04 92 21 08 49.
The national park office is based in a converted 18C military hospital.

▷ *Head towards the Porte d'Embrun and turn right.*

Petite-Gargouille (Rue de la Mercerie)★
Narrower than the Grande and less commercial, it is nonetheless charming with its high austere façades, and stairs leading to doors decorated with ironwork.

Collégiale Notre-Dame
Built in the early 18C, it has a remarkable façade flanked by two high towers decorated with sundials. There is a good view of the fortifications, the modern town below, and the Briançon basin and the Montgenèvre Pass beyond.

EXCURSION
Croix de Toulouse★★
▷8.5km/5.3mi. *Allow 1hr.*
⚠ Make sure you are equipped for the gusts of wind.

▷ *Leave Briançon by the rte de Grenoble and turn left onto D 232T.*

The twisting narrow road rises through pine trees in a series of hairpin bends. Carry on along the unsurfaced part and leave the car near a blockhouse.
🚶 It is also possible to reach the Croix de Toulouse on foot *(2hrs return)* from the Fort des Salettes. A path runs along the cliffside offering fine views. The Croix de Toulouse is a rock spur situated at the end of a ridge separating the Guisane and Clarée valleys and towering over Briançon. The **view** extends to the walled town, and to the Guisane and Durance valleys up to the Col du Lautaret.

🚶 HIKES
Fort des Salettes★
🚶 *From the Champ de Mars – 45min return on foot – along the chemin des Salettes.* 👁‍🗨*Guided tours (about 2hrs) by appointment with the Service du Patrimoine* ✆*04 02 20 29 49 or Club du Vieux Manoir* ✆*04 92 13 64 62.* ✍*5€.*
Built in 1707 and remodelled during the 19C, the fort was intended to guard the access to Briançon from Montgenèvre and Italy.

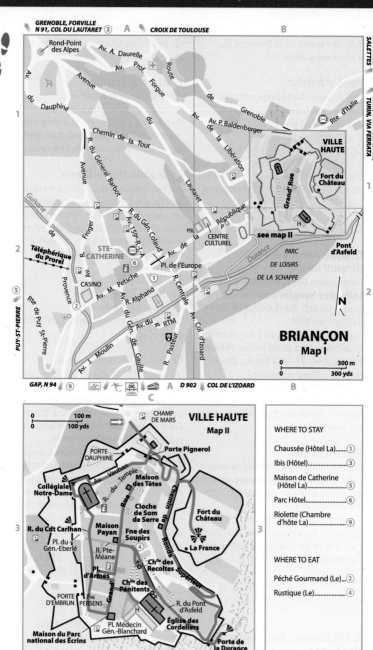

Pont d'Asfeld and Fort des Têtes ★

2hrs there and back. From La porte de la Durance, walk along the chemin du Fort des Têtes, then the pont d'Asfeld and the chemins de Fontchristiane and de la Croix-du-Frêne to the Parc de la Schappe.

The Fort des Têtes is at the centre of Vauban's defence system.

Le Prorel★

🚶 *Start from the cable-car station in the Ste-Catherine district. The journey is in two sections and it is possible to do part of the journey or take a one-way ticket only.* 🚡 *Be prepared to face strong, cold winds blowing continuously at the top.* 🕐 *Open Jul–Aug daily 9.45am–7.30pm, 20min total ride.* 🎫 *11.10€ return, both sections.* 📞 *04 92 25 55 00.*

There are numerous possibilities for fine walks to the surrounding heights offering magnificent **panoramic views**★★.

Chapelle Notre-Dame-des-Neiges

🚶 *15min from the Prorel cable car. Possible to return to Briançon, in around 2hrs 30min, by the marked path going down the alpine pastures.*

Lovely view of the Serre-Chevalier Valley from the chapel (alt. 2 292m/7520ft).

Via Ferrata at the Croix de Toulouse

The path starts between two cafés opposite the Champ de Mars car park *(15min walk)* and ends just east of the Croix de Toulouse.

It is possible to go back along the chemin des Salettes *(4hrs return)*. Ask at the **Bureau des guides**.

🚗 DRIVING TOUR

PUY-CHALVIN AND PUY-ST-PIERRE

Drive of 15 km/9.3mi shown on the regional map (🕐 see p334). Allow 1hr.

▷ *Leave Briançon SW to Puy-St-Pierre.*

The road rises quickly above the the Durance Valley. After **Puy-St-André**, there are views of the Massif de la Condamine and Écrins massifs.

▷ *Park below Puy-Chalvin and continue on foot.*

Puy-Chalvin

The 16C **Chapelle Ste-Lucie** standing in the heart of this hamlet is covered with

murals inside and outside. The front is decorated with scenes from the Passion and representing various saints.

▷ *Return to Puy-St-André and turn left to drive to Puy-St-Pierre along D 335.*

Puy-St-Pierre

Almost completely destroyed during World War II, this hamlet has retained a church offering a splendid **panorama**★★ of Briançon and the Durance Valley. At night, the floodlit church can be seen clearly from the Ste-Catherine district in Briançon.

▷ *Return to Briançon by car, and at the exit of Le Plnet turn left, and park at the end of the road.*

🚶 Around 15min walk to the open-air **Musée des Canaux et des Cultures Anciennes**.

▷ *Continue along D 335 then D 35 to return to Briançon.*

ADDRESSES

🛏 STAY

🍽 **Chambre d'hôte La Riolette** – *38 r. du Mélezin, 05100 Villard-St-Pancrace, 3.5km/2mi of Briançon.* 📞 *04 92 20 58 68. http://gites05.free.fr. Closed 26 Aug–2 Sept.* ♿🅿🚫. *5 rooms, half-board available, restaurant*🍽. Simple rooms in a homely ambience. Dishes use home-grown produce .

🍽 **Hôtel La Maison de Catherine** – *Chemin des Blés, 05100 Puy-St-Pierre, 4.5km/2.8mi from Briançon.* 📞 *04 92 2040 89. www.aubergecatherine.fr. Closed 3–19 Apr, 23 Oct–8 Nov.* 🅿. *Wifi. 11 rooms, half-board available, restaurant*🍽. Friendly family hotel with pretty rooms. Traditional cuisine.

🍽🍽 **Hôtel La Chaussée** – *4 r. Centrale.* 📞 *04 92 21 10 37. www.hotel-de-la-chaussee. com. Closed 26 Apr–24 May, 9 Oct–5 Nov and Mon–Wed lunchtimes. Wifi. 13 rooms* 🍴 *8.50€, half-board available, restaurant* 🍽. Welcoming hotel with cosy rooms. Local cuisine offered.

🍴/EAT

🍴🍴 **Le Péché Gourmand** – *2 rte de Gap. ☎04 92 21 33 21. Closed Easter holidays, 14–21 Sept, Tue lunch, Sun eve and Mon.* 🅿. Sophisticated, authentic cuisine.

🍴🍴🍴 **Le Rustique** – *36 r. du Pont-d'Asfeld ☎04 92 21 00 10. www.restaurantle rustique.com. Closed 2 weeks Nov and Mon–Tue.* ♿. Savoyarde specialities.

🛒 SHOPPING

Le Panier Alpin – *48 Grand' Rue. ☎04 92 20 54 65. www.panieralpin.com. Closed Oct–Nov and Sun–Mon out of season.* Local produce on sale. On the first floor is a *salon de thé*/restaurant.

Market – *ZAC Durance, av. du 4e-RTM (car park).* Every Wednesday morning at the entrance to the Parc de la Schappe.

🍸NIGHTLIFE

Casino Barrière Briançon – *7 av. Maurice-Petsche. ☎04 92 20 66 66. www.lucien barriere.com. Open 11am–late.* Bar, restaurant, slot machines, roulette and diverse entertainment.

🏃ACTIVITIES

Bureau des guides de Briançon – *Parc Chancel. ☎04 92 20 15 73. www.guides-briancon.fr. Open Jul–Aug daily 10am–noon, 3–7pm; Sept–Jun 5–7pm.* Mountain guides for all seasons.

Canoë-Kayak Club Briançon – *R. J.-Moulin. ☎04 92 20 17 56. Closed 30 Oct–1 May.* Various circuits with qualified instructors.

Parc 1326 Briançon – *37 r. Bermont-Bonnet, BP 42. ☎04 92 20 04 04. www.vert-marine.com. Ice skating ⊚6.50€ (4.50€ children under 10).* Leisure park with several outdoor pools, sauna, hammam, ice-skating rink, tennis courts.

Le Briançonnais★★

The geography of the Briançonnais is marked by striking contrasts. In the centre of the area lies Briançon at the intersection of four valleys. During the Middle Ages, the communities of these valleys formed a kind of federation under the terms of the Grande Charte. The large stone-built houses, decorated with arcades and columns, testify to the fact that the inhabitants were relatively well off. The region is well known for its southern mountain climate, clear skies, unmistakable light, and good snow coverage which encouraged the early development of important ski resorts such as Montgenèvre and Serre-Chevalier.

- **Michelin Map:** 77 folds 7, 8 and 18, 189 folds 8 and 9 or 244 folds 42 and 43.
- **Info:** 1 pl. du Temple, 05100 Briançon. ☎04 92 21 08 50. www.ot-briancon.fr.
- **Location:** Great efforts are made to clear the passes of Lautaret and Montgenèvre of snow during the winter, but drivers heading for the Izoard or the valley of the Clarée may encounter snowdrifts in Oct–Jun.
- **Don't Miss:** The valleys of the Guisane and the Clarée, especially the route to Izoard, are spectacular.
- **Timing:** Give yourself two or three days in the Briançonnais.

🚗DRIVING TOURS

VALLÉE DE LA GUISANE★
Drive of 32km/19.9mi. Allow 1hr.

This wide valley, linking the *départements* of Isère and Hautes-Alpes, is well known for cross-country skiing, ski-trekking and alpine skiing at the **Serre-Chevalier** winter-sports complex. The imposing mass of the Meije glaciers comes into view soon after the **Col du Lautaret**. The road goes through a wide valley. On the way down, N 91 skirts the barren slopes of the **Grand Galibier**. The pyramid-shaped Grand Pic de Rochebrune can be seen in the distance, down the valley beyond Briançon. The valley then widens and villages begin to appear. Turn right to rejoin **Le Lauzet**, the highest village of the valley. From here you can appreciate the magnificent jagged peak of Aiguillette du Lauzet.

Le Casset
The elegant steeple rises above the roofs of this hamlet dwarfed by the mighty Glacier du Casset. The Parc national des Écrins information centre is open afternoons in summer (⊘closed Tue).

Le Monêtier-les-Bains★
⌚See Serre-Chevalier p342.
At Villeneuve, turn left after the roundabout and leave the car in the car park.

Villeneuve
⌚See Serre-Chevalier p342.

La Salle-les-Alpes★
⌚See Serre-Chevalier p342.

▷ *Return on D 1091. At Chantemerle, take D 234T, which rises to the Col de Granon.*

Col de Granon★★
🚶 *Leave the car beyond the barracks and climb to a viewing table on the right.*

▷ *Go back along D 234T and detour through the village of St-Chaffrey.*

St-Chaffrey
⌚See Serre-Chevalier p343.

▷ *Take D 1091.*

Briançon★★
⌚See Briançon p336.

BRIANÇON TO THE CHALETS DE LAVAL
Drive of 30 km/18.6mi shown on the regional map (⌚see p335). Allow 2hrs. ⌚See p345.

ROUTE DE MONTGENÈVRE
Drive of 12km/7.4mi shown on the regional map (⌚ see p335). Allow 30min.

▷ *Leave Briançon by the NE.*

The road overlooks the deep valley of the River Durance. Leaving the Clarée Valley road to its right, N 94 rises rapidly, offering glimpses of the Briançon basin and the Clarée Valley. Not far from Montgenèvre, the pine trees give way to the **Sestrière** larch forest.

Montgenèvre
⌚See Montgenèvre p344.

ROUTE DU COL DE L'IZOARD★★
Drive of 27 km/16.8mi shown on the regional map (⌚see p335). Allow 1hr. ⊘The Col de l'Izoard is usually impassable due to snow Oct–Jun.

Briançon★★
⌚See Briançon p336.
The road twists its way above the **Gorges de la Cerveyrette**.

Cervières
Destroyed in 1944 by German bombs, this village was entirely rebuilt on the opposite bank of the river. In an ancient alpine chalet **Maisone Faure-Vincent Dubois** is a collection of household objects which recount 18C village life.

Refuge Napoléon
⌚See Col du Lautaret p344.

Col de l'Izoard★★
⌚See Château Queyras p374.

HAUTE DURANCE
Drive of 17km/10.6mi shown on the regional map (⌚see p335). Allow 1hr.

▷ *Leave Briançon by N 94, then turn left and cross the Durance towards Villard-St-Pancrace.*

Villard-St-Pancrace
Fine houses in typical Briançonnais style. The 15C church has two beautiful south doorways with triple arches resting on

slender columns. The artist's signature (1542 J. Ristolani) is on the left-hand jamb of the right-hand doorway.

▷ *Drive through the village of Villard-St-Pancrace then along D 36 to rejoin N 94.*

Prelles
The **Chapelle St-Jacques** situated in the high street has retained 15C **murals**★ in the chancel.

▷ *Rejoin N 94 and drive S.*

Between Prelles and Queyrières, the road clings to the cliff-side above the gorge through which flows the River Durance.

Belvédère du Pelvoux★
A viewing table placed near the road helps to locate the main summits of the Écrins Massif, which can be seen through the valley of the lower Vallouise.

L'Argentière-la-Bessée
See L'Argentière-la-Bessée p350.

Serre-Chevalier

Situated in the Guisane Valley, Serre-Chevalier is the largest winter- sports complex in the southern Alps. The resort, sheltered by the surrounding mountains, enjoys 300 days of sunshine a year.

SKI AREA
Serre-Chevalier is composed of four resorts: **Briançon**, which is known as **Serre-Chevalier 1200**, **Serre-Chevalier 1350** (Chantemerle-St-Chauffrey), **Serre-Chevalier 1400** (Villeneuve/La Salle-les-Alpes) and **Serre-Chevalier 1500** (Le Monêtier-les-Bains). Traditional houses and churches stand next to modern shops and hotels.
Good facilities for children.
The resort has 68 lifts giving access to 250km/155mi of north-facing runs. In summer, the valley offers outdoor activities.

SIGHTS
Le Monêtier-les-Bains★
Named after a former monastery and its thermal spa dating from Roman times, this village showcases traditional architecture and pretty gardens.
The **Musée d'Art Sacrée** housed in the St-Pierre Chapel has a collection of religious art reassembled from the local villages.

- **Michelin Map:** 334 H3.
- **Info:** Bureau de Cantermerle, BP 20, 05240 Serre-Chevalier. 04 92 24 98 97. www.serre-chevalier.com.
- **Location:** 8.8km/5.5mi NW of Briançon.
- **Don't Miss:** The superb panorama from the Serre-Chevalier summit.
- **Kids:** The resort is part of the "Famille Plus Montagne".

Villeneuve
Installed in the Chapel Ste-Luce, the **Musée Autrefois mon village** exhibits furniture, objects and clothes relating to ancient village life.

La Salle-les-Alpes★
Chapelle St-Barthélemy – The interior of this 15C chapel is decorated with murals recounting the tale of Ste Marthe's exploits.
From the terrace there is a superb **view**★ of the valley.
Église St-Marcellin – Inside the capitals are sculptured with naive motifs, and the 17C wooden altarpiece is framed by a Baroque ensemble with twisted columns and statues of saints.

St-Chaffrey

🐾Follow the road that passes behind the village church and turn right onto the chemin St-Arnoul, which leads to the 11C St-Arnoul Chapel.

🥾 HIKES

Sommet de Serre-Chevalier★★ 🎿

🚶 *Alt. 2 483m/8 146ft. Access from Chantemerle by* **cable car** *(🕐open Jul–mid-Aug daily 9am–5.30pm, last 2 weeks Jun and mid-Aug–mid-Sept 9am–12.30pm, 1.30–5.30pm; 🚠16€ per family, two sections; 📞04 92 24 29 29).* From the upper station, climb to the viewing table: splendid **panorama**★★ of the Oisans Massif, the Aiguilles d'Arves and Pic du Galibier, the Vanoise and the Queyras.

Eychauda Summit★★

🚶 *5hrs on foot. A 1:25 000 map is strongly recommended. The walk starts in Chantemerle and ends in Le Monêtier; return to Chantemerle by coach (information from the tourist office).*
Take the cable car to the top of Serre-Chevalier. From the viewing table, go down towards the Col de Serre-Chevalier and follow tracks to the Eychauda. Walk up to the **Col de la Pisse**.
The path runs across the mountainside, offering lovely **views**★★ and finally reaches the **Col de l'Eychauda**. A wide path leads down to a restaurant. Go to the left, leave the path and take another one to the right *(GR 54, marked in white and red, sometimes in yellow).*
Towards the end of the walk, continue on past a chapel and follow a small road to the left. When you reach a square with a playground, turn right, cross a bridge and walk up rue de la Grande-Turière. As you join the route Nationale, the coach stop is in front of the post office.

Lac du Combeynot★★

🚶 *5hrs return on a path marked in blue. Do not pick flowers, disturb animals or bring dogs into the central zone of the park.*
Start from Les Boussardes, 200m/219yds south of Le Lauzet. On the way up to the lake, you are likely to meet chamois. The Tête de Vallon rises above the lake.

Via Ferrata de l'Aiguillette du Lauzet★

The via ferrata has become very popular, and these high limestone cliffs are the favourite haunt of rock-climbers.

ADDRESSES

🛏 STAY

🛏 **Chambre d'hôte Les Marmottes** – *22 r. du Centre, 05240 St-Chaffrey. 📞04 92 24 11 17. www.chalet-marmottes.com. Wifi. 5 rooms, half-board available, restaurant🛏🛏.* Converted barn houses cosy rooms. Good home cooking.

🛏 **Hôtel Alliey** – *05220 Le Monêtier-les-Bains. 📞04 92 24 40 02. www.alliey.com. Closed end Apr–mid-Jun and early Sept–mid-Dec. Wifi. 22 rooms 🍽15€, half-board available.* Pleasant alpine-style rooms. The chef uses local produce.

🛏 **Hôtel L'Auberge du Choucas** – *17 r. de la Fruitière, 05220 Le Monêtier-les-Bains. 📞04 92 24 42 73. www.aubergedu choucas.com. Closed 3–29 May. 2 Nov–4 Dec. Wifi. 12 rooms 🍽17€, half-board available, restaurant🛏🛏.* Elegant auberge with comfortable rooms. Up-to-date cuisine.

🍴 EAT

🍴 **La Table du Chazal** – *Les Guibertes, 05220 Le Monêtier-les-Bains, 2.5km/1.5mi from Briançon. 📞04 92 24 45 54. Closed 2–25 Jun, Mon and Sept–Jun Tue.* Traditional cuisine revisited.

🛍 SHOPPING

La Maison des Artisans – *3 pl. du Marché, 05220 Le Monêtier-les-Bains. 📞04 92 24 51 11. Open daily 10am–noon, 3–7pm. Closed 1 May–15 Jun, 15 Sept–15 Dec.* Co-op where regional producers sell their creations.

🍷 NIGHTLIFE

Cocoon Café – *C.C. Le Prélong, 05240 La Salle-les-Alpes. 📞04 92 24 92 25. Open 8.30pm–2am. Closed end Apr–mid-Jun and Sept–Nov.* Good choice of tea, coffee, and beer in winter, and cocktails in summer.

Col du Lautaret★★

In spite of its relatively high altitude (2 057m/6 749ft), the Col du Lautaret is the busiest pass of the Dauphiné Alps and the road is now kept clear of snow throughout most of the winter. From July until the beginning of August, wild narcissi, anemones, lilies, gentians, rhododendrons and edelweiss brighten up the rather austere landscape.

SIGHTS

Jardin Alpin★

05480 Villar-d'Arêne. ○*Open Jun–Sept daily 10am–6pm.* ⊜*6€ (children under 12 free; children 12–18 5€).* ℘*04 92 24 41 62.*

A path at the highest point of the pass leads off to the Jardin alpin. This famous garden, created early in the 20C and managed by the University of Grenoble, contains around 2 000 species of wild and medicinal plants from the Balkans, the Himalayas and the Rocky Mountains. From the viewing table, there is a striking **view**★★ of the Meije Massif surrounded by glaciers.

Refuge Napoléon

The Refuge Napoléon is an information and exhibition centre devoted to the local fauna, flora and geology.

- ○ **Michelin Map:** 334 G2.
- **Info:** Access to the Col ℘04 92 21 08 50.
- ◐ **Location:** 28km/17.4mi from Briançon at the gateway to the southern Alps.
- ◎ **Don't Miss:** Panorama of the Massif de la Meije and its glaciers.

🥾 HIKE

Réserve Naturelle du Combeynot★

🥾*At least 7hrs, need to be picked up by car at Casset. Start from the Refuge Napoléon at the Col du Lautaret.*
Suitable only for walkers with stamina and a good head for heights.
◎*Inadvisable to walk when it is raining, or after recent snowfall.*

Head west after crossing N 91, and take the sentier des Crevasses *(marked)*, which enters the Réserve Naturelle du Combeynot. To reach Col d'Arsine take **GR 54** to Casset. After a gentle climb stop to admire the view from the Refuge de l'Alpe de Villar d'Arêne. Take the path heading south. After a halt continue to the Col d'Arsine from where you will be rewarded by a magnificent **view**.

After the Arsine chalets, the path passes the Lac de la Douche, overlooked by the Casset Glacier, then continues along the Vallon du Petit Trabuc to the Guisane Valley (◐*see Le Briançonnais p340*).

Montgenèvre

Situated between Briançon and Italy, Montgenèvre is set among summits approaching 3 000m/9 843ft. This small border town was the birthplace of French skiing: in 1903, the War Ministry founded a school (which later became the École Française de Ski) and ordered all the alpine troops to be suitably equipped. Today the town is one of the biggest skiing centres in the Briançonnais.

- ▶ **Population:** 466.
- ○ **Michelin Map:** 334 I3.
- **Info:** Rte d'Italie, 05100 Montgenèvre. ℘04 92 21 52 52.
- ◐ **Location:** 12.5km/7.8mi NE of Briançon.
- ◎ **Don't Miss:** Panoramas from Le Chalvet and Les Chalmettes.

SKI AREA

Montgenèvre is an important ski resort which forms part of the Franco-Italian **Voie Lactée** (Milky Way) together with the resorts of Clavière, Cesana, San-sicario, Sestrières and Sauze-d'Oulx. The Montgenèvre ski area offers 100km/62.2mi of ski runs and 38 ski lifts. Finally, 17km/10.6mi of marked trails are open to **cross-country skiers**.

In summer, trails welcome hikers and mountain bikers, and the resort offers a swimming pool, tennis, obstacle running, climbing and deltaplaning.

Le Chalvet★★ – *In winter access daily by the Chalvet gondola and chairlift (alt. 2 577m/8 455ft).* ℘04 92 21 91 73.

In summer access on foot: 4hrs 15min there and back. Hike up to the viewing table (check for avalanche hazards). Splendid **panorama**★★ of the Oisans region to the west, including the Bans, the Pointe de Sélé, the Pelvoux, the Barre des Écrins, the Agneaux, the Grande Ruine, the Rateau, the Pic Gaspard and the Meije. The Thabor and Aiguilles d'Arves can be seen to the north while, to the south, the view encompasses the Montgenèvre ski area overlooked by the Janus and Chenaillet summits.

Chalmettes gondola – *Alt. 2 200m/ 7 218ft.* Open 7 Jul–2 Sept. 6€ (children under 12 4€); combined ticket with Aigle chairlift or Observatoire 9€ (children 6€) ℘04 92 21 91 73. **View** to the north of the Chalvet and the Chaberton, to the south of the Anges and the Janus.

🚗 DRIVING TOUR

ROUTE DE MONTGENÈVRE
Drive of 12km/7.4mi shown on the regional map (see p336). See p341.

ADDRESSES

🍴 STAY / EAT

Chambre d'hôte La Maïta – *Les Alberts (Vallée de la Clarée).* ℘04 92 20 29 72. www.gites05.com. Closed mid-Oct–mid-Nov. 6 rooms. Simply furnished rooms, and a gîte in a rustic setting.

Hôtel Valérie – *Pl. de l'Église.* ℘04 92 21 90 02. www.hotel-montgenevre.com. Closed Apr–1 Jul and Sept–20 Dec. 19 rooms, half-board available. Close to the ski lifts, this hotel offers an alpine ambience and comfort.

🏇 ACTIVITIES

Au Pas de l'Âne – *Les Alberts, 05100 Montgenèvre.* ℘04 92 21 30 95. www.ane.fr. Discover the landscape on the back of a donkey.

Vallée de la Clarée★★

This picturesque valley owes its name to the clear waters of the mountain stream running through it. Being unsuitable for ski lifts, the area has retained its lovely villages with houses covered with larch shingles and decorated with sundials. Landscapes change as you drive up the long and narrow valley, fresh and wooded at first, then more open and populated beyond Plampinet, when it suddenly veers to the left.

- 🧭 **Michelin Map:** 334 H/I 2/3.
- ℹ **Info:** La Vachette, 05100 Val-des-Prés. ℘04 92 21 38 19. www.claree.fr.
- 👁 **Don't Miss:** The charming village of Névache.
- 🕐 **Timing:** Allow half a day to do the two drives and a whole day for a hike.

🚗 DRIVING TOURS

BRIANÇON TO THE CHALETS DE LAVAL
Drive of 30km/18.6mi shown on the

regional map (◔ see p335). Allow 2hrs.

Briançon★★ ◔ See p336.

▷ *Leave Briançon by N 94 towards Montgenèvre. At La Vachette turn left onto D 994G.*

Shortly beyond La Vachette, is the confluence of the River Durance and its tributary River Clarée. The road overlooks the valley of the River Durance and the Pont d'Asfeld. The lovely village of **Val-des-Prés** showcases typical houses resting on an arcaded base. The road follows the Clarée through one of the most attractive parts of the valley.

Situated at the top of the village of **Plampinet**, the **Église St-Sébastien** is characteristic of mountain architecture. The **murals**★, circa 1530, are probably the work of an artist from Piedmont.

The **Chapelle Notre-Dame-des-Grâces** has also retained a set of 16C **murals**★.

Névache★
🛈 *Ville Haute, 05100 Névache in season.*
🕑*Open daily 9am–6pm.* ☎*04 92 20 02 20.*
The church of the Ville Haute, **L'Église St-Marcellin et St-Antoine**★ (🛈☎*04 92 21 19 19 or at the tourist office),* was built

---

---

in 1490. Beyond Névache, note the picturesque **Chalets de Fontcouverte et de Laval** (1 857m/6 093ft) and lovely 17C **chapel**.

At the **cascade de Fontcouverte**, the Clarée crosses an important glacial lock. The road ends at the chalets de Laval, at 2 015m/6 611ft. Excursions leave from here, including one to **Mont Thabor**.

LA VALLÉE ÉTROITE★
Drive of 17km/10.6mi shown on the regional map (◔ see p335). Allow 2hrs.

▷ *From Plampinet, turn right and take D 1 towards the Col de l'Échelle.*

After threading through the lower Clarée Valley you see in the distance the **Grande Pic de Rochebrune**.

Col de l'Échelle
At 1 766m/5 794ft, this is the lowest border pass in the western Alps. On the Italian side, the road goes steeply towards the Bardonecchia Valley.

Vallée Étroite★
⚠*The road to the Vallée Étroite can only be taken by private cars – open period contact* ☎*04 92 20 02 20.*
This valley was Italian territory from 1713 until 1947, and still retains Italian signposting. It is covered with larch trees.

HIKE
Lacs de Laramon and du Serpent★
🚶 *3hrs return. 500m/547yds gradient to Lac de Laramon and 700m/766yds to Lac du Serpent.*
From Fontcouverte continue on D 301 to La Fruitière. The path continues past the refuge of Ricou and joins GR 57, which leads to Lac Laramon. A fine **panorama**★★ includes the Massif des Écrins.

Lac Vert★
🚶 *1hr return. Leave the car at the CAF refuge and continue along the road until you reach the signpost Lago Verde.*
The small lake suddenly appears framed by larch trees; its colour is due to the profusion of green algae that it contains and its clear, icy water.

Fertile valleys and jagged peaks, alpine pastures and Mediterranean blue skies; this region is full of contrasts. The landscape, sculpted by rivers and glaciers, is a popular year-round destination, drawing hikers and climbers in the summer, and skiers in the winter. The architecture of the traditional houses adds to the charm of the area. White-water rafting, canyoning, climbing and the vertiginous via ferrata trails provide thrills for devotees of energetic sports.

Natural Treasures

The Parc national des Écrins has a wealth of alpine flowers, with over 1 800 different flora specimens, including 40 that are very rare. The flowering period changes due to the altitude and the microclimates created by the valleys. When the snow melts, spring flowers bloom in the meadows and woodlands. Fields of narcissi, fragile alpine snowbells and the star-shaped *bulbocodium* blossom along the gorges, passes and hillsides.

In the lower valleys, in May and June, there are globe flowers, orchids, marguerites and scabiouses, while at higher altitudes gentians will be blooming.

Thistles and lavender thrive on the hotter drier slopes in summer, but the Martagon lily shies away from direct sunlight, preferring damper, shadier areas. Late summer is the time to hunt down the rare and protected *Chardon Bleu*, or "Queen of the Alps".

The vast array of blooming flowers attracts a host of butterflies and moths. 175 species of butterflies and 244 species of moths have been recorded in the Parc national des Écrins. These flutter and hover around the flowers growing on the alpine pastures, or cluster around puddles or pools, great favourites for the dragon- and damselflies.

Underground is also a source of treasure: silver. In the Fournel Valley deep quartz veins with a base layer of silver were mined from the Middle Ages. At the Fournel mines, which offer guided tours, you can see ancient adits, which were essential for draining water and supplying air, dating from the 10C to the 14C. The silver-mining industry peaked in the 19C, when around 20km/12.4mi of shafts were tunnelled. It stopped completely in 1910. The mining museum at L'Argentière-la-Bessée explains the local mining industry.

Highlights

1 Discover the silver-mining heritage of **L'Argentière-la-Bessée** by visiting the museum and the nearby mines (p350)

2 Take in the air and the views from the top of the **Glacier Blanc** and **Glacier Noir** (p353)

3 Enjoy skiing at the **Puy-St-Vincent** and **Orcières-Merlette** ski resorts (p354 and p357)

4 Walk over the alpine seabed along the **Sentier des Alpages** from Champs-Queyras to Dormillouse (p355)

5 Find yourself face to face with a marmot or chamois in the **Park National des Écrins** (p359)

Roche Rousse lift, Orcières-Merlette

© Jean-Luc Armand/Photononstop

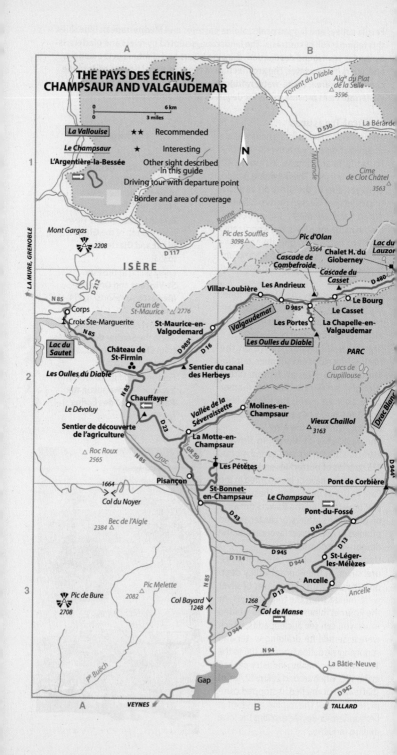

The Pays des Écrins, Champsaur and Valgaudemar

La Vallouise ★★ Recommended
Le Champsaur ★ Interesting
L'Argentière-la-Bessée Other sight described in this guide

Driving tour with departure point

Border and area of coverage

0 ——— 6 km
0 ——— 3 miles

N

ISÈRE

PARC

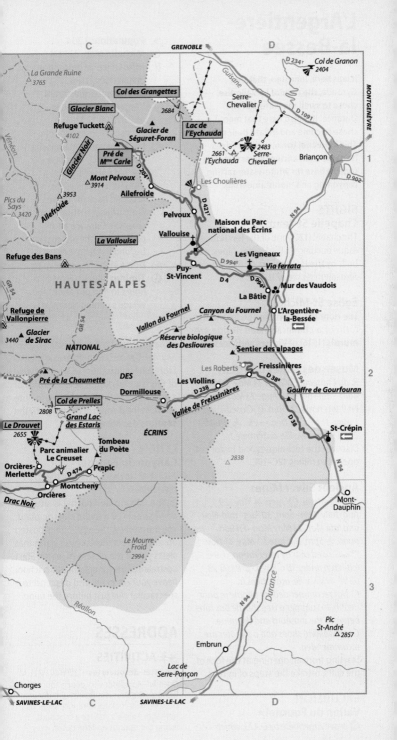

L'Argentière-la-Bessée

It was here, long ago, that the Gyronde, the river of La Vallouise, chose to swell the waters of the Durance. It is also here that men chose to come and inflate their rafts. This industrial town, which derives its name from ancient silver mines, is today a base for white-water rafting, canyoning and mountaineering.

SIGHTS

Chapelle St-Jean

The chapel (12C), one of the few Romanesque buildings in the Hautes-Alpes, was built by the Hospitaliers de St-Jean-de-Jérusalem (⚅ see p71).

Église St-Michel

The door has an ornate 16C lock in the form of a chimera's head. Inside are **murals** (1516) of Virtues and Vices.

Musée des Mines d'Argent

R. du Château. ◷Open 24 May–29 Aug daily 9am–6pm; 30 Aug–23 May Mon–Fri 9am–noon, 2–5pm. ◷Closed 1 Jan, 1 May, 11 Nov, 25 Dec. ⌦2€. ♿ ☏04 92 23 02 94. www.ville-argentiere.fr.
Discover the techniques and history of operating mines 12C–19C.

Ancient Silver Mines

R. du Château. ◷Open 24 May–29 Aug daily 9am–6pm; 30 Aug–mid-Nov and late Mar–23 May Mon–Fri 9am–noon, 2–5pm. ◷Closed 1 May, 11 Nov. ☞Guided tour by reservation. ⌦9€ (children under 18 6.50€). ☏04 92 23 02 94. www.ville-argentiere.fr.
☺Not recommended for people in poor health. In summer a free shuttle bus runs between the museum and the mine. Good walking shoes and a sweater are recommended.
Starting from an opening at the foot of the cliffs, retrace the steps of miners.

EXCURSION

Vallon du Fournel★

◯ Leave Argentière by D 423, which passes through the narrow Vallée du Fournel. ◷Access forbidden in winter. From Eychaillon there is a lovely view of the Fournel gorges and the ruins of a medieval castle. ☞It is a 10-minute return to the bottom of the gorge by the **sentiers des Mineurs**.

🥾 HIKE

Canyon du Fournel

Take D 423 in the direction of the silver mines.
☺The Canyon du Fournel is situated downstream of a hydroelectric plant. You must follow the regulations posted up, and respect the warning alarm that alerts you of the release of water. Start upstream of the mountaineering school (leave your car here), and descend to a spectacular clue just before the mine.

ADDRESSES

🚶 ACTIVITIES

Navettes-découvertes – ☏08 10 00 11 12. Open Jul–Aug. Discovery coach tours through the Pays des Écrins with diverse themes: winemaking heritage, religious heritage, sundials. Ask for a brochure listing the outings and the dates.

▶ **Population:** 2 304.
♿ **Michelin Map:** 334 H4.
ℹ **Info:** Office de promotion du pays des Écrins, 23 r. de la République, 05120 L'Argentière-la-Bessée. ☏0 810 00 11 12. www.paysdesecrins.com.
◖ **Location:** Argentière is the gateway to La Vallouise. The old part of town L'Argentière-Église has retained its rustic charm. From Briançon, turn right, cross the Durance and continue on the left to just beyond the factories.
✦ **Don't Miss:** The silver mine.
🕐 **Timing:** Allow at least two hours to find out about the village's mining heritage.

La Vallouise★★

The valley of an important tributary of the Durance, which penetrates deep into the Écrins Massif, was named Vallouise in the 15C after Louis XI, who was King of France at the time. The lush landscapes are reminiscent of Savoie, but the luminous sky is characteristic of the southern Alps. Large villages and stone-built houses, typical of the Briançonnais region, add to the charm of the area. The ski resort Puy-St-Vincent has contributed to the development of tourism.

A BIT OF HISTORY

The Vaudois – Not to be confused with the Swiss from the Vaud canton, these Vaudois or Waldenses were members of a sect founded in the 12C by a rich merchant from Lyon, **Pierre Valdo** (or de Vaux), who believed that salvation depended on the renunciation of all worldly possessions. As this new sect spread throughout the Lyon region, the Church became worried and the Pope denounced the schismatics, excommunicating Pierre Valdo.

The Vaudois scattered and took refuge in nearby regions, settling in remote valleys where they were forgotten for two centuries. Ultimately, however, the persecution began again in earnest; the campaign led by the Catholics of Grenoble in 1488 inspired merciless crusades against the "heretics", who were rooted out and slaughtered. The valley of the Gyronde, where many of the new sect had settled, was devastated and came to be known as *Val pute*, or "the bad valley". Louis XI brought the grim persecution to an end, and the area was renamed in his honour.

The final blow came after the revocation of the Edict of Nantes: 8 000 soldiers were sent to "cleanse" the Vallouise, Valgaudemar and Champsaur valleys, forcing the Vaudois to take refuge over the border in Piedmont in Italy.

Farmhouses – The three-storey houses still common in Vallouise are a reminder of the region's strong farming traditions.

- **Michelin Map:** 334 G3.
- **Info:** Pl. de l'Église, 05290 Vallouise. ℘04 92 23 36 12. www.paysdesecrins.com.
- **Location:** At l'Argentière, leave N 94, which links Gap and Briançon, cross the Durance and take D 994, which rises up towards the four municipalities in the valley.
- **Don't Miss:** Be sure to see the lovely houses of Vallouise.
- **Timing:** The circuit will take you three hours, and you will want to see the mountains.

The vaulted ground floor would have served as accommodation for the animals; the first floor, often with a larch balcony painted with flowers, provided living quarters for the family; and the top floor, or *baouti* in local dialect, was designed to be used as a grain store.

🚗 DRIVING TOUR

LE CŒUR DES ÉCRINS
38km/23.6mi. Allow 6hrs.

▶ *From L'Argentière, drive along D 994E, following the Vallouise Valley.*

The road crosses the Durance and the Gyronde near their confluence.

Note on the right the ruins of some 14C fortifications improperly called **Mur des Vaudois**, which might equally have been built to keep out marauding mercenaries, or in a vain attempt to halt the spread of the plague.

▶ *Turn right towards Les Vigneaux.*

Les Vigneaux
The outside wall of the 15C **church**, to the right of the traditional porch, is decorated with **murals** on the theme of vices and their punishments.

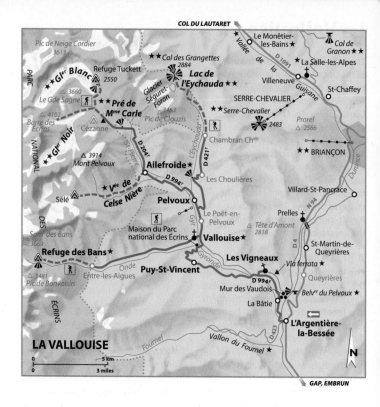

GAP, EMBRUN

Via ferrata des Vigneaux★ – 📷 At the village, on D 4 towards Prelles. Park the car at the entrance to the village. Allow 3hrs there and back, gradient 400m/1 312ft. Facing south, it is the most popular via in the region because it has the most impressive aerial views. From easy to medium difficulty, it comprises two paths: the one on the left (de la Balme) is easier, but does have some spectacular passages. Avoid arriving mid-morning or at the beginning of the afternoon (the queues are long); it is better to get there before 10am or at the end of the day when it is calmer.

▶ At Pont des Vigneaux, follow the road leading to Puy-St-Vincent.

The cliff road rises through a larch forest, opposite the escarpments of the Tête d'Aval and Tête d'Amont.

Puy-St-Vincent
🔗See Puy-St-Vincent p354.

▶ From Puy-St-Vincent, drive down to Vallouise.

👥 The **Maison du Parc national des Écrins** (🕐contact for details; ♿ 𝄐04 92 23 32 31) stands on the left, near the intersection with D 994E. It houses exhibitions relating to the flora, fauna and geology of the area and also to the traditional architecture inside the park. Various activities are designed to make children aware of the environment.

Vallouise★
This picturesque village has retained a wealth of architectural interest, including large houses with arcades.

▶ Continue along D 994T. Beyond Le Poët-en-Pelvoux, turn right towards Les Choulières.

The road climbs in a series of hairpin bends and offers **close-up views★★** of the Grande Sagne, the twin peaks of the Pelvoux, the Pic Sans Nom and the Ailefroide.

▷ *Turn back at Les Choulières and rejoin D 994T.*

Pelvoux

Pelvoux is a family resort with 12 ski runs. A 5km/3.1mi off-piste route is reserved for adept skiers and boarders, as well as cross-country trails.

Ailefroide★

This hamlet, which seems crushed by the Pelvoux foothills, makes an ideal mountaineering base. D 204T follows the bottom of the valley.

Pré de Madame Carle★★

This hollow, once filled by a lake and since planted with larches, is today a stony, avalanche-prone **landscape★★**. Legend has it that the field is named after a local woman whose husband, a rich nobleman, was consumed with anger on returning from his campaigns and learning of her infidelity. He revenged himself by depriving his wife's horse of water before she went on one of her rides. Dying of thirst, the horse plunged into the river and drowned its rider.

▣ HIKES

While the following hikes do not require an understanding of mountaineering techniques, as long as the glaciers are avoided, the correct equipment is essential. Walkers should not attempt the following itineraries without good hiking boots, rainproof clothing and sunglasses.

Glacier Blanc★★

▣ *4hrs return. 676m/ 2 218ft gradient to the refuge. Start from the Pré de Madame Carle, marked path. Average difficulty.*
The path crosses the mountain stream and climbs up the lateral moraine of the glacier, then, leaving the path leading to the Glacier Noir on the left, it winds its way to the Glacier Blanc. Continue to the refuge; difficult sections are fitted with metal ladders.

Glacier Noir★★

▣ *3hrs return. Start from the Pré de Madame Carle. Narrow path not suitable for people prone to vertigo.*
Follow the same itinerary as for the Glacier Blanc, but turn left towards the Glacier Noir and walk alongside it.
It takes its name, the "black glacier", from the thick layer of stones which covers it. The **Pic Coolidge** stands straight ahead with the **Ailefroide** and **Mont Pelvoux** on the left.

Refuge des Bans★

▣ *This walk requires a certain amount of stamina.*
The Sommet des Bans is visible from the car park. There it follows the stream then climbs a rocky escarpment to the refuge; **view★** of the Glacier des Bruyères, the Pic and Glacier de Bonvoisin.

Lac de l'Eychauda★★

From Vallouise, take D 994T towards Ailefroide. At Sarret, turn right at the end, D 421T. Park in the car park. 🡒2hrs 30min for the ascent and 1hr 45min for the descent. Leave early in the morning because the climb on foot, very steep and monotonous, can be extremely tiring in the sun.
You will be rewarded for your efforts by the view of this splendid lake. Held back at 2 514m/8 248ft by a block of granite, it is surrounded by the Crêtes des Grangettes and the Pics de l'Eychauda. To reach the **Séguret-Foran** Glacier, walk along here *(45min)* on the right, towards **Col des Grangettes★★**: from here, there is a magnificent **panorama★★**.

ADDRESSES

⚐ACTIVITIES

Base Écrins Eaux Vives – *Le Rif, 05120 Les Vigneaux. ☎04 92 23 11 94. www.ecrinseauxvives.com.* Various activities: kayaking, rafting, swimming, air boats.

Puy-St-Vincent

The fast-expanding ski resort and the summer walking routes in the nearby Parc national des Écrins have greatly contributed to the development of this village. The Combe de Narreyoux, a lovely pastoral conservation area, also offers fine walks.

PUY-ST-VINCENT 1400

This traditional village comprises the resort's hotel sector.

Chapelle St-Roch – It houses an exhibition: "The Plague and the Penitents".

Point de vue de l'église★ – Go round the Église des Prés for a panorama of the Vallouise, framed by mountains.

Chapelle St-Vincent – *Head in the direction of Puy-St-Vincent 1600 and park at the fork in the road leading to the Vallon de Narreyoux. Climb up on foot.* Open Jul–Aug Thu 3–5pm. 04 92 23 30 66. It is dedicated to the Dominican missionary **St Vincent Ferrier**, who, in 1401, tried to convert the Vaudois (see La Vallouise p351). Beautiful 15C frescoes.

PUY-ST-VINCENT 1600

The modern resort of Puy-St-Vincent 1600, situated above the old village, faces the ski runs on two levels; a gondola gives access to the upper part of the **ski area**. The ski area has good snow cover and there are 30km/18.6mi

- ▶ **Population:** 293.
- **Michelin Map:** 334 G4.
- **Info:** Office du Tourisme de Puy-St-Vincent, Chapelle St-Jacques Les Alberts. 04 92 23 35 80. www.paysdesecrins.com.
- **Location:** Take D 94 from Briançon. At Argentière turn right towards Vallouise; Puy-St-Vincent is just 10km/6.2mi from here.
- **Timing:** Allow two hours to wander around the traditional village.

of cross-country trails. Close to the **Parc National des Écrins** (see Le Valgaudemar p359), Puy-St-Vincent is the departure point for races in summer. Other **summer pursuits** include white-water sports.

ADDRESSES

STAY / EAT

Hôtel La Pendine – Aux Prés. 1km/0.6mi E by D 404. 04 92 23 32 62. www.lapendine.com. Closed 7 Apr–19 Jun, 1 Sept–15 Dec. 25 rooms , restaurant . Perched above the village, this hotel has rustic rooms, some with a balcony. Traditional cuisine.

Vallée de Freissinières★

This small valley, "hanging" 200m/656ft above the River Durance and hidden behind reddish-ochre rocks typical of Mediterranean landscapes, is in fact an alpine U-shaped valley scoured by a glacier, with a flat floor and contrasting sides: the south-facing adret dotted with houses and crops and the north-facing ubac covered with larch and pine woods. The municipality includes 13 hamlets which reflect the importance of sheep-farming in the area.

- **Michelin Map:** 334 H4.
- **Info:** Moulin des Ribes, 05310 Freissinières. 04 92 20 95 49. www.paysdesecrins.com.
- **Location:** The town of St-Crépin is 11km/6.8mi S of Argentière-la-Bessée and 14km/8.7mi N of Guillestre, gateway to the Queyras region.
- **Timing:** Give yourself a half-day to tour the region.

DRIVING TOUR

ST-CRÉPIN TO DORMILLOUSE

Drive of 25km/15.5mi shown on the regional map (see p349). Allow 3hrs.

St-Crépin

This village stands on top of a pink marble rock spur barring the Durance Valley. The D 38 rises along a stony slope dotted with juniper bushes and tufts of lavender. Low stone walls are a reminder of the days when these slopes were covered with crops; the view covers the Guillestre basin and **Mont-Dauphin**★★ standing on top of its promontory.

Gouffre de Gourfouran★

Access is difficult. Leave the car 500m/547yds beyond Le Chambon. Follow the path to a pile of stones. From there, walk across fields to a rocky promontory overlooking the chasm and the Durance Valley.

The River Biaisse joins the Durance Valley via a 100m/328ft-deep gorge. The valley narrows beyond Freissinières. The road leads on through **Les Viollins** (old Protestant church) to the end of the valley, where a number of waterfalls flow together into the Biaisse.

HIKES

Dormillouse★

1hr 30min return. Park in the car park at the end of the valley, or well before the bridge and follow the sentier des cascades. Dormillouse is the only inhabited hamlet in the Parc national des Écrins. In the 16C the Vaudois, after the revocation of the Edict of Nantes, took refuge here.

Sentier des Alpages★

5hrs, no major difficulty; a car is needed for the return journey. Departure from Champs-Queyras, just before the hamlet of Les Aujards. Destination is Dormillouse.

This long hike on the south-facing slope makes use of the old footpaths linking the high-pasture hamlets. The path climbs to Les Garcines then crosses several streams above the tree line. Beyond Les Allibrands, the path overlooks the chalets at La Got before reaching Dormillouse.

Via Ferrata de Freissinières

3hrs return. Contact town hall for details 04 92 20 92 87.

The via ferrata de Freissinières is well equipped and safe for beginners, in spite of some vertiginous sections.

Le Champsaur★

The Champsaur is the area surrounding the upper Drac Valley upriver from Corps. Lying at altitudes often higher than 1 000m/3 281ft it offers spectacular rural landscapes. Several winter-sports resorts have developed in the Champsaur area.

DRIVING TOURS

1 DRAC NOIR★

66km/41mi. Allow 2hrs 30min.
Follow D 13 from Col de Manse.

You drive through pleasant alpine scenery, then the resort of **Ancelle**, before rejoining the bottom of the valley.

- **Michelin Map:** 334 E/F 4.
- **Info:** Maison du Tourisme Champsaur-Valgaudemar, Les Barraques. 04 92 49 09 35. www.champsaur-valgaudemar.com.
- **Location:** Le Champsaur is reached by taking D 1085 (Route Napoléon), between Grenoble and Gap, then D 944.
- **Timing:** It will take you a day to make all excursions, and two days if you want to take the hiking paths.

St-Léger-les-Mélèzes – Refuge des animaux – ⏱Open Tue 2–5pm; school holidays summer and winter Mon–Sat 3–6.30pm; rest of year contact for details. ⏱Closed public holidays. ⊜3€ (children 6–16 1.50€). ☎04 92 21 47 78. A collection of stuffed animals.

Pont-du-Fossé – The old mill in Pont-du-Fossé houses the **Musée des Arts et Traditions du Champsaur**★ (⏱open Jul–Aug Mon–Fri 3–6pm; ⏱closed public holidays; ⊜4€; ☎04 92 51 91 19), displaying objects from traditional rural life.
🛈 Pont-du-Fossé, 05260 St-Jean-St-Nicholas. ☎04 92 55 95 71. www.pont-du-fosse.fr.

▶ In Pont-du-Fossé, turn right onto D 944.

Orcières – On the way to Prapic, note how the houses in Montcheny are adorned with *pétètes*, decorative little heads, unique to the Champsaur.

▶ Continue along D 76, to the resort Orcières-Merlette (⏱opposite).Go E on D 474. Car park uphill from Prapic.

Prapic – This hamlet has retained its heritage of traditional houses; **Musée de la Casse** (⏱open Jun–Oct daily 9am–6pm; ☎04 92 55 62 58) contains a reconstructed interior.

② DRAC BLANC★★
12km/7.4mi from Pont du Fossé to Auberts.

▶ From Pont-de-Corbière turn left (D 944A) to Champoléon.
The Vallée du Drac Blanc is wild.

Walk to the Pré de la Chaumette refuge★ – 🥾 3hrs return via the Tour du Vieux Chaillol GR trail.

Start from the car park, near Les Auberts bridge. Follow the footpath starting just before the second bridge.

The path follows the valley before reaching the Pré de la Chaumette refuge.

③ THE LOWER DRAC
60km/37.3mi. Allow 2hrs.

Between Pont-du-Fossé and St-Bonnet (via D 43, D 945 and D 215), the road follows the Drac.
St-Bonnet-en-Champsaur★ – This small town has retained its medieval appearance and narrow streets.

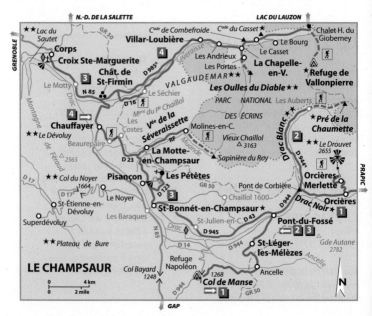

▷ *From St-Bonnet, follow D 23 towards Bénévent, turn right at D 123, then left at the signpost Cimetière.*

A small road leads to a chapel and the Trois Croix viewpoint offering a **panorama**★ of the St-Bonnet Valley.

▷ *Continue until you reach L'Auberie.*

Chapelle des Pétètes – The name means "dolls' chapel". The façade has small recesses with naive statuettes.

Pisançon – Ferme de l'histoire – 🕐*Open Jul–Aug 2–6pm; rest of year contact for details.* 🎫*3€ (children 2€).* 📞*04 92 49 02 30.* The past of Champsaur is explained in a fun way.

La Motte-en-Champsaur – Picturesque village with fine stone houses.

▷ *Take the forest road leading to Molines-en-Champsaur.*

Vallée de la Séveraissette – The road follows the valley to Molines.

▷ *Return to La Motte-en-Champsaur and rejoin D23. At Beaurepaire, between Les Costes and Chauffayer, park on the side by the traffic lights.*

Sentier de découverte de l'agriculture – ⬤⬤*2.5km/1.5mi. The trail has information panels.* Located between Chauffayer and Le Motty is the Séveraisse Valley and the ruins of the **Château de St-Firmin**. At the **Croix Ste-Marguerite** there is a view of the Sautet lake and the Obiou summit.

Corps – 👍*See Le Dévoluy p392.*

ADDRESSES

🍽 STAY

◎◎ **Hôtel La Crémaillère** – *4 rte de la Motte, 05500 St-Bonnet-en-Champsaur.* 📞*04 92 50 00 60. www.cremaillere.eu.* 🅿. *Wifi. 23 rooms* ◻, *restaurant* ◎. This chalet-style inn sits in a pleasant garden. The renovated rooms are best. Local cooking.

Orcières-Merlette

Orcières-Merlette occupies a promontory overlooking the village of Orcières at the heart of the Champsaur Valley, in an austere high-mountain setting. Created in 1962 at an altitude of 1 860m/6 102ft, it has become one of the best ski resorts of the Hautes-Alpes. There is an outdoor leisure centre along the Drac for summer holidaying.

- 📍 **Michelin Map:** 334 F4.
- ℹ **Info:** 05170 Orcières. 📞04 92 55 89 89. www.orcieres.com.
- ▷ **Location:** 5km/3.1mi from Orcières.
- 👁 **Don't Miss:** The cable-car ride to Drouvet in summer.
- 👪 **Kids:** The resort has the designation "Famille Plus Montagne".
- 🕐 **Timing:** You need half a day to see everything.

SKI AREA

Spread over three areas, the resort has two lifts, at Drouvet and Roche Rousse, 52 alpine trails and a snowpark. At 1 350m/4 429ft, the cross-country ski area of Orcières offers 20km/12.4mi of trails. When snow cover is good, cross-country skiers can follow 100km/62.2mi of tracks along the Champsaur promontory. As well as ski-skating trails, there are also 25km/15.5mi of groomed trails for walking in the Roche Rousse area.

Station 1850

Orcières has activities for all the family. 👪**Le Palais des sports** – This futuristic building houses three swimming pools, an ice-skating rink, a fitness club and a bowling alley. There are outdoor activities as well – downhill mountain-bike trails from Drouvet, and several hikes.

Le Drouvet★★
Access via the cable car in two sections.
🕙*Open Dec–Apr 9am–4.30pm; school holidays 9am–5pm.* 💶*9€ (children under 6 7€).* ℘*04 92 55 89 89. www.orcieres.com.*
From the viewing table there is a remarkable **panorama**★★ of the Olan, the Sirac and Ailefroide to the north, the Vieux Chaillol, the Pic de Bure and Gapeçais to the west, the Grande Autane to the south, and the Grand Pinier and the Font Sancte to the east.

🚶 HIKE
Grand Lac des Estaris★
🔺*Alt. 2 558m/8 392ft.*
1hr walk from the Drouvet summit.
Beautiful lake that is worth taking the time to walk around. Experienced walk-

ers can reach the Col de Freissinières, or **Col des Prelles**★★ in 45 minutes for a fine view★★ of the Massif de Pelvoux.

ADDRESSES

🏃 ACTIVITIES

👥 **Base de loisirs** – *"Le Château", 05170 Orcières.* ℘*04 92 55 76 67. www.labelle montagne.com. Open Jul–Aug 7am–10pm.* Vast range of activities: quad-biking, riding, archery, minigolf, go-karting, paint-balling, an adventure park, and also watersports.

Roll'Air Cable – *Sommet du Drouvet.* ℘*06 84 44 88 10. www.latyrolienne.fr. Open end Jun–end Aug and mid-Dec–mid-Apr 9am–4pm; Sept–Oct by reservation only. Summer 29.50€; winter 38€.* The longest Tyrolienne (zip line) in Europe: about 2km/1.2mi of cable.

Le Valgaudemar★★

The Séveraisse, a clear mountain stream, penetrates deep into the Écrins Massif; this is the reason why the Valgaudemar Valley is such a popular mountaineering area. The scenery changes dramatically at Villar-Loubière.
Downstream, the deep pleasant valley is covered with pastures and dotted with picturesque villages; upstream, the valley becomes almost oppressively narrow.

- ♿ **Michelin Map:** 334 E/F4.
- 🛈 **Info:** Pont-des-Richards, 05800 St-Firmin. ℘04 92 55 23 21. www.champsaur-valgaudemar.com.
- ▶ **Location:** At 30km/18.6mi N of Gap, turn E on D 985A to climb into the Valley of the Séveraisse.

🚗 DRIVING TOUR

THE UPPER SÉVERAISSE★★
Drive of 27km/16.8mi from the Route Napoléon on Le Champsaur map, ④ (▶ see p356).

▶ *Leave N 85 3km/1.9mi N of Chauffayer, on the first road right after the bridge spanning the Séveraisse, to the sign marked Le Pont-des-Richards.*

Sentier du Canal des Herbeys
🔺*1hr return. Start from Séchier.*
You stroll along the sides of this 18C canal. At Ubac village, cross over the Séveraisse and turn right.
Villar-Loubière – The village clinging to the rockside forms a picturesque setting with the heights of the Écrins Massif in the background. Villar-Loubière is also the site of Valgaudemar's last **working mill**, dating back to 1838, the thatched mill was restored in 1979. The Aiguille du Midi des **Andrieux** deprives it of

any sun for **100 days every year**, from November to February.

La Chapelle-en-Valgaudemar – This mountaineering centre is ideally located beneath the Pic d'Olan, where there is the **Maison du Parc national des Écrins**.

Les Oulles du Diable★★ – From La Chapelle it is easy to walk to **Les Portes**, *(1hr return)*; fine **view★** of the Pic d'Olan and of the Cime du Vallon. Beyond the hamlet, a path leads down to the bridge spanning the **Oulles du Diable★★**, a series of potholes carved by erosion.

Bridge of the Oulles du Diable

© Jean-Luc Armand/Photononstop

▶ *Return on D 480 and continue in the direction of Casset.*

After the **cascade de Combefroide** *(on the right)*, you arrive at an untamed part of the valley. Continue to **Casset**, where there is an ancient farmhouse which has preserved its thatched roof, and then to the **cascade du Casset★**. Past the junction leading to **Bourg** hamlet, the road, which is very steep and twisting, climbs up the Gioberney Valley. It leads to the **Chalet Hôtel du Gioberney** (alt. 1 700m/5 577ft), situated in a beautiful mountain **cirque★★**.

▶ *Return to St-Firmin on D 985A.*

Look out for the Romanesque **St-Maurice-en-Valgodemard** church.

Parc National des Écrins

Created in 1973, this is France's largest national park, and has been crowned the Parc Européen de la Haute Montagne by the European Council. This high-mountain region includes numerous peaks above 3 000m/9 843ft, including Meije, Pelvoux and Agneaux and the highest of them all, the Barre des Écrins, which reaches 4 102m/13 458ft. Within the park there are glaciers covering an area of 12 000ha/29 652 acres, such as the Glacier Blanc on the north side of the Barre des Écrins, and lakes such as Lac Lauvitel and Lac de l'Eychauda.

The Massif du Pelvoux, situated at the heart of the park, offers marvellous possibilities for mountain climbing, whereas the diverging Vénéon, Valgaudemar and Vallouise valleys are ideal for hiking. More than 1 000km/622mi of footpaths are available inside the park, including the GR 54 "Tour de l'Oisans" and the "Tour du Vieux Chaillol", which leads through Champsaur.

A combination of alpine and Mediterranean climates encourages a varied flora. 1 800 different species of flowering plants grow here. This habitat also supports 7 000 chamois as well as golden eagles. More than 50 000 sheep spend the summer in the area; in October, their trek down from the pastures is marked by fairs in the villages of La Chapelle-en-Valgaudemar and St-Bonnet.

The High-Pasture Lookout

Marmots, who live in colonies above 1 000m/3 281ft, have evolved an unusually exact warning system: one single cry announces the presence of a bird of prey, whereas a series of cries warns of a fox or a dog. Marmots lead a strictly regulated family life. The colony, which forms the social unit, includes several families living in burrows. At the end of the mating season, which lasts from mid-April to mid-May, three to four baby marmots are born to every pair. The species is protected throughout the alpine nature parks and reserves.

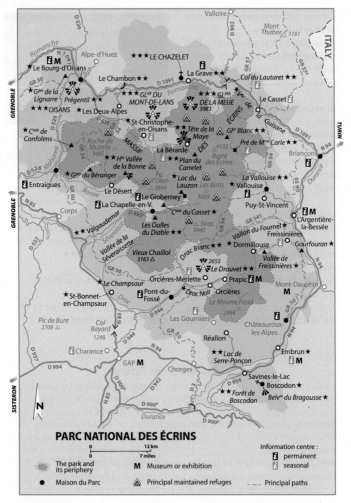

PARC NATIONAL DES ÉCRINS

| | 12 km |
| 0 | 7 miles |

The park and its periphery

● Maison du Parc

M Museum or exhibition

🏔 Principal maintained refuges

Information centre :
🅸 permanent
🅸 seasonal

--- Principal paths

🚶 HIKES

Lac du Lauzon★

🏔 *2hrs 30min return on foot; start upstream of the Chalet Hôtel du Gioberney, on the left.*

From the lake there is a splendid **view**★★ of the glacial cirque.

Refuge de Vallonpierre★

🏔 *Walkers wishing to continue beyond the refuge will need experience of crossing névés and scree.*

The relatively easy walk offers a good view of the **Glacier de Sirac**. The "Sentier du Ministre" joins GR 54, which in turn leads to the Lac de Vallon-

pierre; the pleasant refuge on the shore is a relaxing place to stop in summer.

ADDRESSES

🛏 STAY

😊😊 **Ferme-auberge Les Clarines** – *Entrepierres, 05800 St-Jacques-en-Valgaudemar. 1 km/0.6mi S of St-Jacques-en-Valgaudemar. ✆04 92 55 20 31. www. auberge-clarines.com. � ♿ 🅿. 6 rooms 😊.* This farm-inn offers accommodation and meals. You can choose from a studio, a gîte for six people, and simple, clean rooms with a mountain view.

The Queyras is an isolated, unspoiled region between the Durance Valley and the Italian border. Sheltered to the west by the jagged peaks of the Écrins, and a wall of peaks to the east, this is said to be the route Hannibal took with his elephants when he crossed the Alps. Today the stunning landscape, centred around the Guil Valley, enchants visitors with its woodland glades, steep gorges and airy summits. The region has two fine examples of military architecture: the picture-postcard Château-Queyras, and the UNESCO-listed Mont-Dauphin. Aside from honey, woodcrafts and sundials, the landscape is criss-crossed with walking trails, and has an outstanding ski resort at Vars.

Sundials

Sundials crop up everywhere in the Queyras. They first appeared in the late Middle Ages, and were originally influenced by the Italian school of art. Apart from the sunny climate, there are three main reasons for the presence of sundials here: for telling the time, as a decorative feature, and in memory of an occasion or a person. Due to the development of the watch and clock industry in the 19C, interest in sundials declined, but over the last 20 years they have become popular again and many have been restored.

Sundials fixed to the walls of houses and churches have beautiful panels painted with folk art, representing landscapes, birds and animals, and are inscribed with a motto or a proverb. In the 19C, a famous Italian sundial painter called Zarbula travelled from village to village carrying all his materials on the back of a donkey. Many of his sundials can still be seen today. A fine example can be found on a southwest-facing wall in St-Véran. The panel depicts an imperial eagle rather than the Republican *coq*, and the motto reads "The sun rules me, you are determined by the shadow."

Fustes

Another regional architectural feature is the "fuste", a steep-roofed house, built in the 17C to 18C, with a tall, multi-terraced wooden attic. The ground floor has thick stone walls, while the upper floor (fuste) is made of stacked larch logs. At St-Véran there are several fine fuste houses, one of which, dating from 1641, has been converted into a museum open to visitors. Inside, traditional ancient Queyras life is reconstructed. On the ground floor it shows how people and animals slept

Highlights

1   The hike to the summit of the **Pain de Sucre** and the breathtaking panorama (p367)

2   The colourful **markets** at Guillestre on Mondays and Abriès on Wednesdays (p368 and p377)

3   Imagine life inside the garrison town of the UNESCO-listed **Mont-Dauphin** (p370)

4   Cross over the drawbridge and step into the **Château-Queyras**; discover how the Alps were formed at the **Espace Géologique** (p374)

5   Time stands still at the pretty high-altitude village of **St-Véran** (p375)

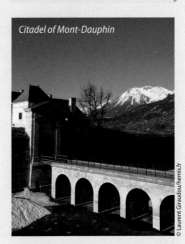
Citadel of Mont-Dauphin

© Laurent Giraudou/hemis.fr

together for warmth; upstairs there are workshops, and the "fuste" on the top floor, which was used to store and dry hay and grain.

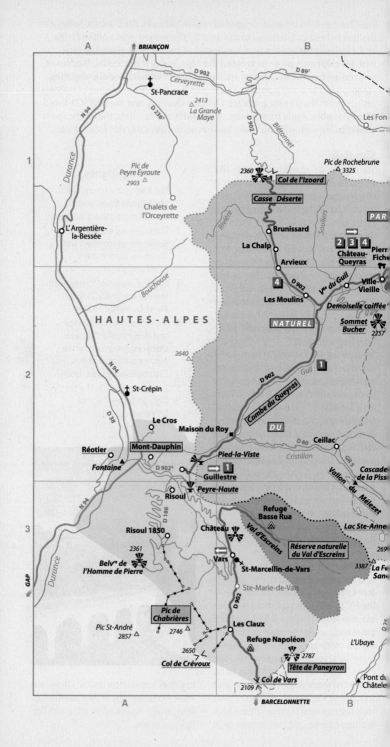

BRIANÇON

St-Pancrace

Cerveyrette

D 902

D 236

2413
La Grande
Maye

D 89'

Les Fon

Pic de
Peyre Eyraute
2903

Chalets de
l'Orceyrette

L'Argentière-
la-Bessée

Durance

N 94

Bouchouse

HAUTES-ALPES

2640

2360
Col de l'Izoard

Casse Déserte

Brunissard

Pic de Rochebrune
3325

Souliers

PAR

2 3 4
Château-
Queyras

Pierr
Fiche

La Chalp

Arvieux

4
D 902

Les Moulins

Vn du Guil

Ville-
Vieille

Demoiselle coiffée

NATUREL

Sommet
Bucher
2257

D 902

Guil

1

Combe du Queyras

St-Crépin

D 38

Le Cros

Maison du Roy

DU

D 60

Ceillac

Cristillan

GR 5

Vallon du Mélezet

Cascade
de la Piss

Réotier

Mont-Dauphin

D 902h

Pied-la-Viste

1

Guillestre

Fontaine

Risoul

Peyre-Haute

Refuge
Basse Rua

Val d'Escreins

Lac Ste-Anne

Risoul 1850

2361

Belvº de
l'Homme de Pierre

Château

Réserve naturelle
du Val d'Escreins

269

Vars

St-Marcellin-de-Vars

3387
La Fe
Sane

GAP

Durance

N 94

Ste-Marie-de-Vars

D 902

Pic St-André
2857

2746

Pic de
Chabrières

Les Claux

Refuge Napoléon

L'Ubaye

D 2

2650

Col de Crévoux

2787

Tête de Paneyron

Col de Vars
2109

BARCELONNETTE

Pont du
Châtel

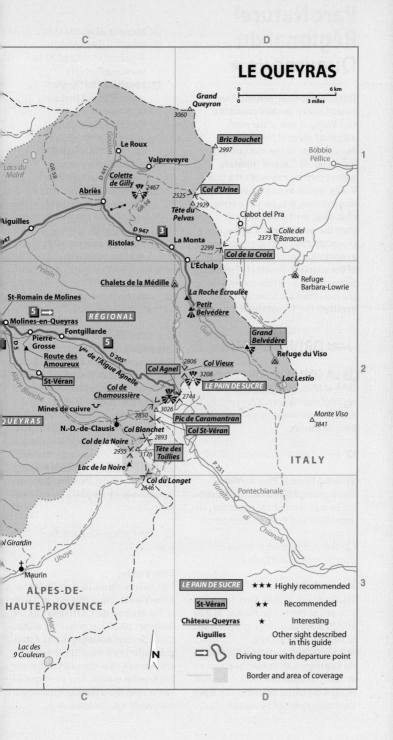

LE QUEYRAS

0 — 6 km
0 — 3 miles

Grand Queyron △ 3060

Bric Bouchet △ 2997

Bòbbio Pèllice

Le Roux

Valpreveyre

Goulon

GR 58

Lacs du Malrif

D 441

Colette de Gilly ☼ 2467

Abriès

Col d'Urine △ 2525
△ 2929

Tête du Pelvas

Ciabot del Pra

Pèllice

Colle del Baracun △ 2373

Aiguilles

947

GR 58

D 947 [3]

Ristolas

La Monta

L'Échalp

L'Échalp △ 2299

Col de la Croix

Refuge Barbara-Lowrie ▲

Pelvin

Chalets de la Médille ⌂

La Roche Écroulée

Petit Belvédère ▲

St-Romain de Molines

RÉGIONAL

[5] ⇨

Molines-en-Queyras

Fontgillarde

Guil

Grand Belvédère ▲

Refuge du Viso ▲

Pierre-Grosse

[5]

Vte de l'Aigue Agnelle

D 205^T

Route des Amoureux

D 5

Col Agnel

Col Vieux △ 2806
☼ 3208

Lac Lestio

St-Véran

Aigue Blanche

Col de Chamoussière

L ☼ △ 2744
△ 3026

LE PAIN DE SUCRE

Mines de cuivre

2850 ✕

Pic de Caramantran

Monte Viso △ 3841

QUEYRAS

N.-D.-de-Clausis ✝

Col Blanchet ✕ 2893

Col St-Véran

Col de la Noire

2955 ✕

Tête des Toillies △ 3176

Lac de la Noire ▲

ITALY

Col du Longet ✕ 2646

P 251

Pontechianale

Varaita di Chianale

ol Girardin

Ubaye

Maurin ✝

ALPES-DE-HAUTE-PROVENCE

Mary

Lac des 9 Couleurs

N

LE PAIN DE SUCRE ★★★ Highly recommended

St-Véran ★★ Recommended

Château-Queyras ★ Interesting

Aiguilles — Other sight described in this guide

⇨⬭ — Driving tour with departure point

▬▬ — Border and area of coverage

C | D

Parc Naturel Régional du Queyras★★★

This geographical, historical and human entity, centred round the Guil Valley, is one of the most authentic areas of the southern Alps, and one of the most culturally independent. Several tributary valleys converge towards the Guil Valley, which, as one follows it downstream, is in turn imposing, charming, restful and austere. Even the weather has a distinctive character: the Queyras region has a reputation for blue skies and one of the sunniest climates in France, tempered by a certain coolness in the mountain air. Snow cover is excellent for six months of the year.

- **Michelin Map:** 334 I/J 4/5.
- **Info:** Pl. J.-Léa, 05470 Aiguilles. &04 92 46 70 34. www.aiguilles.com.
- **Location:** The Queyras region is an isolated area, accessible all year via the Combe de Queyras, and in summer by Col de l'Izoard and Col Agnel.
- **Kids:** There are several nature walks in the Parc régional. Older children can learn rock-climbing at "La Roche Écroulée" near l'Échalp.
- **Timing:** Allow two days or a long weekend.

🚗 DRIVING TOURS

1 LA COMBE DU QUEYRAS★★
Drive of 17km/10.6mi shown on the regional map (see p362). Allow 1hr, not including drive to Sommet-Bucher.

▶ *From Guillestre, drive along D 902.*

Viewing Table at Pied-la-Viste
The imposing **Pelvoux-Écrins Massif**★ can be seen through the gap of the Durance Valley and Vallouise depression.

▶ *The road becomes narrower and goes through several tunnels.*

Maison du Roy
Tradition has it that King Louis XIII stopped at this inn on his way to Italy in 1629. A painting hanging inside is said to be a gift from the king.
At 300m/328yds away from the **Maison du Roy** there is a fossilised beach found vertically on a wall overlooking the road. At the time of the dinosaurs this was a sand bank caressed by waves!

▶ *Leave the rte de Ceillac (see p372) and continue along D902.*

The road enters the **Combe du Queyras**★★, a long steep gorge. The narrowest part lies between La Chapelue and L'Ange Gardien. Beyond this point, the road offers a fine view of the splendid Château-Queyras.

Château-Queyras
see Château-Queyras p373.

2 ROUTE DE ST-VÉRAN★★
Drive of 15km/9.3mi shown on the regional map (see p362). Allow 30min.

▶ *From Château-Queyras, drive E along D 947.*

Ville-Vieille
This village forms part of **Château-Ville-Vieille**. Inevitably you will stop at the **Maison de l'Artisanat** (see Addresses, p368). Just before the village, the **Sentier écologique des Astragales** offers a pleasant *(1hr 30min)* walk. There are views of the valley and of the Bric Bouchet summit. Rare plant species can be seen along the way, in particular milk-vetch and Ethiopian sage.

Le Queyras

Unusual relief – The Queyras region is divided into two distinct areas. To the east, the Haut Queyras consists of folded sedimentary schist – made from deposits which once formed a **prehistoric seabed** – mixed with layers of volcanic rocks; these were shaped into jagged summits and ridges overlooking rounded glacial valleys. The limestone that predominates in the Bas Queyras to the west produced impressive but austere landscapes like those of the Casse Déserte near Col de l'Izoard or Combe du Queyras.

A land apart – The natural seclusion of the mountains has always encouraged a sense of independence from the world beyond; the medieval confederation of seven towns in the Aiguilles canton preserved a degree of autonomy until the 18C. During the 19C the Queyras remained almost untouched by the Industrial Revolution; the region's first surfaced road, between Guillestre and Château-Queyras, was built only in 1856.

Arts and crafts – The Queyras region is rich in folk art, comprising mainly objects made by peasants during long evenings. Pieces of **furniture** made of larch wood or arolla pine are particularly famous; they include box beds, wedding chests, spinning-wheels and cots, all decorated with carved motifs.

There are many sundials in this exceptionally sunny region. They were the work of travelling artists, often natives of Italy, and are decorated with mottos which express popular wisdom. There are also numerous wooden **fountains**, with a rectangular basin and a circular bowl.

Croix de la Passion (or Croix des Outrages) – Queyras is famous for these crosses, usually found in front of churches, sometimes inside; fine examples of this devotional art can be seen at St-Véran and Ceillac.

The Tour du Procureur – Several villages in the Haut Queyras region have a characteristic campanile, dating from the Middle Ages and built of larch logs and crowned with a bell, known as the Tour du Procureur.

Parc naturel régional du Queyras – By the mid-20C isolation and depopulation had considerably slowed down the region's economy so that, in the 1960s, it was decided to modernise traditional agriculture, to develop handicrafts and above all tourism. The **Parc naturel régional du Queyras** was created in 1977 to provide information on the area, mark hiking routes and maintain refuges, as well as preserving the landscape and endangered plant and animal species. The **flora** displays a great variety of Mediterranean and alpine species, and the **fauna** includes the usual mountain-dwellers such as the chamois and black grouse as well as rarer animals like the black salamander.

The **mouflon**, a wild sheep which can weigh up to 50kg/110pounds, is another example of a successful newcomer; the 12 animals brought from Corsica in 1973 increased to over 300 in a little over 20 years. Their splendid horns grow during their first year and, by the third year, curve right round to their neck. In winter, the search for food brings mouflon down to the villages, where hay is often provided for them. These are timid animals; be careful not to alarm them.

The **bouquetin** (ibex) disappeared from the Alps during the 17C. At the beginning of the 19C, there were fewer than 100 in the Grand Paradisio Massif on the Italian side. Reintroduction in the Parc naturel régional du Queyras took place in 1995 when 12 animals were transferred from La Vanoise. The animals are given electronic chips to make it possible to locate them.

The road rises along the slope, and just beyond a hairpin bend, it enters the Aigue Blanche Valley. At the exit of the Prats Ravine, note the **Demoiselles coiffées** (👣 *see p385*), a strange rock formation.

Molines-en-Queyras★
👣 *See Excursion, opposite.*

The road continues to climb through a pastoral landscape, and the houses of St-Véran suddenly appear, scattered over the sunny side of the valley.

St-Véran★★
👣 *See St-Véran p375.*

③ LE HAUT QUEYRAS
CHÂTEAU-QUEYRAS TO THE MONTE VISO BELVEDERE
Drive of 30km/18.6mi shown on the regional map (👣see p362). Allow 1hr.

This itinerary takes you through the most open and pleasant part of the Guil Valley, between Château-Queyras and Abriès, and offers views of Monte Viso.

▶ *From Château-Queyras, follow D 947 towards Abriès.*

The road runs up the Guil Valley, densely forested with larches and pines on the north-facing side. There is a clear **view** ahead towards the soaring Bric Bouchet (alt. 3 216m/10 551ft).

Aiguilles★
Aiguilles is the liveliest resort of the Queyras region. A large number of local inhabitants emigrated to South America at the beginning of the 19C; most of them returned, fortune made, at the end of the century (👣see Barcelonnette box, p399).

Abriès
👣 *See Abriès p377.*

▶ *Continue along D 947.*

The Guil Valley changes its course and becomes more austere. After **La Monta** stands the Grande Aiguillette and its glaciers. To the right the aptly named La Taillante ridge is remarkable for its distinctive sharp tapered peak.

L'Échalp
This is the last village in the valley and the starting point for excursions to the Monte Viso belvederes. 🥾 The walk to the **Chalets de la Médille**★ *(1hr 30min return on foot)* affords a fine view of Monte Viso; take the first bridge over the Guil upstream of L'Échalp and follow the path which rises towards the charming Plateau de la Médille.
The road continues up the Guil Valley, passing near a huge rock, known as 🧗🧗 **"La Roche écroulée"**, used for rock-climbing practice (🕐 *open Jun–Sept; ☎04 92 46 72 26*). The road is closed to traffic at the point where it crosses the Guil. Continue on foot, in order to get a close-up view of the rocky ridge of Monte Viso.

Petit Belvédère du Monte Viso
Sentier écologique du Pré Michel★
🚶 *45min walk and about 1hr for a halt.*
The information centre near the car park (🕐*open in season*) sells a booklet, which is also available in local tourist offices. In July you can admire an array of wild plants such as the martagon lily, *Delphinium dubium* and *Fritillaria*. 👣*For the Grand Belvédère, see* Hikes.

④ ARVIEUX VALLEY
Drive of 10km/6.2mi shown on the regional map (👣see p362). Allow 1hr.

▶ *2km/1.2mi beyond Château-Queyras, turn right onto D 902 to the Col de l'Izoard.*

Arvieux
In the hamlet of **Les Moulins**, below Arvieux *(left after 1km/0.6mi on D 902)*, you can visit the restored mill (🕐*open Jul–Aug Mon–Sat 2–6pm; 👛2€ (children under 16 free); ☎04 92 46 88 20*).
This village, and the surrounding hamlets, are interesting for their houses cov-

ered in larch shingles. The 16C church has preserved its 11C door and porch, and has naive figure carvings.

👥 La Chalp

Situated above Arvieux, this village has been a toy-making centre since the 1920s, set up to give inhabitants a trade to follow in winter; the wooden toys are decorated by hand. The centre offers a museum, demonstrations and a shop where you can purchase local products.
🏠 ℘04 92 46 73 86.

Brunissard

This village has a curious **bell tower**, which looms over the ancient communal oven. In winter, you can indulge in cross-country skiing, and in fine weather enjoy the **sentier de lecture** (🚶‍♂️1hr; start from the car park at Jamberoute).

EXCURSION
Molines-en-Queyras★

🏠 Clot-la-Chalpe, 05350 Molines-en-Queyras. ℘04 92 45 83 22. www.molinesenqueyras.com.
Not far from St-Véran lie the seven hamlets of Molines. Their picturesque old houses are surmounted by grain lofts, where crops continue to ripen after the harvest. Molines offers a small ski area, which is linked to that of St-Véran.

5️⃣ ROUTE DU COL AGNEL★★

Drive of 15km/9.3mi to the Col Agnel shown on the regional map (⬅ see p363). Allow 30min.
🚗 *Road closed in winter.*

Drive to Pierre-Grosse, which owes its name to the **erratic blocks** of igneous rock scattered over the surrounding pastures, then on to Fontgillarde. Beyond here, the road offers a fine **view** of Pic de Château Renard. The armies of both Hannibal and Caesar marched through here on their way across the Alps.
The road continues to climb, offering **views** of the snow-covered Pelvoux Massif to the northwest. It finally reaches the Agnel Pass on the Italian border. Walk up to the **viewing table** (alt. 2 744m/9 003ft) for a splendid **panorama**★★.

Col Agnel

© Dean Moriarty/Fotolia.com

🥾 HIKES
Le Pain de Sucre★★★

🚶 *Leave the car between the refuge and the Col Agnel. This itinerary is suitable for experienced walkers equipped with climbing boots; dry weather essential.*
The **Col Vieux**★ is reached in 30 minutes; another 15-minute climb takes you to a ledge; carry straight on to a path which winds up to the Pain de Sucre (☺ very steep climb, caution is recommended).
The magnificent **panorama**★★★ includes Monte Viso to the east, the Brec and Aiguille de Chambeyron to the south and the Oisans Massif to the west. To the north, the view extends as far as Mont Blanc in clear weather. Starting near the cross take the path leading back to the Col Vieux.

Grand Belvédère, Lac Lestio and Viso Refuge★★

🚶 *5hrs 30min there and back. Gradient 700m/2 297ft. This round tour is varied and pleasant but does not offer outstanding panoramas. Leave your car at l'Échalp car park.*
You will reach the Grand Belvédère after a walk (1hr 45min) along a landscaped path running parallel to the road. From here the **view**★ extends to **Monte Viso**. After climbing a few moments take a path on the right, recognisable by yellow markings, which follows a stream; after the path to the refuge and crossing the stream, you reach **Lac Lestio**. Retrace your steps and take the path, indicated by white and red markings, back down to Grand Belvédère and the car park.

♿*Other hikes can be discovered at Abriès, Ceillac and St-Véran.*

BIKE TOURS★★ 🚴

The most interesting tours start from Abriès and climb up to La Monta. Other options include a one-day excursion up to the **Col de la Croix** (alt. 2 298m/ 7 539ft) or a longer, more thrilling ride through the Val Pellice to the refuge **Barbara-Lowrie** (alt. 1 753m/5 751ft). The ascent to the **Col du Baracun** (alt. 2 380m/7 808ft) is reached after a succession of gruelling hairpin bends.

ADDRESSES

🛏 STAY / 🍴EAT

🖙🍲🛏 **Hôtel La Ferme de l'Izoard** –*La Chalp, 05350 Arvieux. Rte du Col.* 📞*04 92 46 89 00. www.laferme.fr. Closed Apr and 29 Sep– 19 Dec.* ♿🖥. *Wifi. 23 rooms.* 🍽*11€, half- board available, restaurant*🍲🍲. Comfortable hotel, built in a traditional style, offering spacious bedrooms with either a terrace or a balcony. The restaurant serves local specialities.

🖙🍲🛏 **Chambre d'hôte La Girandole** – *Brunissard, 05350 Arvieux.* 📞*04 92 46 84 12. www.lagirandole.fr. Closed 5 Apr–20 May, 15 Sept–15 Dec.* 📇🚫. *5 rooms*🍽. This cosy

guesthouse is full of antique furniture and ornaments, soft sofas and a piano. In the rooms there is a prevailing lack of fuss or frills. Two gîtes available.

🛍 SHOPPING

Fromagerie de la Durance et du Queyras – *05350 Arvieux.* 📞*04 92 46 72 34. www.fromageriedeladurance.fr. Open 9.30am–noon, 3–6.30pm. Closed Apr–Jun, Sept–Nov and Sun.* A small shop with produce made from local Queyras milk.

La Maison de l'Artisanat – *Charpenel, 05350 Château-Ville-Vieille.* 📞*04 92 46 75 06. Contact for opening times.* Discover traditional furniture, wooden toys, jewellery, leather goods and more.

🏃ACTIVITIES

🪂👥**École de parapente en Queyras** – *La Chalp, 05350 Arvieux.* 📞*06 08 01 27 27. www.parapente05.com. 72€ discovery flight.* Paragliding centre.

Winter sports – A pass "Tout Queyras" is valid for the ski domaines of Aiguilles, Abriès-Ristolas, Arvieux and Molines.

TRANSPORT

Navettes de l'Escarton – In season, a shuttle bus (free with the **Carte d'hôte**) runs a service between the villages of Haut Guil and L'Echalp.

Guillestre★

Le Guillestrois is a magnificent mountain cirque bordered by the Écrins, Queyras and l'Embrunais. Guillestre is doubly lucky: its mountains protect it from rain (the rainfall level of 30cm/12in per year is one of the lowest in France); and located at a natural crossroads, every Monday the town hosts the principal market in Queyras – evidence of the fact that trade has existed among the neighbouring valleys since the Middle Ages.

VISIT

🔎**Good to know** – A brochure describ- ing the ancient town centre is available from the tourist office.

▶ **Population:** 2 273.
♿ **Michelin Map:** 334 H5.
🛈 **Info:** Office du tourisme du Guillestrois, pl. J.-Salva, 05600 Guillestre. 📞04 92 45 04 37. www.pays-du- guillestrois.com. Office du tourisme de Risoul, 05600 Risoul. 📞04 92 46 02 60. www.risoul.com.
🧭 **Location:** On the Grandes Alpes route, between the Col de l'Izoard and Col de Vars, Guillestre is also midway between Gap and Briançon.
🕐 **Timing:** Around three hours to look around.

Pass under one of four gateways and wander through the narrow streets and small squares. The Eygliers tower is all that still stands of the ramparts that were built to protect the medieval centre. The Renaissance church possesses a beautiful porch supported by four columns, two of which have crouching lions at the base, vestiges of an ancient priory. Lean over the wrought-iron lock: you will see the grim portrait of an archbishop!

EXCURSIONS
Table d'Orientation de Peyre-Haute
2 km/1.2mi S of Guillestre, on the Vars road. At 100m/109yds upstream of the hamlet (signposted), climb the slope on the left. 15min there and back.
View★: from left to right, Allefroide, separated from the Pic Sans Nom by Coup de Sabre breach, Pelvoux, Pic Neige Cordier and the Blanc Glacier.

Réotier★
10km/6.2mi from Guillestre. Take D 902 to N 94, turn right then left just before Mont-Dauphin railway station.
Follow the signposts for **Fontaine Pétrifiante de Réotier**. Mineralised water formed by concretion folds.

Risoul 1850
14km/8.7mi S along D 186.
On the winding road from the ancient village, halfway to the ski resort, there is a **superb panorama★★**.
The resort has been awarded the "Famille Plus Montagne" label (*see p30*). The Plate-de-la-None ski lift goes up to the summit of the ski slopes and connects the modern resort of Risoul with Vars 1850 creating **Domaine de la Forêt Blanche**, one of the largest Alpes du Sud ski areas (18 km/115mi of ski slopes). Other winter sports are not overlooked; a snowpark and superpipe have both been installed. In summer, two chairlifts take you to the summit, from where there is a good choice of pleasant walks.
An unsurfaced road leads to the Col de Cherine and continues to the **Belvédère de l'Homme-de-Pierre** (alt. 2 374 m/

7 789ft). Fine **panorama★★** (orientation table) of the Massif de la Vanoise, the Lake Serre-Ponçon and, in the distance, Mont Ventoux.

🚗 DRIVING TOUR

LA COMBE DU QUEYRAS★★
Drive of 17km/10.6mi shown on the regional map, 1 (see p362). See p364.

🚶 HIKES
Rue des Masques
2hrs. Difference in altitude 250m/820ft. From the tourist office, take r. des Champs-Élysées to the police station; at this point, turn right onto chemin d'Eygliers. Carry on to the end of the plateau. The path is signposted.
You will find yourself standing between two high walls: this "rue", which lacks only the houses, is a natural phenomenon, a void 5m/16ft wide and 600m/656yds long hollowed from the rocks. Walk back along the top path, at the plateau's edge, that follows an irrigation canal.

Balade à Mont-Dauphin★★
2hrs. Orange markers.
Leave Guillestre taking the direction for Briançon (D 902) and continue until you arrive at Quartier des Chapelles. Cross the Chalp Plateau and take the footbridge over Le Guil.
On this walk you can admire Mont-Dauphin (*see p370*).

ADDRESSES

🛏 STAY
🛏 **Camping St-James-les-Pins –**
Rte des Campings, 1.5 km/0.9mi W along rte de Risoul and take a right-hand turning. 04 92 45 08 24. www.lesaintjames.com. Closed early Nov–mid-Dec. 100 pitches.
Pleasant campsite located at an altitude of 1 000m/3 281ft on the banks of a stream, surrounded by pine trees. Various watersports on offer.

⊝⊝ **Hôtel La Bonne Auberge** –
*05600 Risoul. ℰ04 92 45 02 40. www.bonne
auberge-risoul.com. Closed 1 Jun–15 Sept,
26 Dec–31 Mar.* ▣. *25 rooms* ⊡*8€, half-
board available, restaurant* ⊝⊝.
Chalet offering well-maintained rooms
with lovely views of the Mont-Dauphin
fortress. Family guesthouse ambience in
the restaurant.

⊌/ EAT

⊝⊝ **Dedans Dehors** – *Ruelle Sani.
ℰ04 92 44 29 07. albandedansdehors@
yahoo.fr. Closed end Sept–mid-May.* ⊡.
Situated in a vaulted cellar in a deserted
medieval alley this eclectic bistro serves
sandwiches, salads and several dishes
cooked *à la plancha.*

⊟ SHOPPING

Market – On Monday mornings, it seems
that the whole village meets at this market.
Among with fresh produce you will also
find an old book or soap.

⚔ ACTIVITIES

Base de loisirs – *D 994. 05600 St-Clément-
sur-Durance. 7.5 km/4.7mi SW of Guillestre on
D 902 then N 94 and D 994. ℰ04 92 45 04 35.
Closed 16 Sept–14 Apr.* Leisure centre
on the riverbank with a large choice of
watersports. Also nature walks, bike tours
and paragliding.

Mont-Dauphin★★

**Mont-Dauphin is a mighty citadel
situated on top of a promontory,
commanding a superb view**★★
of the Durance and the Guil.

A BIT OF HISTORY

When the Duke of Savoie's troops seized
the towns of Gap, Embrun and Guillestre
in 1692, King Louis XIV of France ordered
Sébastien Le Prestre de Vauban to build
fortifications along the border.
Mont-Dauphin was one of nine strategic places where Vauban chose to build
not just a fortress, but a fortified settlement from which the king's troops could
guard the Queyras region, the Durance
Valley and the road leading across the
Col de Vars. Vauban's garrison town
began to take shape, but the 1713 Treaty
of Utrecht modified the borders and the
menace from Savoy invaders declined.
The defences were less important and
interest in finishing waned.
The citadel failed to attract 2 000 residents as predicted.

VISIT
Citadel

🔍 *Guided tours of the citadel (2hrs)
Jul–Aug daily 10am, 3pm, 4pm;
Jun and Sept daily 10am; Oct–May
Tue–Sun 3pm.*

▸ **Population:** 136.
🖎 **Michelin Map:** 334 H4.
🖹 **Info:** Quartier des Artisans
d'Art, 05600 Mont-Dauphin.
ℰ04 92 45 17 80.
▶ **Location:** Mont-Dauphin
sits on the Plateau des
Mille Vents, above the
town of Guillestre.
👁 **Don't Miss:** The citadel,
and the views of Mont-
Dauphin from Le Cros.
🕐 **Timing:** You'll need
one to two hours to
see the citadel.

🕐*Closed 1 Jan, Easter Mon, 1 May,
1 Nov, 11 Nov, 25 Dec.* ⊜*7€.*
Vauban named the citadel in honour of
the king's eldest son, the dauphin, and
the historic province of Dauphiné.
Since 2008 Mont-Dauphin has been
included on the World Heritage list, by
UNESCO, along with Briançon and 10
other major Vauban sites.

Moat – There is a **view** of the moat
from the bridge joining the gate and the
guardhouse; note the scarp and counter-
scarp, the bastions and the lunette which
communicates with the outside through
an underground passage.

The town – The residential area of the citadel is split into four square blocks. Its buildings are built of Guillestre pink marble.

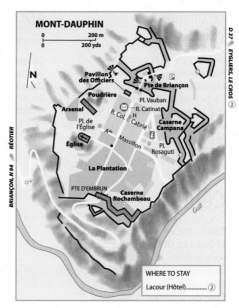

MONT-DAUPHIN

Pavillon des Officiers
Poudrière
Arsenal
R. Col
Cabrié
Pl. de l'Église
Église
La Plantation
PTE D'EMBRUN
Massillon
Pl. Vauban
R. Catinat
Pte de Briançon
Caserne Campana
Pl. Rosaguti
Caserne Rochambeau
Guil

BRIANÇON, N 94   RÉOTIER
D 37   EYGLIERS, LE CROS ②

WHERE TO STAY
Lacour (Hôtel).............. ②

Powder Magazine★ – Only an earth mound and a few air pipes are seen from the outside. Inside, the upper room is covered with pointed vaulting, and the lower with a larch framework. A gallery provided ventilation and light, as a naked flame from a lamp could have devastated the town.

Arsenal – Decorated with ox-eye windows, it houses exhibitions in the rooms that once stocked artillery.

Church – It has bizarre proportions since, of the original design, only the choir has been completed. The transept walls and the first bays were erected, but their stones were taken away and used for the construction of ammunition bunkers in 1873. Just before the first pew on the right look out for an ammonite in the stone floor.

Caserne Rochambeau – Outside, these large barracks form a defence wall overlooking the porte d'Embrun and the ramparts.

Inside is a wooden **framework**★, which dates from 1820, based on a design by King Henri II's architect, Philibert Delorme (1512–70).

Caserne Campana – Several craftsmen (leather, terracotta, silk, sundials) exhibit their work. This has helped to revive the village after the departure of the army in 1980.

Vauban or the Military Genius

Sébastien Le Prestre (1633–1707) was known as the Marquis de Vauban. Tireless and brilliant, he was a soldier, engineer, architect and urban planner. He personally led 53 sieges, created the Army Engineering Corps, redesigned ports, built canals, constructed the Maintenon Viaduct, remodelled 300 strongholds and edified 33 new ones. He was active in Flanders, Ardennes, Alsace, Franche-Comté, Les Pyrénées, Les Alpes and the coast.

Commissaire Général des Fortifications, he was inspired by the works of his predecessors, such as Errard in the southern Alps. He perfected his own work not only by referring to new inventions and tactics, but by improving on them by adding defensive half-moons, deep ditches, counterguards and bastioned ramparts. On top of that, his works had an invaluable aesthetic value. He built and restored no fewer than 12 strongholds from Briançon to Nice and Antibes.

EXCURSION
Le Cros
▶ *5km/3.1mi NW. Cross Eygliers and carry on to Le Cros. Difficult road.*
Remarkable **views**★ of Mont-Dauphin and its fortress, and beyond Cros, the Gorges du Guil. You can travel to St-Crépin, 4km/2.5mi north on N 94, and discover the **Vallée de Freissinières** (&*see p354*).

ADDRESSES

🛏 STAY / 🍽 EAT

🍴🍴 **Hôtel Lacour et Restaurant Gare** – *℘04 92 45 03 08. www.hotel-lacour.com. Closed Sat, 20 April–30 Jun and 1 Sept–26 Dec. Wifi. 46 rooms, half-board available, restaurant🍴.* A friendly hotel and annexe, below the fortress, with comfortable rooms; those overlooking the garden are quieter. The restaurant serves regional cuisine.

Ceillac

This pretty village is the phoenix of Queyras. Devastated by fire several times, its traditional character has been preserved after each resurrection.
Even the ski resort, hidden in a gully, remains discreet. Nothing spoils the beauty of the landscape, a vast cirque reaching up to an altitude of 1 650m/5 413ft.

▶ **Population:** 297.
& **Michelin Map:** 334 I4.
🛈 **Info:** Office du tourisme de Ceillac, pl. Ph.-Lamour, 05600 Ceillac. ℘04 92 45 05 74. www.ceillac.com or www.queyras.com.
▶ **Location:** Ceillac is 14km/8.7mi E of Guillestre along D 60.
😊 **Don't Miss:** The walk to Lac Ste-Anne.
🕐 **Timing:** Allow one day to visit Ceillac and take a good walk.

SIGHTS
Village
At the edge of Ceillac stands the bell tower of **Église Ste-Cécile** (14C–15C). In the village centre, **Église St-Sébastien**★ is outstanding for its 16C belfry with five bells under an abat-son. Inside, the choir is decorated with murals.
The **Chapelle des Pénitents** houses a museum of religious art and exhibitions.

Ski Domaine 🎿
This resort will satisfy the most demanding holidaymakers. It has 14 downhill ski slopes; no less than 35km/21.8mi of great snow for cross-country skiers; great opportunities for alpine tour skiing; and there are three footpaths and 25km/15.5mi of cross-country trails.
In summer, the town is a great base for hikers. You can also practise climbing, cycling, paragliding and horse riding.

🥾 HIKES
Vallon du Mélezet★
Alt. 1 967m/6 453ft.
You can also drive the 5km/3.1mi.

Scattered with recently restored hamlets and strange chapels, it has larch-covered slopes rising to over 2 000m/6 562ft! On the right can be seen the snow-capped **Font Sancte** (alt. 3 387m/11 112ft). Opposite the Pied-du-Mélezet hamlet tumbles the **Cascade de la Pisse**.

Lac Ste-Anne★
🚶 *Alt. 2 415m/7 923ft. 2hrs 30min return. Park at the end of Vallon du Mélezet. Possible to follow the 5hr loop (GR 5), which passes by the Lac Miroir.*
A walk through the larch trees and alpine pastures. Suddenly, without warning appears the Lac Ste-Anne. The water, an extraordinary blue-green colour, is held back by a moraine dam, left behind by an ancient glacier. The reflection in the waters of the Font Sancte peak is breathtaking. On the lakeside is a chapel which hosts a pilgrimage on 26 July.

Château-Queyras ★

Impressive Fort Queyras is perched on a rugged knoll that almost completely blocks the entrance to the Guil Valley, leaving only a narrow pass. Without doubt it is the most photogenic place in Queyras. It provided the perfect setting for Philippe de Broca's film *Le Bossu*, based on the novel by Paul Féva.

VISIT

Fort Queyras ★

Open daily Jul–Aug 9am–7pm; May–Jun and Sept 10.30am–5pm.
Guided tours Jul–Aug daily 10.30am, 2.30pm, 4.30pm. See website. ℘04 92 46 86 72. www.fortqueyras.com.
See Architecture p71.

In 1310 and 1334 great festivals were held here for the Dauphins Jean II and Humbert. The Protestant Lesdiguières seized it in 1587, and afterwards the fort nearly became derelict. It found favour again, in 1690, when the Duc de Savoie's army began to menace the French borders. The army was beaten back two years later due to the strength of the fort's garrison, but not without paying a price: the village was destroyed by flames. A few months later Vauban was sent to inspect the damage. He conceived an advance observation post, and reinforced the fort by adding scarps, ditches, counterscarps and half-moons.

- **Michelin Map:** 334 I4.
- **Info:** Chateau-Queyras, 05350 Château-Ville-Vielle.
- **Location:** Château-Queyras is 17km/10.6mi SW of Guillestre, and 38km/23.6mi NW of Briançon along D902.
- **Don't Miss:** A guided tour of the fortress.
- **Kids:** Discover the geological riches of the region at the Espace Géologique.
- **Timing:** Half a day to visit Château-Queyras, and walk up to the Bucher summit.

Meanwhile the Sun King's garrison became bored, while waiting for the Duke of Savoie to attack again, and gave the inhabitants a hard time: their complaints are stored in the town's archives in the **Armoire aux Huit Serrures**, which stands in the Ville-Vieille town hall.

Crossing the drawbridge, you enter into a maze of passages, stairs, casemates and bastions, which were still under construction up to the 19C; a marked path shows you the way *(free map at the fort reception)*.

From the **tower**, which houses exhibitions in season, you have a fine view of the Guil Valley.

Fort Queyras

©Jean-Luc Armand/Photononstop/Tips Images

DISCOVERING LE QUEYRAS

👥 Espace Géologique★

At the church, take the road on the left. Leave the car near the river, and walk back on foot and go through the porch. 🕐 *Open Jul–Aug Sun–Fri 10am–noon, 2–6pm.* 💶 *3.50€ (children 6–16 2.50€).* 📞 *04 92 46 88 20.*

In the church's crypt, the origin of the Alps is explained through interactive information panels. This initiation will enable you to better understand the region's geological phenomenas. You'll smell a 170-million-year odour after banging together pebbles: that of seaweed decomposed in mud.

EXCURSION
Sommet Bucher★

🔵 *11km/6.8mi – about 1hr there and back.* ⚠️ *The road is very difficult – please drive carefully.*

The narrow road, shaded by larches and pines, climbs in a series of hairpin bends, offering fine glimpses of Château-Queyras and the Guil Valley. From the end of the road, climb to the viewing tables on either side of a military building. The panorama includes Mont Viso and St-Véran village, framed by the Pic de Châteaurenard.

🚗 DRIVING TOURS

ROUTE DE ST-VÉRAN★★
Drive of 15km/9.3mi shown on the regional map, 2 *(🕐 see p362).* 🕐 *See p364.*

LE HAUT QUEYRAS
Drive of 30km/18.6mi shown on the regional map, 3 *(🕐 see p362).* 🕐 *See p366.*

ROUTE DU COL DE L'IZOARD★★
Drive of 22km/13.7mi shown on the regional map, 4 *(🕐 see p362).* 🕐 *See p366.*

Casse Déserte★★
The ragged spires are due to a local geological phenomenon causing layers of ground limestone and gypsum to be bonded into a yellowish conglomerate, known as *cargneule*.

Col de l'Izoard★★
Built by the Armée des Alpes this pass is the highest point of the Route des Grandes Alpes, after le Galibier.
Musée-relais – 📞 *04 92 46 76 18.* This museum recounts the saga of cycling; look out for an unusual 1869 velocipede. Two plaques commemorate rival cycling heroes: Fausto Coppi, winner of the Tour de France in 1952, and Louison Bobet, who triumphed in 1953, 1954 and 1955.

Table d'Orientation
🚶 *15min there and back.*
Climb to the orientation tables set slightly above the road. Here you will find a beautiful, rugged panorama; to the north the Briançonnais mountains and beyond Le Thabor, to the south the summits of Queyras, the Houerts and Font Sancte peaks, and the Massif de Chambeyron. The path continues to Briançon.

ADDRESSES

🏃 ACTIVITIES

Bike rides – There are several bike trails in the region. Topo-guides on sale in the tourist office *(7€).*

Sentier écologique des Astragales – From Ville-Vieille, may be extended by including GR 5 and GR 58; go past La Pierre Fiche (menhir), and continue to Meyries and then walk back down to Château-Queyras *(booklet sold at the tourist office).*

🎭 EVENT

Life in the Middle Ages at Fort-Queyras – *Fort Queyras. Details from tourist office.* In August, at weekends, the medieval ambience of the fort is re-created by Les Voyageurs du Temps acting troupe.

TRANSPORT

In season, a shuttle bus *(free with the Carte d'hôte)* runs between Château-Queyras and La Monta-L'Échalp.

St-Véran★★

St-Véran is "the highest village where one eats the bread of God", reads an inscription on one of the 15 sundials. But don't just consider the village a mere curiosity. The presence of humans at 2 040m/ 6 693ft is an undeniable fascination. It is these people you need to meet to understand the lives they led before the famous fuste chalets transformed the village into a museum.

▶ **Population:** 296.

Ⓖ **Michelin Map:** 334 J4.

🄸 **Info:** Office du tourisme de St-Véran. ℰ04 92 45 82 21. www.saintveran.com.

◖ **Location:** At 2.5km/1.5mi from Château-Queyras, take D 5 to St-Véran.

◉ **Don't Miss:** A walk around the old village.

SIGHTS

Old Village★★

Built entirely of wood and stone, the village is considered one of the prettiest in France: south-facing alpine farmhouses with long galleries in front of their storage lofts, where cereals go on ripening after the harvest. Each of St-Véran's six districts – set well apart as a fire precaution – has its own wooden fountain, *Croix de la Passion* and communal oven. Many houses are decorated with elaborate sundials.

The church, the town hall and the tourist office are found at the village square.

Church

Encircled by its cemetery, the church was constructed in the 17C. The entrance is guarded by two weary lions, originating from a previous church. The one on the left holds down a child in its paws.

Inside the surprisingly vast nave has a magnificent Baroque **alterpiece**★: where would the churches of the alpes be without Italian artists?

Musée du Soum★★

🕐*Open Jul–Aug daily 9.30am–6.30pm; Sept–Jun contact for details.* ⊛*3.80€ (children 6–16 1.90€).* ℰ*04 92 45 86 42.* The museum illustrates traditional life in St-Véran through a succession of furnished rooms. Installed in the oldest house in the village, built in 1641, it has typical local features: an outside pig pen; an inner courtyard for cattle, floored with tree trunks; and on the

St-Véran

© Gérard Labriet/Photononstop

The Dragon Hunter

Véran, patron saint of shepherds, was a 6C archbishop who fought a dragon that was terrorising the region. While the wounded dragon was flying to Provence 12 drops of blood dripped from its wounds. These later symbolised the places where shepherds stopped when moving their livestock from Luberon to summer pastures in Queyras.

ground floor, a "shepherd's room" for seasonal workers.

In the living room, note the box bed (1842), the fireplace – an unusual feature as the kitchen would normally be the only room to have one – and the hay rack, which is a reminder that humans and cattle cohabited in winter. Upstairs, the joiner's and the lapidary's workshops have been reconstructed.

Ancienne Maison Traditionelle

Guided tour available (30min) daily 10am–noon, 2–6pm. 2.50€. 04 92 45 82 39.

Until 1976, the residents shared this house with their animals, in the traditional way. Former residents guide visitors around their old home.

HIKES

Route des Amoureux★

Around 2hrs.

Leaving St-Véran this path has views of the northern slopes of the valley and the Pic de Rochebrune, then penetrates the larch forest and continues to the **Pierre-Grosse** hamlet.

Chapelle Notre-Dame-de-Clausis

In Jun–Aug the road is closed to motor vehicles. Access is by shuttle (paying: the trip takes 20min then 15min on foot) or on foot (3hrs return).

As the road runs past disused marble quarries and copper mines, spare a thought for the miners who worked here at high altitude, on meagre rations, and who would get so covered in verdigris during their shift that they were known as "diables verts" ("green devils"). Colonies of marmots live in the area.

Tête des Toillies Round Tour★★

A splendid but taxing walk offering varied scenery: allow 5hrs 30min for the walk and at least 1hr 30min for the breaks. Leave early in the morning, catching the shuttle to Notre-Dame-de-Clausis no later than 10am.

Leave the road on the last bend before a chapel and follow a path straight ahead, which leads to the Lac du Blanchet. Turn right before the refuge towards the **Col de la Noire** affording **views**★ of the Tête des Toillies.

The path drops steeply to the **Lac de la Noire**; walk past the lake for another 10 minutes and turn left then immediately head for the bottom of the valley.

Shortly afterwards, there is a tricky passage through the rocks then the path runs along the mountainside to the Lac du Longet and disappears. Join another path leading to the **Col du Longet**, set in a wild landscape of screes and lakes. Walk down for 10 minutes and turn left towards the **Col Blanchet**.

Allow 45 minutes to climb up to the pass through pastures: striking **panorama**★★ of the Tête des Toillies soaring up to the sky, of the Pelvoux, Pic de Rochebrune, Monte Viso and the Italian Alps.

Allow 1hr 15min to return to the shuttle.

Col St-Véran and Pic de Caramantran★★

Allow 3hrs 30min. Take the shuttle to the Chapelle de Clausis. Walk along the road for 5min. Before the bridge, take GR 58 (signposted).

It takes 1 hour 30 minutes to get to the pass: **view**★ of Monte Viso and Lake Castello.

Follow the ridge line on the left, which leads in 30 minutes to the **Pic de Caramantran**: superb **panorama**★★ of the surrounding peaks.

Follow a path running between the two Caramantran peaks to the **Col de Chamoussière**★ offering a view of the Pain de Sucre, and return to the shuttle along the marked path.

ADDRESSES

STAY

Hôtel L'Astragale – *04 92 45 87 00. www.astragale.eu. Closed 1 Apr–17 Jun, 1 Sept–17 Dec. Wifi. 21 rooms, half-board available, restaurant.* Rustic décor, large, comfortable, well-equipped rooms. Cosy dining room with open fire.

ACTIVITIES

The resort **St-Véran/Molines** has 36km/22.4mi of **downhill ski slopes**, 25km/15.5mi of **cross-country trails**, three paths for **snowshoeing** and two for **nordic skiing**.

Abriès★

Abriès is a ski resort-village at the gates of the Réserve Naturelle de la Haute Vallée du Guil. It is equally renowned for its colourful market, held every Wednesday, as well as its peaks along the Italian border, that form a vast terrain for nature lovers.

VISIT

The village has been the victim of several fires and floods throughout its history. The floods of 1728 carried away the cemetery, the church porch and the stone lions, later found swimming in the floodwaters.

Don't waste any time taking the **Circuit des Pierres Ecrites**; follow the stones, engraved with inscriptions, which line the streets of Abriès.

Guide published by the Parc on sale at tourist office (4.50€). Guided tours in season Wed 6pm.

Maison du Costume d'Autrefois

Open Mon–Fri except public holidays 2–6pm; school holidays 10am–noon, 3–5pm Guided tours (1hr) by appointment. 3€ (children under 6 free). 04 92 46 87 32. www.maison ducostume.com.

This museum displays traditional costumes of the Queyras region.

EXCURSIONS
Valpreveyre

Climb to the, now abandoned, alpine hamlet: this is a pleasant walk of 6km/3.7mi along the banks of the Bouchet river. Ancient houses have preserved their authenticity.

La Maison de la Nature à Ristolas

Phone for times and fees. 04 92 46 86 29 or 04 92 46 88 20.

This ecologically themed exhibit highlights the natural heritage of the area.

HIKES
Colette de Gilly★

Take the Gilly chairlift, leaving Abriès in the direction of Ristolas.

- **Population:** 377.
- **Michelin Map:** 334 J4.
- **Info:** Office du tourisme d'Abriès, Quartier Le Bourg, 05460 Abriès. 04 92 46 72 26. www.queyras-montagne.com.
- **Location:** To reach Abriès follow D 947 and continue through the Vallée du Guil. *In season, a shuttle (charge) runs between Château-Queyras and La Monta.*
- **Kids:** The Maison de la Nature at Ristolas.
- **Timing:** Allow two hours to discover the village and follow the Pierres Ecrites, and half a day if you go up to the alpine hamlet of Valpreveyre.

Open Jul–Aug, request details on times. 5.50€. 04 92 46 72 26. On arrival (alt. 2 150m/7 054ft) take the GR 58 *(white-and-red markers)*, which is found just in front of you, and continue to climb for around 45 minutes until you reach the Colette de Gilly. Just another 15 minutes, and you arrive at the summit of Gilly (alt. 2 467m/ 8 094ft), from where you can admire the fine **panorama**★.

Tour du Bric Bouchet★★

Allow 8hrs, marked path all the way; spend the night at the Refuge du Lago Verde (Italy).

The **first option** (also a ski touring path) is the shorter and more challenging, it takes you to the border pass of Valpreveyre, which affords close-up views of Bric Bouchet (alt. 2 997m/9 833ft). Descend to the Refuge du Lago Verde. The rest of the circuit is the same as the second option.

On this longer **second option** enjoy the diversity of the landscape and admire the traditional architecture.

From **Valpreveyre**, go to the **Roux** hamlet downstream, then go past the Pra Roubaud chalets (beautiful wooden fountain) before coming to the border pass of Abriès or of St-Martin (alt. 2 657m/8 717ft); a four-hour walk without difficulty. Super **view**★★ of the **Val Germanisca** (Italy) and the well-defined summit of Bric Bouchet. A one-hour walk brings you to the Refuge du Lago Verde (alt. 2 583m/8 474ft). In the north, peaks of the **Cime du Grand Queyron** (alt. 3 060m/10 039ft) can be seen.

After a good meal, make the most of your trip to the lovely Italian Vallée de Pignerol by visiting **Prali** and its Musée d'Ethnologie du Val Germanisca. Take the path to the Bout du Col, where you see the start of a surfaced road. Don't take this, but follow the path that borders the river, until the first houses at **Pomieri**. It takes around three hours to get to **Ghigo di Prali**. Several routes are available to return to Queyras, either by the Col de la Croix or by the Col d'Urine, which bypasses the Tête du Pelvas (♧ *below*). These walks necessitate one or two nights' stay in the Italian refuges, at Villanova or at the Refuge Jervis (*near the Col de la Croix*).

Tour of the Col de la Croix and Col d'Urine via the Ciabot del Pra (Italy)★★

• *2 days, with an overnight stay at the Refuge Jervis.*

From **La Monta**, a two-hour walk brings you to the Col de la Croix (alt. 2 299m/

7 542ft): take GR 58C, which leads to a wood, climbing up the right bank of the Combe Morelle stream. After walking for 1 hour 30 minutes you reach the Refuge Jervis *(refreshments available in season)*. The steep trail descends to **Ciabot del Pra**: just at the exit turn right; take the path heading north, which skirts round a small hill before reaching the valley.

After walking for three hours, maximum, you arrive at the **Col frontière d'Urine** (alt. 2 525m/8 284ft).

On the left the imposing mass of the **Tête du Pelvas** (alt. 2 929m/9 610ft) dominates the pass and valley, which carry on westwards. Descend from here, and emerge from a wood into the Valpreveyre Valley *(2hrs from the Col)*. There is the option of continuing on GR 58B to Abriès *(30min)*.

ADDRESSES

🛒 SHOPPING

Market – *Mon mornings.* Don't miss this lively food and produce market.

Le Plantivore – *Au Roux.* ☎04 92 46 76 54. www.plantivore.fr. Open in season Mon–Fri 8–11.45am, 2–5pm, Sat–Sun 8–11.45am. Produce from local mountain plants. The jams are popular, but it is the hyssop, larch, queyrassine and *génépi* liqueurs and aperitifs called "amours", that top them.

Vars

Situated between Guillestre and Barcelonnette, near the pass (2 109m/6 919ft) that links l'Ubaye and the Haut-Embrunnais, Vars is one of the main winter and summer resorts of the southern Alps, highly regarded for its sunny climate, the quality of its facilities and the beauty of its natural environment.

THE RESORT

Chalets are scattered among the larches; **Les Claux** is the centre of the resort. **Ste-Marie-de-Vars** and **Les Claux** alone offer direct access to the ski runs.

▶ **Population:** 941.
☿ **Michelin Map:** 334 I5.
🔲 **Info:** Cours Fontanarosa, 05560 Vars. ☎04 92 46 51 31. www.vars-ski.com.
◐ **Location:** The resort is spread over three traditional hamlets and a modern resort at altitudes ranging from 1 600m/5 249ft to 1 800m/5 906ft.
☺ **Don't Miss:** The wild scenery of the Col de Vars.
◷ **Timing:** A half-day at the Réserve naturelle du Val d'Escreins.

Ski Area

Linked to the slopes of **Risoul** under the name of **Domaine de la Forêt Blanche**, the resort includes 56 ski lifts and 180km/112mi of runs.

Its gentle slopes are ideal for intermediate skiers who love fine scenery. Vars also boasts a number of high-speed runs on which the **Speed-Skiing** World Cup is held.

In summer, Vars is an excellent walking base. In addition, the choice of activities include skating, snowmobiling, swimming, riding and squash. Mountain bikers can try the longest course in Europe (32km/19.9mi).

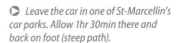

DRIVING TOURS

COL DE VARS ROUTE

Drive of 9km/5.6mi shown on the regional map (see p362). Allow 30 min. **Good to know** – *In Dec–Apr the Col de Vars may be impassable due to snowfall.*

From Vars to the pass, the road runs along the foot of the slopes, equipped with ski lifts going from Ste-Marie to the **Refuge Napoléon**.

Col de Vars – Alt. 2 109m/6 919ft.
In the middle of meagre pastures dotted with blocks of sandstone stands a monument commemorating the renovation of the road by alpine troups. On the way down to l'Ubaye, the pastoral landscape remains austere. The summit of the Brec de Chambeyron can be seen to the east.

VAL D'ESCREINS★★

Drive of 7km/4.3mi shown on the regional map (see p362). Allow 1hr.

▷ *From Vars, drive down towards Guillestre along D 902; turn right.*

St-Marcellin – This ancient hamlet has retained its mountain-village atmosphere. ⓧ A pleasant **walk to the castle ruins**★ starts in St-Marcellin.

Fast Run

The **Piste de Chabrières** is the most impressive in the world: some 1 400m/4 593yds of slope at a gradient of 52 percent on average and 98 percent maximum! It's understandable that, at the lower section, the area of deceleration and braking measures 850m/930yds. It's in this section that you could start speed-skiing.

▷ *Leave the car in one of St-Marcellin's car parks. Allow 1hr 30min there and back on foot (steep path).*

Walk along the right side of the church. The path is marked in yellow. After the first bend to the left, carry straight on *(do not go towards the house up on the right)*. The path crosses a small road. Continue to the summit, where you will enjoy an extended **view**★ of the various hamlets around Vars.

▷ *Rejoin D 902 towards Guillestre and turn right.*

Réserve Naturelle du Val d'Escreins★★

ⓞ*Open May–Oct, contact for details.* ℘*04 92 46 51 31. www.vars-ski.com.*
La Vallée de Rif Bel, inaccessible eight months of the year, has been a natural reserve since 1964. Part of the **Parc Naturel Régional du Queyras** *(see p364)*, it covers a third of the territory of the commune of Vars, that is 2 500ha/6 177acres.

The larch-covered slopes give way to barren summits, including the **Pic de la Font Sancte** (alt. 3 387m/11 112ft). Its name "holy fountain", according to a legend, comes from a spring discovered by a shepherdess. Experienced walkers now grace the summit to admire the most beautiful view of the area.

The reserve, rich in flora and fauna, has 37km/23mi of marked footpaths. The climb to the Col des Houerts is only suitable for experienced walkers *(walking guide on sale at tourist office)*.

Identify the Conifers

In Haute Provence, there are five species to recognise:

- The **pin noir d'Autriche** is used for reforestation. It is recognisable by its dark green needles about 10cm/4in long, hard and spiky, and its resinous buds;
- The **pin à crochets** owes its name to the curved hooks on its cones. Its needles are short, shiny and rigid;
- The **pin d'Alep**, with reddish-brown bark-rouge, and twisted trunk, adores dry soils, but at no higher than 500m/1 640ft . Its bright green needles, durable and supple, are grouped in pairs;
- The **pin sylvestre** grows here naturally, especially at high altitude. Its bark peels off in thin strips, and its sturdy needles, grouped in pairs and often twisted, are dark green.
- The **larch**, with a reddish cracked bark, is the only one to change colour in autumn and lose its needles in winter. Soft to the touch, the needles are grouped together into bright green rosettes.

A **botanical path** *(600m/656yds)* and the **Tétras discovery path** *(1hr 15min, brochure on sale at tourist office)* offer educational walks. Accommodation and camping are available *(caravans forbidden)* at the Refuge de **Basse Rua** *(reservation advisable; ☎06 09 31 62 18; www.basserua.com).*

🥾 HIKES

Pic de Chabrières★★

In winter, access via the 🚠**Chabrières gondola** *(☎04 92 46 51 04; www.sedev.fr), the Crévoux and Chabrières chairlifts. In summer, access via the Chabrières gondola, then on foot (3hrs 30min there and back). It is advisable to wear walking boots.*

The upper station of the **Télécabine de Chabrières** stands at the foot of the **Kilometre lancé** speed-record trial run; view of Ste-Marie, Ste-Catherine, Col de Vars and Crêtes de l'Eyssina.

The **Pic de Chabrières** offers a magnificent **panorama★★** of the Forêt Blanche ski area backed by the Pic de la Font Sancte, the Queyras Massif, the snow-capped Pelvoux and the peaks surrounding the Lac de Serre-Ponçon, which is visible from the **Col de Crévoux★**.

Tête de Paneyron★★

🥾 *Leave the car at the Col de Vars. 3hrs 30min there and back on foot. It is advisable to wear walking boots.*

Walk down towards Barcelonnette for a few minutes and turn left onto a path which leads to a shepherd's house; above and to the right are some cairns which mark the way. After a 10-minute walk, you will find a clearer path which climbs steeply as it nears the summit. Beautiful **panorama★★** of the ski area from the Pointe de l'Eyssina to the Val d'Escreins and of the road to the Col de Vars, from Guillestre to the River Ubaye.

ADDRESSES

🛏 STAY

😊😊 **Hôtel Alpage** – *05560 Ste-Marie-de-Vars. ☎04 92 46 50 52. www.hotel-alpage.com. Closed 16 Apr–14 Jun, 2 Sept–14 Dec. 🅿. 17 rooms ⌂, half-board available, restaurant😊😊.* Ancient village farm now houses this hotel. Spacious, pleasant rooms with cute regional décor. Traditional cuisine served in the former barn.

🍴 EAT

😊 **La Passerelle** – *Les Claux. ☎04 92 46 53 28. passerelle05560@free.fr. Closed May–Jun and Sept–Nov. ♿.* Local specialities, *pierrades*, fondues and pizzas, served in this bar-restaurant with a sunny terrace facing the ski slopes.

😊😊 **Chez Plumot** – *☎04 92 46 52 12. dominique.lallez@wanadoo.fr. Closed May–Jun and Sept–Nov.* Rustic restaurant serving traditional dishes.

Alpine landscapes are tamed by touches of Provence in this region of the southern Alps. The scenery is diverse; ranging from the immense man-made Lac de Serre-Ponçon in the east, to the barren limestone escarpments shadowed by the Obiou mountain in the northwest. In the centre sits the lively town of Gap, which makes a great base for exploring the surrounding countryside. Whether sipping a cool drink in a pretty village square, or quizzically admiring the Demoiselles Coiffées, this region gives you a hint of the Mediterranean while remaining firmly planted in the Alps.

Follow the Eagles

The Route Napoléon follows the emperor's route on his return from Elba. It runs the length of his journey, from where he landed in Golfe-Juan with 1 000 troops, through to his triumphant arrival in Grenoble. The route is lined with plaques and monuments bear the flying eagle symbol inspired by Napoleon's remark: "The eagle will fly from steeple to steeple until he reaches the towers of Notre-Dame." The emperor and his troops covered this journey in five days, much of it on foot since the poor road conditions made it impossible to travel by carriage.

On 6 March 1815, travelling along a coach road, he reached Gap, where he was warmly welcomed. Leaving Gap he climbed up the Col Bayard, passed through the Champsaur and stopped for the night at Corps, where General Combronne had reserved a room for him at the Auberge Dumas. A commemorative marble plaque marks the occasion.

The Emperor's Legacy

As a sign of gratitude to the people who offered hospitality to him along this route, the emperor bequeathed a sum of money to the region, intended for the construction of refuges at the top of the passes for travellers taken by surprise in bad weather conditions. Work began in 1854. Originally eight refuges were planned, but only six were finished due to lack of funds.

Now most of the refuges have fallen into ruin, or have been replaced by hotels, restaurants and bars, such as the ones at the Col du Noyer and the Col de Manse.

Highlights

1 Take to the water at Europe's largest artificial lake, **Lac de Serre-Ponçon** (p384)

2 Visit the **Abbaye de Boscodon**, and then enjoy a walk along the botanical path in its ancient forest (p385)

3 Stroll around the pretty village of **Embrun**, and admire its fine church (p388)

4 Try your hand at boarder cross-racing or snowscootering at the ski resort of **Superdévoluy** (p392)

5 The view from the basilica **Notre-Dame-de-la-Salette** (p395)

Village of Embrun

© Franck Guiziou/hemis.fr

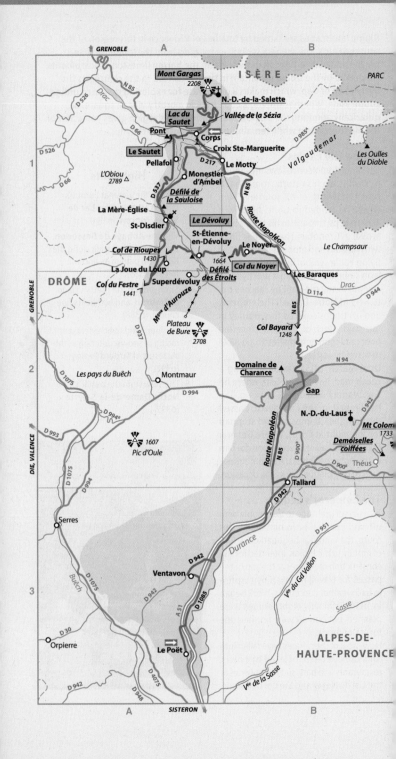

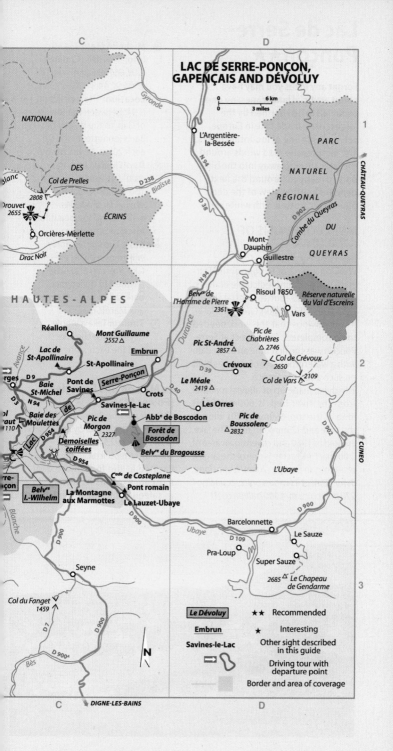

LAC DE SERRE-PONÇON, GAPENÇAIS AND DÉVOLUY

6 km
3 miles

Gyronde

NATIONAL

L'Argentière-la-Bessée

PARC

DES

Col de Prelles
2808

Biaisse

D 238

D 38

N 94

NATUREL

RÉGIONAL

Drouvet
2655

ÉCRINS

Orcières-Merlette

DU

Mont-Dauphin

Guillestre

Col du Queyras

D 902

blanc

Drac Noir

Combe du Queyras

CHÂTEAU-QUEYRAS

QUEYRAS

1

HAUTES-ALPES

Belvᵉ de
l'Homme de Pierre
2361

Risoul 1850

Réserve naturelle
du Val d'Escreins

Réallon

Mont Guillaume
2552 △

Vars

Pic de
Chabrières
△ 2746

Avance

Lac de
St-Apollinaire

Embrun

Durance

Pic St-André
2857 △

Col de Crévoux
2650

rges

D 9

St-Apollinaire

Serre-Ponçon

D 39

Crévoux

2109

Baie
St-Michel

Pont de
Savines

N 94

Le Méale
2419 △

Col de Vars

D 3

Crots

D 40

Les Orres

de

Savines-le-Lac

ol
aut
110

Baie des
Moulettes

Lac

D 954

Pic de
Morgon
2327

Abbᵉ de Boscodon

Pic de
Boussolenc
△ 2832

D 902

CUNEO

Demoiselles
coiffées

Forêt de
Boscodon

L'Ubaye

D 954

Belvᵉ du Bragousse

re-
nçon

Blanche

Belvᵉ
l.-Wilhelm

La Montagne
aux Marmottes

Cᵈᵉ de Costeplane

Pont romain

Le Lauzet-Ubaye

D 900

Ubaye

Barcelonnette

Le Sauze

D 900

D 109

Super Sauze

Pra-Loup

2685 △ Le Chapeau
de Gendarme

Seyne

D 7

D 900

Col du Fanget
1459

Bès

D 900A

N

Le Dévoluy   ★★ Recommended

Embrun   ★   Interesting

Savines-le-Lac   Other sight described
                        in this guide

                    Driving tour with
                    departure point

                    Border and area of coverage

DIGNE-LES-BAINS

3

C   D

383

Lac de Serre-Ponçon★★

Forget any ideas you may have about artificial landscapes; no one could fail to be charmed by the largest man-made lake in Europe, set against a line of mountain peaks. The picturesque road winds around the lake, turning away into the hills, only to reappear around the next bend for another view of the deep blue water, dotted with white sails.

METAMORPHOSIS OF A VALLEY

Barrage★★

Work on a project to control the Durance, this most unpredictable of rivers, began in 1955, but torrential floods devastated the region two years later. It was obvious that the work needed to be completed. The project at Serre-Ponçon was the first time an earth dam with a waterproof core of clay was built on such a scale in France.

The dyke, made up of alluvial material from the river bed, is 600m/1 969ft long at the top, 650m/2 133ft wide at the base and 123m/404ft high. The lake, created in 1960 and covering an area of 3 000ha/7 413 acres, is one of the largest reservoirs in Europe *(20km/12.4mi long, 3km/1.8mi at its widest point; capacity: 1 270 million cu m/4 500 million cu ft).*

- 🕭 **Michelin Map:** 334 F6.
- 🛈 **Info:** 9 av. de la Combe d'Or, 05160 Savines-le-Lac. ☎04 92 44 31 00.
- ▶ **Location:** The lake lies on N 94; between the towns of Gap, to the W, and of Barcelonnette, to the E, each 20km/12.4mi away.
- ☺ **Don't Miss:** The huge dam is an amazing sight. You will also want to see Les Demoiselles coiffées and the beautiful forest of Boscodon.
- 👫 **Kids:** The whole family will enjoy a dip in the lake. You can also take children to the animal park called La Montagne aux Marmottes.
- 🕐 **Timing:** Take a whole day to enjoy the lake and the excursions.

La Maison des Énergies (Power Station)

🕐*Open Jul–Aug 9am–12.30pm, 1.30–5pm; rest of year by appointment.* ☞*Free.* ☎*04 92 54 58 11.* *www.ot-serreponcon.com.*

Located at the foot of the dam, this museum explains its history. As well as safeguarding the lower valley and

View of the Lac de Serre-Ponçon from near Pontis

S Sauvignier/MICHELIN

A Dam of Good Fortune

At the inauguration of the dam, in the late 1950s, the Serre-Ponçon lake was of little interest to tourists, and the 800m/875yd band of land around its waters – then controlled by the EDF – was non-constructable. The dam's hydroelectric power station saved the lakeside, better than a financial investor in any development plan could have done. With its 80km/49.7mi of preserved shoreline and waters at 23°C/75°F in summer, it has become a paradise for watersports enthusiasts: six beaches patrolled by lifeguards, with 800 mooring rings. Fishing is authorised all year round. In 2010, the lake celebrated its 50th anniversary, with a firework display and various exhibitions.

improving irrigation, the dam is also an energy provider. Its power station can produce 720 million kw per year.

The Lake★★

The curved shape of the lake, its indented shores and the promontory marking the confluence of the Durance and the Ubaye blend with the natural scenery, and offer at the same time a variety of watersports.

The lake has a multitude of activities on offer: canoeing, waterskiing, windsurfing, kitesurfing, jet-ski, etc.

EXCURSIONS
Demoiselles Coiffées★

From the dam, take D 900B towards Tallard, then right towards Théus. Continue for 5km/3.1mi to the car park. The path, steep in places, veers to the right, 50m/55yds further on.

This geological curiosity is the strangest in the area. The **salle de bal**★ has the largest number of columns. The summit of **Mont Colombis** has a fine **panorama**.

Abbaye de Boscodon★

Between Savines and Embrun, turn right onto D 568. ⏱*Open Jun–Aug Mon–Sat 10.30am–noon, 2.30–6.30pm; rest of year contact for details.* *Guided tour (1hr 30min) by appointment.* ⊗6€ *(children under 12 free).* ☎04 92 43 14 45. http://abbayedeboscodon.fr.

The pale stone architecture of this abbey is striking in its purity.

The refectory houses exhibitions. It is now home to a small community of Dominican nuns.

Forêt de Boscodon★★

From the abbey, take the rte de la Fontaine-de-l'Ours.

This forest extends over 850ha/2 100 acres. Inside a chalet there is a map of the forest trails, including the **botanical trail**, which has identification panels along its route to help identify 24 different species of trees. From the **Belvédère du Bragousse**★ there is a fine view of the gullied Bragousse cirque.

🚗 DRIVING TOURS

1 FROM THE LOWER DAM TO EMBRUN
39km/24.2mi. Allow 1hr 30min.

▷ *D 3 to Chorges follows the downstream reservoir before rising sharply within sight of the dam.*

Belvédère Ivan-Wilhelm★★
Alt. 847m/2 779ft.

This viewpoint, built along the axis of the ridge line of the dam and named after the engineer who designed it, offers a fine overall view.

Muséoscope du Lac

Guided tours (1hr), times vary, contact for details. ⊗9€ *(children 7.10€).* ☎04 92 54 50 00. www.museoscope-du-lac.com.

Films and models offer reminders of the villages which were submerged under the lake.

▷ *Beyond the tunnel, the road veers away from the lake.*

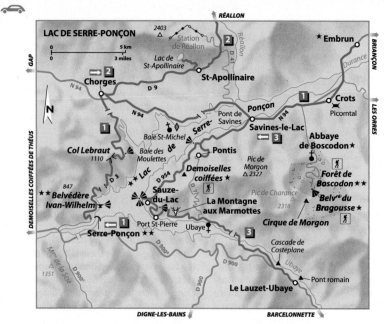

Col Lebraut

From the pass, there is a view of the Gap basin to the west and of the lake to the east. Further on *(1.2km/0.7mi)*, the **panorama**★ extends to the whole northeast arm of the lake.

Chorges

The village has retained a few old houses, a lovely 16C fountain and a hill-top church with a rounded 12C porch; to the right stands an imposing pink-marble stela, known as "Nero's stone", which may well be the pedestal of a Roman statue. Also noteworthy is the 14C bell tower.

From Chorges, the Savines road runs east towards the lake; note, on the right, a chapel standing on a tiny island in the **Baie St-Michel**. Further on, N 94 runs across the lake over the **pont de Savines**, almost level with the water.

Savines-le-Lac

This village, rebuilt in the 1960s on the banks of the lake, is the successor of Savines village which was submerged by the dammed waters. The church of **St-Florent** (1962), designed by the architect De Panaskhet, has remarkable stained-glass windows.

There are numerous watersports on offer here. The beach has a lifeguard in summer. It is also the principal point of embarkation for **boat trips**.

Crots

Lying on the edge of the lake, this ancient village and its 14C church are overlooked by the 13C **Château de Picomtal**, extended in the 16C.

The beach has a lifeguard in summer Just before Embrun, the road crosses the Durance near the expanse of water reserved for sailing and watersports.

Embrun★

See Embrun p388.

2 VALLÉE DE RÉALLON

18km/11.2mi. Allow 1hr. Two alternative access roads: D 41 N from the pont de Savines or D 9 from Chorges; choose the second one in preference.

From Chorges, D 9 offers lovely views on its way to **St-Apollinaire**, a picturesque village overlooking the Lac de Serre-Ponçon; this section of the route sometimes forms part of the Monte-Carlo Rally. The Lac de St-Apollinaire can be reached along a road on the left.

Réallon

Réallon has been a famous archaeological site since the discovery last century of Bronze Age precious objects, exhibited in the Gap Museum.

This village has become a winter and summer family resort. Throughout the year the **chairlift** climbs up to an altitude of 2 135m/7 005ft (viewing table). There are 19 downhill ski runs, and 25km/15.5mi of marked trails for nordic skiers. In summer, there is a large choice of mountain-bike trails, and hikes.

3 FROM SAVINES-LE-LAC TO LE LAUZET-UBAYE
25km/15.5mi. Allow 1hr.

Savines-le-Lac

From Savines, D 954 winds along the indented shore of the lake; the **view**★ becomes gradually broader, embracing the wild southern part of the lake.

▶ *A small road branching off to the left leads to Pontis.*

Pontis

The old school houses the **Musée de la Vallée** (open 6 Jul–31 Aug daily 10am–noon, 2.30–7pm; 3.30€ (children 1.80€); 04 92 44 26 94), a museum illustrating school life in the 19C.

▶ *Turn back towards D 954.*

Demoiselles Coiffées de Pontis★
30min return.

A path climbs up to the moraine glaciers, also called *cheminées de fées*. They are protected from erosion by an umbrella-shaped rock.

Sauze-du-Lac

This is a picturesque **site**★★, on top of a promontory overlooking the lake, at the confluence of the Durance and Ubaye. There is a fine **view**★ back towards Le Sauze from the road beyond.

The beach at **Port St-Pierre** is patrolled by a lifeguard in summer. The road winds steeply down the slope, offering a clear view of the Ubaye arm of the lake.

La Montagne aux Marmottes

 Open Jul–Aug daily 10am–7pm; May–Jun and Sept Wed–Mon 10am–6pm; Oct–Nov Wed–Mon 11am–5.30pm 13€ (children under 15 9€). 04 92 44 32 00. www.parc-animalier-montagnemarmottes.com.

The "Marmot Mountain" is an educational centre, studying and protecting animals from nature reserves and private collections. At certain hours, birds of prey and marmots are presented for close inspection. Also on show are a prehistoric cave dwelling, a beehive with a glass wall and a mountain fauna museum.

After **Ubaye** (the church and the cemetery are all that remain of the flooded village), D 94 runs across a bridge at the extremity of the lake. At the intersection with D 900, on the left, is the **Cascade de Costeplane**.

▶ *Continue along D 900 towards Barcelonnette.*

Le Lauzet-Ubaye

The village lies next to a small lake (*lauzet* in local dialect) where you can swim or hire a canoe.

In the village centre is a small museum of hunting and local flora **Musée de la Vallée** (contact for details; 2€, children free; 04 92 81 00 22).

A Roman bridge spans the river near the modern one.

HIKE
Belvédères de l'Embrunais

Embrun tourist office sells guides detailing the itineraries of the Belvédères de l'Embrunais.

The magnificent Lake Serre-Ponçon is surrounded by easily accessible mountains with fine views.

After a three-hour walk, you reach the **Mont Guillaume** (alt. 2 552m/8 373ft), where there is a chapel, and a panorama of the Durance and the lake. The route de Boscodon (*start from the Ours car park*) leads to the **Pic de Morgon** (alt. 2 324m/7 625ft) in 2 hours 30 minutes with a view of the Lac de Serre-Ponçon.

Embrun★

Embrun is picturesquely perched on a rocky ledge, above the Durance and the Lac de Serre-Ponçon. Its church, the finest in Dauphiné, testifies to its past influence as a religious centre. The town is a pleasant resort offering a wide choice of watersports on the lake as well as the Durance, and walking in the surrounding area. In winter, it is a centre of cross-country and alpine skiing at Les Orres and near the mountain village of Crévoux.

- ▶ **Population:** 6 345.
- **Michelin Map:** 334 G5.
- **Info:** Place Gén.-Dosse, 05200 Embrun. ℘04 92 43 72 72. www.ot-embrun.fr.
- **Location:** Embrun lies on N 94, between Gap and Briançon, close to the lake of Serre-Ponçon.
- **Kids:** The Orres resort, which has the designation "Famille Plus Montagne".
- **Timing:** Allow one hour for a stroll around the town, and two hours to visit the cathedral and Tour Brune.

SIGHTS

The old town evokes Provence: it's hard to imagine that the peaks of Queyras are only a matter of miles away.

Cathédrale Notre-Dame-du-Réal★

"Réal" is a distortion of "royal": the church was once Notre-Dame-des-Rois, or kings. The edifice reflects the transitional period from the Romanesque style to the Gothic style (late 12C–13C). **Portail "le Réal"**★ – This is a remarkable example of Lombard art. The arch of the doorway is supported by pink marble columns.

Interior – ⏱Open daily 9am–6pm. ⏺Guided tours of cathedral and treasury (1hr 15min) Jul–Aug Tue 9pm and Thu 10am, on request at the tourist office. ⬧4.50€. ℘04 92 43 72 72.
The Byzantine influence explains the absence of a transept. The late-15C organ is one of the oldest in France.

Treasury★ – ⏱Open Jul–Aug Wed 10am–noon, Sun 3.30–5.30pm; rest of year contact the tourist office for information. ⬧3€. ℘04 92 43 72 72.
It was one of the richest in France before being plundered in the 16C. However, it still contains an important collection.

Place de l'Archevêché

The Belvédère du Roc offers a fine view of the Durance Valley and Morgon mountains. The 13C **Maison des Chanonges** is a rare example of Medieval domestic architecture.

Tour Brune★

⏱Open mid-Jun–mid-Sept Tue–Sat 10am–noon, 3–7pm, Sun 3–7pm; rest of year contact for details. ⬧Free. ℘04 92 43 49 48.
This 12C tower, the former keep of the episcopal castle, houses a **Musée du Paysage**, devoted to the Parc national des Écrins.

A Religious Centre

Ebrudunum was a small Gallic village that resisted Caesar. Finally defeated, it was, however, made capital of the Alpes Maritimes under Nero. Later, the village became part of the Holy Roman Empire. Its archbishops were granted joint temporal power of Embrun with the dauphins, and the right to mint their own money. From the 14C onwards, the pilgrimage to Notre-Dame-du-Réal attracted large crowds including Louis XI and Louis XIII. The rank of canon conferred on Louis XI during his visit was passed on to his successors. Embrun struggled for centuries against invasions, but only the Revolution deprived it of its status.

Rue de la Liberté and Rue Clovis-Hugues★

At no. 6 rue de la Liberté, the governor's palace boasts a beautiful wooden **doorway**★ in Renaissance style. Admire the 12C carved façade between no. 29 and no. 31 rue Clovis-Hugues. There is a 16C fountain in red marble on the place St-Marcellin.

Chapelles des Cordeliers

Houses the tourist office.
The side chapels of the former Franciscan church are decorated with 15C and 16C **murals**★.

EXCURSIONS
Les Orres★ 🎿🏂

▶ *17km/10.6mi SE of Embrun. Leave Embrun along N 94 towards Gap, drive for 2km/1.2mi and turn left onto D 40. The twisting road rises up the Vallée de l'Eyssalette.* 🏠 *05200 Les Orres.* ℘*04 92 44 01 61. www.lesorres.com.*
This winter resort, created in 1970, developed to form one of the main winter-sports resorts.
The **Orres resort** (alt. 1 650m/5 413ft) and its annexes of Le Pramouton (alpine skiing) and Champs-Lacas (cross-country skiing) offer a wide choice of activities including snowmobiling, paragliding and snowboarding.

Gap★

The austere valleys are behind us. Arriving at Gap, one is first struck by one of the largest valleys in the Alps. The snow glistens for a long time on the surrounding peaks, but the blue horizons reach far into the distance towards Provence. The most vibrant town of the southern Alps does not have spectacular monuments, but it has a pleasant southern feel to it with pedestrianised streets, lively squares and colourful houses. As a tourist centre, Gap takes advantage of its situation near the Lac de Serre-Ponçon, and ski resorts such as Orcières-Merlette.

Prelongis and Fontaine Chairlifts★

From the top there is a view of the Lac de Serre-Ponçon and the Embrun area.

Crévoux

▶ *13km/8.1mi E of Embrun. Leave at the eastern end of Embrun on the rte du Coin; join the rte du Col de Parpaillon.*
Between the **Montagne du Méale** and the **Pic St-André**, this small family resort has 13 alpine ski runs and 45km/28mi of cross-country ski trails.

🚗 DRIVING TOUR

FROM THE LOWER DAM TO EMBRUN

Drive of 39km/24.2mi shown on the Lac de Serre-Ponçon map, 1 (&*see p386).* &*See p385.*

ADDRESSES

🏠 STAY

🛏 **Camping Les Esparons** –
Rte de la Madeleine. 05200 Baratier. N on D 40 or D 340. ℘*04 92 43 02 73. www.lesesparons.com. Closed end Aug–mid-Jun.* &🛏. *83 pitches.* This simple campsite offers spacious pitches, bounded by apple trees.

▶ **Population:** 37 785.
- **Michelin Map:** 334 E5.
- **Info:** 2A cours F. Mistral, 05002 Gap. ℘04 92 52 56 56 www.gap-tourisme.fr.
- **Location:** Gap lies at the intersection of the Route Napoléon (Grasse to Grenoble) and D 994 (Valence to Briançon).
- **Don't Miss:** The Musée Départemental.
- **Kids:** The Domaine de Charance.
- **Timing:** Allow three hours for the town, museum and Domaine de Charance.

SIGHTS

Few architectural traces remain of Gap's ancient past. The town was destroyed on several occasions, one of them being during the Wars of Religion in 1692.

The Old Town★

Few traces of the original medieval architecture remain, but the pattern of streets has changed little. The pedestrian area, lined with colourful houses, comes alive during the Saturday market.

Cathedral – The 19C passion for Historicism was given full rein in this fusion of neo-Romanesque and neo-Gothic styles. Note the use of white, red and grey stone from the area, reminiscent of Embrun's cathedral.

Musée Départemental★

6 av. Mar.-Foch. ⏰*Open Jul–mid-Sept Wed–Mon 10am–noon, 2–6pm; mid-Sept–Jun Mon and Wed–Fri 2–5.30pm, Sat–Sun 2–6pm.* ⏰*Closed public holidays except 14 Jul and 15 Aug.* ⊚*3€.* ♿*04 92 51 01 58.*
Situated inside the public gardens of **La Pépinière**, this museum houses fine archaeological collections and antique earthenware. Among the local finds in the archaeology section (basement) are a **double bust of Jupiter Ammon**★, the **stelae**★ of Briançon, a Roman bas-relief from the 2C and some remarkable pieces of **jewellery**★ dating from the Late Bronze Age. The **display of local ethnography**★ illustrates traditional daily life in the **Queyras** region from the 17C onwards, with carved **furniture**★★ and beautifully decorated objects.
Don't miss the **mausoleum**★ of the Duc de Lesdiguières, sculpted by Jacob Richier (1585–1640). It comprises four bas-reliefs describing the capture of Grenoble, the victory of Pontcharra, the meeting of Moulettes and the taking of Barraux.

EXCURSION
Domaine de Charance★

▶*3km/1.8mi W of Gap. From Gap, drive W along D 994 (towards Veynes) and turn right. In Jul–Aug, a navette bus*

"Linea" runs here. 📷*Guided tour (1hr 30min), details at tourist office.* ⊚*5€ (children free).* ♿*04 92 52 56 56.*
Overlooking the valley, on the site of the old castle, destroyed by successive wars and replaced by a gracious 18C château, these English-style **gardens** occupy some 220ha/544 acres.
After the French Revolution, rich owners embellished the gardens, which now include lawns, a forest, waterfalls, a lake and, most spectacularly, a **garden** on four terraces with a view of surrounding mountains. Gap purchased the estate in 1973 and has developed it into an environmental centre.
Footpaths include a tour of the lake *(30min)*, nature trails and a more ambitious climb up to the Pic de Charance *(3hrs)*. The **Conservatoire botanique alpin** has a large collection of rare and exotic plants, as well as old roses, fruit trees – including 550 varieties of apples – and local wild plants.

Notre-Dame-du-Laus

▶*23km/14.3mi SW of Gap. From Gap, drive S (D 942A) towards Valserres then turn left onto D 11 and left again onto D 211.*
In 1664 the Virgin Mary appeared to the shepherd **Benoîte Rencurel** (1647–1718). In 1666 a shrine was erected inside the small chapel and the hamlet became a place of pilgrimage.

ADDRESSES

🏠 STAY / 🍴 EAT

⊚⊚**Hôtel Le Clos** – *Par N 85, rte de Grenoble and private road.* ♿*04 92 51 37 04. www.leclosfr. Closed all saint holidays, Mon (except hotel) and Sun eve.* 🅿. *Wifi. 29 rooms* ⊐*9.50€, restaurant* ⊚⊚. This hotel, on the outskirts of Gap, has well-equipped rooms (Wifi, flat-screen TV), some with balconies. Rustic dining room.

⊚**Le Tourton des Alpes** – *1 r. des Cordiers.* ♿*04 92 53 90 91. Closed 1st 2 weeks Jul.* ♿. The best place to taste the local speciality, the *tourton*, a sort of deep-fried pastry with various fillings.

Route Napoléon★

From Le Poët to Corps

You are following the footsteps of Napoleon: did you know that, in his era, this pass was inaccessible to carriages, and that he had to cross these peaks on horseback or on foot? Today, even if the journey is easier, the landscape has hardly changed: the road passes through the Gapençais region with its spectacular panoramas over the valleys of the Durance and Drac.

🚗 DRIVING TOURS

THE CROSSING OF PRÉALPES DE DIGNE

Drive of 100km/62.1mi from Castellane to Poët. Allow half a day. See p446.

THE CROSSING OF THE GAPENÇAIS

Drive of 79km/49.1mi shown on the regional map (see p382). Allow half a day.

Le Poët

Fifteen minutes from the exit of the village of **Poët** (on the ancient N 85), stop off at the **viewing table** to admire the wonderful panorama of the Gapençais, Embrunais and Écrins summits.

▷ *Return on N 85. At the entrance to Valenty, turn left onto D 21.*

Ventavon

Built upon the ruins of an 11C fortress, this pleasant village has a Provençal style. From the top of the modern belfry *(58 steps, viewing table)* is a **panorama★** over the pink-tiled roofs, the Durance valley and, to the northeast, the Monts de l'Embrunais, the Pic d'Aujour and Crête de Selles to the northwest and the Gache and Lure mountains to the south.

▷ *Return to N 85 towards Gap.*

Michelin Map: X341 A/B 5 and 334 D/H 3/10.

Info: Palais des Congrès, 22 cours H.-Cresp, 06130 Grasse. ☎04 93 40 04 34. www.route-napoleon.com.

Location: Covers the section from Poët to Corps.

Don't Miss: The town of Gap; and also the lovely villages of Ventavon and Tallard.

Timing: Leave a day for the journey from Castellane to Corps.

Tallard

This old village is surrounded by orchards and vineyards.

Église St-Grégoire – Reconstructed in the 17C, inside there is a 15C **baptismal font** supported by lions.

Château – *Open 1 Jul–15 Sept 10.30am–12.30pm, 2–6pm; rest of year contact for details. Guided tour (1hr), reserve at town hall (☎04 92 54 10 14) or tourist office (☎04 92 54 04 29). 4.50€(children 2.50€).* Constructed between the 14C and the 16C it suffered serious damage in 1692 when the Savoie troops seized the region. It has since been restored. Admire the Renaissance **corps de logis** and the Flamboyant-style **chapel**.

Gap★

See Gap p389.
After Gap, N 85 climbs to **Col Bayard** (alt. 1 248m/4 094ft) and continues to **Le Champsaur** (see p355).

Les Baraques

From Baraques there is a fine **view★** of the escarpments of Dévoluy (Montagne de Féraud), then the peaks of Olan, in the gap at **Valgaudemar** (see p358), and at l'Obiou, dominant citadel of the Lac du **Sautet**.

Le Dévoluy★★

Rising to nearly 3 000m/9 843ft, Dévoluy is impressive. Legend has it that the Obiou, Grand Ferrand, Pic de Bure and Féraud clashed together to form this wild, isolated region. Today the eroded cliffs of these four mountains are reflected in the peaceful waters of Sautet lake.

EXCURSIONS
Station
Superdévoluy is distinguishable by its architecture. Houses and shops on two levels wind up the Aurouze mountain, their wooden balconies facing south-west. **Joue du Loup** has the charm of a traditional resort-village.

Ski Area
The **ski area** includes a variety of ski runs down the northern slopes of the Sommarel and the Pic Ponçon, totalling 100km/62.2mi. The link with the Joue du Loup ski area is accessible to inter-mediate skiers; those more experienced prefer the Pierra, Sommarel and Mur red runs. Cross-country skiers have access to 14 circuits. Superdévoluy is also the place to try something new, be it slalom, boarder cross, snowscooter-ing (a cross between snowboarding and BMX biking) or even a dog-sled ride. There are 31km/19.3mi of marked trails for walkers.
For children there is a pony-sledge (details from the tourist office).

🚗 DRIVING TOURS

1 ROUTE DELS COLS★
Drive of 81km/50.3mi shown on the local map (opposite). Allow 3hrs 30min.

Corps
The capital of Beaumont, the historic region of the middle valley of Drac, is a lively summer resort and a convenient meeting place for pilgrims on their way to Notre-Dame-de-la-Salette. The Obiou towers over the delightful valley **land-scape**★★. Wander through its narrow

● **Michelin Map:** 334 D4.
● **Info:** 05250 St-Étienne-en-Dévoluy. ℰ04 92 58 91 91. www.ledevoluy.com.
● **Location:** The Dévoluy is a limestone massif isolated between Buëch and Champsaur.
● **Don't Miss:** Be sure to see the dam on the Sautet with the lake behind it; the mountain passes of the Noyer and Rioupes; the impressive gorges of the Souloise and the Étroits.
● **Timing:** The two proposed excursions, the round tour of the Cols and the circuit around the Lac du Sautet, will take you a day.

medieval streets and along the ruined ramparts (*15min return*). At the end of the village, towards Gap, there is a small path on the right leading to the **St-Roch** chapel.

▷ *Leave Corps drive W on D 537.*

Before the **pont du Sautet** (*see tour 2, p394*), take a few minutes to appreci-ate the Dévoluy lake and its surrounding mountains.

▷ *Leaving the dam, continue on D 537.*
To the west the imposing **Obiou** summit looms over the Drac Valley.

Défilé de la Souloise★
The road runs between splendid lime-stone escarpments.

▷ *Continue S along D 937.*

St-Disdier
Park at the village centre and continue on foot. 20min climb.
The **Mère-Église** (11C) was the first church in Dévoluy. Inside, notice the decoration with the royal fleurs de lys (1783) and the sun, moon and Maltese cross of the Templars.

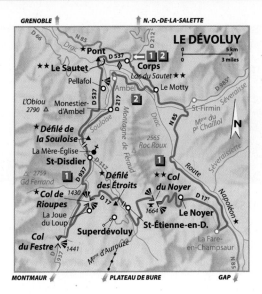

▶ *Turn right after 7km/4.35mi to Gap.*

Col du Festre
Alt. 1 441m/4 728ft.
Fine views from this pass below the desolate heights of the Montagne d'Aurouze.
From the Col du Festre, you can reach **Montmaur**★ (*◉ see Les Pays du Buëch p413*) by following the deserted landscape of the Vallée de la Béoux. From Potrachon there is a view to the left of the Bure Plateau.

▶ *Turn around; take D 17 on the right.*

The road winds through larch trees.

Col de Rioupes★
This pass offers **views** of a vast ring of barren mountains: Crêtes des Aiguilles, Grand Ferrand, Obiou and Montagne de Féraud separated by the Col du Noyer from the Montagne d'Aurouze, which is riddled with sink-holes.

Défilé des Étroits★
Stop the car between the two bridges which D 17 crosses.
The road overlooks the River Souloise, which has carved a passage through the rock. The via ferrata is guaranteed to set the pulse racing.

St-Étienne-en-Dévoluy
This green oasis in the barren Dévoluy landscape was once virtually self-sufficient, cut off from the rest of the world until the connecting road was opened in 1872.

Col du Noyer★★
The pass is closed early Nov–mid-May.
Both sides of the pass offer contrasting **landscapes**: the barren ridges of the Dévoluy on one side and, on the other, the broad Drac Valley (Bas-Champsaur), framed by the heights of the Vieux-Chaillol Massif, the Gapençais mountains, and beyond the Écrins Massif.

Le Noyer
👤👥 **Maison de la botanique** –
🕐*Open Jul–Aug daily 2–6pm; school holidays except Christmas Wed 2–6pm; rest of year contact for details.* 🎟3€ *(children 2€).* 📞*04 92 23 28 02.*
Behind the church, this "Maison" houses one of the écomusées of Champsaur-Valgaudemar. Discover the flora and fauna of the region.

▶ *The road which descends to the Drac is difficult (especially the first 5km/3.1mi). It leads to La Fare-en-Champsaur on D 1085, which continues to Corps.*

Barrage du Sautet

© F. Scholz/age fotostock

[2] LAC DU SAUTET★★

Drive of 35km/21.8mi from Corps, [1]
(see p392) shown on the local map
(see p393). Allow 2hrs.

▶ *Leave Corps on D 1085 towards Gap.*

This road overlooks the lake. At **Motty**, turn right onto D 217, after a bridge crossing the Drac.
At a left-hand bend, as well as from the terrace in front of the Ambel church, there is a magnificent **panorama**★ of the Obiou, the Vercors, Corps, Salette and the peaks overlooking the entrance to Valgaudemar. After **Monestier-d'Ambel** the road descends to the bottom of the Souloise Valley.

Barrage du Sautet★★

Just after the bridge, there is a tourist kiosk, where you can walk down stairs to view the vault close up.
This elegant dam, 126m/413ft high, has created a reservoir capable of containing 115 million cu m/4060 million cu ft of water.

The Legend of the Pucelle

Three centuries ago, the Lord of Malmort tried to take advantage of a young Dévoluarde girl on the eve of her wedding. Terrified, but strong-willed and reckless, she escaped by jumping across the narrowest point in the Souloise gorges, which has since been known as the "**Saut de la Pucelle**" ("the maiden's jump").

ADDRESSES

🏠 STAY

🛏 **Gîte Le Beau Rêve** – *Le Pré, 05250 St-Étienne-en-Dévoluy. 04 92 58 96 38. www.lebeaureve.com. 🚗. 4 rooms ⏢6€.* These four gîtes, sleeping 2 to 8 people, are ideal for families.

🛏🍽 **Hôtel du Tilleul** – *R. des Fosses. 38970 Corps. 04 76 30 00 43. www.hotel-restaurant-du-tilleul.com. Closed 1 Nov–20 Dec. 🅿. Wifi. 18 rooms ⏢8€, restaurant🍽.* Well-maintained rooms, those in the annexe are quieter. Simple rustic restaurant serving traditional fare.

🛏🍽🍽 **Hôtel La Neyrette** – *05250 St-Disdier 04 92 58 81 17. www.la-neyrette.com. Closed 13–24 Apr, 11 Oct–5 Feb 🅿. 12 rooms ⏢9€, restaurant🍽🍽🍽.* Lovely auberge with prettily decorated rooms. The restaurant is housed in the ancient mill. Copious regional dishes.

🍽 EAT

🍽🍽 **Château d'Aspres** – *05800 Aspres-lès-Corps. 04 92 55 28 90. www.chateau-d-aspres.com. Open Christmas. Closed 13 Nov–end Feb and Sun eve except public holidays. ♿. 7 rooms ⏢12€, restaurant🍽🍽🍽.* Elegant dining room serving traditional dishes.

🏃 ACTIVITIES

👫 **Base nautique du pays de Corps** – *Lac du Sautet. 38970 Corps. 04 76 30 02 01. www.lacdusautet.com. Closed mid-Sept–mid-Jun. 5€ per hr electric boat 4–5 people (children 5€).* Various watersports on offer, including the hire of boats to cruise the Souloise gorges.

Notre-Dame-de-la-Salette★

This basilica, a pilgrimage destination, is built on a splendid site: an alpine cirque, the perfect setting for great walks.

 DRIVING TOUR

FROM CORPS TO NOTRE-DAME-DE-LA-SALETTE

Drive of 15km/9.3mi shown on the regional map (see p382). Allow 1hr.

Corps
See Le Dévoluy p392.

Leave Corps at the NW edge on D 21.

Between Corps and La Salette-Village, you climb the **Vallée de la Sézia**. The road passes the graves of the passengers of a Canadian plane which crashed into the Obiou on 13 November 1950.
Between La Salette-Village and the sanctuary the road rises steeply facing the **Cime de l'Obiou**★★ (alt. 2 789m/9 150ft).

Notre-Dame-de-la-Salette★
Open 4 Apr–mid-Nov. *Guided tour (30min), contact for details. Free. 04 76 30 00 11. http://lasalette.cef.fr.*
On 19 September 1846, in the guise of a weeping lady, the Virgin Mary appeared to two children: Maximin Giraud, aged 11, and Mélanie Calvat, 14 , who were tending cows. She spoke to them in French and the native dialect, then disappeared in a halo of light.
After five years of investigations, controversy and trials, the Church formally approved the testimony of these two children, and a basilica was constructed. Today, the sanctuary receives from 150 000 to 200 000 pilgrims each year. Besides the film about the apparition at 9am and 2pm, there is: the Mass at the basilica at 10.30am, the pilgrim meeting at 3pm, the rosary at 6pm and the torchlight procession at 8.30pm. There are organised pilgrimages; the main ones take place on 15 August and 19 September.

- **Michelin Map:** 333 I8.
- **Info:** Mairie, 38970 La Salette-Fallavaux. 04 76 30 01 72.
- **Location:** 15km/9.3mi N of Corps. The road may be closed in winter.
- **Don't Miss:** Besides the basilica, there is a fine view from the Planeau mound and a panorama from Mont Gargas.
- **Timing:** Allow one hour to visit the basilica and to walk to the Planeau; the hike to Mont Gargas takes around two hours.

HIKES
Walking around the Planeau, a mound surmounted with a cross, you have a fine circular **view**★ of the Oisans, the Dévoluy and the Beaumont.

Mont Gargas★★
2hrs return.
Climb to the north, on marked paths going up to slopes overlooking the sanctuary, to the Col de l'Éterpat; from here, follow the ridge on the left.
At the summit, a viewing table indicates the most important destinations for Christian pilgrimages (Lourdes, Jerusalem, etc.), and also Lhasa. Superb **panorama**★★.

ADDRESSES

STAY
Hôtellerie du Sanctuaire – *Sanctuaire de la Salette, 38970 Salette-Fallavaux. 04 76 30 32 90. http://lasalette.cef.fr. Closed 15 Oct–4 May. 228 rooms* *.*
Write or telephone the sanctuary to reserve.

The valley of the River Ubaye forms the most northern region of the Provençal Alps. The landscape is a patchwork of rocky peaks, wide valleys carved out of layers of flysch, and fine conifer forests creating an impression of spaciousness that contrasts with the deep valley scenery of the northern Alps. Valley life centres around Barcelonnette, its capital since 1230 – a lively market town worth visiting for its Mexican-style villas. A major ski destination, it is also a paradise for walking, cycling and white-water sports.

Highlights

1. Eclectic-style architecture of **Barcelonnette** (p398)
2. The gentle ski slopes of **Le Sauze**, or, for advanced skiers, the **Pra-Loup** area (p399 and p400)
3. A hike up the amusingly named **Chapeau de Gendarme** (p400)
4. The splendid view from the single-arched bridge **Pont du Châtelet** (p403)

Surviving the Long Winters

Prior to 1883, the Ubaye Valley was cut off during the harsh winter months. The resourceful inhabitants developed their own survival methods for resisting the long winter. The women and young children stayed in the valley and tended to the livestock and the house, while the elder male members found work elsewhere. The opportunities were sparse; some found work as shepherds on the lower-altitude plains, but most left the valley with a bundle of textiles on their backs. Itinerant pedlars sold locally produced fabrics, and finer cloth purchased from factories – Jausiers was a centre for silk production. They trekked the roads in Piedmont, Provence, the Rhône Valley, the Saône and even as far as Flanders.

The economy of the valley relied for a long time on the textile industry, which led eventually to the emigration of the trade; first to Louisiana, then to Mexico, where the Arnaud brothers established a textile business in the 19C.

History of the Ski Resorts

The first winter ski club was founded in Barcelonnette in 1910. It was only after the Couttolenc family from Le Sauze

Barcelonnette

© Franck Guiziou/hemis.fr

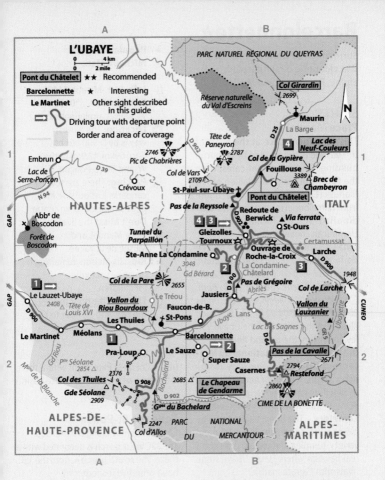

L'UBAYE

0	4 km
0	2 mile

Pont du Châtelet ★★ Recommended

Barcelonnette ★ Interesting

Le Martinet Other sight described in this guide

⇒ Driving tour with departure point

Border and area of coverage

PARC NATUREL RÉGIONAL DU QUEYRAS

Réserve naturelle du Val d'Escreins

Col Girardin 2699

Maurin
La Barge

4 **Lac des Neuf-Couleurs**

Tête de Paneyron

2746 Pic de Chabrières 2787

Col de la Gypière

Fouillouse

3389 Brec de Chambeyron

Embrun
Lac de Serre-Ponçon

D 39

Col de Vars 2109

St-Paul-sur-Ubaye

Pont du Châtelet

ITALY

Crévoux

Pas de la Reyssole

Redoute de Berwick

Via ferrata

St-Ours

Certamussat

HAUTES-ALPES

Abbᵉ de Boscodon

Forêt de Boscodon

Tunnel du Parpaillon

4 **3** Gleizolles

Tournoux

Ouvrage de Roche-la-Croix

Larche

1948

Ste-Anne La Condamine

3048 Gd Bérard

2 La Condamine-Châtelard

3

Col de la Pare 2655

Le Tréou

Pas de Grégoire

Abriès

Col de Larche

GAP

Le Lauzet-Ubaye

2408 Tête de Louis XVI

Vallon du Riou Bourdoux

Jausiers

Faucon-de-B.

St-Pons

Ubaye Lans

Vallon du Lauzanier

CUNEO

Les Thuiles

Lac des Sagnes

Le Martinet Méolans

1 Barcelonnette

Pas de la Cavalle 2671

Pra-Loup

Le Sauze

2

Super Sauze

2794

Mᵐᵉ de la Blanche

Pᵗᵉ Séolane 2854

2376

Col des Thuiles

Casernes

Le Chapeau de Gendarme

Restefond

2860

Gde Séolane 2909

D 908

2685

CIME DE LA BONETTE

ALPES-DE-HAUTE-PROVENCE

Gᵉˢ du Bachelard

2247 Col d'Allos

PARC NATIONAL DU MERCANTOUR

ALPES-MARITIMES

---

proposed the use of their hillsides to the club that the resort really became popular. The first ski lift made its appearance in 1935 on the slopes of Le Sauze. This "monte-skieurs" took skiers on a type of sledge, which was pulled up to the top of the slopes.

It was in the late 1950s that Pra-Loup was created under the initiative of Pierre Grouès, with the help of the famous Alpine skier Emile Allais, and Honoré Bonnet, coach of the French alpine skiing team. In the 1970s a major decision was taken to link Pra-Loup to Foux d'Allos, making this one of the largest ski areas in the southern Alps. The combined domain is called "l'Espace Lumière". In 2011 Pra-Loup celebrated its 50th anniversary.

White-water rafting on the Ubaye

Barcelonnette★

Surrounded by white rocky slopes,
Barcelonnette is multifaceted:
alpine, Provençale and Mexican.

SIGHTS
Place Manuel
This vast open space at the heart of
the *bastide* is surrounded by colourful
buildings and pavement cafés. Note
the **fountain** with a medallion of J.A.
Manuel (1775–1827), a political figure
from Barcelonnette, and the **Tour Cardinalis** (15C), the former belfry of a
Dominican convent.

Villa La Sapinière – Houses the **Musée
de la Vallée**★ *(10 av. de la Libération;
☉open Jul–Aug daily 10am–noon, 2.30–
7pm, rest of year Tue–Sat 2.30–6pm;
☉closed public holidays; ⇔3.30€, under
20 1.80€; ♿ ℘04 92 81 27 15)*, which
illustrates the history of the Ubaye Valley. In season, the ground floor houses
the **Maison du Parc national du Mercantour** *(☉open Jul–Aug daily 10am–
noon, 3–7pm, last half of Jun and first half
of Sept 3–6.30pm; ⇔free; ℘04 92 81 21
31)*, with information on guided **walks**.
Cemetery – The burial vaults made by
Italian artists are striking in their size and
variety: temples, shrines, a chapel and a
real pavilion where Haute Ubaye stone
rivals with Carrara marble.

🚶 HIKE
Vallon du Riou Bourdoux★
*3hr hike from the Le Tréou car park.
From Barcelonnette, follow D 900
towards Gap then turn right onto D 609
to La Frâche. Pass the aerodrome and,
leaving the access road to La Frâche on
your left, cross the Riou Bourdoux and
continue along the forest road.*
Stop by the Tréou forest lodge and follow
the **marked nature trail**.

Col de la Pare★
🚶 *4hrs 30min there and back from
Les Dalis car park. For the section to
Le Tréou, ☉see above.*
To the right, the trail leads through a forest to a cottage. A path goes up to an
altitude of 2 000m/6 562ft, and contin-

▶ **Population:** 2 766.
🗺 **Michelin Map:**
Local Map L'Ubaye.
ℹ **Info:** Pl. F.-Mistral, 04400
Barcelonnette. ℘04 92 81 04
71. www.barcelonnette.com.
▷ **Location:** The easiest
way is by D 900 out of
Gap, 69km/42.9mi to the
W, and Serre-Ponçon.
🅿 **Parking:** There are several
car parks just outside the
pedestrianised town centre.
👁 **Don't Miss:** The lively
place Manuel, and
Musée de la Vallée.
👫 **Kids:** La Maison du Rafting
organises activities
for children.
🕐 **Timing:** One hour to see
the city, and an hour to visit
the Musée de la Vallée.

ues to Col de la Pare, from where there
is a **view**★ of the Barcelonnette basin.

EXCURSION
Église de St-Pons★
▷ *2km/1.2mi W along D 9 or D 900.*
The 12C **west porch** is decorated with a
frieze. The **south porch**★, from the 15C,
has a primitive iconography.

🚗 DRIVING TOURS

ROUTE DU COL D'ALLOS★★
*Drive of 20km/12.4mi shown on the
regional map (☉see p397). Allow 1hr.*

▷ *Leave Barcelonnette on D 902 going S.*

The road rises above the **Gorges du
Bachelard**★. After the Fau bridge the
Brec de Chambeyron summit is in view.
The D908 road travels through the Agne-
liers Valley, overlooked by the **Grande
Séolane rocks**. The road then runs
along the top of the Bachelard Valley
with vertiginous views of the river.

Col d'Allos★★ (☉*See Val d'Allos p479)*

The "Barcelonnettes" in Mexico

It all started in Jausiers (9km/5.6mi NE of Barcelonnette) in 1805, when two brothers, Jacques and Marc-Antoine Arnaud, decided to leave the family business and try their luck in America. In Mexico, Marc-Antoine opened a fabric store known as "El cajón de ropas de las Siete Puertas" (a craft centre in Barcelonnette now bears the same name). The success of the business was such that by 1893 there were more than 100 fabric stores in Mexico owned by natives of the Ubaye region. Some tried their hand at other businesses (paper, breweries and finance, including the London and Mexico Bank). Most of the emigrants were country folk who, except for the Arnaud brothers, eventually returned to their native country, and built sumptuous villas to mark their success in the New World. These opulent houses built between 1880 and 1930 have various architectural styles: Italian, Tyrolean, Baroque, but not Mexican. Notice fine examples on avenue des Trois-Frères-Arnaud and avenue de la Libération. One of the last to be built was the Villa Bleue (1931), avenue Porfirio-Diaz.

CIME DE LA BONETTE★★★
Drive of 31km/19.3mi shown on the regional map (see p397). Allow 1hr 30min.

◗ *Leave Barcelonnette on D 900, towards Italy.*

Leaving Jausiers, turn right onto the route de Nice. The road passes Abriès Valley on the left, and then goes up the **Pentes du Restefond**. Continue up to the Col de la Bonette and you arrive at the foot of the Cime de la Bonnette.

ADDRESSES

STAY
 Chambre d'hôte Le Bosquet – *2av. Mme Watton-de-Ferry.* 📞*04 92 81 41 28.*
www.ubaye.com. Closed end Oct–early Feb. ♿📶 ⛖. *3 rooms* ⛖. An agreeable house with large rooms furnished with lovely old furniture.

EAT
⊜⊜ **Le Gaudissart** – *Pl. Aimé-Gassier.* 📞*04 92 81 00 45.* ♿📶. Good-value menu and daily specials. Pleasant dining room and shady terrace.

SHOPPING
Market – *Pl. Aimé-Gassier.* This food market runs every Wednesday and Saturday mornings.

ACTIVITIES
Brevet des 7 cols – 📞*04 92 81 04 71.12€.* A book of tickets, on sale at the tourist office, for bike rides to seven peaks.

Le Sauze and Super Sauze

Le Sauze and Super Sauze shelter at the foot of the Chapeau de Gendarme and the Pain de Sucre. These two resorts, the oldest in the Alps, are known for their family atmosphere, and gentle slopes that are ideal for skiing and snowshoeing.

- **Michelin Map:** 334 I6.
- **Info:** Immeuble La Perce-Neige, 04400 Le Sauze. 📞04 92 81 05 61. www.sauze.com.
- **Location:** 5km/3.1mi from Barcelonnette.
- **Kids:** The resort has the designation "Famille Plus Montagne" (see p30).

⚡ HIKE

Le Chapeau de Gendarme★★

4hrs 30min there and back.

From the Raquette car park a path follows the ski runs then goes through the woods to a stream. The path continues alongside the stream before heading due west to a ridge.

Follow the ridge towards the southwest, then go round a rock spur and join up with another trail at Collet du Quieron. Continue south towards the east face of the Chapeau de Gendarme and take the right-hand fork to the Col de Gyp, where there is a fine **view**★ of the valley.

Pra-Loup

The resort of Pra-Loup is one of the most popular in the Alpes-de-Haute-Provence, owing its fame to its wonderful position in a larch forest on the edge of a plateau, and its vast ski domain.

THE RESORT

Pra-Loup 1500 has relatively traditional architecture, while, linked by a free shuttle bus, Station 1600 is marked by a lively ice-rink and shopping centre.

The **station** is linked with that of La Foux d'Allos (⊙ *see Val d'Allos p479*). Known as **L'Espace Lumière**, it has 50 ski lifts and 180km/112mi of runs. Pra-Loup boasts the most spectacular *big air* in France, a snowpark and four avalanche-free zones. In summer, there are a range of bike routes, white-water sports, paragliding guides and walks.

⚡ HIKE

Col des Thuiles★

This Pra-Loup itinerary *(6hrs)* is suitable for experienced walkers. The ascent to the pass is arduous but the walk down is pleasant.

Take plenty of drinking water. Return by the lake, and then the ski lift.

A path running along the mountain slope offers a fine **view**★ of the Agneliers area, the Gorges du Bachelard, the Cimet and Chapeau de Gendarme, even-

There is a splendid **view**★★ of the Barcelonnette basin and the **Gorges du Bachelard** from the summit.

ADDRESSES

🏨 STAY

⊖⊖ **Les Flocons** – *Super Sauze, 04400 Le Sauze.* ☏*04 92 81 05 03. www.lesflocons.com. Closed 16 Apr–14 Jun and 16 Sept–mid-Dec.* 🅿. *17 rooms* ⊑. At the edge of the village, this hotel has comfortable non-smoking rooms for two to six people.

- 🕤 **Michelin Map:** 334 H6.
- ℹ **Info:** Maison de Pra-Loup, 04400 Pra-Loup. ☏04 92 84 10 04. www.praloup.com.
- ▶ **Location:** Pra-Loup is 8.5km/5.3mi SW of Barcelonnette by D 902 and D 109.

---

tually reaching the Col des Thuiles. From here, cross the Torrent de Langail and follow the yellow markings. A path leads downhill for 100m/328ft, then turn right onto a path which crosses the Torrent des Bruns. Beyond the woods, a broad path leads to the Pas Lapeine.

Carry on through the Gimette Forest, across the stream and then head towards Grande Séolane and the Col des Thuiles (2 376m/7 795ft). The path opposite the Grande Cabane leads to the Lac de Pra-Loup.

ADDRESSES

🏨 STAY

⊖⊖⊖**Hôtel Le Prieuré des Molanès** – *Les Molanès.* ☏*04 92 84 11 43. www.prieure-praloup.com. Closed 21 Apr–4 Jun, 22 Sept–14 Dec.* 🅿. *13 rooms* ⊑, *half-board available, restaurant* ⊖⊖. Near the ski lift. This former priory has rustic rooms. Regional mountain food.

L'Ubaye★★

Not so long ago this remote valley was cut off from the rest of France: D 900 to Barcelonnette was only completed in 1883. Until then crossing between the snow-capped peaks of the Cols de Vars, de Larche and d'Allos, was made by perilous mule tracks. This isolation has influenced the political history of the valley. It had closer links with Piedmont and remained in the sphere of influence of the Comtes de Savoie (14C–18C). Ubaye offers an unspoiled paradise for hiking, skiing and white-water sports.

🚗 **DRIVING TOURS**

① **LOWER UBAYE VALLEY**
Drive of 21km/13mi from Le Lauzet-Ubaye to Barcelonnette shown on the regional map (see p397). Allow 30min.

The vast horizons of Serre-Ponçon are long gone. The gorges become narrower and the spirit of the landscape changes entirely. After a turning, first surprise: in the distance stands Les Séolanes and La Roche Bénite. Just before the Martinet, on the left, there is a rocky summit aptly named "La Tête de Louis XVI".

▷ *Turn right.*

Le Martinet
As you drive through the village, look right up the Grand Riou Valley sloping down from the Montagne de la Blanche. Before the bridge, a road runs down to an important watersports park.
The landscape becomes more open beyond Les Thuiles and the view embraces the Barcelonnette basin at the heart of the valley. To the right, the ski resort of **Pra-Loup** (*see opposite*) can be seen clinging to the steep slopes of the Péguieu. On its way to Barcelonnette, the road runs between the tributary valleys of the Riou Bourdoux (*see p398*) and of the Bachelard.

- 🐾 **Michelin Map:** 334 H/I 6/7.
- ℹ **Info:** R. Principale, 04850 Jausiers. ℘04 92 81 21 45. www.jausiers.com.
- ▷ **Location:** The Barcelonnette basin lies at the intersection of the international Gap–Cuneo route (D 900–S 21) and the Route des Grandes Alpes (D 902), between the Col de Vars and the Col de la Cayolle.
- 🐾 **Don't Miss:** Be sure to visit the Musée de la Vallée, the Fort de Tournoux and the remarkable pont du Châtelet.
- 🕐 **Timing:** It will take you a day to complete all the excursions.

② **BARCELONNETTE BASIN**
Drive of 15km/9.3mi from Barcelonnette to Gleizolles shown on the regional map (see p397). Allow 1hr.

▷ *D 900 runs across the Barcelonnette basin.*

Faucon-de-Barcelonnette
This ancient village going back to Roman times is said to owe its name to the numerous birds of prey (falcons) inhabiting the area. It was the home of St Jean de Matha, who founded the Order of Trinitaires, charged to recover the Christian prisoners from the Muslims. The **Tour de l'Horloge** (12C) dominates the village. Notice at the right of the church a Gallo-Roman sarcophagus lid covered with sculptured scales.

Jausiers
The Arnaud brothers, who pioneered the mass emigration of locals to Mexico in 1805 (*see box, p399*), were natives of this village, which has been twinned with Arnaudville in Louisiana since 1995. Several buildings testify to the success of the emigrants in the New World (Villa Morélia, Villa Manon).

The artist **Jean Caire** (1855–1935) was also a native of Jausiers, and it was in the family house, in 1889, that he settled permanently with his companion, the artist **Marie Tonoir** (1860–1934). Some of their work is on display at the Villa La Sapinière in Barcelonnette (*see p398*).At the entrance to the village, the gourmets should stop at the **Maison des Produits de Pays** (*see Addresses, p404*).

Behind the beautiful carved larch door, the Jausiers church reveals a wonderful Baroque interior with a strange altar of the dead: it is decorated with sculptures of skulls and human bones.

Like at Méolans, a campanile sitting high on a rock overlooks the village, on the site of a former church. Follow the chemin de Croix; you'll get there in 45 minutes. From there, you will appreciate the panorama (*orientation table*).

At the exit, the **Plan d'eau de Siguret** is a pleasant place to swim, climb and eat a picnic.

Musée de la Vallée★ – www.ubaye. com/musees. In a house on the main square, this branch of the Museum offers information on the area, including geologic and fossil displays, winter sports, and the story of the development of hydraulic works that tamed the floods.

Moulin d'Abriès★ – *Leaving Jausiers, take D 64 to Restefond, then turn right after 600m/656yds.* Open Jul–Aug Tue and Fri 4–5pm; Apr Fri during school holidays 2–3pm; rest of year contact for details. Closed 15 Dec–15 Mar. *Guided tour (1hr).* 5.50€ (children under 7 free). 04 92 81 11 42. http://robert.martin9.free.fr. A miller's son revived this marvellous wooden machine turned by water. The guided tour includes the attic, which houses the grinding stone and amazing silk sieve.

Fragile Beauty

Caution: In the absence of oxygen rubbish can take several years to decompose. A high-altitude lake is a very vulnerable environment.

Return to D 900 and turn right.

Beyond Jausiers, wooded basins alternate with deep gorges. The strategic importance of the narrow **Pas de Grégoire** and **Pas de la Reyssole** (*see opposite*) was at the origin of the construction of the Fort de Tournoux.

Turn left.

Ste-Anne La Condamine
Alt. 1 800m–2 400m/5 906ft–7 874ft. If you have bought the "Ski-Pass 3 stations", this relaxing, small ski resort with 30km/18.6mi of downhill ski runs has all you need.

Return to D 900. 1km/0.6mi after La Condamine-Châtelard, turn left before the bridge; park the car in open space.

Fort de Tournoux★
The walk up to the fort can only be made on the days when there are guided tours. Make sure you have walking boots. Registration required at the tourist office 04 92 81 03 68. www.ubaye.com. Open Jul–Aug Tue and Thu–Sat 10am, 12.30pm, Wed, Sun and public holidays 2.30pm; mid–end Jun and early–mid-Sept Tue and Sat 2.30pm; public holidays contact for details. Guided tours (1hr 30min) by reservation. 6.50€ (children under 12 3.50€). 06 87 35 93 99.

Clinging to the rocks these fortifications, built from 1843 to 1865, are a real feat of engineering. The different batteries are linked by underground passages and steps (including a flight of 808 steps). The upper fort has a pink marble façade, and from its batteries there is a fine **view**★ of the valleys.

7km/4.3mi along a forest road branching off D 900 to the right, just before the intersection with D 902.

Ouvrage de Roche-la-Croix
This fort, built between 1931 and 1940, formed part of the Maginot line of defence. The tour illustrates the fighting here in 1940 and 1945.

D 900 disappears deep into the Vallée de l'Ubayette, and D 902 leads to the Haute Ubaye. This area provides a condensed history of military architecture.

③ UBAYETTE★

Drive of 11km/6.8mi from Gleizolles to the Col de Larche (on the Italian border) shown on the regional map (see p397). Allow 30min.

D 900 follows the Ubayette Valley lined with villages destroyed in 1944 and rebuilt after the war.

St-Ours

A narrow twisting road, branching off D 900, leads to this isolated hamlet, famous for its fortifications which withstood attacks by the Italians in 1940. The fort of **St-Ours-Haut**, an infantry and artillery station, forms the central part of the fortifications. It was used together with the Roche-la-Croix Fort to block the Col de Larche. At St-Ours-Bas is a branch of the **Musée de la Vallée★**, which describes military life.
On the north side of the Rochers de St-Ours, a path gives access to the base of the **Via ferrata de St-Ours** offering rock-climbers two different courses, L'Ourson and L'Aiguille de Luce.

Larche

This is the last French village before the Italian border. There are 30km/18.6mi of ski runs and two snowshoe trails and in summer it is ideal for hiking. Beyond the Col de Larche, on the Italian side is the lovely Lac de la Madeleine.

④ UPPER UBAYE VALLEY★★

Drive of 28km/17.4mi from Gleizolles to Maurin shown on the regional map (see p397). Allow 3hrs.

The Briançon road (*D 902*) follows the upper Ubaye Valley. The **Redoute de Berwick** on the right formed part of fortifications built at the beginning of the 18C in anticipation of the union of the Ubaye region with France. The road and the river then go through the corridor formed by the **Pas de la Reyssole**.

St-Paul-sur-Ubaye★

This village is the starting point of numerous excursions. The **church★** dates from the Early Middle Ages but the chancel was rebuilt in the 15C and the vault in the 16C.
The former barn of the Maison Arnaud houses the **Musée de la Vallée** (open Jul–Aug daily 2.30–6.30pm, Easter holidays Tue–Sat 3–6pm, Jun and Sept Tue–Sat 2.30–6.30pm; 2€; 04 92 84 36 23), whose collection is devoted to agriculture and forestry. It displays tools and machinery from the Ubaye region and illustrates traditional techniques, some of which are also demonstrated at a fair of local produce which takes place on the third Sunday in August.
In winter, the nordic ski centre offers 17km/10.6mi of trails and a 3km/1.8mi snowshoe track.

▷ *From St-Paul, continue along D 25 and the River Ubaye.*

The road goes through a succession of small hamlets overlooked by the slender steeples of their churches, in particular the façades, often decorated with frescoes.

Pont du Châtelet★★

This site is famous throughout the region; the single-arched bridge, built in 1880, spans the gorge 100m/328ft above the stream. On the way up, there are splendid **views★★** of the Tête de Panyron and the Pic de la Font Sancte.

Fouillouse

This high-mountain hamlet lies on the edge of a desolate glacial cirque overlooked by the Brec de Chambeyron, (alt. 3 389m/11 119ft); 24 houses compose the hamlet, where there are five permanent residents.

▷ *Return by the Vallée de l'Ubaye.*

The road rises towards Maurin through a lonely mountain landscape, enhanced by the Mediterranean light, until suddenly the view opens onto the valley, framed by rocky slopes. A hike *(3hrs)* from La Barge and Maljasset leads to the **Col Girardin**★★.

Maurin

The church stands on an isolated site, surrounded by an old cemetery.

HIKES
Vallon du Chambreyon and the Lac des Neuf-Couleurs★

🚶 *6hrs there and back starting from Fouillouse. Leave the car at the entrance of the village. It is possible to make it a two-day trip by booking a night in the Refuge du Chambeyron. It may be necessary to cross névés (glacial snowpacks). It is therefore essential to wear appropriate boots.*

Go through the village and take the path on the left winding its way through a pine wood to a ledge. After two hours you will reach the **Refuge du Chambeyron** and **Refuge Jean-Coste** overlooking Lac Premier. The superb mountain landscape is framed by the Aiguille de Chambeyron to the north and the Brec de Chambeyron to the east. The Brec de Chambeyron was always regarded as impossible to climb until two climbers from Fouillouse reached the top in 1878, to be followed the next year by the American mountaineer **William A.B. Coolidge**.

The path runs northeast to Lac Long. From the top of a mound on the left there is a fine view of Lac Noir. Continue along the path which goes past the Lac de l'Étoile before reaching **Lac des Neuf-Couleurs**★★.

You could continue climbing for another hour to the **Col de la Gypière**, in clear weather only; walkers must be used to crossing steep screes.

▷ *Return to Fouillouse by the same route.*

Vallon du Lauzanier★

🚶 *In Larche, turn right after the border post and leave the car in the Pont Rouge car park, 6km/3.7mi further on. 2hr walk to the Lac de Lauzanier along GR 5-56.*

Continue along the green valley, past a series of waterfalls. The **lake** fills one of the finest glacial depressions in this part of the Alps. Experienced walkers can take the trail passing the Lac de Derrière-la-Croix to join the **Pas de la Cavalle**★★ *(2hrs there and back; ⏱see Route de la Bonette p500).*

Mountain Bike Circuit du Parpaillon★

🚵 *1 000 m/3 281ft gradient over 30km/18.6mi. Start from the Ste-Anne resort and go in the direction of the Chapelle Ste-Anne and Bérard bridge.*

This tough trail goes along the Parpaillon military route, dug by the alpine troops at the end of the 19C, and then reaches the famous **Tunnel du Parpaillon**, 500m/547yds long. Unsurfaced, it links the valleys of Haute Ubaye and l'Embrunais, and La Condamine-Châtelard to Crévoux, then Embrun.

ADDRESSES

🏠 STAY / 🍴 EAT

😐😐 **Bourillon "Les Granges" Gîte-Auberge** – *Fouillouse, 04530 St-Paul-sur-Ubaye. 7.5 km/4.7mi NE of St-Paul-sur-Ubaye along D 25 and GR 5. ☎04 92 84 31 16. www.gitelesgranges.com. Closed May and 3 Nov–12 Jan. 🅿 🍴. 5 rooms ⚲, half-board available.* This restored ancient farm building has lovely views of the Brec de Chambeyron. Stay in either a dorm or a private room. Homely welcome. Eat and drink while basking in the sunshine on the terrace.

🛒 SHOPPING

Maison des Produits de Pays – *Rte de Barcelonnette, 04850 Jausiers. ☎04 92 84 63 88. www.produitsdepays.fr. Open daily 10am–noon, 2.30–6.30pm.* Run by a group of 52 local producers.

🏃ACTIVITIES

Cycling – *Guide VTT de 20 circuits en Ubaye (8€)* is on sale in local bookshops. Information is available from tourist offices: a guide for cyclists *Vallée de l'Ubaye, faire ou ne rien faire,* and for mountain-bike enthusiasts a detailed map with marked circuits.

LE DIOIS, *Le Buëch and Les Baronnies*

Majestic alpine scenery provides the backdrop to rolling hillsides swathed in lavender, olive trees and vines. This is the point at which the cool forests and jagged peaks of the northern Alps meet the hot scrublands and blue horizons of the southern Alps. Although access via the Drôme Valley is the easiest route to take, a more spectacular entrance via one of the high-altitude passes is worth the effort. A new Parc naturel regional des Baronnies Provençales is to be inaugurated in 2012. It covers 220 000ha/543 632 acres from Nyons, in the west, to Serres, in the east.

The Local Wines

South of the Col de Rousset you start to see the vineyards, clustered mainly around the villages of Die and, slightly higher, Châtillon en Diois. Growing at altitudes of 400m–700m/1 312ft–2 297ft, on predominantly chalky soils, these are some of the highest vineyards in France. According to Pliny, wine has been made here since Roman times. Located at the northern tip of the Mediterranean region and close to the lofty Alps, the climate ranges from hot dry summer days, to cool nights. The most prestigious wines fall under the Clairette de Die AOC, made using the Méthode Ancestrale Dioise, where low-temperature fermentation begins in the vat, and continues in the bottle. The AOC permits a blend of Muscat and Clairette grapes; the better wines, however, are made from 100 percent Muscat.

The more ordinary brut version, Crémant de Die, is made by the champagne method, using a blend of mainly Clairette grape, with some Aligoté and Muscat added.

Highlights

1 The delightful drive along to the **Col de Menée**, through lavender fields and vineyards (p409)

2 The stunning panorama from the **Plateau de Bure** (p414)

3 Stroll round the maze of narrow streets and *drailles* at **Orpierre** (p417)

4 Test your olfactory skills at the **Maison des Plantes Aromatiques** (p419)

5 Enjoy the view from the jacuzzi on the terrace at the spa baths in **Montbrun-les-Bains** (p422)

Coteaux de Die is a still, dry white version made from 100 percent Clairette. Châtillon en Diois AOC includes wine in all three colours, made from various combinations of grapes. The Cave de Die Jaillance coop, on the outskirts of Die, offers a tour and a visitors centre. The local wine festival takes place in September.

Diois vineyards in autumn

© Gérard Labriet/Photononstop

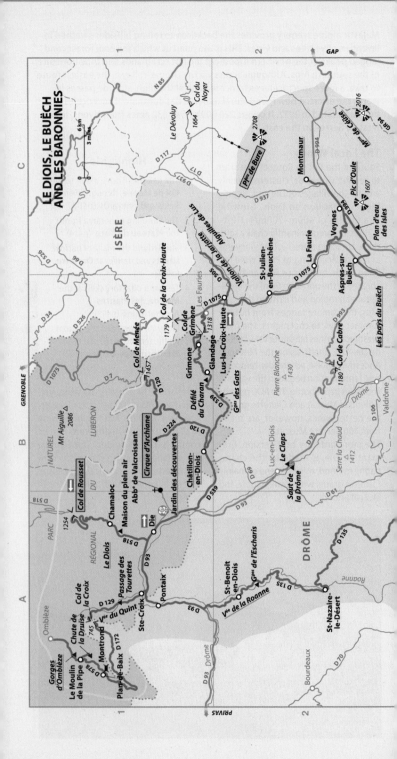

LE DIOIS, LE BUËCH
AND LES BARONNIES

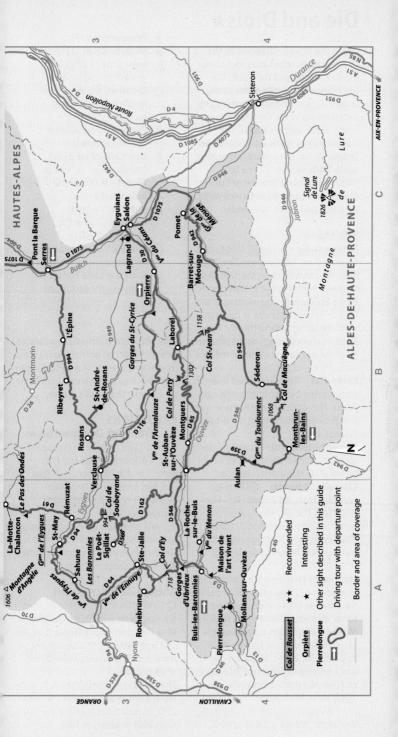

HAUTES-ALPES

ALPES-DE-HAUTE-PROVENCE

Durance

Sisteron

AIX-EN-PROVENCE

A 51

A 51

V 85 N

D 951

D 4085

D 4075

D 951

Route Napoléon D 4

D 4

D 942

D 1085

D 948

Signal
de Lure
1826

Montagne
de
Lure

Jabron

D 946

Pont la Barque

D 994

Serres

D 1075

Buëch

Eyguians
Saléon

D 1075

Lagrand

Vée du Céans

Orpierre

D 30

D 1075

Pomet

Gge de la Méouge

Barret-sur-
Méouge

D 942

L'Épine

D 994

Montmorin

D 26

Ribeyret

Rosans

St-André-
de-Rosans

Gorges du St-Cyrice

D 949

Laborel

1158

Col St-Jean

D 942

Sederon

Col de Macuègne

1068

D 542

D 546

Montbrun-
les-Bains

N

St-Auban-
sur-l'Ouvèze

Col de Perty

1302

Montguers

Ouvèze

D 65

Gges du Toulourenc

D 72

D 942

La-Motte-
Chalancon

D 61

Le Pas des Ondes

Rémuzat

St-May

D 94

Gae de l'Eygues

Montagne
d'Angèle
1606

Vée de l'Eygues

Eygues

Col de
Soubeyrand
994

D 162

Vée de l'Armalauze

D 116

Verclause

Sahune

Les Baronnies

Le Poët-
Sigillat

D 568

Col d'Ey

D 64

Ste-Jalle

Vée de l'Ennuye

718

Gorges
d'Ubrieux

Vée du Menon

La Roche-
sur-le-Buis

D 546

Aulan

D 359

D 70

D 94

Rochebrune

Nyons

D 538

D 94

D 46

Buis-les-Baronnies

Pierrelongue

Maison de
l'art vivant

Mollans-sur-Ouvèze

D 5

D 40

D 13

D 538

D 938

ORANGE

CAVAILLON

Col de Rousset ★★ Recommended
Orpierre ★ Interesting
Other sight described in this guide
Driving tour with departure point
Border and area of coverage

Pierrelongue

407

Die and Diois★

Life in the Diois is sustained by the Drôme and its tributaries, including the Bez, the Rif and the Boulc. Die lies hidden in the hills of the sunny Diois Valley, overlooked by the shiny escarpments of the Glandasse range south of the Vercors Massif. The easiest way to reach Die is along the Drôme Valley, but a more interesting route leads over the Col de la Chaudière, Col du Rousset or Col de Menée and down through vineyards, orchards and fields of lavender.

▶ **Population:** 4 375.
- **Michelin Map:** 332 F5.
- **Info:** ℘04 75 22 03 03. www.diois-tourisme.com.
- **Location:** Situated in the heart of a valley, Die is built on a slight slope.
- **Parking:** Leave your car near the ramparts.
- **Don't Miss:** Fête de la Transhumance in June or the Fête de la Clairette in September.
- **Kids:** The Jardin des découvertes near Die on the road to Gap.
- **Timing:** You will need a half-day to visit the town, and a day and a half to complete the excursions.

SIGHTS

Roman walls – In the 3C these walls measured 3m/10ft thick and 2km/1.2mi long. You can walk along the ruins, from the tourist office to the St-Marcel gate.

Porte St-Marcel – The vaulting of this Roman arched gateway is decorated with interlacing and rosettes; the friezes illustrate chariot racing and the prosperity of the *pax Romana* symbolised by a tamed lion and dancing.

Cathedral – The massive bell tower is surmounted by a wrought-iron campanile. The south wall and Romanesque porch tower belonged to the original 12C–13C church.

Ancien hôtel de ville – *Now the Espace social et culturel de Die et du Diois.* Exhibition of art in this bishop's palace.

Chapelle St-Nicolas – *Open Apr–Sept Wed 11am, Sat 2.30pm; Jan–Mar Wed 11am; Oct–Dec Mon–Sat except public holidays 9am–noon, 2–6pm. Guided tour (30min) by appointment. 2€ (children under 12 free); ℘04 75 22 03 03.*

The interior features a 12C oratory, and magnificent 12C **mosaics** which depict the universe. On the walls, there are still traces of frescoes from the Middle Ages.

Musée d'Histoire et d'Archéologie – 11 r. Camille-Buffardel. *Open Jul–Aug Mon–Sat 2.30–5.30pm; Apr–Jun and Sept–mid-Oct Wed and Sat 2–5pm; end Dec–Mar contact for details. Closed public holidays. Guided tours available (1hr 10min). 3€ (children under 16 free). ℘04 75 22 40 05.*

This 18C *hôtel particulier* houses an eclectic collection which includes some interesting pieces. The Gallo-Roman period is well represented with some exceptional **taurobolic stelae**.

EXCURSIONS

Jardin des Découvertes★

3km/1.8mi to the SE on the road to Gap. Open daily Jul–Aug 10am–6pm; May–Jun 10am–noon, 2–5pm. 6.50€ (children under 10 4€). ℘04 75 22 17 90. www.jardin-decouvertes.com.

In a vast greenhouse, exotic plants grow without soil; protected from wind and weather, hundreds of gorgeous butterflies flutter about in liberty.

Abbaye de Valcroissant

6km/3.7mi on D 93 to Sisteron, then the road on the left. Open Jul–Aug Mon, Wed and Fri 5pm; May Fri 3pm; Jun and Sept Wed 5pm. Guided tour on request. 3€ (children under 12 free). ℘04 75 22 12 70.

The road climbs the gorge finally arriving at a cirque at the foot of the Vercors cliffs; an isolated spot where the Cistercians built an abbey in 1188.

Le Claps
▶ *20km/12.4mi SE along D 93, just beyond Luc-en-Diois.*
This pile of rocks is the result of a huge landslide which occurred in the 15C. It formed two natural dams and two lakes which have now dried up.

🚗 DRIVING TOURS

A drive through the narrow gorges of the Diois leads past clusters of houses, perched high on the hillsides. These little villages offer tourists a welcome break between such impressive landscapes as the Cirque d'Archiane.

1 COL DE ROUSSET TO DIE
22km/13.7mi. Allow 1hr.

Col de Rousset★★
This peak marks the transitional point from the northern to the southern Alps. After the dark misty forests of the Vercors you pass through a tunnel and drive out, at an altitude of 1 254m/4 114ft, into another landscape: the south – rocks, bright sunshine, and an endless blue horizon. The road below twists and turns in sharp hairpin bends. The **ski resort** at Rousset has 25 ski runs, 25km/15.5mi of cross-country ski trails, and 15km/9.3mi of paths for hiking or snowshoeing.

Chamaloc
The mellow-stone houses, roofed with curved tiles, add a Provençal air to the village. Just past Chamaloc, at the Baise farm, there is the **Maison de plein air**, which has a botanical trail.

2 ROUTE DE MENÉE★★
45km/28mi. Allow 2hrs. ☹ The pass is usually blocked by snow in Dec–Mar.

▶ *From Die, follow D 93 towards Gap.*

The road runs through the Die basin, among vineyards overlooked by the limestone cliffs.

▶ *In Pont-de-Quart, turn left onto D 539.*

Châtillon-en-Diois★
🏠 *Square J.-Giono, 26410 Château-en-Diois. ℘04 75 21 10 07.*
Built around a castle that is now gone, the village has retained its medieval character. A network of streets, lanes and covered passages, known as *viols*, surrounds place Reviron.

▶ *Turn left onto D 120 towards the Col de Menée. Take D 224 to Archiane.*

Cirque d'Archiane★★
The upper end of the Archiane Valley is barred by escarpments forming a splendid amphitheatre split in two by a huge promontory, the "Jardin du Roi". Ideal for mountaineering and hiking.
Beyond Les Nonières, the road rises in a succession of hairpin bends; the barren landscape gradually gives way to pine woods and pastures.

▶ *Return on D 224 and turn left.*

Col de Menée★
From the southern end of the tunnel, the view extends to the Montagne de Glandasse, and from the northern end, there is a **panorama** of the Mont Aiguille.

3 VILLAGES OF YESTERYEAR★
14km/8.7mi. Allow 1hr 30min.

From Die to Châtillon-en-Diois
🚶*See 2, above.*

▶ *Leave Châtillon-en-Diois along D 539.*

Gorges des Gats★

Prior to the building of the road in 1865, travellers had to cross several fords in order to go up this narrow gorge.

Glandage and Grimone

The closely grouped houses of these hamlets with large steep roofs, well adapted to heavy snows, give an idea of the hardships of life at high altitude a few generations ago.

Beyond the **Col de Grimone**, the view extends southeast to the Montagne de Garnesier and Crête des Aiguilles.

▷ *Drive S on D 1075.*

Lus-la-Croix-Haute

See Les Pays du Buëch p412.

4 GORGES D'OMBLÈZE★
48km/30mi. Allow 2hrs 30min.

▷ *Leave Die by D 93 towards Crest then turn right onto D 129 to Ste-Croix.*

Ste-Croix

Built on a narrow ridge, the village is overlooked by 13C ruins.

The ancient monastery has a **garden** of medicinal plants and herbs. There is also a **botanical trail** (*1hr 30min*) that starts from here. The road climbs the **Vallée du Quint** and passes through the narrow **Passage des Tourettes**.

▷ *Turn left onto D 172.*

The narrow twisting road leads through oak and pine woods to the **Col de la Croix**, then down the Sépie Valley to Beaufort-sur-Gervanne.

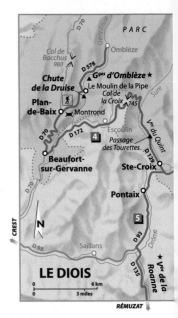

Beaufort-sur-Gervanne

The way offers a spectacular view which includes what remains of the fortifications now turned into a pleasant walk.

▷ *Follow D 70 to Plan-de-Baix.*

Plan-de-Baix

Built on a hillside, the village is overlooked by the Rochers du Vellan cliffs. The 13C–14C **Château de Montrond** towers over the Gervanne Valley.

At first D 578 follows the Gervanne Valley, then it runs down the slopes.

▷ *Turn right in Le Moulin de la Pipe towards Ansage and drive for 1km/0.6mi to the car park.*

Chute de la Druise

1hr return on foot.

A marked path leads to the top of the waterfall; from there, another steep and stony path leads down to the bottom.

The **Gorges d'Omblèze**★ start beyond Le Moulin de la Pipe.

The Petite and the Grande Cascades de la Pissoire fall by the roadside; la Grande Cascade often dries up in summer. There are glimpses of the Col de la Bataille to the north.

What is Clairette de Die?

Crémant de Die (a sparkling dry white wine) is made using a blend of Clairette, Aligoté and Muscat, while the **Coteau de Die** (still dry white wine) is vinified using only Clairette. Châtillon-en-Dios appellation comes in all three colours: red, white and rosé.

410

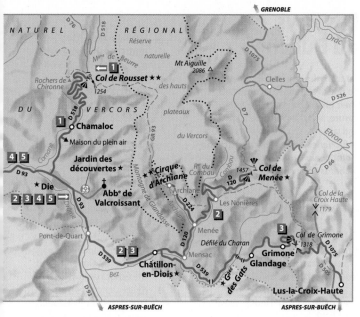

GRENOBLE

NATUREL   RÉGIONAL
Réserve
naturelle
Mt Aiguille
2086 △
Rochers de
Chironne
1 Col de Rousset ★★
1254
des hauts
Clelles
D U   V E R C O R S   plateaux
1 Chamaloc   du Vercors
Maison du plein air
Jardin des
découvertes ★   ★ Cirque
d'Archiane   **1457** ★ Col de
Menée ★
Col de la
Croix Haute
4 5   Archiane   1179
★ Die   Abb° de   D 224   Les Nonières
Valcroissant   **2**
Menée   Col de Grimone
Pont-de-Quart   **3** 1318
Défilé du Charan   Grimone
Mensac   Glandage
2 3   Châtillon-   Lus-la-Croix-Haute
en-Dios ★
Bez
ASPRES-SUR-BUËCH   ASPRES-SUR-BUËCH

5 DIOIS TO BARONNIES★

Drive of 78km/48.5mi shown on the local map (☞see above) and the regional map (☞see p406). Allow 4hrs.

▷ *Leave Die on D 93 heading W to Valence.*

Pontaix

Built on a beautiful **site**★, the main street of this village is lined with 15C and 16C houses. The **chapel** has 15C and 17C frescoes.

▷ *Continue on D 93 for 6km/3.7mi and then follow directions to St-Nazaire-le-Désert. The D 135 climbs above the* **Vallée de la Roanne**★.

St-Benoît-en-Diois

Perched on a rocky ridge is a lovely **church**. The village below has **lintels** dating from the Middle Ages. Beyond St-Benoît the road passes by a waterfall and through the **Gorges de l'Escharis**.

St-Nazaire-le-Désert

A pretty village full of charm. Take D 135 on the left. The road climbs to the Col de Guillens, which affords a view of the **Montagne des Trois Becs**, and

continues to the Col des Roustans, from where there is a view of the **Montagne d'Angèle**. There is a splendid **view**★ at the gorge entrance.

La Motte-Chalancon

A circular village perched on a hill, with small flower-filled lanes, or **calades**. At the church there is a beautiful **view**.

Rémuzat

The association **Vautours en Baronnies** holds an exhibition at the tourist office, and organises discovery trails to observe the vultures at the Rocher du Caire.

ADDRESSES

🛏 STAY

🛏 **Camping Le Glandasse** – *Quartier de la Maldrerie. 1km/0.6mi SE of Die on D 93 (rte de Gap), take the turn on the right. ☎04 75 22 02 50. www.camping-glandasse.com. Closed Oct–early Apr. ♿. 120 pitches.*

🏃 ACTIVITIES

Aloa'venture – *Les Chaussières. 26410 Châtillon-en-Diois. ☎04 75 21 13 63. www.aloaventure.com. Descend the Rio Sourd and in a kayak, and explore or climb the Vallon de Baïn.*

Les Pays du Buëch★

Far from the city crowds, the pays du Buëch are unjustly forgotten. Their green valleys are havens of nature, and the welcome is warm and sincere. You are now in the Alps of Provence, where sharp crests and gaunt peaks provide a backdrop to orchards and lavender fields.

🚗 DRIVING TOURS

THE HAUT-BUËCH AND THE VEYNOIS

Drive of 52km/32.3mi shown on the regional map (see p406). Allow 2hrs.

The **Col de la Croix-Haute**, above Lus, marks the border between the cool, green northern Alps and the dry, barren southern Alps. It is just at the outskirts of Le Faurie hamlet that the Provençal landscape starts to claim the territory.

Lus-la-Croix-Haute – The village is set in a vast alpine basin crossed by the Haut-Buëch.

At the **Maison du patrimoine** there are exhibitions explaining how life was in former times. *Open Jul–Aug Mon and Wed–Sat 10am–noon, 4–7pm, Tue and Sun 10am–noon. ✆04 92 58 52 94.* The **resort** (alt. 1 150m/3 773ft) is near to Vallon de la Jarjatte (*below*).

▷ *From the Grand-Place, go E on D 505.*

Vallon de la Jarjatte★

The road enters the upper Vallée du Buëch, which soon after becomes narrower. Near to Jarjatte is the **winter resort**, which has six alpine ski runs, 18km/11.2mi of trails for cross-country skiing, and one trail for snowshoeing. You will shortly see the sharp outlines of the **Aiguilles de Lus**.

The **view**★★ extends over the barren peaks between the summit of Vachères (alt. 2 400m/7 874ft) and the Tête de Garnesier (alt. 2 368m/7 769ft).

⚓ **Michelin Map:** 334 C5/6.

🔲 **Info:** Office du tourisme d'Aspres-sur-Buëch, av. de la Gare, 05140 Aspres-sur-Buëch. ✆04 92 58 68 88. www.buech.com. Office du tourisme de Veynes, av. Cdt-Dumont, 05400 Veynes. ✆04 92 57 27 43. www.tourisme-veynois.com.

▷ **Location:** Le Buëch is a tributary of the Durance. The pays du Buëch encompass the Veynois and the Haut-Buëch, the Serrois and the Rosanais (*see Serres p415*), Orpierrois and the Gorges de la Méouge (*see Orpierre p417*). From Lus-la-Croix-Haute, you can return to Die (*see p409, follow the route the opposite way round, tour ③*).

🕐 **Timing:** Allow at least half a day to explore Veynois.

👪 **Kids:** The écomusée at Veynes retraces the life of the railway workers.

The route continues through the pine trees to a mountain **cirque** at the end of the Vallée du Buëch.

▷ *Return on D 505.*

The D1075 twists and turn around the stony bed of the Buech: on the right are the **serres**, a succession of long sharp ridges. On the left rise the wooded slopes of the Durbonas mountain.

Beyond **St-Julien-en-Beauchêne**, the mountains, dotted with pine and oak trees, are capped with sharp-pointed peaks, which sometimes overlook a ruined castle, such as the one at La Rochette, the remains of a 12C fort.

▷ *4km/2.5mi past La Faurie, turn left onto D 994B. The road goes through a small pass.*

Veynes

Situated at the axis on the Gap–Die route, this village has suffered successive attacks from the Huguenots, and the troops of the Duke of Savoy. In 1875 the arrival of the railway made it an important rail hub in the Alps.

Écomusée – R. du Jeu-de-Paume. ⏰Open Jun–Sept Wed–Sat 2–6pm. 👓3.50€ (children under 12 1.50€, under 4 free). 📞04 92 58 00 49. www.ecomusee-cheminot.com.

The collection retraces the life of the railwaymen. After wandering the lovely streets of the **old town**, you can set out for one of the pleasant walks, or rides, or enjoy one of the numerous watersports on offer at the **Plan d'eau des Isles**.

▷ Leave Veynes going E on D 994. After 2km/1.2mi, turn left onto D 937.

Montmaur★

This village nestles under the protective gaze of the Aurouze mountain and Pic de Bure. In the 14C, the Montaubans constructed a fortress with four towers and ramparts. Today this château, which was added to in the 16C, has only two towers standing.

Château – ⏰Open Jul–Aug Wed and Fri 3–6pm. 💬Guided tour available (1hr 30min) Tue, Thu and Sat 3pm, 5pm. 👓4€ (children 2€). 📞04 92 58 02 42.

The interior is decorated with monumental fireplaces, ornate beamed ceilings, frescoes and friezes depicting war or mythological scenes. In 1930 it became a vegetarian hostelry, owned by an Englishman. And from 1942 to 1944 the château housed the Resistance.

▷ Return to D 994 and pass again through Veynes. After 5km/3.1mi, turn right onto D 994A.

Aspres-sur-Buëch

This lively Provençal village encircles an ancient feudal motte topped by a clock tower. From here, the **view** extends over the village and the surrounding mountain cirque.

The strong air thermals make Aspres an ideal haunt for those who are passionate about paragliding and **gliding**.

After the **Pont la Barque**, the valley becomes extremely narrow.

Serres★

👣See Serres p415.

THE ROSANAIS REGION

Drive of 93km/57.8mi shown on the regional map (👣 see p407). 👣See p415.

THE ORPIERRE AND THE GORGES DE LA MÉOUGE

Drive of 61km/37.9mi shown on the regional map (👣 see p407). 👣See p417.

🥾 HIKES

Pic d'Oule★

3hr climb. Gradient 800m/2 625ft.

From Veynes, cross the Petit Buëch at the pont de la Morelle then take the path that leads to the farms and crosses a small river. Climbing south to the Col d'Oule, the path passes through a maple

---

"The Light from Above Tells You to Go Even Higher"

This energetic motto derives from one of the 400 sundials in the Hautes-Alpes, illustrations of a vivid imagination and lively pictorial art in the region during the 18C and 19C. The sundials are widespread in Queyras and Briançonnais, but Buëch also possesses some fine examples.

At **St-Julien-en-Beauchêne**, the Maison Forestière in the Durbon Forest has two 18C sundials. The town hall at **Aspres-sur-Buëch** has a contemporary one made by the Orthodox monks. Near La Beaume, at the **Col de Cabre**, a sundial is carved into the rock, at the west entrance of the tunnel, in memory of Ladoucette, the first Préfet of the Hautes-Alpes. Finally, at the primary school at **Serres**, there is a meridian showing the sun's course and the positions of the equinox.

and beech tree forest. The summit is reached after following the line of crests. The summit (alt. 1 607m/5 272ft) affords a magnificent **panorama**★★ of the Val d'Oze and the Massif de Bure.

Montagne de Céüse★

⬛ The isolated and tabular relief landscape of the Montagne de Céüse is astonishing. Several departure points exist.

▶ *From Veynes, from the N side, take D 20 towards Châteauneuf-d'Oze then, at the junction, turn left onto the forest road going to the Col des Guérins.*

Rejoin **GR 94**, which goes around the Céüse mountain easterly. A section of this trail follows a forest route leading to Manteyer on the northeast slope.

▶ *From the Céüse 2000 resort, take the run opposite the hotel which leads to flat ground, then follow the steep run of the Marseillais ski lift until the end.*

Walk up to the Torrent ski lift to where there is a signposted pole and take the path that goes along a ridge. From the Pic de Céüse there is a magnificent **panorama**★★ stretching to the Massif des Écrins and de Bure in the north, and to the Ubaye in the east.
The return can be made by taking a different itinerary to the west, which passes along the top of the climbing site, then the Vallon d'Aiguebelle. Then, follow the trail signposted Céüse 2000 back to the departure point.

Plateau de Bure★★

⬛ 4hrs 30min climb. From Montmaur, take D 937 in the direction of Col de Gaspardon (5km/3.1mi). Park at the Maison Forestière des Sauvas (alt. 1 320m/4 331ft).
A wide gravel path rises to the north to the Bure cliffs, on the right bank of the river. In one hour, you arrive at the Roc

des Hirondelles at the bottom of the Aurouze Valley, from where there is a path marked in blue. After a small pass, you reach the Bure Plateau (*in total, 3hrs 30min walk*).
Continue west to reach the summit, in 45 minutes, of the Pic de Bure (alt. 2 708m/8 885ft). On a clear day, it is one of the most beautiful **panoramas**★★★ of the Alps, extending from the foothills of Mont Blanc in the northeast to the Cévennes (*to the right of Mont Ventoux*) and to the Italian massifs.

ADDRESSES

🛏 STAY

😋😋 **Chambre d'hôte Le Relais de St-Géraud** – *Rte de Grenoble, 05140 Aspres-sur-Buëch. ℘04 92 58 76 55. www.relaisdesaintgeraud.com.* 🅿 🚭. *4 rooms ⌂, half-board available.*
A former coaching inn (1830) with comfortable rooms.

🍽 EAT

😋😋 **La Sérafine** – *Les Parois. 05400 Veynes. 2 km/1.2mi E by rte de Gap and D 20. ℘04 92 58 06 00. Closed Mar and Mon.* Friendly restaurant serving local produce. Terrace for fine weather.

🛒 SHOPPING

Pâtisserie Gondre – *Pl. de la République, 05400 Veynes. ℘04 92 57 26 12. Open Tue–Sat 9am–noon, 3–7pm, Sun 9am–noon. Closed mid-Sept–early Oct and Mon.* Taste the local specialities such as seille, or the pic de bure.

🏃 ACTIVITIES

Base du Chevalet – *Aérodrome, 05140 Aspres-sur-Buëch. ℘04 92 58 61 22.* Gliding at all levels. Also a campsite, restaurant and pool at the base.

Serres★

One of the best-preserved villages in the pays du Buëch, Serres shelters under the pointed La Pignolette rock. A stroll through its maze of streets in the footsteps of the Lesdiguières will bring to life the village's turbulent past.

VISIT

From the car park, turn left and take the rue Varanfrain to the arcaded **placette de la Fontaine**.

Turn right and admire the Renaissance-style façade of the **town hall**, with its veneer of pebbles collected from the Buëch. Its 17C porch has a coppery-red wooden door.

Rue Henri-Peuzin

On the right, the square belfry is called the **Portalet**. Along the street notice the carved **doorways** dating from the 15C to 18C; especially the one at no. 56, with a stone balcony above.

No. 39 is the **Maison de Lesdiguières**★. On the Renaissance façade, there is a carved portrait of Marie Vignon, mistress, then wife, for whom this Medieval house was renovated in 1585.

Typical of rich Protestant mansions, the rustications (rock imitations) are encrusted with galena, which makes

- ▶ **Population:** 1 322.
- **Michelin Map:** 334 C6.
- **Info:** Office du tourisme de Serres, pl. du Lac, 05700 Serres. ℘04 92 67 00 67. www.montagne-en-provence.com.
- **Location:** Between Gap (41km/25.5mi NE on D 994) and Sisteron (34km/21.1mi SE on D 1075).
- **Parking:** Car park near Buëch, by the tourist office.
- **Timing:** Allow 1 hour 30 minutes to walk around the village.

Serres Shipwreck

Le Radeau de la Médus was painted by Géricault in 1819. We can spot, among the survivors of the shipwreck, **Alexandre Corréard**, born at Serres, and a friend of the painter.

the walls sparkle at night. Galena was extracted from the mines at Sigotier. Opposite the church, a passage disappears under the houses and branches off. The **ancient Jewish quarter** is

Village of Serres by the Buëch

© Hervé Lenain/hemis.fr

A Protestant Stronghold

In 1576 the Protestant **François de Bonne**, **Duc de Lesdiguières**, bought the Seigneurie de Serres. It was here that he installed his headquarters, his arsenal, his foundry and built beautiful houses. After the death of Henry IV, the religious conflicts resumed and in 1633 Richelieu ordered the destruction of the citadel and ramparts of Serres.

remarkable for the height of the houses, some of which have six floors.
Return to the car park by the r. des Remparts. 15min.
From the church continue climbing to reach the upper part of the village. Past the Chapelle de Bonsecours, you reach the **tomb of the Jew** (14C).
Continue *(30min)* to reach the good view at **Rocher de La Pignolette**.

🚗 DRIVING TOUR

THE ROSANAIS REGION
Drive of 93km/57.8mi shown on the regional map (see p407). Allow 3hrs.

▷ *Leave Serres on D 994.*

L'Épine
This small village has some interesting lintels and *soustets* (covered passages) on the main street. On the hill stands a windmill dating from 1800.

Ribeyret
Small Provençal village, with a sundial on the village square.

Rosans
This most westerly village in the Hautes-Alpes has a truly Provençal character. Its 16C and 17C houses spiral around the foot of a square 13C **tower** (*guided tours in summer*, 📞04 92 66 66 66).

▷ *Leave at the E side on D 994 and take D 949 on the right.*

St-André-de-Rosans
In the 10C a Cluny monastery was founded on the route linking the Rhône to the Durance. The Wars of Religion have left only a ruined **church**, with a few ancient ornate relics.

▷ *Return to Rosans, and continue on D 994.*

Verclause
This hilltop fortified village was a fief of the dauphins in the 13C. Among the ruins, notice the bell tower. At the promontory there is an exceptional **view**★ of the Eygues Valley and the Clavelière mountain.

▷ *Leave Verclause in a southerly direction (D 116).*

The road follows the Eygues. Just beyond Laux-Montaux, at a bend, there is a view of the **Vallée de l'Armalauze**, and further on the **Gorges du St-Cyrice**.

Orpierre★ *See opposite.*

▷ *Continue on D 30 to return to Eyguians and then D 1075 to Serres.*

ADDRESSES

🏠 STAY / 🍴 EAT

🛏 **Camping Domaine des Deux Soleils** – *05700 Serres. 0.8km/0.5mi SE on N 75 (rte de Sisteron), then 1km/0.6mi on the road on the left, at Super-Serres. 📞04 92 67 01 33. http://perso.wanadoo.fr/2soleils. 72 pitches.* Campsite with a lovely view of the Buëch Valley.

🛏🛏 **Hôtel des Alpes** – *R. du Lac. 📞04 92 67 00 18. http://hoteldesalpes05.fr. Closed 11 Nov–15 Dec. 6 rooms, half-board available.* Small family hotel with simple rooms. Good-value food.

🏃 ACTIVITIES

👥 **Domaine de Germanette** – *Rte de Sisteron. 3km/1.8mi S of Serres on D 1075 then D 50A. 📞04 92 67 03 77. http://germanette.over-blog.com. Open Jun–Aug daily 10am–6.30pm.* Numerous watersports available.

Orpierre★

When he saw this village, situated between Buëch and Baronnies, Giono enthused: "Orpierre where the golden stones stand under a sky of lavender". Sheltered by Quiquillon mountain and its cliffs, much appreciated by climbers, the old streets and restored houses recount a piece of France's history.

VISIT

Wander through the maze of streets and **drailles**, covered passages, of the **old village**. Pass the Café des Alpes, and go along the **Grand-Rue**, which is lined with beautiful doorways, the relics of Renaissance *hôtels particuliers* at Chalon-Arlay, Autard de Bragard and Bozonier. Retrace your steps and walk, on the right, under Cassettes Boureynaud, a *draille* leading to the Jewish quarter. This leads you to the place de la Fontronde, where there is an octagonal **fountain** from the Middle Ages. Turning left takes you to the bottom of the village. Cross the Céans over a footbridge leading to the orchards, then follow the river to come back on the other bank by a wooden bridge. Opposite, you continue along the Grand-Rue then the **Bourgade** quarter.

A road on the right climbs above the village: you can see over the rooftops.

Botanical trail – *Leave the village in the direction of the Belleric waterfall, near the river, at the foot of the Quiquillon. There are around fifty different species of trees growing along here.*

NEARBY SIGHTS

The Cliff Dancers

A real choreography takes place up and down the cliffs of Orpierre. There are 400 climbing routes (from level 3 to 8C), which appeal to climbers from near and far.

The **Quiquillon**★ offers more than 200 equipped climbing routes. You can walk to the **Cascade de Belleric**, where there are climbing trails for beginners. To the north is the Quatre-Heures cliff, which has secure climbing routes.

▶ **Population:** 323.

Michelin Map: 334 C7.

Info: Office du tourisme intercommunal des Baronnies, pl. du Village, 05700 Orpierre. ℘04 92 66 30 45. www.orpierre.fr. Office du tourisme Laragnais-Gorges de la Méouge, pl. des Aires, 05300 Laragne-Montéglin. ℘04 91 65 09 38. www.ot-laragne.fr.

Location: On the banks of the Céans, in the E corner of the Baronnies, Orpierre is overlooked by the Suillet (alt. 1 324m/4 344ft) and the Grand Puy. At 19km/11.8mi S of Serres, you return to the Vallée du Buëch.

Parking: Park near to the church or close to the Belleric river.

Don't Miss: A walk around the old town with its covered passages, and the botanical trail.

Kids: Climbing courses at the Quatre-Heures du Quiquillon cliff.

Timing: Allow at least one hour to stroll around.

🚗 DRIVING TOUR

THE ORPIERRE AND THE GORGES DE LA MÉOUGE

Drive of 61km/37.9mi from Orpierre to the gorges shown on the regional map (see p407). Allow 1hr 30min.

▶ *Take D 30 heading to Eyguians.*

After a short distance, the **Vallée du Céans** widens suddenly: this is where Lagrand towers above the confluence of the rivers Buëch, Céans and Blaisance.

▶ *Turn left.*

A Catholic Baron in a Protestant Region

In the 13C, the dauphin gave Orpierre to Jean Chalon, Lord of Orange, who established his fief here. The Nassau, who ruled Holland, succeeded Chalon. Their successor, **Guillaume le Taciturne**, raised as a Catholic, tried in vain to halt the progress of the reform. Finally, he had to convert to Protestantism. In 1713, under the Treaty of Utrecht, Orpierre was reintegrated into the royal domain. A page in history was turned, but the main route to Orange kept the name "Route des Princes d'Orange".

The town hall in **Lagrand** is a typical 18C Provençal *bastide*.
Église Romane – 📞 *04 92 66 25 35*. 🕐*Open Jul–Sept all day.* This is all that remains of a priory which belonged to the order of St-Sépulcre-de-Jérusalem.

 *Rejoin D 30.*

The village of **Eyguians** is a former *seigneurie* of the Mevouillon barons.

 *Rejoin D 30, cross the pont Lagrand to the roundabout and take the exit to Saléon.*

Buis-les-Baronnies★

This little town on the Ouvèze looks south in more ways than one. Vines, olives, apricots and almonds flourish in the valley and fields of lavender supply many family-run distilleries.
Some 80 percent of France's lime blossom tea comes from this area; on the first Wednesday in July, traders gather along the river bank for the **Foire au Tilleul**★, the largest market of its kind in Europe.

From **Saléon**, which is named after a saltwater fountain, there is a remarkable **view** of the Buëch Valley.

 *Take D 330 then, near to Laragne-Montéglin, turn right onto D 942. Pass through Le Plan and continue on D 942.*

This Buëch tributary has formed the **Gorges de la Méouge**★ for more than 4km/2.5mi. There is a succession of waterfalls and a lovely view of the gorge from the top of **Pomet**.
At **Barret-sur-Méouge**, leaving by the the west exit of the gorges, continue up on the right to Barret-le-Haut and the ruins of an 11C chapel. Leave by the road that goes to the Calandre hamlet, then turn right onto D 170 and climb up to the **Col St-Jean**. You will reach the Céans Valley at **Laborel**, which you follow down to Orpierre. At the exit of the gorges, you can also follow the road to **Montbrun-les-Bains** (🕐*See p422*).

ADDRESSES

🛏 STAY

🏕 **Camping Les Princes d'Orange** – Le Flonsaine. 300m/328yds S of the village, 150m/164yds from Céans. 📞*04 92 66 22 53. www.campingorpierre.com. Closed mid-Oct–early Apr.* ♿ 🍽. *100 pitches.* Campsite perched at 700m/2 297ft.

▶ **Population:** 2 290.
⚙ **Michelin Map:** 332 E8.
🚏 **Info:** 18 b. M.-Esséric, BP 18, 26170 Buis-les-Baronnies. 📞04 75 28 04 59. www.buislesbaronnies.com.
▶ **Location:** Buis stands away from the Rhône Valley, while remaining easy to reach. The A 7 is 60km/37.3mi to the W.
🕐 **Timing:** The old town is well worth an hour or two; an excursion will take about three hours.

⚡WALKING TOUR

The city originated in the shadow of a large boxwood tree, next to a spring. Perhaps that is the reason why the inhabitants of Buis-les-Baronnies have such a passion for trees, which are admired and loved here.

The Brotherhood of the Knights of Linden, along with the Knights of the Olive Tree, are fiercely committed, with a sense of humour, to save these wonderful trees.

OLD TOWN★
Esplanade

This alleyway, shaded by plane trees, runs along the Ouvèze, where the town walls once stood; it is a typical Provençal *cours*, particularly lively on market days (*Wed mornings*).

Opposite the *cours*, on the left bank, looms the **Rocher St-Julien** (767m/ 2 516ft), a limestone outcrop renowned as a climbing site.

◖ *Pass through the porte de Ste-Euphémie leaving on your left the pl. du Marché.*

Rue de la Conche

The shopping street has retained a few fine doorways.

◖ *Turn left onto the r. de la Commune.*

Former Dominican Monastery

The restored 16C building has been turned into holiday accommodation. Note the staircase and the cloisters.

◖ *Left of the convent, pass through the gate and take the vaulted passage called the r. de la Cour-du-Roi-Dauphin.*

Notre-Dame-de-Nazareth

The choir and stalls deserve a look.

◖ *Walk along the left side of the church.*

Ancien Couvent des Ursulines

Only the finely sculpted Renaissance doorway remains from the original chapel. It houses a cultural centre and a library (whose entrance is found on the rue de Beauvoisin).

◖ *Take the r. du Paty to the Jardin des senteurs, behind the Maison des Plantes Aromatiques.*

Maison des Plantes Aromatiques

⏱*Open Mon–Sat all day.* ⏱*Closed public holidays.* ✎*2.50€ (children under under 18 1€, under 12 free).* ♿ ☎*04 75 28 04 59. www.maisondes plantes.com.*

With a **jardin des senteurs** and an amazing collection of aromatic and medicinal plants, the Maison houses exhibitions and organises events and seminars, with a gift shop too.

From the terrace you can admire the view over part of the town.

◖ *Take the Grand-Rue, then cross the pl. aux Herbes and continue down the r. Notre-Dame-la-Brune on the right.*

Place du Marché

This "square", looking more like a wide street, is lined with slightly pointed stone arcades dating from the 15C.

◖ *Take the bottom right-hand corner of the square to return to the esplanade.*

From the esplanade, you can rejoin the promenade de la Digue, which goes along the right-hand bank of the Ouvèze where the **tour de Saffre** (12C) stands, once part of the ancient wall.

EXCURSIONS
La Roche-sur-le-Buis

◗ *3km/1.8mi E on D 159.*

You climb up the charming **Vallée du Menon** surrounded by lime and olive trees. Here is the small chapel which houses the **Musée Layraud**. ⏱*Open Jul–Aug Sun and public holidays 4–7pm; rest of year by reservation.* ✎*Free.* ☎*04 75 28 01 42.*

An interesting signposted trail from Buis to La Roche (⚡*12km/7.4mi – allow 3hrs there and back*) is described in a booklet sold by the Buis tourist office.

Pierrelongue

◑ *7km/4.3mi S on D 5.*

Towering over the village, an incongruous sight in this landscape, the **Église Notre-Dame-de-la-Consolation** is the dream of a priest who, in the late 19C, at the peak of anticlericalism, insisted on building a chapel on a rocky outcrop.

🚗 DRIVING TOURS

LES BARONNIES DU BUIS★
91.5km/56.9mi. Allow half a day.

Between the **Diois** (*see p408*) in the north and the **Montagne de Lure** (*see p432*) to the southeast, these high hilltops and valleys stretch languidly in the sun, sometimes aromatic and fruity, sometimes furrowed by the rivers that swell the Eygues and Ouvèze.

Villages perch along the flanks of the rocky cliffs. This is the perfect terrain for medicinal plants and lavender, olive trees and orchards. This is also the country of **lime** trees, whose leaves compose the *tilleul* infusion.

Harvesting of tilleul, Buis-les-Baronnies

© Camille Moirenc/Photononstop

◑ *From Buis-les-Baronnies drive NE along D 546.*

You follow the Route de l'Olivier to Ste-Jalle. The road follows the Ouvèze amid olive groves and goes through the picturesque **Gorges d'Ubrieux**.

◑ *Turn left onto D 108.*

Olive groves, pine trees and broom cling to the sunny slopes. Climbing up to the Col d'Ey, there are lovely views of the Ouvèze Valley, Buis-les-Baronnies, St-Julien and Mont Ventoux.

From the **Col d'Ey** pass, flanked by the Montagne de Montlaud to the east and the Montagne de Linceuil to the west, the view extends to the Ennuye Valley and the Montagne de Buisseron.

◑ *Take D 528 left to Rochebrune.*

The village of **Rochebrune** stretches over a rock spur; its only street leads to a round tower (all that remains of the 13C castle) and to the 12C church remodelled in the 15C.

◑ *Return to D 108 and turn left.*

The **old town**★ of **Ste-Jalle** has retained part of its walls and two of its gates.

The **castle** consists of a massive square keep (12C–13C), a round tower with Renaissance windows, and living quarters (17C–18C) looking more like a large house.

The size of its bell tower spoils the otherwise fine proportions of the 12C church of **Notre-Dame-de-Beauvert**. The unusual carved **doorway** has a tympanum depicting a rooster and three figures of differing social class.

◑ *Follow the River Ennuye along D 64 then turn right onto D 94 after Curnier.*

The road runs through the pleasant valley of the Eygues, planted with vines and with peach, cherry and olive trees.

The old village of **Sahune** lies on the left bank of the Eygues. Beyond Sahune, the road makes its way through the deep **Gorges de l'Eygues**★.

St-May village is perched on a promontory overlooking the gorge. Beyond St-May, the Eygues flows between brightly coloured limestone cliffs.

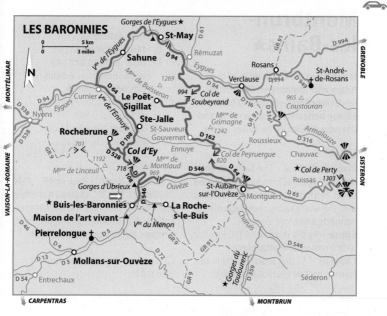

LES BARONNIES

Gorges de l'Eygues ★

St-May

Sahune

Rémuzat

Rosans

Verclause

St-André-de-Rosans

Col de Soubeyrand

Coustouran

Le Poët-Sigillat

Ste-Jalle

St-Sauveur-Gouvernet

M^{gne} de Grimagne

Rochebrune

Roussieux

Col de Peyruergue

Chauvac

Col d'Ey

M^{gne} de Montlaud

Col de Perty

Ruissas

Gorges d'Ubrieux

St-Auban-sur-l'Ouvèze

Montguers

★ Buis-les-Baronnies

La Roche-s-le-Buis

Maison de l'art vivant

V^{ée} du Menon

Pierrelongue

Gorges du Toulourenc

Mollans-sur-Ouvèze

Entrechaux

Séderon

CARPENTRAS

MONTBRUN

Turn right onto D 162.

The road rises through orchards to the **Col de Soubeyrand** (alt. 994m/3 261ft) set among fir trees.

Take a right onto D 568.

The fortified medieval village of **Le Poët-Sigillat**, where the ramparts are still visible, is one of the four *poëts* (promontories) of the Drôme. It has a Romanesque church.

Continue on D 568 to D 162 and turn right to St-Sauveur-Gouvernet.

On the way down, the view extends over the Massif du Ventoux.

Beyond St-Sauveur-Gouvernet, continue on D 64 in the direction of St-Auban-sur-l'Ouvèze. Turn right onto D 546, which leads to Buis-les-Baronnies.

HAUTE VALLÉE DU TOULOURENC

Drive of 80km/49.7mi shown on the regional map (see p407). See p422.

ADDRESSES

🏠 STAY

⌂ **Camping Les Éphélides** – *Quartier Tuves. 1.4 km/8.7mi SW on av. de Rieuchaud.* ✆*04 75 28 10 15. www.ephelides.com. Closed early Sept–mid-May.* ♿*. 40 pitches.* Warm welcome at this campsite at the river's edge.

⌂⌂⌂ **Chambre d'hôte L'Ancienne Cure** – *2 r. du Paroir.* ✆*04 75 28 22 08. www.ancienne-cure.com. Closed 6–30 Jan, 16 Nov–22 Dec.* 🅿 ⊟. *5 rooms* ⊟*, half-board available.* This 16C bishop's house has elegant rooms.

🏃 ACTIVITIES

Mountaineering – Buis-les-Baronnies is an internationally known site.
Walking and bike trails – Several walking trails and marked mountain-bike trails.

🎭 EVENT

Tilleul en Baronnies – Takes place in mid-July, along with the lime tree market.
Routes de l'olivier – *See p11. Route de l'olivier en Baronnies* is available online.

Routes de la lavande – The trail Les Préalpes Provençales, Les Baronnies du Buëch. Free guide available at tourist offices.

Montbrun-les-Bains★

Standing at the confluence of the Anary and Toulourenc, Montbrun-les-Bains comprises the old hillside village beneath the castle ruins, and the new district in the valley below.

VISIT

Place du Beffroi – The belfry, or **tour de l'Horloge** (14C), is a high crenellated tower. From the terrace a **view** stretches over the Anary Valley, the village of Reilhannette and Mont Ventoux.

Église – Richly decorated 17C interior with a remarkable **altarpiece★**.

Château – All that remains of this vast fortress are the four round towers.

🚗 DRIVING TOUR

HAUTE VALLÉE DU TOULOURENC

Drive of 80km/49.7mi shown on the regional map (&see p407). Allow 2hrs 30min.

▷ *Leave Montbrun and join D 159.*

Gorges du Toulourenc★
Squeezing between the Montagne de l'Ubac and the Montagne du Buc, the Toulourenc rushes over rocks.

▷ *Take D 359 on the left.*

Aulan
Château d'Aulan – 🚶*Open Jul–Aug daily; guided tours only 10am–noon,*

Water of Youth

The sulphur waters are excellent for the treatment of rheumatism, bronchitis, skin diseases and ear, nose and throat complaints, and in the late 19C, Montbrun was a popular spa town. However, WWI put an end to this activity, which was only resumed much later, in 1987.

▶ **Population:** 448.
🚗 **Michelin Map:** 332 F8.
ℹ **Info:** ℘04 75 28 82 49. www.montbrunlesbains officedutourisme.fr.
📍 **Location:** 12km/7.4mi N of Sault on D 942.
🕐 **Timing:** Allow half a day, including the drive.

2–7pm. 🕐*Closed 15 Aug.* ∞*4€.* ℘*04 75 28 80 00.* The 19C château has a fine collection of furniture and mementoes.
Église – 🕐 *As above.* Although altered, it retains its 12C apse and 18C altar.

▷ *Continue on D 359; then turn left onto D 546.*

St-Auban-sur-l'Ouvèze
🚶Walk up to to the **place Péquin**: fascinating view of the Rocher du Rang fault. Nearby, the **serre de Rioms** offers a walk through chestnut trees.

▷ *Return on D 65, turn right to reach the Col de Perty.*

Passing through **Montguers**, take a peek at the chapel on the plateau. After the hamlets of Ruissas and La Combe, the road winds up in hairpin bends offering marvellous **views** of the Baronnies.

Col de Perty★
🚶A path to the right leads to the viewing table from where there is a splendid panorama.

▷ *Continue down Vallon du Céans. Turn right at Laborel and take D 170.*

Climb up towards the **Col St-Jean** with the Montagne d'Herc to the west and that of Chabre to the east.

▷ *Turn right onto D 542.*

Beyond **Séderon**, you reach the **Col de Macuègne** (alt. 1 068m/3 504ft), then return to Montbrun by the Vallon de l'Anary.

LA MOYENNE DURANCE, *Les Préalpes de Digne*

This region has a definite southern appeal. Sisteron is often referred to as the "Gateway to Provence" because it perches on a rocky knoll in a narrow gap between two long mountain ridges: the Lure and Baume/Gache. The deceptively docile Durance river flows down a wide valley to the Serre-Ponçon lake. Aside from the lovely landscape of lavender fields, olive trees and river valleys there are the lively towns of Dignes and Forcalquier to explore. Outdoor activities include good hiking trails, and canoeing, canyoning and rafting on one of the Durance tributaries.

Local Specialities

The local producers are particularly proud of their home-raised lamb, which has achieved a quality label status, "Red label". The appellation is only granted to lambs from Merino Arles, Mourérous and south Préalp ewes nursed by their mothers for at least two months on the pastureland around Sisteron. The meat is refined and tender, best eaten simply roasted with herbs. You will find it on many restaurant menus in the region. The Fête d'Agneau takes place over the Ascension weekend in Sisteron. The people of Sisteron believe in making the most of their local lamb. *Pieds et parquets* are a speciality, consisting of stuffed mutton tripe cooked with lard in a rich tomato sauce, seasoned with herbs and pepper and served with grilled sheep's feet.

The local cheese, banon, is made in the village of Banon, near Forcalquier. It is an unpasteurised cheese made from goat's milk. The ripening period lasts two weeks. After this it is dipped in *eau de vie* before being wrapped in chestnut leaves that have been softened in a vinegar–water mixture, then tied up with string.

Highlights

1. Quaint narrow streets of Sisteron's **old town** (p426)

2. Hear the buzz of the cicadas on the drive through **Pays de Contadour** (p432)

3. The towns of **Forcalquier** and **Dignes-les-Bains**, the first hosts a music festival, and the latter a lavender fair (p436 and p438)

4. The fascinating geological reserve of the **Haute-Provence**, and butterfly garden (p441)

5. Take a walk with a mule at **Seyne** (p442)

This AOC cheese is best between spring and autumn. The Fête de Fromage takes place in Banon each May.

Other regional delights include the *miel de lavande* (lavender honey), *fougasse à l'anchois* (a lattice-shaped flat loaf flavoured with anchovies), *callissons* (oblong-shaped biscuits), nougat made with honey and almonds from Provence, and olive oil from the Durance Valley.

Forcalquier with Notre-Dame Cathedral

© Franck Guiziou/hemis.fr

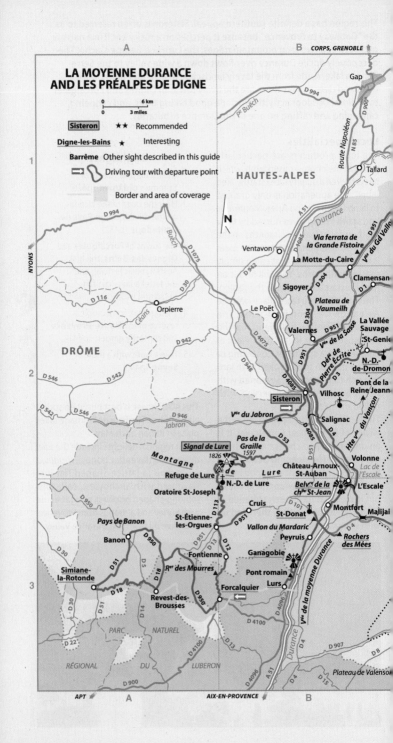

LA MOYENNE DURANCE AND LES PRÉALPES DE DIGNE

0   6 km
0   3 miles

Sisteron ★★ Recommended

Digne-les-Bains ★ Interesting

Barrême Other sight described in this guide

Driving tour with departure point

Border and area of coverage

CORPS, GRENOBLE

Gap

Tallard

HAUTES-ALPES

Route Napoléon
N 85

Pt Buëch

D 994

D 900

A 51

Durance

Via ferrata de la Grande Fistoire

La Motte-du-Caire

Ventavon

Sigoyer

Plateau de Vaumeilh

Le Poët

Valernes

Clamensan

D 1

La Vallée Sauvage
St-Genie

Déft de Pierre Écrite

N.-D.-de-Dromon

Vilhosc

Pont de la Reine Jeann

Salignac

DRÔME

Orpierre

Buëch

Nyons

Céans

D 994
D 116
D 1075
D 30
D 942

D 546
D 542
D 546
D 542
D 546
D 946
D 4075
D 248
D 4085
D 304
D 304
D 951
Vte de la Sasse
D 3
D 4085
D 951
D 4

Sisteron

Vte du Jabron
Jabron

Pas de la Graille 1597

Signal de Lure 1826

Montagne de Lure

Refuge de Lure

N.-D. de Lure

Oratoire St-Joseph

Pays de Banon

Banon

Simiane-la-Rotonde

St-Étienne-les-Orgues

Cruis

Fontienne

Rer des Mourres

Revest-des-Brousses

Forcalquier

Château-Arnoux-St-Auban

Belvr de la chlle St-Jean

L'Escale

Lac de l'Escale

Montfort

Malijai

St-Donat

Vallon du Mardaric

Peyruis

Ganagobie

Pont romain

Lurs

Rochers des Mées

Vte de la moyenne Durance

Volonne

Hte vte du Vançon

Vte du Jabron

D 53
D 951
D 113
D 951
D 13
D 12
D 950
D 30
D 51
D 5
D 18
D 14
D 950
D 22
D 30
D 51
D 18
D 107
D 4
D 4096
D 4100
D 13
D 4
D 4
D 907
D 8
D 15
D 900
D 4096
A 51

PARC NATUREL RÉGIONAL DU LUBERON

Plateau de Valenso

APT

AIX-EN-PROVENCE

A   B

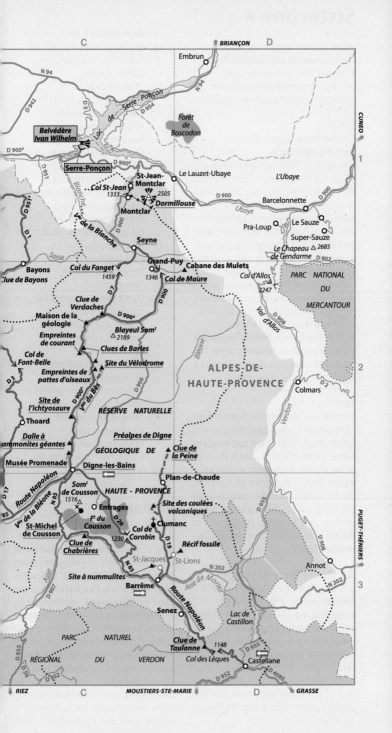

Sisteron★★

In the vibrant light of the Haut Pays Provençal, you discover firstly a citadel, then the mysterious *andrônes* (covered passages) that climb between the narrow houses.

SIGHTS
Cathédrale Notre-Dame-des-Pommiers★

This church, built between 1160 and 1220, is a fine example of Provençal Romanesque architecture. As so often in Provence, the influence of Lombard style is immediately apparent: an elegant doorway has alternate black-and-white voussoirs extended by half-rounded arches leaning against strong buttresses. The main pediment is also flanked by two half-pediments; jambs and slender columns are decorated with carvings and capitals forming a continuous frieze representing a bestiary.

With its three naves, Notre-Dame is one of the largest churches in Provence. The square bell tower is surmounted by a spire in the shape of a pyramid.

Towers

Sisteron has retained five towers from 1370, which formed part of the town's fortifications; four stand just south of Notre-Dame, the fifth guards the foot of the citadel. Each bears an evocative name: during the Wars of Religion, the Protestants fled the town through the Porte Sauve, the "escaping gate"; women used to gather for a gossip at the Porte de la Médisance, or "scandal-mongers' gate".

▲▮ Musée Terre et Temps★

6 Pl. Gén-de-Gaulle. ◑Open Feb–Nov Tue–Sat. ◻Free. ℘04 92 61 61 30.

In the Visitandine Chapel, this museum set up by the Réserve Géologique de Haute-Provence explores the development of the idea of time, from geological time to modern timepieces.

A Foucault's pendulum shows the rotation of the Earth. The museum is the starting point of the **Route du Temps** (◑*see p429*).

- ▶ **Population:** 7 288.
- **Michelin Map:** 334 D7.
- **Info:** Pl. de la République, 04200 Sisteron. ℘04 92 61 36 50. www.sisteron.fr.
- **Location:** Sisteron is located on the Route Napoléon (N 85) between Gap, 50km/31.1mi to the N, and Digne, 39km/24.2mi to the SE. Two tunnels facilitate passage through the village, one under the hill and its citadel, the other under the rock face opposite, on A 51.
- **Parking:** Free parking beneath the citadel, near the river.
- **Don't Miss:** Be sure to see the citadel, impressive in itself and which offers views over the town and countryside.
- **Kids:** Children will enjoy the Musée Terre et Temps at Sisteron and the animal park at La Vallée Sauvage.
- **Timing:** Give yourself a half-day to see the town; each one of the suggested routes requires another half-day.

Old Sisteron★

The old town lies between rue Droite and the Durance; narrow streets running down to the river are lined with tall houses. Note the elegant carved doorways (16C, 17C and 18C) along the way. Walk along **rue Deleuze** to the **Tour de l'Horloge★** surmounted by a magnificent wrought-iron campanile bearing Sisteron's motto: *"Tuta montibus et fluviis"* ("Safe between its mountains and its rivers"). The **Longue-Andrône**, a narrow arcaded passageway, branches off rue Mercerie. Continue along **rue du Glissoir**, which has retained a 13C Romanesque façade (no. 5). Beyond the square, rue Basse des Remparts leads

Sisteron with its citadel and the Durance

© Peter and Georgina Bowater/Tips/Photononstop

to **rue Font-Chaude** then through a covered passageway up to **rue Saunerie**; Napoleon had lunch at no. 64, the old **Hostellerie du Bras d'Or**. Note the attractive 16C door at no. 2, rue Mercerie; the **porte d'Ornano** takes its name from the noble family who once lived here, and whose arms it bears

The Citadel★

Open Apr–11 Nov daily. 5.80€.
04 92 61 27 57. www.sisteron.com.
There is nothing left of the 11C castle. The keep and the watch-path are late 12C and the mighty walls set around the rock are the work of **Jean Errard**, Henri IV's chief military engineer. New defences, designed by **Vauban**, Louis XIV's military engineer, in 1692, were added to the powerful 16C fortifications. Part of the citadel was bomb-damaged in 1944 but later tastefully restored.

A marked tour leads up a succession of steps and terraces, offering views of the town and the Durance Valley, and on to the watch-path. Walk on below the keep, where Jan Kazimierz, Prince of Poland, was imprisoned in 1639, to reach the terrace and enjoy the bird's-eye **view**★ of the lower part of town, the reservoir and the mountains dominating the horizon to the north. The 15C **chapel** is an exhibition centre.

Walk to the north side of the citadel, to the "**Guérite du Diable**" offering an impressive **view**★ of the Rocher de

Tales of Sisteron

A prehistoric village 4 000 years ago, a stopover for the Romans along the **Domitian Way**, a bishopric in the 6C, a fortified site of the Lords of Forcalquier in the 11C, Sisteron has seen a long line of influential guests. After unification with Provence, the stronghold guarded the territory's northern border, until Provence itself was ceded to the King of France in 1483. The citadel was built during the Wars of Religion (late 16C). It was the engineer **Jean Errard** who designed the citadel. In 1815 Napoleon passed through Sisteron, before marching on to Grenoble. On 15 August 1944 the French–American airforce bombarded bridges, and damaged the citadel and the town. The Americans liberated it on 22 August 1944. Today, the town boasts a 5 600sq m/6 700sq yd reservoir with **beaches**, and since 1977, an underground factory, the Salignac Dam and a hydroelectric plant.

la Baume. The steps were once part of an underground staircase, built to link the citadel to the Porte de Dauphiné, destroyed in 1944.

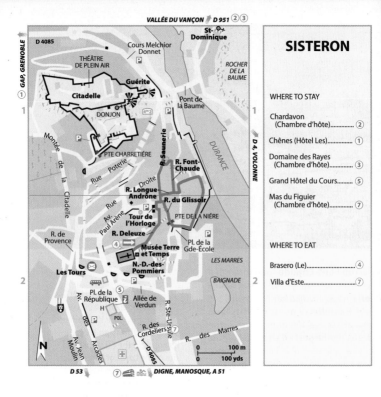

SISTERON

WHERE TO STAY

Chardavon
 (Chambre d'hôte)................ ②

Chênes (Hôtel Les)................ ①

Domaine des Rayes
 (Chambre d'hôte)................ ③

Grand Hôtel du Cours.......... ⑤

Mas du Figuier
 (Chambre d'hôte)................ ⑦

WHERE TO EAT

Brasero (Le)............................ ④

Villa d'Este............................. ⑦

Église St-Dominique

🕐*Open Jul–Aug Mon–Tue 2pm,
4pm, Wed–Sun 10am, 2pm and 4pm;*
🔊*guided tour of the town which ends
at the church (1hr 30min).* 🕐*Closed
public holidays.* 📞*04 92 51 54 50.*
At the foot of the Rocher de la Baume,
it hosts summer concerts and literary
evenings. It is from here that you have
the best **view**★ of the citadel.

EXCURSION
Rieuré de Vilhosc

▶ *10km/6.2mi E along D 4 towards
Volonne. Drive 5km/3.1mi then turn
left onto D 217; 4km/2.5mi further on,
cross the Riou de Jabron and follow the
signposted road on the right.*
The three-naved **crypt** of an ancient
monastery is a rare example of 11C Early
Romanesque art.

Penned Novels

Paul Arène led a bohemian life. Writing for the Paris newspapers he met his
true love; but the father of this pretty Provençal girl refused for them to marry.
Paul returned to Sisteron where he wrote *La Chèvre d'or*, *Domnine*, *Jean des
Figues* and many others. He is buried under an almond tree in Sisteron.

The plot for the *Secret des andrônes*, a novel by **Pierre Magnan**, from
Manosque, unfolds in the citadel: "By the bastions, the redoutes and the
posterns shaped like bayonets, sweating and panting, but still with a cigarette
between his lips, Laviolette began to climb to the keep. The crisp air whipped
him in the face when he got to the top. From the Lure summit to the Pic
d'Olan, the Drôme hills to the Brec de Chambeyron, one hundred kilometres of
windswept horizon unfurled all around."

Continue along D 217 for 5km/3.1mi to reach the pont de la Reine Jeanne spanning the Vançon. Cross the bridge over the Durance and drive NE along D951.

🚗 DRIVING TOURS

HAUTE VALLÉE DU VANÇON★
92km/57.2mi round tour. Allow 3hrs.

This route follows a part of the **Route du Temps**, organised by the Réserve géologique de Haute-Provence, which is signposted from the departure point in Sisteron.

If you wish to follow the complete route, continue along south towards Thoard. The road rises, offering interesting **views**★★ of Sisteron and of the Buëch Valley in the foreground, with the Montagne de Lure to the southwest.

Défilé de Pierre Écrite
The rock face of this deep gorge, on the left of the road near a small bridge, bears a Roman inscription celebrating Dardanus, a prefect of Gaul who converted to Christianity and ordered the building of the first road through the gorge in the 5C AD.

🚶La Vallée Sauvage
⏰*Open 10am–7pm Apr, Jul–Aug and end Oct–early Nov daily; May–Jun and Sept–Oct Wed, Sat–Sun and public holidays.* ⬤*9.80€ (children 3–16 7.90€).* ☎*04 92 61 52 85. www.lavalleesauvage.com.*
Just outside the gorge, this animal park provides a nice stop for children, who can see wild boars, mountain sheep, deer and farm animals along a 2km/1.2mi circuit.

Notre-Dame-de-Dromon★
🚶*15min round trip. Park near a farm and continue on foot.*
A modest building that is a pilgrim site. Fine **view** of the Mélan mountain opposite, and to the left, of the Monges. The road overlooks the bottom of the higher Vançon Valley. The view extends over the Luberon and Ste-Victoire mountain.

Beyond Authon, the narrow road passes over the **Col de Font-Belle**.

▷ *At Le Planas, follow the small road to Thoard.*

The old village of **Thoard** has retained part of its medieval walls and a Romanesque keep is now the bell tower.

▷ *Continue along D 17 to reach N 85 and follow the Route Napoléon (☎see p446) back to Sisteron.*

PAYS DE LA MOTTE-TURRIERS
85km/52.8mi round tour. Allow 3hrs.

▷ *From Sisteron, drive N along D 951.*

The Sasse Valley, lying northeast of Sisteron, is an area modelled by erosion into a route of ravines and gorges.

🚶Sentier des Contes★
The whole family can discover the Sasse Valley by following the trails marked Route des Rochers qui parlent. With a copy of the "magic booklet", which has text and images on the history of the Middle Ages and the Renaissance (sold at tourist offices, hotels and town halls), go by car, then on foot to the fake rocks where there are directions for following the trail.

▷ *Turn right onto D 1.*

Pass **Clamensane**, a village perched on a rocky spur. The landscape becomes gradually wilder and more austere. Beyond the **Clue de Bayons**, the road enters an open basin.

In **Bayons**, a large and beautiful abbey **church** overlooks the square. Built in the 12C and 13C, it is a harmonious mix of Romanesque and Gothic art.

▷ *Turn left towards Turriers.*

The road rises in a series of steep hairpin bends, known locally as "tourniquets", to the Col des Sagnes, in its setting of gullied mountain slopes, before running down to Turriers and Bellaffaire (18C castle).

▶ *Beyond Bellaffaire, turn left onto D 951.*

The road follows the **Grand Vallon** Valley, famous for its orchards.

La Motte-du-Caire
In Provençal, *caïre* means "rock", and this one towers high above the village.
Via ferrata de la Grande Fistoire – 2km/1.2mi before the village, on the right *(length of trail 500m/547yds; La clue de la Fistoire;* ⏱*open Jul–Aug 8.30am–5.30pm, rest of year 8.30am– noon, 2–5.30pm, public holidays 8.30am–5.30pm;* ↝*guided tours and hire of equipment available, book in advance;* ⊚*5.50€;* ✆*04 92 68 40 39; www.viaferrata-alpes.com or www.hautesterresprovence.com)*, allows you to practise climbing in safety.

▶ *Beyond La Motte, turn right onto D 104 to Melve then left onto D 304.*

The road crosses a plateau and the **view** extends to Champsaur in the north.

Sigoyer
From the partly restored 15C castle, the **view**★★ extends to the Durance and, beyond, to the Baronnies and the Montagne de Lure. At the side door of the church there is a tactile **computer screen** where you can take a virtual tour of the château in 3D images.
The vast **Plateau de Vaumeilh**, on the left of the road, a popular place for gliding, is overlooked by the peak of the Pied de Hongrie.
The road runs down to **Valernes** through lavender fields. This hilltop village has retained part of its fortifications and offers a view of the Sasse Valley.

▶ *Return to Sisteron along D 951.*

ALONG THE VALLEY★
33km/20.5mi from Sisteron to Lurs.
⏱*See p433.*

LE PAYS DU CONTADOUR★
74km/46mi from Forcalquier to Sisteron.
⏱*See p432.*

ADDRESSES

🛏 STAY

🍽 **Chambre d'hôte Chardavon** – *04200 St-Geniez. 17km/10.5mi NE of Sisteron on D 3.* ✆*04 92 61 29 04. www.chardavon.be* 🅿. *5 rooms* ⊠. Lovely renovated 18C sheepfold with spacious and well-maintained rooms.

🍽 **Chambre d'hôte Mas du Figuier** – *La Fontaine. 04200 Bevons. 7km/4.3mi W of Sisteron on D 4085, D 946 and D 553.* ✆*04 92 62 81 28. www.masdufiguier.fr. Closed Nov– Jan.* 🅿↝. *6 rooms* ⊠, *half-board available.* Pretty 17C *mas* with pleasant Provençal-style rooms decorated in sunny colours.

🍽 **Hôtel Les Chênes** – *300 rte de Gap. 2km/1.2mi NW via D 4085.* ✆*04 92 61 13 67. leschenes.hotel@wanadoo.fr. Closed 24 Dec–31 Jan, Oct–Mar Sat and Oct–May Sun. 23 rooms* ⊠*8.50€, half-board available, restaurant* ⊚🍽. The rooms are small but functional. The swimming pool and garden are shaded. Enjoy local cuisine on the terrace in fine weather.

🍽🍽 **Chambre d'hôte Domaine des Rayes** – *Domaine des Rayes, 04200 St-Geniez. 17km/10.5mi NE of Sisteron, rte de St-Geniez by D 3.* ✆*04 92 61 22 76. www. lesrayes.fr. Closed Oct–May except school holidays.* ♿🅿. *5 rooms* ⊠, *restaurant* ⊚🍽. Beautifully restored 17C sheepfold. Large rooms decorated in Provençal colours.

🍽🍽 **Grand Hôtel du Cours** – *Pl. de l'Église.* ✆*04 92 61 04 51. www.hotel-lecours.com. Closed 6 Nov–end Feb.* ♿. Wifi. *45 rooms* ⊠*10€, half-board available, restaurant* ⊚🍽. Family-run hotel in the historic centre. Bedrooms are more spacious and quieter at the rear. Their speciality is Sisteron lamb.

🍴 EAT

🍽 **Le Brasero** – ✆*04 92 61 56 79.* ♿. In a Far West décor, this restaurant offers a vast choice of meat dishes. The speciality is the *braserade*.

🍽 **Villa d'Este** – ✆*04 92 31 86 76.* ♿. Generous portions served in this contemporary restaurant: large salads, pasta, pizza, entrecôte steak with *cèpes*.

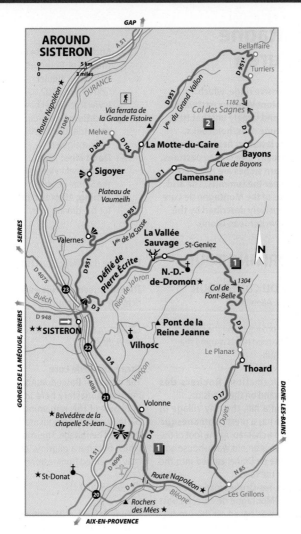

AROUND SISTERON

GAP

A 51

DURANCE

Route Napoléon

D 1085

D 951

Via ferrata de
la Grande Fistoire

Melve

D 304

D 104

La Motte-du-Caire

Vⁿᵉ du Grand Vallon

Col des Sagnes   1182

D 1

Bellaffaire

D 951

Turriers

Bayons

Clue de Bayons

Sigoyer

D 1

Clamensane

Plateau de
Vaumeilh

D 951

Vⁿᵉ de la Sasse

Valernes

**La Vallée
Sauvage**

St-Geniez

1

N

D 951

Défilé de
Pierre Écrite

**N.-D.
de-Dromon** ★

Col de
Font-Belle   1304

Riou de Jabron

SERRES

D 4075

Buëch

23

D 3

★★ SISTERON

D 948

22

D 4

† **Vilhosc**

▲ **Pont de la
Reine Jeanne**

D 3

Le Planas

Thoard

DIGNE-LES-BAINS

GORGES DE LA MÉOUGE, RIBIERS

21

D 4085

Volonne

Vançon

D 17

Duyes

★ **Belvédère de la
chapelle St-Jean**

A 51

D 4096

★ **St-Donat**

D 4

20

1

Route Napoléon ★

Bléone

N 85

Les Grillons

▲ **Rochers
des Mées** ★

AIX-EN-PROVENCE

🛒 SHOPPING

Pâtisserie Les Amandines – *131 r. de Provence.* ☎*04 92 61 02 49. Open Tue–Sat 7am–12.30pm, 2.30–7.30pm, Sun 7am–1pm. Closed Mon.* Large selection of local specialities on offer like the *brioche sisteronnaise* and aujoras.

🧗 ACTIVITIES

👥 **Parcours Aventures** – *Montée de la Citadelle.* ☎*06 18 67 50 34. Mon–Sat 9am–7pm. Closed Sept–Jun and Sun.* This adventure park just under the citadel offers four obstacle courses for all levels, from beginner to accomplished alpine commando.

👥 **Water Reservoir** – *Les Marres. www.sisteron.fr.* ∞*Free.* Swimming and picnics are the order of the day here (*patrolled mid-Jun–mid-Sept*).

🎭 EVENTS

Fête de l'agneau – *Information and reservation at the tourist office (mid-May Sat).* Flocks of sheep pass through the streets of Sisteron, accompanied by Provençal singing and dancing; there's also a local market.

Foire aux santons et aux crèches – *Early Dec–early Feb.* There are over a hundred Christmas cribs, complete with santons, exhibited at this fair.

Montagne de Lure★

This impressive ridge, which prolongs Mont Ventoux eastwards, is austere and largely uninhabited; as the altitude rises, holm oaks, scrubland, lavender fields and cedar trees gradually give way to pastures. The northern slopes are forested with firs near the summits. The arid landscapes of the Montagne de Lure were extensively described by the Provençal writer Jean Giono.

- **Michelin Map:** 334 C/D8.
- **Info:** 13 pl. Bourguet, 04300 Forcalquier. 04 92 75 10 02. www.forcalquier.com.
- **Location:** Lure mountain sits under the Bassin de Forcalquier.
- **Don't Miss:** The magnificent view from the Signal de Lure.
- **Timing:** Allow two hours for the driving tour.

🚗 DRIVING TOUR

LE PAYS DU CONTADOUR
74km/46mi. Allow 2hrs.

▷ *Leave Forcalquier on the NW side on D 12. The road twists around the Lure mountain.*

The rock formations **Rochers des Mourres** stand on the roadside. Perched on a hill, the tiny village of **Fontienne** has a pretty **Romanesque chapel** and a château. At the foot of the village there is an old wash-house and the fontaine de Diane, carved into the rock under the road.

St-Étienne-les-Orgues marks the gateway of the Montagne de Lure. Its past prosperity was based on the production of numerous remedies based on aromatic and medicinal plants, which were sold by pedlars as far away as the Auvergne and Bourgogne regions. The 16C houses have mullioned windows.

Jean Giono

The vast wilderness bewitched **Jean Giono**, who spent his summers at Contadour (from 1935 to 1939) with a group of friends, students, communist sympathisers and pacifists. These meetings resulted in the writing of *Les Cahiers du Contadour*.

▷ *Leave the village E on D 951.*

The little streets of **Cruis** lead you to the richly decorated **church**.

▷ *Return to St-Étienne-les-Orgues and turn right.*

Notre-Dame de Lure

The monks of Boscodon Abbey built a modest monastery here in 1165. The only part of this remaining is a large barrel-vaulted room located beneath the small hermitage. The abbey church, which became a pilgrims' chapel, has now benefited from restoration work.

▷ *Return to D 113.*

Refuge de Lure 🎿 ski centre is equipped with a few ski lifts and cross-country trails offer a wide **view**. A memorial to the 17C Belgian astronomer Wendelin, who set up the **first observatory in France**, stands at the roadside 1.5km/1mi further on.

The mountain's highest summit **Signal de Lure**★★ offers a **panorama** of Monte Viso, Mont Pelvoux, the Vercors Massif, the Cévennes range, Mont Ventoux and the Mediterranean coast.

⚠ *Access is restricted in winter – enquire in St-Étienne-les-Orgues.*

Beyond the Pas de la Graille, the road goes down to the Jabron Valley.

▷ *Follow D 53 to Sisteron.*

Vallée de la Moyenne Durance★

The Durance river creates a bright breach in the mountains of the southern Alps. For a long time this river taunted engineers and refused to be tamed. The former "scourge of the Provence" is now the source of fertility for villages along its banks.

🚗 **DRIVING TOUR**

ALONG THE VALLEY★
33km/20.5mi. Allow 2hrs.

▷ *Leave Sisteron to the S by N 85.*

The road follows the Durance harnessed by the **Salignac Dam**, passes the mouth of the Jabron winding between the river and the steep edge of the Montagne de Lure and skirts the **Lac de l'Escale Dam** as it reaches Château-Arnoux.

Château-Arnoux-St-Auban
The town hall is housed in the Renaissance **château**.
Its lovely park leads to the Font-Robert farm *(tourist office)*. This small town is especially lively during the Sunday markets and festivals. 👪 **Reservoir of water** (with a slide) at St-Auban.

- **Michelin Map:** 334 B/C/D 8/9/10/11.
- **Info:** La Ferme de Font-Robert, 04160 Château-Arnaud-St-Auban. ✆04 92 64 02 64. www.valdedurance-tourisme.com.
- **Location:** This valley is bordered to the E by the cliffs of the Valensole Plateau, and to the W by the hillsides of the Lure and Luberon.
- **Timing:** Two hours for the drive along the Durance.

▷ *2km/1.2mi further on, along D 4096, turn right along the road signposted Route touristique de St-Jean.*

Belvédère de la Chapelle St-Jean★
There is a fine **panoramic** view of the Montagne de Lure, the Durance Valley, Sisteron, the Lac de l'Escale Dam and the Rochers des Mées.

▷ *Return to D 4096 and continue S.*

In sight of St-Auban, you pass in front of the major Atochem chemical complex and the **National Gliding Centre**. Beyond is the concourse of the Bléone.

Montfort is the hilltop *village perché* in a charming **site**★ overlooking the Durance. It is very picturesque with

---

The Taming of the Durance

The River Durance, which is the last main tributary of the Rhône, has its source near Briançon and flows along a 324km/201mi course before joining the Rhône. Frédéric Mistral, the famous Provençal poet, used to say: "The mistral (a strong wind), Parliament and the Durance are the curses of Provence."
The most unpredictable major river of the southern Alps certainly proved a real threat to local people and, for a long time, defied all attempts to harness it. Since the 1960s, however, the river has become one of the great economic assets of the region, a source of urban water supply and hydroelectricity. South of Sisteron, the river has been regulated by a network of canals built along its course or that of its tributaries. New ecosystems have been able to flourish in the river valley.

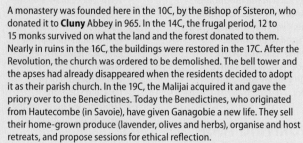

A Millennium Retreat

With its rock caves, springs and abundant vegetation, the Plateau de Ganagobie has been a sought-after site since prehistoric times: megalithic monuments and traces of a Roman oppidum under the ruins of a 15C village have been discovered. The caves, which are found on the plateau hillsides also served as shelter during the Saracen invasions, and hideouts during World War II.

A monastery was founded here in the 10C, by the Bishop of Sisteron, who donated it to **Cluny** Abbey in 965. In the 14C, the frugal period, 12 to 15 monks survived on what the land and the forest donated to them. Nearly in ruins in the 16C, the buildings were restored in the 17C. After the Revolution, the church was ordered to be demolished. The bell tower and the apses had already disappeared when the residents decided to adopt it as their parish church. In the 19C, the Malijai acquired it and gave the priory over to the Benedictines. Today the Benedictines, who originated from Hautecombe (in Savoie), have given Ganagobie a new life. They sell their home-grown produce (lavender, olives and herbs), organise and host retreats, and propose sessions for ethical reflection.

stepped streets lined with charming houses climbing to the restored 16C castle. A fine view of the Durance Valley and Valensole Plateau.

▷ *2km/1.2mi further on, turn right onto D 101.*

The road returns through the **Vallon du Mardaric**, once the route of the ancient Domitian Way.

Église St-Donat★

Built in the 11C on the site where St Donat, the religious recluse, had settled in the 6C, the church is a rare specimen of early Romanesque style in Provence.

▷ *Rejoin D 4096 and cross it to take D 4A across the River Durance.*

Rochers des Mées★

These 100m/328ft-high conglomerate rocks, towering over the village of Les Mées and eroded into strange shapes, are known as the "**Pénitents des Mées**" and make a particularly striking sight when illuminated at night.

▷ *Return to D 4096 and drive towards Manosque.*

The old part of the village of **Peyruis**, once guarded by a drawbridge, is still standing. The 16C church has a six-sided bell tower, built in tufa, with gargoyles in the shape of a lion's head.

▷ *Turn right onto D 30 6km/3.7mi beyond Peyruis.*

Monastère de Ganagobie★

The monastery stands on top of the Ganagobie Plateau. The 1 000-year-old building, restored and reinhabited in the 19C, houses one of the finest mosaics in the West.

The presence of **megaliths** shows that the site was already inhabited in prehistoric times. From its medieval past it has retained the traces of a walled village (Villevieille), abandoned in the 15C, the remains of a Carolingian chapel and above all the Monastère de Ganagobie. The Bishop of Sisteron was the first to found a community on the site in the 10C, but the present **monastery** was built in the 12C. ⏱*Open Tue–Sat 3–5pm, Sun 11am–noon, 3–5pm.*

Church – The decoration of the **doorway**★ is the most noticeable feature of the façade. On the tympanum, a formal, rather stern Christ in Glory contrasts with the freer representations of the adoring angels. Another curious feature of the church is the double transept. Admire the nine **stained-glass windows** designed by Kim En Joong, and especially the marvellous polychrome **mosaics**★★ in the choir and transept.

▶ *Return towards D 4096 but take the little road for Lurs just before joining it.*

The road follows an ancient Roman road and crosses the Buës over a single-arched **Roman bridge**.

Lurs★
🛈 *Pl. de la Fontaine, 04700 Lurs.*
🕾 *04 92 79 10 20.*
This village occupies a remarkable **position**★ on top of a rocky spur overlooking the Durance and the area around Forcalquier. Once a medieval stronghold, it was gradually deserted and became derelict until it was "revived" by a group of graphic designers. It is the setting for **Rencontres internationales de Lurs**. Go through the clock gate, past the church and along the winding streets; there are traces of the old fortifications. Note the **chancellerie des compagnons de Lure**, the rustic open-air theatre, the restored **priory**, and the rebuilt bishops' castle.
Walk along the **promenade des Évêques**, lined with 15 oratories, to the Chapelle Notre-Dame-de-Vie offering fine **views**.

🥾 HIKE
Walk over the Pénitents des Mées★
🚶 *3hrs. After the Notre-Dame-de-la-Salette chapel, on D 101, park at the side of the road and start from the campsite.* Return to the bottom of the Vallon de la Combe. Cross the wall of the second reservoir to reach the north bank. From there, the Pénitents path, marked in green, climbs *(keep right)* to the Pénitents forest. At the pass (alt. 600m/1 969ft), to your left is a view of the Pénitents. Return to the pass and go down the rocky ridge, and take the path that goes along the foot of the Pénitents. Continue on the left to the road which leads to Mées village.

"Pénitents des Mées"
E. Baret/MICHELIN

ADDRESSES

🛏 STAY

⊜⊜ **Auberge de l'Abbaye** – *04230 Cruis.* 🕾 *04 92 77 01 93. http://monsite.wanadoo.fr/ auberge-abbaye-cruis. Closed Feb, All Saints and Christmas holidays. 8 rooms ⊑10€, restaurant*⊜⊜⊜. Rustic interiors, well-kept rooms. Simple dining room serving regional cuisine.

⊜⊜ **Chambre d'hôte Campagne du Barri** – *La Croix, 04190 Les Mées. 2km/1.2mi NE of Mées by D 4 in direction of Digne-les-Bains and turn left.* 🕾 *04 92 34 36 93. www.guideweb.com/provence/bb/ campagne-barri.* 🖥. *5 rooms* ⊑. An 18C manor house with pretty rooms. Table d'hôte, reservation only in winter.

🍽 EAT

⊜ **La Magnanerie** – *04200 Aubignosc. 1.5 km/1.2mi N on N 85.* 🕾 *04 92 62 60 11. www.la-magnanerie.net. Closed 20–30 Dec. 9 rooms* ⊑9€, *half-board available.* Contemporary décor and inventive cuisine. Modern rooms.

⊜⊜ **L'Oustaou de la Foun** – *04160 Château-Arnoux-St-Auban. 1.5km/1mi N of Château-Arnoux-St-Auban by N 85.* 🕾 *04 92 62 65 30. Closed 1–9 Jan, 22–30 Jun, All Saints holiday, Sun eve and Mon.* This former coaching inn serves regional cuisine.

🛒 SHOPPING

François Doucet confiseur – *Zone artisanale, 04700 Oraison.* 🕾 *04 92 78 61 15. Open Mon–Fri 8.30am–noon, 2–6pm. Closed Sat–Sun.* Try the *pralino* (almonds, nougat and vanilla).

Forcalquier★ and Le Pays de Banon

Once the capital of flourishing *comté* (county) *florissant*, Forcalquier is today the cultural capital of the region: the starting point for several excursions, it is a busy tourist centre; every summer, the town vibrates to the sounds of jazz and chamber music. Lovers of good food and literature will love Banon: perched on the heights of the plateau, with the Lure mountain on the horizon, this area is reputed for its cheese, cured meats, biscuits and bookshop.

SIGHTS

Notre-Dame Cathedral

This former co-cathedral offers an interesting contrast between the Romanesque character of its massive rectangular tower and the slender appearance of its steeple crowned by a lantern. A lofty nave in typical Provençal Romanesque style dates from the same period as the transept and the chancel, which, built some time before 1217, are the oldest examples of Gothic style in the area.

Musée Municipal

Pl. du Bourguet. ⚬━Closed for inventory – for temporary exhibitions contact for details. ☎04 92 70 91 19.
The museum is located on the top floor of the Visitandines convent, opposite the cathedral. Antique furniture and objects from everyday life, Moustiers and Apt faïences, and archaeological finds make up the main part of the collection.

▶ *Walk round the cathedral by the bd des Martyrs; turn to face the Couvent des Cordeliers opposite.*

Couvent des Cordeliers

Franciscan friars settled in Forcalquier in 1236. Their monastery, one of the first of its kind in Provence, was occupied until the 18C. It now houses a training centre for the **European University for**

▶ **Population:** 4 649.
⚙ **Michelin Map:** 334 C9.
🅸 **Info:** 13 pl. du Bourget, 04300 Forcalquier. ☎04 92 75 10 02. www.forcalquier.com.
▶ **Location:** 47km/29.2mi S of Sisteron, it is an ideal base for exploring the surrounding area.
😊 **Don't Miss:** The panorama from the Notre-Dame-de-Provence, the Simiane rotunda, banon goat's cheese and the Oppedette rooftops.
🕐 **Timing:** The best time to visit is Tuesday morning, which is when the market, one of the largest in Provence, takes place. To fill in the rest of the morning take a stroll through town. The afternoon can be spent discovering the Pays de Banon.

Scents and Flavours, who organise courses and workshops for the public. ☎04 92 72 50 68. www.uess.fr.
The **cloisters** have a lovely garden with clipped boxwood. The Lords of Forcalquier were buried in these Gothic crypts. The chapter house has twin bays which frame a Romanesque doorway.

Cité Comtale

The **Porte des Cordeliers** gate is all that remains of the town's fortifications and marks the beginning of the medieval town. The narrow streets were laid out to offer the best protection from the mistral. Some houses have kept their paired windows and Gothic, Classical or Renaissance doorways. A 16C **Renaissance fountain**, in the shape of a pyramid crowned by St Michael slaying the dragon, decorates place St-Michel.

Cimetière★

The yews have been clipped into amazing arched shapes in the cemetery.

🚗 DRIVING TOURS

LE PAYS DU CONTADOUR
FORCALQUIER TO SISTERON
Drive of 74km/46mi shown on the regional map (see p424). See p432.

LE PAYS DE BANON
Drive of 69km/42.9mi shown on the regional map (see p424). Allow 3hrs.

▶ *At Forcalquier, take the route for Avignon, then D 950 at the roundabout at the edge of town.*

Banon
🏛 *Pl. de la République, 04150 Banon.*
📞*04 92 72 19 40. www.village-banon.fr.*
At the upper part of the village stands a 14C **machicolation gateway** and the restored Hôtel-Dieu. From near the church there is a pleasant **view**. Banon is known for its **goat's cheese**, wrapped in fresh chestnut leaves.
Le Bleuet – *R. St-Just, 04150 Banon.*
📞*04 92 73 25 85.* 🕐*Open daily.* 🕐*Closed 1 Jan.* Two giant cornflowers are painted on the façade and there is a 4m/13ft wooden sculpture of a pile of books. You can't miss this **bookshop** during your visit to Banon. Inside there are over 100 000 titles and 180 000 volumes!

▶ *Leaving Banon, take D 51 towards Apt.*

Simiane-la-Rotonde★
🏛 *La Rotonde, 04150 Simiane-la-Rotonde*
📞*04 92 73 11 34. www.simiane-la-rotonde.fr.*
This is one of the loveliest hilltop villages in Haute-Provence; perched on the edge

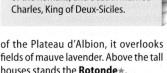

The City of Four Queens
The daughters of **Raymond Bérenger V** all became queens. Marguerite married St Louis, King of France, Éléonore married Henry III, King of England, Sanche married Richard of Cornwall, King of the Romans, and Beatrix married Charles, King of Deux-Siciles.

of the Plateau d'Albion, it overlooks fields of mauve lavender. Above the tall houses stands the **Rotonde★**.
The houses have retained 17C and 18C carved doors. There is a fine **view** of the region from the covered **market**.
Rotonde★ – Just before entering the rotunda, stop for a moment to appreciate the archaeological finds that were excavated in 2001. This 12C keep has been constructed with immense originality. The inside reveals a beautiful Romanesque hall. On the first floor there are 12 alcoves decorated with grimacing sculpted heads, and the leaves of water plants.
To finish your visit, stop off at the **Laboratoire d'aromathérapie** in the former living quarters of the Sault family.

ADDRESSES

🛒 SHOPPING

Market – *Mon 8.30am–1pm.*
Monday morning, this celebrated market attracts locals and tourists alike. Among the regional produce, there is the banon goat's cheese wrapped in chestnut leaves. In summer, get there early to avoid the crowds.

Forcalquier the Capital

At the end of the 11C, the fortified town of Forcalquier became the capital of a *comté* (county) created by a branch of the Comtes de Provence dynasty and extending along the Durance from Manosque north to Sisteron, Gap and Embrun. The bishopric of Sisteron was split into two and the church of Forcalquier became a co-cathedral, a unique precedent in the history of the Church. The Comté de Forcalquier and the Comté de Provence were united at the end of the 12C, under the leadership of **Raimond Bérenger V**. The two territories were eventually bequeathed to the French Crown in 1481.

Digne-les-Bains★

This town by the banks of the River Bléone is a sought-after spa resort. Capital of the "Alpes de la lavande", it is surrounded by lavender fields; in August there is a procession of flower-covered floats, and in September a major lavender fair.

SIGHTS

Route starts at the pl. C.-de-Gaulle. Allow half a day.

Digne was the former capital of Bodiontici and an important medieval bishopric. The town grew up around the Notre-Dame-du-Bourg quarter. In the 14C, it moved to the hill where there was once a castle (now a prison). Pedestrian shopping streets at the foot of the mound have been painted in pleasant pastel colours. The boulevard Gassendi is the liveliest part of town.

Works in Carrara marble from an international **sculpture exhibition** organised in Digne decorate public spaces.

Jardin Botanique des Cordeliers

Pl. de Cordeliers. ◑*Open Mon–Fri Jul–Aug 9am–noon, 3–7pm; 15 Mar–Jun and Sept–15 Nov 9am–noon, 2–6pm.* ◉*Free.* ♿ ℘*04 92 31 59 59.*

This pretty medieval garden in the courtyard of the former convent has been planted with medicinal herbs.

Musée Gassendi★

64 bd Gassendi. ◑*Open Wed–Mon Apr–Sept 11am–7pm; Oct–Mar except public holidays 1.30–5.30pm.* ◉*4€.* ♿ ℘*04 92 31 45 29.*

Founded in 1889 it is both a natural history and a fine arts museum. Artworks include paintings by 19C Provençal artists: Martin, Mayan, Guindon, Ponson, Nardi and watercolours by Paul Martin, the founder of the museum.

The stock of older works is rich in Italian paintings: the major work is the *Virgin with a Missal* by the 17C Roman artist **Carlo Maratta**. A large collection of

- ▶ **Population:** 17 455.
- **Michelin Map:** 334 F8.
- **Info:** Pl. du Tampinet, 04000 Digne-les-Bains. ℘04 92 36 62 62. www.ot-dignelesbains.fr.
- ▶ **Location:** Digne is located at the junction of three valleys on D 4085 (the Route Napoléon), 39km/24.2mi SE of Sisteron and 52km/32.3mi NW of Castellane.
- **Parking:** Parking spaces in the town centre are all paying.
- **Don't Miss:** See the Alexandra David-Néel Museum in the house where she lived between her two trips to Tibet. The Gassendi Museum is also worth a visit.
- **Kids:** The Réserve géologique de Haute-Provence has an interesting nature trail, and, for fun, visit the outdoor sports park Les Ferréols.
- **Timing:** Count on a half-day to tour the town and visit at least one of the several museums.

19C scientific instruments is displayed, as a reminder of the town's association with the astronomer **Pierre Gassendi** (1592–1655). The museum also houses the **Cairn**, a contemporary art centre.

Grande Fontaine

The 19C fountain situated at the end of boulevard Gassendi consists of two Doric porticoes and limestone concretions covered with moss.

Musée de la Seconde Guerre Mondiale

Pl. Paradis. ◑*Open Jul–Aug Mon–Thu 2–6pm, Fri 2–5.30pm; Sept–Jun Wed 2–5pm by reservation.* ◑*Closed public holidays.* ◉*Free.* ♿ ℘*04 92 31 28 95.*

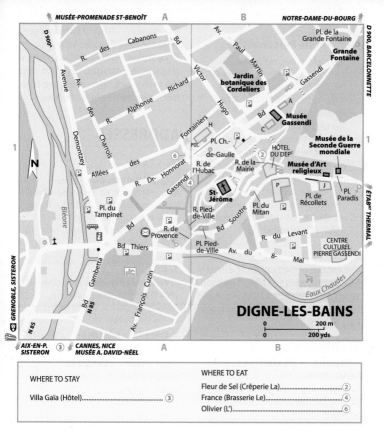

DIGNE-LES-BAINS

0   200 m
0   200 yds

WHERE TO STAY	WHERE TO EAT	
Villa Gaïa (Hôtel)........................ ③	Fleur de Sel (Crêperie La)................ ②	
	France (Brasserie Le)..................... ④	
	Olivier (L')...................................... ⑥	

This small museum is housed in a former air-raid shelter.

In the **old town**, south of the boulevard Gassendi, a network of twisting lanes and stairs surrounds the mound crowned by the **Église St-Jérôme**.

It is possible to reach the cathedral by walking up the Montée St-Charle.

Musée d'Art Religieux

Pl. des Récollets. ⏱*Open Jul–Sept 10am–6pm.* 🎟*Free.* ☎*04 92 32 35 37.*

The **Chapelle des Pénitents** houses a collection from neighbouring parishes, a religious exhibition and a video.

ADDITIONAL SIGHTS
Cathédrale Notre-Dame-du-Bourg★

⏱*Open Jun–Oct daily 3–6pm; Nov–May Sun 3–6pm.* 📷*Guided tours on request.* 🎟*Free.* ☎*04 92 32 06 48.*

This vast Romanesque church, built between 1200 and 1330, has an elegant Lombard doorway. This cathedral was badly damaged in the late 15C. Excavations have revealed construction from the 1C AD, and traces of a 5C church.

The blown and stained glass is the work of Canadian-born artist David Rabinowitch (1943–).

Musée Alexandra David-Néel★

Along the road to Nice, left just after the petrol station, 27 av. Mar.-Juin. ⏱*Open all year.* 📷*Guided tours (2hrs) 10am, 2pm, 3.30pm.* 🎟*Free.* ☎*04 92 31 32 38. www.alexandra-david-neel.org.*

In 1924 Alexandra David-Néel crossed the Himalayas in disguise and reached Tibet and its capital Lhasa, the Forbidden City. On her return, she wrote *Voyage d'une Parisienne à Lhassa.*

In 1927, David-Néel bought a house in Digne which she called Samten-Dzong

Digne Personalities

The philosopher, mathematician and astronomer **Pierre Gassendi** (1592–1655) was born near here. It was as Descartes' rival that he became famous.

The bishop in *Les Misérables*, Bienvenu Myriel, was modelled on the **Bishop de Miollis** of Digne.

Alphonse Beau de Rochas (1815–93), born at Digne, proposed a channel tunnel project, and urged on the local republican resistance at the *coup d'état* of 2 December 1851.

(the fortress of meditation). She lived in it between travels and filled it with souvenirs. She bequeathed it to Digne, and has become one of Digne's most legendary of personalities.

EXCURSION
Chapelle St-Michel-de-Cousson★

◗ *11km/6.8mi S of Digne. Leave Digne, passing the spa, on D 20 leading to Entrages.*

The charming village of **Entrages** overlooks the Eaux-Chaudes Valley.

🥾 *2hr walk without difficulty.* A few steps from Entrages, turn left onto the path which skirts along the basin formed by the summits of Cousson.

ADDRESSES

🛌 STAY

⊖🍴🛏 **Hôtel Villa Gaïa** – *24 rte de Nice.* ☎*04 92 31 21 60. www.hotel-villagaia-digne.com. Closed 5–11 Jul, 22 Oct–14 Apr.* ♿. *10 rooms* ⊟. Welcoming hotel with individually decorated rooms. Traditional cuisine.

🍽 EAT

⊖ **Brasserie Le France** – *54 bd Gasse-ndi.* ☎*04 92 31 03 70. Closed Sept–Jul.* ♿. Good range of meat and fish dishes in a relaxed setting.

⊖ **Crêperie La Fleur de Sel** – ☎*04 92 35 32 69.* Good buckwheat pancakes.

⊖🍴 **L'Olivier** – ☎*04 92 31 47 41. www.resto-lolivier.fr.* Provençal and Mediterranean menu.

Préalpes de Digne★

The Préalpes de Digne were once the most desolate mountains in the Alps. Today, they are planted with forests of larch and beech which provide a verdant setting for the geological reserve.

🚗 DRIVING TOURS

1 LA VALLÉE DU BÈS AND THE MASSIF DU BLAYEUL★

Drive of 95km/59mi shown on the local map (🛈 see p443) and regional map (🛈 see p425). Allow 3hrs without the walks. Car parks are found all around the site.

- 👣 **Michelin Map:** 334 E/F/G 7/8.
- ℹ **Info:** Réserve géologique de Haute-Provence, Montée B. Dellacasagrande. ☎04 92 36 70 70. www.resgeol04.org.
- ◗ **Location:** From Digne, you venture into the Préalpes on winding roads: D 900A to the N and D 20 to the S.
- 🕐 **Timing:** Allow a day and a half for three drives.

◗ *Leave Digne-les-Bains from the N on D 900A (towards Barles) and, just after the bridge, follow the signposts to the car park.*

Geological Reserve of the Haute-Provence

Founded in 1984, this geological reserve is a protected territory, the largest of its kind in Europe, and offers unique study opportunities, enabling you to follow the evolution of the earth over millions of years.

The strata of transverse valleys – Verdaches, Chabrières and Péroué, for instance – are like an open book of local geology. Looking at the often barren landscape today, it is hard to believe that the reserve lies in what was a vast "alpine sea" during the Secondary Era, a natural habitat for fish, molluscs and coral.

Sedimentary deposits were laid during each era. Plant deposits inform us about the flora of the Primary Era. Relics of the Secondary Era, characterised by a rich marine life, include the skeleton of a large reptile and numerous ammonite fossils, while the Tertiary Era preserved for us the footprints left by birds combing the shores of the alpine sea.

Musée-Promenade de la Réserve Géologique de Haute-Provence★

Open Jul–Aug Mon–Fri 10am–1pm, 2–7pm, Sat–Sun and public holidays 10.30am–12.30pm, 2–7pm; Apr–Jun and Sept–Oct Fri 9am–noon, 2–4.30pm, Sat–Thu 9am–noon, 2–5.30pm; rest of year contact for details. *Closed 1 Jan, 25 Dec.* *Guided tours available (1hr 30min).* 5€ *(children 3€).* 04 92 36 70 70. www.resgeol04.org. Bus: line 2, stop Champourcin.

The centre of geology is situated in the **Parc St-Benoît**, which has been built on tufa formed from deposits of a **petrographic waterfall**★.

Three paths cross through the park *(1km/0.6mi, 70m/230ft gradient):* the sentier de l'Eau, the **sentier de Cairns** and the sentier des Remparts.

The **museum** has temporary exhibitions on the ground level, while on the other levels the reserve is described as it is today, and in the future. The **aquariums** show the last living fossils in their natural environment. At the park entrance stands the **Géodyssée**, which relates the life of Jurassic marine animals.

Jardin des Papillons

At the site of the Musée-Promenade. *Open Jul 11am, 2.30pm, 4pm; Aug 10am, 11.30am, 2.30pm, 4pm; Sept–Jun contact for details.* *Closed public holidays.* *Guided tour (1hr) by reservation.* 5€ *(children 3€).* 04 92 31 83 34.

Over 120 butterflies can be admired.

Dalle à Ammonites Géantes★

This tilted black-limestone slab bears the imprint of ammonites, some of them 70cm/28in in diameter, which lived here 200 million years ago.

▷ *Drive 8km/5mi along D 900A.*

Site de l'Ichtyosaure★

🚶 *2km/1.2mi path to the site in 1hr.*

The path runs along the left bank past the waterfalls of the Bélier Gorge and then climbs the opposite hillside to the Col du Jas. On the plateau, turn left and head down to where the fossil lies. Ichthyosaurus, a 4.5m/15ft-long, fish-like reptile, swam in the sea which covered the whole region 180 million years ago. Its fossilised skeleton has been left in situ under glass.

▷ *Continue for 6km/3.7mi after the junction with D 103.*

Site of the Vélodrome

🚶 *Allow 2hrs there and back on foot.*

The itinerary goes across an area where the reddish soil contrasts with the black pines growing on it. Keep going left until you breast the first rise and proceed towards the ruins of the village of Esclangon; turn right and aim for the Serre d'Esclangon summit.

The panorama to the west reveals the geological phenomenon known as the "**Vélodrome**"★. This fan-shaped natural feature is the result, over a period of 16 million years, of the folding of sandstone layers. Constant erosion dug the Bès Valley and gave the landscape its present appearance.

▶ *Return to the road for 2km/1.2mi.*

Prints of Bird Feet (Empreintes de Pattes d'Oiseau)

🚶 *5min. On the right, follow the path uphill.*

Twenty million years ago, the sea had not retreated from the area and birds pecked away at the sand of the beach.

Clues de Barles★

The road squeezes through these two gorges. The **imprints of water currents** visible further on are evidence of what life was like 300 million years ago.

Halt at the **Maison de la géologie** at the exit to Barles. This information point holds temporary exhibitions.

Afterwards you pass through the **Clue de Verdaches**.

▶ *Continue on D 7.*

Col du Fanget★

There is a fine **view** to the north with the Blanche Valley flanked by the Dormillouse summit and Montagne de la Blanche, with the Parpaillon Massif and Gapençais mountains in the distance.

⛷ Le Fanget offers some 16km/10mi of cross-country ski trails and groomed trails for snowshoers.

Seyne★

A summer and winter resort with a reputation for horse and mule breeding.

▶ *From Seyne, drive SE along D 900.*

Col de Maure★

The pass links the valleys of the River Blanche and River Bès.

🎿 The small ski resort of **Grand-Puy** close to the pass is a winter annexe of Seyne, situated further down.

▶ *Return to the road to get close to the Clue de Verdaches. You have the option to go back to Digne by the Vallée de la Bléone following D 900.*

② ROUTE DU COL DE COROBIN★

Drive of 32km/19.9mi shown on the local map (♿ see opposite) and regional map (♿ see p425). Allow 1hr.

▶ *From Digne, drive along D 20 towards Entrages.*

The road runs through the Cousson Forest, then climbs over the Col de Corobin to join N 85 leading to Barrême.

Barrême

♿ *See the Route Napoléon p446.*

Barrême is situated at the confluence of the three small Asse valleys. Downstream from Barrême, the River Asse flows to the **Clues de Chabrières★**.

③ ASSE DE CLUMANC

Drive of 18km/11.2mi along D 19 shown on the local map (♿ see opposite) and regional map (♿ see p425).
Allow 45min.

The road follows the River Asse de Clumanc from Barrême to Plan-de-Chaude. The valley contains a wealth of fossil-bearing layers. The sites are listed and marked with explanatory panels.

Fossil Nummulites at St-Jacques

🚶 A path leads in 10 minutes to a site where 40-million-year-old fossils can be seen in limestone strata.

Fossil Reef of St-Lions (Récif Fossile de St-Lions)

🚶 A path leads through brushwood in 30 minutes to a site consisting of a coral reef which used be in the alpine sea 35 million years ago.

Clumanc

The village houses covered with *lauzes* are spread out along the stream. The Romanesque Église Notre-Dame houses an interesting tabernacle in gilt wood. 🚶 A path starting north of the village leads in 10 minutes to the **panorama★** of the castle ruins. The hillside illustrates a period in the formation of the Alps.

Land Art at Digne-les-Bains

Since the mid-1990s the Digne region has provided major land artists with an extraordinary opportunity. For these artists who work with the natural elements and expose their works in the natural environment, the geological reserve represents an ideal source of inspiration. Emblematic figure of this movement, the Scot **Andy Goldsworthy**, known for his works of piled stones, made a 150km/93.2mi circuit dotted with "**art shelters**", original art creations installed at the side of the road, on a mountain pass, at a farm or in a chapel *(information from Musée Gassendi in Digne-les-Bains see p438)*. You can already get an idea about land art at the Gassendi Museum and by taking the sentier des Cairns at the Musée-Promenade *(see p441)*.

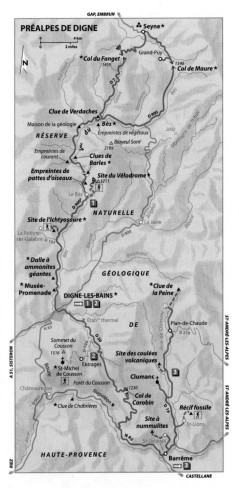

Site des Coulées Volcaniques

15min.
At the junction with D 219, park in front of the post office and take the path.
The only trace of volcanic activity in the region: 60km/37.3mi away, 35 million years ago, the lava and ashes from erupting volcanoes fell to the bottom of the alpine sea and were transported here.
You can cross the Riou des Sauzeries river to return to the **Clastres** hamlet. Return to the road to go back to the town hall at Clumanc.

Clue de la Peine★

1hr 30min return.
Park in the car park by the houses. Marked path leading to the Clue. Take the same path to return to Barrême.
At **Plan-de-Chaude**, in the direction of the Clue de la Peine, you can continue the journey on D 219, returning to St-André-les-Alpes *(see p472)*, and then the Castillon lake.

Seyne★

Seyne, the capital of the Blanche Valley, altitude 1 200m/3 937ft, is a popular summer and winter resort that has held on to its traditions – breeding horses, especially mules.

⚘ WALKING TOUR
Seyne has four **écomusées**.

▷ *Circuit starts at the pl. des Armes. Allow 2hrs.*

Maison de Pays
Musée du Mulet. . ⊙*Open Oct–Nov Mon–Sat 9am–noon, 3–6pm; Dec–Sept Mon–Sat 9am–12.30pm, 2–6.30pm, Sun and public holidays 9am–noon.* ⊙*Closed 1 Jan, Easter Sun–Mon, 1 Nov, 11 Nov, 25 Dec.* ⊗*Free.* ⚫ ℘*04 92 35 31 66. www.fortetpatrimoine.fr.* Exhibiton on "the miracle of the mule".

▷ *Follow Grande-Rue, then take r. du Barri left.*

You pass in front of the **forge** and, at the end of the road, you reach the **Porte de Provence**, which is the only remaining feature of the medieval ramparts. Returning up the rue Basse, you will see the **school** (reconstitution of a classroom) and the **tailor's** shop next to it.

▷ *Continue on Grande-Rue.*

▸ **Population:** 1 427.
▵ **Michelin Map:** 334 G6.
▯ **Info:** Office du tourisme de Seyne/Vallée de la Blanche, Pl. d'Armes, 04140 Seyne-les-Alpes. ℘04 92 35 11 00. www.valleedelablanche.com.
▷ **Location:** On D 900, 41km/25.5mi from Digne and 25km/15.5mi from Lac de Serre-Ponçon, Seyne dominates the Vallée de la Blanche.
▣ **Parking:** Free parking on the place des Armes, at the entrance to the village (coming from Digne).
◔ **Timing:** Allow two hours for a walk around the village and the citadel.

Chapelle des Dominicains
Inside, a painting, *Procession des Pénitents*, illustrates the population of Seyne depending upon their importance of social standing in the village.

Église Notre-Dame-de-Nazareth
◔*See Architecture p71.*
Lovely example of Romanesque mountain architecture. Inside admire the fine

Seyne

© Franck Guiziou/hemis.fr

The Mule Is King

At Seyne, the **mule** reigns. The last national French mule competition was held here *(2nd Sat in Aug)* at the village fair, and there is also the Horse and Mule Fair *(2nd Sat in Oct)*. An honour it well deserves: a pack animal that is sure-footed in the mountains, a draft animal for working in the fields and forests, the mule was also used to carry ammunition and food supplies to the alpine troops at the isolated hilltop forts. Sterile hybrid of the horse and the donkey, the mule is smaller, more resistant and more economic than the horse. The arrival of the tractor is a possible threat to the breeding of mules. But to combat this Seynes has developed green tourism and riding activities.

furniture (stalls, pulpit, altar) and capitals decorated with horrible anthropomorphic monsters.
Return to the rue Haute: next to the wash-house the **bugade** (washing of laundry) is interpreted.

▶ *Go to the citadel.*

Citadelle
🕐*Contact for details.* •*Guided tour available.* ⊛*3€ (children under 10 free).* ☏*04 92 35 31 66.*
The citadel was built in 1693 at the request of **Vauban** and encompasses the 12C watchtower.
After the Treaty of Utrecht, Ubaye was reattached to France, and it no longer held a strategic position. Exhibitions on the citadel and the mule.

EXCURSIONS
Vallée de la Blanche
▶ *This valley stretches over 20km/ 12.4mi from Seyne to the Durance.*
At the **Col de Maure** (🕐*see Préalpes de Digne p442*), in an area bordered by larches and alpine meadows, near to the **Mule hut**, is where the River Blanche takes its source (•*around 3hrs there*). The river crosses the Seyne region diagonally. In the north, downstream from Selonnet, it has furrowed deep gorges before reaching the Durance.
As the valley widens you can see the trace left behind from a glacier that once stood at the **Col St-Jean**.

St-Jean-Montclar
▶ *12km/7.4mi N on D 900.*
This family **winter-sports** resort shares its ski area with **Le Lauzet-Ubaye**, on the other side of Dormillouse.
At **Montclar**, there is a 17C château with two round towers standing on a hill (⊶ *closed to the public*).

HIKE
Walk to Dormillouse★
🥾 *Alt. 2 505m/8 219ft.*
*Leaving St-Jean-Montclar, take the chairlift to the Plateau de la Chau, then start the walk on the forest trail (45min). From the Vauban-period fort (the battery now houses a refuge), there is a lovely **view**★ of the Ubaye Valley. The cliff at the foot of the Dormillouse is popular for gliding.*

ADDRESSES

🛏 STAY
🍴 **Hôtel-Relais de la Forge** – 04460 Seyne. ☏*04 92 35 16 98. www.relaisdela forge.fr. Closed 16–24 Apr, 11 Nov–20 Dec, Sun eve and Mon except school holidays. 14 rooms ⊠, half-board available, restaurant ⊜⊜.* Family hotel with simple rooms. Rustic dining room with traditional menu.

🏃 ACTIVITIES
Hikes – *Guides on sale at tourist offices.* The **Blanche Valley** has three resort villages and alpine ski runs at the Col du Fanget.

Route Napoléon★

From Castellane to Le Poët

You are following the footsteps of Napoleon. However, he would have had to cross the peaks on horseback or on foot since the roads were impassable for carriages in his era. Today, even if the journey is easier, the landscape remains unchanged. The road passes through the narrow valleys of the Préalpes de Digne and emerges onto the Durance plain.

🚗 DRIVING TOURS

THE CROSSING OF PRÉALPES DE DIGNE

Drive of 100km/62.2mi shown on the local map (see opposite) and the regional map (see p425).
Allow half a day.

Beyond the pass, the road goes through the **Clue de Séranon**. Napoleon spent the night (2–3 March) in the village of **Séranon** hidden in a pine forest. On the way down from the Col de Luens, the road affords views of Castellane.

Castellane★

See p470.
On the way up to the **Col des Lèques** there are lovely **views** of Castellane, the Lac de Castillon and the Préalpes de Provence.

Clue de Taulanne★

This opening cut through sheer rock leads from the Verdon Valley to the Asse Valley.

- **Michelin Map:** 341 A/B 5, 334 D/H 3/10.
- **Info:** Association nationale des élus pour la route Napoléon (ANERN – comprising 42 towns situated along the route), Palais des Congrès, 22 cours H.-Cresp, 06130 Grasse. ℘04 93 40 04 34. www.route-napoleon.com.
- **Location:** The route described here goes from Castellane to Le Poët. The first part, from Golfe Juan to the Col de Valferrière, is described in the MICHELIN GREEN GUIDE FRENCH RIVIERA. The part from Le Poët to Corps is described on p391.
- **Don't Miss:** The towns of Castellane, Digne, Sisteron are almost mandatory, but the village of Volonne is also worth seeing, especially for the panorama.
- **Timing:** You could complete the drive in half a day, although you will gain by taking more time. Allow a whole day from Castellane to Corps.

Senez

This Gallo-Roman town was one of the oldest and poorest bishoprics in France, finally dissolved in 1790. It came into the limelight in the 18C, when Bishop **Jean**

Testimony of Las Cases

Regarding the return of the emperor he wrote: "he embarked at Golfe-Juan, and just before nightfall he set up camp. In the middle of the night he broke up camp and set off for Grasse. There, the Emperor counted on finding a road that he ordered to be built; but it had never been completed. Due to the difficult road conditions and the snow, he had to leave his coach and cannons at Grasse … The Emperor continued on like lightning. Victory is mine, France will be mine at Grenoble. We covered a hundred miles in five days, from 2 to 7 March, in such adverse road and weather conditions…" (*Mémorial de Ste-Hélène*).

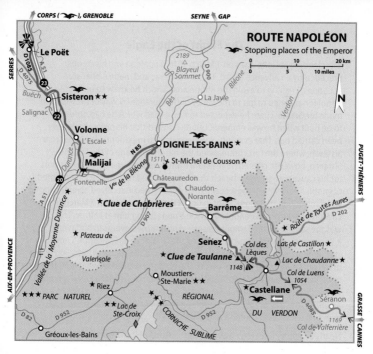

ROUTE NAPOLÉON
Stopping places of the Emperor

Soanen refused to condemn Jansenism and was removed from office.

The **former cathedral** (guided tours by request at the town hall; 04 92 34 21 15) dates from the early 13C. The east end is decorated with arcading in Lombard style. A Gothic doorway gives access to the Provençal Romanesque-style nave.

 Return to D 4085 and continue towards Digne.

Barrême

Napoleon spent the night of 3 March 1815 here *(plaque on a house along D 4085).*

The railway station houses a geology exhibition organised by the Réserve géologique de Haute-Provence (see Préalpes de Digne p441).

The Préalpes de Digne start beyond Chaudon-Norante. Napoleon went to Digne along the route followed by D 20. However, carry on along D 4085.

Driving through the Clue de Taulanne

© Chris Hellier/Alamy

The Flight of the Eagle

After landing at Golfe-Juan on 1 March 1815, Napoleon and his troops, preceded by an advance guard, set up a bivouac and made a brief stop at Cannes. Wishing to avoid the Rhône area, which he knew to be hostile, Napoleon planned to get to the valley of the Durance by way of the Alps and made for Grasse. There he expected to find a road which he had ordered to be built when he was emperor, but discovered that his orders had never been carried out. That evening, Napoleon waited impatiently for news from Sisteron, where the fort commanded the narrow passage of the Durance. Sisteron, however, offered no resistance and Napoleon realised that support for his cause was growing; he felt that France would rally to him if he reached Grenoble. Travelling along a coach road once more, he received an enthusiastic welcome in Gap that night, slept in Corps the next day and on 7 March reached La Mure, only to find Grenoble garrison troops facing him at Laffrey. This was the setting for the famous episode which turned events in his favour. It happened on what came to be called the "Prairie de la Rencontre", now commemorated by a monument. Seeing the road blocked by a battalion which greatly outnumbered his own escort, the emperor walked forward and, pulling open his greatcoat, declared: "Soldiers, I am your emperor! If anyone among you wishes to kill his general, here I am!" In spite of being ordered to fire by an officer, the troops rallied to Napoleon shouting: "Vive l'Empereur!" and marched with him in triumph to Grenoble.

Nearly a century later N 85 was named the **Route Napoléon** in 1913.

Digne-les-Bains★
See Digne-les-Bains p438.

Leave Digne by the SW.

The road (N 85) continues along the **Bléone Valley**. The imposing Château de Fontenelle stands on the right-hand side of the road, just before Malijai.

Malijai
Napoléon spent the night of 4–5 March in this elegant 18C **château** (open Mon–Thu 9am–noon, 3–6pm, Fri 9am–noon, 3–5pm; closed public holidays; free; 04 92 34 01 12).
Beyond Malijai, the view embraces the Durance Valley and the Montagne de Lure. The road follows the Canal d'Oraison to L'Escale and the dam.

Leave the bridge to your left and drive N along D 4.

Volonne
This village clings to a rocky spur crowned by two towers. On the northern edge are the remains of the 11C **St-Martin Church**.
Shortly after the Salignac Dam there is a splendid **view**★ of Sisteron.

Sisteron★★ See Sisteron p426.

Le Poët
See Route de Napoléon (from Le Poët to Corps) p391.

THE CROSSING OF THE GAPENÇAIS
Drive of 79km/49.1mi shown on the Lac de Serre-Ponçon, Gapençais and Dévoluy regional map (see p382).
See p391.

THE PAYS DU VERDON

The Gorges du Verdon is one of the most impressive canyons in Europe. The River Verdon, named for its striking blue-green colour, plunges through ragged limestone cliffs, reaching its destination at the Lac de Ste-Croix; the most spectacular section lies between Castellane and Moustiers-Ste-Marie. Driving along one of the roads that follows the rim of the ravine provides vertiginous views. The cliffs attract keen rock-climbers, with over 1 500 climbing routes on good limestone rock. It is also a popular destination for fishing and white-water sports.

Lavender

There are three types of lavender grown on the hillsides.

The high-quality *lavender vrai* produces the best essence, but thrives only between altitudes of 600m/1 969ft to 1 200m/3 937ft. Increasingly the lower-quality *lavandre aspic* and the hybrid *lavandin* are found, since their yield is higher and they are more hardy.

The best time to visit is between July and September when the flower is in full bloom. Local distilleries and markets are the ideal places to buy lavender products.

☺ Useful Tips for a Successful Walk in the Canyon

♦ Study detailed maps of the area and calculate your probable time, allowing for the slowest member in your group. Then add an extra hour (minimum). Follow the itinerary in the direction that is recommended.

♦ Take food and 2 litres (4 pints) of water per person (the river water is not suitable for drinking), one or two torches (with spare batteries),

Highlights

1 The spectacular views driving along the **Route de la Corniche Sublime** (p453)

2 Observe the eagles accompanied by an ornithologist with the association **Le Piaf** (p460)

3 Stroll around the pretty historic village of **Riez** (p465)

4 Discover the secrets of **Moustiers-Ste-Marie**'s ceramics trade at the Musée de la Faïence (p466)

5 After a drive around the **Gorges du bas Verdon**, stop for a picnic on the shores of the immense **Lac de Ste-Croix** (p468)

additional clothing and strong walking boots.

♦ Strictly prohibited: camping on unauthorised sites, lighting a fire, digging up fossils. Walkers are also asked to refrain from taking shortcuts

Lavender fields, Plateau de Valensole

© Andreas G. Karelias/Fotolia.com

THE PAYS DU VERDON

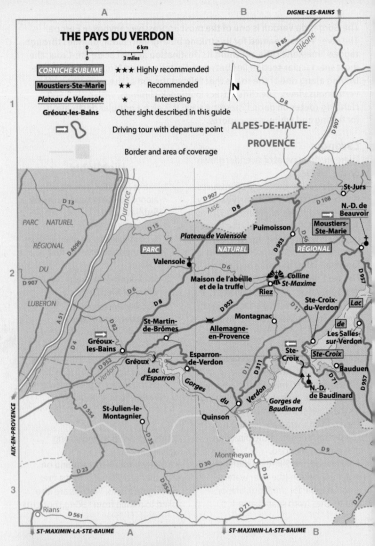

THE PAYS DU VERDON

0		6 km
0	3 miles	

CORNICHE SUBLIME	★★★ Highly recommended
Moustiers-Ste-Marie	★★ Recommended
Plateau de Valensole	★ Interesting
Gréoux-les-Bains	Other sight described in this guide
	Driving tour with departure point
	Border and area of coverage

DIGNE-LES-BAINS

N 85

Bléone

N

ALPES-DE-HAUTE-PROVENCE

St-Jurs

N.-D. de Beauvoir

Moustiers-Ste-Marie

Puimoisson

Plateau de Valensole

PARC   **NATUREL**   **RÉGIONAL**

Valensole

Maison de l'abeille et de la truffe

Colline St-Maxime

Riez

Ste-Croix-du-Verdon

Lac

Montagnac

St-Martin-de-Brômes

Allemagne-en-Provence

Les Salles-sur-Verdon

Gréoux-les-Bains

de

Ste-Croix

Gréoux

Lac d'Esparron

Esparron-de-Verdon

Ste-Croix

Bauduen

Gorges

du

Verdon

N.-D. de Baudinard

Gorges de Baudinard

St-Julien-le-Montagnier

Quinson

Montmeyan

Rians

ST-MAXIMIN-LA-STE-BAUME

ST-MAXIMIN-LA-STE-BAUME

PARC NATUREL

RÉGIONAL

DU

LUBERON

AIX-EN-PROVENCE

Making Moustiers faïence, Moustiers-Sainte-Marie

D. Pazery/MICHELIN

(which increases the erosion of slopes), crossing the river, except via bridges, and picking flowers. Dogs must not be taken along the footpaths in the gorges.

◆ Going into the gorges with children under 10 is not recommended; the sentier Imbut is too difficult for them.

◆ Water released by the Chaudanne or Castillon plants can cause a sudden rise in the level of the Verdon. The EDF recorded information (℘04 92 83 62 68) only lists forecast rates of flow, so it is essential, when stopping for any

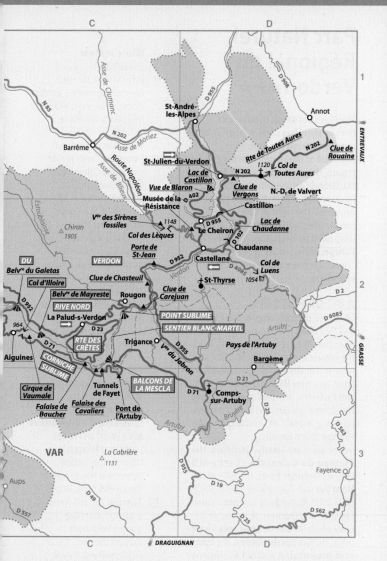

length of time, to choose a few rocks at water level as markers and watch them carefully. Releases from the dams are not preceded by warning signals.

◆ **Maps and topo-guides** –
In addition to the local maps included in this chapter, it would be useful to buy the Moustiers-Ste-Marie local map (1:50 000) and the Grand Canyon du Verdon map by A. Monier. *Le Guide du Verdon* by J.F. Bettus is on sale in La Palud-sur-Verdon; another useful

guide is *Randonnées pédestres dans le pays du Verdon*, published by Édisud.
◆ Exploration of the bottom of the gorge – It can be done mostly on foot, but swimming is necessary in places, so it is closer to canyoning and requires a thorough knowledge of the techniques of white-water sports.
◆ Rock-climbing sites – The main one is the Belvédères de la Carelle; there is also the Belvédère de Trescaire and the Falaise de l'Escalès.

Parc Naturel Régional du Verdon★★★

The River Verdon, a tributary of the Durance, has carved magnificent gorges through the limestone plateaux of the Haute-Provence region, the most spectacular being the Grand Canyon, which extends for 21km/13mi from Rougon to Aiguines. The sight of this vast furrow lined with sheer walls in wild unspoiled surroundings is unique in Europe; in the words of Jean Giono: "Here, it is more than remote, it is elsewhere …."

A BIT OF HISTORY

Since 1997, the park comprises 180 000ha/ 444 774 acres over 46 *communes* surrounding the Verdon. Springing from the mountains at 2 500m/8 202ft altitude and finally tumbling into the Durance, this river links together the Alps and Provence. The park centres around the Verdon gorges, but it also encompasses a mosaic of landscapes with strong cultural identity.

Seven units are clearly identified: the **Plateau de Valensole** (see p463) with its lavender fields, the hills of the **Haut Var** with Aups (see GREEN GUIDE CÔTE D'AZUR), the **deep gorges** around Esparron and Quinson (see Lac de Ste-Croix p468), the **Lac de Ste-Croix** (see p468), the **Gorges du Verdon**, the **lakes and mountains** around Castellane (see p470) and the region of **Artuby** near Bargème (see p470).

Its average altitude is around 700m/ 2 297ft with the highest peak, the **Mourre de Chanier**, at 1 930m/6 332ft. The rapid succession of the diverse levels of vegetation, from alpine to southern, results in a wide variety of species over a limited area: cicadas chirr in the heathland and olive groves, the wild boar rustles through the undergrowth, the chamois climbs the crests, the black grouse clatters through the larch forests and the marmot stands amid the

- **Michelin Map:** 334 D/H10/11.
- **Info:** Maison du Parc naturel régional du Verdon, Domaine de Valx, 04360 Moustiers-Ste-Marie. ℘04 92 74 68 00. www.parcduverdon.fr.
- **Location:** On its N side, the Grand Canyon can be followed on D 952 and D 23, while D 71 runs along the S side.
- **Don't Miss:** The Verdon is a paradise for outdoor activities; its rich archaeological past can be discovered at Quinson; admire the faïence at Moustiers-Ste-Marie; take the waters at Gréoux-les-Bains; and inhale the lavender on the Valensole Plateau.
- **Kids:** Take children to the Maison des gorges du Verdon and on the nature walks of Châteauneuf-les-Moustiers at La Palud and of Les Lézards at Rougon. Observe the Griffon vultures at Rougon with the Le Piaf Association.
- **Timing:** You will need a day to follow the gorges from both sides of the river. If you enjoy walking, stay at least another day.

fields of gentian. Circling the peaks are the golden eagle, the short-toed snake eagle, and the griffon vulture, which has been successfully reintroduced into the region. And that highly protected rarity: the hairy-backed snail.

Sport and leisure activities are well represented around the five artificial lakes, on the hiking paths, the mountaineering trails, and on the white waters of the Gorges du Verdon.

Les Gorges du Verdon

175km/109mi long, from the summits of Mercantour to the Durance river banks, the Verdon derives its name from the Gallic tribe of *Verguni*.

Taming the Verdon – Over three decades, at least **five dams** have been built across the Verdon. The first was at Castillon in 1947, followed by the one at Chaudanne (🦽*see Castellane, p470)*; then came those of Gréoux, and Quinson and to finish that of Ste-Croix (🦽*see p468)*. The Verdon can have sharp variations in water levels, but thanks to the precious reserves, the Provence no longer suffers from water shortage.

Birth of a giant – Why has the Verdon carved out such a deep gorge in such hard rocks, rather than skirted around them? The reason is that when the alpine area folded, and the limestone deposits rose, the existing river bed sank deeper. The Verdon widened and intense erosion carved huge caves and hollowed out a vast network of underground caves and galleries.

Exploration and development – Until the beginning of the 20C, access to the bottom of these gorges was deemed impossible. In 1896 Janet probed at the entrance to the gorges, but didn't go much further. In 1900 the need to develop the hydroelectrical resources of the region led the government to begin on the project of damming the Verdon. A founder of speleology, **É.A. Martel** (1859–1938), after a survey of the Grand Canyon, began his exploration in August 1905 with two teams, **Isidore Blanc**, a

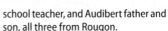

Green Waters and Purple Shadows

In 1959 Jean Giono wrote: "Nothing is more romantic than the combination of these rocks and abysses, of these green waters and purple shadows, of this sky that resembles Homer's sea and the wind that speaks with the voice of dead gods."

school teacher, and Audibert father and son, all three from Rougon.

Isidore Blanc led É.A. Martel on his expeditions, but he mainly pioneered local tourism by developing pathways and making them accessible to walkers. From 1928 the Touring Club de France took over the task of developing the belvederes.

The main viewpoints were signposted. In 1947 the Corniche Sublime road (D 71) opened the south bank to motorists. On the north bank, the Route des Crêtes (D 23) was only completed in 1973.

🚗 DRIVING TOURS

1 LA CORNICHE SUBLIME★★★
81km/50.3mi. Allow half a day.

The road twists and turns to reach the most impressive viewpoints. Beyond the passage of **Porte de St-Jean**★, the river turns and flows south.

Clue de Chasteuil★ is a long transverse gorge lined with vertical rock strata.

View of the Gorges du Verdon from the Col d'Illoire

S. Sauvignier/MICHELIN

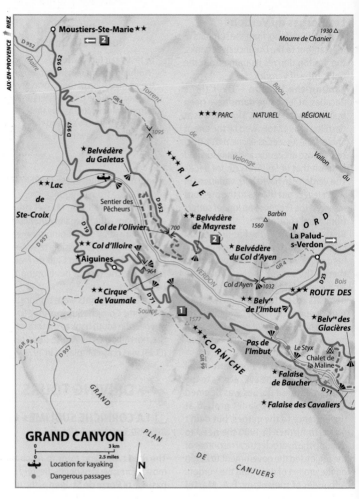

Moustiers-Ste-Marie ★★

1930 △
Mourre de Chanier

★★★ PARC   NATUREL   RÉGIONAL

★ Belvédère
du Galetas

R I V E

★★ Lac
de
Ste-Croix

Sentier des
Pêcheurs

Col de l'Olivier

★★ Belvédère
de Mayreste

Barbin
1560

N O R D
La Palud-
s-Verdon

★★ Col d'Illoire

★ Aiguines

★ Belvédère
du Col d'Ayen

★★ Cirque
de Vaumale

Source

Col d'Ayen   1032

★★ Belv.re
de l'Imbut

ROUTE DES

★ Belv.re des
Glacières

1577

CORNICHE

Pas de
l'Imbut

Le Styx
Chalet de
la Maline

★ Falaise
de Baucher

★ Falaise des Cavaliers

GRAND CANYON

0   3 km
0   2.5 miles

Location for kayaking

Dangerous passages

PLAN

DE

CANJUERS

N

GR 99

D 957

GRAND

▷ *In Pont-de-Soleils, turn left into D 955.*

Leaving the Verdon, the road passes the foot of the Défends Forest.

▷ *Turn right onto D 90.*

An imposing medieval castle, remodelled in the 16C (now a hotel–restaurant), overlooks the village of **Trigance**. From here there are historical and botanical trails *(map at the entrance to the village)*. The road follows the green **Jabron** Valley.

▷ *Return to D 955.*

Comps-sur-Artuby sits at the foot of a rock crowned by the 13C **Église St-André**. From here is a **view** of the Plans de Provence and the Artuby gorges.

▷ *From Comps, drive W along D 71.*

A bend in the road affords a **view**★ of the Préalpes de Castellane and Préalpes de Digne.

Balcons de la Mescla★★★
On the right side of the road and on either side of the Café-Relais des Balcons.
From these rock terraces, there are views of the Mescla 250m/820ft below, the name given to the confluence of

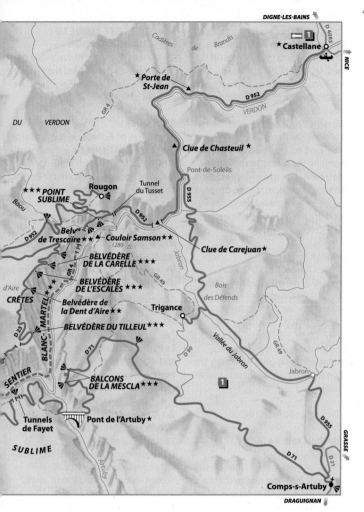

the Verdon and the Artuby. The Verdon takes a sharp bend and the view embraces the upstream part of the gorge, 400m–500m/1 312ft–1 640ft deep.

▶ *Follow D 71.* ❄ *Snow and landslides may block the road in Dec–Mar.*

The **Pont de l'Artuby**★ bridge, an ideal spot for bungee jumping, spans two sheer cliffs. The road goes round the Pilon du Fayet, to reach the Verdon Canyon. *Car park at the exit to the bridge.* Between the two **Tunnels du Fayet** and just after, extraordinary **view**★★★ of the curve of the canyon at the Étroit des Cavaliers. After leaving behind the

gorges, the road runs along the edge of the cliff. At a fork in the road, turn right; this takes you to the Restaurant des Cavaliers.

From the terrace there is a splendid **view** of the **Falaise des Cavalier**★ (300m/984ft).

There is a lovely view upstream of the Bassin du Pré Raucher from **Falaise de Baucher**★.

At **Pas de l'Imbut** there is a vertiginous view of the Verdon, which disappears under a blockfield of rocks, 400m/1 312ft below. The road veers from the gorges, and after two hairpin bends affords a view of the Falaises de Barbin.

A left-hand bend marks the entrance to the wooded **Cirque de Vaumale**★★; the view extends to the exit point of the gorges. At 700m/2 297ft above the Verdon the road reaches its highest point at 1 202m/3 944ft; vast panorama of the Source of Vaumale.

Leaving the cirque; **view**★ over the Verdon and the Ste-Croix lake.

At the exit to the gorge, stop for a moment for a last look from **Col d'Illoire**★★. The **view**★ embraces a horizon of blue ridges; notice the peak of the Ste-Victoire mountain. In the foreground are the Valensole Plateau and the Ste-Croix lake.

Aiguines★

🏠 *Allée des Tilleuls, 83630 Aiguines.*
🖉 *04 94 70 21 64. www.aiguines.com.*
🕐 *Open 1 Jul–30 Aug Mon–Fri 8.30am –6.30pm, Sat–Sun 9am–12.30pm, 2–5.30pm; 31 Aug–30 Jun Mon–Fri 9am–12.30pm, 2–5.30pm.* 🕐 *Closed 23 Dec–2 Jan and public holidays.*

Continue climbing until you reach the St-Pierre Chapel, where there is a viewing table.

▷ *Turn right onto the D 957.*

Lac de Ste-Croix ★★

🔔 *See p468.*

The D 957 borders the lake, then crosses the Verdon; from the bridge there are **views** of the canyon entrance. After, the road climbs the Vallée de la Maire and passes the leisure park of Moustiers.

Moustiers-Ste-Marie★★

🔔 *See Moustiers-Ste-Marie p466.*

2 NORTH BANK★★★

73km/45.4mi. Allow half a day.

The road *(D 952)* from Moustiers to Castellane only runs close to the Grand Canyon at each end. However, the "Route des Crêtes" *(D 23)* offers a round tour from La Palud-sur-Verdon via a number of viewpoints. There are three sections to the tour: from Moustiers to La Palud; the Route des Crêtes loop; from La Palud to Castellane.

MOUSTIERS-STE-MARIE TO LA PALUD-SUR-VERDON

On the way down the Maire Valley the view embraces the edge of the Plateau de Valensole, overlooking the vast expanse of the Lac de Ste-Croix.

Belvédères

From that of **Galetas**★, view of the gateway of the Grand Canyon, uphill of the rue d'Eau de St-Martin, and downhill of the Lac de Ste-Croix. From the Cirque de Mayreste the road climbs steeply. From the **Belvédère de Mayreste**★★ *(signposted – 🚶 15min there and back along a marked path on a stony ridge that is sometimes slippery)* – View uphill over the gorges.

Belvédère du Col d'Ayen★ *(not signposted – 🚶 15min on foot there and back)* – Upstream view of the twisted course of the canyon. The road veers away from the Verdon towards the area around La Palud-sur-Verdon. The family resort of **La Palud-sur-Verdon** is ideal for walks and rock-climbing. A 12C Romanesque **bell tower** is all that remains from the church. The 18C **castle** and its four corner towers overlook the village.

👥 **Maison des gorges du Verdon**★ – *Le Château, 04120 La Palud-sur-Verdon.* 🕐 *Open Wed–Mon 15 Jun–15 Sept 10am–1pm, 4–7pm; mid-Mar–mid-Jun and mid-Sept–mid-Nov 10am–noon, 4–6pm.* 🕐 *Closed 1 May.* 💶 *4€ (children 2€).* 🖉 *04 92 77 32 02. www.lapaludsurverdon.com.*

This is an essential stop for the information you need to appreciate the Verdon Gorges. On the first floor there is an **écomusée**. On the second floor there is a library, and on the top floor there is a climbing wall.

🚶 **Châteauneuf-les-Moustiers nature trail** – *1hr 30min. Booklet on sale at the Maison des gorges or the Maison du Parc régional du Verdon.* 💶*4€.*

A trail that is enjoyable for families, with the guide, to explore the ruined village which testifies to life in former times.

ROUTE DES CRÊTES★★★
(Round tour starting from La Palud-sur-Verdon)

A succession of belvederes or viewing points line this itinerary.

 *From La Palud, take D 952 towards Castellane then turn right into D 23.*

First is the **Belvédère de Trescaire★★**. Looking upstream, the Verdon is seen to flow through a jumble of fallen rocks and disappear under the Baulme aux Pigeons Cave, in the Samson Corridor. From the **Belvédères de la Carelle★★★** is a bird's-eye view of the river. To the left is the Auberge du Point Sublime and, above it, the hilltop village of Rougon. From the **Belvédère de la Dent d'Aire★★** (alt. 1 238m/4 062ft), on the left, are the golden cliffs of the Dent d'Aire and of the Barre de l'Escales; ahead is the narrow corridor of the Baumes-Frères with the Arme Vieille peak towering above.

The road reaches 1 320m/4 331ft. At the **Belvédère du Tilleul★★★** the confluence of the Verdon and Artuby, known as the "Mescla", lies ahead and the pont de l'Artuby behind, and beyond the Plan de Canjuers. The Verdon changes course to the northwest.

At the **Belvédère des Glacières★** there is a view of the Mescla and its enormous promontory, of the Verdon and, in clear weather, the Mediterranean. And finally, the **Belvédère de l'Imbut★★**: the Verdon disappears under a pile of fallen rocks and the sentier Vidal and sentier de l'Imbut can be seen on the opposite bank. There is a **view** of the Baou Béni cliffs. Upstream, from the "**Passage du Styx**" there are glimpses of the Pré Baucher.

The road returns to La Palud-sur-Verdon.

LA PALUD-SUR-VERDON TO CASTELLANE

Don't miss the fine **view** on the next bend: the hilltop village of **Rougon** suddenly appears ahead.

Point Sublime★★★

15min return. Leave from the car park near the Auberge du Point Sublime. Follow the marked path on the right across the Plateau des Lauves to the belvedere 180m/591ft above the confluence of the Verdon and the Baou.

 *Return to the car and follow D 17 to Rougon.*

The "eyrie" of **Rougon**, overlooked by medieval ruins, affords a fine **view★** of the entrance of the Grand Canyon. It is from here that you can observe the griffon vultures that have been reintroduced to the region.

Return to D 952 and follow it towards Castellane.

Couloir Samson★★

Just before the Tunnel du Tusset, a dead-end road branching off to the right leads to the confluence of the Verdon and the Baou (car park); it meets the path running along the river from the Chalet de la Maline.

The Birds of the Verdon

The Verdon has an **ornithological atlas** after the vast survey carried out in 2004 and 2005, which was conducted for an atlas of a similar nature for the Provence-Alpes-Côte d'Azur region. One hundred and fifty-five species of nesting birds have been recorded on this territory, which includes **four "ornithological landscapes"**: the confluence Durance–Verdon, the Plateau de Valensole, the Grand Canyon and the Préalpes in the Haut Pays.

The **vulture** is in the process of being reintroduced in the Verdon. In 1999 12 griffon vultures were released in the *communes* of Rougon. Now there are nearly one hundred. The monk vulture is also being reintroduced. *Information from Castellane tourist office (see p470). For further details: http://verdon.lpo.fr.*

From this spot, the narrowing of the Grand Canyon downstream looks wild.

The limestone strata at **Clue de Carejuan**★ are strangely coloured.

▷ *Return to D 952 and Castellane.*

⚑ HIKING IN THE GRAND CANYON
① SENTIER BLANC-MARTEL★★★

A shuttle bus for hikers runs from Castellane.

⚑ Between the Chalet de la Maline and the Point Sublime, GR 4, known as the sentier Martel, offers an unforgettable experience with the Grand Canyon.

Chalet de la Maline to the Point Sublime

⚑ *5hr hike, plus resting time, along a difficult itinerary; ⏱see map opposite – torch essential, a headlamp even better. GR 4 is marked in white and red.*
From the steps going down to the river, there are fine views of the Pas de l'Estellié.

▷ *Ignore the path branching off to the right towards the Estellié Footbridge; it leads to the Corniche Sublime.*

View of the Grand Canyon du Verdon from Sentier Martel

J. Malburet/MICHELIN

At the Pré d'Issane *(after 1hr 30min walking)*, the path runs close to the river and follows it through the Étroit des Cavaliers. The gorge widens and the path reaches the Talus de Guègues. Continue upstream past the Baumes-aux-Bœufs Cave and take the second path to the right leading to the **Mescla**★★★ *(30min return)*, from where there is a view upstream of the Défilé des Baumes-Frères.

▷ *Retrace your steps to the intersection and turn right.*

The path winds its way up to the Brèche Imbert *(steps)*: superb view of the Baumes-Frères and the Barre de l'Escalès. The canyon becomes wider and the extraordinary jumble of the Chaos de Trescaïre, on the right, comes into view. Next come two tunnels; inside the second, metal steps lead to the **Baume-aux-Pigeons**★, a vast cave, 30m/98ft high. From the last opening, there is a view of **Couloir Samson**★★. Beyond the tunnel, the path climbs to **Belvédère du Point Sublime**★★★.

▷ *Walk to the inn, where you can call a taxi, or catch the shuttle.*

② SENTIER DE DÉCOUVERTE DES LÉZARDS

⚑⚑ From Point Sublime★★★
⚑ This well-marked trail starts from the Plateau des Lauves. Pick up a booklet at the Auberge du Point Sublime or at the tourist office in La Palud-sur-Verdon.

③ BELVÉDÈRE DE RANCOUMAS★★
East Bank Starting from the Point Sublime★★★
⚑ *3hrs 30min return. It is possible to start from the Point Sublime car park and to walk S, following GR 49 markings, or to drive towards the Couloir Samson (D 23B) and park the car 500m/547yds after the junction.*

2km/1.2mi before reaching the car park, take GR 49 on the left; it leads through

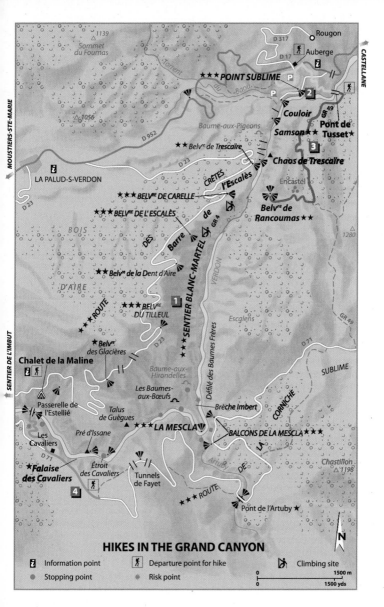

HIKES IN THE GRAND CANYON

🅘	Information point	🚶	Departure point for hike		Climbing site
●	Stopping point	✳	Risk point		

an oak forest down to the 17C **Pont de Tusset**★.

Turn right onto the track; it crosses a stream before reaching the ruins of Encastel. From the edge of the cliff the Belvédère de Rancoumas offers a **panorama**★★ of the Falaise de l'Escalès, and below, the sentier Martel. The **Mourre de Chanier** soars in the distance to the northwest.

▶ *Return along the same route.*

4 SENTIER DE L'IMBUT★★

🚶 *This walk is for experienced walkers only, or walkers accompanied by a guide. Due to the difficulty it is unsuitable for children.* ⏱ *See Hiking map above. 6km/3.7mi. Allow 4hrs 30min. From the Auberge des Cavaliers you follow the left bank along a path*

which is equipped with handrails and ladders at the narrower points.
You walk alongside the Couloir de Styx, and, after 2 hours 30 minutes, reach the Imbut beach.

5 SENTIER DES PÊCHEURS

See Hiking map p459. 6.5km/4mi. Gradient 300m/984ft. Allow 2hrs 30min. Depart from Col de l'Olivier, on D 952 (car park). Check if there is going to be a release of water at the Maison des gorges du Verdon.
A looped hike of medium difficulty. After a steep short descent you continue the walk along the river banks.

ADDRESSES

STAY

There are environmentally friendly places to stay. Two gîtes designated **gîtes Panda** by the WWF: one at St-Jurs (*04 92 74 44 18; www.ferme-de-vauvenieres.fr*) and the other at Trigance (*04 94 76 91 23; http://saintmaymes.multimania.com*). Three **hôtels au naturel** at St-Laurent-du-Verdon, Moissac-Bellevue, La Palud-sur-Verdon.

Chambre d'hôte La Valdenay – *Rte des Crêtes, 04120 La Palud-sur-Verdon. 2km/1.2mi E of La Palud by D 952 (Route de Castellane) and D 23 (Route des Crêtes). 04 92 77 37 92. www.provenceweb.fr/04/valdenay. Closed Oct–Easter.* 5 rooms. Modern house with quiet rooms. Regional cuisine.

Chambre d'hôte Mme Colombéro – *Campagne L'Enchastre. 04120 La Palud-sur-Verdon, 12km/7.4mi N of La Palud by D 123 (towards Châteauneuf) then D 17. 04 92 83 76 12. Closed Oct–May.* 5 rooms. Modern house on a farm estate, with plain but comfortable rooms decorated in colourful tones.

Hôtel Les Gorges du Verdon – *04120 La Palud-sur-Verdon. 1km/0.6mi by rte de la Maline Sud. 04 92 77 38 26. www.hotel-des-gorges-du-verdon.fr. Closed 18 Oct–1 Apr. Wifi. 27 rooms, restaurant.* Gaily decorated rooms in this hotel perched on a hillside. Menu inspired by the region.

EAT

Auberge du Point Sublime – *D 952, 04120 Rougon. 04 92 83 60 35. pointsublime@nordnet.fr. Closed 3 Nov–24 Apr.* 13 rooms. Family auberge serving regional dishes in a rustic dining room, or on shady terrace. Simple rooms.

Lou Cafetié – *04120 La Palud-sur-Verdon. 04 92 74 41 65.* Tourist and locals alike frequent this restaurant to enjoy a simple grilled steak, or a regional dish such as ravioli, or swiss chard lasagne. Sandwiches and bruschetta served all day.

SHOPPING

Exposition-Atelier La Sagne – *Ferme de la Sagne, SW of Trigance on D 955, rte de Comps-sur-Artuby, 83840 Trigance. 06 82 17 49 92. Open Jul–Aug 3–7pm; rest of year by reservation. Closed Nov–Apr.* Craft and contemporary art exhibition in an old farmhouse.

Maison des Produits du Pays du Verdon – In Allemagne-en-Provence (*see Plateau de Valensole p463*).

Market – Wednesday at La Palud-sur-Verdon.

ACTIVITIES

Sortie de découverte des vautours du Verdon – *04120 Rougon. 06 26 47 50 00. www.voirlepiaf.fr. 10€ per 2hrs (children 6€).*
The **Le Piaf association** organises discovery trails for observing the vultures of the Verdon, accompanied by an ornithologist (loan of binoculars and telescopes). Meeting point at the Point Sublime car park.

EVENTS

Fête du Parc – Late September, every year in the communes of the Parc naturel régional du Verdon, craft fair, conferences and various activities centred around the local heritage.

Gréoux-les-Bains

Jean Giono described Gréoux, located deep in the Provence, as the "romantic oasis of Verdon". Today, this very popular ancient spa town, already famous in Roman times for the healing virtues of its waters, is favoured for its setting, near the Lac d'Esparron, and its lavender fields.

SIGHTS

Vieux village – The old village centre nestles at the foot of the castle.

Start with a climb up to the **château des Templiers**, with its massive square keep. It houses exhibitions in the guardroom and, in summer, festivals are staged in the courtyard. And next, stroll through the "**andrônes**", covered passages that weave their way under the houses.

At the other end of the **rue Grande**, the main shopping street, stands the Notre-Dame-des-Ormeaux church. Rebuilt over the centuries, the belfry was added in the 19C.

Troglodytic baths – To the east of the town, opened in 1968, are the present-day spa baths. Not far away, the archaeologists uncovered a pool dating from the 1C AD: the Romans were already coming here to recover. They dedicated a stela (inscribed stone) to the water nymphs, which was discovered last century.

The **Source de Gréoux**, the only one, releases 2.5 million litres/550 000gals of hot (42°C/108°F) sulphurous water used

- ▶ **Population:** 2 459.
- ◔ **Michelin Map:** 334 D10.
- **Info:** 7 pl. de l'Hôtel de Ville, 04800 Gréoux-les-Bains. ✆04 92 78 01 08. www.greoux-les-bains.com.
- ◑ **Location:** Gréoux is 14km/8.7mi E of Manosque. Lac Ste-Croix is 20km/12.4mi NE by D 952, passing through Riez.
- **P Parking:** Car parks are found at av. Pierre-Brossolette, esplanade C.-de-Gaulle, and at the upper end of the village.
- **Kids:** Musée des Miniatures, Poupées et Jouets du Monde has hundreds of dolls to admire in thematic settings.
- ◷ **Timing:** Count one hour to see the town, and another to drive to St-Julien-le-Montagnier and admire the view.

for the treatment of rheumatism, arthritis and respiratory complaints.

Oliva, Thermal and Morelon parks – ◷*Open May–Oct. Map identifying the exhibits available at the tourist office.* From the Oliva Park, on the avenue des Thermes, to the Morelon Park, which overlooks the banks of the Verdon, dis-

Gréoux-les-Bains

© phbcz/Bigstockphoto.com

cover the works of around 40 artists and sculptors dotted around the parks.

👤👤Musée des Miniatures, Poupées et Jouets du Monde – Le Petit Monde d'Émilie en Provence

16 av. des Alpes. ✎🔍*Guided tours 5 Apr–15 Nov Mon–Fri 3.30–6.30pm.* ⊜*7.50€ (children under 12 6€, under 4 free).* ☎*04 92 78 16 52. http:// pageperso.aol.fr/petitmondemilie.* Hundreds of dolls and toys, arranged in thematic scenes, fill 12 rooms.

EXCURSION
St-Julien-le-Montagnier

▶ *14km/8.7mi S of Gréoux on D 8 and D 35.* 🏛*15 r. de l'Hôtel de Ville, 83560 St-Julien-le-Montagnier.* ⏱*Open May–Oct Tue–Sat 9am–12.30pm, 3.30–6.30pm, Sun 10.30am–12.30pm; Nov–Apr Tue and Sat 9am–12.30pm, 2–6pm.* ⏱*Closed 1 Jan, 1 May, 8 May, 15 Aug, 11 Nov, 25 Dec.* ☎*04 94 77 20 95. www.ot-stjulien83.com.*
Wonderful **view**★ of the Plans de Provence, the Durance Valley, the Plateau de Valensole, Ste-Baume and Ste-Victoire from what used to be the village threshing floor.
The square, lantern-shaped bell tower of the 11C **village church** is a hallmark of traditional Haute-Provence architecture. Inside, a carved, gilded altar from the 17C and a well-preserved rood beam still survive.
The 13C **ramparts** are all that remains of the medieval stronghold. Follow the road to the point where it enters the village; there is a good view of the area from the fortified gate.
⏱*Open Sat–Sun 9am–5pm, contact M or Mme Nicaud.* ☎*04 94 80 02 52.*

🚗 DRIVING TOURS

PLATEAU DE VALENSOLE★
Drive of 74km/46mi shown on the regional map (⊙see p450).
⊙*See opposite.*

GORGES DU BAS VERDON AND THE LAC D'ESPARRON
Drive of 41km/25.5mi shown on the regional map (⊙see p450). ⊙*See p469. Follow route in the opposite direction.*

ADDRESSES

🛏 STAY
⊜🏨**Hôtel Villa Castellane** – *Av. des Thermes.* ☎*04 92 78 00 31. www.villa castellane.com. Closed late Nov–early Mar.* 🅿️. *10 rooms* ⊑*11€.* This old hunting pavilion stands in the centre of a park. Comfortable bedrooms and apartments. Both restaurant and swimming pool are for guests only.

⊜⊜🏨**Chambre d'hôte Bastide St-Donat** – *Rte de Vinon, 4km/2.5mi SW of Gréoux-les-Bains by D 952.* ☎*04 92 76 56 71. www.bastidesaintdonat.com. Closed 2 weeks in Dec.* 🅿️ ⇋. *4 rooms* ⊑. The rooms in this former fortress are decorated in Provençal colours.

⊜⊜🏨**Hôtel La Chêneraie** – *Les Hautes-Plaines, by av. des Thermes.* ☎*04 92 78 03 23. www.la-cheneraie.com. Closed mid-Nov–mid-Mar.* 🅿️. *Wifi. 20 rooms* ⊑*11€, half-board available, restaurant* ⊜⊜.
This modern hotel on the hillside above town has spacious, functional rooms. Hearty Provençal cuisine.

⊜⊜🏨**Hôtel Les Alpes** – *Av. des Alpes.* ☎*04 92 74 24 24. www.hoteldesalpes04.fr. Closed Jan. Wifi. 26 rooms* ⊑, *half-board available, restaurant* ⊜⊜. This hotel offers modern, practical rooms. Provençal cuisine.

🍴 EAT
The **rue Grande** is lined with agreeable restaurants, crêperies and snackbars such Myriam Miam.

⊜⊜**La Marmite Provençale** – ☎*04 92 77 66 62.* Traditional Provençal cuisine.

⊜⊜**Les Oliviers** – ☎*04 92 75 24 27.* ♿🅿️. Tasty, well-prepared Provençal cuisine.

🏃 ACTIVITIES
Établissement thermal – *Les Hautes-Plaines.* ☎*0 826 468 184. greouxlesbains@ chainethermale.fr. Open Mon–Sat 6am–4pm. Closed Nov–Mar and Sun. Reservation advised.* A range of treatments: one-day cure, or several days' cure.

Plateau de Valensole ★

This region is a vast plateau sloping from east to west and towering above the Durance. The Asse Valley splits it into two: the north includes arid wooded areas and a few inhabited valleys; the south is flatter and more open with vast fields of cereals and lavandin (cultivated lavender), dotted with almond trees. The best time to drive across the plateau is at almond blossom time in March, or in July when the scent of the lavender flowers fills the air.

🚗 DRIVING TOUR

PLATEAU DE VALENSOLE ★
Drive of 74 km/46mi shown on the regional map (🔗 see p450). Allow 1hr 30min.

Gréoux-les-Bains
🔗 *See p461.*

▷ *Leave from the N (D 8).*

Valensole
Take a few moments to admire the **St-Blaise Church** (14C), which has beautiful 16C stalls. The church and the deanery, which house a Benedictine community, form a remarkable site. Valensole is part of the Cluny order, ever since **St Mayeul** (910–94), the fourth Abbot de Cluny in Bourgogne (who was born here), gave the order his family home along with

---

> 📍 **Michelin Map:** 334 D9.
> ▷ **Location:** The plateau is defined by three river valleys: the Bléone in the north, the Durance in the west and the Verdon in the south. The valley of the River Asse runs down the middle.
> 👫 **Kids:** Maison de l'Abeille et de la Truffe at Puimoisson.
> 🕐 **Timing:** Take a day and picnic at the Lac d'Esparron; in the afternoon, plan to visit the château of Allemagne-en-Provence, which has limited visiting hours.

---

the Chapelle Ste-Maxime. On Saturday mornings, there is a Provençal market.

▷ *From Valensole, drive NE along D 8.*

The road runs along the edge of the Valensole Plateau and through fields of wheat and lavender.
At Poteau-de-Telle, fine **view** of the Asse Valley, its villages and the ruins of Bras-d'Asse clinging to the opposite cliff.

▷ *Turn right onto D 953 towards Puimoisson.*

Puimoisson
Behind the 13C fortified gates, the 15C church looks out over a vast square planted with hackberry trees. Here once stood the castle of the powerful

---

The Bee Transhumance

When summer approaches, a fever takes hold of Valensole and the other villages. Aromatic plants flower: the hives need to be installed quickly. The season starts in spring with rosemary and peaks in late June when the lavender fields are in full bloom. The plateau is covered with 250 000 hives, belonging to 500 beekeepers from neighbouring areas, the Var, the Bouches-du-Rhône, the Ardèche, and even abroad. Land is leased by the beekeepers according to the type of honey required and the flowering period. As to the transport of hives by lorry, it must take place at night, not only for safety reasons, but also because many bees play truant and don't return to the house until after sunset….

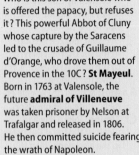

Abbot and Admiral

Who is this son of Valensole who is offered the papacy, but refuses it? This powerful Abbot of Cluny whose capture by the Saracens led to the crusade of Guillaume d'Orange, who drove them out of Provence in the 10C? **St Mayeul**. Born in 1763 at Valensole, the future **admiral of Villeneuve** was taken prisoner by Nelson at Trafalgar and released in 1806. He then committed suicide fearing the wrath of Napoleon.

Knights of the Hospital of St-Jean-de-Jérusalem, who commanded the village until the 12C. During the Revolution it became communal property; it was first abandoned, then destroyed. Its stones have been used to build several of the village houses.

▷ *Continue along D 953.*

Riez★
Riez opposite.

▷ *Leave by the SW (D 952).*

Château d'Allemagne-en-Provence★
Guided tours (50min) Jul–mid-Sept Tue–Sun 4pm, 5pm; Easter–end-Jun and mid-Sept–2 Nov Sat–Sun and public holidays 4pm, 5pm. 7€ (children under 12 free). ☎04 92 77 46 78. www.chateau-allemagne-en-provence.com. See Architecture p71.

During the Wars of Religion, the **Baron d'Allemagne**, allied to the Protestant Lesdiguières, valiantly defended his seat during a siege. Believing he had won, he was caught off guard and was killed by a musket shot. In revenge, his wife sacrificed 12 prisoners at his tombstone, all Catholic.

On the banks of the Colostre stands a 12C crenellated keep. The Renaissance façades of the castle have fine mullioned windows. Part of the park is laid out as a **medieval herb garden**.

Inside, the great hall has a **monumental fireplace**★ decorated with gypsum carvings.

▷ *Continue on D 952.*

The drive continues through lavender and tulip fields.

St-Martin-de-Brômes★
The old houses lining the streets have curious doorways with inscriptions. On the ancient village square stands a moss-covered fountain dating from 1845. Inside the Romanesque **church**, behind the altar, is a curious tabernacle in stucco polychrome. Admire the series of paintings by Esprit Michel Gibelin which recount the life of St Martin.
Tour templière – *Reserve for guided tour at town hall. Free. ☎04 92 78 02 02. http://mairie.wanadoo.fr/mairie-smdb.* This 14C tower houses on the ground floor a small **Gallo-Roman museum**.

▷ *Continue on D 952 to return to Gréoux.*

ADDRESSES

🏠 STAY

🛏️🛏️🛏️ **Chambre d'hôte Le Château d'Allemagne-en-Provence** – 04500 Allemagne-en-Provence. ☎04 92 77 46 78. www.chateau-allemagne-en-provence.com. Closed 5 Nov–22 Mar. 🅿️. **3 rooms.** The château has large rooms. Three nights or more, reservation required.

🏃 ACTIVITIES

Ets Nevière – Rte de Manosque, 04210 Valensole. ☎04 92 74 85 28. www.neviere.fr. Open Tue–Sat 8am–noon, 1.30–5.30pm. Living bee museum.

Riez★

Many paths have crossed at Riez: first Celtic, then Roman. The foundation of a bishopric in the 5C made Riez an economic as well as a religious force in the region. From here, all roads lead into the Parc naturel régional du Verdon.

▶ **Population:** 1 741.
◉ **Michelin Map:** 334 E10.
▯ **Info:** Pl. de la Mairie, 04500 Riez. ℘04 92 77 99 09. www.ville-riez.fr.
◗ **Location:** Between Gréoux-les-Bains and Moustiers.

SIGHTS
Old Town★

Stroll leisurely around the place de Quinconce and de Javelly, typical Provençal squares planted with shady trees.

Enter the old town through the 13C **Porte Aiguière**. The former main street, **Grand-Rue**, is lined with decorated houses: a corbelled house (no. 1), 16C **Hôtel de Mazan** (no. 12), lovely decorated façade (no. 25), windows surrounded by moulded friezes (no. 27). As you reach the 14C **Porte St-Sols**, turn right towards rue St-Thècle; a tiny square on the left offers an interesting view of what remains of the town walls and of the **Tour de l'Horloge**.

◗ *Walk back down towards the Porte St-Sols to the church.*

The bell tower and chapels behind the choir remain from the 15C cathedral. The rest dates from the 19C.
In a field stand the remains of the **Temple of Apollo**: four slender 6m/20ft granite columns with fine marble capitals and architrave, dating from the 1C.

Baptistery★

R. Frédéric-Mistral. ⟜⟞*Guided tour mid-Jun–mid-Sept Tue 10am, Thu and Sat 3pm.* ⧖*Closed public holidays.* ⊛*2.50€.* ℘*04 92 77 89 30. www.ville-riez.fr.*
This small square baptistery, built in the 5C, is one of the earliest known buildings still standing in France. It houses the **lapidary museum**, which has a collection that includes altars, Roman inscriptions, sarcophagi and mosaics. On the other side of the road are the remains of a Gallo-Roman village and 5C palaeo-Christian cathedral.

EXCURSIONS
Colline St-Maxime

◗ *2km/1.2mi NE on the r. du Faubourg-St-Sébastien.*
At the top of this 636m/2 087ft hill sits the **Chapelle St-Maxime**, which is a surprising mix of styles: six ancient columns stand side by side with a 19C décor. From the terrace there is a vast **panorama**★.

Château d'Allemagne-en-Provence★

◗ *8 km/5mi SW on D 952.*
◉*See opposite.*

St-Jurs

◗ *15km/9.3mi NE on D 953 then D 108.*
This village is the highest on the plateau at an altitude of 825m/2 707ft. From the church there is a wonderful **view**★ extending over the plateau. In the 16C building work unearthed the relics of St Nicaire and Restitut.

The Black Gold of Haute-Provence

The truffle is called **rabasse** in regional Provençal. The white, springtime variety serves as "bait" for the training of the truffle-finding dogs. The black, rarer and more refined, is harvested in December. Brillat-Savarin called it "the diamond of the kitchen". Buried under the oak and hazelnut trees, it is in fact a disease of the tree. It is harvested in the *truffières*, fields of trees that are favourable to their slow development. **Montagnac**, near to Riez, is a well-known site for truffles.

In the 19C the gypsum quarries were at their peak. This sedimentary rock was made into plaster that was used in local constructions. You can visit a restored plaster mill here.

 DRIVING TOUR

PLATEAU DE VALENSOLE★
Drive of 74km/46mi shown on the regional map (see p450). See p463.

ADDRESSES

STAY

 Chambre d'hôte Le Vieux Castel – *1 rte des Châteaux, 04500 Roumoules. 4 km/2.5mi NE of Riez, rte de Moustiers-Ste-Marie, on D 952, at the entrance to Roumoules. 04 92 77 75 42. http://vieuxcastel.free.fr. 5 rooms .* 17C building which once belonged to a Moustiers faïence creator. Simple traditionally decorated bedrooms.

EAT

 Le Café – *04 92 72 88 23. www.riez-restaurant-le-cafe.com. .* Bright modern restaurant serving dishes such as red mullet salad, duck breast cooked in Riez honey and flambéed king prawns.

SHOPPING

Le marché provençal – *Allée L.-Gardiol. Wed and Sat morning.*

Truffle market – *Café de France, allée L.-Gardiol. 04 92 77 99 09. Nov–Feb.*

Moustiers-Ste-Marie★★

It's not just Moustiers' amazing setting, at the heart of the Parc naturel régional du Verdon and near to the Lac de Ste-Croix, that has made it popular, but the production, over three centuries, of a fine white faïence (glazed earthenware).

SIGHTS
Church★
 Open Jul–Aug, contact for details. Guided tour possible. 3€ (children under 12 free). 04 92 74 67 84.
Its warm-coloured massive bell tower, characteristic of the Lombard Romanesque style, comprises three storeys with twinned openings and blind arcading resting on pillars or slender columns. Before reinforcement in the 18C, it was a *clocher branlant*, an oscillating bell tower. At the base, a room houses a **collection of religious art** and Moustiers vases.
The Romanesque chancel was replaced in the 14C by a Gothic chancel which forms an angle with the 12C nave. The base of the flat east end is decorated with twinned arcading opening onto rounded arches. Note the beautifully carved 16C and 18C stalls in the chancel.

Musée de la Faïence★
 Open Jul–Aug 10am–12.30pm, 2–7pm; Apr–Jun and Sept–Oct 10am–12.30pm, 2–6pm; Nov–Dec and Feb–Mar contact for details. 3€ (children free). 04 92 74 61 64.
The museum of faïence (glazed earthenware) has displays centred on the craftspeople who made Moustiers ceramics famous (see All Fired Up box, opposite).

- ▸ **Population:** 705.
- **Michelin Map:** 334 F9.
- **Info:** Place de l'Église, 04360 Moustiers. 04 92 74 67 84. www.moustiers.fr.
- **Location:** 15km/9.3mi NE of Riez.
- **Don't Miss:** The Faïence Museum.
- **Timing:** Give yourself half a day to stroll around town.

Chapelle Notre-Dame-de-Beauvoir★

 *30min there and back on foot.*

This chapel has been a place of pilgrimage since medieval times. The wide-stepped path leading to it offers glimpses of the village and of the Notre-Dame Gorge.

At the end of the path, there is a terrace dating from the Middle Ages, planted with trees and ringed by the remains of the old ramparts; from there, the **view**★ takes in the rooftops of Moustiers, the Maire Valley and the straight edge of the Valensole Plateau.

 DRIVING TOURS

GORGES DU VERDON★★★
Drive of 159km/98.8mi shown on the Grand Canyon map, 1 *and* 2 *(see p455). See p453.*

TOUR OF LAC DE STE-CROIX★★
Drive of 70km/43.5mi shown on the regional map (see p450). See p468.

ADDRESSES

🛏 STAY

🍽🍽🍽 **Chambre d'hôte l'Escalo** – *R. de la Bourgade. 04 92 74 69 93. http://lescalo.odepp.org. Closed 15 Jan–15 Mar.* 🅿 🚭. *4 rooms* 🍽.

Typical Provençal village house furnished with antiques. The largest rooms are on the second floor. Breakfast on the terrace.

🍽🍽🍽🍽 **Hôtel Bastide de Moustiers** – *Chemin de Quinson. S of the village, on D 952 and then a minor road. 04 92 70 47 47. www.bastide-moustiers.com. Closed 4 Jan–3 Mar and Nov–Mar Tue–Wed.* ♿. *Wifi. 12 rooms* 🍽 *20€, restaurant* 🍽🍽🍽. 17C *bastide*, once belonging to a faïence manufacturer. Modern, well-equipped rooms decorated in a Provençal style.

🍽 EAT

🍽 **Côté jardin** – *04 92 74 68 91. cjardin.moustiers@free.fr.* Refined cuisine with dishes such as foie gras ravioli, and home-made cannelloni stuffed with goat's cheese.

🍽🍽🍽 **Restaurant La Treille Muscate** – *Pl. de l'Église. 04 92 74 64 31. www.restaurant-latreillemuscate.com. Closed 15 Nov–10 Feb Wed except lunch in winter and Sept–Jun Thu.* Friendly little Provençal bistro serving tasty dishes.

All Fired Up

According to the story, a monk from Faenza came to **Pierre I Clérissy** and revealed to him the secret of making beautiful enamel. He then, in 1679, manufactured the first Moustiers faïence, decorating them with characters and hunting scenes, all in bright blue.

In 1738 **Joseph Olérys** introduced the high-temperature polychrome technique. Applied to small everyday objects, painted birds and flowers, sometimes extraordinary characters, this proved to be a great success.

With the brothers **Ferrat** and **Féraud**, the chinoiserie style and sometimes real-life topics appeared at the end of the 18C. A total of twelve workshops were operating at Moustiers. Then four closed down, the last one in 1874.

It was in 1927 that **Marcel Provence** revived this art. It was his idea to create the Musée de la Faïence de Moustiers. The 1970s and the increase in tourism relaunched this craft. *See opposite.*

Lac de Ste-Croix★★

The Lac de Ste-Croix stretches from the Grand Canyon du Verdon to the Gorges of the Lower Verdon. The turquoise-coloured lake is framed by the heights of the Plateau de Valensole and Plan de Canjuers.

- **Michelin Map:** 334 E10.
- **Info:** Mairie, 04500 Ste-Croix-du-Verdon. 04 92 77 85 29.
- **Location:** The lake, which is as large as Lake Annecy, is situated between the Grand Canyon and the lower Gorges du Verdon.
- **Kids:** The Musée de Préhistoire des Gorges du Verdon at Quinson.
- **Timing:** Give yourself a day to visit the lake, including a picnic and a swim.

🚗 DRIVING TOURS

The valley of Ste-Croix was flooded in 1975, after the dam was built.

TOUR OF THE LAKE★★
Drive of 70km/43.5mi shown on the regional map (♿ see p450). Allow 3hrs. The 2 200ha/5 436 acres can be seen from the plateau.

Ste-Croix-du-Verdon
This old hilltop village, which gave its name to the lake, is today almost level with the water. There is a **beach** along the shore *(patrolled in Jul–Aug)*, and also a watersports centre.

▷ *The road descends to the lake.*

Barrage de Ste-Croix
This dam and its plant produce more than 150 million kw per year.

▷ *Beyond the dam, turn right onto D 71. The road runs through the Gorges de Baudinard.*

Bauduen
The **setting**★ is remarkable. Old houses line the picturesque streets climbing towards the church.

▷ *Take the road going to Aups, then turn left onto D 957.*

Les Salles-sur-Verdon
A few architectural features of the old, now submerged, town were saved and used again in the new village.

Lac de Ste-Croix viewed from Ste-Croix-du-Verdon

© Nicolas Thibaut/Photononstop

GORGES DU BAS VERDON AND THE LAC D'ESPARRON

Drive of 41km/25.5mi from Ste-Croix Dam to Gréoux Dam shown on the regional map (see p450). Allow 1hr 30min.

▶ *After the dam, turn right onto D 71 then D 9. The road runs through the **Gorges de Baudinard.***

▶ *After Baudinard, turn left onto the path leading to the chapel.*

🐾 *1hr return.*

At **Notre-Dame-de-Baudinard★**, the **view** extends over the lake, the plateaux of Valensole and Canjuers, and beyond, the Alps.

▶ *Rejoin D 9 to reach the other side of the Verdon. After St-Laurent-du-Verdon, continue on D 311.*

Quinson

This village, surrounded by limestone cliffs, houses the Musée de Préhistoire des Gorges du Verdon, which retraces the history of our distant ancestors. There is also a reconstruction of a **prehistoric village**.

▶ *Leave Esparron from the northern end and continue on D 315 towards Gréoux-les-Bains.*

Barrage de Gréoux

From the reservoir there is a fine **view★** of Esparron-de-Verdon and the château. The road reaches the lower Verdon Valley and leads to Gréoux.

ADDRESSES

🏠 STAY

⊜ **Camping Le Soleil** – *1000 chemin de la Tuilière, 04800 Esparron-de-Verdon. S by D 82, rte de Quinson, then 1 km/0.6mi along the road on the right. ℘04 92 77 13 78. www.campinglesoleil.net. Closed early Oct–mid-Apr. 100 pitches.* Campsite on the shores of the lake.

⊜⊜ **Chambre d'hôte Les Fenières** – *Le Village, 04500 Ste-Croix-de-Verdon. ℘04 92 77 77 23. www.verdon-chambre-sainte-croix.com. Closed Dec–Feb. 5 rooms.* Tastefully decorated rooms. Breakfast taken within view of the lake.

⊜⊜ **Hôtel Relais Notre-Dame** – *04500 Quinson. ℘04 92 74 40 01. www.relaisnotredame-04.com. Closed 16 Nov–29 Mar and Mon–Tue except in summer. Restaurant closed 15 Dec–15 Feb, Mon eve and Tue. Wifi. 12 rooms 9€, half-board available, restaurant.* Family-run hotel with modern Provençal-style rooms. Regional dishes, truffles in season.

⊜⊜⊜ **Hôtel Le Moulin du Château** – *04500 St-Laurent-du-Verdon. ℘04 92 74 02 47. www.moulin-du-chateau.com. Closed 8 Nov–12 Mar. 10 rooms, half-board available, restaurant.* 17C olive oil mill with well-maintained rooms, run on ecological principles. Breakfast, and Provençal menu.

⊜⊜⊜⊜ **Chambre d'hôte Château d'Esparron** – *Château d'Esparron, 04800 Esparron-de-Verdon. ℘06 64 65 17 00. www.esparron.com. Closed Nov–Easter. 5 rooms.* This château has been in the Castellane family since the 13C. Spacious rooms with four-poster beds, marble fireplaces and period furnishings. Copious breakfast.

🛒 SHOPPING

Marché provençal – *Pl. Ste-Anne. Thu morning at Salles-sur-Verdon (all year), and Sun morning at Ste-Croix (early May–late Sept).*

🏃 ACTIVITIES

Watersports – Several leisure centres along the shore of the lake offering various **watersports:** canoeing, kayaking, pedalos, surfbikes and electric-powered boats. Some organise a descent by canoe of the lower Verdon gorge to Quinson.

Mountain climbing – Quinson offers a vast choice for mountain climbers, with nearly 170 rock-climbing routes.

Bargème★

At an altitude of over 1 000 m/ 3 281ft , the highest village in the Var is also one of the most beautiful. The ruined feudal castle, with its tall white towers, perched on a rocky outcrop, can be seen from afar. Within the ramparts, the village has been carefully restored. Its charming passages and maze of narrow streets immerse the visitor in an authentic medieval atmosphere.

SIGHTS

Passing through the gateway to the village, you will find yourself in the Middle Ages. The narrow streets, connected by vaulted passages, are lined with ancient houses and flowering hollyhocks.

Église St-Nicolas – ⏲*Open Jul–Aug 2–5pm; Sept–Jun by reservation only.* ☞ *Guided tours (15min).* ☞*Free.* ☎*04 94 50 23 00.*
Inside this beautiful Romanesque building there are several paintings and **altarpieces**, including that of **St-Sébastien**★, sculpted on wood.

- ▶ **Population:** 115.
- **Michelin Map:** 334 H10.
- **Location:** 9km/5.6mi NE of Comps-sur-Artuby, at the centre of the **Parc naturel régional du Verdon**. At an altitude of 1 097m/3 599ft, this village stands on the slope of the Brouis mountain.
- **Parking:** Cars are forbidden in the village.
- **Don't Miss:** The St-Nicolas Church, and the castle.
- **Timing:** Allow one hour to wander around the village.

Château – The **castle** comprises four round towers, one square tower and a courtyard. Although in ruins, the staircases, fireplaces and windows leave you to imagine the original grandeur of the castle. From here, the **view**★ extends over the Malay and Lachens mountains, the Préalpes de Grasse, Canjuers plateau, and beyond to the Massif des Maures.

Castellane★

This tourist centre is located in one of the most striking **settings**★ of the Haute-Provence. First, an ancient fort, then a Roman town, **Petra Castellana** occupied the top of the cliff; in the 15C the town was moved to the valley below and surrounded with fortifications. It is an ideal base for visiting the Gorges du Verdon, and enjoying a range of sports.

☞WALKING TOUR
Route shown on the local map (⏲Opposite). Allow half a day.

Place Marcel-Sauvaire
This busy central square is decorated with arcades and a fountain. A market is held here every Wednesday and Saturday.

- ▶ **Population:** 1 604.
- **Michelin Map:** 334 H9.
- **Info:** Office du tourisme, R. Nationale, 04120 Castellane. ☎04 92 83 61 14. www.castellane.org.
- **Location:** Nestled in the mountains along D 4085, the famous Route Napoléon, halfway between Digne-les-Bains and Grasse.
- **Timing:** A half-day to visit the town centre and climb to the terrace of the Notre-Dame-du-Roc Chapel.

▷ *Go back up the r. Nationale.*

At no. 34 on the rue Nationale, Napoleon breakfasted here on 3 March 1815.

▷ *Continue along the bd St-Michel and turn right.*

The chemin du Roc offers a view of the ruined ramparts built in 1359 and the machicolated **Tour pentagonale**.

Chapelle Notre-Dame-du-Roc
1hr return.

An information trail leads up to the chapel: a pleasant **walk**★, with a view over Castellane. You pass the ruins of **Petra Castellana**, and St-André Church. At the summit, the 18C **chapel** overlooks the Verdon. There is a magnificent **view**★★ over the Castellane Valley, the mountains and the entrance to the Gorges du Verdon.

▷ *Go back down to the Ville Basse and take the second on the right after the church.*

Vieille Ville
Enter through the **Porte de l'Annonciade**, and head for the **St-Victor** Church, which has an interesting Lombard bell tower. Continue to the **Porte de l'Horloge**, surmounted by a wrought-iron campanile. Take the rue Nationale and turn immediately onto the **rue du Mitan**, which has a pretty **Fontaine aux Lions**.

▷ *Return to the pl. Marcel-Sauvaire.*

Maison Nature et Patrimoine★
Pl. de l'Église. ◷*Open May–Sept Wed–Mon 10am–1pm, 3–6.30pm.* ⊚*4€ (children 2€).* ℘*04 92 83 19 23 or 04 92 36 70 70. www.parcduverdon.fr.*
This former prison now houses two museums and an information centre. On the first floor is the **Relais du Parc**, where you can find, in summer, information on the park. On the second floor there is a museum dedicated to ancient life in the Verdon, and the top floor houses the **Musée Sirènes et Fossiles** with a collection devoted to manatees.

EXCURSIONS
Musée de la Résistance
▷ *D 4085. La Palud.* ◷*Open Jul–Oct 9.30am–7pm; May–Jun 9.30am–12.30pm, 2–7pm; Nov–Apr open on demand.* ⊚*4€.* ℘*04 92 83 78 25. http://resistancecastellane.free.fr.*
This museum recounts the role of the Resistance in the Haute-Provence.

Chapelle St-Thyrse★
▷ *7km/4.35mi S on D 102 going to Robion.*
A narrow road climbs the gorge, then reaches a plateau. This chapel's bell tower is a good example of Early Romanesque architecture.

Vallée des Sirènes Fossiles
◷ *After 8km/5mi, on D 4085, park the car at Col des Lèques, on the right after the campsite.*

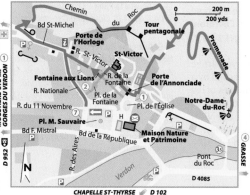

D 4085 DIGNE-LES-B., GRENOBLE
D 955, BARRAGE DE CASTILLON

CHAPELLE ST-THYRSE 🚶 D 102

CASTELLANE	
WHERE TO STAY	
Chasteuil (Chambre d'hôte de)...	①
Levant (Hôtel du).............	⑦
WHERE TO EAT	
Forge (La)...........................	①
Main à la Pâte (La)...........	②
Teillon (Auberge du).........	④

A one-hour walk leads to the "valley of the sea cows", where there is a unique collection of Sirenia fossil remains.

🚗 DRIVING TOURS

CORNICHE SUBLIME ROUTE★★★
Drive of 41km/25.5mi from Castellane to the Balcons de la Mescla shown on the Grand Canyon map, 1 (⏱ see p455). ⏱ See p453.

LAC DE CASTILLON AND LAC DE CHAUDANNE★
Drive of 56km/34.8mi shown on the regional map (⏱ see p451). Allow 3hrs.

▶ *Leave Castellane going E on D 4085 and turn left onto D 102.*

This tour begins at **Barrage de Chaudanne**, which is a 70m/230ft-high and 95m/312ft-long dam. The road then rises to the **Croix de la Mission**, from where there is a fine **view**★★ of the Lac de Castillon. On the way down, there are **views**★★ of the Lac de Chaudanne, and the village of **St-Julien-du-Verdon**. A major part of this village lies submerged. At the lake there is a watersports centre and a beach *(patrolled in Jul–Aug)*.
Follow the route to **St-André-les-Alpes**, a small town dotted with nine information panels explaining the 19C drapers trade. 🚶 *1.5 km/1mi*. The **sentier de la Verdissole** leads to the **Plage du Plan** *(patrolled in Jul–Aug)*.
Take D955, which follows the left shore of the lake. At **Barrage de Castillon**, stop by the belvedere to get a good view of the site.
Turning right onto D402, you arrive in Blaron. From the top, reached by a footpath, there is a **panorama**★ of the Castillon lake, and St-Julien-du-Verdon. From **Col de la Blache**, the view stretches over the Castellane Valley.
At **Cheiron** there is a **beach** *(patrolled in Jul–Aug)*.

ROUTE DE TOUTES AURES★
Drive of 30km/18.6mi from St-Julien-du-Verdon to Annot shown on the regional map (⏱ see p451). Allow 1hr.

This road is a section of the "winter alpine route" (N 202). Running east, the road rises up the gorge to the **Clue de Vergons**★ offering fine views of the lake and St-Julien-du-Verdon. Just after Vergons, on the left, is the **Notre-Dame-de-Valvert** Chapel.
The **Col de Toutes Aures** is an almost vertically tilted rock strata.

Clue de Rouaine★
Beyond Scaffarels, the deep Coulomp Valley widens at the confluence with the Var, the pont de Gueydan. The road then follows the Var Valley.

ADDRESSES

🛏 STAY

🍽 **Hôtel du Levant** – ☎04 92 83 60 05. *www.touring-levant.com.* 🅿. *26 rooms* ⌂*8€, half-board available.* Lovely arcaded building with small, wood-panelled rooms.

🍽🍽🍽 **Chambre d'hôte de Chasteuil** – *Hameau de Chasteuil, 8km/5mi SW of Castellane on D 952, rte de Moustiers and 2km/1.2mi on the right, rte de Chasteuil.* ☎04 92 83 72 45.www.gitedechasteuil.com. *Closed 15 Nov–15 Feb.* 🅿. *5 rooms* ⌂, *half-board available.* This former school house has quiet rooms.

🍴 EAT

🍽 **La Main à la Pâte** – *5 r. de la Fontaine.* ☎04 92 83 61 16. *Closed mid-Dec–mid-Jan.* Salads and pizzas on the menu.

🍽🍽 **Auberge du Teillon** – *Route Napoléon, 04120 La Garde.* ☎04 92 83 60 88. *www.auberge-teillon.com. Closed 16 Nov–14 Mar, Sun eve and Mon except Jul–Aug and public holidays, and Tue lunch in Jul–Aug.* 🅿. *8 rooms* 🍽🍽 ⌂, *half-board available.* Rustic auberge serving traditional dishes.

🍽🍽 **La Forge** – ☎04 92 83 62 61. Traditional dishes.

THE ALPES DU MERCANTOUR

At less than an hour's drive from Nice, and bordering Italy to the east, the Mercantour Alps offer an imposing panorama of peaks, glacial valleys, lakes, mountain cirques and deep gorges. Situated on the transition point between the high Alps and the Mediterranean, there is a vast diversity of habitats, and nature lovers will be dazzled by the diversity of flora and fauna.

The interior harbours animals such as the chamois, ibex, mouflon and the occasional wolf, while the perimeter landscape reveals stunning villages with rich architectural treasures. There are delightful walks across the lower slopes and meadows, or more ambitious hikes.

What's Your Poison?

One day in the 16C, at Villars-sur-Var, a stranger came to the château asking for alms. He looked suspicious and, after torture, he confessed that he had come on a mission to poison the entire household. The rascal had been sent by the Duke of Savoy to prevent Jean-Baptiste Grimaldi giving Nice over to France. Today, far more pleasant beverages can be enjoyed at Villars-sur-Var. Try the local Côtes de Provence AOC wine at the estate of Le Clos St Joseph. Whites and oak-aged reds have been made here for over three generations.

Secure, Free and Beautiful

Entrevaux was originally founded in the 11C by the Glandèves but this ancient city no longer exists. Located on the other bank of the Var it was exposed to the ebb and flow of invaders… and flooding. In 1542, Florent Corelqui sliced the throat of lieutenant Charles Quint, who occupied the city. When the city's inhabitants saw the bloodied cloth they chased the army out of the city, and François I declared it a free town. In 1690, Louis IV, at war with the Savoie, called Vauban in to fortify the city, which was the beginning of 50 years of construction. The result is the magnificent citadel.

Highlights

1 The charismatic old town of **Colmars** (p476)

2 The majestic views from the **Clues de Haute-Provence**, especially the one over the Faye Valley from the Col de Bleine (p487)

3 Discover the architectural riches of the perched village in the **Vallée de la Tinée** (p491)

4 Enjoy a family day out on the **Isola 2000** ski slopes, only a bus ride from Nice (p494)

Sigale, Clues de Haute-Provence

E. Barec/MICHELIN

473

THE ALPES DU MERCANTOUR

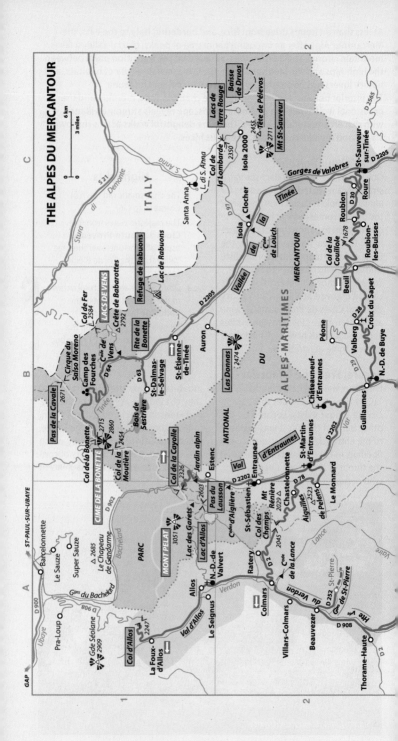

THE ALPES DU MERCANTOUR

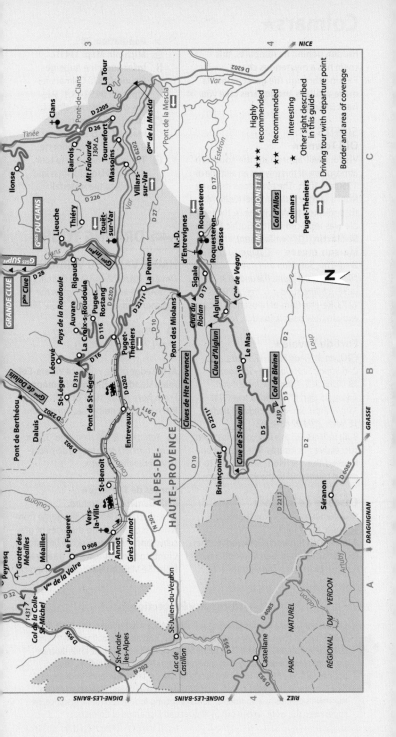

NICE

La Tour

Clans
Pont-de-Clans
D 2205
Bairols
D 26
Ilonse
Tournefort
Mt Falourde
1304△
Massoins
Tinée
Ges du CLANS
Lieuche
Thiéry
Touët-sur-Var
Villars-sur-Var
Gges de la Mescla
Pont de la Mescla
Var
D 6202

GRANDE CLUE
Ptte CLUE
D 28
Gges SUPES
Gges INFes
Auvare
Rigaud
Pays de la Roudoule
La Croix-s-Roudoule
Puget-Rostang
Clans
D 226
D 27
D 17
Roquesteron
N.-D.
d'Entrevignes
Roquesteron-Grasse
Estéron

Gorges de Daluis
Léouvé
St-Léger
D 316
D 116
D 6202
Puget-Théniers
La Penne
D 2211A
Pont des Miolans
Sigale
Clue du Riolan
Cude de Vegay
D 17

Pont de Berthéou
Daluis
D 902
D 2202
Pont de St-Léger
D 16
D 4202
Entrevaux
D 911
D 10
Clue d'Aiglun
Aiglun
Le Mas
Clues de Hte Provence
CIME DE LA BONETTE
Col d'Allos
Colmars
Puget-Théniers

Coulomp
St-Benoît
ALPES-DE-
HAUTE-PROVENCE
D 2211A
Briançonnet
Clue de St-Auban
D 10
D 5
Col de Bleine
1439△
D 5
D 2
Loup

Grotte des Méailles
Peyresq
Méailles
Le Fugeret
D 908
Vers-la-Ville
Annot
Grès d'Annot
Vte de la Vaïre
N 202
D 2
GRASSE

D 32
1431△
Col de la Colle-St-Michel
D 908
D 908

Séranon
D 2211
D 6085
DRAGUIGNAN

Arroux

St-André-les-Alpes
N 202
St-Julien-du-Verdon
Lac de Castillon
D 955
Castellane
D 4085
Artuby
PARC NATUREL RÉGIONAL DU VERDON
D 952
RIEZ

DIGNE-LES-BAINS
DIGNE-LES-BAINS

Highly recommended ***
Recommended **
Interesting *
Other sight described in this guide
Driving tour with departure point
Border and area of coverage

N

475

Colmars★

Hidden behind its ramparts, this town has a mysterious charm. Passing through the great gates, its maze of alleys and squares take you back in time.

SIGHTS
Old Town★★
Visitors will appreciate the southern atmosphere of this town at an altitude of 1 250m/4 101ft. The town took its name from a temple built on a hill (Collis Martis) dedicated to Mars. In the 8C the temple was replaced by the Gothic **Église St-Martin** (⏰*Open Tue–Sun*).
Maison musée – ⏰*Open Jul–Aug Wed–Thu, Sat–Mon and public holidays 10am–noon, 3–6pm, Tue and Fri 3–6pm.* 🎟*3€ (children under 12 free).* ☎*04 92 83 12 73.* Re-creations of household rooms explain how people lived in Verdon.

Fort de Savoie★
⏰*Open Jul–Aug 8am–12.30pm, 2–6.30pm; Sept–Jun Tue–Sat 9am–12.15pm, 2–5.45pm.* ⏰*Closed 1 Jan, 1 May, 25 Dec.* 🚶*Guided tours (1hr 15min) Mon, Sat.* 🎟*2€ (children under 12 free).* ☎*04 92 83 41 92.*
Built in 1693–95 this fort comprises two successive enclosures. The second one housed the garrison. Stairs lead to a round tower and to the vast armoury.

Cascade de la Lance
🚶*40min return. Follow the road opposite the church.*
A path leads through pinewoods to the foot of a cliff, then slips through a narrow gorge to reach the waterfall.

▶ **Population:** 385.
⚲ **Michelin Map:** 334 H7.
🅸 **Info:** Ancienne Auberge Fleurie, 04370 Colmars-les-Alpes. ☎04 92 83 41 92. www.colmars-les-alpes.fr.
▶ **Location:** Colmars is reached by D 908, 44km/27.3mi S of Barcelonnette.
⏰ **Timing:** A half-day to tour the old village, fortress and to walk to the waterfall.

🚗 DRIVING TOURS

HAUTE VALEE DU VERDON★
Drive of 36km/22.4mi from Colmars to St-André-les-Alpes shown on the regional map (⚲see p474). Allow 1hr.

▶ *Follow D 908 going S. After 2km/1.2mi, turn right.*

At the edge of the village of **Villars-Colmars** stands the **Kiosque Demontzey**. From here is the start of a silviculture interpretation trail. 🚶*20min return.*

▶ *Return on D 908 then, after 3.5km/2.2mi, turn left onto the rte de Villars-Heyssier to the car park.*

Gorges de St-Pierre★
🚶*1hr 30min on foot return.*
A marked path leads to the gorge from where it climbs along the sides of grey schist and white-and-ochre limestone. Climb to the old town of **Beauvezer** from the Maison de Produits de Pays car

---

Necessary Protection

Colmars became a border town in 1390 when Allos was annexed to Savoie. In 1528 François I had the ramparts strengthened, and added small square towers that are still standing today. The town was set alight, in 1583 and 1592, during the punitive expeditions against the Protestants hiding in the cellars, then accidentally, in 1672. In 1690 the Duc de Savoie declared war, and the Marquis de Parelli besieged Colmars in vain. In 1692 **Vauban** was commissioned to review the town's defences, without ever actually setting foot here. From a distance, he supervised the work carried out by Niquet and Richerand at Colmars.

park. Continue along the valley to Thorame village and the pont de Villaron. Take D 955 to St-André-les-Alpes and return to Castellane along the Circuit des Lacs de Chaudanne et de Castillon.

ROUTE DU COL DES CHAMPS
Drive of 30km/18.6mi shown on the regional map (see p474). See p480.

ROUTE DU COL DE LA COLLE-ST-MICHEL★
Drive of 46km/28.6mi shown on the regional map (see p475). See p482.

ADDRESSES

🏠 STAY
😊🍽️🍷 **Hôtel Le France** – 📞*04 92 83 42 93. www.hotel-lefrance-colmars.com. 9 rooms ⌒7€.* Family-run restaurant in a 19C

building. Copious hearty dishes. Well-equipped bedrooms.

😊🍽️🍷 **Les Transhumances** – *Les Espiniers.* 📞*04 92 83 44 39. www.lestranshumances.fr.* 🅿️ 🍴. *3 rooms ⌒.* This farm above Colmar has charming rooms. Reserve in advance for meals.

🛒 SHOPPING
Provençal market – Tue and Fri morning.

Maison de produits du pays du haut Verdon – *Rte de Colmars, 04370 Beauvezer.* 📞*04 92 83 58 57. Open mid-Jun–mid-Sept 9.30am–7.30pm; school holidays 9.30am–12.30pm, 2–6pm; rest of year Fri–Sun 9.30am–12.30pm, 2–6pm; public holidays contact for details. Closed last 3 weeks Nov.* A former wool mill which sells local products.

TRANSPORT
A bus service runs from the **Thorame-Haute** station to Allos, via Colmars (📞*04 92 89 02 55; Mon–Sat).*

Val d'Allos★

Deep in the Haut Verdon Valley lies Val d'Allos. The village of Allos, and the nearby ski resorts of Seignus and La Foux, are at the gateway to the Parc national du Mercantour, a paradise for walkers: you will discover the largest high-altitude lake in Europe, perched at over 2 200m/7 218ft. Val d'Allos is also a very popular ski resort and has extensive facilities.

THE RESORTS
Allos★
Alt. 1 400m/4 593ft.
This old village is the starting point for many excursions.
In summer, the **outdoor leisure park**, set in green surroundings round a large expanse of water, offers swimming plus water chutes, canoeing and tennis.
Église Notre-Dame-de-Valvert is an interesting example of 13C Provençal Romanesque art. You will especially appreciate the exterior, its elegant chevet, Lombard arcade and covering of larch shingles. Above the porch notice

▶ **Population:** 676.
⚲ **Michelin Map:** 334 H7.
📋 **Info:** Pl. du Presbytère, Maison de la Foux, 04260 Allos. 📞04 92 83 02 81. www.valdallos.com.
▶ **Location:** From Barcelonnette in the N, the road D 908 is steep and winding. It is easier to take D 955 and N 202 from Castellane in the S, then D 908, via St-André and Colmars. By this route, you cross first Allos (Allos 1400), then Le Seignus (Val d'Allos 1500) and finally La Foux d'Allos (Val d'Allos 1800).
▶ **Don't Miss:** Walk around the old village of Allos, and hike to the splendid Lac d'Allos.
🕐 **Timing:** Spend at least a day in the Val d'Allos.
👫 **Kids:** The ski resorts of Val d'Allos have the designation "Famille Plus Montagne".

Parc National du Mercantour

Founded in 1979, the park's objectives include protecting the natural environment and informing visitors about the fragility of the landscape. The 68 500ha/169 261 acres, which constitute the central zone, straddling the Alpes-Maritimes (22 communes) and the Alpes-de-Haute-Provence (6 communes), were the French part of the **ancient hunting estates** of the Kings of Italy, who before 1861 occupied both sides of the Alps. Since 1987, the Parc national du Mercantour has been twinned with its Italian counterpart the Parco Naturale delle Alpi Marittime, sharing 33km/20.6mi of border. These two organisations associate on different issues: the monitoring of animal species that roam the entire protected area, the establishment of cross-border signposting, etc. They are working on a joint application for classification as a UNESCO World Heritage site. In 2011 they aimed to become the first "**European park**". In July 2007 commenced the largest European inventory on biodiversity over a 10sq-km/2 471-acre area at the border of both parks: it tracks the evolution of listed species over 10 years.

The Mercantour is the only European massif that is home to the three mountain ungulates, lovers of the park's cirques, glacial valleys and deep gorges: chamois (more than 9 000), mouflon (890) and alpine ibex (over 520). Twenty-two ibexes, fitted with transmitters, were reintroduced here in 1994. This is just one of many projects designed to encourage the survival of this species. Mid-altitude wooded areas are inhabited by red deer and roe deer, as well as the hare, the stoat and the marmot. The birds include the black grouse, the snow-partridge and the Lagopus, and a number of birds of prey. The **bearded eagle** was successfully reintroduced during the summer of 1993. For the first time in France since 1942, wolves are also returning to the Massif du Mercantour, crossing over from Italy where they are a protected species.

Besides the **larch**, the most famous among the 2 000 species of plants in the area (including 220 rare species) is *Saxifraga florulenta* (endemic species that blooms just once in its life); it was chosen as the park's emblem.

The altitude of this high-mountain region ranges from 590m/1 936ft to 3 143m/10 312ft, and offers beautiful landscapes. Walkers can choose from 600km/373mi of paths, and nature trails, like those at Lac d'Allos and the Col de la Bonette. Two long-distance hiking routes, the GR 5 and GR 52A (sentier panoramique du Mercantour) also cross park territory.

Regulations in the Central Zone

Information boards and signs remind you of the rules and regulations: vehicles and mountain bikes are forbidden to circulate, no dogs allowed (even on a leash), don't pick the plants or flowers, or pick up samples of rocks or minerals, don't make a lot of noise, take your rubbish away with you, don't light fires, camping prohibited. ⚑ Maison du Parc National, Valberg. ✆04 93 02 58 23. Col de la Cayolle refuge: 15 Jun–15 Sept. ✆04 92 81 24 25.

the stunned faces and animals laughing: what have they seen?

Ski area – Cross-country skiers have 19km/11.8mi of marked trails at their disposal near the village, which is linked by gondola to Le Seignus and the ski runs.

Le Seignus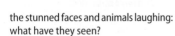
Alt. 1 500m/4 921ft.

This long-established family resort inaugurated the first ski lift of the upper Verdon region in 1936. The gondolas remain open in summer for hikers and mountain bikers.

Ski area – Situated just above Allos village, Le Seignus offers a limited but varied ski area: 12 ski lifts and some 15 runs (including the Valcibière red run) between 1 500m/4 921ft and 2 400m/ 7 874ft. The first section is equipped with snow cannon. There are 42km/26.1mi of marked trails for cross-country skiers. **The gondolas** remain open in summer for walkers and mountain bikers.

La Foux d'Allos

Alt. 1 708m/5 604ft.

La Foux is a modern resort, situated between Allos and the Col d'Allos, whose wooden houses decorated with small balconies blend well with the surroundings.

Ski area – Situated inside a glacial cirque, overlooked by the Trois Évêchés Massif, the ski area is spread over five slopes, which catch the sun in turn. It is linked to that of **Pra-Loup** (*see p400*) to form the **Espace Lumière**, one of the largest ski areas in France with a total of 180km/112mi of runs. The snowfields around La Foux are ideal for advanced skiers, particularly the runs starting from the Observatoire gondola.

Observatoire gondola★ – *Alt. 2 600m/ 8 530ft.* **View** of the Tête de l'Estrop, the Préalpes de Digne, the Grande Séolane and Mont Pelat from the top station.

🚗 DRIVING TOUR

ROUTE DU COL D'ALLOS★★

Drive of 22km/13.7mi from Colmars to Col d'Allos shown on the regional map (see p474). Allow 1hr. Possible to continue the drive, 44km/27mi from

Colmars to Barcelonnette (see p398). Allow 2hrs. 🚸 *Please exercise* **extreme caution** *at crossroads. The Col d'Allos is blocked by snow in Nov–May.*

Through the rugged landscape between Barcelonnette and the upper Verdon Valley the twisting, narrow track clings to a near-vertical rock face. Extra care is needed, but exhilarating views are guaranteed.

Allos★ *See Allos p477.*

Col d'Allos★★

Alt. 2 247m/7 372ft.

From the platform of the refuge situated just below the pass *(viewing table)*, there is a fine **panorama**★.

🥾 HIKES

D 226 climbs for 13km/8.1mi to a car park with an information point for the park.

Lac d'Allos★★

🥾 *This excursion attracts many tourists in mid-Jul–mid-Aug. Leave very early. Drive E along D 226 for 13km/8.1mi. From the car park allow 1hr there and back on foot.*

Situated at the heart of the Parc national du Mercantour, the 60ha/148-acre **lake**, which has a maximum depth of 50m/164ft, is the largest natural lake in Europe at that altitude (2 230m/7 316ft). Phenomena concerning alpine geology and flora are explained on panels dotted along the **nature trail**.

View of the Lac d'Allos from Mont Pelat

Mont Pelat★★★

🚶 *Alt. 3 051m/10 010ft. 5hrs there and back. Leave the car in the same car park as for the previous excursion. The yellow-and-green-marked path is not too taxing, but climbing boots are strongly recommended.*

From the summit, there is a **panoramic view★★★** of the roads leading to the Col d'Allos, Col de la Cayolle and Col de la Bonette and of the surrounding summits. A recently discovered underground glacier runs beneath the surface of Mont Pelat.

ADDRESSES

🏠 STAY

🛏 **Chambre d'hôte La Ferme Girerd Potin** – *Rte de La Foux, 04260 Allos. 1.5km/ 0.9mi S of La Foux d'Allos on D 908. ℰ04 92 83*

04 76. www.chambredhotes-valdallos.com. *Closed out of season.* 🅿 🚭. *5 rooms, half-board only.* 16C farm with five duplex rooms and a gîte. Home-made dishes.

🛏🛏 **Hôtel L'Ours Blanc** – *Le Seignus, 04260 Allos. 4km/2.5mi E of Allos by D 908 then D 26. ℰ04 92 83 01 07. www.hotel-loursblanc.com. Closed Apr–May and mid-Sept–mid-Dec.* 🅿. *15 rooms🛏.* Welcoming hotel, at the foot of the slopes, with comfortable rooms.

TRANSPORT

A shuttle service runs all year between Allos and Seignus and La Foux. In summer, a shuttle runs between Allos and the **Lac d'Allos** nature trail *(reserve at tourist office)*. Bus service from la **gare de Thorame-Haute** to Allos, via Colmars *(Mon–Sat; out of season times contact ℰ04 92 89 02 55).*

Val d'Entraunes★★

Set in the middle of the **Parc national du Mercantour**, the Val d'Entraunes is one of the remotest areas of the Alpes-Maritimes *département*, **even though Nice lies only 100km/62.2mi away.**

🚗 DRIVING TOURS

ROUTE DU COL DES CHAMPS
Drive of 30km/18.6mi from Colmars shown on the regional map (👁 see p474). Allow 1hr. 😟 Take care! The road is narrow.

After several hairpin bends D 2 passes through **La Ratery**, where there is a botanical trail.

The pass of **Col des Champs★** is on the border of the Alpes-de-Haute-Provence and the Alpes-Maritimes. 🚶 *3hrs return. Start from 500m/547yds on the left after the Col. An easy walk going from the Cime de Voya to **Mont Rénière**.*

- 🕐 **Michelin Map:** 334 U7/8/9.
- ℹ **Info:** Tourist office of Guillaumes: Mairie, 06470 Guillaumes. ℰ04 93 05 57 76. www.pays-de-guillaumes.com.
- ▶ **Location:** To get to Entraunes from Barcelonnette, take the route des Grandes Alpes and the Col de la Cayolle, or go by the Col d'Allos, Colmars and the Col des Champs. From Puget-Théniers or Entrevaux, drive through the Gorges de Daluis.
- 🚫 **Don't Miss:** The Gorges de Daluis are spectacular.
- 🕐 **Timing:** A half-day.

🎿 The small cross-country ski resort of **Chastelonnette**, also known as **Val-Pelens**, is overlooked by the **Aiguilles**

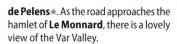

de Pelens★. As the road approaches the hamlet of **Le Monnard**, there is a lovely view of the Var Valley.

St-Martin-d'Entraunes
See below.

FROM COL DE LA CAYOLLE TO PUGET-THÉNIERS
Drive of 51km/31.7mi shown on the regional map (see p474). Allow 3hrs.

Jardin alpin★
1km/0.6mi before Estenc. Car park and picnic area. Obtain a free topo-guide. 1hr 30min. Gradient 50m/164ft. This is an itinerary prepared by the **Parc national du Mercantour**.

The chalets of the hamlet **Estenc** stand on a glacial ridge. This is where the Var has its source. The surrounding peaks are composed of sandstone ridges. Look out for **Cascades d'Aiglière** and Garreton on the right after the pont St-Roch (*accessible by a marked path from Entraunes; allow 3hrs. Gradient 200m/219yds*).

A complete tour of the village of **Entraunes** starts at the ancient communal oven. *Heritage tour – 04 93 05 51 26. Free brochure from the town hall.* The setting of the village of **St-Martin-d'Entraunes** perched on a morainic mound contrasts with the arid landscapes of the Var Valley. The Provençal Romanesque **church** has a fine altarpiece, the **Retable de la Vierge de Miséricorde★**, by François Bréa (c.1555).

▷ *3.5km/2.2mi beyond Villeneuve-d'Entraunes, turn left onto D 74, which rises above the Barlatte Valley.*

Châteauneuf-d'Entraunes lies in a desolate landscape, above the upper Var Valley. The Baroque church has an 1524 altarpiece.

▷ *Return to D 2202 and turn left.*

Guillaumes is overlooked by a ruined castle. Around the **wash-house**, panels illustrate the village's history.

La Vierge de Miséricorde (1555) by François Bréa.

E. Barer/MICHELIN

Musée des Arts et Traditions populaires – Open mid-May–mid-Oct, contact for details. Guided tours. 3€(children under 12 1€); 5€ ticket includes a tour of Guillaumes. 04 93 05 57 76. Discover the life of yesteryear. **Notre-Dame-du-Buyei** – Rte du Plan. Open Jul–Aug Wed and Thu afternoon. Guided tour (reserve 2 days in advance). 04 93 05 57 76. www.pays-de-guillaumes.com. Inside is a painting of the fire of Guillaumes in 1682.

The cliff road between Guillaumes and Daluis affords fine **views★★** of the red-schist gorge. At the **pont de la Mariée** there is bungee-jumping point and nearby the **pont de Berthéou** provides an ideal spot for canyoning. From here there is also the start of a nature trail of the **Gorges de Daluis★★** (*2hrs return; gradient 150m/492ft*).

The hilltop village of **Daluis** (alt. 800m/2 625ft) is overlooked by the ruins of a castle. The **Grotte du Chat** nearby, in which there is an underground river of more than 720m/787yds, is made up of a series of chambers. Between Daluis and Entrevaux, the road follows the river, which veers left at pont de Gueydan. On the way to Puget-Théniers along D 4202, there is a lovely **view★★** of **Entrevaux★**.

Annot★

This small town, lying on the banks of the River Vaire, 700m/ 2 297ft above sea level, is the oldest settlement in the valley, developing as a stopping point on the Roman road that linked Digne and Nice. Annot is surrounded by rocks, known as **grès d'Annot**. These formations, sculpted by erosion into strange shapes and arches, make for interesting walks around the town and earned Annot the nickname "the painters' paradise".

SIGHTS

Old town★ – The old town looks quaint with its steep twisting lanes, arcades, arched alleyways and leaning houses. The **cours Provençal** is the centre of activity, a typical southern avenue lined with plane trees. For an overall view, walk along rue Basse then **Grande-Rue** leading through a fortified gate. Note the **Maison des Arcades**, a 17C mansion; its ground floor houses the **Musée Regain**, a collection of prehistoric objects found in the Méailles Cave.

The Romanesque **church** has a raised apse forming a defence tower. Also remarkable, around the Renaissance belfry, are the statues of four Evangelists. Leave the place de l'Église by the door of the former town hall and turn left onto the rue des Vallasses where there is the ancient **lavoir** (wash-house), and the **Tour du Peintre**.

Continue along the rue Notre-Dame and turn right onto the rue Capone, at the end of which is found the village's communal **oven**.

Chapelle Notre-Dame-de-Vers-la-Ville – *20min there and back. Take the road at the right of the fountain and follow the Vers-la-Ville path, dotted with small oratories.* The chapel (12C) sits among a cluster of ruiniform rocks. Fine **view** of the village and the surrounding mountains.

Les Grès d'Annot★ – *3hrs. From the chapel, take the signposted path Chambre du roi. Topo-guide on sale at tourist office.*

▶ **Population:** 1 019.
Michelin Map: 334 H9.
Info: Pl. du Germe, 04240 Annot. ℰ04 92 83 23 03. www.annot.fr.
Location: The old Roman road, now D 4202, is 2km/ 1.2mi to the S of Annot, by D 908. It leads to the Lac de Castillon and, 17km/10.6mi further, to St-Julien-du-Verdon. By following N 202 7km/4.3mi eastwards, you can link up with D 902, which crosses the gorges of Dalius.
Don't Miss: The reddish colour of the Grès d'Annot rocks contrasts spectacularly with the lush vegetation.
Timing: Give yourself a good hour to tour the village, and another three hours to wander among the rocks.

These rock formations are a paradise for climbers. Walk to the **Rochers de la gare** along a trail marked Chemin des Grès and to watch serious climbers handle the cliffs. The rocks have been given fanciful names: the camel, the face and the king's bedroom, etc. A climbing guidebook is on sale at the tourist office. The Association Vive les Gestes (ℰ06 74 04 76 89) organises climbing sessions.

EXCURSION
St-Benoît
▶ *5km/3mi E along N 202.*
The pont à Becs, called "Pont de la Reine-Jeanne", spanning the Coulomp, existed in Roman times.

🚗 DRIVING TOUR

ROUTE DU COL DE LA COLLE-ST-MICHEL★
Drive of 46km/28.6mi shown on the regional map (see p475). Allow 1hr.

▶ *Head N from Annot by D 908.*

The village of **Le Fugeret** lies in a depression on the left bank of the Vaire. Note the 18C humpback **bridge** spanning the stream. The slopes of the valley have scattered sandstone rocks and lumps of walnut, chestnut and pine trees. **Méailles**★, a hilltop village, is built on a limestone ridge above the left bank of the Vaire. On the way down, there is a contrast between the forested slopes and the barren limestone layer overlooking the **valley of the Vaire**. In the church there is a lovely 16C altarpiece. The pretty villages of the **Vallée de la Vaire** can be discovered by taking the train from Digne-les-Bains (*see p438*) to Nice.

▶ *Beyond the pass, turn left onto D 32 towards Peyresq.*

The old shepherds' village **Peyresq** lies in a picturesque **setting**★ by the Vaire, and was restored to house an international cultural and artistic university centre.

Col de La Colle-St-Michel
Alt. 1 431m/4 695ft.
In winter the 50km/30.1mi of runs are perfect for nordic skiing. The pass La Colle-St-Michel connects the Vallée du Var to the **Vallée du Haut Verdon** (*see Colmars p476*).

⚑ HIKE
Grotte de Méailles
⚑ *From Méailles, drive towards La Combe and, in the first major bend on the right, park the car. Wear non-slip shoes and carry a torch. Allow 4hrs.*
From the parking area, a well-marked path leads north across a ravine then climbs in a landscape of scrub dotted with cairns. The two entrances of the cave are situated beyond the ridge. The main gallery slopes gently down to a stream which has burrowed out a vast chamber partitioned by numerous concretions. The structure of this cave is of particular **geological interest**: its floor is formed by a Cretaceous layer, and the roof Tertiary puddingstone.

Puget-Théniers

This small town nestles beneath a rocky spur crowned with the ruins of a castle, at the confluence of the River Var and River Roudoule.

OLD TOWN★
The west bank of the Roudoule includes place Adolphe-Conil as well as many old houses. ◀*10min return.* At the end of the rue Casimir-Boucher, follow the **irrigation canal** towards the Gorges de la Roudoule. Step inside the church and admire the richly decorated interior.

🚗 DRIVING TOURS

PAYS DE LA ROUDOULE
Drive of 45km/28mi round tour shown on the local map (see p484). Allow 3hrs.

▶ **Population:** 1 822.
🍴 **Michelin Map:** 334 J9.
🅸 **Info:** Maison de Pays, N 202 (former train station), 06260 Puget-Théniers. ✆04 93 05 05 05. www. provence-val-dazur.com.
▶ **Location:** The old town is on the right (west) bank of the Roudoule river.
🚸 **Kids:** The steam train.
🕐 **Timing:** One hour to see the town and three hours the Pays de la Roudoule.

To the north of Puget-Théniers, an unusual landscape begins; the Roudoule has scoured narrow gorges through limestone, red sandstone and black marl. The road rises above Puget and offers a lovely view of the old town.

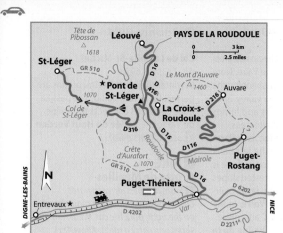

○ Turn right onto D 116 towards Puget-Rostang.

The road follows the Mairole Valley and goes through a landscape with black marl formations, known as *robines*.
The hilltop village of **Puget-Rostang** is overlooked by the square tower of a restored castle.
The **Écomusée du Pays de la Roudoule** (○*open May–Sept daily 10am–noon, 2–6pm; Oct–mid-Dec and mid-Jan–Apr Mon–Fri except public holidays 10am–noon, 2–6pm;* ✆*4.50€;* &. ✆*04 93 05 07 38; www.ecomusee-roudoule.fr*) was created to preserve and develop the area's heritage. From Puget-Rostang, take the twisting road to Auvare *(13km/8.1mi return).*

No God No Master

Born in 1805, **Louis Auguste Blanqui**, professional revolutionary, was present at all the uprisings and he spent more than 36 years in prison. Liberated, he founded his last newspaper, and gave it as a title his own life's maxim: "Ni Dieu ni maître." He died a year later, at the age of 76. **Aristide Maillol** dedicated to him **L'Action enchaînée**★, a female nude. First unveiled in 1911 – to the outrage of the pious – near the church, the statue was moved to a less contentious spot on the Grand-Place beside D 6202!

Below is the Roman bridge **pont de St-Léger**★ with the paved Roman road at each end.

○ Continue towards Léouvé and turn right onto D 416.

La Croix-sur-Roudoule

In a picturesque **setting**★, this village is still guarded by an old fortified gate. The altarpiece inside the church has two panels by **François Bréa**.

○ Return to D 16 and turn right.

The **Léouvé** Cirque is carved out of red sandstone; copper was mined here from 1861 to 1929. **Maison de la mine** – (○*open May–Oct Tue–Sun except public holidays 10am–noon, 2–5.30pm, Nov–Apr contact for details;* ✆*2.50€ (children under 8 free);* ✆*04 93 05 14 64*) retraces the difficult conditions of mining.

○ Return to the pont de St-Léger and cross over.

The road rises to the Col de St-Léger, from where a totally different landscape unfolds.

○ Turn back towards Puget-Théniers.

Just before the pont de St-Léger, there is a fine view of the Roman bridge and the village of La Croix-sur-Roudoule.

CLUE DU RIOLAN★

Drive of 23km/14.3mi shown on the Clues de Haute-Provence map, ①
(see p487). See p486.

FROM COL DE LA CAYOLLE TO PUGET-THÉNIERS

Drive of 51km/31.7mi shown on the regional map (see p474). See p481.

Villars-sur-Var

Set in the midst of rocks, vines and olive groves, Villars-sur-Var was once a stronghold of the mighty Grimaldi family. The remains of the old walls and the Porte St-Antoine bear witness to the important role of this village in the Middle Ages. Perched on a mountain terrace above the Var, this peaceful village is only 40 minutes' drive from Nice.

VISIT

A walk along the cobbled streets, closed to traffic, leads past a number of doorways with carved 18C and 19C porches. **Church** – The highlight of the rich interior decoration is a large **high-altar retable**★ made up of 10 panels in Franciscan style, painted by an unknown artist; the central panel represents the **Entombment**★★.

EXCURSION
Thiéry★

14km/8.7mi NW along D 226.
A place of narrow streets, this isolated village overlooking the Gorges du Cians has stood on the hilltop since the 11C.

🚗 DRIVING TOUR

ROUTE DE TOURNEFORT★

Drive of 12km/7.4mi shown on the regional map (see p475). Allow 1hr.
D 25 links the River Var and River Tinée across the Pointe des Quatre-Cantons. 11km/6.8mi west of the Pont de la Mes-cla, the road branches off from N 202 and climbs towards Villars.

ADDRESSES

🏃 ACTIVITIES

Steam tourist train – *Information at chemins de fer de Provence, at Nice. 04 97 03 80 80, or at Puget-Théniers train station 04 93 05 00 46.*

▶ **Population:** 650.
Michelin Map: 334 K9.
Info: Pl. L.-et-V. Robini, 06710 Villars-sur-Var. 04 93 05 32 32.
Location: From Villars, you can drive to the Vallée de la Tinée by way of Tournefort; alternatively, you can head for the Gorges du Cian through Touët-sur-Var, 9km/5.6mi to the E.
Parking: The old town is closed to cars; park just above the village.
Timing: Leave time to relax at a café and sample a glass of Clos-S.-Joseph, the only wine in the Alpes-Maritimes with an AOC designation.

Massoins
From this mountain village, there is a fine **view** of the Var Valley. The ruins of a 14C castle stand above the centre. The road winds up the slopes of **Mont Faloude**; beyond the Tinée is the Chapelle de la Madone-d'Utelle.

2km/1.2mi further on, turn right onto a small road.

Tournefort
The village clings to a steep rock spur. The **view**★ embraces the valleys framed by mountains, the Madone d'Utelle and the village of La Tour (see p492).

Return to D 26 and follow it down to the Tinée Valley.

Clues de Haute-Provence★★

Located south of Puget-Théniers, only 40km/24.9mi from the busy coast, rushing rivers have cut their way across the mountains, forming narrow *clues*, the transverse valleys which are typical of this region. In the heart of this mountain mosaic lie hidden villages set in terraced fields or surrounded by untouched nature.

- ⊙ **Michelin Map:** 334 I/J 9/10.
- ⓘ **Info:** Maison de Pays, D 6202, 06260 Puget-Théniers. ☎04 93 05 05 05.
- ◑ **Location:** S of Puget-Théniers, this is a region of mixed landscapes ranging from cultivated terraces to untamed woodlands.
- ⊙ **Don't Miss:** The majestic sites of Sigale; the view of the Faye ravine from the Col de Bleine.
- ◷ **Timing:** Allow three hours to do all suggested tours.

🚗 DRIVING TOURS

1 CLUE DU RIOLAN★
23km/14.3mi. Allow 1hr.

Puget-Théniers
⊙*See Puget-Théniers p483.*

◑ *Cross the River Var for D 2211A.*

The road rises in wide hairpin bends above Puget-Théniers to the Col de St-Raphaël; beautiful view of Roudoule and the Mercantour region beyond.

La Penne
A **square keep** overlooks the village clinging to a rocky ridge (🚶30min return). Walk up through the pretty streets to a viewpoint of the Vallée du Miolans and Montagne du Cheiron.

◑ *At pont des Miolans, take D 17 on the left towards Sigale.*

Clue du Riolan★
This is an impressive gap cut across the mountain range by a tributary of the Estéron. From the road there is a fine **view** of this famous canyoning area.

Sigale★
Sigale is a former stronghold that has retained two fortified gates, several Gothic houses and a 16C fountain.
From the terrace there is a **panorama** of the surrounding mountains. To the north, small fields are located on a succession of terraces.
To the right, towards Roquesteron, there is the Chapelle **Notre-Dame-d'Entrevignes**. Rebuilt in the 15C, it is decorated with murals. ⊙*Open on request, contact town hall ☎04 93 05 83 52.*

Roquesteron
The River Estéron divided the village into two municipalities: Roquesteron in the north, and Roquesteron-Grasse in the south, where there stands a 12C **fortified Romanesque church**.

Geological Formation

Clue comes from the Latin *clusa*, "closed". In the Secondary Period, fine calcareous particles settled at the bottom of the alpine sea. Sixty million years later, the Alps were formed by the folding and thrusting of the plates. Then erosion released the band of limestone rocks. Finally, the river dug out a deep vertical gap, over several million years, and the final result is a magnificent clue.

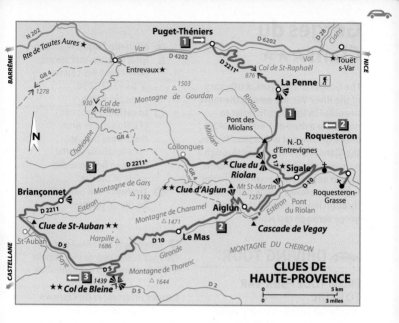

[2] CLUE D'AIGLUN★★

33km/20.5mi from Roqueston to the Col de Bleine. Allow 1hr.

From the pont du Riolan, there are **fine views**★ of the gorge and its emerald river. Further on is the **Vegay Waterfall**. Then D 10 crosses the hilltop village of **Aiglun**, celebrated by Frédéric Mistral.

Clue d'Aiglun★★

The road, which crosses the Estéron, offers a striking view of the most secluded *clue* in the area.

Le Mas

This village, built on the edge of a beak-shaped limestone spur, has a 13C Romanesque **church**. D 10 meanders along the hillside, then D 5, on the left, rises to the **Col de Bleine**★★ (alt. 1439m/4 721ft). Magnificent **view** of the deep Faye Valley, the Harpille Peak, the Charamel mountain and the Grandes Alpes du Sud in the distance.

[3] CLUE DE ST-AUBAN★★

36km/22.4mi from Col de Bleine (see above) to pont des Miolans. Allow 1hr.

▶ *5km/3.1mi beyond the Col de Bleine, turn left onto D 5, which runs along the Faye and joins D 2211.*

Clue de St-Auban★★

The Estéron, a tributary of the River Var, goes through this impressive gorge with vertical sides hollowed out in places and forming huge caves.

Briançonnet

This tiny village lies in a strange setting, beneath a huge rock. The houses were built with stones from an earlier Roman settlement.

From the cemetery, which is adjacent to the apse of the church, there is a **view**★ of the summits of the Alps.

Beyond Briançonnet, the **view** embraces the Montagne de Gars and the Montagne de Charamel on either side of the River Estéron.

Soon after Collongues, the Clue d'Aiglun can be seen on the right, and further on, the Clue du Riolan.

From the **pont des Miolans**, it is possible to return to Puget-Théniers along D 2211A.

Gorges du Cians★★★

The Gorges of the Cians, a tributary of the River Var, are among the most beautiful in the Alps. In order to negotiate a drop of 1 600m/5 249ft over a distance of only 25km/15.5mi, the Cians has hewn its way through a narrow cleft. The superb sheer cliffs vary in appearance according to the terrain, the lower gorge being cut through limestone and the upper gorge through red schist.

🚗 **Michelin Map:** 334 J/K 8/9.

🛈 **Info:** Quartier du Passaire, 06470 Beuil-les-Launes. ✆04 93 02 32 58. www.beuil.com.

▷ **Location:** Like those of Daluis to the west, the Gorges du Cians cut a southern swathe between Beuil and the valley of the Var.

🕐 **Timing:** Allow half a day for the driving tour.

 **DRIVING TOUR**

FROM TOUËT-SUR-VAR TO BEUIL

Drive of 38km/23.6mi shown on the regional map (🕐 see p475). Allow 2hrs.

Touët-sur-Var★

🅿 *Park at the bottom of the village and climb the stairs on r. Armand-Faillères.* 🥾*10min climb.*

The tall narrow village houses, backing onto the rocky slope, line the partially covered streets. Nearly all have a south-facing galleried loft, known as the *soleil-loir*, used for drying fruit. The 17C church is built on an arch spanning the river, which you can see from a small window made in the floor of the central aisle.

▷ *Leave Touët on D 6202 going W. The road passes near to the Chapelle N.-D.-du-Cians. Turn right onto D 28.*

Gorges Inférieures du Cians★★

Water oozes from every crack in the spiky rock face. The road winds its way through the tortuous gorge.

▷ *Turn right onto D 128, which rises sharply; caution is recommended.*

Lieuche

Black schist forms the impressive **setting★** of this tiny mountain village. From the church terrace there is an overall **view★** of the Gorges du Cians, overlooked by the Dôme de Barrot, and part of the Var Valley.

The Return of the "Bone Breaker"

The **bearded vulture**, the largest alpine bird with an impressive 2.8m/9ft wingspan, is typical of Europe's endangered species. Decimated throughout the alpine region during the 19C, it survived in the Pyrenees and in Corsica. This vulture has a strange lifestyle: it flies over almost inaccessible high pastures and feeds on dead chamois and ewes, ripping off large bones from their carcasses and dropping them from a great height onto the rocks below in order to break them, hence its nickname. In 1993 the Parc national du Mercantour and the Parco Naturale delle Alpi Marittime joined forces to attempt the reintroduction of the bearded vulture into the area. The operation was highly successful. Young birds (90 days old) are placed in caves and usually fly away 30 days later. However, it takes eight years for the vultures to be fully grown and they have a life expectancy of 40 years.

To date, over 100 bearded vultures have been reintroduced into the whole alpine range from Austria to France, as part of a unique international programme.

▶ *Return to D 28, turn right then 1km/0.6mi further on left onto D 228.*

The road overlooks the superb Vallée du Cians.

Rigaud
This hilltop village overlooking the Cians Valley nestles below the ruins of its medieval Templar fortress in a very attractive **setting**★. In the fortified **church**, lovely Baroque décor and several 17C pictures, notably *La Descente de Croix* at the high altar.

▶ *Return to D 28 and turn left.*

Gorges Supérieures du Cians★★★
From the entrance of the gorge, the road rises progressively following the mountain stream that drops down to the valley in a series of steps. The narrowest passages, known as the **Petite Clue**★★ and the **Grande Clue**★★★, where the

Gorges du Cians
© Camille Moirenc/hemis.fr

road has been hewn out of the rock, are the most picturesque. The Grande Clue can only be seen on foot *(park before the tunnel)*. The cliff-faces are only 1m/3.28ft apart at their narrowest point.
Beuil in its striking **setting**★ suddenly appears on a bend.

Beuil★

Exiting the Cians gorges, an elegant church steeple emerges from the valley, covered with snow in winter, and perfumed by lavender in summer. This pleasant resort is best explored on a mountain hike, a rafting excursion, a skiing trip, or by strolling through the narrow medieval streets with their allure of Provence.

SKI AREA
Lovers of winter sports have been meeting in Beuil-les-Launes, the oldest resort in the Mediterranean Alps, since 1910 and the architecture keeps its turn-of-the-century style.
Despite being only an hour from the coast, Valberg (◉ *see p491*) also enjoys good snow conditions. Linked to Beuil, it offers 50 ski runs and a snow park. Cross-country skiers have 25km/15.5mi of trails at their disposal, and a groomed trail 10km/6.2mi long is reserved for snowshoes.

▶ **Population:** 491.
◉ **Michelin Map:** 334 J8.
▮ **Info:** Quartier du Passaire, 06470 Beuil-les-Launes. ℘04 93 02 32 58. www.beuil.com.
▷ **Location:** Beuil, perched on a hill, is located between the valleys of Entraunes and of La Tinée; the town of Guillaumes is 20km/12.4mi to the W, St-Sauveur-sur-Tinée is 24km/14.9mi to the E.
◴ **Timing:** A walk around the village will take about one hour.

VISIT
The upper part of Beuil, around the main shopping street, contrasts with the lower part, around the rue Napoléon-III. There, you wander through a maze of small streets and covered passages.

Church
⏱ *Open 10am–5pm.*
Rebuilt in the 17C, it has retained a 15C Romanesque bell tower and some fine **paintings**★. Bottom right is the *Adoration of Magi* by the Veronese school. At the high altar is an altarpiece of the rosary, primitive, in 16 panels. On the left side, a predella features the Resurrection, and a panel of the altarpiece shows St Catherine de Sienne.

🚗 DRIVING TOURS

ROUTE DU COL DE VALBERG★
Drive of 20km/12.4mi W along D 28 shown on the regional map (👣see p474). Allow 45min, not including walks.

This road links the **Gorges du Cians**★★★ (👣see p488) and the **Gorges de Daluis**★★ (👣see p481) via the Valberg Pass.

Valberg 🎿🏂
👣*See opposite.* On the way down from the **Col de Valberg** to Guillaumes, the scenery is varied.

Guillaumes
👣*See Val d'Entraunes p481.*

ROUTE DU COL DE LA COUILLOLE★
Col de la Couillole
Drive of 1 678m/5 505ft shown on the regional map (👣see p474). Allow 2hrs.

▷ *Leave Beuil on D 30 going E.*

Extended view on either side of the pass. This is a popular vantage point for fans of the Monte-Carlo Rally.
Shortly the village of **Roubion**★ perched on top of a red-schist ridge comes into sight (👣see p493); wonderful waterfall after the fourth tunnel.
The road winds above the raging torrent of the Vionène river in a striking **countryside**★ where green trees contrast with red schist.

Roure★ 👣*See Roure p494.*

▷ *Return to D 30.*

The road plunges into the valley. A series of tight hairpin bends take you through landscape of wild beauty enhanced by the contrasting colours of the rocks.

St-Sauveur-sur-Tinée
👣*See Vallée de la Tinée p492.*

ADDRESSES

🛏 STAY
🍽🍽 **Hôtel L'Escapade** – *At the village.* 📞*04 93 02 31 27. www.monsite.wanadoo.fr/ hotelescapade. Closed 12–25 Apr, 1 Oct– 26 Dec. 11 rooms ⬚, half-board available, restaurant ⬚⬚.* Small, well-maintained bedrooms with rustic furnishings. Some, facing south, have balconies. The restaurant is decorated with ancient farm tools, and serves generous regional dishes.

Conquered by the Felons

"I am the Count of Beuil, I do what I like", proclaimed the last Count of Beuil, **Annibal Grimaldi**. Beuil belonged to this powerful family from the 14C to the 17C. The Dukes of Savoie often resorted to treachery against them: they bribed Lord Beuil's barber, and one day, his chin pointing up waiting to be shaved, he collapsed in his chair with his throat slit; and a valet stabbed his master as he was putting on his doublet. The Grimaldis at times sought the support of Spain, and at other times France. In 1617 Louis XIII granted them protection. But soon after, he made a truce with Charles-Emmanuel de Savoie, forgetting "his dearly beloved Annibal"! The count took refuge in his fortress at Tourette-du-Château, but the Duke de Savoie didn't need to assault the walls of the castle: it was again betrayal that opened the gates.

Valberg

Lying amid larch forests and green pastures, Valberg is only 80km/49.7mi from the coast and is the starting point for round tours of the Gorges du Cians and Gorges de Daluis as well as hikes to Mont Mounier.

SKI AREA

The resort has 90km/55.9mi of alpine ski runs, a snowpark, 25km/15.5mi of cross-country ski trails, 10km/6.2mi of snowshoeing trails, also an ice-skating rink and swimming pool. In summer, there are lovely walks to enjoy.

VISIT

Chapelle Notre-Dame-des-Neiges – *Contact for times.* 04 93 23 24 24. Modern church with a colourful **interior**★ evoking a ship's hull.

Sentier des Oursons – *1hr 30min return. Starts at the end of the resort.* A forest walk with information panels.

Croix de Valberg or Croix du Sapet – *Follow the sentier des Oursons and continue up after the Sénateur lake. You can also take the chairlift.* The cross, made of wooden skis, is illuminated at night. **Panorama**★★ from Grand Coyer to Mont Pelat.

Vallée de la Tinée★★

Passing through this green valley covered with forests of larches and chestnuts, you will appreciate the exceptional scenery. The spectacular twisting, winding roads lead you to adorable villages, perched higher and higher. These pockets of civilisation, hidden deep in the countryside, reveal simple little churches brightened on the inside with frescoes and altarpieces worthy of the Louvre. The pathways of Mercantour are lined with sacred art.

Michelin Map: 334 J8.

Info: Pl. C.-Ginesy, 06470 Valberg. 04 93 23 24 25. www.valberg.com.

Location: 80km/49.7mi from Nice on D 6202, and D 28, which crosses the Gorges de Cians.

Timing: Valberg is best enjoyed for its outdoor activities. For a more cultural visit go directly to Péone.

EXCURSION
Péone★

8.5km/5.3mi N on D 29.

The maze of narrow streets takes one past *trompe-l'œil* house façades in this ancient village. The promenade des Demoiselles leads to the **Cheminées de calcaire**★, striking rock formations.

DRIVING TOUR

ROUTE DU COL DE VALBERG★

Drive of 20km/12.4mi from Beuil (7 km/4.4mi E) to Guillaumes shown on the regional map (see p474). See opposite.

Michelin Map: 334 J/K 7/8/9.

Info: Maison du Tourisme, r. des Communes-de-France, 06660 St-Étienne-de-Tinée. 04 93 02 41 96. www. stationsdumercantour.com.

Location: The villages of the Tinée Valley are often perched at the end of winding roads that branch off D 2205.

Don't Miss: Try to stop at a few of the *villages perchés*.

Timing: To visit each village, you need two days.

 **DRIVING TOUR**

THROUGH THE GORGES
*116km/72.1mi from Pont de la Mescla
(135km/83.9mi from Villars-sur-Var on
D 6202) to St-Étienne-de-Tinée.
Allow 1 day.*

This itinerary begins at the confluence
of the Tinée and the Var.

▷ *From the pont de la Mescla,
drive along D 2205.*

Gorges de la Mescla★
The road runs along the bottom of the
gorge, beneath overhanging rocks.

▷ *At the pont de la Lune, turn
right onto D 32.*

The isolated village of **La Tour**, perched
above the Tinée Valley, has retained
its medieval character and boasts a
square lined with arcades, a fountain
and *trompe-l'œil* façades.
Church – ℘04 93 02 04 84 – *ask at the
presbytery.* Inside there are three beautiful Renaissance altarpieces.
The **Chapelle des Pénitents-Blancs**
stands along D 32. The side walls are
covered with **frescoes**★ by Brevesi and
Nadale dating from 1491.

▷ *Return to D 2205 and drive N to
pont-de-Clans then turn left onto D 56.*

The road winds its way to the village of
Bairols in a series of hairpin bends.
Bairols (alt. 830m/2 723ft) is surrounded
by olive groves, and oak and chestnut
forests, and has been tastefully restored.
Bird's-eye **views**★ of the valley.

▷ *Rejoin D 2205 and turn immediately
right onto D 55 to Clans.*

Clans, overlooking the steep Clans Valley on one side and the Tinée on the
other, is surrounded by a forest. Note
its medieval fountains.
The Romanesque **church** was rebuilt in
Baroque style, so the doorway, dating
from 1702, is preceded by a portico.

Inside the decoration is overwhelming:
beautiful altarpieces; organ (1792) by
Honoré Grinda, famous Niçois organ-
maker; and the ancient **frescoes** (11C)
of the Count de Nice.
Outside on the left, look for the house
called the"Reine-Jeanne", which has a
mullioned window. On the left of the
pont-de-Clans road stands **Chapelle St-
Antoine**. The small rustic chapel has a
wall-belfry and the interior is extensively
decorated with 15C **frescoes**★. The
view embraces Clans, the Tinée Valley
and the Pointe des Quatre Cantons. *The
churches and chapels are open on request;
contact the town hall for the key. ℘04 93
02 90 08.*

▷ *Return to D 2205 turn left to Ilonse.*

Ilonse lies in a beautiful mountain setting, at an altitude of 1 210m/3 970ft.

▷ *Continue on D 2205 towards
St-Sauveur-sur-Tinée.*

The Valdeblore road on the right links
the Tinée and Vésubie valleys.

St-Sauveur-sur-Tinée is a maze of
lanes lined with tall buildings with
projecting roofs. The 15C **church** has
a Romanesque bell tower. Inside is the
Retable Notre-Dame (1483) by Guillaume Planeta.
Beyond St-Sauveur, D 30 winds westwards along the Vionène and across
the Col de la Couillole (*see Beuil p490*).
D 2205 follows the Tinée through the
Gorges de Valabres★.

In **Isola** the Romanesque bell tower of
the church, destroyed by a flood of the
Guerche, stands at the entrance of the
village. The road on the left leads to the
Cascade de Louch★.

▷ *To reach Isola 2000 (see p494),
turn right onto D 97 and follow the
Vallon de Chastillon. To reach Auron
(see p498), turn left onto D 39.*

St-Étienne-de-Tinée★
See St-Étienne-de-Tinée p496.

Roubion★

This village perched above the deep Vionène Valley is an impressive sight. Overlooked by a rocky ridge, it clings to a cliff-face and seems to be suspended in mid-air. It has retained its authenticity, its narrow shady streets, and its ancient houses.

VISIT

The main road passes through an arch-way under a house and emerges at the church square. Here, a **tunnel** pierces the cliff, the start of a trail (9km/5.59mi), which leads to **Vignols**, a charming, well-preserved alpine hamlet.

Inside the **church**, the chapel on the right is crammed with decoration: geo-metric motifs in yellow, blue and red, and carved angels playing trumpets. From the top of the village there is a fine **panorama**.

Chapelle St-Sébastien★ –

Below the village, at the first bend in the road (D 38), going in the direction of St-Sauveur-sur-Tinée (see opposite), to the right you'll see a small path sloping down. The key is available on request from the tourist office, 04 93 02 10 30, or at the Auberge du Moulin.

Twelve 16C frescoes, naive and realistic, illustrate the legend of St Sébastien. The chapel also features the Vices and Vir-tues: on the left, a dragon, mouth agape,

> - **Population:** 108.
> - **Michelin Map:** 334 K8.
> - **Info:** Le Village, 06420 Roubion. 04 93 02 10 30. www.roubion.com.
> - **Location:** Between Beuil and Roure, overlooked by the Col de la Couillole, at 1 300m/4 265ft.
> - **Timing:** Allow one hour to walk around the village.

swallowing chained sinners, straddling monstrous chimeras.

EXCURSION
Roubion-les-Buisses
2km/1.2mi on D 30 to Beuil.

This small winter resort (alt. 1 410m –1 920m/4 626ft–6 299ft) has 30km/18.6mi of alpine ski runs and 12km/7.4mi of cross-country ski trails. In summer take the chairlift up and ride down the slopes on mountain bikes.

🚗 DRIVING TOUR

ROUTE DU COL DE LA COUILLOLE
Drive of 35km/22mi from Beuil to St-Sauveur-sur-Tinée shown on the regional map (see p474).
See p490.

Frescoes in the Chapelle St-Sébastien

S. Sauvignier/MICHELIN

Roure★

Perched high at the heart of a beautiful mountain setting, overhanging the Vinène and Tinée valleys, this ancient village has retained a wealth of interesting 17C and 18C architecture.

The houses are partly built of red schist and their roofs are covered with red-schist slabs *(lauzes)*. Some have walls made of hewn larch trunks. Climb the rock opposite the church to appreciate the captivating charm of the village.

▶ **Population:** 204.
⚙ **Michelin Map:** 334 K8.
ℹ **Info:** Mairie, Pl. A.-Ségur, 06420 Roure. ✆04 93 02 00 70.
◖ **Location:** Between Roubion and St-Saveur-sur-Tinée, at 1 132m/714ft altitude.
◷ **Timing:** You'll need around two hours to stroll through the steep lanes and to admire the architecture of the village.

VISIT
Church
The **altarpiece of St Laurent**★ (16C), in beautiful green and red colours on a background of gold, is framed by twisted columns. The altarpiece of the Assumption is in the style of Bréa.

Chapelle St-Bernard-et-St-Sébastien★
◷*Open Mon–Tue and Thu–Fri 9am–1pm, 2–6pm.* ☞*Free. Collect key at the town hall,* ✆*04 93 02 00 70.*
This chapel is decorated with remarkably well-preserved naive frescoes, the work of Andre de Cella. They illustrate hallucinating devils with long red tongues. The friezes separating the panels date from the Renaissance.

High-Altitude Arboretum Marcel-Kroenlein★
🥾*Access from trail (2km/1.2mi) above the village.* ◷*Open daily summer 10am–6pm; winter 10am–4pm.*
🥾*Guided tours Jul–Aug.* ☞*5€.*
✆*04 93 35 00 50. www.arboretum-roure.org or www.no-made.eu.*
Created in 1988 by botanist **Marcel Kroenlein**, its 6ha/14.82 acres, in a magnificent altitude of 1 150m/3 773ft, are planted with mountain trees from around the world.

Four à Bois
◷*Open Sat 6–8pm, Sun 8am–noon.*
Near to the Auberge Le Robur, a wood-fired oven is still in use. You'll find freshly baked bread, as well as croissants and brioche.

Isola 2000

Isola 2000, in a beautiful mountain setting close to the Italian border, is the nearest alpine ski resort to the Côte d'Azur region. It owes its popularity to its sunny climate and to its good-quality snow cover.

⚙ **Michelin Map:** 334 K7.
ℹ **Info:** Espace Mercantour, Immeuble Le Pévelos, 06420 Isola 2000. ✆04 93 23 15 15. www.isola2000.com.
◖ **Location:** Isola 2000 is less than 100km/62.2mi from Nice and 5min from Italy.
◷ **Timing:** Spend some time in the village of Isola before exploring the resort and its sports facilities.

VISIT
Honoré Bonnet created the resort in 1972.
Ski area – It extends from an altitude of 1 800m/5 906ft to 2 600m/8 530 ft and has exceptional snow cover. There are

42 downhill ski runs (120km/74.6mi), as well as a halfpipe and snowpark.

Summer resort – Isola is the starting point for numerous hikes and mountain-bike trails; also golf, tennis, swimming, horse riding and fitness centre.

HIKES

Tête de Pélevos★

Alt. 2 455m/8 054ft. Take the cable car. Open Jul–Aug 9–11.45am, 1.45–4.30pm. 3.70€ (children under 16 3.30€), return 5.50€ (children under 16 3.70€), mountain-bike passes 6.80€ half-day, 9.50€ full day.
04 93 23 15 15.

From the upper station, follow a path on the right which climbs towards the Marmottes lifts. Bear left at the second lift and go to the summit for a fine **panorama★**.

Lacs de Terre Rouge★★

4hrs return. Gradient 650m/2 133ft.
Start from La Bergerie at the end of the resort and climb to the Hôtel Diva. From there, a marked path leads to the lakes at the foot of the Cime de Tavels and Mont Malinvern. Climb to the **Baisse du Druos★★** (alt. 2 628m/8 622ft) ; from where there is a lovely **view** of the Parc de l'Argentera in Italy; to the south is the Lac Valscura and the Cime Valrossa. On the French side, notice the Mont St-Sauveur and the Mont Mounier.

Mont St-Sauveur★★

3hrs 30min return.
Gradient 400m/1 312ft.
Go up to the Marmottes 2 lift, as for the Tête de Pélevos, and continue to the Col Valette. From there, take a narrow path that runs along the mountainside towards Mont St-Sauveur. Turn left at marker 89 and follow the short path along the crest of the mountain. The **panorama★★** stretches out over a large part of the Mercantour, the Gorges de Valabrès and the domain of Valberg to the south, the Mont Mounier and Auron to the west and, further north, the Terre Rouge lakes, overlooked by the Cimes de Tavels, de Vermeil and de la Lombarde, Monte Viso and the Pelvoux Massif.

Col de la Lombarde (Italian Border)

Alt. 2 350m/7 710ft. 3hrs return walk without difficulty along a marked path, after the Belvédère chairlift.

The peak is framed by the Cime de la Lombarde on the right and the Crête de la Lausetta on the left. Fine view of Isola 2000 overlooked by the Tête Mercière.

EXCURSION

Santuario di Santa Anna★★ (Italy)

12km/7.4mi to the N. 45min drive and 45min walk return.
Have identification with you.

From the Col de la Lombarde, the road runs through a rocky landscape, skirts Lake Orgials and goes down through larch woods. In a bend, turn left towards Santa Anna.

As you reach the sanctuary, turn left and continue to the end of the surfaced road. **View★** of the sanctuary and of the mountains towering over it. Leave the car and walk for 40 minutes to the **Lago di Santa Anna★**.

ADDRESSES

STAY

Camping Le Lac des Neiges – *06420 Isola, 0.5km/0.3mi W of the centre, on the D 2205 (rte d'Auron), near to La Tinée and a lake. 04 93 02 18 16.www.lacdes neiges.com. 98 pitches, restaurant.*
Campsite located at the lakeside.

EAT

The resort has a vast choice of restaurants. There are also restaurants at the top of the cable car and St-Sauveur surface lift.

ACTIVITIES

Snow-scooter trips – *Le Front de Neige, 04 93 23 91 32. www.isola2000.com.*
Drive along the forest paths, or ski runs on a snow scooter.

St-Étienne-de-Tinée★

This charming alpine town in the heart of the Mercantour region was rebuilt after a devastating fire which occurred in 1929. In summer, St-Étienne-de-Tinée is the ideal starting point of very pleasant walks, in particular from the Route de la Bonette. In winter, it offers a small **ski area** – highest point: **Cime de la Berchia**, alt. 2 274m/7 461ft – linked to that of Auron by cable car and chairlift.

SIGHTS

A pass, the **Passeport Loisirs**, offering reductions on several activities at St-Étienne-de-Tinée and Auron, is sold at the ski lift ticket booths.

Church

The most striking feature is the four-tiered **steeple**★ in Lombard Romanesque style, surmounted by a tall octagonal stone spire surrounded by four gargoyled pinnacles; the date inscribed on the base of the steeple is 1492.

The Chapels

Open Tue–Sat 9am–noon, 2–6pm. Guided tours organised by the tourist office. ℘04 93 02 41 96.

▶ **Population:** 1 320.
Michelin Map: 334 J7/C2.
Info: 1 r. des Communes de France, 06660 St-Étienne-de-Tinée. ℘04 93 02 41 96. www.stationsdumer cantour.com.

▶ **Location:** St-Étienne-de-Tinée lies on the banks of a fast-flowing river, in a pleasant setting of pastures and terraced fields surrounded by mountains. Many people here still speak a Provençal dialect, called *gavot*.

▶ **Timing:** If you visit the town and take one of the suggested walks, you'll need a whole day.

Well-preserved frescoes by Baleison and Canavesio in the **Chapelle St-Sébastien** include the creation of Adam and Eve on the vaulting, Jesus between the two thieves on the back wall and scenes from the life of St Sebastian on the right.

The Chapel **St-Michel** houses a small museum dedicated to the penitents.

The **Chapelle des Trinitaires**, which belonged to the former monastery, is decorated with fine carved wood panel

Frescoes on the ceiling of the Chapelle St-Sébastien

©World Pictures/Photoshot

17C frescoes. The **Chapelle St-Maur** was decorated in the 15C with picturesque frescoes depicting the legends of St Maur and St Sebastian.

Museums

🕐 *Open Tue–Sat except public holidays.*
🗨 *Guided tour (1hr), on request with the Maison du tourisme, contact for details.*
🎟 *Free.* 📞 *04 93 02 41 96.*

Three small museums illustrate aspects of traditional life. The **Musée des Traditions**, housed in the former village bakery, explains the process of making rye bread, and the **Musée du Lait** displays the equipment used in cheese-making. Finally, the **Musée de l'École** tells about school life in past days.

🗨 *Start from the campsite.*
Small water **interpretive trail** with five information panels along the way.

EXCURSIONS
St-Dalmas-le-Selvage★

🛈 *06660, St-Dalmas-le-Selvage.*
📞 *04 93 02 46 40.*

St-Dalmas, situated at the top of the upper Tinée Valley, is the highest village of the Alpes-Maritimes *département*.
The tall, Lombard-style steeple of the village **church** (🕐 *open by appointment with tourist office*), built in Romanesque Revival style and covered with larch shingles, stands out against the splendid wild setting of the Jalorgues Valley. The west front is decorated with *trompe-l'œil* **paintings**: one of these depicts St Dalmas, a 3C martyr who preached the gospel in the Alps.
The narrow streets are lined with stocky houses built of dark schist, covered with shingles and adorned with numerous sundials.

🥾 There is an interesting three-hour hike, le sentier de découverte, sketched out by the tourist office to explore village life in former days.

⊙ *Continue on D 63 after St-Dalmas.*

Col de la Moutière★

⊙ *12km/7.4mi NW along a narrow road.*

The Energy Trail

In the 1930s plans were drawn up to install a high-altitude penstock here, on incredibly difficult terrain. The water from the lakes was meant to feed a hydroelectric plant at St-Étienne-de-Tinée, but this was never completed: at the time, each region had to produce its own electricity. Today, this path at 1 300m/4 265ft looks out over the Tinée Valley, and provides an 8km/5mi-long trail, almost horizontal between St-Étienne-de-Tinée and the Lac de Rabuons.

The road offers bird's-eye views of the village and goes through a splendid larch wood, known as the Bois de Sestrière. Beyond the refuge of the same name, the road enters the central zone of the Parc national du Mercantour. You can observe colonies of marmots near the pass below the Cime de la Bonette.

🥾 HIKE

🌸 The picking of certain endangered species of alpine flowers is severely restricted in the nature reserves and parks: cyclamen, large blue thistle, lis martagon and edelweiss.

Refuge de Rabuons★★

🗨 *Around 5hrs walk. Marked path from the Refuge des lacs de Vens (🕐 see Route de la Bonette p500).*

The main attraction of this walk which connects the two shelters, the highest in the **Parc national du Mercantour**, is the stunning **panorama** from the path which looks out over the Tinée Valley. Initially, walk along the right side of the lakes, and after crossing a footbridge, walk up to the large **Crête des Babarottes**.
The path, on the descent, goes along a section of the "chemin de l'énergie", dotted with retaining walls and tunnels, which leads to the glacial rock bar of the **Lac de Rabuons**, overlooking the shelter.

Auron

This ancient alpine hamlet, which was formerly the grain store for St-Étienne-de-Tinée, is today a dynamic winter and summer resort, at just over an hour from Nice and at the edge of the Parc national du Mercantour.

SKI AREA

This sunny resort, a favourite with the Niçois, has 135km/83.9mi of ski runs over four areas. For those who practise snowboarding there is also a snowpark. As an alternate to skiing, you can choose to take a trip in a sleigh, or a turn at the ice-rink.

Cross-country skiers can enjoy 50km/31.1mi of trails at **St-Dalmas-le-Selvage** (*see St-Étienne-de-Tinée p497*). In **summer**, the terrain is ideal for mountain-biking enthusiasts with 150km/93.2mi of marked trails. After an exhilarating mountain ride go and relax at the swimming pool.

Chapelle St-Érige

Guided tour – contact the tourist office for information ℘04 93 23 02 66. Romanesque, the nave with a double apse is covered by a larch framework. Its **decoration**★, painted in tempera in 1451, is teeming with lively scenes. Between the two apses, in a recess, Mary Magdalene is welcomed to heaven by two angels; on the dais, above, she is preaching to the Provençal people in a flower-filled field.

On the left wall a giant St Christopher is carrying the Infant Jesus. There is a **view**★ of the mountain ridge from the chapel.

Las Donnas★★

○*Open mid-Dec–mid-Apr 9am–4.30pm.* ○6.50€. ℘04 93 23 00 02. The **cable car** transports you in five minutes to the foot of the Rocher de Las Donnas at 2 256m/7 402ft. From here, there is a **panorama** of the Haute Tinée and the French–Italian Alps.

▶ **Population:** 320.
⚅ **Michelin Map:** 334 J7.
▯ **Info:** Office du tourisme d'Auron, La Grange-Cossa, av. de Malhira, 06660 Auron. ℘04 93 23 02 66. www.auron.com.
◗ **Location:** Auron, at an altitude of 1 600m/5 249ft, lies on a sunny plateau overlooked by the Cime de Las Donnas. You reach here by passing through the Vallée de la Tinée.
○ **Timing:** The Pinatelle cable car runs every day to the ski domain of Auron.

ADDRESSES

⌂ STAY

😐😐😐 **Hôtel L'Écureuil** – *Bd G.-Pompidou.* ℘04 93 23 02 72. www.lecureuil.com. Closed mid-Apr–early Jun and Nov. ⌨▯. 19 rooms ⌂10€, half-board available.* One of the rare hotels to stay open for most of the year in Auron. The functional rooms have been tastefully renovated retaining some of the rustic features. Regional cuisine offering inventive dishes (*pot-au-feu, crozet gratin* in winter, stuffed vegetables, swiss chard tart in summer) served in a mountain setting.

🏃 ACTIVITIES

A pass, the **Passeport Loisirs**, is available offering reductions on several activities at St-Étienne-de-Tinée and Auron (*details at tourist office*).

Via ferrata d'Auron – ℘04 93 23 02 66. www.auron.com. Entrance fee.* For further information contact the tourist office. Seven sections, that can be completed independently (*3–4hrs in total*). Due to the level of technical difficulty people with limited experience need to be accompanied by a guide.

Route de la Bonette★★

Each summer the snow finally melts from these rocky summits and leaves uncovered for a few months the highest road in France. Long ago this strategic pass was used by the Spanish troops, during the Austrian War of Succession (1740–48), and more recently the Germans, until the end of World War II. It used to be a mere mule track; widened in 1832, the present road was only completed in 1964. Today, abandoned by armed troops, it leads those people seeking wild mountain landscapes to the heart of the Parc national du Mercantour.

- ⚐ **Michelin Map:** 334 I6.
- ▷ **Location:** When clear of snow that blocks passage from November to June, the second-highest road in Europe brings Barcelonnette to within 149km/92.6mi of Nice.
- ⚑ **Don't Miss:** The 18 viewing tables explain the main features of the extraordinary countryside between the Casernes de Restefond and St-Étienne-de-Tinée.
- ⏱ **Timing:** Give yourself half a day, counting stops at the La Bonette peak and the old military camp at les Fourches.

🚗 DRIVING TOUR

ROUTE DE LA BONETTE★★★

Drive of 25km/15.5mi from St-Étienne-de-Tinée to the Cime de la Bonette shown on the regional map (⚐ see p474). Allow 1hr 30min.

The road follows a river in an impressive rocky landscape.

▷ *At the Pont-Haut, turn left onto D 63 in the direction of St-Dalmas.*

St-Dalmas-le-Selvage★

⚐*See St-Étienne-de-Tinée p497.*

▷ *Rejoin D 2205; turn left.*

3km/1.8mi beyond the pont-Haut, you can see the **Cascade de Vens**. On the climb up larches are replaced by the grassy alpine pastures.

Camp des Fourches

These barracks at 2 250m/7 382ft, fallen into ruin, were occupied from 1912 until the end of World War II by the 11th Alpine Infantry Batallion.

It was established shortly after the breakthrough of the strategic road connecting the Vallée de l'Ubaye to that of the Haute Tinée via the Col de Restefond.

🔺*30min there and back.* A path leads to the Col des Fourches: lovely view of the vast **Cirque du Salso Morenoa** surrounded by the Cimes de la Tête de l'Enchastraye and Mont Aiga, the natural border with Italy *(viewing table).*

The road then follows along the crest tops encircling the cirque, where the Tinée has its source.

Cime de la Bonette★★★

Alt. 2 862m/9 390ft. 🔺*From the highest point of the road, 30min there and back on foot. Viewing table.*

The breathtaking **panorama** embraces most of the mountain ranges of the southern Alps: the Queyras (Font Sancte), Monte Viso and the Ubaye (Brec de Chambeyron and Tête de Moïse) to the north, the Pelvoux to the northwest; then the upper Verdon (Grande Séolane and Mont Pelat) and the southern Alps to the west, the Préalpes de Digne to the south and the Corborant and Argentera to the east. A special viewing table explains the formation of the Alps.

▷ *This drive can be continued to Barcelonnette (⚐ see p398).*

Route de la Bonnette

© J.-M. Richard/Fotolia.com

🚶 HIKES

The Pas de la Cavale★★

🚶 *3hrs 30min there and back. Gradient around 750m/2 461ft. Start from Col des Fourches. Walking boots advised.*

Walk down a narrow path to an old shack just below the **Salso Moreno Cirque**★. The splendid landscape is interesting from a geological point of view: sinkholes have resulted from the action of water and snow erosion. Colonies of marmots inhabit the area.

From waymark 37 onwards, the stony, slippery path climbs steadily to the Pas de la Cavale framed by the Rocher des Trois Évêques and the Tête Carrée. The **view**★★ embraces the Lacs d'Agnel, the heights lining the Italian border and the Auron ski area to the south, the Vallon du Lauzanier and the Brec de Chambeyron to the north. The Lac de Derrière la Croix lies just below.

The Lacs de Vens★★★

🚶 *6hr walk in a loop passing by the Col de Fer. Gradient 940m/3 084ft. Leave the car at Pra. Easy but long and taxing itinerary.*

The path goes through a larch forest to the Plateau de Morgon, then past waymark 33 to the Tortisse Forest lodges.

From there it is possible to go straight to the Refuge de Vens, but the detour via the **Col de Fer** (alt. 2 584m/8 478ft) is recommended for the **view**★.

Experienced walkers can climb Cime de Fer, where a splendid **panorama**★★ includes Mont Vallonnet and the Lacs de Vens in the foreground, the road to the Col de Larche and the Tête de Moïse summit further north.

From the Col de Fer, the path leads to the refuge and **Lacs de Vens**★★. The reflection of the mountains and of the sky in the clear waters of the lakes enhances the beauty of the landscape.

Skirt the first lake and part of the second then turn right beyond a pile of huge rocks. The path divides several times; keep left every time in order to reach the top of the ridge.

Go up the path, running just below, to waymark 23 and turn towards Le Pra. The path runs along the mountain slope in a splendid **setting**, then down to the Tortisse Forest lodges. From there, retrace your steps to Le Pra.

INDEX

INDEX

INDEX

INDEX

INDEX

🏠 STAY

INDEX

⚲/ EAT

COMPANION PUBLICATIONS

REGIONAL AND LOCAL MAPS

For each of the sites listed in *The Green Guide French Alps*, **map references are indicated which help you find your location on our range of maps. You may use:**

◆ the regional maps at a scale of 1:275 000 **nos 523 and 527,** which cover the main roads and secondary roads, and include useful indications for finding tourist attractions. These are good maps to choose for travelling in a wide area. In addition to identifying the types of road ways, the maps show castles, churches and other religious edifices, scenic viewpoints, megalithic monuments, swimming beaches on lakes and rivers, swimming pools, golf courses, racetracks, airfields, and more.

◆ the latest edition of the map of France **no 721** gives an overall view of the Alpine region and the main access roads which connect it to the rest of France (1 : 1 000 000 scale).

◆ Atlas formats are also available, spiral bound, paperback, hardback and the new, convenient Mini France (all including the Paris region, 50 town plans and an index of place names).

INTERNET

Michelin is also pleased to offer an online route-planning service:
www.viamichelin.com
www.travel.viamichelin.com

MAP LEGEND

	Sight	Seaside resort	Winter sports resort	Spa
Highly recommended ★★★		���	✱✱✱	♯♯♯
Recommended ★★		��	✱✱	♯♯
Interesting ★		�	✱	♯

Additional symbols

🛈		Tourist information
═══ ═══		Motorway or other primary route
❶	❶	Junction: complete, limited
▭▭▭ ═══		Pedestrian street
ɪ═════ɪ		Unsuitable for traffic, street subject to restrictions
▭▭▭ ----		Steps – Footpath
🚆	🚉	Train station – Auto-train station
🚌	S.N.C.F.	Coach (bus) station
──•──		Tram
Ⓜ		Metro, underground
🅿		Park-and-Ride
♿		Access for the disabled
✉		Post office
☎		Telephone
✉		Covered market
•×•		Barracks
△		Drawbridge
∪		Quarry
✗		Mine
Ⓑ	Ⓕ	Car ferry (river or lake)
🚢		Ferry service: cars and passengers
🚤		Foot passengers only
③		Access route number common to Michelin maps and town plans
Bert (R.)...		Main shopping street
AZ **B**		Map co-ordinates

Sports and recreation

🏇		Racecourse
⛸		Skating rink
≋	≋	Outdoor, indoor swimming pool
🎥		Multiplex Cinema
⛵		Marina, sailing centre
⛺		Trail refuge hut
□─■─■─□		Cable cars, gondolas
□+++++□		Funicular, rack railway
🚂		Tourist train
◆		Recreation area, park
🐎		Theme, amusement park
⚲		Wildlife park, zoo
⚘		Gardens, park, arboretum
☘		Bird sanctuary, aviary
🚶		Walking tour, footpath
☺		Of special interest to children

Selected monuments and sights

Tour - Departure point

Catholic church

Protestant church, other temple

Synagogue - Mosque

Building

Statue, small building

Calvary, wayside cross

Fountain

Rampart - Tower - Gate

Château, castle, historic house

Ruins

Dam

Factory, power plant

Fort

Cave

Troglodyte dwelling

Prehistoric site

Viewing table

Viewpoint

Other place of interest

Abbreviations

A	Agricultural office (Chambre d'agriculture)
C	Chamber of Commerce (Chambre de commerce)
H	Town hall (Hôtel de ville)
J	Law courts (Palais de justice)
M	Museum (Musée)
P	Local authority offices (Préfecture, sous-préfecture)
POL.	Police station (Police)
	Police station (Gendarmerie)
T	Theatre (Théâtre)
U	University (Université)

The Michelin Adventure

It all started with rubber balls! This was the product made by a small company based in Clermont-Ferrand that André and Edouard Michelin inherited, back in 1880. The brothers quickly saw the potential for a new means of transport and their first success was the invention of detachable pneumatic tires for bicycles. However, the automobile was to provide the greatest scope for their creative talents. Throughout the 20th century, Michelin never ceased developing and creating ever more reliable and high-performance tires, not only for vehicles ranging from trucks to F1 but also for underground transit systems and airplanes.

From early on, Michelin provided its customers with tools and services to facilitate mobility and make traveling a more pleasurable and more frequent experience. As early as 1900, the Michelin Guide supplied motorists with a host of useful information related to vehicle maintenance, accommodation and restaurants, and was to become a benchmark for good food. At the same time, the Travel Information Bureau offered travelers personalised tips and itineraries.

The publication of the first collection of roadmaps, in 1910, was an instant hit! In 1926, the first regional guide to France was published, devoted to the principal sites of Brittany, and before long each region of France had its own Green Guide. The collection was later extended to more far-flung destinations, including New York in 1968 and Taiwan in 2011.

In the 21st century, with the growth of digital technology, the challenge for Michelin maps and guides is to continue to develop alongside the company's tire activities. Now, as before, Michelin is committed to improving the mobility of travelers.

MICHELIN TODAY

WORLD NUMBER ONE TIRE MANUFACTURER

- 70 production sites in 18 countries
- 111,000 employees from all cultures and on every continent
- 6,000 people employed in research and development

Moving
for a world

Moving forward means developing tires with better road grip and shorter braking distances, whatever the state of the road.

CORRECT TIRE PRESSURE

RIGHT PRESSURE

- Safety
- Longevity
- Optimum fuel consumption

-0,5 bar

- Durability reduced by 20% (- 8,000 km)

-1 bar

- Risk of blowouts
- Increased fuel consumption
- Longer braking distances on wet surfaces

forward together
where mobility is safer

It also involves helping motorists take care of their safety and their tires. To do so, Michelin organises "Fill Up With Air" campaigns all over the world to remind us that correct tire pressure is vital.

WEAR

DETECTING TIRE WEAR
The legal minimum depth of tire tread is 1.6mm. Tire manufacturers equip their tires with tread wear indicators, which are small blocks of rubber moulded into the base of the main grooves at a depth of 1.6mm.

Tires are the only point of contact between the vehicle and road.

The photo below shows the actual contact zone.

If the tread depth is less than 1.6mm, tires are considered to be worn and dangerous on wet surfaces.

NEW TIRE

WORN TIRE
(1,6 mm tread)

Moving forward
means sustainable mobility

By 2050, Michelin aims to cut the quantity of raw materials used in its tire manufacturing process by half and to have developed renewable energy in its facilities. The design of MICHELIN tires has already saved billions of litres of fuel and, by extension, billions of tons of CO_2.

Similarly, Michelin prints its maps and guides on paper produced from sustainably managed forests and is diversifying its publishing media by offering digital solutions to make traveling easier, more fuel efficient and more enjoyable!

The group's whole-hearted commitment to eco-design on a daily basis is demonstrated by ISO 14001 certification.

Like you, Michelin is committed to preserving our planet.

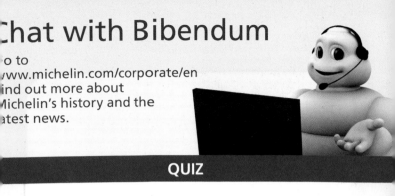

Chat with Bibendum

Go to
www.michelin.com/corporate/en
to find out more about
Michelin's history and the
latest news.

Michelin develops tires for all types of vehicles.
See if you can match the right tire with the right vehicle…

Michelin Apa Publications Ltd

A joint venture between Michelin and Langenscheidt

58 Borough High Street, London SE1 1XF, United Kingdom

No part of this publication may be reproduced in any form
without the prior permission of the publisher.

© 2012 Michelin Apa Publications Ltd
ISBN 978-1-907099-53-3
Printed: December 2011
Printed and bound in Germany